OXFORD STUDIES ON THE ROMAN ECONOMY

General Editors

ALAN BOWMAN   ANDREW WILSON

OXFORD STUDIES ON THE ROMAN ECONOMY

This innovative monograph series reflects a vigorous revival of interest in the ancient economy, focusing on the Mediterranean world under Roman rule (*c.* 100 BC to AD 350). Carefully quantified archaeological and documentary data are integrated to help ancient historians, economic historians, and archaeologists think about economic behaviour collectively rather than from separate perspectives. The volumes include a substantial comparative element and thus will be of interest to historians of other periods and places.

Roman Coin Hoards Across Frontiers

Edited by

BENJAMIN D. R. HELLINGS,

MARGUERITE SPOERRI BUTCHER

and

CHRIS HOWGEGO

OXFORD
UNIVERSITY PRESS

OXFORD
UNIVERSITY PRESS

Great Clarendon Street, Oxford, OX2 6DP,
United Kingdom

Oxford University Press is a department of the University of Oxford.
It furthers the University's objective of excellence in research, scholarship,
and education by publishing worldwide. Oxford is a registered trade mark of
Oxford University Press in the UK and in certain other countries.

Published in the United States of America by Oxford University Press
198 Madison Avenue, New York, NY 10016, United States of America

British Library Cataloguing in Publication Data
Data available

Library of Congress Control Number: 2025948466

ISBN 9780198986447

DOI: 10.1093/9780198986478.001.0001

Printed and bound by
CPI Group (UK) Ltd., Croydon, CR0 4YY

The manufacturer's authorized representative in the EU for product safety is
Oxford University Press España S.A. of Parque Empresarial San Fernando de Henares,
Avenida de Castilla, 2 – 28830 Madrid (www.oup.es/en or product.safety@oup.com).
OUP España S.A. also acts as importer into Spain of products made by the manufacturer.

MIX
Paper | Supporting
responsible forestry
FSC
www.fsc.org
FSC® C013604

Contents

PART III. EVIDENCE AND INTERPRETATIONS: THE EAST

PART IV. EXPANDING EXPLANATORY FRAMEWORKS

List of Figures

List of Tables

List of Contributors

Donald T. Ariel, Head (emeritus) of the Coin Department of the Israel Antiquities Authority, Jerusalem, and co-editor of *Israel Numismatic Research*. He has written four books, edited four volumes, and authored over 200 chapters and articles. He is also a major contributor to the 2023 Tel Kedesh archive volume. He serves as numismatist for many archaeological expeditions in Israel and as stamped amphora expert for a similar number of teams. Most recently he has become head of the Maresha archive publication project.

Jérémie Chameroy, Research Associate and Curator of the coin collection at the Roman Archaeology Department, Leibniz-Zentrum für Archäologie (LEIZA), Mainz. His research interests focus on counterfeiting coins in the Roman Empire through two research programmes dedicated to the study of coin moulds found in Qasr-Qarun (Egypt) and Trier (Germany) and on Hellenistic to Byzantine coin production and coin finds in Asia Minor. He serves as numismatist for the German excavations at Pergamum and is a corresponding member of the German Archaeological Institute.

Vincent Drost, Curator of Roman and Iron Age coins at the Bibliothèque nationale de France, département des Monnaies, médailles et antiques, Paris. He specializes in the field of coin finds through collaborations with French archaeological units and with the Portable Antiquities Scheme at the British Museum.

George A. Green, Associate Professor in Classical and Scientific Archaeology (Senior Research Fellow), School of Archaeology, University of Oxford, and Cultural Heritage Researcher at the ISIS Neutron and Muon Source. The research presented in his chapter was supported by a Leverhulme Trust Early Career Fellowship at the Ashmolean Museum (University of Oxford), where he was the Principal Investigator of the Determining the Flow of Gold in Ancient Africa, Asia and Europe Project, and by the Lavery-Shuffrey Early Career Fellowship in Roman Art and Archaeology at Lincoln College, Oxford.

Pierre-Marie Guihard, Research Engineer at the University of Caen Normandie and Head of the numismatics department at the Centre Michel de Boüard-CRAHAM (UMR 6273) within which he coordinates the Nummus database (https://mrsh.unicaen.fr/nummus/) for recording coin finds from archaeological contexts in France. His work focuses on ancient monetary practices (Celtic and Roman) and counterfeiting in the Roman period through two research programmes dedicated to the study of coin moulds found in Qasr-Qarun (Egypt) and Trier (Germany).

Benjamin D. R. Hellings, Jackson-Tomasko Associate Curator and Head of Numismatics at the Yale University Art Gallery, New Haven, CT. He holds MPhil and DPhil degrees from the University of Oxford, where his research focused on coin-find patterns and the use of Roman coins in northern Europe. He has published on ancient Greek and Roman coins to colonial and modern American coins, and banknotes and related material.

In 2024, he published *The Naseby Cup: Coins and Medals of the English Civil War*, distributed by Yale University Press, and in 2025, *Coin Finds and Monetization in the Roman Northwest*, with the American Numismatic Society.

Helle W. Horsnæs, Assistant Keeper and Senior Researcher in the Royal Collection of Coins and Medals at the National Museum of Denmark, Copenhagen. Her current research focuses on the interaction between archaeology and numismatics, particularly the interpretation of coin finds made during metal detector surveys in Denmark.

Chris Howgego, Research Keeper of the Heberden Coin Room in the Ashmolean Museum, Oxford, and Professor of Greek and Roman Numismatics at the University of Oxford. He was the founding Director of Roman Provincial Coinage Online and, with Professor Andrew Wilson, of Coin Hoards of the Roman Empire. He has written widely on Roman coinage and history. His publications include *Greek Imperial Countermarks* (London, 1985), *Ancient History from Coins* (London, 1995), and *Roman Provincial Coinage vol. IV.4 (From Antoninus Pius to Commodus: Egypt)* (London, 2023), and he co-edited *Coinage and Identity in the Roman Provinces* (Oxford, 2005) and *Coin Hoards and Hoarding in the Roman World* (Oxford, 2022).

Marek Jankowiak, Researcher at the Institute of History, Polish Academy of Sciences, Warsaw, and Visiting Professor at the Institute for the History of Ancient Civilizations (IHAC), Northeast Normal University, Changchun, China, was formerly Associate Professor in Byzantine History at the University of Oxford. He was the co-investigator of the AHRC Dirhams for Slaves Project (2013–17) and co-editor of *The Archaeology of Slavery in Early Medieval Europe. The Invisible Commodity* (with F. Biermann, Cham, 2021) and *Viking-Age Trade: Silver, Slaves and Gotland* (with J. Gruszczyński and J. Shepard, London, 2021). In addition to early medieval slavery and slave trade, he works on various aspects of Byzantine, Islamic, and northern European history in the seventh to eleventh centuries.

Anahide Kéfélian, Research Fellow at the CNRS, UMR 5648 CIHAM, CNRS/Lyon 2, former postdoctoral Marie Skłodowska-Curie Fellow at the Ashmolean Museum of Oxford University and Junior Research Fellow at Wolfson College (2020–3), as PI of the RoCAA project. Her research interests include the study of the Greater Armenian Kingdom, its interactions with the Roman Empire, and interdisciplinary research to bring new data to the study of ancient Armenia.

Kyrylo Myzgin, Associate Professor at the Faculty of Archaeology, Head of the Department of Numismatics and Museology, University of Warsaw. His research interests are Roman coin finds from central and eastern Europe and archaeology of the Late Roman period and the Great Migration period. He is corresponding member of the German Archaeological Institute and has held post-doctoral fellowships at the Institute of Pre- and Protohistoric Archaeology, Bonn University (DAAD programme), at the Institute of Archaeology, University of Warsaw (Polish National Science Centre FUGA programme), and at the Zentrum für Baltische und Skandinavische Archäologie (LEIZA-ZBSA) (Alexander von Humboldt Foundation).

Rasmus Holst Nielsen, former curator and currently external researcher at the Royal Collection of Coins and Medals at the National Museum of Denmark, Copenhagen, is a DPhil student in Classical Archaeology at the University of Oxford. His research focuses on the methodological implications of the use of the metal detector in generating large-scale datasets regarding Roman coin finds in Denmark.

Emilia Smagur, Assistant Professor in Archaeology, in the Department of Greek, Roman, and Byzantine Culture Studies, Polish Centre of Mediterranean Archaeology, University of Warsaw. Her work focuses on the movement of coins in the Indian Ocean world, Indian Ocean trade, agency of imports, and archaeology of port cities. Recent publications include 'Indian imitations of Roman aurei reconsidered', *Numismatic Chronicle* 182 (2022), and '"Romano-Sasanian" imitations from India: Notes on their life histories and the Indo-Sasanian Trade', *South Asian Studies* 38.2 (2022).

Irene Soto Marín, Assistant Professor of Classics in the Department of the Classics at Harvard University, Cambridge, MA. Her research focuses on the economy of Late Roman Egypt, particularly on aspects regarding trade, economic integration, taxation, and monetary supply. She has been working in the Dakhleh Oasis of Egypt at the site of Amheida (ancient Trimithis) since 2008.

Marguerite Spoerri Butcher, Senior Research Fellow at the Heberden Coin Room, Ashmolean Museum, University of Oxford, co-Director of the Roman Provincial Coinage Online project, and Scientific Member of the Swiss School of Archaeology in Greece. Her research interests cover a range of subjects pertaining to Greek and Roman coinage, with a focus on the eastern part of the Mediterranean. She has published on Roman provincial coinages, coin finds from Eretria (Euboea), the coinage of Juba II of Mauretania, and the quantification of the Roman imperial coinage (with Benjamin D. R. Hellings).

Ludovic Trommenschlager is Project Manager of the 'Trouvailles monétaires' programme at the Bibliothèque nationale de France, département des Monnaies, médailles et antiques, Paris. He holds a PhD in Roman Archaeology and specializes in the field of coin finds and hoards with French archaeological units.

David G. Wigg-Wolf, Honorary Professor at the School of Archaeology and Ancient History, University of Leicester, was until August 2024 a Senior Researcher at the Römisch-Germanische Kommission des Deutschen Archäologischen Instituts, Frankfurt am Main. His research interests include the production, circulation, and use of coinage in western and central Europe from the late pre-Roman Iron Age to the early medieval period, and digital numismatics. He is a member of the steering committee of nomisma.org, co-chair of the DARIAH-EU Digital Numismatics Working Group, and convenor of the European Coin Find Network.

Andrew Wilson, Professor of the Archaeology of the Roman Empire, Faculty of Classics, University of Oxford, and Fellow, All Souls College. His research interests include the economy of the Roman Empire, ancient technology, ancient water supply and usage, Roman North Africa, and archaeological field survey. Recent co-edited publications include *Recycling and Reuse in the Roman Economy* (with Chloë Duckworth; Oxford, 2020), *Coin Hoards and Hoarding in the Roman World* (with Jerome Mairat and Chris Howgego; Oxford, 2022), *Simulating Roman Economies: Theories, Methods, and Computational Models* (with Tom Brughmans; Oxford, 2022), and *The Economy of Roman Religion* (with Nicholas Ray and Angela Trentacoste; Oxford, 2023).

Bernhard E. Woytek, Professor of Ancient Numismatics and Monetary History at the Department of Numismatics and Monetary History, University of Vienna. He has published widely on the coinage of the Roman Republic and the High Empire as well as on the ancient economy and on the history of classical scholarship. He is a corresponding member of the Austrian Academy of Sciences and the German Archaeological Institute.

1

Introduction: Roman Coins across Frontiers

Chris Howgego, Benjamin D. R. Hellings, Marguerite Spoerri Butcher, and Andrew Wilson

This is the second volume in this series under the auspices of the Coin Hoards of the Roman Empire Project (CHRE). It stems from a conference held on 21–22 April 2022 in Oxford. Its purpose is to begin to capitalize on the opportunity that the Coin Hoards of the Roman Empire Project now provides to study the Empire together with the full reach of Roman material culture beyond the frontiers through the lens of coin hoards. In the past, Roman coin hoards within and outside the Roman Empire have rarely been studied together. Comparison with patterns inside the Empire may be critical for understanding what is going on outside. An inspirational start in consolidating research on Roman coin finds from beyond the frontiers was made by the publication in 2008 of *Roman Coins outside the Empire. Ways and Phases, Contexts and Functions.*[1] Since then the subject has moved rapidly in certain areas. The current volume seeks to capture some of the best current research and to recontextualize it. It is intended to be read in conjunction with our first volume, *Coin Hoards and Hoarding in the Roman World*, which concentrated on the Empire alone.[2]

THE COIN HOARDS OF THE ROMAN EMPIRE PROJECT

This international collaborative initiative, to create an online database of all known hoards containing Roman coinage from Augustus to the death of Anastasius, was the idea of Baron Lorne Thyssen-Bornemisza and has received generous support from the Augustus Foundation since 2013. It is structured as a joint venture between the Ashmolean Museum and the Oxford Roman Economy Project under the direction of Chris Howgego and Andrew Wilson. The small core team currently

[1] Bursche, Ciołek, and Wolters (2008).

[2] Mairat, Wilson, and Howgego (2022).

consists of Marguerite Spoerri Butcher as Senior Research Fellow and Cristian Găzdac as Consultant.

The core team supports an extensive collaborative network, so far including 50 institutional collaborative partners in 25 countries, as well as individual collaborators. It particularly encourages the participation of researchers in the early stages of their careers. Already 20 graduate students have been involved internationally. Some of these graduate students have since gone on to hold academic posts at a variety of institutions, and further supported the Project. In addition, several funded opportunities have been generated at Oxford itself. As doctoral students, Matthew Ball has been supported by the Leverhulme Doctoral Centre, as part of their Publication Beyond Print initiative, and Anni Byard by the Arts and Humanities Research Council under its Collaborative Doctoral Partnership scheme. Among early career researchers, George A. Green, as Leverhulme Trust Early Career Fellow, and Anahide Kéfélian, as Marie Curie Research Fellow, are now in a position to share some of their results in the present volume. In addition, the Project has formed the basis of a master's course on Roman coinage at Leiden (with Liesbeth Claes), been utilized for a Security Studies course in Cluj (with Cristian Găzdac), and been the subject of study for a Digital Humanities course in Houston (with Kristina Neumann).

The Project's aim in its first phase (2013–18) was to collect summary hoard data of all coinages in use in the Roman Empire between *c.* 30 BC and AD 400, or later where appropriate.[3] In its second phase (2019–), the Project has aimed to improve geographical coverage, to extend coverage systematically to the death of Anastasius in AD 518, and to begin to undertake the daunting task of recording hoards at the level of the coin (including standard references, such as *RIC* numbers, and full descriptions), where such data are available. At the time of writing (March 2025), data have been collected for *c.* 18,200 hoards, comprising *c.* 7 million coins from an area embracing 73 modern countries. All validated data are made available online under a Creative Commons CC BY-NC-SA 4.0 licence.

In the second phase a strategic decision was taken to extend the geographical coverage to include hoards of Roman coins and their imitations from outside the Roman Empire to demonstrate Rome's economic and cultural reach. This enhanced scope underpins the vision for the current volume.

THIS BOOK

We aim to promote debate by exposing divergent ideas about apparently similar phenomena in different contexts, and indeed by juxtaposing divergent interpretations of material from the same context. The contributions in this book cross

[3] Howgego and Wilson (2022: 3–5).

literal and academic frontiers. At the beginning and the end, we have deliberately pushed the boundaries. The first part comprises three enlightening chapters on deposition *within* the Empire, to underpin debate about motivations for hoarding outside. Indeed, the later chapters by David Wigg-Wolf and by Jérémie Chameroy and Pierre-Marie Guihard go on to demonstrate just how important it is to compare hoards inside and outside the Roman Empire if one is to begin to understand the hoarding patterns beyond the frontiers. At the end of the book, a final section seeks to expand explanatory frameworks by the inclusion of later periods and alternative sources of evidence. A chapter on the spectacular later export of Islamic silver dirhams northwards to Russia, Ukraine, the Baltic, and Scandinavia in the ninth and tenth centuries AD hints at the possible relevance for the Roman period of interpretative modes advanced for later periods; a chapter based on metallurgical analysis suggests how movements of Roman coin can be tracked where the reworking of metal in antiquity deprives us of the direct evidence of Roman finds; and a final chapter presents an analysis of the key textual evidence for the export of coin outside the Empire.

Sandwiched between the expansive introductory and concluding material are two parts devoted to evidence and interpretation, in north, central, and eastern Europe, on the one hand, and in the East on the other. A degree of unevenness in treatment is inevitable. For some regions the evidence is well known and published, so contributors can focus more on the reasons behind the export of coins, on when they were exported and deposited, and on differences from coin circulation and use within the Empire. For other regions, the chapters in this volume are the first to present the sources in a systematic way, so that inevitably the focus is more on presenting the evidence and less on analysis.

We do not seek in this introduction to summarize the complexity of the hoard data presented in this book, or the bewildering variety of contexts in which they need to be interpreted. The chapters speak eloquently enough of such diversity. Rather, we seek to draw out some of the shared themes in relation to export, use, and deposition.

The one thing on which we do wish to insist is the importance of the sheer extent of the spread of Roman material culture. It was this which led Mortimer Wheeler to write *Rome Beyond the Imperial Frontiers* in 1954.[4] The evidence base has radically shifted since then, not least for coinage.[5] A glance at the map of hoard distribution (Figs 1.1 and 1.2) makes clear the advantages of a holistic approach. One cannot help but be struck by the quantity of hoards in Scandinavia (particularly the Baltic islands) or in Ukraine; one can begin to discern early traces of the so-called 'Silk Road';[6] and India almost looks like a Roman province. The map of this form of Roman material culture and its imitations thus makes an impression entirely different from a modern political map of Roman provinces,

[4] Wheeler (1954). [5] Whittaker (2004: 20–2); Wells (2013). [6] Graf (2017).

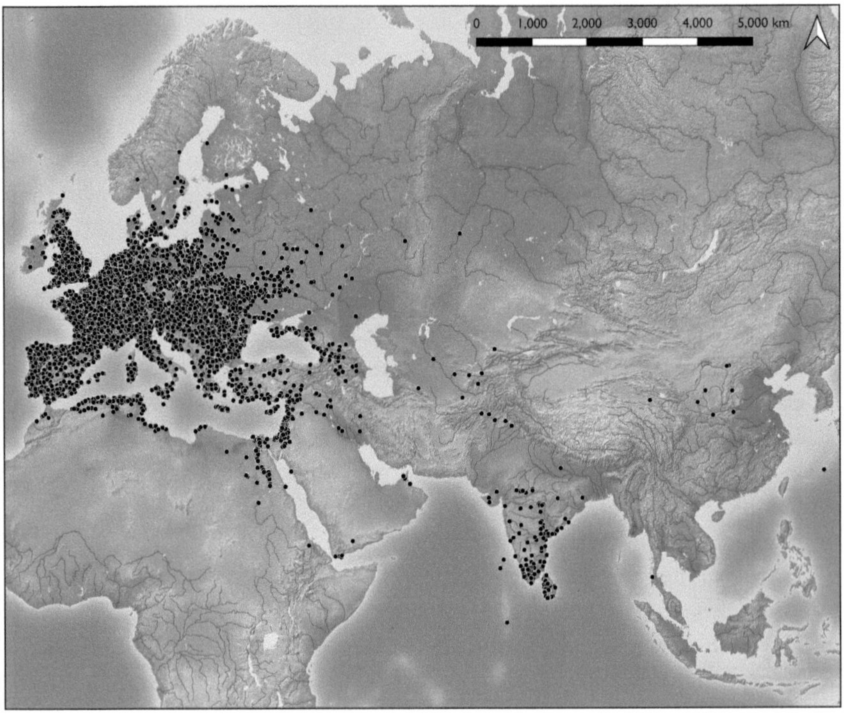

Fig. 1.1. Distribution of all hoards with coordinates entered into the Coin Hoards of the Roman Empire Project database, as at 5 March 2025 (n = 17,712).
Map: A. Wilson/Coin Hoards of the Roman Empire Project.

illustrating what David Mattingly calls the 'long reach of the Roman economy'.[7] It is worth recalling the Roman perspective, embodied in Agrippa's map, that India might indeed be considered a province, in other words a 'field of action' over which the Romans claimed control (*imperium*).[8] So, in some ways maps of Roman material culture help us to see the world more as the Romans themselves did. Frontiers as limits to empire are largely absent from Roman cartographic or chorographic sources.[9] The map of hoards presented here thus raises questions about the nature of Roman imperialism, the importance of commerce, and the significance of frontiers. We note, as Bowman once drily observed, 'War and imperialism were good for business and economic activity, then as now'.[10] Whatever the mode of export of Roman coin, the distribution of Roman coinage and its imitations demonstrate connectivity with regions way beyond the Mediterranean core of the Roman Empire.[11]

[7] Mattingly (2017a: 20).

[8] Whittaker (2004: ch. 7, at 145); cf. Virgil, *Aeneid* 6.794–5 (of Augustus): *super et Garamantas et Indos proferet imperium*, 'he shall extend control over the Garamantians and the Indians'.

[9] Whittaker (2004: 79–80).

[10] Bowman (2006: 83).

[11] For Mediterranean connectivity: Horden and Purcell (2000).

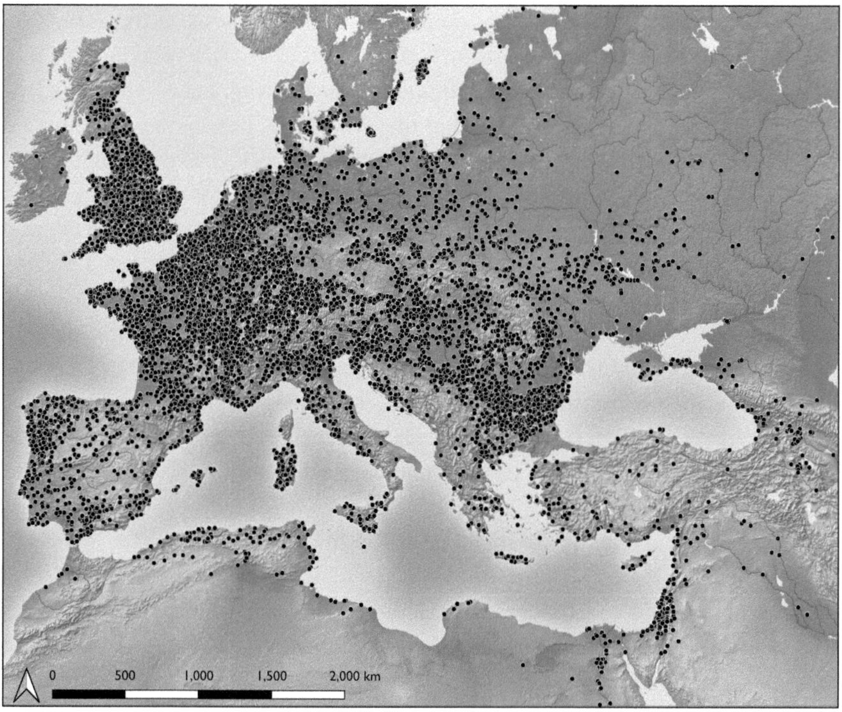

Fig. 1.2. Distribution of all hoards with coordinates in Europe and the circum-Mediterranean region entered into the Coin Hoards of the Roman Empire Project database, as at 5 March 2025. Map: A. Wilson/Coin Hoards of the Roman Empire Project.

SCOPE

Definition of a Hoard

As discussed in our earlier volume, *Coin Hoards and Hoarding in the Roman World*, the Project pragmatically defines a hoard as *any group of coins which appear to have been deposited together.*[12] It is essential for the database not to rely on a definition involving intentionality (especially the intention or not to recover, as implied by terms such as 'savings hoard', 'emergency hoard', or 'ritual deposit'), as that is based on subjective interpretation, which varies between scholars and with academic fashion. Similarly, in a legislative context in England, Wales, and Northern Ireland, it was the need to remove intention from the definition that led to the change from the old common law of Treasure Trove to the more archaeologically coherent 1996 Treasure Act.[13] Thus, the Project includes

[12] Howgego and Wilson (2022: 4–5).

[13] Bland *et al.* (2020: 2–3).

hoards where there was evidently no intention to deposit, as in the case of lost purses or groups of coins from shipwrecks. Nonetheless, as several authors note, it is important to bear in mind the different definitions of 'hoard' that have been used in different countries over time, as they have had a bearing on recording and interpretation.[14] And, as David Wigg-Wolf discusses, consideration of intentionality is inevitable when it comes to the interpretation of patterns of deposition.[15]

It is important to recognize that even our pragmatic definition may be problematic to apply in the field, not least as it can be difficult to distinguish between multiple single finds and a hoard scattered by agricultural work. Helle Horsnæs and Rasmus Nielsen have a careful discussion of this issue and possible methodologies to address it, drawing on some very high-quality recording in Denmark. Regrettably, the precision required will present too high a barrier in many cases. And, as they note, there is the additional challenge that future finds from repeated metal detector visits to a site may change the interpretation of what has already been found.

The Project systematically includes single finds of gold coins, as their high value and archaeological behaviour (i.e. they may behave more like hoards than other single finds) merit their consideration as hoards in their own right.[16] Horsnæs and Nielsen point out that single Roman silver coins might also be valuable and conscious deposits in certain contexts, and, we might add, in some cases also individual bronze coins. A grand unified database of all Roman coin finds, including hoards and single finds in all metals, would provide a means to test such hypotheses systematically, but that is a long way off. In the meantime, within the Project database a 'single gold coin' is recorded as such under 'data type', so that researchers may include or exclude them according to their research questions. Single finds of silver and bronze coins are omitted.

Chronology

The Project aims to record all hoards deposited between 30 BC and AD 518. Chronological limits for interpretation are inevitably more flexible. The chapters in this book range into the Byzantine period, and we have included a consideration of Viking-age finds to obtain a valuable comparative perspective. For late hoards, researchers may also consult the Framing the Late Antique and Early

[14] Horsnæs and Nielsen (this volume, chapter 5); Myzgin (chapter 8).

[15] Wigg-Wolf (this volume, chapter 7).

[16] Howgego and Wilson (2022: 5); also Horsnæs and Nielsen note here in chapter 5 that the topography of single finds of Roman gold coins in Denmark often suggests that the coin was deposited deliberately.

Medieval Economy project (FLAME), which seeks to reconstruct the early medieval economy for the period AD 325–725 in western Afro-Eurasia.[17]

Geography

Discussion is inevitably complicated by the nature of Roman frontiers. These were more like dynamic, ill-defined zones of power than closed, linear, and defensive barriers, although there is inevitably debate about this, and variation by place and time.[18] It is not yet possible to produce a complete synopsis of the hoarding of Roman coin 'outside' the Empire. In some regions there is little to say, or little to add to what has already been published. Rather, we have attempted to commission a representative range of illuminating discussions, drawing on recent research. We note here some obvious omissions.

To the north-west, we have not sought to add to the interpretations of Roman coin in Scotland and Ireland, although hoards continue to emerge, particularly in Scotland. Except for periods of Roman incursion into Scotland, finds are dominated by silver coin, but with some gold, variously interpreted as exported through subsidies and diplomatic gifts, military pay, trade, and gift exchange.[19] In Ireland, the 18 bronze coins from Domitian to Antoninus Pius found at the promontory fort of Drumanagh, on the east coast of Ireland, stand out from this pattern.[20] They may have resulted from trade contact.

The numerous *denarius* hoards from the Swedish islands of Gotland and, to a lesser extent, Öland in the Baltic are not directly covered here, as the evidence has not changed substantially.[21] They do, however, provide a precursor to the Viking-age hoards of Islamic dirhams, also found there in quantity, which are discussed here.[22]

Nor have we included a systematic consideration of the limited export of coin southwards from the Empire. In the conference, Antony Hostein and Laurent Callegarin outlined their project to tackle circulation in the Maghreb (Morocco, Algeria, Tunisia), but they felt that it would be premature for them to publish a survey that their own project will render obsolete.[23] Daniel Hoyer has generously

[17] https://coinage.princeton.edu/ (accessed 23 November 2023). [18] Whittaker (2004: 1–27).

[19] Scotland and Ireland: Hanson (2020). Scotland: Robertson (1975; 1978); Hunter (2007; 2009); Abdy (2002)—an exemplary study of a period of Roman incursion in relation to the Antonine Wall; Hunter and Painter (2013)—Traprain Law treasure. Ireland: Bateson (1971; 1976).

[20] Bland (2015).

[21] Lind (1981). For a recent map see https://www.su.se/numismatiska-forskningsgruppen/om-forskningsgruppen/romerska-denarer-1.592797 (accessed 22 November 2023).

[22] Jankowiak (this volume, chapter 12).

[23] MONOM. La monnaie dans l'Occident méditerranéen: https://www.efrome.it/en/research/research-themes/program-detail/monom; https://www.casadevelazquez.org/recherche-scientifique/programmes-scientifiques-de-lehehi/axe-ii-circulations-echanges-reseaux/monom/presentation-generale/.

made his data and interpretation of hoards and single finds for the period 23 BC to AD 275 from Roman Africa, defined as modern-day Morocco, Algeria, Tunisia, and Libya, freely available online.[24] His database, which includes fewer than 8,000 coins between 23 BC to AD 235, readily exposes the challenges of reporting and publication for the region, but in any case his data do not cover export of coin from the Empire to the south.[25] We note, however, that finds of silver *denarii* from a metalworking site near Jarma, the capital of the Garamantian Kingdom in the Libyan Sahara, may suggest some reworking of Roman *denarii* into silver artefacts there, and the presence of brass, almost certainly of Mediterranean origin, in Fazzan from the first to fourth centuries AD might hint at the recycling of Roman base metal coinage too.[26] Brass even made its way to the sub-Saharan Sahel.[27] Nonetheless, the Garamantes do not appear to have been major users of coins themselves, and there is no evidence that coins as such were a significant feature of any onward trans-Saharan contact in the Roman period.

As regards eastern Africa, the evidence for the movement of Roman coin southwards beyond the Horn of Africa is limited and unsatisfactory.[28] It is confined to base metal coinage and does not include hoards. There is a coin of Severus Alexander from Mogadishu and a (decidedly suspicious) group of Roman coins from the first to the fourth centuries AD, found alongside Hellenistic and later coins, recorded from Burgabo, a port town in southern Somalia near the border with Kenya, also known by the early twentieth-century name Port Dunford.[29] There is also a scatter of individual Roman coins from Nairobi and even further south, including Madagascar, some of which may be secondary finds deposited in modern times.[30]

The main evidence for the export of coin from Egypt eastwards is the literary and documentary evidence reviewed here by Bernhard Woytek, and the coin finds from India, discussed here by Emilia Smagur. We look forward to the results of Smagur's research project on the use and value of coins in the ancient western Indian Ocean ports.[31] The *Periplus Maris Erythraei*, written in the middle of the first century AD, notes that there was a market for Roman money in some port cities south along the Red Sea on both the African and Arabian coasts, and on the south Arabian coast, as well as on the Indian subcontinent.[32] There is also some,

[24] Hoyer (2018). See also Nizolek (2015).
[25] Hoyer (2018: map 1).
[26] Sauer (2007); Mattingly (2017a: 26, table 1.1; 31). Presence of brass: Mattingly *et al.* (2017c: 436). Reworking of metal in Fazzan: Leitch *et al.* (2017: 321–2).
[27] Magnavita (2017).
[28] We are grateful to Emilia Smagur for references.
[29] González-Ruibal *et al.* (2022: 106); Mogadishu: Freeman-Grenville (1963: 181); Burgabo: Mattingly (1932); Wheeler (1954: 112–14); Casson (1989: 95–7).
[30] Charlesworth (1949).
[31] https://pcma.uw.edu.pl/en/2023/04/17/project-history-from-coins/ (accessed 5 December 2023).
[32] Casson (1989); references are to sections in the text, the pages of the translation are given in brackets afterwards: Adulis 6 (53); Malaô 8 (55); Muza 24 (63–4); Kanê 28 (67); Barbarikon 39 (75); Ozênê 49 (81); Bakarê (85).

as yet very limited, physical evidence to support such movement. The Coin Hoards database includes *aurei* from Eritrea and Yemen towards and beyond the mouth of the Red Sea, and from the UAE at the mouth of the Gulf, and also late Roman gold from Yemen and Aden. Aksumite and Roman gold coins were hoarded together in Yemen around AD 520, and the Roman gold seems to have been in use there earlier.[33]

There are hints of an early start to the overland Silk Routes in western Central Asia in the form of an aureus of Tiberius in a female burial in the princely necropolis of Tillya-tepe (Afghanistan),[34] and a hoard of approximately 300 Roman *denarii* from Vespasian to Commodus from Mujum (Tajikistan).[35] There are also finds of Roman bronzes from the fourth to the first half of the fifth century from Merv (Turkmenistan) and elsewhere.[36] Roman and Byzantine gold arrived again in western Central Asia from the fifth to the seventh century onwards.

There is also late evidence from the Far East for the transport of Roman gold by overland routes, and for its further transmission. We have not sought to duplicate here the studies in an important recent book on the movement eastward of Byzantine gold coins and their imitation there.[37] Over one hundred Byzantine gold coins, imitations, and single- and double-sided bracteates have been found in China, mainly in the crescent extending from Xinjiang in the north-west to Liaoning in the north-east.[38] They largely date to the fifth to seventh centuries. The same book also includes a discussion of the remarkable bracteates from the seventh-century Shoroon Bumbagar Tomb in Bayannuur Soum (Mongolia), some of which imitate Byzantine coins from the fifth to the early seventh centuries AD.[39] It also covers Byzantine gold coins from India,[40] and the heterogeneous scatter of Roman coins found in South-East Asia (Thailand, Malaysia, Cambodia, and Vietnam).[41]

DATA

There are substantial geographical and chronological disparities in the data available to us, which have come through many filters.[42] These include the processes of hoarding and deposition, variable recovery in antiquity, modes of discovery in 'modern' times (principally chance, agricultural and building activity, archaeological investigation, and the use of metal detectors), the vagaries of reporting and publication as influenced by national legislation, institutions, and practice, and, finally, the unevenness of data entry within the Project itself.

33 Munro-Hay (1989); Dowler (2018). 34 CHRE 18817. 35 CHRE 17586.
36 Hobbs (1995). 37 Günther *et al.* (2021). 38 Guo (2021a).
39 Guo (2021b). 40 Darley (2021). 41 Borell (2021).
42 Howgego and Wilson (2022: 11–12); Howgego (2025).

It is important to try to understand the factors involved, and to interpret the data in the light of them. Several chapters here make significant contributions in this direction. The impact of archaeological investigation and publication is most readily apparent here through Irene Soto Marín's analysis of the excavations at Karanis, which were a game changer for the data from Egypt. Kyrylo Myzgin carefully analyses the 'dynamics of gathering information' over time for eastern Europe. Key to the recent explosion of data for Ukraine in particular are both the use of metal detectors and the onset of widespread online communication, that is the publicizing of finds by metal detectorists on Facebook and the like. What Myzgin modestly fails to emphasize is his own immense effort in gathering and making available that data. Scholarly effort is another filter. In a similar vein, Horsnæs and Nielsen analyse the history of information for Denmark, where records go back to the seventeenth century, much earlier than in most countries. They thoughtfully begin to address the impact of metal detecting over the last 40 years on the nature and scale of the data available to us. Also enlightening is Donald Ariel's account of the physical and institutional background to why we have relatively greater knowledge of hoards from shipwrecks in the Levant than elsewhere. Such mature reflections help us to come to terms with our data. Unevenness of data is not a vitiating characteristic of numismatic evidence in particular but a feature common to many of the 'big data' projects within digital humanities. We will clearly need to explore statistical techniques designed to address disparities of evidence.[43]

Coin hoards can give only a partial view of the original reach of Roman coinage, especially where the coin arriving was melted down or traded onwards. The chapters here seek to mitigate such gaps in the evidence by using various proxies for the movement of coin beyond the frontiers: literary and documentary sources (discussed here by Woytek), struck or cast imitations and copies, and metallurgy.

The local production of imitations or copies of Roman coins implies some contact with the originals which they copied, albeit possibly at some remove, and is also indicative of some need for coin, although that need might be, say, decorative or social, as well as monetary.[44] Imitations, identified as such, are included in the Project database, where they occur in hoards or as single gold finds. There is no separate treatment of imitations here, but they are discussed by contributors where appropriate.

Metallurgy can in principle trace the movement of coin which has been melted down, although much remains to be done. Indicative here of its potential for tracing the export of coin is George Green's demonstration that the recycling of Roman gold coin was a major (although not the exclusive) factor in the notable shift in the chemical composition of Kushan gold *c.* AD 150–250 in what are now

[43] Howgego and Wilson (2022: 6).

[44] Imitations: Dymowski (2019), with bibliography there. Copies: Dymowski (2021).

parts of Uzbekistan, Tajikistan, Turkmenistan, Afghanistan, Pakistan, and northern India. The techniques and the potential for sourcing gold have been discussed in the context of the AVREVS project, as well as in Green's work, and for silver in the context of analyses by Kevin Butcher and Matthew Ponting.[45] All of these studies emphasize the care required to interpret the analytical data, especially given the complexity which arises from refining processes and the mixing of metal from different sources. We should also pay greater attention to the recycling of base metal. There is evidence for the recycling of Roman bronze in 'Free Germany', as well as of Roman silver, including *denarii*.[46] Recycling may have been particularly attractive for brass, given its golden appearance. The reuse of Roman brass should be relatively easy to trace through its zinc content and the lack of local traditions of brass production. By way of spectacular example only, there is evidence for the reworking of Roman brass coinage on the Baltic and in north-western Russia, and possibly also in Saharan and sub-Saharan Africa.[47]

We need to remain alert to the possible gaps in our evidence caused by the reworking or trading on of coinage. A striking instance is noted by Smagur. Whereas the *Periplus Maris Erythraei* records the considerable profit to be gained from exporting Roman gold and silver coinage to the trading port of Barygaza on the western coast of India, the finds of Roman coins are actually rather scarce on the territory of Gujarat. There is also the major question of what happened to the Roman coinage, if any, which reached China. As Woytek discusses, Pliny's *Naturalis Historia* records the drain of capital to Arabia, India, and China,[48] but the evidence for Roman and Byzantine coin in China comes only much later, in the form of gold coins of the fifth to seventh centuries AD.[49]

EXPORT

Woytek's masterly analysis of selected textual sources, both literary and documentary, provides the background for considerations of the export of coin from the Empire.[50] We have sought to provoke further debate about the role of trade, which is clearly the main mechanism by which Roman silver and gold coin reached India. Trade to the south and the east by the Red Sea routes was underpinned by heavy Roman state investment in physical infrastructure and protection.[51]

[45] Green (2020); Suspène *et al.* (2023); Butcher and Ponting (2014). Note the increased awareness of the difficulties in sourcing silver by metallurgical analysis, owing to the addition of lead and copper (and their associated impurities) during silver refining and debasement, and by ancient recycling of coinage: Wood, Ponting, and Butcher (2023).

[46] Voß 2013.

[47] Baltic: Zapolska and Dymowski (2021); north-western Russia: Myzgin (this volume, chapter 8, on the Koporje hoard); Saharan and sub-Saharan Africa: see above, p. 8.

[48] *N.H.* 12.84.

[49] Guo (2021a).

[50] Woytek (this volume, chapter 14).

[51] Wilson (2015).

The situation is more complicated for exports northwards. We have juxtaposed the chapter by Wigg-Wolf (chapter 7), who emphasizes the most current view of the dominance of diplomatic payments there, with that by Chameroy and Guihard (chapter 6), who see a greater role for trade. We have also included a later perspective in the form of Jankowiak's treatment of the Viking-age export of Islamic dirhams to the north (chapter 12), where the dominance of trade, principally in slaves and furs, is seen as relatively unproblematic. There is not a simple dichotomy between the two explanations, as the payment of 'subsidies' may itself have promoted trade.

We echo Aleksander Bursche's call, endorsed here by Woytek, for the need to unpack the use of the term 'subsidies' as shorthand for a variety of mechanisms, including army pay for soldiers from beyond the frontiers fighting in Roman auxiliary forces, single and periodic payments to peoples across the borders, the ransoming of captives, the *annonae foederaticae* of Late Antiquity, and diplomatic gifts.[52] We also need to reckon with booty. Perhaps the best-documented example is the outflow of Roman coin in gold, silver, and bronze associated with incursions by the Goths into the Empire, and in particular with their victory over the army of Trajan Decius at Abritus in AD 251, which seems to have resulted in the loss of the imperial treasury.[53]

The integration of a vast mass of Roman coin hoard data for central and eastern Europe, provided by many contributors, into a single database, and the ability to map it comprehensively offer new perspectives on the scale, and perhaps even the motivation, for the export of Roman coins across the northern frontiers of the Roman Empire (Fig. 1.3).[54] What is striking is not only the geographical extent of the phenomenon but also the superficial similarity between the density and overall pattern of distribution between Roman coins in central and eastern Europe and early Islamic dirhams in the same region. Particularly notable are the concentrations in both periods on the Baltic islands of Gotland, Öland, and Bornholm. Marek Jankoviak has proposed a model of 'dirhams for slaves' to explain the high quantities of silver coinage in ninth-century central and eastern Europe, as the result of a slave trade from the north towards the Byzantine and particularly early Islamic world.[55] James Howard-Johnston, in response, proposed an alternative: 'dirhams for furs'.[56] Might a similar explanation work for the Roman period—are some of the Roman silver, and gold, coins in hoards across Europe to the north and east of the Roman frontier the result of trade, whether for slaves or furs or both? Or is there a two-stage process at work, only the second part of which accounts

[52] Bursche (1996: 101–23).
[53] Bursche and Myzgin (2020); Myzgin (this volume, chapter 8).
[54] See also the Antike Fundmünzen in Europa project: http://afe.dainst.org/ (accessed 9 February 2024).
[55] Jankowiak (2016); Gruszczyński, Jankowiak, and Shepard (2020); and Jankowiak (this volume, chapter 12).
[56] Howard-Johnston (2020).

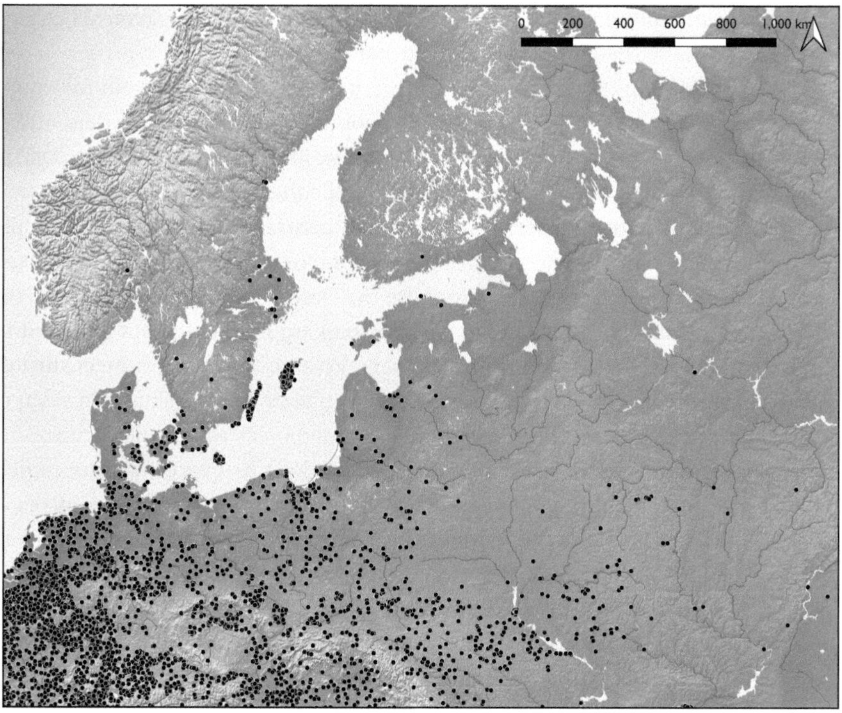

Fig. 1.3. Distribution of all hoards found in the Baltic region and northern eastern Europe (30 BC–AD 518), and entered into the Coin Hoards of the Roman Empire Project database, as at 5 March 2025, for comparison Fig. 12.5. Map: A. Wilson/Coin Hoards of the Roman Empire Project.

for the similarities in the dense concentrations on the islands off Scandinavia, while the first may differ between periods? Specifically, was the export of large quantities of coin to mainland central Europe from the Roman Empire on the one hand, and from the early Islamic world on the other, perhaps driven by different factors, but the arrival of coin on Gotland, Öland, and Bornholm a result of a long-continued practice of the islanders raiding the mainland of what is now Germany and Poland, perhaps, for example, to amass wealth for dowries?[57]

The overall drain of Roman gold coin to the north, by whatever mechanism, seems to have been significant. Production, as measured by the numbers of obverse dies used each year, did not fall between the second and third centuries AD, whereas finds of gold coin within the Empire fall sharply, at least for *aurei* produced within the Central Empire. Drain to the north is likely to be one of the

[57] For the importance of dowries on early medieval Gotland, see Jankowiak (this volume, chapter 12).

explanations.[58] In the first half of the fifth century, substantial payments of gold were also made to the Huns.[59]

When considering the reasons for export, it is important to bear in mind that one cannot assume that Roman coin invariably reached the places where it was deposited directly from the Empire. For example, Myzgin argues that the Roman *denarii* found within the Chernyakhiv culture of eastern Europe (associated with the Goths) in the third century derived from central Europe, where they had arrived earlier, probably as a result of the Marcomannic wars under Marcus Aurelius. Similarly, the majority of finds on the Danish island of Bornholm in the Baltic are of second-century *denarii*, but Horsnæs argues that the main influx was derived from the Vistula estuary in northern Poland, and came only in the late fifth or early sixth century.[60] The *denarii* seem to have arrived with gold *solidi* of that date, with which they were sometimes hoarded.

There were both push and pull factors involved in the export of coin: motivations for exporters to choose to export coin in the first place and for recipients to want coin, and choices to be made about what coin to take and what coin to accept. An advantage of the holistic approach adopted here is to expose the significance of monetary reform within the Empire for these processes. It is surely no coincidence that the debasement of the *denarius* down to 80% fine in AD 64 (combined with a weight reduction from 84 to 96 to the pound) influenced the outflow of Roman silver to India, and that its debasement down to 50% or 45% in AD 194 influenced the outflow to the north.[61] In both cases it has been argued that the recipients wanted the earlier, finer coin, and continued to accept them after the debasements, while not accepting the more debased later coins.[62] The 'push' factor may have been there too, if the earlier, finer coins became undervalued after the debasements (i.e. the silver in them was worth more than a *denarius*), so that it was profitable for merchants to select these for export to places where the silver content rather than the face value mattered. Wolters has made the plausible suggestion that some such thing had happened earlier, arguing that the debasement of Mark Antony's legionary *denarii* down to *c.* 83% led the Germani next to the Roman Empire to prefer old, fine Republican *denarii* (*serrati* and *bigati*).[63] The tendency for recipients to prefer particular, trusted types of coin may be traced later too. A preference for the Gaius and Lucius *denarii* of Augustus and the PONTIF MAXIM *denarii* of Tiberius is obvious in India, and the contents of the early Nedumkandam hoard suggests the avoidance of the debased legionary *denarii* of Mark Antony.[64] Gaius and Lucius *denarii* were

58 Bland (2013). 59 Guest (2008). 60 Horsnæs (2013: 94–5).
61 As argued by Howgego (1995: 104–5).
62 India: MacDowall (1991); Burnett (1998: 181–2; 184–5). North: the careful chronological analysis by Chameroy and Guihard (this volume, chapter 6) is decisive.
63 Wolters (2021), cited by Woytek (this volume, chapter 14).
64 Smagur (this volume, chapter 11).

popular in ancient Armenia and Caucasian Iberia too, and their later scarcity led to the production of imitations of them in Iberia in the first half of the third century.[65]

USE

It is, of course, abundantly clear that the exported coinage was put to many different uses, which varied according to the many cultural contexts covered by this book. Reading Myzgin's chapter (chapter 8), one cannot help but be struck by the sheer complexity of ethnocultural processes in eastern Europe alone. That complexity is multiplied across the full reach of Roman material culture. Nonetheless, common themes emerge.

In default of documentary evidence, coin use is best investigated through combining considerations of hoard evidence and single finds. The scale of the combined task is not to be underestimated, but the recent book by Hellings attempts this for the north-west.[66] Hellings investigates the close relationship between military and civilian populations within the Empire that was wholly dependent upon 'state' administrative and monetary policy and Empire-wide events. This, in turn, had ramifications beyond the Empire, where an intimate connection can be observed through coin finds.

There can be no doubt that inclusion within the Roman Empire affected the nature of coin use, although distinctions are not hard and fast. The Roman way of using coin to some extent spread to the north-west prior to formal incorporation into the Empire, a sequence suggestive of the role of Roman merchants in advance of provincialization.[67] Equally, coin use might change or disappear altogether following the departure of Rome: witness the radical diminution of coin over a generation or two following the abandonment of Britain or of northern Gaul.[68] It is reasonable to conclude that the use of small change, at least, was largely characteristic of the Empire. Thus, the decline in coin use in northern Gaul between AD 390 and 450 is probably to be linked with the abandonment of military camps along the *limes* and the withdrawal of Roman troops. There is no sign of late imitations to fill gaps in supply, and no bronze coins were produced by the rulers who took over from the Romans, suggesting that small change was no longer needed.[69]

Dacia also makes an interesting test case: during the course of the imperial period, it began outside the Roman Empire, was conquered and became a province

[65] Kéfélian (this volume, chapter 10).
[66] Hellings (2025); see also Hellings (2020).
[67] Howgego (2013).
[68] North Gaul: van Heesch (2022).
[69] van Heesch (2022: 302–3, 307).

(and subsequently provinces), was abandoned, and then partially reoccupied.[70] In the imperial period prior to the Roman conquest in AD 106, Republican and imperial silver *denarii* dominated the finds. After conquest, we find the introduction of the signature Roman trimetallic system of gold, silver, and bronze, mostly hoarded separately, with a few mixed hoards. Following the Roman withdrawal from *c.* AD 270 to 300, there were few hoards of any kind in the area abandoned.[71] After the reconquest of the southern regions under Constantine I, the difference between the areas under Roman control and those with Germanic incomers in the fourth and fifth centuries may be characterized as 'gold and silver for the incomers, bronze [mostly *nummi*] and old coins for the locals'.[72] Again, it is clear from the entire history that inclusion within the Empire affected coin use, and, in particular, that small change was characteristic of the period of Roman control.

The degree to which the use of small change extended beyond frontiers will have varied by region and over time, according to local circumstances. In default of documentary sources, careful analysis of site finds is likely to offer the best approach to this question. Detailed mapping of Augustan *aes* coinage and its imitations throughout the Roman continental north-west shows how it spilled out across the frontier.[73] Exemplary here is Fleur Kemmers' study of the Lower Rhine region.[74] Perhaps surprisingly, she was able to show that the native settlements outside the Empire to the north of the frontier initially had greater access to coinage from the Roman auxiliary forts on the Rhine than did the native settlements within the Empire to the south. This remained true until the establishment of Germania Inferior as a province in its own right, with clearly defined borders, in the Flavian period. This is a subject which will clearly need to be explored on a local basis, where the find evidence is available to do so, and in the light of the evolving nature of frontiers.

Beyond the border regions, the proportion of bronze coinage was generally low to the west and the north, decreasing with distance from the Empire.[75] The formerly Hellenistic east beyond the frontiers behaved rather differently, as some areas already had a long tradition of coinage, including bronze, and continued to use Parthian and, later, Sasanian coinages, both of which again included base metal denominations.[76] The situation is complicated by multiple episodes of Roman influence or expansion. At any rate, Roman provincial bronze coin, especially Antiochene SC bronzes, was exported into some adjacent regions, and—to judge from circulation, countermarking, and imitation—also used there. Such regions include Armenia and northern Mesopotamia.[77] In Colchis, by contrast, Roman bronze, consisting of provincial issues and later *nummi*, seems to have

[70] Găzdac (2022; 2023). [71] Găzdac (2023: 233–5 with fig. 12).
[72] Găzdac (2023: 234 with fig. 13). [73] Hellings (2020). [74] Kemmers (2008).
[75] Horsnæs (2013: 73); Hedeager (1978). [76] Sinisi (2018); Schindel (2018).
[77] Kéfélian (this volume, chapter 10); Spoerri Butcher (chapter 9); Butcher (2017).

been confined to the Roman forts on the coast, although provincial silver produced in Caesarea in Cappadocia and Severan *denarii* did penetrate into the hinterland.[78]

The long-distance export of Roman base metal currency in quantity was exceptional. Two instances stand out: Roman brass coinage from the first to third centuries is found on the Baltic coast, especially in the West Balt region, where *sestertii* are the dominant denomination encountered in hoards and graves.[79] In addition to ceremonial use, there is evidence for the melting of brass to make jewellery and other elements of attire. One suspects that merchants exploited an opportunity to take Roman brass coin to a region where it would be valued more highly, perhaps because of its colour, in the context of the trade in amber from the Baltic to the Roman world.[80] The other instance is the substantial influx of late Roman bronze into Sri Lanka *c.* AD 425 to 450, perhaps via south India.[81] This may be a case of the profitable export of junk coinage for use elsewhere. In Sri Lanka itself the Roman coins seem to have played a limited economic role with a religious component, and some need for coinage there is also implied by the striking of imitations in the extreme south of the island.

In relation to precious metal coinage, to the north of the Empire there is a debate to be had about use, again exemplified by the chapters by Wigg-Wolf on the one hand and Chameroy and Guihard on the other. Wigg-Wolf argues for what has now become almost the orthodox view that, except in the vicinity of the *limes*, coinage functioned as special-purpose or social money. He also emphasizes the role of silver *denarii*, in particular, as a store of wealth. The case that coinage in the north served special purposes in a prestige economy, and circulated as means of payment in socially or politically motivated transactions, has been set out clearly by Bursche, drawing on anthropological theories regarding non-market economies.[82] By contrast, Chameroy and Guihard view the hoarding practice to the north of the Empire as proof that silver coins had economic value, alongside social, political, and religious functions. They argue that 'the Germans had an economic use and conception of the Roman silver coins through the influence of Roman habitus, even if their use of small change was more limited than in the Empire'. The paucity of base metal 'small change' certainly does not rule out a monetary or economic function of some kind, as is evident from the monetary economies based solely on silver coinage prevalent for considerable periods in the Middle Ages. The comments by Jankowiak here may be relevant, despite the fact that they relate to a later period. He argues that use of silver in northern Europe in the ninth and tenth centuries AD became increasingly diversified and that it is

[78] Spoerri Butcher (this volume, chapter 9).
[79] Zapolska (2013); Zapolska and Dymowski (2021).
[80] Amber routes: Horsnæs (2010: 183–5).
[81] Burnett (1998: 185–6); Walburg (2008); Darley (2015).
[82] Bursche (2008).

not necessary to draw a sharp distinction between 'monetary' and 'non-monetary' uses. Bursche himself allowed that within centres of trade and power, or early 'ports of trade', *denarii* may have played an economic role as means of exchange.[83]

There is no doubt that *denarii* 'circulated' in the vast area between the Danube and Scandinavia and between the Rhine and the Black Sea. Although interregional circulation is difficult to prove from finds of centrally produced official Roman *denarii*, the movement of locally produced *denarius* imitations circulating alongside them acts like a tracer dye.[84] *Denarii* might be subject to considerable intermixing, and the coins themselves might be intensively used. Such circulation might have been social (as in gift exchange) or economic, or, as may well be the case, a combination of both, but the weight of new evidence increasingly supports the idea that there was at least 'something like a monetary circulation'.[85] We note in this context the striking observation by Jankowiak in relation to Islamic dirhams that imitations were mostly made at the two main markets where Scandinavian and Muslim merchants met to trade.

On the other hand, it seems that the *aurei* captured by the Goths after the Battle of Abritus were treated in a more symbolic way, as the majority were pierced, mostly above the image of the emperor's head.[86] There is, indeed, no doubt that in some contexts coinage beyond the frontiers was treated in a non-monetary way, sometimes being holed, fitted with a loop or mount, otherwise turned into jewellery, or ritually cut or damaged.[87] Of course, such treatments reflect only one aspect of the life history of the coins concerned and they do not *necessarily* mean that such coins, or indeed other coins, had no monetary role beforehand.

Turning towards the east, we should like to know more about how the Roman monetary system interacted with the Parthian and Sasanian systems.[88] One has the impression that the frontier was, for the most part, permeable to coinage in one direction only. Little Parthian or Sasanian coinage was hoarded within the Roman Empire. On the other hand, there are mixed hoards of Roman and Parthian silver from Armenia and Mesopotamia.[89] Such mixing may be suggestive of monetary use, although it might also be interpreted as a way to store silver of whatever kind. A hoard from the Kingdom of Albania (in Azerbaijan) even mixes earlier Roman *denarii* and Parthian drachms with Sasanian drachms from the last quarter of the third century.[90] There are hints that Late Roman *nummi* and Sasanian bronzes could have belonged to the same circulation pool, as suggested by a late fourth-/early fifth-century hoard from Kish (in Iraq).[91]

[83] Bursche (2008: 398). [84] Stribrny (2003); Dymowski (2019).
[85] Dymowski (2019: 163). [86] Myzgin (this volume, chapter 8); Bursche and Myzgin (2020).
[87] Including Denmark: Horsnæs and Nielsen (this volume, chapter 5).
[88] Sinisi (2018); Schindel (2018).
[89] Kéfélian (this volume, chapter 10); Spoerri Butcher (chapter 9).
[90] Chukhur Gabala: CHRE 4008. [91] Milne (1934).

There are also mixed hoards in India, with *denarii* alongside Indian punch-marked silver. Local imitation *denarii* account for 13% of the contents of hoards there and were hoarded alongside Roman *denarii*. Coins were also counter-marked. All this suggests some kind of monetary function within India. On the other hand, it is abundantly clear that the uses of coin again extended beyond the monetary. Double piercings or loops show that coins might be used as ornaments or amulets. In sum, it is striking that many of the phenomena seen to the north of the Roman Empire are also seen in India, with variations, although that does not automatically mean that they are to be interpreted in the same way.

DEPOSITION

Intellectual trends in the interpretation of reasons for the deposition of hoards have, to some extent, been shared by studies within and beyond the frontiers. So, to promote discussion, we have included three important chapters on deposition within the Empire, all of which bring to bear contextual evidence which can act as a control on *a priori* interpretation. The extent of ritual deposition, where there was no intent to recover, has been a major topic of debate. This question lay behind a recent major reassessment of hoarding in Britain, where the discovery of the Frome hoard re-energized an approach which had originated in the late 1980s.[92] To broaden this debate, we elicited the chapter by Vincent Drost and Ludovic Trommenschlager (chapter 2) on how the topic of ritual deposition might be approached from a Continental perspective. Their carefully considered criteria for how to recognize a ritual deposit and their taxonomy of such deposits in a Gallo-Roman context are of wider relevance. The chapter by Donald Ariel on hoards from shipwrecks along the eastern Mediterranean coast (chapter 3) not only shows how such evidence may be brought to bear on patterns of trade but also reminds us that not all deposition is deliberate. Finally, there has been an awareness that monetary reform and coinage withdrawal may lie behind some major late third-century hoards in Britain and elsewhere (including, indeed, the Frome hoard, which renewed the debate about ritual deposition).[93] This subject could benefit from greater awareness of the extraordinary hoard context revealed by the excavations at Karanis.[94] Egypt underwent a major coinage reform under Diocletian, which ended the closed currency system there and replaced the earlier tetradrachm coinage with imperial currency. It has been suggested that the demonetization of the old coinage may have been one cause for a revolt there. Irene Soto Marín argues here that the building complex in which the majority of

[92] Moorhead, Booth, and Bland (2010: 36).
[93] Bland (2018: 89–96); Bland *et al.* (2020: 314–17; 321).
[94] Soto Marín (this volume, chapter 4); cf. de Callataÿ (2017: 326–7).

the hoards were deposited may have acted as a tax office where people turned in their pre-reform coinage, or it may have been related to slightly later requisitions for metal bullion. It is hard to imagine a more relevant archaeological context for assessing the relationship between monetary reform and hoarding.

A corollary of the rigorous criteria required for the kind of analysis undertaken by Drost and Trommenschlager is that the intention behind the deposit of the majority of individual hoards cannot be categorized at all. An alternative approach is to analyse overall patterns of hoarding. From a diachronic review of hoarding from *c.* 400 BC to AD 1950, François de Callataÿ concluded that 'What emerges . . . is the link between hoarding and general fear, mostly generated by political trouble and civil wars but also including financial violence caused by unfavourable monetary reforms.'[95] He argues that there was a background level of hoarding at all times, but that the chronological pattern which we have (by definition, of hoards that were not recovered in antiquity) is dominated by the requirement for safe-keeping in times of crisis. Recovery was thwarted, typically as a result of the crises themselves. This picture does not deny a place to ritual deposition, but it does imply that it was of secondary importance. The clarity of this analysis is helpful, although at times both economic and ritual motivations may have been at play, and, indeed, some episodes of ritual deposition may themselves have been motivated by crisis. A strong connection between the pattern of coin hoards and crisis in the Roman world is explicit in the title of a recent book: *Group and Individual Tragedies in Roman Europe*.[96] This includes a convincing case made by van Heesch that the concentration of hoards in the north of Gaul *c.* AD 260 is to be connected with invasions from the sea and along rivers.[97] Readers are also referred to Howgego and Wilson's earlier brief discussion of the connection between hoarding patterns and invasion and warfare, where it was also suggested that it is worth considering a relation between episodes of plague and the non-recovery of hoards.[98]

This debate is highly relevant to considerations of deposition beyond the frontiers, where ritual deposition has often been seen as dominant. As Colin Haselgrove observes, 'modern ideas of economic sense and rational behaviour may offer little clue to the motivation behind Iron Age coin deposition.'[99] Progress can be made by setting the numismatic evidence within the theoretical framework of archaeology and material-culture studies,[100] but, of course, it is even more challenging to use the material culture of past societies as evidence for their social practices and traditions where there is no written evidence to provide a control. The call for a 'systematic and objective analysis of the evidence' by Peter Guest, in his important general review of why Roman coin hoards were

[95] de Callataÿ (2017: quotation at 335). [96] Găzdac (2020). [97] van Heesch (2020).
[98] Howgego and Wilson (2022: 8). [99] Haselgrove (2005: 173).
[100] Kemmers and Myrberg (2011).

deposited, applies as much to deposition as part of ritual and ceremonial practices as to any other explanatory model.[101] Archaeological context, associated material, and landscape settings are critical to interpretation. The burial of coins in funerary contexts constitutes a distinct form of ritual deposition, the original meanings of which will have varied by context.[102] To the extent that funerary deposits were intended to provide for the needs of the dead, they may be interpreted as a mirror of the use of coins in life.

As Drost and Trommenschlager argue for Gaul, 'Taking the context into account can sometimes turn an apparently "regular" hoard into a ritual deposit.' No systematic analysis of contexts has been undertaken for the regions beyond the frontiers, such as has recently been attempted for Britain.[103] Beyond the frontiers, probably the best archaeological data for surveying deposition practices is to be found in Denmark, analysed here by Horsnæs and Nielsen (chapter 5). One important observation is that hoards containing *denarii* there may have been deposited considerably later than the date of the latest coin in them, and long after they had ceased to circulate within the Empire. Despite the prevalence of *denarii* struck during the Flavian to Antonine periods, the influx of *denarii* into Denmark took off only in the third century, and in some cases they were not deposited until at least the early sixth century. The careful analysis by Horsnæs and Nielsen shows just how difficult it is to pin down reasons for deposition even with good archaeological evidence. *Denarius* hoards are known from central locations (religious and/or administrative centres), but also from wet areas or territorial borders. In terms of associated objects, *denarii* were on occasion mixed with hacksilver or gold, and in the fifth and sixth centuries it looks as though gold coins, coin imitations, and bracteates shared the same significance. This suggests that such hoards may be interpreted as accumulations of 'value'. Coins were sometimes deposited in purses for personal belongings, presumably in a display of wealth and status. But Horsnæs and Nielsen do not seek to impose an overarching interpretative model, and we salute their caution.

In India, as Smagur argues, regional variation is apparent, and ritual and economic rationalities were sometimes intertwined. For example, she observes that while there is evidence for the use of individual Roman coins as ritual offerings in monastic compounds, those offerings were intended for subsequent reuse. An *aureus* from the excavations of a stupa, a Buddhist dome-shaped structure usually containing relics, is pretty obviously a ritual deposit, but the single example suggests that the practice of depositing coins in stupas was less common than in the Kushan realms. Then again, only one hoard has been recovered during excavations of an ancient Indian settlement (in one of the residential buildings

[101] Guest (2015).

[102] See, for example, Fabian (2019: 49–51) on the use of coins in mortuary practice in Caucasian Iberia.

[103] Bland *et al.* (2020).

outside the citadel). Archaeological evidence is sparse. Association of Roman coins with Indian punch-marked coins suggests a monetary context, but association with jewellery is more indicative of personal valuables. Here, as elsewhere, we need to remain alert to complexity.

QUANTIFICATION?

Much remains to be done in the recording and analysis of the export of Roman coin beyond the frontiers, but perhaps the greatest need is for a sense of scale. One could begin from the conventionally round and morally loaded numbers for trade with the East given by the Elder Pliny, or from the documentary evidence of the Muziris papyrus, both critiqued here by Woytek, or from the literary sources for the scale of payments to peoples beyond the frontiers. However, greater scope for future progress lies in the material evidence. Relevant here is Jankowiak's chapter (chapter 12), with his estimations of the size of the inflow of Islamic silver to the north. The methodology which he adopts is to estimate the survival rate of the dirham imitations from a die study, to use that as a proxy for the survival rate of all dirhams, and finally to sense-check the results against an estimate of the size of the monetary stock within the Islamic world, again based on die studies. There are many assumptions and approximations involved in these calculations, which are intended to give only a sense of the orders of magnitude.

Further, de Callataÿ has underscored the need to take total population into account when interpreting the significance of hoarding patterns.[104] Again, this is not an easy thing to do, but Jankowiak does attempt to contextualize the number of numismatic finds on Gotland in terms of an estimate of the number of farmsteads there, with which the coin finds were largely associated. This again suggests possible ways forward.

The constraints on the structure and availability of the evidence required for such calculations are demanding, as indeed is the work involved in die studies, although that will be eased in future by the use of AI-based systems.[105] For all the reservations and challenges, methodologies such as these offer hope of progress.

ACKNOWLEDGEMENTS

As always, we are grateful to Baron Lorne Thyssen-Bornemisza, and to the Augustus Foundation, for his support for the Oxford Roman Economy Project since 2010, and for coming up with the idea for the Coin Hoards of the Roman Empire Project and generously supporting it since 2013. The conference in Oxford on 'Crossing Frontiers: the Evidence of

[104] de Callataÿ (2017: 317).

[105] Heinecke *et al.* (2021).

Roman Coin Hoards' was conceived by Chris Howgego, and developed with advice from Aleksander Bursche, Bernhard Woytek, Benjamin Hellings, and Marguerite Spoerri Butcher. Marguerite Spoerri Butcher undertook by far the greatest part of the organization, with good-humoured efficiency. The conference had to be postponed by a year owing to the Covid-19 pandemic, and even at the time of its organization difficult circumstances and uncertainties remained. Andrew Wilson hosted in All Souls College, Oxford, and we are grateful to the staff of the College for ensuring that all ran smoothly. The majority of the work of editing the volume was undertaken by Marguerite Spoerri Butcher and Benjamin Hellings, with support from Chris Howgego and advice and supplementary editing by Andrew Wilson. We thank Robert Bennett for the careful preparation of the indices.

REFERENCES

Abdy, R. (2002). 'A survey of coin finds from the Antonine Wall', *Britannia* 33: 189–217.

Bateson, J. D. (1971). 'The finding of Roman silver coins in the vicinity of the Giant's Causeway', *Ulster Journey of Archaeology* 34: 50–7.

Bateson, J. D. (1976). 'Further finds of Roman material from Ireland', *Proceedings of the Royal Irish Academy: Archaeology, Culture, History, Literature* 76: 171–80.

Bland, R. (2013). 'What happened to gold coinage in the 3rd c. A.D.?', *Journal of Roman Archaeology* 26: 263–80.

Bland, R. (2015). 'Roman contacts with Ireland in the light of the coins from Drumanagh', in R. Bland and D. Calomino (eds), *Studies in Ancient Coinage in Honour of Andrew Burnett*. London, 167–79.

Bland, R. (2018). *Coin Hoards and Hoarding in Roman Britain, AD 43 – c.491*. London.

Bland, R., Chadwick, A., Ghey, E., Haselgrove, C., Mattingly, D. J., Rogers, A., and Taylor, J. (2020). *Iron Age and Roman Coin Hoards in Britain*. Oxford and Philadelphia.

Borell, B. (2021). 'Coins from western lands found in Southeast Asia', in Günther *et al.* (2021), 277–314.

Bowman, A. K. (2006). 'Outposts of empire: Vindolanda, Egypt, and the empire of Rome', *Journal of Roman Archaeology* 19: 75–93.

Burnett, A. (1998). 'Roman coins from India and Sri Lanka', in O. Bopearachchi and D. P. M. Weerakkody (eds), *Origin, Evolution and Circulation of Foreign Coins in the Indian Ocean*. New Delhi, 179–89.

Bursche, A. (1996). *Late Roman-Barbarian Contacts in Central Europe: Numismatic Evidence*. Berlin: Studien zu Fundmünzen der Antike vol. 11.

Bursche, A. (2008). 'Function of Roman coins in Barbaricum of Later Antiquity. An anthropological essay', in Bursche, Ciołek, and Wolters (2008), 395–416.

Bursche, A. R., Ciołek, R., and Wolters, R. (eds) (2008). *Roman Coins outside the Empire. Ways and Phases, Contexts and Functions*. Wetteren and Warsaw.

Bursche, A. and Myzgin, K. (2020). 'The Gothic invasions of the mid-3rd c. A.D. and the Battle of Abritus: coins and archaeology in east-central Barbaricum', *Journal of Roman Archaeology* 33: 195–229.

Butcher, K. (2017). 'From the Achaemenids to the Arsacids', in S. Heidemann and K. Butcher, *Regional History and the Coin Finds from Assur. From the Achaemenids to the Nineteenth Century. Regionale Geschichte und Münzfunde aus Assur. Von der Zeit des Achämeniden bis zum neunzehnten Jahrhundert* (Wissenschaftliche Veröffentlichungen der Deutschen Orient-Gesellschaft 148). Wiesbaden, 7–81.

Butcher, K. and Ponting, M. (2014). *The Metallurgy of Roman Silver Coinage. From the Reform of Nero to the Reform of Trajan*. Cambridge.

Casson, L. (1989). *The Periplus Maris Erythraei: Text with Introduction, Translation, and Commentary*. Princeton.

Charlesworth, M. P. (1949). 'A Roman imperial coin from Nairobi', *Numismatic Chronicle* 6th series 9: 107–10.

Ciołek, R. and Chowaniec, R. (eds) (2021). *Aleksanderia: Studies on Items, Ideas and History Dedicated to Professor Aleksander Bursche on the Occasion of his 65th birthday*. Wiesbaden.

Darley, R. (2015). 'Self, other and the use and appropriation of Late Roman coins in south India and Sri Lanka (4th–7th centuries A.D.)', in H. P. Ray (ed.), *Negotiating Cultural Identity: Landscapes in Early Medieval South Asian History*. London and New Delhi, 60–84.

Darley, R. (2021). 'Byzantine gold coins and peninsular India's Late Antiquity', in Günther *et al.* (2021), 135–70.

de Callataÿ, F. (2017). 'Coin deposits and civil wars in a long-term perspective (*c.*400 BC–1950 AD)', *Numismatic Chronicle* 177: 313–38.

Dowler, A. (2018). 'The interaction of Aksumite and Roman gold coins in South Arabia in the 6th century CE', *Journal of the Oriental Numismatic Society* 233 (Autumn 2018): 5–28.

Dymowski, A. (2019). 'The problem of the presence of Barbarian imitations of Roman denarii in the lands of present-day Poland: An attempt at a balance', *Notae Numismaticae-Zapiski Numizmatyczne* XIV: 149–82.

Dymowski, A. (2021). 'Barbarian copies of Roman imperial denarii', in Ciołek and Chowaniec (2021), 111–16.

Fabian, L. (2019). 'The meanings of coins in the ancient Caucasus', *Historische Anthropologie* 27.1: 32–51.

Freeman-Grenville, G. S. P. (1963). 'Coins from Mogadishu, c. 1300 to c. 1700', *Numismatic Chronicle* 7th series 3: 179–200.

Găzdac, C. (ed.) (2020). *Group and Individual Tragedies in Roman Europe. The Evidence of Hoards, Epigraphic and Literary Sources*. Cluj-Napoca.

Găzdac, C. (2022). 'Coin hoards from Roman Dacia', in J. Mairat, A. I. Wilson, and C. Howgego (eds), *Coin Hoards and Hoarding in the Roman World*. Oxford, 130–96.

Găzdac, C. (2023). 'In-out and near. Patterns of hoarding in pre-, during- and post-Roman Dacia. The benefits of using a large database – Coin Hoards of the Roman Empire project (CHRE)', *Journal of Ancient History and Archaeology* 10.1: 222–36.

González-Ruibal, A., Torres, J. de, Martínez Barrio, C., Franco Fernández, M. A., Fernández Fernández, A., Gutiérrez de León Juberías, P., Yravedra Sainz de Los Terreros, J., Gaudiello, M., and Jama, A. D. (2022). 'Nomads trading with empires: intercultural trade in Ancient Somaliland in the first to seventh centuries CE', *American Journal of Archaeology* 126: 103–38.

Graf, D. F. (2017). 'The Silk Road between Syria and China', in Wilson and Bowman (2017), 443–530.

Green, G. A. (2020). *Gold Coinage in the Roman World: Function and Production.* PhD thesis, University of Warwick.

Gruszczyński, J., Jankowiak, M., and Shepard, J. (eds) (2020). *Viking-Age Trade: Silver, Slaves and Gotland* (Routledge Archaeologies of the Viking World). London.

Guest, P. (2008). 'Roman gold and Hun kings: the use and hoarding of solidi in the late fourth and fifth centuries', in Bursche, Ciołek, and Wolters (2008), 295–307.

Guest, P. (2015). 'The burial, loss and recovery of Roman coin hoards in Britain and beyond: past, present and future', in J. Naylor and R. Bland (eds), *Hoarding and the Deposition of Metalwork from the Bronze Age to the 20th Century: a British Perspective* (BAR British Series 615). Oxford, 101–16.

Günther, S., Qiang, L., Ying, L., and Sode, C. (eds) (2021). *Byzantine Gold Coins in the World of Late Antiquity. Papers Read at the International Conference in Changchun, China, 23–26 June 2017*, Supplement to Journal of Ancient Civilizations 8. Changchun.

Guo, Y. (2021a). 'Classification of Byzantine gold coins and imitations found in China', in Günther *et al.* (2021), 207–40.

Guo, Y. (2021b). 'Features of coins and bracteates from the Shoroon Bumbagar Tomb in Mongolia', in Günther *et al.* (2021), 259–76.

Hanson, W. S. (2020). 'Roman relations with Ireland: a Scottish perspective', *Scottish Archaeological Journal* 42.1: 91–106.

Haselgrove, C. (2005). 'A new approach to analysing the circulation of Iron Age coinage', *Numismatic Chronicle* 165: 129–74.

Hedeager, L. (1978). 'A quantitative analysis of Roman imports in Europe north of the limes (0–400 AD), and the question of Roman-Germanic exchange', in K. Kristiansen and C. Paludan-Müller (eds), *New Directions in Scandinavian Archaeology.* Copenhagen, 191–216.

Heinecke, A., Mayer, E., Natarajan, A., and Jung, Y. (2021). 'Unsupervised statistical learning for die analysis in ancient numismatics', https://arxiv.org/abs/2112.00290 (accessed 7 December 2022).

Hellings, B. D. R. (2020). 'Further considerations on the circulation of Augustan bronze coins in the Roman northwest', in Stroobants and Lauwers (2020), 203–22.

Hellings, B. D. R. (2025). *Coin Finds and Monetization in the Roman Northwest.* New York.

Hobbs R. (1995). 'Roman Coins from Merv, Turkmenistan', *Oxford Journal of Archaeology* 14.1: 97–102.

Horden, P. and Purcell, N. (2000). *The Corrupting Sea: A Study of Mediterranean History*. Oxford.

Horsnæs, H. W. (2010). *Crossing Boundaries: An Analysis of Roman Coins in Danish Contexts.* Vol. 1: *Finds from Sealand, Funen and Jutland* (Publications of the National Museum, Studies in Archaeology and History 18). Copenhagen.

Horsnæs, H. W. (2013). *Crossing Boundaries: An Analysis of Roman Coins in Danish Contexts.* Vol. 2: *Finds from Bornholm* (Publications of the National Museum, Studies in Archaeology and History 18). Copenhagen.

Howard-Johnston, J. (2020). 'The fur trade in the early Middle Ages', in J. Gruszczyński, M. Jankowiak, and J. Shepard (eds), *Viking-Age Trade: Silver, Slaves and Gotland* (Routledge Archaeologies of the Viking World). London, 57–74.

Howgego, C. (1995). *Ancient History from Coins.* London.

Howgego, C. (2013). 'The monetization of temperate Europe', *Journal of Roman Studies* 103: 16–45.

Howgego, C. (2025). 'Coin Hoards of the Roman Empire: the shape of the evidence', in O. Tekin and R. Boyraz Seyhan (eds), *Proceedings of the Third International Congress on the History of Money and Numismatics in the Mediterranean World (April 1–4, 2024 – Antalya).* Istanbul, 49–72.

Howgego, C. and Wilson, A. (2022). 'Introduction: Coin hoards and hoarding in the Roman world', in Mairat, Wilson, and Howgego (2022), 3–22.

Hoyer, B. (2018). 'An overview of the numismatic evidence from imperial Roman Africa', http://dlib.nyu.edu/awdl/isaw/isaw-papers/13/ (accessed 7 March 2024).

Hunter, F. (2007). 'Silver for the barbarians: interpreting denarii hoards in north Britain and beyond', in R. Hingley and S. Willis (eds), *Roman Finds: Context and Theory. Proceedings of a Conference held at the University of Durham.* Oxford, 214–24.

Hunter, F. (2009). 'Denarius hoards beyond the frontier. A Scottish case study', in A. Morillo, N. Hanel, and E. Martín (eds), *Limes XX: XX congreso internacional de estudios sobre la frontera romana.* Madrid, 1619–30.

Hunter, F. and Painter, K. S. (eds) (2013). *Late Roman Silver: The Traprain Treasure in Context.* Edinburgh.

Jankowiak, M. (2016). 'Byzantine coins in Viking-Age northern lands', in F. Androshchuk, J. Shepard, and M. White (eds), *Byzantium and the Viking World.* Uppsala, 117–39.

Kemmers, F. (2008). 'Interaction or indifference? The Roman coin finds from the Lower Rhine delta', in Bursche, Ciołek, and Wolters (2008), 93–103.

Kemmers, F. and Myrberg, N. (2011). 'Re-thinking numismatics. The archaeology of coins', *Archaeological Dialogues* 18.1: 87–108.

Leitch, V., Duckworth, C., Cuénod, A., Mattingly, D., Sterry, M., and Cole, F. (2017). 'Early Saharan trade: The inorganic evidence', in Mattingly *et al.* (2017b), 393–413.

Lind, L. (1981). *Roman Denarii found in Sweden: 2, Catalogue. Text* (Stockholm Studies in Classical Archaeology 11.2). Stockholm.

MacDowall, D. W. (1991). 'Indian imports of Roman silver coinage', in A. K. Jha (ed.), *Coinage, Trade and Economy: January 8th–11th, 1991, 3rd International Colloquium*. Bombay, 145–63.

Magnavita, S. (2017). 'Track and trace. Archaeometric approaches to the study of early trans-Saharan trade', in Mattingly *et al.* (2017b), 393–413.

Mairat, J., Wilson, A. I., and Howgego, C. (eds) (2022). *Coin Hoards and Hoarding in the Roman World*. Oxford.

Mattingly, D. J. (ed.) (2007). *The Archaeology of Fazzan*. Volume 2, *Site Gazetteer, Pottery and other Survey Finds*. London.

Mattingly, D. J. (2017a). 'The Garamantes and the origins of Saharan trade. State of the field and future agendas', in Mattingly *et al.* (2017b), 1–52.

Mattingly, D. J., Leitch, V., Duckworth, C. N., Cuénod, A., Sterry, M., and Cole, F. (eds) (2017b). *Trade in the Ancient Sahara and Beyond*. Cambridge.

Mattingly, D. J., Leitch, V., Duckworth, C. N., Cuénod, A., and Sterry, M. (2017c). 'Concluding discussion', in Mattingly *et al.* (2017b), 433–40.

Mattingly, H. (1932). 'Coins from a site-find in British East Africa', *Numismatic Chronicle* 5th series 12: 175.

Milne, J. G. (1934). 'Late Roman coins from Mesopotamia', *Numismatic Chronicle* 14: 132–4.

Moorhead, S., Booth, A., and Bland, R. (2010). *The Frome Hoard*. London.

Munro-Hay, S. (1989). 'The al-Madhāriba Hoard of gold Aksumite and Late Roman coins', *Numismatic Chronicle* 149: 83–100.

Nizolek, A. (2015). *Coin Circulation in Roman North Africa: An Examination of Coin Hoards*. MStud thesis, University of Oxford, https://chre.ashmus.ox.ac.uk/reference/1614.

Robertson, A. S. (1975). 'The Romans in North Britain: the coin evidence', *Aufstieg und Niedergang der Römischen Welt* II 3: 364–426.

Robertson, A. S. (1978). 'The circulation of coins in North Britain: the evidence of hoards and site-finds from Scotland', in R. A. G. Carson and C. M. Kraay (eds), *Scripta Nummaria Romana. Essays Presented to Humphrey Sutherland*. London, 186–216.

Sauer, E. (2007). 'The coins', in Mattingly (2007), 463–4.

Schindel, N. (2018). 'Sasanian mints – where and why?', in Woytek (2018), 497–517.

Sinisi, F. (2018). 'Some remarks on the patterns of coin production in the Parthian Empire', in Woytek (2018), 473–96.

Stribrny, K. (2003). *Funktionsanalyse barbarisierter, barbarischer Denare mittels numismatischer und metallurgischer Methoden. Zur Erforschung der sarmatisch-germanischen Kontakte im 3. Jahrhundert n. Chr.* (Studien zu Fundmünzen der Antike 18). Mainz am Rhein.

Stroobants, F. and Lauwers, C. (2020). *Detur dignissimo. Studies in Honour of Johan van Heesch*. Brussels.

Suspène, A., Blet-Lemarquand, M., Duyrat, F., and Nieto-Pelletier, S. (eds) (2023). *AVREVS. Le Pouvoir de l'or/The Power of Gold*. Bordeaux.

van Heesch, J. (2020). 'Coin hoards as evidence of tragedies. Some general remarks on the north of Gaul (3rd century AD)', in Găzdac (2020), 263–75.

van Heesch, J. (2022). 'The end of the small change economy in Northern Gaul in the fourth and fifth Centuries AD', in Mairat, Wilson, and Howgego (2022), 294–312.

Voß, H. U. (2013). 'Roman silver in "Free Germany": Hacksilber in context', in Hunter and Painter 2013: 305–19.

Walburg, R. (2008). 'Rome beyond its eastern frontiers: "Chicken feed copper" in ancient Śrī Laṅkā. The impact of a foreign currency on the local economy', in Bursche, Ciołek, and Wolters (2008), 355–62.

Wells, P. S. (ed.) (2013). *Rome beyond its Frontiers: Imports, Attitudes and Practices*. (Journal of Roman Archaeology). Portsmouth, RI.

Wheeler, R. E. M. (1954). *Rome beyond the Imperial Frontiers*. London.

Whittaker, C. R. (2004). *Rome and its Frontiers: The Dynamics of Empire*. London.

Wilson, A. I. (2015). 'Red Sea trade and the state', in F. De Romanis and M. Maiuro (eds), *Across the Ocean: Nine Essays on Indo-Mediterranean Trade*. Leiden and Boston, 13–32.

Wilson, A. I. and Bowman, A. K. (eds) (2017). *Trade, Commerce, and the State in the Roman World*. Oxford.

Wolters, R. (2021). 'The Serrati of Niederlangen and Tacitus' Germania', in Ciołek and Chowaniec (2021), 415–22.

Wood, J. R., Ponting, M., and Butcher, K. (2023). 'Mints not Mines: a macroscale investigation of Roman silver coinage', *Internet Archaeology* 61, https://doi.org/10.11141/ia.61.10.

Woytek, B. (ed.) (2018). *Infrastructure and Distribution in Ancient Economies. Proceedings of a Conference held at the Austrian Academy of Sciences, 28–31 October 2014*. Vienna.

Zapolska, A. (2013). 'The influx of Roman coins to the West Balt Culture environment', *Notae Numismaticae* VIII: 105–16.

Zapolska, A. and Dymowski, A. (2021). 'Roman imperial bronze coins from the 1st–3rd centuries AD on the southern and eastern Baltic coast', in Ciołek and Chowaniec (2021), 429–34.

Chris Howgego, Benjamin D. R. Hellings, Marguerite Spoerri Butcher, and Andrew Wilson, *Introduction: Roman Coins across Frontiers* In: *Roman Coin Hoards Across Frontiers*. Edited by: Benjamin D. R. Hellings, Marguerite Spoerri Butcher, and Chris Howgego, Oxford University Press.
DOI: 10.1093/9780198986478.003.0001

PART I

DEPOSITION WITHIN THE ROMAN EMPIRE: SOME ALTERNATIVE MODELS

2

Identifying Ritual Deposition of Coins: A Gallo-Roman Perspective

Vincent Drost and Ludovic Trommenschlager

INTRODUCTION

As more data is collected through various projects,[1] the more the question why hoards were deposited and never recovered arises. Thorough studies of very large hoards of low-value coins raise even more questions. This is the case, for example, with the recently published Saint-Germain-lès-Arpajon hoard (Essonne), which consists of 34,000 coins dating up to the end of the third century.[2] The similar and even bigger Frome hoard (Somerset), meanwhile, was one of the triggers for a major research programme on ancient coin hoards in Britain.[3] This programme has recently resulted in an extensive publication that offers new perspectives.[4] On the basis of a colossal work of inventory and contextualization, Roger Bland, Adrian Chadwick, Eleanor Ghey, Colin Haselgrove, and David Mattingly explore all the avenues, case by case, to try to explain the multitude of ancient coin hoards in Britannia. They confirm that the military or event-based explanation cannot be generalized and that it only applies to specific cases (the Boudican revolt, for example). On the other hand, economic factors and monetary reforms clearly provoked many waves of burials. The authors also emphasize throughout the book the ritual/sacred character of many—Celtic, but also Roman—hoards not only on religious sites but also regularly in domestic and landscape contexts or in urban and military settlements.

The aim of this chapter is to shed a 'Continental' light on this issue, using Gaul as a case study. The essential question is the following: is it possible to identify the ritual character of a coin deposit and, if so, on what criteria? To answer this

[1] See, for instance, the database of the Coin Hoards of the Roman Empire Project, based at the University of Oxford and the Ashmolean Museum (https://chre.ashmus.ox.ac.uk).

[2] Drost (2020).

[3] 'Crisis or continuity? Hoards and hoarding in Iron Age and Roman Britain', a collaborative project between the British Museum and the University of Leicester, funded by the Arts and Humanities Research Council (AHRC).

[4] Bland *et al.* (2020).

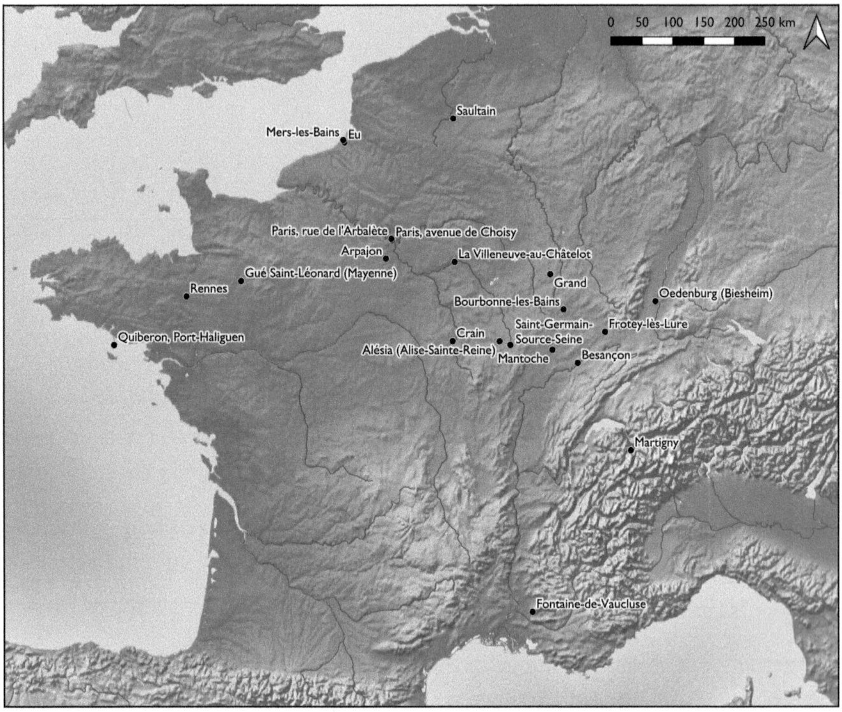

Fig. 2.1. Map of hoards and sites mentioned in the chapter. Map: Andrew Wilson.

question, we will rely on concrete examples from recent publications as well as on the inventory of coin finds that is currently being carried out within the framework of the research programme 'Trouvailles monétaires' managed by the département des Monnaies, médailles et antiques of the Bibliothèque nationale de France (see Fig. 2.1 for the examples cited below).[5]

To date (April 2022), this inventory includes 8,252 hoards and single finds of gold coins from all periods. The dataset is already very complete for antiquity, but it must be conceded that the British data are superior with regards to well-identified context. Of the 3,716 Roman hoards recorded from France, only 871 come from a site with a known or suspected socio-economic function. This is mostly due to the fact that a large proportion of these finds predate the mid-twentieth century. Approximately 40% (348) of these 871 deposits come from identifiable ritual or funerary contexts. Such a proportion must be qualified because it is easier to identify a funerary context, for example, than other types of contexts. Nevertheless, it can be stated that ritual deposit of coins was a relatively common practice in Roman Gaul.

[5] For an introduction to the 'Trouvailles monétaires' research programme, see Drost (2019).

THE RITUAL APPROACH TO COIN HOARDS IN FRANCE

In Britain, the idea that ritual practices play a significant role in hoarding in the Roman period was introduced in the late 1980s and early 1990s.[6] In France, one should mention the pioneering work of Jules Toutain, an archaeologist who was for a long time the director of excavations in Alésia. As early as 1918, he postulated the sacred nature of some Iron Age and Roman coin hoards.[7] The problem is that he had very little information about archaeological contexts to do so, and thus relied on vague indications (in a marsh, on the edge of a lake, under a rock, near a dolmen, in a fountain, at the foot of a tree, in a river, in a tumulus,...) or on the association with other types of objects to suggest the sacred nature of a hoard and often to link it to the cult of water and forest. He systematized the ritual interpretation of coin hoards, as Adrien Blanchet had done previously for the barbarian invasions.[8] Today we know that such systematization should be avoided.

Traditional explanations have long prevailed in France. The ritual nature of some Iron Age hoards has, of course, been recognized, but this is less frequently the case for hoards from the Roman period. In an important paper on ancient coin hoards, Gérard Aubin gives some examples of well-characterized Iron Age and Roman ritual deposits, but does not make a specific category of them.[9] He distinguishes between ritual deposits corresponding to sealed assemblages (funerary deposits, foundation deposits, temple treasures, coins from shrines) or to accumulations (offering boxes, chests and fountains, ford deposits), although he does not push the votive interpretation beyond these explicit cases. Several excellent recent studies have focused on ritual coin deposits, but they only consider places of worship.[10]

The development of 'archéonumismatique' and the consideration of the archaeological context of coin finds have made it possible to increase the number of obvious examples of coins deposited as part of ritual practices on various sites.[11] 'Anthroponumismatique', a term suggested by Jean-Marc Doyen,[12] is a new branch of numismatics. Its aim is to study coins through their precise context in order to trace all behaviours and ritual practices they may have undergone and to suggest a social interpretation (the 'archéologie du geste').[13] Günther Thüry identifies a multitude of coin uses (ritual or otherwise) by illustrating each use with an example from a precise archaeological context. Without going as far

[6] For a summary, see Bland *et al.* (2020: 56). [7] Toutain (1918).
[8] Blanchet (1900). [9] Aubin (2007).
[10] In particular, Popovitch (2012); Izri and Nouvel (2015); Golosetti (2019).
[11] 'Archéonumismatique' refers to an approach, developed since the end of the 1950s, which consists in studying coins in close connection with their archaeological context. See Doyen (2021: 73–6).
[12] Doyen (2021); Doyen (2022).
[13] The expression 'archaeology of gesture' is used by Duchemin (2019) to describe each action in a practice or ritual in relationship with the deposition of coins. We are using the more general term 'practices' here.

interpreting the function of a coin and its use, it is appropriate to interrogate the presence in large numbers of unrecovered ancient coin hoards in Gaul.[14] Ritual deposition is one of the factors of permanent concealment, but in what proportion? The difficulty lies in identifying ritual deposits.[15]

COIN MUTILATIONS AS EVIDENCE OF RITUAL DEPOSITION

Defaced coins that are sometimes found at worship places testify to the ritual nature of deposits. Several groups of notched or hammered coins have been discovered in sanctuaries in Gaul. Among the most spectacular finds are those from La Villeneuve-au-Châtelot, Aube (more than a thousand Iron Age, Republican, and Augustan silver and bronze coins, most of them affected by chisel marks in the form of a cross on the portrait),[16] and Port-Haliguen, Morbihan (450 coins from the same period, almost all hammered or notched).[17] Another example of a smaller-scale, but slightly later, find is the group of 12 bronze coins from Augustus to Claudius found in Alésia (Côte-d'Or), which bore one or more notches on the obverse or reverse.[18] Such practices are generally interpreted as evidence of a will to demonetize the coins and to perpetuate them as offerings.[19] It is generally considered that this practice does not extend beyond the Julio-Claudian period, although it may have occasionally continued slightly later, as shown, for example, by two mutilated coins of Titus and Hadrian found at Grand, Vosges (Fig. 2.2).[20] Such mutilations suggest the ritual nature of these deposits, but they are not necessarily of a religious nature.[21] The methods of mutilation can vary from one region to another, and sometimes even within a single sanctuary. This demonstrates that there was no standardization of this rite in Gaul in the Iron Age and the early Roman Empire.[22]

Fig. 2.2. Notched bronze coins from Grand. Left: as of Titus (10.85 g, 29 mm). Right: as of Hadrian (11.05 g, 26 mm). © L. Trommenschlager.

[14] Thüry (2016).
[15] Bürstrom and Ingvardson (2021) address the question of coin use as part of rites and demonstrate how difficult it is to determine the exact function of coins within the ritual.
[16] Zehnacker, Richard, and Barrandon (1984: 85–7). [17] Giard (1967: 121).
[18] Popovitch (1995). [19] Popovitch (2012: 32). [20] Trommenschlager (2013).
[21] Wigg-Wolf (2021). [22] Wigg-Wolf (2021).

Cutting coins, a practice generally associated with the need for small change, can sometimes also have the objective of 'sacrificing' money. Among the numerous coins discovered at one of the *fana* (i.e. Romano-Celtic temples) of Martigny (Valais, Switzerland), many coins of the early Empire were voluntarily cut into halves, thirds, quarters, or even smaller fractions, while others were hammered.[23] In this case, the quasi-systematic cutting of the coins, sometimes into very small fractions, has been interpreted as a ritual gesture.[24] In a funerary context, coins may also have been sacrificed by fire. This is the case, for example, with the six coins from tomb 10 discovered at the *rue Henri-Barbusse* site in Saultain (Nord).[25] Finally, pierced coins can be linked to ritual deposits in burials or serve as *ex-votos* in sanctuaries, as at La Villeneuve-au-Châtelot (Aube).[26]

However, such practices remain quite uncommon and limited in time. Their absence does not mean, of course, that there was no ritual gesture. Of course, coins may also have been used in sanctuaries for other purposes, such as purchasing offerings, paying for services, or even financing the sanctuary and its priests.[27] It is difficult to determine the original purpose of single finds from sanctuaries from an archaeological perspective. Only the study of the context, combined with the analysis of the composition of an assemblage, can possibly lead to the conclusion that a coin was permanently deposited without any intention of recovery, which is a definition of a ritual deposit.

MIXED ASSEMBLAGES: LONG-TERM OFFERINGS?

Heterogeneous assemblages accumulated over a long period of time through multiple individual behaviours also correspond to the practice of monetary offering. Outside sanctuaries, these accumulations are generally found in watery contexts and are linked to the rite of *iactatio stipis*, which consists of throwing coins as an offering. This is evidenced by important assemblages found on the site of an ancient ford crossing, including, for instance, the tens of thousands of coins discovered in the beds of the River Mayenne in Saint-Léonard (Mayenne) and the River Vilaine in Rennes (Ille-et-Vilaine).[28] Coins from the first century AD are particularly numerous there, partly because of the early occupation of the town and the initial presence of troops.[29] The Bourbonne-les-Bains hoard (Haute-Saône) is an early example of coin depositions in springs. Around 10,000 coins were discovered in the sump of the thermal spring. The 3,701 that have been

[23] Wiblé (1996: 327–30). [24] Wiblé (1996: 330).
[25] Henton (2011: 21) (study of the coins by E. Louis); Henton (2014: 188–91).
[26] Piette and Depeyrot (2008: nos 1350, 1889, 2657, 3926, and 3927). However, Kiernan (2001) considers that piercing coins is not related to a ritual act for the Roman period.
[27] Malrieu (2005); Doyen (2022). [28] Besombes (2005); Besombes and Morin (2007).
[29] Besombes and Morin (2007: 6).

studied include mostly Augustan coins but also Republican *denarii*, Iron Age bronze coins, a number of *quadrantes* and half-*dupondii*, as well as a few gold coins.[30] However, the practice of throwing coins into springs seems to have continued until the fifth century. This is illustrated by the example of the Fontaine-de-Vaucluse spring (Vaucluse), where 1,624 coins from the first to fifth centuries AD were found in the crevices of the rock, along with iron nails, and bronze and silver objects.[31] The ritual nature of such assemblages is obvious, even if it is difficult to distinguish the voluntarily discarded coins from those lost.

In sanctuaries, various structures could be used as offering receptacles. The first type of structure that comes to mind is the offering box (*thesaurus*). Of the rare offering boxes found in Gaul, most were empty. Indeed, many of the coins 'offered' in sanctuaries could be put back into circulation, but only in the context of the sanctuary economy. However, an offering box discovered at Crain (Yonne) still contained 207 coins from Augustus to Commodus (Fig. 2.3).[32] At the Oedenburg sanctuary (Haut-Rhin), the offerings were placed in amphorae. Nine amphora bottoms were found in front of the entrance to a building, which still contained 31 Julio-Claudian coins.[33] When these amphorae were broken, they were replaced, and the coins they contained were recovered. The absence of

Fig. 2.3. View of the fanum of Crain; in the foreground, the upper part of the money box. © Jean-Bernard Devauges, April 1971 (with thanks to Jacques Meissonnier).

[30] Sauer (2005).
[31] For a summary, see Golosetti (2019: 13–14).
[32] Meissonnier (1973).
[33] Popovitch (2011).

coins of the third century onwards in these offering structures is notable. William Van Andringa also notes that in northern Gaul the practice of sacred coin deposits, unknown in Roman religion, tended to fade during the early Empire.[34] Nevertheless, examples of later offerings do exist. A heterogeneous group of 836 coins from Augustus to Maximus was found in a small vase at Saint-Germain-Source-Seine (Côte-d'Or). This small vase was itself placed, along with metallic *ex-votos*, in a larger pot inscribed with a dedication to Sequana and sealed by a lead plate (Fig. 2.4). This assemblage would have consisted of at least four different hoards put together at the end of the fourth century.[35]

The ritual nature of these assemblages from fords, springs, or shrines seems obvious. Their interpretation would probably be quite different if the context did not allow us to associate them with a sacred place. Indeed, without a precise context these coins could then be considered as single finds suggesting intense monetary exchanges, given their number and variety. The composition of these assemblages is indeed closer to groups of single finds than to proper 'hoards' as sealed accumulations with a coherent structure. However, some hoards with a

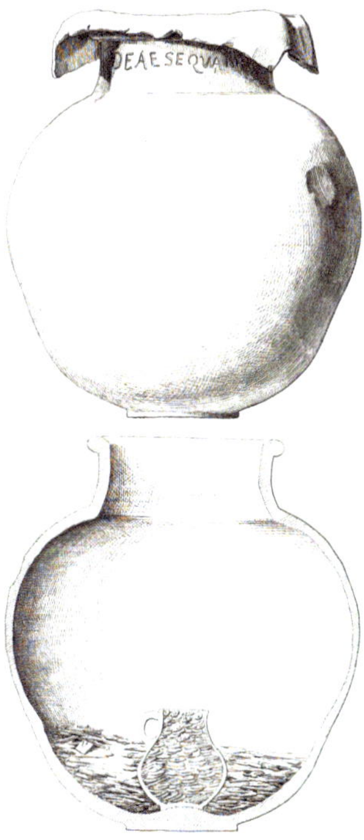

Fig. 2.4. The Saint-Germain-Source-Seine 'hoard'. From Baudot (1842–6), pl. X.

[34] Van Andringa (2017: 135).

[35] Baudot (1842–6); Chauvot (1981).

more classical profile may also have a ritual character. Here again, the context is essential to determine whether this can be the case.

HOMOGENEOUS SEALED ASSEMBLAGES: HOARDING OR RITUAL DEPOSITION?

Although funerary deposits are ritual offerings by nature, their profile can be very similar to what we would expect for traditionally identified safekeeping or emergency hoards. For instance, the hoard from the *avenue de Choisy* in Paris, discovered in a tomb, combines 75 radiates and barbarous radiates of Tetricus I and II, and surgical instruments (Fig. 2.5).[36] Without knowledge of the funerary context and the associated material, nothing would distinguish this group of coins from an ordinary late third-century hoard of radiates. Similarly, the *rue de l'Arbalète* hoard, also in Paris, consists of 307 radiates dated from AD 253 to 270.[37] These coins were placed in a small *ampulla* made of brick-red earth deposited on the side of a skeleton buried in the ground without a coffin. The vessel has no opening and appears to have been fired with the coins inside. Again, the composition of this group of coins is identical to that of usual hoards of the early 270s. The Saintes hoard (Charente-Maritime) in a tomb excavated in 1981 includes 57 barbarous radiates and one official radiate to the period *c.* AD 260–74.[38] Once again, there is nothing to distinguish it from a regular hoard other than its presence in a grave.

The profile of some important foundation deposits is very similar to classical hoards as well. The foundation deposit discovered in Besançon (Doubs), in a pit under the floor of a large room of a presumably public building, is a good example.[39] It consists of eight Augustan *aurei* and four gold rings in a bronze case. Although safekeeping is a possible explanation for this deposit, the context observed by the archaeologist clearly links it to the foundation of the building. Moreover, the difficulty in recovering the coins supports the idea of a foundation deposit. This assemblage is quite similar to the Mers-les-Bains (Somme) hoard consisting of two *aurei*, three gold rings, and four silver spoons, all also contained in a bronze box.[40] However, in the absence of a context, one would tend to consider by default the Mers-les-Bains hoard as family savings.

Taken as a whole, the hoard discovered in 1993 at Frotey-lès-Lure (Haute-Saône), consisting of 27 copper-alloy coins, would fit among a series of hoards buried in Gaul and Germany under the rule of Magnentius, AD 350–3 (Table 2.1).[41] Nevertheless, its context suggests that it is a foundation deposit. The coins were found in a foundation slab that supported a column base. They were thrown in

[36] Hollard (1988). [37] Toulouze (1882). [38] Surmely (1990: 71).
[39] Giard (1992). [40] Broustet and Drost (forthcoming). [41] Mazimann (1995).

Fig. 2.5. Coins and surgical instruments from a tomb, *rue de Choisy*, Paris. © Musée Carnavalet, Patrick Pierrain.

together with nails, ceramics, and animal bones in a gesture of *iactatio* that was supposed to bring prosperity to this rural building. The foundation deposit of Mantoche (Haute-Saône), found in the remaining bottom of a pottery, consists of one radiate and 29 *nummi* up until the monetary reform of AD 318.[42] This profile

[42] Bonvallot and Amandry (2009).

Table 2.1. Composition of the Frotey-lès-Lure hoard (after Mazimann 1995) and other contemporary hoards from Gaul and Germany (after Bastien 1983).

	Frotey-lès-Lure	Soest	Bengel II
First-/second-century bronzes	1	0	2
Third-century radiates	0	0	1
Fourth-century *nummi* (294–348)	16	15	255
Aes 1/2 (348–53)	8	2	10
Illegible coins	2	0	0
Total	27	17	268

is also typical of the many hoards buried in reaction to the reform of AD 318. However, its presence along a wall, under the floor of the room, implies that it would not have been possible to recover it and therefore that it was permanently abandoned. Finally, the hoard found in the Roman theatre of Eu (Seine-Maritime), consisting of 1,616 radiates up to Probus, is a particularly meaningful example of the importance of the context for interpretation.[43] The coins were found at the base of a doorpost inside the theatre itself, opposite the *orchestra*. This assemblage was interpreted by Laurent Cholet, the archaeologist who made the discovery, as a foundation deposit made during a late renovation phase of the theatre. Given the terminal date of the hoard, which coincides with the date of abandonment of the site, Étienne Mantel and Stéphane Dubois suggest instead that it was an offering made as part of a closing ceremony, or even an emergency hoard, which in this case would not have been ritual.[44]

Taking the context into account can sometimes turn an apparently 'regular' hoard into a ritual deposit. What about similar assemblages for which we have no context and which represent the majority of finds? By default, we tend to consider them as temporary deposits intended to be recovered. It should be noted, however, that very large finds such as the Frome or the Saint-Germain-lès-Arpajon hoards would have been very difficult to recover. To do so, it would have been necessary to remove by hand the tens of thousands of small copper-alloy coins placed in bulk in a pot that would break if one tried to lift it. These hoards have sometimes been interpreted as accumulations of discarded coins. Another explanation has been suggested about the Frome hoard, which is considered as a possible permanent ritual deposit.[45] It raises the possibility that these coins may have acquired a sacred value greater than their exchange value, that they became 'money for the gods' permanently deposited as part of ritual practices.[46] To have proof of this, it would ideally be necessary to have a large hoard in which the

[43] Hollard (2000). [44] Mantel and Dubois (2017: 14).
[45] Moorhead (2019: 296–8). [46] Bland *et al.* (2020: 316).

depositor(s) would have placed an explicit votive mention, such as a dedication to a deity. The only case of which we are aware, the hoard of the Saint-Germain-Source-Seine with its dedication to the goddess Sequana, is obviously the result of different offerings that were collected, not a proper hoard. It seems difficult to generalize this type of ritual interpretation and to apply it to 'classical' hoards in the absence of a specific context, associated material, or an obvious act.

CONCLUSION

This chapter has offered several examples to demonstrate that ritual interpretation cannot be excluded *a priori* when it comes to interpreting Roman coin hoards. Similarly, it cannot be favoured on principle either. One must avoid any systematization and, as British scholars have recently suggested, keep an open mind. The interpretation of a hoard must certainly be free of preconceived ideas, but it must be based on tangible elements, such as an analysis of the context of the discovery, and on a comparison with other contemporary deposits. In some cases, it must be admitted that we simply do not know why a hoard was buried and never recovered, and that we may never come to a definitive determination.

REFERENCES

Aubin, G. (2007). 'Les trésors (monétaires) antiques: le mot, les choses et les chercheurs', in F. Baratte, M. Joly, and J.-C. Béal (eds), *Autour du trésor de Mâcon. Luxe et quotidien en Gaule romaine*. Mâcon, 49–73.

Bastien, P. (1983). *Le monnayage de Magnence (350–353)*, 2nd edition. Wetteren.

Baudot, H. (1842–6). 'Rapport sur les découvertes archéologiques faites aux Sources de la Seine', *Mémoires de la Commission des Antiquités du département de la Côte-d'Or* 2: 95–144.

Besombes, P.-A. (2005). *Le dépôt des 22 438 monnaies du gué de Saint-Léonard (Mayenne)* (Trésors monétaires 21). Paris.

Besombes, P.-A. and Morin, É. (2007). 'Le dépôt de la Vilaine à Rennes', *Trésors monétaires* 22: 1–35.

Blanchet, A. (1900). *Les trésors de monnaies romaines et les invasions germaniques en Gaule*. Paris.

Bland, R., Chadwick, A., Ghey, E., Haselgrove, C., and Mattingly, D. J. (2020). *Iron Age and Roman Coin Hoards in Britain*. Oxford and Philadelphia.

Bonvallot, N. and Amandry, M. (2009). 'Un dépôt constantinien découvert à Mantoche (Haute-Saône) en 1993', *Trésors monétaires* 23: 95–9.

Broustet, M. and Drost, V. (forthcoming). 'Le coffret de Mers-les-Bains (Somme)', *Trésors monétaires* 31.

Bürstom, N. M. and Ingvardson, G. T. (2021). *Divina Moneta. Coins in Religion and Ritual*. London and New York, 2021.

Chauvot, A. (1981). *Le trésor monétaire des Sources de la Seine*. Master's degree dissertation, Université de Dijon.

Doyen, J.-M. (2021). *Pour une anthropologie de la monnaie*. Brussels.

Doyen, J.-M. (2022). 'Coins and ancient cult places: from "archaeonumismatics" to "anthroponumismatics"', *Journal of Archaeological Numismatics* 12: 7–43.

Drost, V. (2019), 'Les trésors au Cabinet des médailles et le programme "Trouvailles monétaires"', in 'L'Antiquité à la BnF', 6 August 2019, https://antiquitebnf.hypotheses.org/8256 (accessed 1 October 2022).

Drost, V. (2020). *Le trésor de Saint-Germain-lès-Arpajon (Essonne), un dépôt géant du IIIe siècle après J.-C.* (Trésors Monétaires 29). Paris.

Duchemin, J.-P. (2019). 'Coins in funerary contexts: towards a paradigm shift. Contribution of recent excavations to the redefinition of a concept', in J.-M. Doyen, J.-P. Duchemin, and P. P. Iossif (eds), *Proceedings of the International Conference 'A Coin for the Dead. Coins for the Living. Charon's Obol: The End of a Myth?' (Journal of Archaeological Numismatics* 9). Brussels, 27–44.

Giard, J.-B. (1967). 'Le trésor de Port-Haliguen. Contribution à l'étude du monnayage d'Auguste', *Revue Numismatique* 6.9: 119–39.

Giard, J.-B. (1992). 'Un trésor à Vesontio', in J.-O. Guilhot and C. Goy (eds), *20 000 m^{3} d'histoire. Les fouilles du parking de la mairie à Besançon*. Besançon, 128.

Golosetti, R. (2019). 'La *stips* des Alpes à la Méditerranée: interpréter la présence des monnaies dans les sanctuaires d'époque romaine', Gallia 76.2, http://journals.openedition.org/gallia/5054 (accessed 29 September 2022).

Henton, A. (2011). *Saultain (59), 'Rue H. Barbusse-Le Champ du Pont de Curgies'. Occupations protohistorique et gallo-romaine en bordure d'un ancien talweg*, 1 (Rapport de diagnostic, Service régional de l'archéologie Nord-Pas-de-Calais).

Henton, A. (2014). *Nord-Pas-de-Calais, Saultain, Rue H. Barbusse. Résidence 'Champ du Pont de Curgies'. Une nécropole à hypogées et un atelier de forge gallo-romains*, 1 (Rapport Final d'Opération d'Archéologie Préventive, Service régional de l'archéologie Nord-Pas-de-Calais).

Hollard, D. (1988). 'Le dépôt monétaire de l'avenue de Choisy, à Paris (1880)', *Trésors monétaires* 10: 59–66.

Hollard, D. (2000). 'Le dépôt monétaire du théâtre du sanctuaire gallo-romain d'Eu "Bois-l'Abbé" (Seine-Maritime)', *Trésors monétaires* 19: 33–55.

Izri, S. and Nouvel, P. (2015). 'Les monnaies sur les sanctuaires', in J. Kaurin, S. Marion, and G. Bataille (eds), *Décrire, analyser, interpréter les pratiques de dépôt de l'âge du Fer* (Bibracte 26). Glux-en-Glenne.

Kiernan, P. (2001). 'Ritual mutilation of coins on Romano-British sites', *British Numismatic Journal* 71: 20–4.

Malrieu, A. (2005). 'Le rôle économique des sanctuaires romains : thésaurisation et investissement des fonds sacrés', *Topoi* 12.1: 95–116.

Mantel, É. and Dubois, S. (2017). 'L'agglomération de *Briga* (Eu, Bois-l'Abbé, Seine-Maritime): premières données sur l'occupation durant l'Antiquité tardive', *Gallia* 74.1, http://journals.openedition.org/gallia/2427 (accessed 29 September 2022).

Mazimann, J.-P. (1995). 'Le dépôt de fondation de la villa gallo-romaine de Frotey-lès-Lure (Haute-Saône)', *Bulletin de la Société française de numismatique* 50.4: 1034.

Meissonnier, J. (1973). 'Le fanum de Crain (Yonne): les monnaies', *Revue archéologique de l'Est et du Centre-Est* 24.2: 215–48.

Moorhead, S. (2019). 'The Frome Hoard. How a massive hoard changes everything', in B. Callegher (ed.), *Too Big to Study? Troppo grandi da studiare?* (Polymnia Numismatica Antica e Medievale, Studi 11). Trieste, 281–304.

Piette, J. and Depeyrot, G. (2008). *Les monnaies et les rouelles du sanctuaire de La Villeneuve-au-Châtelot (Aube) (2e s. av. J.-C. – 5e s. ap. J.-C.)* (Moneta 74). Wetteren.

Popovitch, L. (1995). 'Un nouvel ensemble de monnaies romaines entaillées à Alésia (Alise-Sainte-Reine, Côte-d'Or)', *Revue archéologique de l'Est et du Centre-Est* 46: 361–7.

Popovitch, L. (2011). 'Les offrandes monétaires du sanctuaire', in M. Reddé (ed.), *Oedenburg. Fouilles françaises, allemandes et suisses à Biesheim-Kunheim (Haut-Rhin, France)*, 1. *Les camps militaires julio-claudiens*. Mainz.

Popovitch, L. (2012). 'Les offrandes monétaires en Gaule romaine', in O. de Cazanove and P. Méniel (eds), *Étudier les lieux de culte en Gaule romaine, Actes de la table-ronde de Dijon, 18–19 septembre 2009*. Montagnac, 29–36.

Sauer, E. (2005). *Coins, Cult and Cultural Identity: Augustan Coins, Hot Springs and the Early Roman Baths at Bourbonne-les-Bains* (Leicester Archaeology Monographs 10). Leicester.

Surmely, M. (1990). 'Les monnaies antiques de Saintes', *Trésors monétaires* 12: 69–99.

Thüry, G. E. (2016). *Die antike Münze als Fundgegenstand. Kategorien numismatischer Funde und ihre Interpretation*. Oxford.

Toulouze, É. (1882). 'Fouilles dans le Vieux Paris, découverte d'un tribut au nocher du Styx, époque gallo-romaine', *Revue archéologique*, 3rd series, 7.1: 301–2.

Toutain, J. (1918). 'Le caractère sacré de certains trésors de monnaies celtiques et de monnaies romaines', *Pro Alesia* 4: 81–108.

Trommenschlager, L. (2013). 'Les monnaies entaillées de Grand : gestes religieux et/ou politiques', *Bulletin de la Société française de numismatique* 68.4: 69–75.

Van Andringa, W. (2017). *La religion en Gaule romaine. Piété et politique (Ier–IVe siècle apr. J.-C.)*, 2nd edition. Arles.

Wiblé, F. (1996). 'Martigny, lieu-dit "Coin de la Ville"', *Vallesia* 51: 322–30.

Wigg-Wolf, D. (2021). 'Death by deposition?', in N. M. Bürstom and G. T. Ingvardson (eds), *Divina Moneta. Coins in Religion and Ritual*. London and New York, 13–29.

Zehnacker, H., Richard, J.-C., and Barrandon, J.-N. (1984). 'La trouvaille de la Villeneuve-au-Châtelot (Aube)', *Trésors monétaires* 6: 9–92.

Vincent Drost and Ludovic Trommenschlager, *Identifying Ritual Deposition of Coins: A Gallo-Roman Perspective*
In: *Roman Coin Hoards Across Frontiers*. Edited by: Benjamin D. R. Hellings, Marguerite Spoerri Butcher, and Chris Howgego, Oxford University Press. © Oxford University Press 2026. DOI: 10.1093/9780198986478.003.0002

3

Roman Coin Hoards from Shipwrecks along the Eastern Mediterranean Coast

Donald T. Ariel

INTRODUCTION

Thirteen Roman coin hoards deemed to have derived from shipwrecks in the Mediterranean along its eastern littoral are the subject of this chapter. Most were found in the sea, while a few came from its immediate shoreline in places without evidence of ancient occupation and thus are likely to have washed up on shore. These 13 hoards are compared with land-based hoards along the same shoreline. Although some shipwreck hoards included coins attesting to long-distance travel—from Egypt in the south to Greece in the west—most are similar to their terrestrial counterparts.

This study originates from the realization that there is a near dearth of hoards available for study from the important frontier to the east of the southern Levant in general, and east of Israel in particular. I therefore chose to examine what, if anything, can be learned from a different kind of frontier, the sea as a frontier—in this case the Mediterranean Sea as a means of accessing very distant points, both on the frontier of the Roman world and within it. After all, when one boards a ship at its point of origin, or in the middle of its voyage, there are likely to be many points of disembarkation that are both foreign and exotic, and even threatening, just as land frontiers can be. In the Roman period I venture that most maritime travel in the Mediterranean was commercial in nature, and military-oriented seafaring, albeit important, was less prevalent. In the course of Mediterranean sea journeys, even if most ports of call were friendly, frontier regions were often not very far away.

The basis of maritime commercial activity was the exchange of goods. Although money was transported on ships, it is likely that the goods in the ships' holds were the primary bases for exchange en route, and monetary components were secondary. One may ask how sailors or merchantmen, or their fellow travellers, related to the money they encountered at their destination, or on the way to their destination?

Did they hold on to small change for future visits, or keep some coins as keepsakes or mementoes?

In the early imperial period, 38 first-century BC and first-century AD Jerusalem-minted coins arrived at nine sites in Spain.[1] Judaean coins are not attested over most of the long distance from Judaea to Hispania. Therefore, it is most probable that the Jerusalem-minted coins did not travel over land but, rather, on ships. The same is certainly true for Roman coins that arrived in southern India and many other regions.

Shipwreck hoards from the Mediterranean's eastern littoral bring us in contact with Egypt in the south, with the coastline of Anatolia, and almost to the Peloponnese in the west. Their composition has common features with coin hoards from the Black Sea—a distant region accessible to the Mediterranean primarily through seafaring. To my knowledge there is no material evidence in Roman coin hoards found in frontier regions that included coins from as far as the southern Levant—although occasionally Levantine coins are documented as individual finds at sites, as in distant Hispania, just mentioned.[2]

Although the southern Levant is on the eastern periphery of the Empire, its inhabitants consistently looked to the west.[3] Even the land-based hoards and isolated finds in Israel have few connections to the eastern frontier. Despite all of the Nabatean trade on the spice route, no coins from the east (Arabia, India) made their way from there, either on land or in any underwater hoards wrecked along the Levantine coast. At best, shipwreck coin hoards can only attest to the geographical extent of maritime activity/trade inside the Empire, a subject that is broadly covered by written sources.

The shoreline of Israel is 273 km long, very close in length to the shorelines of Lebanon or even Montenegro. Because it was once estimated that 200 shipwrecks covering thousands of years of sailing were known along the Israel coastline,[4] my sense had been that 13 shipwrecks with Roman coin hoards was a small number. In retrospect, however, 13 underwater Roman coin deposits is not small. At the time of writing, the website of the Coin Hoards of the Roman Empire Project (CHRE) attests to 21 Roman coin hoards from shipwrecks from the entire Mediterranean—including nine under consideration here.[5] Four new hoards bring the southern Levant total to 13 (Table 3.1: Hoards 3, 6, 9, and 12).

[1] Zorea (2018).

[2] On file at the Israel Antiquities Authority (IAA) is documentation of coins minted in the southern Levant but provenanced throughout the ancient world, from the British Isles in the west to Tamil Nadu state in southern India. None of these finds is as robust as the coins from Spain.

[3] Against an earlier non-maritime view generated by a focus on the insularity of Judaea, among other reasons, see Kingsley (2004: 23–34).

[4] Galili (1992: 26).

[5] https://chre.ashmus.ox.ac.uk (accessed 7 July 2022).

Table 3.1 Roman coin hoards from shipwrecks along the eastern Mediterranean coast (hoards 1–12) followed by 21 Roman land-based coin hoards (Hoards 13–33) collected for comparison. Summaries of the three late Hellenistic comparanda (Hoards A–C) appear at the bottom of the table. For each hoard, the CHRE or, alternatively, the internal IAA reference (Coin Department Hoard No.) reference is given. Further details on Hoards 5–9, 12, and 13 can be found in the main text, including remarkable mints (cited for Hoards 6, 7 and 8). References including a full catalogue of coins are noted with a superscript, bold letter **c**.

	Sea-based Hoards		
No.	**Hoard**	**Content**	**Reference(s)**
1	Caesarea 1968 (CHRE 9012)	39 *aurei* (38 documented); Augustus (1); Tiberius (5); Claudius (1); Nero (6); Vespasian (6); Titus (2); Domitian (2); Nerva (1); *t.p.q.* Trajan (13)	Kindler (1969)[c]; Warner and Safrai (2001)
2	Caesarea South 1993 B, south anchorage (CHRE 8149)	Unspecified numbers of bronze coins (Tiberius–Trajan)	Galili, Dahari, and Sharvit (1993: 67)
3	Carmel Coast, Assemblage 13 or 14, sector IV (N/A)	'dozens' of *denarii* of Hadrian	Galili and Sharvit (1999: 17*)
4	Carmel Coast, Assemblage 11, sector IV (CHRE 8445)	'hoard' of *denarii*	Galili and Sharvit (1999: 17*)
5	Carmel Coast 1990 A (CHRE 7713)	162 coins (Tiberius–Severus Alexander, possibly two hoards): 68 *denarii*, 9 imperial bronzes, 6 provincial silver coins, 76 provincial bronze coins, and 3 lead *tesserae*; additional remarkable mints: Berytos, Tyre, Yafo, Antipatris, Ascalon, Alexandria	Galili, Dahari, and Sharvit (1993: 69); Meshorer (2010)[c]
6	Caesarea 2020 ('Cloaca') (IAA E.-R. 67)	423 coins (*t.p.q.* Trebonianus Gallus): 81 Syrian tetradrachms, 341 *sestertii*, 1 *antoninianus*	Ariel (in prep.)

(*Continued*)

Table 3.1 (Continued)

	Sea-based Hoards		
No.	**Hoard**	**Content**	**Reference(s)**
7	Carmel Coast 1990 B (CHRE 7665)	75 *nummi* (*t.p.q.* early 320s)	Ariel (2010)[c]; Galili, Dahari, and Sharvit (1993: 72)
8	Caesarea 2016, north entrance to harbour (CHRE 8454)	*c.* 6,874 *nummi* (*t.p.q.* 318)	Sharvit and Buxton (2022)
9	Ma'agan Michael 2015 (N/A)	245 *nummi* (*t.p.q.* 341–6, or 364–75?)	Cvikel (2021: 58*); Cohen *et al.* (2018: 543)
10	Caesarea South 1993 A, south anchorage (CHRE 8148)	*c.* 1,500 *nummi* (*t.p.q.* 363?)	Galili, Dahari, and Sharvit (1993: 68)
11	Carmel Coast, Assemblage 21, sector III (CHRE 8447)	'dozens' of fourth century bronze coins	Galili and Sharvit (1999: 18*)
12	Tell Nami 2021 (N/A)	3.161 kg lump (*t.p.q.* end fifth century? (Only identifiable coin: 383–95)	Sharvit (in prep.)
13	Kfar Samir (Ḥishule Carmel) (CHRE 7683)	6 bronze coins (*t.p.q.* sixth century?)	Unpublished

	Land-based Hoards		
No.	**Hoard**	**Content**	**Reference(s)**
14	'Akko-Ptolemais 2003 (CHRE 7726), 760 m from shore	46 Syrian tetradrachms (*t.p.q.* 119)	Tepper (2010); Syon and Tepper (2021)[c]
15	'Akko-Ptolemais 1980 (CHRE 7909)	35 *aurei* (Nero–161), 1 *denarius* and 29 Syrian tetradrachms (Nero–Trajan)	Burnett (1985: 157–9, no. 243)[c]
16	Tel Ashkelon (CHRE 7738), 240 m from shore	13 bronze coins (*t.p.q.* mid-third century)	–
17	Rafih-Yam (CHRE 7689), 1,000 m from shore	138 coins: 43 Syrian tetradrachms (*t.p.q.* Trebonianus Gallus) and 95 *antoniniani* (*t.p.q.* Quietus, AD 261)	Cited by Ariel and Sokolov (2018: 163)
18	Ḥorbat Qastra 1994 (CHRE 7711), 240 m from shore	19 *antoniniani* (*t.p.q.* 272)	–

19	Tel Ashkelon (IAA E.-R. 20)	14 bronze coins (*t.p.q.* second–third century) ; remarkable mint: Tyre (×1)	–
20	Yavne-Yam (North) (CHRE 8467), 50 m from shore	7 (or 9) *nummi* (*t.p.q.* 317)	Ariel (2015: 117*: 'possible hoard that was subsequently scattered')[c]
21	Apollonia 2006 A (CHRE 7643), 150 m from shore	21 *nummi* (*t.p.q.* Leo I)	Tal and Bijovsky (2017)[c]
22	Caesarea Synagogue (CHRE 7565), 30 m from shore	3,700 *nummi* (1,453 registered) (*t.p.q.* 363)	No author (1962); Raphael and Bijovsky (2014)[c]
23	Caesarea 1995 (CHRE 7638), 80 m from shore	19 *nummi* (*t.p.q.* 383)	–
24	Yafo 1970 (CHRE 7636), 125 m from shore	12 *nummi* (*t.p.q.* 383–95)	–
25	Caesarea 1996 (CHRE 7639), 90 m from shore	103 *nummi* (*t.p.q.* 383–95)	–
26	Caesarea 1993 (Millstone hoard) (CHRE 4394), 90 m from shore	99 *solidi* (*t.p.q.* 402)	Lampinen (1999)[c]
27	Ashkelon 1994 Smadar Hotel (A) (CHRE 7672), 400 m from shore	65 *nummi* (*t.p.q.* Zeno)	Bijovsky (2004)[c]
28	Ḥorbat Qastra 2000 (CHRE 8799), 780 m from shore	117 *nummi* (*t.p.q.* Zeno)	–
29	Ashkelon 1994 Smadar Hotel (B) (CHRE 7673), 400 m from shore	89 *nummi* (*t.p.q.* 498)	Bijovsky (2004)[c]
30	Naḥal Tanninim Dam (CHRE 7679), 500 m from shore	123 *nummi* (*t.p.q.* 498?)	Ariel (2023)[c]
31	Caesarea 1992 L.Q13 (CHRE 8797), 90 m from shore	100 *nummi* (*t.p.q.* 450–7)	–
32	Caesarea 1992 L.H16, 90 m from shore	7 *nummi* (*t.p.q.* 534–9)	Bijovsky (2012: 466, no. 41); Bijovsky (forthcoming)[c]

(*Continued*)

Table 3.1 (Continued)

	Land-based Hoards		
No.	**Hoard**	**Content**	**Reference(s)**
33	Ashqelon, Barnea 2003 (IAA Byz. 29), 640 m from shore	7 gold coins (*t.p.q.* 527–65)	Bijovsky, Sandhaus, and Milevski (2014)
	Hellenistic comparanda		
No.	**Hoard**	**Content**	**Reference(s)**
A	Carmel Coast	*c.* 3,500 (1,755 registered) Ptolemaic tetradrachms (*t.p.q.* 72/1 BC)	Ariel and Sokolov (2002); Olivier (2012: 29–293, no. 36)
B	Megadim IV, hoard in Rhodian amphora (IAA E.R. 24)	7 Hellenistic bronze coins (*t.p.q.* 138–29 BC)	Misch-Brandl (1985: 14); Galili and Sharvit (1999: 17*); Syon, Lorber, and Galili (2013: 68,[c] 'Hoard 3')
C	Ashkelon 1988, 'Periplous hoard' (IAA P.-H. 26)	49 bronze coins and 1 silver coin (*t.p.q.* 100 BC); remarkable mints: Teos, Samos, Rhodes, Kos, Knidos, Sardeis, Side, Antioch, Tyre, Paphos?, Ascalon	Gitler and Kahanov (2002; 2008)[c]; Ariel (2022: 391–7)[c]

To this I was able to add another shipwreck hoard recently found on the Turkish coast,[6] yielding a total, without the Israeli material, of 14 Mediterranean shipwreck hoards (CHRE 4780, 4848, 4962, 4963, 4973, 5381, 5399, 6801, 6803, 6921, 7478, 14414, and 17654, plus the one mentioned in note 6).

In other words, 48% of the shipwrecked Roman coin hoards in the Mediterranean are from the Israeli coast. Along the coastlines of neighbouring Syria, Lebanon, Gaza, the Sinai Peninsula, or Egypt, no coin hoards from Roman shipwrecks are documented on the CHRE website or are otherwise known to me. It is also noteworthy that the numbers of shipwrecks with Roman hoards in Italy and Greece, the countries with the longest Mediterranean coastlines, lag behind the 13 from Israel.

The large quantity of maritime Roman coin hoards off the coast of Israel is doubtless due to the country's strong archaeological institutions that have enabled

[6] This is a coin hoard from a shipwreck in the Kızlar Hamamı Bay, Turkey; see Dumankaya and Açar (2019).

the documentation of its provenanced coin hoards. In 2017, Joshua Goldman, an Oxford University MPhil student, came to Israel to collect Roman hoard data amassed there from Israel and the Palestinian territories for the CHRE project. He documented and uploaded 227 Roman hoards to the CHRE site.[7] Many of these hoards were physically available for examination; others could not be located but had been published on one level or another. The Israel national coin collection alone has some 310 physical coin hoards in its collection, from earliest times to AD 1700, and it is fair to estimate that at least 500 pre-modern coin hoards are known from the area of what was Mandatory Palestine.[8] This is but a fraction of the over 14,000 validated coin hoards listed by CHRE, but the advantage of the Israeli data is that a majority of the hoards were retrieved from licensed archaeological excavations and surveys, both underwater and on land.

I am wary of delving too deeply into this analysis of only 13 maritime hoards. Instead, this chapter will add qualitatively to our understanding of these underwater hoards by bringing them into the context of the 20 Roman coin hoards found near them—less than 1 km from the shoreline in Israel (Table 3.1, Hoards 14–33).[9] These land-based hoards come from archaeological contexts with architecture, unlike the 'beach hoards' without architectural context that were included together with the underwater hoards.[10] Unlike the shipwreck hoards, they are not presented in a detailed discussion. Rather, they constitute the basis for the comparisons in a later section below ('Comparison with Roman proximate land-based hoards'). All 33 hoards appear on the map (Fig. 3.1).

In order to contextualize the Roman underwater coin hoards, two underwater hoards that immediately predate the Roman period and one land-based hoard of the same time frame are also included in the discussions of this chapter (Table 3.1, Hellenistic comparanda A–C, and in the section below, 'Presentation of the Roman shipwreck hoards and their Hellenistic comparanda').

In general, throughout antiquity the southern Levant was a multidirectional transportation hub. In the Roman period, however, the general direction seems only to have been the movement of goods from east to west, to the many ports and anchorages of the southern Levant. Most of the coins from underwater hoards in the Roman period do not enable researchers to uncover the starting and ending points of those journeys. In some cases, we can see in the coins from shipwrecks hints of some major ports of call along those routes, and in a very few cases we are

[7] Despite the dates in Goldman's thesis title, the date range employed by Goldman was 125 BC to AD 300 (2017: 103). A chapter derived from the thesis was published as Goldman (2022).

[8] Incidentally, these do not include single finds of Roman gold coins found underwater, because no such finds were attested.

[9] Only one hoard was rejected by me as being far too dubious even to appear in Table 3.1: it is CHRE 8093. It is not an underwater hoard but one in close proximity (365 m) to the coastline. The 'hoard', reported by Schumacher (1900: 359), is attributed to Kefr es-Samir, a village at the foot of Mount Carmel. It was also reported in Noe (1937: 147, no. 544). Another roughly 170 Roman-period hoards deriving from further inland are registered in the Israel national coin collection.

[10] A case justifying this approach is Table 3.1, Hoard 9.

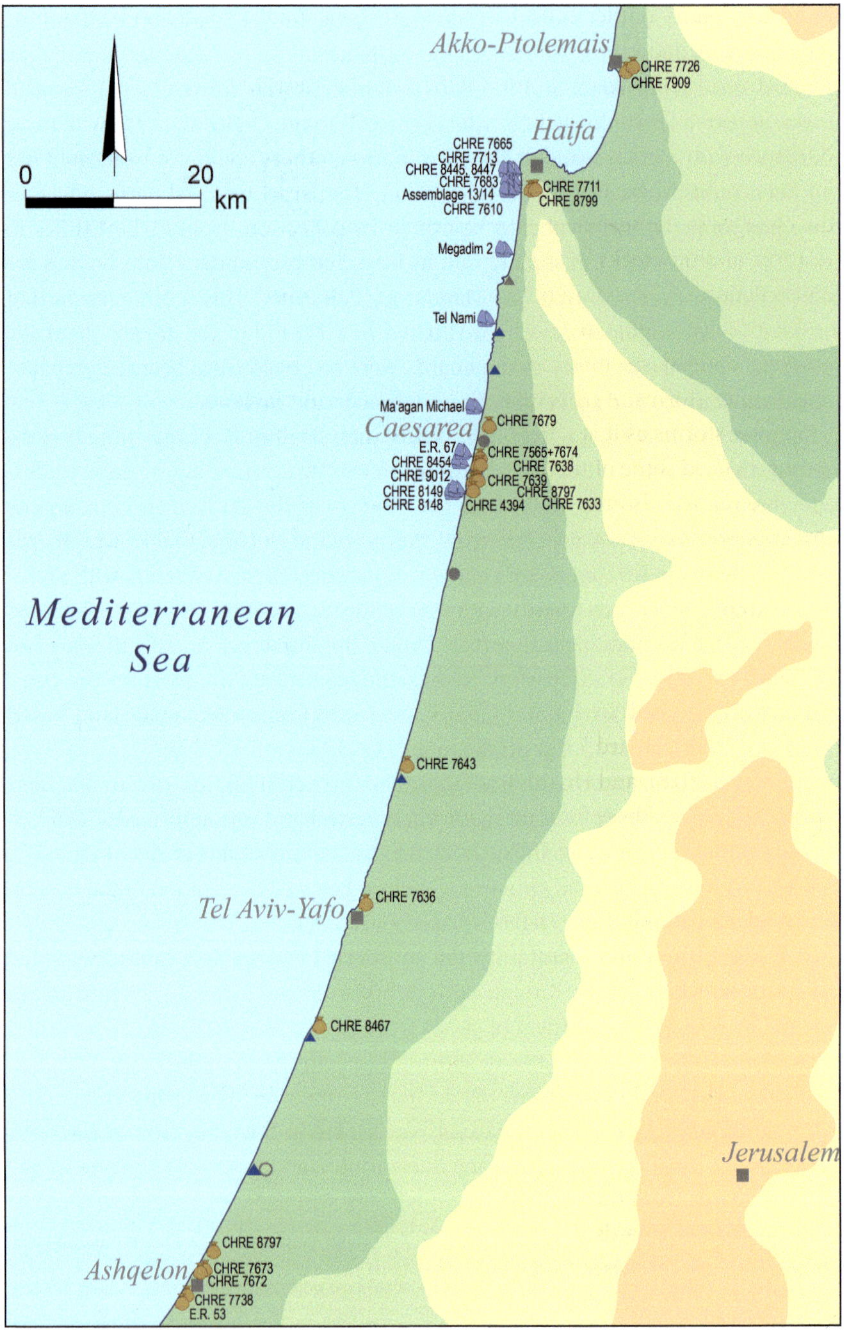

Fig. 3.1. Map of the Roman coin hoards from the 13 shipwrecks presented in this chapter (Table 3.1: Hoards 1–13) and the 20 Roman land-based coin hoards found less than 1 km from the coast (Table 3.1: Hoards 14–33). Map: Slava Pirsky.

lucky to identify outlier coins that attest to stops along a route and hint of more far-flung destinations.

Uncovering shipwrecks in the southern and eastern Mediterranean is a daunting enterprise. Those coastlines are characterized by fine-grained sand, which during violent storms can quickly erode, exposing some sunken ships and burying others. Elsewhere in the Mediterranean Sea, in areas with coarse-grained sand, the changes in the seabed are less extreme. Other factors complicating the identification of shipwrecks in the region are the effects of sand quarrying and the construction of breakwaters and marinas. These obstacles change the currents and expose sites long covered by layers of sand. Another additional factor is the growing enthusiasm of recreational divers to go treasure hunting immediately after winter storms. As a result, the IAA Marine Archaeology Unit must dive as soon after storms as it is safe, to surveil the treasure-hunting activity. These dives have produced some of the hoards considered here.

Sometimes finds are identified, only to be covered up again in a subsequent storm. In those cases, an exact GPS measurement enables the Marine Archaeology Unit to monitor the site. One example of this is the pre-Roman tetradrachm hoard from the Carmel coast (comparandum A). A few tetradrachms had been unearthed at the site in the early 1990s,[11] but it was a storm in 1994 which revealed the major portion of the hoard. Other underwater hoards have been similarly 'harvested' over multiple years, for example Hoard 5 (CHRE 7713; in 1990 and 1998), Hoard 7 (CHRE 7665; in 1990 and 1998), Hoard 8 (CHRE 8454, in 2016 and 2018), and Hoard 6, the Caesarea 'Cloaca' underwater hoard (in 2016 and 2020). When these finds are reported in their first year of discovery, and then additional finds turn up in subsequent years, those finds can be misconstrued as coming from different wrecks, when in fact they are from the same wreck.

The composition of the eastern Mediterranean hoards is sometimes enlightening; at other times they merely provide all-important dates for other objects from the same wreck.

PRESENTATION OF THE ROMAN SHIPWRECK HOARDS AND THEIR HELLENISTIC COMPARANDA

The 13 hoards from the shipwrecks are summarized in chronological order at the top of Table 3.1 (Hoards 1–13). Those available for study or for which enough details are known are discussed here. The other shipwreck hoards (current dispositions unknown or too few details) have basic information on the table but are not covered below. This section also includes a discussion of the three Hellenistic comparanda mentioned above (Table 3.1, comparanda A–C).

[11] Olivier (2012: 293).

Hoard 1 (CHRE 9012): Caesarea 1968

In an article published in Hebrew in 1969, Arie Kindler reported the find of an underwater hoard from the vicinity of Caesarea.[12] Found in August 1968, the hoard was discovered 100 m from the Caesarea coastline by an unnamed diver. Thirty-nine *aurei* were found, but Kindler was able to document only 38 of them. Based on the profile of the assemblage and the wear on the oldest issues, Kindler was convinced that the coins indeed comprised a hoard. At the time, it was the largest gold hoard found in the region.[13]

Hoard 5 (CHRE 7713): Carmel Coast 1990 hoard A

The publication of the Carmel Coast 1990 hoard A (Fig. 3.2) by the late Ya'akov Meshorer appeared soon after his passing. In his analysis of the assemblage, he wrote, 'I will analyse the group as if all indeed belonged to one hoard and shall suggest some solutions to problems in the hoard's composition.'[14] He then proceeded to present the assemblage's trimetallic (silver, bronze, and lead) 'diversified composition of coins' as one hoard. However, Meshorer did not, in my view, convincingly show that all the coins indeed constituted only one hoard. He reasoned that the *denarii*, whose range extends from the reign of Augustus to that of Faustina Junior (AD 176), circulated alongside provincial bronzes that started later and continued until the reign of Severus Alexander. He argued that this was because the *denarii* were valued for their high silver content, based upon a feature of the land-based Mamshit hoard (CHRE 7616). In that hoard, found on land in a large bronze jar, between 10,320 and 10,500 silver coins were found. The hoard had two main components—early coins through the reign of Trajan and later coins. The emperor with the largest number of coins in the early component was Trajan himself, with 2,042 drachms, one *denarius*, and 554 tetradrachms. The later coins begin again with low quantities, from Hadrian through Commodus and then very high numbers from Septimius Severus all the way through the reign of Elagabalus, all tetradrachms. Meshorer reasoned that the huge spike of Trajanic silver was included in the Mamshit hoard because of its high silver content. That may be. Because the Mamshit hoard is without doubt one hoard (it was found in the same container), in a sense there is no need to argue whether the early silver and especially the Trajanic silver was in the hoard for its silver content or for some other reason.[15]

[12] Kindler (1969). The hoard went unnoticed in English publications until Waner and Safrai (2001: 327, no. 54) cited it—and there, the reference (Oestreicher 1962) was incorrect.

[13] For more on Hoard 1, see below, notes 32 and 33.

[14] Meshorer (2010: 111).

[15] One such reason could be that the Mamshit hoard was two very separate hoards that were combined in antiquity.

Fig. 3.2. Hoard 5, Carmel Coast 1990 A. © Dafna Gazit, Courtesy of the Israel Antiquities Authority.

For the 'Carmel Coast 1990 hoard A', Meshorer took his theory about the Trajanic silver from the Mamshit hoard and applied it to the coins from the shipwreck, because the excavators also believed it to be one hoard and because he 'preferred' that option to one where 'the group of denars from the reigns of Claudius to Trajan originates from a different wreck'.[16] In my view there is no reason to build a case for joining the 68 *denarii* from Hoard 5 with an assemblage of bronze coins (and lead *tesserae*), from a generally different time period,[17] especially as another hoard, the 'Carmel Coast 1990 hoard B' (see below and Table 3.1, Hoard 7) was also found at exactly the same findspot.

Meshorer's argument that Trajanic coins had silver contents 20–30% higher than the later silver in the Mamshit hoard should not be applied to a shipwreck site. It is eminently possible that the 68 *denarii* found at the 'Carmel Coast 1990 A' site came from the same shipwreck, but from another hoard located there.[18]

[16] Galili, Rosen, and Sharvit (2010: 61); Meshorer (2010: 112).

[17] The *denarii* in the 'Carmel Coast 1990 A' hoard range from Tiberius (AD 14–37) to Faustina Jr (AD 161–76), while (with one exception) the Roman bronzes span the reigns of Antoninus Pius (AD 140–3) to the latest coins in the hoard, those of Severus Alexander (AD 222–35)—in line with the Roman provincial bronzes in the hoard.

[18] van Alfen (2016): 'a single wreck might contain dozens of separate hoards'. In 1932 Shirley Weber made a similarly convoluted argument that an Egyptian hoard of the second century AD also contained a few second- and first-century BC Peloponnesian and Rhodian silver coins (Weber 1932). She (and Edward Newell himself) accepted this claim by an antiquities dealer citing a 'certain fellahin' in the Egyptian Nile Delta. They were convinced by the coins' patina and the fact that, in two cases, an early coin was still adhering to a second-century AD coin. I do not believe that such an apparent ruse

Meshorer thought that as one hoard, with its 68 *denarii*, nine imperial bronzes, six provincial silver coins (Lycia, Antioch, and Alexandria), 76 provincial bronzes from various cities, and three lead Egyptian *tesserae*, it could reflect a port-hopping coastal voyage. Based upon five Alexandrian coins and the three Egyptian lead *tesserae*,[19] Meshorer construed that the ship plied a route from Egypt to possibly Greece (based on a unique bronze coin of Corinth).[20]

Although the provincial issues from Caesarea and 'Akko-Ptolemais predominate in this hoard, other unusual single specimens are from Corinth, Miletus, Cyzicus, and Lycia (Xanthus?). Those and a provincial coin of Antioch (*RPC* III, 3575) and another one minted in Rome for circulation in Cyrene/the East (*RPC* III, 7), both formerly attributed to Caesarea in Cappadocia and published as such by Meshorer, definitely hint at a northern and western extent for the voyage. Because Meshorer wished to add the Roman *denarii* of different dates, he also added Rome to the route,[21] concentrating on tracing the ship's route and not on identifying its most recent departure. The excavators correctly argued, however, that the large percentage of Roman provincial issues from Caesarea Maritima and other eastern Mediterranean mints attested to a strong local component to the hoard.[22]

Hoard 6 (IAA E.-R. 67): Caesarea 2020

The next hoard, 'Caesarea 2020', found just north of the Caesarea harbour, is also named the 'Cloaca' hoard after the main Byzantine-period sewerage outlet at that point on land (Fig. 3.3). It comprised 423 coins: 81 were provincial tetradrachms, one was a poorly preserved *antoninianus*, and the rest were *sestertii*. All the tetradrachms were cleaned, as were half of the bronzes. The latest coin in the debased silver category was issued by Trebonianus Gallus, while the latest *aes* was of Volusian. The debased silver coins all appear to have been issued in Antioch. Because Antioch was the only mint to issue provincial tetradrachms between Gordian III and the father–son reigns of Trebonianus Gallus and Volusian (AD 251–3), it is

would be accepted today. Moreover, I believe Weber felt challenged by Newell to explain the 'curious and unusual association' of the two groups of very different date.

[19] Although Alexandrian coins of Trajan and Hadrian are rather common finds on land in the southern Levant, the later Alexandrian coins are not.

[20] A hoard the likes of what Meshorer reported, but without the Roman silver, is a *periplous* hoard not dissimilar to the one deposited on the coast of Ashqelon some three centuries earlier. I will discuss that below (comparandum C; also listed at end of Table 3.1).

[21] As noted above, from the point of view of the excavators, Galili, Rosen, and Sharvit (2010: 61), there also were two assemblages: 'the artefacts were scattered over an area measuring 50 × 50 m and located 75–125 m offshore…Although the finds were scattered throughout the site, two major artefact concentrations were discerned, corresponding to the two coin hoards mentioned above. The third-century assemblage was mainly distributed in the western, deeper part of the site; while the fourth-century assemblage was concentrated in the eastern, shallower area of the site.'

[22] Galili, Rosen, and Sharvit (2010: 106).

Fig. 3.3. Hoard 6, Caesarea 2020 ('Cloaca' hoard). © Dafna Gazit, Courtesy of the Israel Antiquities Authority.

possible that the date of the shipwreck in which this hoard was found falls after the mid-third century AD. This aligns well with the latest dated *aes* in the hoard. It is not possible to know from which direction the ship had come to harbour. One could suppose that, had the ship departed from Caesarea, there might have been some provincial tetradrachms from that mint itself in the assemblage. However, because only a small number of tetradrachms roughly contemporary with the Caesarean tetradrachm emission under Caracalla, Macrinus, and Diadumenianus were attested, there is actually very little reason to expect any of the very rare Caesarean tetradrachms in the hoard.[23]

Hoard 7 (CHRE 7665): Carmel Coast 1990 B

The coins comprising this hoard were uncovered at exactly the same spot where 'Carmel Coast 1990 A' was found (Fig. 3.4). There is no doubt, however, of the integrity of this hoard. It has a very restricted range, roughly a decade. Interestingly,

[23] On bimetallic hoarding in Roman Palestine, see Goldman (2022: 218): 'Mixed metal hoards, e.g. silver-bronze, were rare in Roman Palestine. Thirteen such assemblages were deposited during the Bar Kokhba Revolt, 45 suggesting reduced monetary discrimination during periods of crisis. Only two mixed metal hoards are known from the First Jewish Revolt.'

Fig. 3.4. Hoard 7, Carmel Coast 1990 B. © Dafna Gazit, Courtesy of the Israel Antiquities Authority.

85% of the coins derive from western mints—especially Rome (43%)—not uncommon for mint distributions in hoards of this time frame.[24]

That distribution should therefore not be taken to argue forcefully for a decidedly western origin for the voyage. That said, with only two coins from Antioch and one from Alexandria, the hoard's owner is nevertheless more likely to have originated from the West. This will be further addressed below, in the conclusion.

Hoard 8 (CHRE 8454): Caesarea 2016

Hoard 'Caesarea 2016' was discovered by recreational divers near the eastern corner of the northern breakwater reef of the Herodian harbour at Caesarea (Fig. 3.5). The shipwreck remains were exposed when a large amount of sand (*c.* 3 m) was scoured away from the seafloor after a winter storm created a shallow crater.

[24] Ariel (2010: 137).

Fig. 3.5. Hoard 8, Caesarea 2016. © Dafna Gazit, Courtesy of the Israel Antiquities Authority.

Almost all the coins from the shipwreck come from two large lumps preserving the shape of their original containers, which may have been amphorae. The coins are extremely homogeneous, with latest dates *c.* AD 318. These coins may have been intended to be melted down for scrap metal, but it is more probable that they were in the merchantman for their purchasing value.

Besides the two amphora assemblages, a number of earlier coins were excavated from the site. The excavators believed that they probably derived from the same shipwreck because of their great quantity and their contemporaneity with the two large lumps.[25] Many of them were cleaned, and four of the five of these coins raise the possibility that the merchantman made a call at the port of Alexandria. Another rare coin comes from Tarsus in Cilicia.

Hoard 9: Ma'agan Michael beach 2016

Sixty-one coins were found on the Ma'agan Michael beach north of Caesarea in July 2016 by a teenager (Fig. 3.6). Their chronological distribution covered no more than 16 years, placing the hoard in the first half of the fifth decade of the fourth century AD.

The year before, 150 m from the beach, a mid-seventh-/mid-eighth-century AD Umayyad shipwreck was discovered and first excavated. In its 2020 publication, a 'collection of 184 copper-lead alloy coins dated to the mid-fourth century CE' was reported.[26] It is clear that the teenager's 61 coins and the excavated

[25] Sharvit and Buxton (2022: 85*–86*). [26] Cvikel (2021: 58*).

Fig. 3.6. Hoard 9, Ma'agan Michael 2015. © Dafna Gazit, Courtesy of the Israel Antiquities Authority.

assemblage derive from the same hoard of very restricted date.[27] Despite the excavators' attribution of the fourth-century coins to the Umayyad shipwreck,[28] the hoard in all probability belonged to another shipwreck at the same spot as the excavated wreck.

Hoard 12: Tell Nami 2021

This is the newest underwater Roman coin hoard found on Israel's shoreline (Fig. 3.7). Discovered roughly 100 m in the sea near Tel Nami in August 2021 by a tourist,[29] the hoard represents a couple of thousand coins; however, the lump was barely dismantled and, of the few coins that were cleaned, only a single identifiable one dates to AD 383–95, making the hoard's date in the fifth century AD uncertain.

[27] The metallurgical report of the excavated coins cited one coin of AD 364–75; see Cohen *et al.* (2018: 543, no. 4).

[28] Cvikel (2021: 58*) argued that the fourth-century coins were most likely valued for their metal content.

[29] The hoard has an interesting backstory. The IAA Marine Archaeology Unit discovered that a diver found the (3.161 kg) lump of corroded coins the day before, 100 m from the shoreline. The diver did not understand that what he found was made up of coins; he therefore brought it to the coast and left it there, until the tourist identified it as ancient coins and notified the IAA.

Fig. 3.7. Hoard 12, Tell Nami 2021. © Dafna Gazit, Courtesy of the Israel Antiquities Authority.

Hoard 13 (CHRE 7683): Ḥishule Carmel

The last underwater hoard, from Ḥishule Carmel, is small—only seven extant coins, all minute. It has parallels on land but—except for the Tel Nami hoard recently discovered—no parallel in underwater shipwreck hoards. Its sixth-century AD date is only a guess.

Hellenistic Comparandum A: Carmel Coast

The first comparandum, a late Ptolemaic silver hoard from the Carmel coast, was composed at least of roughly 40 kg of tetradrachms from the reigns of Ptolemy IX to XII. Half of the hoard was a 20.646-kg lump still bearing the shape of its container. The rest of the hoard was found in smaller lumps, of which all but one were separated and cleaned. The hoard's deposition date is 72/71 BC, the year Tigranes the Great (of Armenia) was in ʿAkko-Ptolemais, 22 km up the coast. The ship apparently departed from Alexandria and was heading further north when wrecked. To my knowledge, no first-century BC Ptolemaic tetradrachm has ever been found along the eastern littoral of the Mediterranean Sea on land. This demonstrates that coin hoards from ships, perhaps unlike coins carried overland, can include items completely different from the material culture circulating on land. No doubt, however, this phenomenon is very rare.

Hellenistic Comparandum B (IAA E.R. 24): Megadim IV

The remains of the cargo of this wreck, including a Rhodian amphora hoard containing *c.* 100 kg of scrap bronze and seven bronze coins, was found off the coast of Megadim, alongside a huge Mamluk-period shipwreck, also with a scrap metal cargo. The seven coins, of which five were identified (now called the 'Megadim IV' hoard), attest to mints in Lycia, Cyprus, Antioch, and Tyre. Like Hoard 8, this shipwreck carried scrap metal, an important commodity which will be considered in the conclusion.

Hellenistic Comparandum C (IAA P.-H. 26): Ashkelon 1988 ('Periplous hoard')

A third comparandum for the 13 Roman underwater hoards does not originate from a shipwreck, but is an on-land hoard, probably brought by a sailor from a ship anchored off Ashqelon to the Tell around 100 BC. Found as a lump and amounting to 50 small coins, one silver, and the rest bronze, the recorded mints were Teos, Samos, Kos, Rhodos, Sardeis, Knidos, Antioch, Paphos, and Tyre. There is no doubt that the hoard comprised a purse of someone who had travelled along the Anatolian coast. It was thus called the Periplous hoard. The hoard reflects the coast-hugging sea routes of the late Hellenistic period, inspiring Meshorer to label his much later Roman hoard (Hoard 5) a periplous hoard as well.

COMPARISON WITH ROMAN PROXIMATE LAND-BASED HOARDS

In order to enlarge the scope of this analysis, 20 land-based hoards (Table 3.1, Hoards 14–33), all found less than 1 km (a mean distance of 250 m) from the shoreline in Israel, have been included for comparison, with the purpose of investigating whether they differ from shipwreck coin hoards in any significant way. With one exception (Hoard 15), they come from contexts with archaeological structures.

The dramatic settings of many shipwrecks may foster the impression that the uncovered hoards are different from what is found on land. A faulty impression of exceptionality is amplified because shipwreck finds that receive media coverage are often those that contain exceptional finds, such as items made of precious materials, or 'hoards' with large quantities of commonplace items are exaggerated for their uniqueness. There are undoubtedly true exceptions, such as the hoard from before the Roman imperial period noted above (Comparandum A, deposited 72/71 BC), which consisted entirely of Ptolemaic tetradrachms that have never turned up in the vicinity as provenanced finds on land.

Since the shipwreck and land-based hoards presented have only been included due to their findspots and their Roman date, statistically speaking one cannot claim that they are specially selected for exceptionality. When comparing the two groups, it is clear that prosaic coin hoards are found in both settings. The coins in maritime Hoards 12 and 13 are similarly unobtrusive except that Hoard 12 contained thousands of coins while Hoard 13 was comprised of only seven coins. They are similar to terrestrial Hoards 22 and 32 from Caesarea, one large like Hoard 12 and the other small like Hoard 13.

There are, no doubt, more significant commonalities and differences between maritime and land-based coin hoards that deserve our attention.

Dates of deposit

The most important commonality of terrestrial and maritime hoards is their chronology. In the survey region, neither first-century BC nor first-century AD coin hoards are attested. Sea and land hoards first appear in the east in the second century AD, with four maritime hoards (Hoards 1–4) and two land-based hoards (Hoards 14–15).[30] The earliest date to Trajan (Hoards 1–2) and Hadrian (Hoards 3 and 14). The next period of deposition clustering is the third quarter of the third century AD, with two maritime hoards (Hoards 5–6) and four land-based hoards (Hoards 16–19). This is followed by close correspondences in the first two thirds of the fourth century AD: two maritime hoards (Hoards 7–8) and one land-based hoard (Hoard 20) in the period AD 317–19; three maritime hoards (Hoards 9–11) and two land-based hoards (Hoards 21–2) in the years between AD 341–6 and the AD 363 earthquake.

For the last quarter of the fourth century and the last quarter of the fifth century, the symmetry ends. There are no underwater hoards, while on land those periods are well represented, with three hoards (Hoards 23–5) from AD 383–95, the gold Caesarea Millstone hoard (Hoard 26), dated by three *solidi* from AD 395–402, and two hoards (Hoards 27–8) dating to Zeno's reign. The asymmetry with the Millstone hoard is particularly striking because that hoard—covering the second

[30] All three have unknown dispositions and two few details. Hoard 2 was designated as a 'Roman collection' attesting to emperors from Nero to Trajan, i.e. a profile that harmonizes with many land-based hoards from around the time of the Bar Kokhba revolt.

half of the fourth century AD—is the largest Roman gold coin hoard in the region, with 99 *solidi*. The chronological correspondences are again restored between the sea and land hoards in the sixth century AD, with two maritime hoards (Hoards 12–13) and two land-based hoards, one *aes* (Hoard 32) and one gold hoard (Hoard 33).

Metallic composition

Another important commonality between maritime and land-based hoards is that their composition is very similar. This is undoubtedly because, generally, preferences in hoarding would have been the same regardless of the deposition method. In our small sample of maritime hoards and land-based hoards, the common compositions apply only to silver and bronze, but not to gold. One wonders why only one gold hoard (Hoard 1) was found in our maritime hoard sample, while three hoards with gold coins (Hoards 15, 26, and 33) were found in the 20 proximate land-based hoards.[31] One explanation may be found in an observation by Kingsley, who noted that the waters off the coast in this region are shallow, on account of the mild east–west gradient of the continental shelf. The shallow waters allowed many valuable cargos and other items (such as gold coins) to be salvaged soon after a ship went down.[32]

Hoarding rationale

Two commonalities between maritime and land-based coin hoards have thus far been identified. It is time to point out an important difference between the two categories with regard to their rationales in hoarding. Setting aside savings hoards and purse hoards, the overwhelming number of land-based Roman hoards were hidden—or other catastrophic events caused them to be 'closed'. Examining coin hoards from a longue durée perspective, François de Callataÿ found a general 'link between hoarding and general fear, mostly generated by

[31] Ignoring the 1-km restriction and adding the chronological limit of coins deposited no later than the Bar Kokhba revolt, no hoards are found in territories contiguous with Israel (Lebanon, Palestinian territories, and Jordan), but in Israel Hoard 1 is comparable to seven hoards (CHRE 7596, 7617, 7618, 8013, 8043, 8173, and 18787)—of which most are associated with the Bar Kokhba revolt. This suggests that, although the deposit of Hoard 1 should not be related to 'fear' (see the following subsection, 'Hoarding rationale'), it may nevertheless relate to the arrival of Roman legionaries to suppress the revolt.

[32] Assuming the gold coins were securely kept in identifiable containers. Once receptacles of gold coins are damaged underwater and the coins dispersed, it would be nigh impossible to retrieve them all. As there is no way to know the original composition of Hoard 1, we cannot know whether the 39 *aurei* were a large or small proportion of the hoard, Kingsley (2000: 60).

political trouble and civil wars'.[33] If one agrees with de Callataÿ's link, then the dates of deposit of a preponderance of the 14,000 Roman coin hoards available on CHRE ought to relate to fear. Coin hoards from shipwrecks, however, do not appear to have any connection to fears of the kind described by de Callataÿ, and it is very probable that the coin hoards found in the maritime sample are the result of their ships having sunk by inclement weather or navigation error entering, or setting sail from, a port.

COMPARISON WITH SHIPWRECK HOARDS FROM OTHER REGIONS OF THE MEDITERRANEAN

According to my calculation, 27 Roman coin hoards derive from Mediterranean shipwrecks (see the section 'Introduction' and note 5, above). I compared the deposit dates of the 13 hoards from the sea's eastern littoral with the 14 other shipwreck hoards, and discovered that—unlike the chronological consilience between the maritime and land-based hoards above—the 13 hoards are significantly different than hoards from the non-Israeli Mediterranean shipwrecks. Hoards 1–13, with no representation in the first century AD and with significant gaps until the mid-fourth century AD, were followed by a certain regularity until the mid-sixth century AD. That is quite unlike the 14 other Mediterranean shipwreck hoards. There, 12 of the 14 hoards are tightly clustered in the period between AD 212 and 317/18. That leaves two outliers: one from the first century AD and the other dating to AD 355–67. This divergence between the eastern Mediterranean shipwrecks and the other more scattered group of 14 requires more study.

DISCUSSION

Scrap metal

Two of the shipwrecks (Hoard 8 and the Hellenistic Comparandum B) contained scrap metal in their cargos when they sank. In shipwreck B the only coins attested (now called a hoard) were found in a Rhodian amphora which contained roughly 100 kg of scrap metal. Of the seven coins found, five were identified and provide a *c*. 100 BC date for the journey. Two of them (both of Ptolemy VIII Euergetes, produced on Cyprus) may also hint at a Cypriot source for the scrap metal. The cargo of the other wreck, Hoard 8 of the early fourth century AD, included, besides

[33] de Callataÿ (2017: 335).

scrap metal (bronze, iron, and lead), hundreds of kilograms of raw glass.[34] In a maritime context, the scrap metal (and the glass) served a number of functions. If the large money-making items were delivered in one direction, then the scrap metal etc. would improve the voyage's profitability by filling its hold with less valuable cargo for the return voyage. It could also add to (or fully function as) the ballast. Owing to its weight, scrap metal was probably much more economically transported by sea than over land. That idea could also feed into Suzanne Frey-Kupper and Clive Stannard's idea of the movement of blocks of foreign and obsolete bronze coins from place to place.[35]

Salvaging

The 13 underwater hoards discussed here derive from shipwrecks from the surf zone. Because most of the maritime travel that I examined here appears to have been commercial in nature, when a heavy sailing vessel with amphorae, cereals, or raw materials such as glass or scrap metal is wrecked, the question must be asked—why would one expect to find a hoard buried several metres under the sea's surface together with its cargo? In the region that I have covered, with its shallow waters off the coast, their cargos—or much of them, including their coin hoards—would, if at all possible, have been salvaged soon after the ships went down (see above, 'Metallic composition' subsection).[36]

Besides the proactive salvaging of the most valuable cargo, passive depletion of the wrecks could also have taken place. The livestock on the ships, and various objects with wooden parts attached to them, would wash ashore on their own. Ceramic amphorae as well would either drift ashore or roll on the sea bottom for some distance from the wreck site. Only the heavy metallic or stone objects would sink into the sediment and remain at wreck sites in the surf zone.[37]

As the sea bottom becomes deeper, shipwrecks exhibited 'remarkable preservation and intact cargos'.[38] Those wrecks are now more accessible thanks to remotely operated vehicles (ROVs). They are also immune to amateur treasure hunting, leaving a possibility for carefully planned, well-funded recovery of shipwreck coin hoards in the future.

[34] Raw glass was also contextualized with Hoard 5 (CHRE 7713) and Hoard 7 (CHRE 7665); see Galili, Gorin-Rosen, and Rosen (2015).

[35] Frey-Kupper and Stannard (2018). Their idea of the movement of blocks of foreign and obsolete bronze coins, however, does not suit their suggestion that another hoard discussed here, the so-called Periplous hoard, was 'probably a block of scrap coins'; Frey-Kupper and Stannard (2018: 289). Rather, as common sense would have it, the Periplous hoard was composed of 'casual and sporadic [finds], for example, when a traveller or soldier returned home with a coin or two in his purse'; Frey-Kupper and Stannard (2018: 285). Viewing the Periplous hoard as a sailor's purse, and Hoard 5 as a merchant's or shipowner's purse, is more likely than an undefined block of scrap.

[36] Kingsley (2000: 60).

[37] Galili, Rosen, and Sharvit (2010: 106).

[38] Kingsley (2004: 131).

CONCLUSIONS

Unfortunately, the subset of Roman coin hoards on shipwrecks is too small for us to draw definitive conclusions. Although it is not possible for underwater archaeologists to fully predict when hoards will turn up, they now have ways to increase the chances that hoards will appear. Regular use of metal detectors is one way. Archaeologist divers have also learned how and when the seabed changes, and better understand where and when shipwrecks may appear. They can recognize the storms that change the sandy seabed along the coast of Israel, which reveal, with increasing frequency, shipwrecks or the artefactual remains of shipwrecks.[39]

The IAA Underwater Archaeology Unit has capitalized on the observation that a number of ships often sink at the same place. Examples of such collocated hoards in our sample are Hoards 5 and 7 (which, if I am correct, are actually three hoards), Hoard 9 (collocated with an Umayyad wreck), and B, the Megadim IV amphora hoard (mixed with a Mamluk-period hoard). It is thrilling to find large numbers of coins in the sea, but the excitement continues when numismatists come into the picture and try to explain the meaning of what has turned up. Sometimes that means that two hoards, and not one, can be identified. When one adds to this the practice of returning to an underwater site after a violent storm to find additional coins, it becomes clear how the ability to establish the integrity of hoards can depend on the perspicacity of the numismatist.

Serendipity also plays a role. The hoard brought up to land and deposited in a lump at the top of Tell Ashqelon (Comparandum C: Ashkelon 1988 'Periplous hoard'), 35 years before Pompey the Great's arrival at Jerusalem, has demonstrated how someone on a ship, more likely a sailor than a member of the senior staff (based upon the low value of the coins), could have collected small bronze coin issues from a number of ports of call on his journey or journeys, and that collection could shine a light on the ship's route. Hoard 5, identified by Meshorer as another, Roman, Periplous hoard, is a much larger assemblage of coins, and it is thus more difficult to tease out the hoard's 'periplous' character.[40]

Amphorae also were involved in two of these hoards (Hoards 8 and B). In one case (B) the amphora was a storage container for scrap metal, but in the other case (Hoard 8) the amphorae(?) were more probably used to store coins to be spent. Most commonly, however, amphorae found in shipwrecks contained wine, oil, or other wet and dry foodstuffs, which, like scrap metal, raw glass, and other heavy commodities such as marble, were generally transported on ships and not over land. In those cases, what was inside the amphorae was the commodity and not the amphorae themselves. On the CHRE website, amphorae on ships functioned as hoard containers: off the coast of Spain an amphora was found to contain 967

[39] Climate change is likely to increase the number of discoveries of underwater hoards.
[40] See above, note 36.

bronze coins, almost all *sestertii.*[41] Another amphora-bearing shipwreck off the Italian coast was found to have around 1,200 *antoniniani.*[42] Amphorae also functioned as coin hoard containers on land, for example for the very large Misrata hoard.[43]

Determining the normal routes of these ships—when they did not sink en route—is perhaps the most interesting challenge regarding these wrecks. This subject was previously examined through a small literary genre of historical records called a *periplous* (or *periplus*). An early one (fourth century BC) was ascribed to a Skylax (now pseudo-Skylax), and another is Hellenistic: the *Periplous* of Pseudo-Skymnos, now dated to *c.* 100 BC and ascribed to Pausanias of Damascus (most recently by Joseph Geiger),[44] placing that Levantine historian in Bithynia.[45] A later dated periplous—with a very different route—is the *Periplus Maris Erythraei* ('Circumnavigation of the Red Sea'), composed in the first century AD by a Greek merchant or skipper.[46]

Using coin finds from wrecks to reconstruct maritime travel is not unknown, but it took the excavation of the Ashkelon Periplous hoard (Comparandum C) to bring that idea to the forefront.[47] That same hoard induced Abramzon to claim that certain foreign coins belonging to two enormous Hellenistic hoards found in Phanagoria on the northern coast of the Black Sea (one from 2003 and one from 2007) were in fact two distinct 'Periplous assemblages' collected by two sailors—and that those hoards attested to two separate maritime routes.[48] The foreign coins from the 'Phanagoria 2003' hoard traced a route from the Bosporus to Crete, with an itinerary of more than 2,300 km.[49] The 'Phanagoria 2007' hoard indicated that the other sailor's voyage also included the Bosporus but continued to Lycia. In that case, Abramzon's reconstruction of the route is even longer, as the mints of those coins attested to a route some 2,600 km long.

I am not suggesting that these proposed itineraries should be accepted. But what can be said with certainty is that the constellation of bronze coin mints in both the Mediterranean region and north to the Black Sea basin enables such proposals. My sense is that a century later, during the Roman Principate, Roman provincial coinage did not circulate as far. To my knowledge, few assemblages of provincial bronze coinage have geographical spreads as great as the Ashkelon Periplous hoard and the two Phanagoria hoards. Mining the CHRE website may

[41] CHRE 4780; Martínez Mira (1995–7: 130, no. 27).

[42] CHRE 14414; Arslan (1997).

[43] CHRE 4836.

[44] Geiger (2016: 15).

[45] Diller (1955: 278); Bravo (2009).

[46] Casson (1989).

[47] Gitler and Kahanov (2002; 2008). In Gitler and Kahanov's chapters they did not attest any coins from shipwrecks as evincing trade connections between western Anatolia and the southern Levant in the Hellenistic period. Rather, as a proxy for that, they listed 'large numbers of imported stamped amphorae in excavations throughout Israel'; Gitler and Kahanov (2008: 394). For an updated discussion of the Ashkelon Periplous hoard (Comparandum C) see Ariel (2022: 391–7).

[48] Abramzon (2018); Abramzon and Kuznetsov (2021: 64–7).

[49] This is much longer than the route that can be reconstructed by the coins from the Ashkelon Periplous hoard (1,400 km).

serve as a corrective for my admittedly myopic point of view. In the meantime, however, the geographical spread of the mints in first-/second-century AD underwater hoards presented here is less robust.

Looking beyond the period of Roman provincial minting of city coins, in the fourth and fifth centuries AD, one's ability to discern 'exotic' (distant) mints is much more difficult. The coins themselves are easy to identify and the mints are often clear. But the number of mints is restricted to between 16 and 18 in number. Still, one can get a sense if a shipwreck originated from the east from the mint profile of the coins from a hoard that was aboard. I believe I see this in Hoard 7, where over 85% of the hoard derives from western mints—particularly Rome (32 coins, or 43%), although one cannot be certain.[50] It should be noted that the distinguished numismatist Anne Robertson made the converse argument based upon the high number of eastern mints found in some hoards uncovered in the British Isles.[51]

Hoard 5 attests to nine mints outside of the southern Levant. There were ten mints represented in the Ashkelon 1988 'Periplous hoard' (Comparandum C).[52] The Phanagoria 2003 hoard also attests to ten mints, while the Phanagoria 2007 hoard shows 12 mints—after one justifiably discounts the many thousands of homogeneous, local coins in the two Phanagoria hoards.

ACKNOWLEDGEMENTS

I am grateful to Christopher Howgego for inviting me to participate in the Crossing Frontiers conference, to Marguerite Spoerri Butcher for aid in mining the CHRE website and providing revised identifications of two coins in Meshorer (2010), to Jack Nurpetlian for information about coin hoards off the coast of Lebanon, and to Lena Kupershmidt (IAA metals laboratory), Dafna Gazit (IAA photography studio), and Shai Hendler, who assisted in locating the first publication of Hoard 1. Special thanks go to Jacob Sharvit, current head of the IAA Marine Archaeology Unit, who, despite his primary function in managing underwater cultural resources, was instrumental in providing important contextual information about the underwater coin hoards presented here, as well as supplying pinpointed findspot coordinates and images of artefacts relating to the shipwrecks.

[50] For two unpublished hoards from land excavations in the region—at Sepphoris and Qazrin—the mint distribution is similar.

[51] Robertson (1989).

[52] The Megadim IV Amphora 'hoard' (Comparandum B) had five foreign mints, and the Caesarea 2016–18 hoard (Hoard 8, CHRE 8454) had two foreign mints.

ABBREVIATIONS

RPC III Amandry, M. and Burnett, A. (2015). *Roman Provincial Coinage III. Nerva, Trajan and Hadrian (AD 96–138).* London and Paris.

REFERENCES

Abramzon, M. G. (2018). 'Numismatic evidence for ancient seafaring between the Levant, Western and Southern Asia Minor and the Northern Black Sea', *Israel Numismatic Research* 13: 55–72.

Abramzon, M. G. and Kuznetsov, V. D. (2021). *Coin Hoards* XI: *Greek Hoards. The Cimmerian Bosporus* (Colloquia Antiqua 32). Leuven, Paris, and Bristol, CT.

Ariel, D. T. (2010). 'Coin hoard from a fourth-century CE shipwreck off the Carmel Coast', *'Atiqot* 63: 137–45.

Ariel, D. T. (2015). 'The coins from from Yavne-Yam (North)', *'Atiqot* 81: 43–8, 117.

Ariel, D. T. (2022). 'Coins', in K. R. Birney, *Ashkelon,* vol. 9: *The Hellenistic Period.* University Park, PA, 373–432.

Ariel, D. T. (2023). 'The coins', in Y. Porath, U. 'Ad, and 'A. a-S. Sa'id (eds), *Excavations at the Nahal Tanninim Dam and its Vicinity: Final Report of the 2000–2005 Excavation Seasons* (IAA Reports 71). Jerusalem, 249–54.

Ariel, D. T. and Sokolov, H. (2002). 'No title', *International Numismatic Newsletter* 39: 16.

Ariel, D. T. and Sokolov, H. (2018). 'The Kafr Bara hoard', *Israel Numismatic Research* 13: 151–94.

Arslan, E. A. (1997). 'Albino (1961): uno o due ripostigli monetali di III–IV secolo?', *Notizie Archeologiche Bergomensi* 5: 273–307.

Bijovsky G. (2004). 'Coins from Ashqelon, Semadar Hotel', *'Atiqot* 48: 111–21.

Bijovsky G. (2012). *Gold Coin and Small Change: Monetary Circulation in Fifth–Seventh Century Byzantine Palestine* (Polymnia: Numismatica antica e medievale. Studi 2). Trieste.

Bijovsky G. (forthcoming). 'The coins from Insula W2S3 in Caesarea', in Y. Porath (ed.), *IAA Excavations in Caesarea* II: *the Insula W2S3.*

Bijovsky, G., Sandhaus, D., and Milevski I. (2014). 'A Byzantine hoard of gold coins from Ashqelon, Barnea B–C neighborhood', *Israel Numismatic Research* 9: 193–211.

Bravo, B. (2009). *La Chronique d'Apollodore et le Pseudo-Skymnos : érudition antiquaire et littérature géographique dans la seconde moitié du IIe siècle av. J.-C.* (Studia Hellenistica 46). Leuven.

Burnett, A. M. (1985). 'Roman hoards', *Coin Hoards* 7: 147–75.

Casson, L. (1989). *The Periplus Maris Erythraei: Text with Introduction, Translation, and Commentary.* Princeton.

Cohen, M., Ashkenazi, D., Bijovsky, G. I., Inberg, A., Klein, S., and Cvikel, D. (2018). 'Bronze coins from the Byzantine-period Ma'agan Mikhael B shipwreck, Israel: Metallurgical characterization', *Microscopy Microstructure and Analysis* 7.5: 542–60.

Cvikel, D. (2021). 'The Ma'agan Mikha'el B shipwreck, Israel: Summary of six underwater excavation seasons', in K. Covello-Paran, A. Erlich, and R. Beeri (eds), *New Studies in the Archaeology of Northern Israel*. Jerusalem, 49*–61*.

de Callataÿ, F. (2017). 'Coin deposits and civil wars in a long-term perspective (*c*.400 BC–1950 AD)', *Numismatic Chronicle* 177: 313–38.

Diller, A. (1955). 'The authors named Pausanias', *Transactions and Proceedings of the American Philological Association* 86: 268–79.

Dumankaya, O. and Açar, E. (2019). 'Kızlar Hamamı Bay underwater hoard', *Journal of Archaeology & Art* 162: 1–32.

Frey-Kupper, S. and Stannard, C. (2018). 'Evidence for the importation and monetary use of blocks of foreign and obsolete bronze coins in the ancient world', in B. Woytek (ed.), *Infrastructure and Distribution in Ancient Economies. Proceedings of a Conference Held at the Austrian Academy of Sciences, 28–31 October 2014*. Vienna, 283–354.

Galili, E. (1992). 'Navigation and commerce along the Israeli coast in antiquity: Finds from underwater surveys', in *The Maritime Holy Land, Mediterranean Civilizations in Ancient Israel from the Bronze Age to the Crusades*. Haifa, 21–30.

Galili, E., Dahari, Y., and Sharvit, J. (1993). 'Underwater surveys and rescue excavations along the Israeli coast', *International Journal of Nautical Archaeology* 22: 65–8.

Galili, E., Gorin-Rosen, Y., and Rosen, B. (2015). 'Mediterranean coasts, cargoes of raw glass', *Hadashot Arkheologiyot – Excavations and Surveys in Israel* 127, http://www.hadashot-esi.org.il/report_detail_eng.aspx?id=24846&mag_id=122 (accessed 3 March 2022).

Galili, E., Rosen, B., and Sharvit, J. (2010). 'Artifact assemblages from two Roman shipwrecks off the Carmel Coast', *'Atiqot* 63: 61–110.

Galili, E. and Sharvit, Y. (1999). 'Haifa, underwater surveys', *Hadashot Arkheologiyot – Excavations and Surveys in Israel* 110: 15*–20*.

Geiger, J. (2016). 'Some Greek intellectuals in the Decapolis', *ARAM* 28: 11–16.

Gitler, H. and Kahanov, Y. (2002). 'The Ascalon 1988 hoard (*CH* 9, 548): A periplus to Ascalon in the late Hellenistic period?', in A. Meadows and U. Wartenberg (eds), *Coin Hoards*, vol. 9: *Greek Hoards* (Royal Numismatic Society Special Publication 35). London, 259–68.

Gitler, H. and Kahanov, Y. (2008). 'A late Hellenistic coin hoard', in L. E. Stager, J. D. Schloen, and D. M. Master (eds), *Ashkelon* 1: *Introduction and Overview (1985–2006)*. Winona Lake, IN, 385–95.

Goldman, J. (2017). *The Coin Hoards of Roman Palestine: 63 BC–AD 300*. M.Phil. Thesis, University of Oxford.

Goldman J. (2022). 'Coin hoarding in Roman Palestine: 63 BC–AD 300', in J. Mairat, A. Wilson, and C. Howgego (eds), *Coin Hoards and Hoarding in the Roman World* (Oxford Studies on the Roman Economy). Oxford, 208–20.

Kindler, A. (1969). 'Hoard of Roman gold coins from the first and second century [*sic*] CE', *Alon: Internal Quarterly of the Israel Numismatic Society* 3.3: 69–78 (Hebrew).

Kingsley, S. (2000). 'Shipwreck archaeology in Israel: An undeveloped historical resource', *Bulletin of the Anglo-Israel Archaeological Society* 18: 57–72.

Kingsley, S. (2004). *Shipwreck Archaeology of the Holy Land: Processes and Parameters* (Debates in Archaeology). London.

Lampinen, P. (1999). 'The gold hoard of 4th-c. solidi found in 1993', in K. G. Holum, A. Raban, and J. Patrich (eds.), *Caesarea Papers*, vol. 2: *Herod's Temple, the Provincial Governor's Praetorium and Granaries, the Later Harbor, a Gold Coin Hoard, and Other Studies* (Journal of Roman Archaeology Supplement 35). Portsmouth, RI, 368–88.

Martínez Mira, I. (1995–7). 'Tesorillos del s. III d.C. en la Península Ibérica', *Lvcentvm* 14–16: 119–80.

Meshorer, Y. (2010). 'Coin hoard from a third-century CE shipwreck off the Carmel Coast', *'Atiqot* 63: 111–36.

Misch-Brandl, O. (ed.) (1985). *From the Depths of the Sea: Cargoes of Ancient Wrecks from the Carmel Coast* (The Israel Museum, Catalogue no. 263). Jerusalem.

No Author (1962). 'A hoard of 3,700 Late-Roman coins from Caesarea,' *Israel Numismatic Bulletin* 3–4: 106.

Noe, S. P. (1937). *A Bibliography of Greek Coin Hoards* (Numismatic Notes and Monographs 78). New York.

Oestreicher, B. (1962). 'A contemporary picture of Caesarea's ancient harbour', *Israel Numismatic Bulletin* 2.2: 44–7.

Olivier, J. (2012). *Archè et chrèmata en Égypte au IIe s. avant J.-C. (204–81 av. J.-C.). Étude de numismatique et d'histoire*, PhD thesis, Université d'Orléans.

Raphael, K. and Bijovsky, G. (2014). 'The coin hoard from Caesarea Maritima and the 363 CE earthquake', *Israel Numismatic Research* 9: 173–92.

Robertson, A. S. (1989). 'Evidence for the transport of Roman coins from the Mediterranean to Britain', in V. A. Maxfield and M. J. Dobson (eds), *Roman Frontier Studies. Proceedings of the XVth International Congress of Roman Frontier Studies*. Liverpool, 114–16.

Schumacher, G. (1900). 'Reports from Galilee', *Quarterly Statement of Palestine Exploration Fund* 33: 355–60.

Sharvit, J. and Buxton, B. (2022). 'A Roman merchant ship cargo of scrap metal and raw materials in the Caesarea Harbor: Preliminary report', in *Centro, Collected Papers*, vol. 1: *Motion, Movement, and Mobility*. Tel Aviv, 75*–91*.

Syon, D., Lorber, C., and Galili, E. (2013). 'Underwater Ptolemaic coin hoards from Megadim', *'Atiqot* 74: 1–8.

Syon, D. and Tepper, Y. (2021). 'A hoard of Syrian *tetradrachms* from a mass burial in 'Akko-Ptolemais', *Israel Numismatic Research* 16: 125–41.

Tal, O. and Bijovsky, G. (2017). 'A hoard of fourth–fifth century CE copper coins from Sozousa', *Israel Numismatic Research* 12: 147–201.

Tepper, Y. (2010). 'A pagan cemetery from the Roman period at the foot of Tel Akko: Evidence of the burial of Roman soldiers and citizens of Colonia Ptolemais', in A. E. Killebrew and V. Raz-Romeo (eds), *One Thousand Nights and Days: Akko through the Ages* (Hecht Museum Catalogue 31). Haifa, 33*–39*.

van Alfen, P. (2016). *Shipwrecked: The Challenges and Details of Large Quantity Coin Finds*. Paper Delivered at the International Meeting on Underwater Cultural Heritage and Site Protection, in Support of the Implementation of the 2001 Convention on the Protection of the Underwater Cultural Heritage, UNESCO Headquarters, 22 September 2016.

Waner, M. and Safrai, Z. (2001). 'A catalogue of coin hoards and the shelf life of coins in Palestine hoards during the Roman and Byzantine periods', *Liber Annuus* 51: 305–36.

Weber, S. H. (1932). *An Egyptian Hoard of the Second Century A.D.* (Numismatic Notes and Monographs 54). New York, 1–41.

Zorea, C. (2018). 'Judean coins unearthed in Spain: First century BCE to first century CE', *Israel Numismatic Research* 13: 101–20.

Donald T. Ariel, *Roman Coin Hoards from Shipwrecks along the Eastern Mediterranean Coast* In: *Roman Coin Hoards Across Frontiers*. Edited by: Benjamin D. R. Hellings, Marguerite Spoerri Butcher, and Chris Howgego, Oxford University Press. © Oxford University Press 2026. DOI: 10.1093/9780198986478.003.0003

4

Rethinking the Karanis Hoard Evidence

Irene Soto Marín

INTRODUCTION

A large part of Romano-Egyptian monetary history has been written based on the hoard evidence from the site of Karanis, an ancient village located in the Fayum Oasis in Egypt. While 42 hoards are known to have come from Karanis, this chapter will focus on those with a documented archaeological context, namely those excavated by the University of Michigan.[1] The goal of revisiting these hoards is to highlight differences in their composition and archaeological contexts, which in turn reveal aspects of the nature of currency in third-century Egypt. Hoards found in building C401 especially complicate the standard account, showing a potential relationship between civil unrest and recalled coinage around the time of Diocletian's currency reform.

HISTORY OF EXCAVATIONS AT KARANIS

The site of Karanis, located in the Fayum oasis of Egypt, was first excavated by Bernard Grenfell and Arthur Hunt in the winter of 1895/6. Both were originally hunting for more papyri in the Fayum and thus focused more on the procurement of texts than properly excavating structures, though the archaeological context of certain papyri can nonetheless still be ascertained from these early retrieval efforts. Karanis was then excavated (more) systematically by the University of Michigan from 1924 to 1935.[2] During the latter years of excavation, tens of thousands of objects were recovered. Following the rules of the partage system common at the time, many objects stayed in Cairo and *c*. 44,000 went to the

[1] One hoard was also found during the excavation of the site by Grenfell and Hunt in 1896 and initially published in Milne (1898), unfortunately without an archaeological context. The hoard appears in Table 4.1 as Noeske 8 and CHRE 7805. Milne (1898) initially reported the hoard to contain 91 coins, which was repeated by Milne (1900), though Noeske (2006: 80) lists 98 coins.

[2] See Montserrat (1996) for a more detailed description of this first season in Karanis.

University of Michigan where they are now housed at the Kelsey Museum of Archaeology and in the Papyrology Collection in the Hatcher Graduate Library.

Karanis is thought to have been founded in 250 BC, a time when the Ptolemaic dynasty ruling in Egypt resettled much of the land in the Fayum with Greek mercenaries, aiming to profit from the fertile land of the oasis. The Ptolemies used the Fayum as royal lands for important agricultural products and to cultivate novel crops such as the durum wheat commonly planted in mainland Greece and surroundings.

Accordingly, Karanis has been broadly dated from the Hellenistic period to the end of the fifth century AD, reliant largely upon the papyrological evidence,[3] while its archaeological contexts have only haphazardly provided coins, textiles, and sometimes also excavated papyri to refine dating further. While two volumes of the excavations and finds were published in 1931 and 1933, a final report of the excavation was never completed, and thus we lack a holistic view of the 11-year excavation.[4] Furthermore, archaeological contextualization of the objects is not straightforward given the incoherent and disorganized surviving archival record. During the 11 years of excavation a significant archive of documentation was created and brought back to Michigan, though it was never systematically organized.[5] Nevertheless, excavation archives are remarkably rich, including reports, maps, photographs, letters, and even film. Most of the archives are housed at the Kelsey Museum of Archaeology, though several letters are at the Bentley Historical Library and in the Papyrology Collection housed in Hatcher Graduate Library, where Karanis papyri, some ostraca, and writing tablets are kept. While aspects of the archival record have been used for publications and dissertations, Karanis archives housed at the Kelsey have never been properly organized as a whole, and thus making sense of the archaeological contexts of objects is not always possible. This means that understanding the circulation patterns and composition of the hoards from the site is often the only clue for dating the stratigraphy itself.

This chapter presents a list and discussion of the hoards found at Karanis by the excavations conducted by Michigan, but an in-depth analysis of the composition of each hoard is outside its scope. Key hoards are identified to better understand patterns of circulation within the province of Egypt, and the hoards are recontextualized within their archaeological findspot as well as within the wider

[3] The papyri come from excavations by Michigan though, there are many texts mentioning the village which come from unsourced papyri purchased in Egypt at the time, see Haug (2021).

[4] Boak and Peterson (1931) cover the first four seasons of excavation. The first three hoards, temples, and archaeobotanical material were published two years later; see Boak (1933). Husselman and Peterson (1979) deal with the topography and architecture of the site, though as pointed out by van Minnen (1994: 227), the book was 'a summary' of the unpublished report on the excavations compiled by Peterson, which covers the last seven seasons of excavations.

[5] A new project led by Dr Laura Motta and Dr Tyler Johnson has been systematically creating a digital platform for the archives.

monetary practices of Egypt. Tying aspects of the papyrological evidence to the context of the hoards serves to illuminate the function of the building complex C401, where most of the hoards were found. In the end, my aim is to introduce two points that will undoubtedly necessitate further discussion. First, I will discuss why so many hoards from Karanis were found in one building, and whether the fate of the building could ultimately be related to the coin hoards concealed within it. The second point is to demonstrate a trend in the hoards excavated by the University of Michigan in building complex C401, namely that the closer to the date of Diocletian's reform the coin hoards were buried, the higher the quantity of coins there were in them, perhaps indicating a relationship between the reforms of Diocletian and the function of the building complex.

PUBLICATION OF THE KARANIS HOARDS

Archaeologists claimed to have found over 30,000 coins during the excavations conducted by the University of Michigan, though the corrosion on several thousands of them meant that they were impossible to identify.[6] Exactly 26,796 coins were recorded as accessioned specimens at the Kelsey Museum of Archaeology, representing seemingly 1,745 different coin types. Of these, 2,049 are said to be stray finds and 24,747 were found in 37 hoards (Fig. 4.1). Thus, the analysis of the coins performed by the Michigan team pertains specifically to the accessioned specimens at the Kelsey and not those that remained in Cairo. The catalogue also does not include illegible coins, though according to the authors the illegible coins found in hoards 'numbering close to 5,000, are noted in order to give as nearly as possible the total number in the original hoard'.[7] In 2006, Hans-Christoph Noeske also pointed out that the way in which the catalogue had been arranged by Rolfe Haatvedt, Enoch Peterson, and Elinor Husselman, summarizing coins from hoards and single finds into a single type list, made it impossible to distinguish the single finds from the total amount of excavated coins.[8]

Confusion in the accounting of the coins is due in part to the complicated history of their publication. The original analysis of the 1930s Karanis hoards was prepared as a doctoral dissertation by Rolfe Haatvedt in 1939, but the project was never completed. Years later, responsibility for the publication of the book was given to Enoch Peterson, director of the Kelsey Museum of Archaeology at the time. Peterson worked on the book but retired in 1964 before the publication was completed, and the project was finally seen through by Elinor Husselman, Curator of Manuscripts and Papyrology at the University of Michigan Library and Curator

[6] Haatvedt, Peterson, and Husselman (1964: 1): 'Many were so eroded and defaced that identification was impossible, and many in the hoards disintegrated at the touch as they were being counted.'

[7] Haatvedt, Peterson, and Husselman (1964: 1).

[8] Noeske (2006: 278).

Fig. 4.1. Map of Karanis where hoards were found. From: Haatvedt, Peterson, and Husselman (1964: plate X). Karanis, Egypt. University of Michigan excavations. With permission of the Kelsey Museum of Archaeology.

of the Museum of Archaeology.[9] Having gone through several different hands over the course of three decades caused the publication to contain numerous inconsistencies. Some of them were admitted and corrected by Husselman, but several problems remained with the book. Erik Christiansen noted, for example, that some obvious inconsistencies were changed only in the list of types presented in pages 361–89 of the volume, but that 'several incorrect transcriptions of the legends were not corrected at all'.[10]

Since these coins were published prior to the creation of the *Roman Provincial Coinage* catalogues, in addition to the fact that Husselman was a papyrologist, not a trained numismatist, there are many errors in coin types listed as well as misreadings of legends. Thanks to the work of Noeske in 2006, typology numbers

[9] Haatvedt, Peterson, and Husselman (1964).

[10] The errors were already noted, albeit vaguely, by Husselman in Haatvedt, Peterson, and Husselman (1964: V) and were cited by Christiansen (2004: 60–1). It is unclear which corrections Husselman thought obvious enough to fix and which were left as is in the manuscript.

(e.g. references to Milne, Geissen, etc.) were added to all the coins from Karanis,[11] including to any additional hoards that were not uncovered by the Michigan excavations.[12] According to Noeske's calculations, the finds include 282 Ptolemaic coins, 24,257 Roman provincial coins from Alexandria, 1,321 Roman imperial coins, 509 Egyptian imitation coinages, and two coins from the Byzantine period.[13] A large part, though not all, of the numismatic evidence was also analysed by Christiansen in his important contribution *Roman Egypt: The Hoard Evidence* published in 2004.

THE HOARDS IN CONTEXT

The hoards published by Haatvedt, Peterson, and Husselman were numbered by the order in which they were discovered. In the discussion that follows, hoards will be referred to by the numbers that were given to them by Haatvedt, Peterson, and Husselman. In 2006, Noeske organized them by *terminus post quem (t.p.q.)*, as seen in Table 4.1. Hoard 4, the only hoard of *aurei*, will be addressed first, since gold coinages in Egypt have their own special significance. For the purpose of this chapter, 11 of the first 12 hoards, which in most cases were found in separate archaeological contexts, will be discussed individually and by *t.p.q.* Hoards 13–36 will be discussed together since they were found in the same building complex, have a relatively tight chronology, and may suggest different historical implications from the first 12.

The gold hoard (Hoard 4)

Hoard 4 (Table 4.2) is the most remarkable, as it raises an important question for understanding the relationship of the monetary systems between Egypt and the Roman Empire: gold coinage. The hoard contained 60 Roman *aurei* and was found in a courtyard of B11—in what is thought to be a second-century house at the site.[14] The hoard had originally been stored in a cloth bag whose only remnants were traces of mesh weave left in the soil around it. Some textile remains from a cloth bag were found nearby, possibly part of the original bag which held the coins (Fig. 4.2).[15]

Haatvedt, Peterson, and Husselman reported that 22 coins of the 60 *aurei* were retained by the Department of Antiquities in Cairo (those of Hadrian, Antoninus Pius,

[11] Milne (1971); Geissen (1974–83).

[12] Noeske (2006: 71–278).

[13] Noeske (2006: 278).

[14] Again, the coins themselves were the ones used to date the archaeological contexts.

[15] The hoard was initially reported in Boak and Peterson (1931: 38) but then more thoroughly analysed in Haatvedt, Peterson, and Husselman (1964: 14–15).

Table 4.1. Summary of all Karanis hoards by *t.p.q.*, with references to Noeske (2006: 71–2), the Michigan hoard numbering according to Haatvedt, Peterson, and Husselman (1964), *IGCH* for Ptolemaic hoards, and CHRE for Roman hoards.

Noeske	Michigan	*IGCH*/CHRE	Excavation year	*t.p.q.*	No. of coins	Context
1	10	*IGCH* 1715	1924–35	164/163 BC	12	House C137
2	11	*IGCH* 1716	1924–35	164/163 BC	35	House C137
3	13	CHRE 7758	1933–4	AD 52/3?[a]	33	C401 complex
4	12	CHRE 7759	1924–5	AD 65/6	50	House B11
5	N/A	CHRE 18825	1967	AD 67/8	1,005	N/A
6	37	CHRE 7791	1924–5	AD 152/3	7	Granary C123
7	27	CHRE 7793	1924–5	AD 154/5	55	C401 complex
9	4	CHRE 5473	1926	AD 157	60	House B11
8	N/A	CHRE 7805	1896	AD 169/70	91	N/A
10	30A	CHRE 7868	1933–4	AD 257/8	40	House C137
11	14	CHRE 7883	1933–4	AD 262/3	76	C401 complex
12	32	CHRE 7881	1933–4	AD 262/3	747	C401 complex
13	15	CHRE 7884	1933–4	AD 264/5	57	C401 complex
14	1	CHRE 7886	1925	AD 268/9	860	House B501C
15	28	CHRE 7891	1933–4	AD 270/1	36	C401 complex
16	5	CHRE 7912	1924–35	AD 272/3	31	House C45
17	6	CHRE 7917	1933–4	AD 274/5	192	House C45
18	7	CHRE 7918	1924–35	AD 274/5	22	House C55A
19	31	CHRE 7931	1933–4	AD 282/3	416	C401 complex
20	20	CHRE 7930	1933–4	AD 282/3	127	C401 complex
21	26	CHRE 7934	1933–4	AD 285/6	102	C401 complex
22	36	CHRE 7936	1933–4	AD 287/8	2,891	C401 complex
23	30	CHRE 7937	1933–4	AD 288/9	1,001	C401 complex
24	25	CHRE 7938	1933–4	AD 289/90	2,329	C401 complex
25	N/A	CHRE 7952	1972	AD 292/3	1,500	Found in the basement of a house, NW part of Karanis
26	22	CHRE 7949	1933–4	AD 292/3	523	C401 complex
27	29	CHRE 7954	1933–4	AD 293/4	4,500	C401 complex
28	33	CHRE 7961	1933–4	AD 294/5	59	C401 complex
29	17	CHRE 7978	1933–4	AD 295/6	379	C401 complex
30	16	CHRE 7989	1933–4	AD 295/6	1,102	C401 complex
31	19	CHRE 7980	1933–4	AD 295/6	1,439	C401 complex
32	18	CHRE 7979	1933–4	AD 295/6	2,484	C401 complex
33	21	CHRE 7981	1933–4	AD 295/6	762	C401 complex
34	23	CHRE 7982	1933–4	AD 295/6	1,486	C401 complex
35	24	CHRE 7983	1933–4	AD 295/6	1,489	C401 complex
36	35	CHRE 7987	1933–4	AD 295/6	1,499	C401 complex
37	34	CHRE 7986	1933–4	AD 295/6	2,944	C401 complex
38	9	CHRE 18823	1924–35	AD 302–3	11	House B188
39	N/A	CHRE 4328	1974	AD 367–75	29	N/A
40	8	CHRE 18681	1927	AD 395	2	House C56
41	2	CHRE 7992	1925	AD 450	1,074	House 137
42	3	CHRE 18826	1925	AD 455	582	House 113D

[a] As mentioned in the discussion of the hoards, this date is based on the only legible coin of the hoard and I am inclined to think this hoard dates to the third century, as the rest of the hoards found in C401.

Table 4.2. Coins from Hoard 4, after Noeske (2006: 85–6), with the *aureus* of Faustina II (*RIC* III, 679) redated to AD 157 instead of AD 161–76.

Issuing Authority	*RIC* Number	Date	No. of coins	Mint
Hadrian?	?	AD 117–38	1	Rome
Antoninus Pius	*RIC* III 177d	AD 148–9	1	Rome
Antoninus Pius	*RIC* III 226C	AD 152–3	1	Rome
Antoninus Pius	*RIC* III 255a	AD 155–6	4	Rome
Antoninus Pius	*RIC* III 255b	AD 155–6	12	Rome
Antoninus Pius	*RIC* III 266a	AD 156–7	10	Rome
Antoninus Pius	?	AD 138–61	11	Rome
Diva Faustina	*RIC* III 348a	AD 141–61	2	Rome
Diva Faustina	*RIC* III 356a	AD 141–61	1	Rome
Diva Faustina	?	AD 141–61	4	Rome
Marcus Aurelius Caesar	*RIC* III 427B	AD 145–60	1	Rome
Marcus Aurelius Caesar	*RIC* III 469B	AD 156–7	2	Rome
Marcus Aurelius Caesar	?	AD 140–61	3	Rome
Faustina II	*RIC* III 494A	AD 145–61	3	Rome
Marcus Aurelius for Faustina II	*RIC* III 679	AD 157	1	Rome
Antoninus Pius or Marcus Aurelius for Faustina II	?	AD 145–76	3	Rome

Fig. 4.2. Photograph of Hoard 4 in situ. Karanis, Egypt. University of Michigan excavations. © Kelsey Museum of Archaeology, KM 5.2421.

Marcus Aurelius, Faustina the Elder, and three of Faustina the Younger), although Evaristo Breccia listed only 21 specimens and 18 types.[16] The remaining 38 coins, now in the Kelsey Museum, are all dated from the fourth consulship of Antoninus Pius (AD 156–7), leading Haatvedt, Peterson, and Husselman to conclude that this is when the hoard was concealed.[17] Although the 1964 publication of the hoard did mention the *aureus* of Hadrian,[18] Christiansen seemingly only accounted for the coins at the Kelsey, given his statement that all coins from this hoard came from the reign of Antoninus Pius.[19] One of the latest coins was seemingly an outlier: an *aureus* from the reign of Marcus Aurelius in the name of Faustina II dated to the period between AD 161 and 176 (*RIC* III, 679), but Beckmann recently and convincingly used die links and this hoard itself to show that this type of *aureus* ought to be redated to AD 157, a date thus much more consistent with the rest of the hoard.[20]

Throughout the Roman period, Egypt remained a separate currency zone, meaning that only Egyptian coinage was officially minted and circulated in the province.[21] Yet at least eight hoards of *aurei* are known from Egypt including Hoard 4 from Karanis, and they were all briefly discussed by Christiansen in 2004.[22] So what were these *aurei* doing at Karanis? The *aureus* was part of the traditional Roman monetary system, and thus it was not part of the Egyptian Greek system of denominations still in place during this time. Nevertheless, the numismatic record seems to point to the hoarding and active use of *aurei* in Egypt during the Roman period.[23] The mint at Alexandria did not habitually mint gold coins during the Roman period; it was only when emperors visited the province that special coinages for their expenditure would be made.[24] Small issues of gold Alexandrian coins have been identified for Vespasian, Septimius Severus, the usurper Pescennius Niger, as well as Domitius Domitianus, Maximian, Diocletian, Licinius, Justin II, and Heraclius.[25] There was minting of *aurei* in Alexandria during the reign of Septimius Severus, but according to Christiansen this issue was limited and intended only for outside payments, not to be specially (or rather officially) used in Egypt.[26] With the Egyptian closed currency system, in theory

[16] These were reported and listed by type in Breccia (1932: 66).

[17] Haatvedt, Peterson, and Husselman (1964: 14–15).

[18] Haatvedt, Peterson, and Husselman (1964: 14–15).

[19] Christiansen (2004: 46).

[20] Beckmann (2021: 53).

[21] Geissen (2012: 1).

[22] Christiansen (2004: 46–7): the other seven are 26 *aurei* found in Alexandria (CHRE 7873); 600+ in Abu Qir (CHRE 4155); 38 near Suez (CHRE 20936); 800 in Mallawi (CHRE 7809); 'thousands' in Tell Sakha (CHRE 7810); four in Minya (CHRE 7849); and 1,800+ from Karnak (CHRE 6259). Hoard 4 was also detailed and described by Noeske (2006: 85–6).

[23] Christiansen (2004).

[24] For a useful bibliography to the production of the Alexandrian mint during the Roman period, see Geissen (2012).

[25] See *RIC* II^2, 45–6, for Vespasian; Bland, Burnett and Bendall (1987), for Pescennius Niger; Geissen (1976), Thomas (1976) and Staffieri (2005), for Domitius Domitianus; *RIC* VII, Alexandria.

[26] Christiansen (2004: 46).

only billon tetradrachms minted on the Greek standard were to be utilized and circulated though clearly this was not the case in practice, and this hoard exemplifies the porosity of Egypt's (not so isolated) monetary zone. Christiansen hypothesized that these gold coinages present in the province were meant to be used eventually in the active Indo-Roman and sub-Saharan trade, which flowed through Egypt.[27] This hypothesis is supported by thousands of Roman *aurei* which have been found on the Indian coasts. Literary evidence from the *Periplus Maris Erythraei*, too, makes consistent reference to the availability of Roman coinage in different ports and trading cities in sub-Saharan Africa.[28]

The archaeological and literary evidence seems to point to the movement of precious metal currency within and through Egypt, even if it was not part of its official currency. The types from Hoard 4 are also commonly found in excavations from India, e.g. Penuganchiprolu (CHRE 15778), Kumbalam (CHRE 18046), Vinukonda (CHRE 18578), and Mattadakere (CHRE 18594),[29] but whether the gold coins from Karanis were destined to go to India remains unknown.[30]

Bronze hoards (Hoards 1–3 and 5–12)

The bronze hoards are listed by *t.p.q.*, based on Noeske 2006. Hoards 13 and 27, however, will be discussed by their joint archaeological contexts in C401 rather than by *t.p.q.* order. Hoards from complex C401 (namely Hoards 13–36) are discussed separately, following a chronological order by *t.p.q.*

Hoards 10 and 11 are the only Ptolemaic hoards from the site and were both found in Room A in House C 137. Hoard 10 consisted of 12 bronze coins which were found in a small clay pot, and the pot itself was found inside a basket. According to Haatvedt, Peterson, and Husselman, the two identifiable coins in Hoard 10 were 'barbarous' issues minted by Ptolemy X during a native revolt in

[27] Christiansen (2004: 47).

[28] *PME* 8, *PG* 55 Casson (1989). There is mention of coins and Roman money imported from Egypt available in the region of Adulis (53), and the port cities of Malaô (55), Muza (63–4), Kanê (67), Barbarikon (75), Ozênê (81), and Bakarê (85).

[29] I thank Emilia Smagur very much for this important information. The information was obtained from the online database of the Coin Hoards of the Roman Empire Project (accessed October 2023). For bibliography on these hoards and coins see Subrahmanyam, Rama Krishna Rao, and Brahmācāri (2008); Sathyamurthy (2011); Smagur and Romanowski (2020).

[30] There is one more important gold hoard from Karanis, which was recovered in 1974 from either uncontrolled excavations or a looting attempt. This hoard contained 29 *solidi* dating to the second half of the fourth century, with an estimated closing date during the reign of Valens after AD 367–75. The latest coin is *RIC* IX 25b. At this time Egypt was already well integrated monetarily with the rest of the Empire, and thus the occurrence of a gold hoard is perhaps less significant than during the earlier Roman period, though still relevant for understanding circulation patterns. Unfortunately, the archaeological findspot within the site is not known. The hoard was published by Arce (1987: 181–7) and is listed in Noeske (2000: 258–9).

86–84 BC.[31] This classification is erroneous and Noeske restudied the coins and assigned them the date of 170–164/163 BC.[32]

Hoard 11 was found in the same context in a small wooden box. Initially only one coin was said to be legible and was assumed to be from the same period during the reign of Ptolemy X. Noeske restudied the coins and dated the hoard also to 164/163 BC based on the legible coin, but he also thinks the illegible coins are of the same type as the legible coin.[33]

Hoard 12 is the only first-century hoard which was found in House F28 within the precinct of the temple of Penepheros and Petesouchos. Forty coins were found in a storage jar dating to the reigns of Claudius (AD 44/5) and Nero (AD 65/6).[34]

Noeske lists Hoard 13 as having an end date in AD 52/3, yet this is based on the fact that the only legible coin dates to this year. Given the archaeological context of the hoard in building C401, I am inclined to believe that the disintegrated coins in the hoard actually date to the latter half of the third century, and thus I will discuss Hoard 13 alongside the hoards found in C401.

The last hoard presented by Haatvedt, Peterson, and Husselman is Hoard 37, which is a small hoard containing seven coins. All the coins date to the late first century and first half of the second century.[35] The hoard was found in the wall of a vaulted storage room CCH in C123 identified as the granary.[36]

The first three hoards excavated at Karanis were published in 1933. Hoard 1, found below the floor of an underground room in House 4028, was studied by Milne, who argued for AD 268/9 as an end date given the date of the latest coin. It is uncertain whether it was purposely hidden beneath the floor or forgotten and then unintentionally covered by a later floor levelling or construction.[37] The hoard contained 860 Alexandrian tetradrachms, which Husselman listed by type. The earliest coins date to year 10 of Marcus Aurelius, AD 169/70,[38] and the latest coins date to over a hundred years later, to year 2 of Claudius II, AD 268/9.[39] Milne noted that House 4028 was one of the many houses known to be in use during a late period of occupation, namely the late fourth and fifth centuries,[40] yet using the

[31] Haatvedt, Peterson, and Husselman (1964: 18).

[32] Noeske (2006: 72). The coins were identified as *Sv.* 1917, *SNG Cop.* 695–6.

[33] Noeske (2006: 73). The coins were identified as *Sv.* 1698, *SNG Cop.* 695–6.

[34] The earliest coins are Haatvedt, Peterson, and Husselman (1964) nos 77–9 (*RPC* I, 5162) and no. 5163 from year 4 and 5 of Claudius, and the latest are from year 12 of Nero, Haatvedt, Peterson, and Husselman (1964) no. 108 (*RPC* I, 5289). Haatvedt, Peterson, and Husselman (1964: 110; 115). Noeske (2006: 74–5) identified the earliest coins in the hoard as Geissen 81, dated to AD 43/4, and the latest as Geissen 172, dated to AD 65/6.

[35] Milne 1253 is dated to AD 127/8, Milne 1868 to AD 145/6, Milne 2058 to AD 149/50, and Milne 2193 to AD 152/3.

[36] The papyri from this context, as well as a useful introduction to the archaeological contexts, were published by Claytor and Verhoogt (2018: 9–28).

[37] Milne and Hayter (1933: 59).

[38] Milne 2598; Haatvedt, Peterson, and Husselman (1964: 161, no. 418).

[39] Milne 4227; Haatvedt, Peterson, and Husselman (1964: 247, no. 1052).

[40] Milne gives no reason for this dating in Milne and Hayter (1933: 59).

tetradrachms themselves he argued for an earlier construction date and concluded that 'on the basis of the tetradrachms in the hoard we may assign the building of this house to the early part of the B period, that is, not long after AD 250'.[41] Milne thought the hoard was buried about AD 268/9, since the latest coin in it is one of Claudius Gothicus of that year. He also posited that the change in the currency standard might have had something to do with the composition of the hoard, since older coins would have been preferred to newer ones.[42] He furthermore argued that the hoarder could have started amassing coins *c.* AD 234/5, since there are coins from almost every year of Severus Alexander's reign in good condition, in addition to die-linked coins in a great state of preservation belonging to the sixth year of Gordian III. The group seems to have continued over the course of thirty years, though there are fewer coins representing the last eight years of collecting.

Hoards 5 (17 coins) and 6 (9 coins) were found in a 'late third-century house' which has been dated by the coins themselves. Hoard 5 was found in a pottery jar buried beneath the floor of room N. The latest coins in these hoards date to year 6 of the reign of Aurelian, i.e. AD 274/5.[43]

Hoard 7 (22 coins), whose last coin also dates to year 6 of Aurelian,[44] was found in House C55, where many papyri and ostraca were found which dated to the late third and early fourth century, seemingly even in the same archaeological layers as the hoard. Husselman pointed out specifically O.Mich. 502, an ostracon dated to 23 October AD 302, which was found 'rather high in the filling of the room'.[45] The only depositional information we have on the hoard was that it was found on the sill of the niche in the east wall of room A of House C55. The hoard was not buried but, rather, simply placed on the sill, which could indicate that the coins were circulating at least during AD 302, when the text of O.Mich. 502 was composed. While it remains a possibility, it seems unlikely for the hoard to have been dug out in later periods when the house was abandoned, and then simply discarded on the niche.

Hoards 2, 3, 8, and 9 are the only ones with coins issued after Diocletian's reform excavated in Karanis by Michigan. Hoard 9 was found fused together, underneath the floor of room D in House B188; 11 coins were recovered but the hoard was larger. The latest identified coins are of Constantius Chlorus dating to AD 306.[46] It seems that all the coins are post-reform and dated to the Tetrarchic period, with no earlier pre-reform coinage identifiable. The 1964 publication does not specify the size or weight of the fused hoard, so it is not clear what percentage

[41] Milne and Hayter (1933: 59). [42] Milne and Hayter (1933: 60).

[43] Milne 4453 with Severina obverse; Haatvedt, Peterson, and Husselman (1964: 254, no. 1106).

[44] Milne 4456; Haatvedt, Peterson, and Husselman (1964: 253, no. 1097).

[45] Haatvedt, Peterson, and Husselman (1964: 17).

[46] Haatvedt, Peterson, and Husselman (1964: 303). Based on the description and the mint mark, the only option is *RIC* VI Heraclea 3.

of the total hoard the 11 identified coins could represent. Given that there is no other hoard that contains both pre- and post-reform coinage on the site, it is most likely that the unidentifiable coins are also from the Tetrarchic period and later. Noeske identified the earliest coin as one of Constantius Chlorus as Caesar (*RIC* VI, 21a), dated to AD 295–6 and minted in Alexandria. This type of *nummus* with the reverse type GENIO POPVLI ROMANI demonstrated the transition from Greek- to Latin-style coinage. We know the reform did not take place in Egypt until AD 297/8, so, if correct, the coin is an example of the first Latin-style coins minted in Alexandria that could have potentially been part of the reason for the revolt of L. Domitius Domitianus in 297.[47]

Hoard 8, containing only two coins, was found in House C56 and dates to at least after the reign of Arcadius in the late fourth century.[48] The coins were found in the debris that filled the former stairway of a house, and the editors have posited the idea that these repairs were made then to match the level of the street and represent the last occupation level of this house.

Hoard 2, which was also published by Milne in 1933, dates to the early fifth century.[49] It was found in a long-necked footed pot found in the filling of room D at floor level of House 137. The hoard contains 1,074 coins, which Milne categorized into five groups: autonomous Greek, Lycian city issues from the first century BC (2); Alexandrian issues of Trajan and Hadrian (2); imperial coins datable to the period AD 335–430 (606), with dozens of the latest coins dated to the reign of Theodosius II, AD 402–50; local copies of imperial coins (303); and illegible coins (126). Milne rightly pointed out first that a large portion of the hoard consisted of coins which were not 'official currency' during the fifth century. This is a common numismatic trend in Egypt, and elsewhere, during the fourth and fifth centuries, when non-official and foreign coins circulated freely within the province.[50]

Hoard 3 contains nearly 600 small copper *nummi*, the latest dated to the early to mid-fifth century. The hoard was found in a small water jar with a stopper of palm fibre in House 113D. These hoards seem to have been found at habitational level, apparently not concealed within the ground or a wall, which could potentially point to a sudden abandonment rather than a purposeful concealment.

The hoard evidence thus far from around the site seems to point to large hoarding occurring during the late third century. Hoards 1, 5, 6, and 7 all date to the period between AD 268/9 and 292. Hoards 9, 8, 2, 3 are all post-reform but more chronologically scattered with a range for deposition between AD 306 and the late fifth century.

[47] Geissen (2012: 576).

[48] Catalogue number 1732 which has the obverse of no. 1710 and reverse of no. 1711 in Haatvedt, Peterson, and Husselman (1964: 342–54). Based on the description and the mint mark, the only option is *RIC* IX Alexandria 20C.

[49] Milne and Hayter (1933: 71).

[50] See Soto Marín (2020) for an analysis of coin moulds and documentary sources that point to a clear lack of precious metal in the hands of official authorities.

THE HOARDS FROM COMPLEX C401 (HOARDS 13–36) AND THEIR INTERPRETATION

Finds from C401 emphasize this pattern of intense hoarding during the latter part of the third century in Karanis. During one of the last seasons of Karanis (1933–4), Hoards 13 to 36 were found in one complex, comprising four houses (Fig. 4.3). The hoards represent about 27,000 coins. No clear explanation was given or hypothesized as to why so many coins were found in one complex, and the archaeological context of the series of houses, blocked off by streets, makes quite clear that it was in fact one building unit.[51] The excavators commented that the

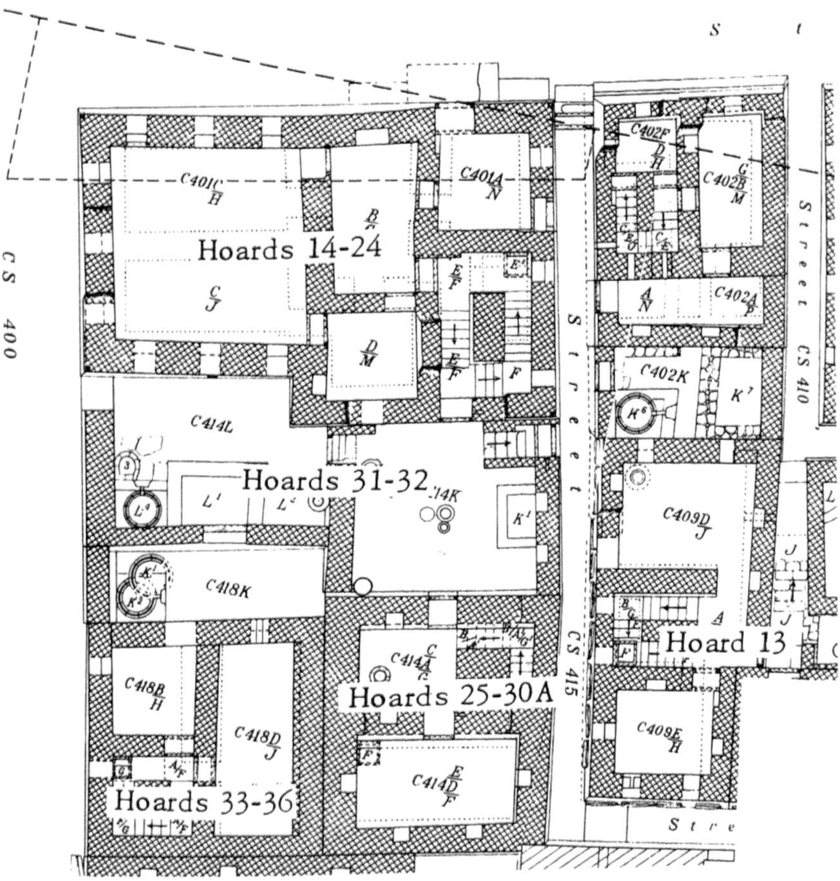

Fig. 4.3. Plan of C401. From: Haatvedt, Peterson, and Husselman (1964: plate Xia). Karanis, Egypt. University of Michigan excavations. With permission of the Kelsey Museum of Archaeology.

[51] Haatvedt, Peterson, and Husselman (1964: 19).

Fig. 4.4. Photograph of façade of building C401. From: Haatvedt, Peterson, and Husselman (1964), plate XIb. Karanis, Egypt. University of Michigan excavations. © Kelsey Museum of Archaeology, KM 5.4247.

principal house of the complex, C401, had a stone entranceway that was unusual, as well as stone steps above street level and leading up to its entrance (Fig. 4.4). Heavily scorched walls present clear signs of a significant fire in the building. Ten of the hoards were found in storage jars, four in cloth bags, and eleven in unprotected heaps. Table 4.3 summarizes the location and context of the hoards found in complex C401, which encompasses buildings B501, B514, C414, and C418.

If we consider the hoards from building C401, a pattern emerges. There are two types of hoard: smaller hoards, with a wide range of coins (namely Hoards 13–15, 17, 27, 28, 30A, and 33) and larger hoards with a tighter chronology (Hoards 16, 18–26, 29, 31, and 34–6). Hoards 30 and 32 count in this latter category due to their size, even though they possess earlier coinage. Most of the hoards have a *t.p.q.* in the late third century AD, already pointing to a caesura in the hoard evidence. But the nature of hoarding seems different between these groups. While Hoards 13–36 were all found in the same complex of buildings which were clearly connected to each other, the location within the buildings and even the diverse ways they were stored (some in jars, others in cloth bags, others exposed) point to potentially different periods, though relatively close in time to each other, and different people who stored and deposited these coins within this building.

Table 4.3. Hoards found in complex C401 with information on their archaeological context and references to the Michigan hoard numbering according to Haatvedt, Peterson, and Husselman (1964).

Michigan	Archaeological context	Storage	No. of coins
13	Floor level, Underground Room C House B501	Cloth bag	32
14	Floor level, Underground Room C House B501	Cloth bag	76
15	Heap on floor, Underground Room G House B501	Unprotected heap	57
16	Floor level Underground Room G House B501	Cloth bag	1,103
17	Floor level Underground Room G House B501	Small amphora	379
18	Floor level Underground Room G House B501	Large storage jar	2,484
19	Floor level Underground Room G House B501	Unprotected heap	1,439
20	Floor level Underground Room G House B501	Unprotected heap	127
21	Floor level, Underground room H House B501	Jar	762
22	Hole beneath floor Underground room H House B501	Jar	523
23	Floor level, Underground room J House B501	Cloth bag	1,486
24	Floor level, Underground room N House B501	Unprotected heap	1,489
25	Under doorway between Room A and courtyard House B514	Jar	2,329
26	Floor level Along wall of Room A House B514	Unprotected heap	102

(*Continued*)

Table 4.3. (Continued)

Michigan	Archaeological context	Storage	No. of coins
27	Floor level Room A House B514	Unprotected heap	55
28	Beneath floor level, Room A House B514	Jar, rim exposed in floor level	36
29	Floor level Room A House B514	Unprotected heap	4,500
30	Foot of stairway from Room A to 2nd floor House B514	Heap	1,001
30A	Floor level Room D House B514	Heap	40
31	Base of bin and oven, Corner of courtyard House B514	Small amphora	416
32	Floor level, Underground room F House C414	Unprotected	747
33	Beneath floor Passageway E House C418	Heap	59
34	Beneath floor Passageway E House C418	Amphora	2,944
35	Beneath floor Passageway E House C418	Amphora	1,419
36	Beneath floor Passageway E House C418	Amphora	2,891

When we plot the quantity of coins and the date of the latest coins in a scatter plot, we find a correlation between the date of the latest coin and the number of coins in each hoard. The scatter plot (Fig. 4.5) clarifies that the closer the date is to AD 297/8, the higher the quantity of coins in the hoard. AD 297/8 is a particularly important date for the monetary history of Egypt, as it is the year of the revolt of Domitius Domitianus.

Contextualizing the hoarding right before the revolt could also explain the abandonment of the hoards, as well as the traces of fire in C401 noticed by the excavators. If there was a massive fire that caused structural damage to the building, the second (and potentially third) floor would have collapsed inward, as is commonly

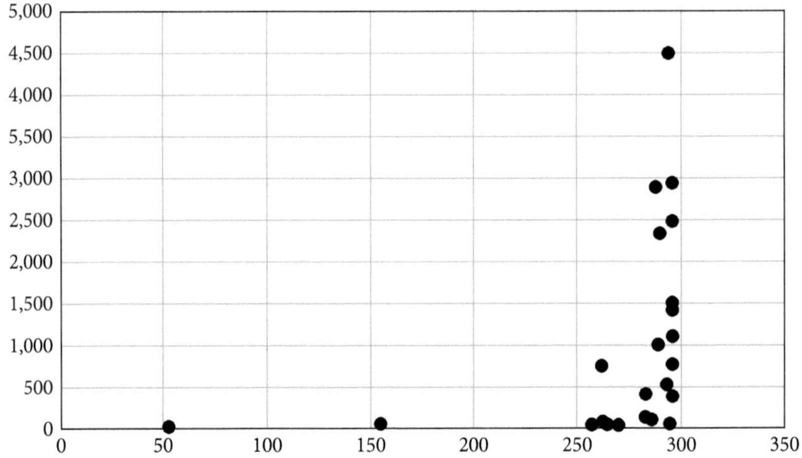

Fig. 4.5. Hoards from C401. Scatter plot of size of hoards in number of coins compared to their *t.p.q*.

observed in the decomposition of Roman sites in Egypt.[52] The fire itself could have been the result of civil unrest, especially since part of the assumed reasons for the revolt were the abolishment of Egypt's closed currency system and the institution of a new monetary system Empire-wide.[53]

Although Diocletian's coinage reform took place in earlier years (AD 294–5) in other provinces of the Empire, Schwartz initially argued that in Alexandria the reform took place in August AD 296 based on his analysis of the coinage issued by the usurper L. Domitius Domitianus. Using papyri, ostraca, and literary evidence, however, Thomas convincingly argued for a revolt in AD 297/8 and this latter date is now widely accepted.[54]

The larger hoards at Karanis could represent recalled coinage, meant to be used for the new coins minted in Alexandria. This responsibility could have fallen to the office of the tax collectors, which could explain the main function of the building as a tax office. This would also explain the presence of other types of smaller hoards with a wider range of coinage. They too could represent tax levies taken in coin or recalled coinage paid by individuals. There is a clear hoard discontinuity even within Karanis that could point to the active hoarding of pre-reform coinage, or maybe even a state-mandated recalling of coinage. Could the complex C401 be a tax office of sorts where people turned in their pre-reform coinage? This could explain the heterogeneity of the hoards as well as the different ways the coinage

[52] There are other sites in Roman Egypt that show a similar pattern of building decay—for example, building B10 in Amheida, where the roof collapsed inwards, burying the roof cellar with *c.* 57 jars of wine, and the kitchen below it, preserving all furniture and archaeobotanical material. See Bagnall *et al.* (2017).

[53] See Geissen (2012: 576); see also Schwartz (1975) for a full investigation into the sources around the revolt of Domitius Domitianus.

[54] Thomas (1976); Estiot (2012).

was stored, though it does not explain the abandonment of these 27,000 coins. I will return to this discussion alongside the papyrological evidence below.

The composition of the hoards varies as well. Hoard 14 contained 76 coins ranging from Nero (AD 54–68) to Gallienus (AD 262/3), including coinage from the emperors Nero, Galba, Vespasian, Nerva, Hadrian, Antoninus Pius, Marcus Aurelius, Commodus, Severus Alexander, Maximinus, Maximus, Gordian III, Philip I, Philip II, Decius, Trebonianus Gallus, Valerian, Gallienus, and Valerian II—a range of over 200 years for the coins in the hoard. Similarly, the much larger and heterogeneous composition of Hoard 17 also led Haatvedt, Peterson, and Husselman to point out that there are coins of nearly 'every emperor and other members of the imperial families. Over two thirds of the types of coins in this hoard are represented by one specimen.'[55] This heterogeneity of the hoard stands out from the more homogeneous compositions of other hoards yet still fits within the wider hoarding patterns of Roman Egypt.[56]

In contrast, there were also hoards which had a much tighter chronology. All the coins in Hoards 20 to 26, for instance, could be dated to the late third century. The earliest coins in these hoards date to Claudius II (AD 268–70), while the latest coin dates to Diocletian (AD 295/6), which means on average a 25-year range for the composition of the hoards. What all of these hoards do have in common is that they contain pre-reform late third-century coins.

The evidence from Karanis represents over 33% of the total numismatic material we have from Roman Egypt.[57] Yet, since 25 of the 37 hoards were found in a single complex of buildings, and several of them were relatively large, this creates a hoard bias and over-representation for coin types in these hoards that need to be addressed to better understand coinage circulation and production in the province, and in some cases might even lead to reassessing the dating of the parts of the site of Karanis.

Several of the hoards were remarkably heterogeneous, and initial scholars placed their closing date in the late third century because of the latest coins they contained. As we have seen from other hoards in Karanis, such as Hoard 14, coinage in Roman Egypt had a long circulation life, where tetradrachms of Nero, for example, are found in tandem with coinage dating to the late third century.[58] Hoard 2 of Karanis contained coins from the first century BC as well as coins dating to the fifth century AD. This is not a phenomenon unique to Karanis: hoards from all over Roman and Late Roman Egypt also often show the same

[55] Haatvedt, Peterson, and Husselman (1964: 27).

[56] See Noeske (2008: 126) for a discussion on the longevity of certain issues of Marcus Aurelius and Nero in second- and third-century hoards.

[57] Noeske (2008: 124). Specifically, billon tetradrachms. Other types of hoard of later dates were not counted in Noeske's total.

[58] The most updated and detailed analysis to date of Nero's reform of Egyptian tetradrachms can be found in Butcher and Ponting (2014: 625–46). For previous scholarship on the monetary reforms of Nero see Christiansen (1988; 2004) and Gölitzer (2004: 84). Noeske (2008: 125–6) traces the presence of Neronian tetradrachms in hoards down to the third century as well.

heterogeneity. Just to give a couple of salient examples: a hoard from Meydum (ancient Moithymis) contained three coins which were described as Ptolemaic or Alexandrian and were broadly dated from the second century BC to the second century AD, while the rest of the hoard contained fourth- and fifth-century coins;[59] and Hoard 6 from Hawara (ancient Averis) had coins ranging from the reign of Antiochos IV (175–164 BC, *BMC* 41) to the reign of Theodosius II (AD 402–8, *LRBC* 2922/2928).[60] Especially in times of high debasement and political turnover, people were more inclined to hoard earlier coinage or, rather, were disinclined to use newer coinages.

The circulation of Hellenistic coinages alongside third-century and post-reform coinage provides some colourful evidence for a debate between scholars of the phrase *παλαιὸν Πτολεμαϊκὸν νόμισμα* and *παλαιὸν νόμισμα* seen in third-century papyri.[61] This phrase, meaning 'old Ptolemaic coins', can be found in sales contracts, loans, receipts for payments, and even leases, all dated between AD 266 and 289.[62] Kruse and Woytek have recently argued that the number of Ptolemaic coins in third-century Roman hoards in Egypt are low and thus rare exceptions. While I agree with the authors that the quantity of Ptolemaic coinage in circulation during the third century was not high, coins were probably encountered by people more often than has been allowed, and thus the memory of a good, heavy tetradrachm acted as reference in contrast to the highly debased, poor-quality coinage that was being minted in the third century.[63] Nevertheless, the authors' conclusions are convincing: in the third century AD people were aware of the difference in the quality of Egyptian billon tetradrachms, and they recognized that the older a coin, the better its quality.[64] This view has rather important implications for understanding the Karanis hoard evidence.

To summarize, first we know it was a common practice in Egypt to utilize coins with a long circulation life. Second, the papyrological evidence from the third century AD does show that people understood the difference between older coins and newer ones, and thus the hoarding of them seems much more purposeful. The preference for older coinages with higher metal content is also highlighted in

[59] CHRE 18827. See Noeske (2000: 289), referencing MacIsaac (1972: 59–66). The hoard initially contained 2,570 bronze coins and was discovered in 1932 by Dr Rowe as part of the expedition by the University of Pennsylvania.

[60] CHRE 18834. See Noeske (2000: 293–315), referencing Milne (1920: 169; 1926: 43). The hoard initially contained 3,119 bronze coins.

[61] Kruse and Woytek (2020: 341).

[62] See Kruse and Woytek (2020: 343) for a full list of texts and references. Respectively, the texts I allude to are *P. Ryl.* II, 165, 18–19; *P. Coll. Youtie* II, 71, 24–5; *P.Oxy.* XXI, 2587, 5–7; *P. Stras.* VI, 539, 5–6. Reinard (2016) argues, erroneously I believe, that the term is a monetary fiction and does not represent physical coins, a hypothesis that is readily disproven with a quick glance at the numismatic record.

[63] *P. Oxy.* 12. 1411, note from the *strategos* to bankers to accept the newly debased coinage under Quietus and Macrianus, AD 260.

[64] Kruse and Woytek (2020: 363).

the well-known *P. Oxy.* 12. 1411, dated to AD 260, where bankers and traders in Egypt are commanded to accept the newly minted coinage, showing a deep distrust of the debased currency in circulation.[65]

ECONOMIC REFORMS: EGYPT AND ELSEWHERE IN THE EMPIRE IN THE LATE THIRD CENTURY

In order to stabilize the economy of the Empire and to assert himself as its new leader after civil unrest, Aurelian (AD 270–5) implemented a monetary reform that included measures to cap inflation and a reorganization of the Empire's mints.[66] The Alexandrian tetradrachms were reformed in AD 273, preceding the official imperial reform of 274, when Aurelian's year 5 tetradrachms had a 15% reduction in weight. Therefore, the weight reduction of the tetradrachm in AD 273 anticipated the reform of Aurelian in 274. Diocletian's currency reform expanded the previous system instituted by Aurelian in the AD 270s, whose coinage reform had limited durability. The coinage had been heavily debased by the time of Diocletian, since it had been affected by the policies instituted by his predecessors.

In conjunction with other reforms, Diocletian abolished Egypt's closed currency system and in AD 295 instituted a new coinage reform throughout the provinces. For over 600 years, the Egyptian territory had required currency exchange at its borders for the purchase of goods, which allowed very close control of the metal supply and the minting schedule, as well as the extraction of coinage within the province.[67] This also separated Egypt in some respects from the rest of the Empire, however, giving it a partially isolated economic status relative to the rest of the provinces, a characteristic that strongly challenged Diocletian's efforts to streamline integration of the Empire. After AD 296, all of the Empire, including Egypt, had a gold coin of 5.45 g (scholars prefer the term *aureus*), which was

[65] Bagnall, Bransbourg, and Soto Marín (2021: 7, n. 25).

[66] Estiot (2012: 546). Aurelian also reorganized the imperial mints, instituting eight official mints and 39 *officinae* along with a clearer and more systemic method of marking mints on coins. The marking of bronze coinage has been recognized as one of the main merits of his reforms.

The reform of Aurelian had regional disparities and was not applied uniformly throughout the Empire. Aurelian managed to recall debased *antoniniani* to make way for his new coinage in the economic channels of the Empire. However, the results in the western part of the Empire were not very successful. For more on the Gallic empire and its issuing of imitation coinages during the third century see Estiot (2012) and Estiot, Amandry, and Bompaire (1994). According to Estiot, the symbols used record the silver content of the coins, stating that 20 bronze reformed *antoniniani* (now termed *aureliani*) would be (by fiat rather than the market value of the metals) equivalent to one *argenteus* of pure silver. This recognized the fiduciary nature of the reformed *antoninianus*, a coin type originally issued under Caracalla. This interpretation, however, is not widely accepted, since the silver coin was never produced. The more traditional view is that it represented the value of 1 part of silver in 20 parts of copper/bronze.

[67] Christiansen (2004).

reduced to a weight of 5.3 g in short order.[68] There was also a silver *argenteus* at 3.4 g, minted only very briefly, and three denominations of billon coins, with the largest at 10 g.[69] For the first time, Egypt utilized the same coinage as the rest of the Mediterranean world, and Roman Egyptian coinage ceased to be made.

Diocletian's economic reforms naturally took some time to take effect, and much of what we see monetarily in the early fourth century seems to be a continuation of the high debasement of the third century. After the revolt of Domitius, production of the Alexandrian mint seems to have been low, while the now-legal utilization of outside mints seems to have taken immediate effect. If we use traditional chronologies and numismatic boundaries, we have only six hoards from this period in Egypt, which were published by Metcalf in 1974. According to Metcalf, the hoards seem to have been deposited sometime between AD 297/8 and 317.[70] The Alexandrian mint represents 50% of the composition of these hoards. Therefore, if Metcalf is correct about the deposition date, this would mean that, immediately or very soon after the abolition of the closed currency system, Egypt was already dependent on outside coinage. This trend seems to continue for the rest of the fourth century, when the Alexandrian mint continuously loses its dominance in hoards and represents about 18% of the numismatic material in hoards.[71] Furthermore, to my knowledge, there are only eight coins as single stray finds that can be attributed to the Alexandrian mint from the first two decades of the fourth century.[72] The evidence for lack of bronze, or precious metal in general, is further reinforced by the archaeological record in Egypt, which shows thousands of used coin moulds near known military camps, showing that the army had to manufacture its own coins for payments to the soldiers during this time.[73] Besides the hoards from Karanis, the papyrological evidence from the site sheds further light on the matter.

P. Columbia VII 138, 139, 140, and 141, dated to AD 307/8, are receipts for the sale of gold, silver, and bronze bullion to the Roman state. The texts referencing gold and silver were originally edited and published by Roger Bagnall,[74] who recognized them as requisitions of precious metal from wealthy landowners. These sales of precious metal were compulsory and represented a kind of levy. In the fourth century, taxes could be commuted to monetary payments (*adaeratio*),

[68] Abdy (2012: 589) notes that the gold coin was already known as the *solidus* by AD 301, but the scholarly custom has preferred to save this name for the reduced gold coin introduced by Constantine, calling the coin an *aureus* until AD 309. The Edict of Maximum Prices (AD 301) offers the value of 1,200 *denarii* per one gold coin. Constantine reduced the gold coin to 4.5 g, a weight that was maintained for the rest of the Late Antique period, until the tenth century, cf. Porteus (1969: 14–33).

[69] Estiot (2012).

[70] Metcalf (1974).

[71] Soto Marín (2018).

[72] Bagnall, Bransbourg, and Soto Marín (2021: 246). See also accompanying table in that article listing Abu Mena, Kom El-Ahmar, Minshat Abu Omar, Clysma-Qolzum, Saqqara, Armant, and Umbarakab-Taphis.

[73] For evidence of lack of bronze in circulation, see Bagnall, Bransbourg, and Soto Marín (2021: 247). For a more in-depth discussion of coin moulds in Egypt, see Soto Marín (2020).

[74] Bagnall (1977).

meaning that the collection did not necessarily have to be in kind.[75] These compulsory sales in the Karanis papyri are different, though, since what was being requested was specifically the precious metal bullion rather than coins. Bransbourg states: 'in the case of P. Col, 7, 141, cols. iii and iv, bronze represented the explicit good that the state sought to acquire, that is, there was an explicit levy of bronze as raw metal, rather than simply a tax to be discharged using bronze currency...'.[76] It is unclear if the bullion meant was melted-down metal, or perhaps could it have been referring to old coinage? The fact that these texts also come from Karanis, though admittedly a decade after the revolt was quelled, shows nonetheless the close control the state sought over coinage and metal bullion.

Could the hoarded pre-reform coinage in Karanis' building complex C401 be related to these requisitions for metal bullion? If the hoards represent recalled coinage, they could have been handed in to this putative tax collection office at a time when they no longer represented the imperial currency (*c.* AD 307/8) and thus were valued both by their owners and by the state for the precious metal bullion in them. If, on the other hand, there is no relationship with these texts and the hoards, the option remains for the material to represent recalled coinage. The intense and heterogeneous yet *consistent* hoarding that we see in the building complex C401 alone indicates monetary friction between the state and the population of Egypt. There are no coins of Domitius Domitianus in the hoards, and thus the hoarding could have taken place prior to the reform and represent one of the last stages of recalled coinage before the introduction of the new currency system. The hoards could also have been deposited during the reforms of Diocletian as part of the recall of the coinage, which caused civil unrest in several areas of Egypt, including the Fayum. The much older coins in the hoards seem to suggest not only a long circulation life for specific issues but trust in and preference for the higher quantity of precious metal that these coins contained.

Continuous changes of imperial power, revolts, and the debasement of Alexandrian tetradrachms did not help to solidify trust in newer currency. As we see in *P. Oxy.* 12.1411, dated to AD 260, the extreme suspicion of the new coinage provided by the state reached a point where bankers no longer accepted the new tetradrachms, as they were disinclined to accept the new, debased currency in exchange for an older issue with a higher silver content.

In addition to having a tradition for utilizing earlier tetradrachms, pre-reform coinage (whether before Aurelian's or Diocletian's new debased coinage) apparently had a particular appeal to be hoarded for its precious metal content. While it is simply a hypothesis, the complex C401 could be identified as the office of a bank, moneylender, or tax collector in charge of collecting taxes, recalling coinage, and eventually putting new coinage into circulation. Another possibility, though

[75] Bagnall, Bransbourg, and Soto Marín (2021: 243).
[76] Bagnall, Bransbourg, and Soto Marín (2021: 243).

perhaps less likely, is that it represents one of the distrusting banks that decided to hoard as much of the 'old coinage' once the reform was announced, keeping tetradrachms with higher silver content because of a lack of trust in the currency reform.

Another important aspect for reanalysing the hoard evidence is to understand the development of the site. Most of the dates we have from the site come either from the coinage themselves or the papyri. According to https://papyri.info (accessed June 2022), so far 3,848 dated texts have been recovered which are known to be from Karanis. Of these, 13 texts belong to the Ptolemaic period (300–50 BC), 122 date to the first century AD, 1,083 to the second century, 985 to the third century, 1,401 to the fourth century, 123 to the fifth century, 28 to the sixth century, 5 to the seventh century, and 4 to the eighth century. There are also 890 undated texts. The concentration of these 3,848 dated texts falls between the late second and the late fourth century (75.2%).[77] We cannot always trace papyrological texts to the same contexts as the coins, but the overall distribution of the dates of the papyri retrieved by Michigan implies high activity during the aforementioned time period.

Recent archaeobotanical analyses of 13 specimens of the site has further reinforced the view of active habitation in the fourth, fifth, and sixth centuries. African Red Slip ware and amphorae found throughout the site suggest active participation in Mediterranean-wide market trends, and archaeobotanical analyses also hint at periods of activity in the fourth to sixth centuries.[78] Unfortunately none of the archaeobotanical specimens come from the same contexts where the hoards were found. Although three of them could potentially belong to the same layer (level C), the confidence in correlating structures with one another is not high, since 'the continuous transformations, abandonment, and reconstruction of standing structures 51 occurred simultaneously with the building of new ones'.[79] Unfortunately, the current state of the archival record of Karanis does not allow us to use other objects that could help to date stratigraphic layers, such as ceramics. The organic material published by Motta *et al.* is the most reliable scientific analysis of the site to date.

The hoard evidence from Karanis contains Alexandrian coins representing every single third-century emperor—even short-lived rulers like Gordian II, with a recorded reign of 22 days. The most frequent types found in the third-century hoards belong to long-ruling emperors like Valerian, Probus, and Diocletian and to short-ruling emperors such as Carus.

[77] Some papyri of Karanis also have a date and an archaeological context which can further shed some light on the chronology of the hoards, but unfortunately the analysis of those dates will have to wait until the archaeological context of these objects is better understood.

[78] Motta *et al.* (2024) notes the archaeological evidence which seems to suggest a period of high activity in the fourth century.

[79] Motta *et al.* (2024). The seeds from level C date to the late fifth and sixth centuries.

The quantity of coins present in just one area of Karanis seems to indicate that the presence of, and presumably access to, coins was common at least in the Fayum, although, as Noeske has pointed out, this could also be due to the more intensive archaeological activity that has taken place there compared to other areas of Egypt, particularly during the earlier twentieth century when papyri were actively sought after and excavated.[80] Karanis is considered a village town—it was not a nome capital and never obtained the designation of *polis* or had a city council. Yet the site shows that it had a familiarity with the usage of coins, a complex and diversified economic system, as is evident from the tax records, and frequent connectivity to Alexandria and other areas beyond in the Mediterranean.[81]

ABBREVIATIONS

BMC	*British Museum Catalogue of Greek Coins*. London (1873–1927).
CHRE	Coin Hoards of the Roman Empire Project (https://chre.ashmus.ox.ac.uk).
Geissen	see Geissen (1974–83).
IGCH	Thompson, M., Mørkholm, O., and Kraay, M. (1973). *An Inventory of Greek Coin Hoards*. New York.
LRBC	Hill, P. V., Kent, J. P. C., and Carson, R. A. G. (1960). *Late Roman Bronze Coinage, AD 324–498*. London.
Milne	see Milne (1971).
RIC II^2	Carradice, I. A. and Buttrey, T. V. (2007). *The Roman Imperial Coinage*, vol. II, Part 1, 2nd fully revised edition: *From AD 69–96, Vespasian to Domitian*. London.
RIC III	Mattingly, H. and Sydenham, E. A. (1930). *The Roman Imperial Coinage*, vol. III: *Antoninus Pius to Commodus*. London.
RIC VI	Sutherland, C. H. V. (1967). *The Roman Imperial Coinage*, vol. VI: *From Diocletian's Reform (A.D. 294) to the Death of Maximinus (A.D. 313)*. London.
RIC VII	Bruun, P. M. (1966). *The Roman Imperial Coinage*, vol. VII: *Constantine and Licinius A.D. 313–337*. London.
RIC IX	Pearce, J. W. E. (1933). *The Roman Imperial Coinage*, vol. IX: *Valentianian I —Theodosius I*. London.

[80] Noeske (2008: 125).

[81] It was argued by Berlin in Gazda and Wilfong (2004: 14) that 'farmers had little hard currency', though I believe this statement is not very accurate given that the example the authors gave was the fact that taxation took place in kind, from a receipt in AD 313. While it is clear there was a need for currency during the early fourth century, we simply do not know the exact level of monetization in Karanis because the single finds from the site have never been analysed. The quantity of bronze coins alone in Karanis, in addition to the papyrological record, could imply that the site was monetized, though the quantity of coins from hoards found in C401 plays a substantial role in this hypothesis. This has been already proven and discussed by Rathbone (1991). The Karanis tax records are perhaps some of the best-known texts from the sites, which were originally published by Youtie, Schuman, and Pearl (1936). Alan Bowman has created a useful online database for these records as part of the Oxford Roman Economy Project, which can be found at http://oxrep.classics.ox.ac.uk/databases/karanis_tax_rolls_database/ (accessed October 2023).

RPC I	Burnett, A., Amandry, M., and Ripollès, P. P. (1992). *Roman Provincial Coinage* I: *From the Death of Caesar to the Death of Vitellius (44 BC–AD 69).* London and Paris.
SNG Cop.	Christiansen, E. and Kromann, A. (1974). *Sylloge Nummorum Graecorum. The Royal Collection of Coins and Medals, Danish National Museum, Part 41: Alexandria-Cyrenaica.* Copenhagen.
Sv.	Svoronos, I. N. (1904). *Τα νομίσματα του κράτους των Πτολεμαίων.* Athens.

REFERENCES

Abdy, R. (2012). 'Tetrarchy and the House of Constantine', in W. E. Metcalf (ed.), *The Oxford Handbook of Greek and Roman Coinage.* Oxford and New York, 585–98.

Arce, J. (1987). 'A solidus hoard from the vicinity of Karanis', *Revue Suisse de Numismatique* 66: 181–91.

Bagnall, R. S. (1977). 'Bullion purchases and landholding in the fourth century', *Chronique d'Égypte* 52: 322–36.

Bagnall, R. S., Bransbourg, G., and Soto Marín, I. (2021). 'State collection of bronze in early fourth-century Egypt', *Zeitschrift für Papyrologie und Epigraphik* 220: 241–8.

Bagnall, R. S., Caputo, C., Casagrande-Kim, R., and Soto, I. (2017). 'New evidence from ostraka for the dating of fourth-century AD ceramic assemblages', *Bulletin de liaison de la céramique égyptienne* 27: 195–211.

Beckmann, M. (2021). *Faustina the Younger : Coinage, portraits, and public image.* New York.

Bland, R. F., Burnett, A. M., and Bendall, S. (1987). 'The mints of Pescennius Niger in the light of some new aurei', *Numismatic Chronicle* 147: 65–83.

Boak, A. E. R. (ed.) (1933). *Karanis: The Temples, Coin Hoards, Botanical and Zoölogical Reports, Seasons 1924–31.* Ann Arbor.

Boak, A. E. R. and Peterson, E. E. (1931). *Karanis: Topographical and Architectural Report of Excavations during the Seasons 1924–1928.* Ann Arbor.

Breccia, E. (1932). *Le Musée Gréco-Romain 1931–1932.* Alexandria.

Butcher, K. and Ponting, M. (2014). *The Metallurgy of Roman Silver Coinage: From the Reform of Nero to the Reform of Trajan.* Cambridge.

Casson, L. (1989). *The Periplus Maris Erythraei: Text with Introduction, Translation, and Commentary.* Princeton.

Christiansen, E. (1988). *The Roman Coins of Alexandria. Quantitative Studies.* (2 vols). Aarhus.

Christiansen, E. (2004). *Coinage in Roman Egypt: The Hoard Evidence.* Aarhus.

Claytor, G. and Verhoogt, A. (eds) (2018). *Papyri from Karanis: The Granary C123.* Ann Arbor.

Estiot, S. (2012). 'The later third century', in W. E. Metcalf (ed.), *The Oxford Handbook of Greek and Roman coinage*. Oxford and New York, 538–60.

Estiot, S., Amandry M., and Bompaire, M. (1994). 'Le trésor de Sainte-Pallaye (Yonne): 8, 864 antoniniens de Valérien à Carin', *Trésors Monétaires* 14: 39–124.

Gazda, E. K. and Wilfong, T. G. (2004). *Karanis, an Egyptian Town in Roman Times: Discoveries of the University of Michigan Expedition to Egypt (1924–1935)*. Ann Arbor.

Geissen, A. (1974–83). *Katalog Alexandrinischer Kaisermünzen der Sammlung des Instituts für Altertumskunde der Universität zu Köln* (Sonderreihe Papyrologica Coloniensia V. Abhandlungen der Rheinisch-Westfälischen Akademie der Wissenschaften). Opladen.

Geissen, A. (1976). 'Numismatische Bemerkung zu dem Aufstand des L. Domitius Domitianus', *Zeitschrift für Papyrologie und Epigraphik* 22: 280–6.

Geissen, A. (2012). 'The coinage of Roman Egypt', in W. E. Metcalf (ed.), *The Oxford Handbook of Greek and Roman Coinage*. Oxford and New York, 561–83.

Gölitzer, E. (2004). *Entstehung und Entwicklung des alexandrinischen Münzwesens von 30 v. Chr. bis zum Ende der julisch-claudischen Dynastie*. Berlin.

Haatvedt, R. A., Peterson, E. E., and Husselman, E. M. (1964). *Coins from Karanis: The University of Michigan Excavations, 1924–1935*. Ann Arbor.

Haug, B. (2021). 'Politics, partage, and papyri: Excavated texts between Cairo and Ann Arbor (1924–1953)', *American Journal of Archaeology* 125.1: 143–64.

Husselman, E. M. and Peterson, E. E. (1979). *Karanis Excavations of the University of Michigan in Egypt, 1928–1935: Topography and Architecture: A Summary of the Reports of the Director, Enoch E. Peterson*. Ann Arbor.

Kruse, T. and Woytek, B. E. (2020). '"(Old) Ptolemaic" and "new" coins in 3rd-century AD Egypt: A reassessment of the papyrological and numismatic evidence', in T. Faucher (ed.), *Money rules! The Monetary Economy of Egypt, from Persians until the Beginning of Islam*. Cairo, 341–66.

MacIsaac, J. D. (1972). 'The weight of the late 4th and early 5th century nummus (AE 4)', *American Numismatic Society, Museum Notes* 18: 59–66.

Metcalf, W. E. (1974). 'The "Cairo" hoard of Tetrarchic folles', *Revue belge de numismatique et de sigillographie* 120: 73–107.

Milne, J. G. (1898). *A History of Egypt under Roman Rule*. London.

Milne, J. G. (1900). 'The coins', in B. P. Grenfell, A. S. Hunt, and D. G. Hogarth, *Fayum Towns and their Papyri*. London, 64–74.

Milne, J. G. (1920). *Two Roman Hoards of Coins from Egypt*. London.

Milne, J. G. (1971). *Catalogue of Alexandrian coins (in the Ashmolean Museum)*. 1st edition repr. with a supplement by C. M. Kraay. London.

Milne, J. G. and Hayter, A. G. K. (1933). 'Three-coin hoards', in Boak (1933), 59–84.

Montserrat, D. (1996). '"No papyrus and no portraits": Hogarth, Grenfell and the first season in the Fayum, 1895-6', *Bulletin of the American Society of Papyrologists* 33: 133–76.

Motta L., Johnson T. D., Burton S., Reimer P. J., Erdkamp P., and Heinrich F. (2024). 'Re-dating Roman Karanis, Egypt: radiocarbon evidence for prolonged occupation until the seventh century AD', *Antiquity* 98 (400): 954–72.

Noeske, H.-C. (2000). *Die Münzfunde des ägyptischen Pilgerzentrums Abu Mina und die Vergleichsfunde aus den Dioecesen Aegyptus und Oriens vom 4.-8. Jh. n. Chr. Prolegomena zu einer Geschichte des spätrömischen Münzumlaufs in Ägypten und Syrien.* Berlin.

Noeske, H.-C. (2006). *Münzfunde aus Ägypten* II: *Die griechisch-römischen Münzfunde aus dem Fayum.* Mainz am Rhein.

Noeske, H.-C. (2008). 'Der Münzschatz von Abu al-Gud und einige Überlegungen zum Hortungsverhalten im kaiserzeitlichen Ägypten', in D. Gerin, A. Geissen, and M. Amandry (eds), *Aegyptiaca serta in Soheir Backhoum memoriam: mélanges de numismatique, d'iconographie et d'histoire* (Collezioni numismatiche 7). Milan, 113–53.

Porteus, J. (1969). *Coins in History: A Survey of Coinage from the Reform of Diocletian to the Latin Monetary Union.* London.

Rathbone, D. (1991). *Economic Rationalism and Rural Society in Third-Century A.D. Egypt: The Heroninos Archive and the Appianus Estate.* Cambridge.

Reinard, P. (2016). 'Altes ptolemäisches und neues kaiserliches Geld in den Papyri des 3. Jh. n. Chr. Beobachtungen zum Verlust der Geldillusion', in K. Martin and B. Eckhardt (eds), *Eine neue Prägung. Innovationspotentiale von Münzen in der griechisch-römischen Antike.* Wiesbaden, 115–49.

Sathyamurthy, T. (2011). *Catalogue of Roman Gold Coins in the Collections of Department of Archaeology, Kerala*, 2nd rev. edition. Thiruvananthapuram.

Schwartz, J. (1975). *L. Domitius Domitianus: Étude numismatique et papyrologique* (Papyrologica Bruxellensia 12). Brussels.

Smagur, E. and Romanowski, A. (2020). 'Review: B. SUBRAHMANYAM, G.V. RAMA KRISHNA RAO and P. BRAHMA CHARY, P. CHENNA REDDY (ed.), Roman Gold Coins. A Treasure Trove from Penuganchiprolu, Museum Series No. 31, Hyderabad (Department of Archaeology and Museums, Government of Andhra Pradesh), 2008, 36 pages (plus front matter not paginated). ISBN 978-81-920727-1-5', *Numismatic Chronicle* 180: 484–90.

Soto Marín, I. (2018). *The Economic Integration of a Late Roman Province: Egypt from Diocletian to Anastasius.* PhD dissertation, New York University.

Soto Marín, I. (2020). 'Coin molds and a decentralized monetary policy in Tetrarchic Egypt', *American Journal of Numismatics* 32: 313–38.

Staffieri, G. M. (2005). 'Testimonianze sulla fine della monetazione autonoma alessandrina (296-298 d.C.)', in C. Alfaro, C. Marcos, and P. Otero (eds), *XIII Congreso Internacional de Numismática, Madrid 2003.* Madrid, 937–45.

Subrahmanyam, B., Rama Krishna Rao, G. V., and Brahmācāri, P. (2008). *Roman Gold Coins: A Treasure Trove from Penuganchiprolu.* Hyderabad.

Thomas, D. J. (1976). 'The date of the revolt of L. Domitius Domitianus', *Zeitschrift für Papyrologie und Epigraphik* 22: 253–79.

van Minnen, P. (1994). 'House-to-house enquiries: An interdisciplinary approach to Roman Karanis', *Zeitschrift für Papyrologie und Epigraphik* 100: 227–51.

Youtie H. C., Schuman, V. B., and Pearl, O. M. (1936). *Tax Rolls from Karanis*. Part I. *Text* (Michigan Papyri. Volume IV, Part I). Ann Arbor.

Irene Soto Marín, *Rethinking the Karanis Hoard Evidence* In: *Roman Coin Hoards Across Frontiers*. Edited by: Benjamin D. R. Hellings, Marguerite Spoerri Butcher, and Chris Howgego, Oxford University Press.
 DOI: 10.1093/9780198986478.003.0004

PART II

EVIDENCE AND INTERPRETATIONS: NORTH, CENTRAL, AND EASTERN EUROPE

5

Roman Coin Hoards from Southern Scandinavia: Reflections in Light of Recent Finds

Helle W. Horsnæs and Rasmus Holst Nielsen

INTRODUCTION

The movement, use, and deposition of Roman coins outside the Empire differs significantly from the patterns within the Empire. There is, however, not a homogeneous pattern that fits all areas in Barbaricum. Multiple factors combine to reveal a diverse picture. Some of these factors are no doubt rooted in phenomena inside the Empire and the story of Imperial Rome. Among these we should count changes in the Roman monetary system, not least the profound changes taking place in the wake of the Diocletianic and Constantinian reforms, the division of the Empire, and the later breakdown of the centralized Western Empire, which facilitated a growth of several independent successor kingdoms. Other factors may be found in the individual cultures of non-Roman Europe.

The modern handling of Roman coins as archaeological artefacts differs widely depending on the findspot within Europe. Although the borders of modern states normally have very little in common with territories inhabited by pre- or proto-historical communities in non-Roman Europe, we need to study the coin finds on the level of modern nation states, as each modern state has its own legal structures as well as its own geographical and topographical conditions and its own modern history. All these factors must be taken into consideration before we can form a coherent interpretation of the use, movement, and deposition patterns of Roman coins outside the Empire in the first five centuries AD.

The Danish treasure legislation in its original form goes back at least to law compilations from the early thirteenth century. This means that information on even very early finds has been preserved in state archives, and finds of Roman coins in the modern state of Denmark have been discussed at least since the seventeenth century.[1] There has, however, been a surge of new finds during the last

[1] Horsnæs (2010; 2018); Holst Nielsen (2021).

40 years due to the extended use of metal detectors by amateur archaeologists.[2] After some initial concerns from professional archaeologists, collaboration between amateurs and authorities has grown, and the present practice today is generally considered to function well in most cases,[3] though some professionals hold reservations.[4]

The finds from Sweden and Norway are, of course, very important for the understanding of the Roman coin finds from Scandinavia in general. The differences between the modern legislations regarding the use of metal detectors make direct comparison arduous. While metal detector surveys have provided extremely high numbers of finds in Denmark, the ban on private detector use in Sweden means that the number of coin finds there has not grown as dramatically as in Denmark. This has ramifications for the total number of Roman coin finds, which has not changed significantly since the publication of Lennart Lind's comprehensive catalogue.[5] Consequently, the distribution of detector finds east and west of Øresund is remarkably uneven.[6] Finds from the few professionally surveyed sites, e.g. Uppåkra in Scania, reveal that the current overarching pattern of Swedish finds is deficient, and in some areas it should probably resemble the Danish pattern. In Norway, detector archaeology developed later than in Denmark, but amateur surveying has taken off since *c.* 2010.[7] Today, the number of finds is rising rapidly in Norway, but no coherent overview has been published so far.[8] It is, however, not only modern legislation and practices but also history, natural resources, and landscapes that differ greatly between these three countries, and we should never expect identical find patterns.

GOLD

Gold coins were found more easily than *denarii* in the pre-detector era, and the number of new gold finds has not grown as much as the finds of *denarii*.[9] The find distribution of gold coins is therefore more easily compared across modern borders and is considered first to illuminate the patterns across Scandinavia (Fig. 5.1).

Gold coins arrived in Denmark from the early first century AD onwards.[10] Many of them have been found as single finds or as part of a larger hoard also consisting of other valuables (such as imported and locally produced jewellery and ingots). In a few instances a single find can be securely related to a burial, most often as part of a necklace, but several finds come without an archaeological

[2] Roman coins: Horsnæs (2010: 32, fig. 7); coin finds in general: Horsnæs (2017).
[3] Baastrup and Feveile (2013); Dobat and Jensen (2016). [4] Ulriksen (2013).
[5] Lind (1981). [6] Feveile (2015). [7] Gullbekk (2019: 175).
[8] Pers. comm. Anette Sættem, June 2022. Skaare (1976) presents the most comprehensive summary but is now outdated.
[9] Horsnæs (2010: 32, fig. 9). [10] Horsnæs (2010; 2013b); Holst Nielsen (2019).

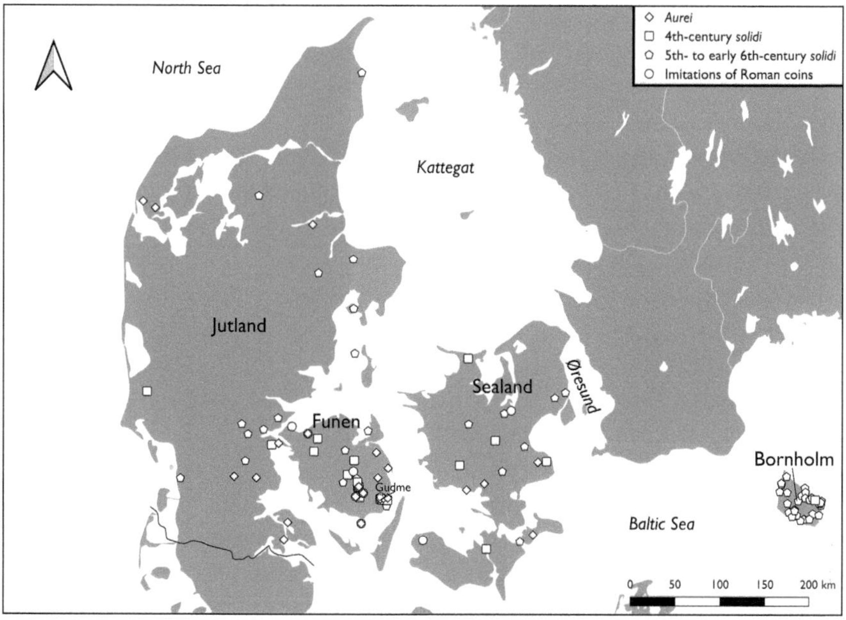

Fig. 5.1. Findspots of Roman *aurei, solidi,* and gold imitations of Roman coins from the second to the early fourth century. Map: Rasmus H. Nielsen.

context. There are several hoards containing coins from the fourth and fifth century from the island of Funen in particular. The finds gravitate towards the Iron Age centre at Gudme on Funen, and Funen is a general hotspot for gold finds.[11] Some of the hoards present remarkable similarities in the composition of coins. This is the case for the two hoards from central Funen, Brangstrup (CHRE 4198, 51 coins), and Boltinggård (CHRE 20009, 15 coins), found only *c.* 700 m apart. They both contain coins from the period from Trajan Decius through Constantine I as well as jewellery. Some of the jewellery in the Brangstrup hoard may indicate an area of origin in south-east Europe. Other examples are the two smaller hoards from the important centre at Gudme in south-east Funen, Gudme I (CHRE 4247) and Bjørnebanke (CHRE 20010). The Gudme I area has yielded 11 *solidi* (one of which is a medallion/multiple of 1½ *solidus*) found over a period of more than 100 years, and the exact composition of the material cannot be ascertained, as *denarii* and *siliquae* as well as a large number of other objects have been found in the same area. The Bjørnebanke hoard consists of three *solidi* and the remains of large late Roman silver platter cut into minute pieces. A fourth *solidus* found in the same general area in the nineteenth century may belong to the same deposition. In both cases the *solidi* are from the mid-fourth century (Gudme I: AD 337–55;

[11] Henriksen (2010).

Bjørnebanke: AD 347–54) and Magnentius' *solidi* are represented in both. These cases seem to indicate that sometimes valuables were assembled elsewhere and imported *en bloc*, only to be split up and/or topped up with objects of other origins before deposition.

While the numbers of gold coins from various periods (*aurei* and *solidi* struck before and after AD 394) are relatively evenly distributed in the parts of Denmark west of Øresund, there is a considerably higher number of fifth-century *solidi* found on the relatively small island of Bornholm compared to all the remaining parts of Denmark combined;[12] but only one earlier gold coin, a *solidus* of Theodosius I (AD 379–88) struck in Milan, was allegedly found on Bornholm, in Østermarie parish (CHRE 14528).[13]

The *solidus* types present on Bornholm, in particular, connect the island to the distribution patterns of the two large Swedish islands of the Baltic Sea—Öland and Gotland—as well as the patterns in eastern Sweden and northern Poland. The gold coins found in the southernmost provinces of Sweden (Scania, Halland, and Blekinge) are also dominated by fifth-century *solidi*, with only a few earlier coins: one *aureus* of Probus and one *solidus* struck for Constantius II in Trier.[14] Not only are there many examples of type identity between finds from these areas, but also die identities have been identified in some numbers. It should, however, be noted that the chronological distribution of the *solidus* finds in the Baltic area shows local differences, and this group of *solidi* continues to attract much attention.[15]

The fifth-century Roman *solidi* found in southern Sweden and in Denmark west of Øresund are not significantly different in types and chronology from the finds on the Baltic islands, but contrary to the material from Bornholm the vast majority of fourth- and fifth-century *solidi* from western Denmark are reworked into jewellery, and much of the material derives from only two hoards, Elsehoved (CHRE 4662) and Rynkebygård (CHRE 4626), on Funen. Furthermore, the Roman fifth-century *solidi* found west of Øresund are supplemented by a disproportionately high number of unassigned and unidentified imitations in gold, based on fifth-century Roman coins.[16]

Contrary to the situation in Sweden the—admittedly few—Roman *solidi* from Norway are dominated by fourth-century coins (four coins from the fourth century and only one from the fifth century).[17] Thus the Norwegian finds conform to the finds from the western parts of Denmark. With the find of the Vindelev hoard in 2020 the number of Roman fourth-century gold medallions found in Denmark

[12] Breitenstein (1944); Horsnæs (2008).
[13] Breitenstein (1944); Klindt-Jensen (1957).
[14] Balling (1966: finds 14 and 17); Fischer (2022).
[15] Fagerlie (1967); Fischer (2022) with references to earlier papers. The critical review by Metcalf (1995) is still valid.
[16] Horsnæs (2009).
[17] In 2013 reports circulated about a *solidus* found at Avaldsnes, the seat of Norwegian Viking Age kings, but this find later turned out to be a hoax (pers. comm. Dagfinn Skre).

has almost doubled, from five to nine specimens,[18] while two specimens have been found in Norway.

The earliest gold imitations found in Denmark are based on Roman coins from the second to early fourth centuries, and they are probably produced within the fourth-century Chernyakhiv culture. The Danish finds are concentrated on Funen and to a lesser degree Sealand, and they reveal connections with south-eastern Europe that can also be seen in imported jewellery (Fig. 5.2). Two new finds from Denmark should be added to those previously listed.[19] The imitations have recently been intensively studied, leading to a surge of new papers on the subject,[20] and since *c.* 2010 Oleg Anokhin has collected information on a large number of finds from Ukraine, as a result of recent private detector surveys.[21] A more heterogeneous group consists of imitations of fifth-century *solidi* distinct from the pseudo-Roman and imitative coinages of the successor kingdoms by being either cast or made as bracteates.[22] The closest parallels can be found in north-west continental Europe.[23]

Imitations of Roman fourth-century gold medallions have been found in Norway (eight specimens), Sweden (five specimens), and Denmark (two specimens). The distribution of the medallion imitations is highly surprising. It differs significantly from the find distribution of official Roman gold medallions in Barbaricum, and even common Roman coins are extremely rarely found in Norway and the parts of Sweden where medallion imitations have been found.[24]

Nordic gold bracteates are known from more than 1,100 specimens. They were clearly inspired by the iconography and general design of the Roman coins and medallions of the mid-fourth century. Their main distribution area is southern Scandinavia, but there are also a number of finds from both the Continent and Anglo-Saxon England, and the bracteates were most likely produced in a number of different centres.[25] The bracteates are found in female burials both on the Continent and in Norway,[26] while in Denmark, where burials are rare in the early Germanic Iron Age, the bracteates have been deposited in hoards. In both hoards and burials the bracteates were deposited in similar circumstances as Roman gold coins and other coin imitations. It seems that coins, coin imitations, and bracteates must have been imbued with the same meaning in fifth- and sixth-century Scandinavia.

A *solidus* was part of the ninth-century Viking Age Hoen hoard,[27] and today the find of this Roman gold coin in the Hoen hoard can be compared to the find

[18] Horsnæs (2023); for a general presentation of the hoard, see Laursen and Ravn (2022).
[19] Horsnæs (2011; 2013a).
[20] See, for example, Bursche and Myzgin (2015); Degler (2015); Bursche and Niezabitowska (2018); Myzgin, Vida, and Więcek (2018).
[21] Anokhin (n.d.).
[22] Horsnæs and Ravn (2021).
[23] Examples in Nicolay (2014).
[24] Horsnæs (2021; 2023).
[25] Pesch (2001; 2007).
[26] Wicker (2005); Pesch (2011).
[27] Fuglesang and Wilson (2006).

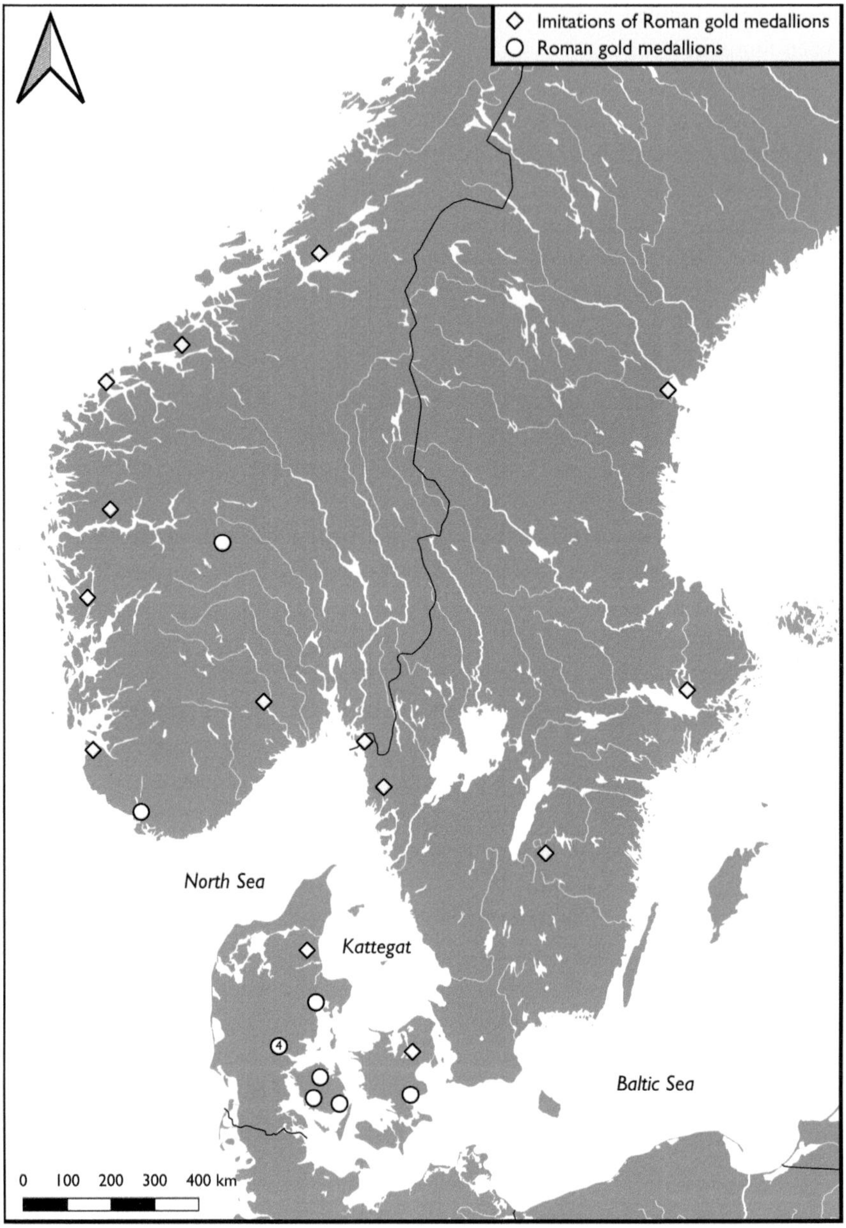

Fig. 5.2. Findspots of Roman gold medallions and medallion imitations. Source for the Norwegian and Swedish data: Skaare (1993: 486). Map: Rasmus H. Nielsen.

of a looped Honorius *solidus* in the Fæsted hoard from the mid-tenth century found in southern Jutland in 2016.[28] Furthermore, a Roman *aureus* struck during the reign of Diocletian was allegedly found in the same field as the Fæsted hoard in 1911 and may derive from the hoard.[29] These examples warn us that Roman gold coins found in the Nordic countries may have been deposited several centuries after they were produced, and only good contextual evidence enables us to date a deposition more precisely than the *terminus post quem* (*t.p.q.*) provided by the end coin.[30]

Denarii

Republican and early imperial coin finds are rare north of the *limes* area.[31] The two earliest coin hoards from Denmark are the Skellerup hoard (CHRE 20011), *t.p.q.* Augustus or Galba depending on interpretation,[32] and the Ginderup hoard (CHRE 13128), *t.p.q.* Vespasian and deposited in an Iron Age house dated *c.* AD 100–50.[33] These hoards testify to the arrival of a restricted number of *denarii* before the end of the first century, and must be seen in connection with the early import of Roman exotics during the Roman Iron Age in Denmark.[34]

The majority of the *denarius* hoards in both Denmark and Sweden consist of coins struck during the Flavian to Antonine dynasties,[35] with no *denarius* hoards reported in Norway. The deposits most often contain *denarii* only, and in these cases the deposition date can only be given by the *t.p.q.* provided by the end coin. However, there is good reason to believe that at least some of the coins may have been deposited later than the end coin. The earliest known contexts for imperial *denarii* in Scandinavia are the Illerup (CHRE 20013) weapon sacrifice dated by dendrochronology to *c.* AD 210 and a few single finds of often reworked coins from burials of Danish Late Roman Iron Age phases C1b-C3 (*c.* AD 210/20–400), whereas the latest contexts travel into the early sixth century.

Scandinavian *denarius* hoards are generally relatively small.[36] The largest known hoards in Denmark—Råmosen (CHRE 13707), Sorte Muld (CHRE 20014), and

[28] Grundvad, Schaadt, and Ejstrud (2017) note that the coin was found after the final manuscript for their book was completed.

[29] Pers. comm. with L. Grundvad and P. Pentz.

[30] See Bogucki, Dymkowski, and Śnieżko (2020) for several articles on the subject.

[31] CHRE search (https://chre.ashmus.ox.ac.uk/search/): *denarius* hoards closing before AD 100; and AFE search (http://afe.dainst.org/en/search-container-en/search): Republican *denarii* (both accessed 12 April 2023).

[32] Horsnæs and Beck (2018); Holst Nielsen (2021).

[33] Bjerg (2007; 2008).

[34] Lund Hansen (1987).

[35] Denmark: Horsnæs (2010; 2013b); Holst Nielsen (2021); Sweden: Lind (1981; 1988; 2013a; 2013 b; 2015; 2018), maps of *denarius* distribution at https://www.su.se/numismatiska-forskningsgruppen/om-forskningsgruppen/romerska-denarer-1.592797 (accessed 3 August 2022).

[36] Lind (1981: 62; 1988: 72) lists 11 Swedish hoards with more than 181 *denarii*.

Smørenge (CHRE 14545)—each contain fewer than 500 coins—exact numbers cannot be given, as none of them were found *in situ*. Most hoards are, however, significantly smaller. *Denarius* hoards have been found in central locations (religious and/or administrative centres), where they may be located in or near a building. An exception is the Præstemosen hoard (CHRE 13706) found in the periphery of the Gudme centre at the edge of a small pond. There are, however, several cases where *denarii* have been the only (or almost only) finds from a site. In some cases, subsequent excavations have revealed building remains on the site, leading to the suggestion that the site had been abandoned without retrieving the *denarius* hoard. In other cases, it is possible to relate *denarius* hoards to wet areas or territorial borders in the landscape and thereby suggest that the deposition may have had a cultic background.

Detector archaeology has had a great impact on the number of *denarius* hoards known from Denmark, and it is very probable that more intensive surveying in Norway and particularly in Sweden would affect the current knowledge of finds there significantly. For example, at least 11 new *denarius* hoards have been identified during the last 15 years in Denmark, where detector archaeology is well established.[37]

The case of many coins in one field presents a particular problem. How do we distinguish between many single finds and a hoard scattered by agricultural works? Strict methodologies must be employed in each individual case. Today, most amateur archaeologists plot each individual find from a field with GPS coordinates, and some even track their search pattern by GPS to ascertain a thorough survey. In this way coins and other objects are mapped on the background of the search pattern that reveals both the true extent of a site and the relationship between coins and other finds.[38]

Special soil conditions have different effects on the preservation of certain coins that may help to identify hoards.[39] In some cases, soil conditions have made the silver of the *denarii* brittle, fragmenting coins in the plough layer. Reassembling these fragments has revealed how far parts of a single hoard can travel by continuous working of the fields with plough and harrow (Fig. 5.3).

While it may be easy to reconstruct a *denarius* hoard if only *denarii* are found on a site, the finds from Skellerup (CHRE 20011) offer a lesson in the difficulties in other circumstances: the Republican and Augustan *denarii* from the site form an ensemble of coin types that is otherwise extremely rarely found in Denmark. What about two Galba *denarii* found in the same field but slightly apart from the earlier *denarii*? They may have been added to the ensemble *en route* to or in Denmark and have been deposited together with the Republican *denarii*,[40]

[37] Holst Nielsen (2021) discussed these hoards. [38] Horsnæs and Beck (2018, pl. 1).
[39] Horsnæs (2006). [40] Holst Nielsen (2021: 35–8).

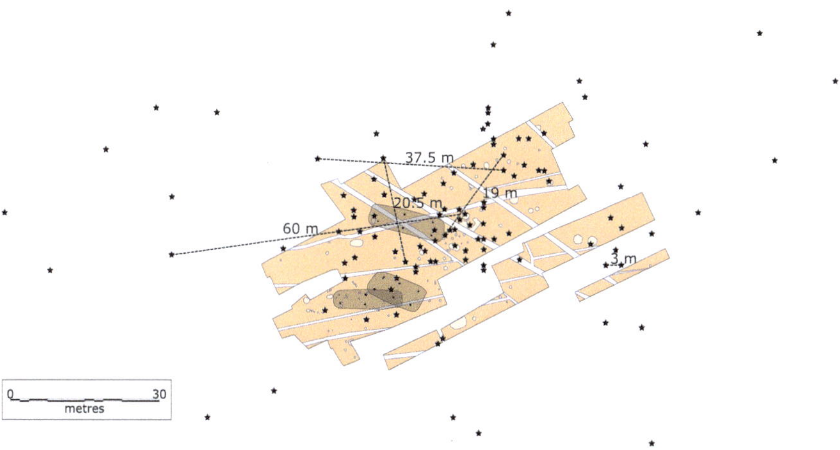

Fig. 5.3. Tagesgård hoard. Position of individual coins in relation to the excavation area. The lines connect two fragments of the same coin and indicate the distance between them. Map: Rasmus H. Nielsen based on distribution and excavations maps by Museum Lolland-Falster.

or they may derive from another deposit in the same area.[41] Furthermore, a single Roman bronze coin was found in the same field, but 15 m from the closest *denarius*. The coin bears faint traces of a portrait and is 29–31 mm in diameter, and can thus be identified as an imperial *sestertius* from the first or second century. The connection of the *sestertius* with the *denarii* is difficult to interpret, in particular as low-denomination coins are rarely found in non-Roman areas. It could be viewed as an independent deposit or the casual loss of a single coin, or as part of a deposit of other coins. A locally produced fibula dating to the pre-Roman Iron Age from the same field presents a similar problem. The uncertainties in the interpretation must be acknowledged, and future finds from repeated metal detector surveys of the field may change interpretations of the site.

Finds of possible treasure in Denmark must be handed in for evaluation at the National Museum via the local museum in charge of the archaeology of the find place. In general, finds from the same field often arrive at the museum in small, uneven streams, and hoards may be identified only after several years of surveying by the amateur detectorists. Indeed, some sites have by now been surveyed repeatedly for up to 40 years, and they still produce new finds. In this way detector archaeology presents a new challenge. It becomes necessary to revisit old registrations, as the repeated surveying, year after year, of the same field may eventually lead to a changed interpretation of a site—from one or a few single finds to a small hoard. Such a revision of sites recently led to the identification of two 'new'

[41] Horsnæs and Beck (2018).

hoards of scattered *denarii*: Eghøj (CHRE 20015) and Maglebro (CHRE 20016), at present consisting of 14 and 17 *denarii* respectively. Previously considered to be single finds, they are now identified as hoards primarily due to the very low number of other find types in the surrounding areas, as well as their composition being very typical of Danish *denarius* hoards.[42] We can never claim that a hoard scattered by ploughing and refound during detector surveys has been completely recovered: for example, more than 30 *denarii* have been found at the site of the Hillested hoard (island of Lolland, CHRE 20017) since its initial publication in 2014.[43] Even recent publications may therefore be outdated in their empirical data. In total, 1,633 *denarii* have been found in hoards from Denmark (excluding Bornholm), and no fewer than 496 of them were found since 2008 (Fig. 5.4).[44]

There are few examples of *denarii* mixed with other precious metals in the form of hacksilver or gold that may be interpreted as a single deposition. One example is a small group of *denarii* and precious metal found in Nr. Fuglesang (CHRE 20019) during a single day of surveying.[45] We suspect that more mixed hoards may exist, but they can only be identified through a close analysis of all finds from the same site.[46]

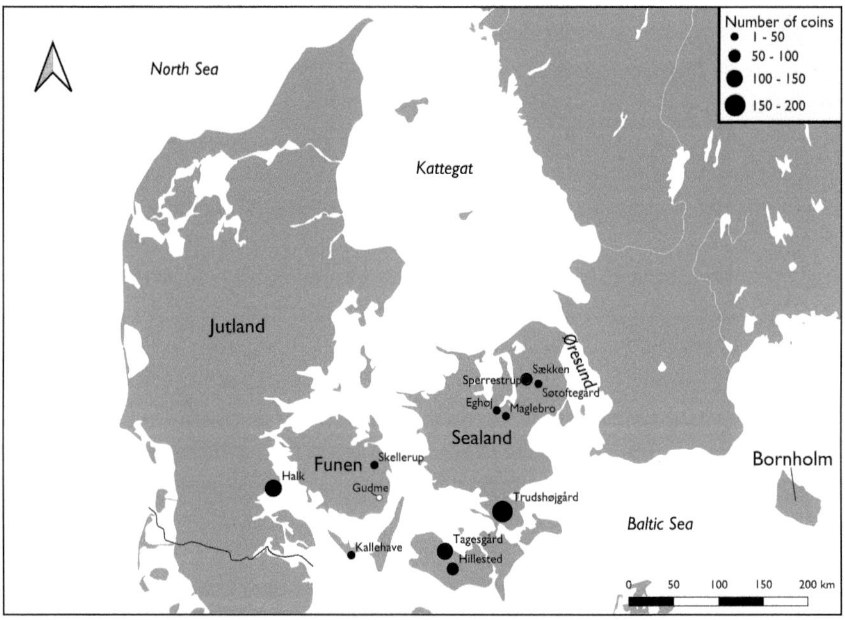

Fig. 5.4. *Denarius* hoards identified between 2009 and 2021. Map: Rasmus H. Nielsen.

[42] Holst Nielsen (2021).
[43] Rasmussen (2014); Holst Nielsen (2021).
[44] Holst Nielsen (2021).
[45] Horsnæs (2013: 44 and 124–5).
[46] This aspect is discussed in an upcoming project by Rasmus Holst Nielsen.

The large and ever-growing number of single finds of *denarii* must be addressed in this connection. In fact, today the number of *denarii* recovered as single finds exceeds the number of *denarii* recovered in circumstances where they are immediately identified as a hoard.[47] In this context, single finds are understood as coins that have been found (often during detector surveys) as the only *denarius* in a site, or as one of few but widely scattered *denarii*. The fact that the majority of them have been found during detector surveys of the plough soil, and thus are deprived of any information about the original deposition circumstances, makes any interpretations of this find group very difficult. Occasionally other finds, whether detector finds or scattered remains of building materials, suggest that the site was a settlement, but some finds are made without any other indication of the nature of the site. Illuminating the impact of detectorists on the data, 1,570 *denarii* are classified as single finds in Denmark (excluding Bornholm), and of those 640 have been found since 2008.[48] This means that more than a third of the total number of *denarii* so far registered from Denmark were found within the last 14 years, which underlines that the high number of finds seen since the 1980s has become a new normal.[49]

For the bulk of the material consisting of imperial *denarii* struck in Rome, it is very difficult to map the route from mint to Scandinavia, and it is, indeed, hard to tell the number of exchanges of each individual coin *en route*. There are few *RIC* types of *denarii* represented by more than one specimen or a couple of specimens in Denmark, suggesting that they were already heavily mixed when arriving. We propose that at least some mixing took place within the Empire. The study of *denarius* imitations has provided die links between coins found in hoards across Barbaricum,[50] indicative of chains of redistributions also existing outside the Empire, but only a limited number of *denarius* imitations have been identified in Denmark.[51] Apart from four die-identical imitations found together in the same purse as part of the Illerup Ådal weapon sacrifice,[52] only one imitation from Bornholm has been die-linked to another specimen, suggesting that the reverse of the coin from Bornholm may be linked to the Ceres-Mulde Group with specimens from Gotland, Ukraine, and Hungary,[53] although Arkadiusz Dymowski has rejected that possibility, favouring the idea that the obverse of this coin is die-linked to a *denarius* imitation from Poland.[54] However, imitations may hide among coins previously classified as Roman, perhaps even with a type reference, and the definition of a coin as official or imitative is clearly a matter of subjective judgement. The known distribution of *denarius* imitations points to their belonging to the pattern of exchange from the northern part of Ukraine towards Poland and the Baltic.[55]

[47] Holst Nielsen (2021); Horsnæs (forthcoming).
[48] Holst Nielsen (2021).
[49] Horsnæs (2010: figs 7 and 9).
[50] Lind (1988; 2018; 2020); Stribrny (2003); Dymowski (2019).
[51] Horsnæs (2010; 2013b: 55–6).
[52] Bursche (2011).
[53] Lind (2018: 8–9).
[54] Dymowski (2019: 159).
[55] Dymowski (2019).

FOURTH-CENTURY SILVER

While second-century *denarii* all derive from the same mint, the mint-marked coins struck after the reforms of Diocletian offer excellent possibilities for more in-depth analysis of the routes of late Roman coinages. Although fewer fourth-century coins have been found when compared with *denarii*, they provide important information on the movement of Roman coins into the non-Roman areas and the use of them locally.

Siliquae found in Denmark can be divided into two groups.[56] One consists of the 293 coins from the Gudme III hoard (CHRE 4326), and other eastern *siliquae* struck in the mid-fourth century. These types are in general very rare in northern Europe, but they have a marked concentration in and around Gudme (*c.* 350 coins in total), with only a couple of finds more than a couple of kilometres away from this centre (Fig. 5.5). All coins of the same types as the ones in the Gudme III hoard may ultimately derive from the same batch of coins.[57] Some of these coins were found in Gudme IV area in connection with

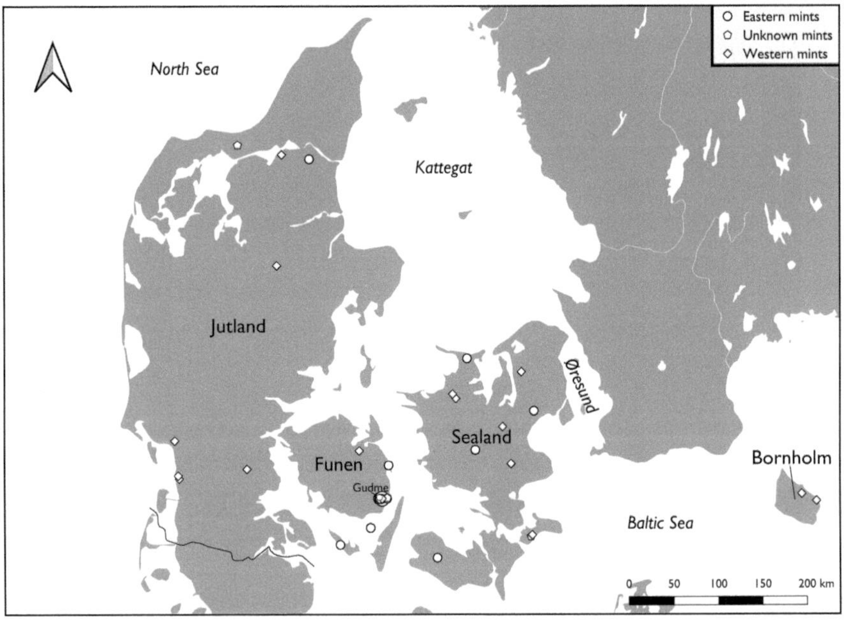

Fig. 5.5. Findspots of Roman *siliquae*. The two hoards from Gudme are indicated by a larger circle. Map: Rasmus H. Nielsen.

[56] Horsnæs (2010, 138–44).
[57] Horsnæs (2010, 143).

second-century *denarii*. Although it is difficult to prove, these coins may have belonged to one hoard, which would make it comparable to the Laatzen hoard (Germany, CHRE 17135) and the recently located hoard from Niederdorfelden (Germany) that is most probably a new mixed hoard containing both *denarii* and *siliquae*.[58]

The other group of *siliquae* consists of coins struck in western mints during the Valentinian dynasty, with Trier as the main mint. The distribution of these *siliquae* is comparatively more dispersed in Denmark, and there are even two specimens found on Bornholm (Fig. 5.5). A single *siliqua* struck by Arcadius in Milan has been found on the western coast of Scania,[59] and two of the three *siliquae* known from Norway seem to belong to the Valentinian dynasty.[60] Many of these coins have been clipped, and a few have also been cut or pierced. In several cases they have been found in hoards with hacksilver of both local and imported objects, including Roman silver plate, the deposition of which is normally dated to the period around AD 500. Although much smaller in weight and scale, these hoards can to some degree be compared with post-Roman British hoards such as the Trapain Law hoard.[61]

ARRIVAL IN SCANDINAVIA

The number of finds in Scandinavia gradually diminishes with the growing distance from the ultimate source, the Roman Empire. This may be an effect of the distance itself, but changes in the topography and vegetation of the inner and mountainous areas of Scandinavia should also be considered, along with modern jurisdiction and recording practices. Still, comparing the distribution of different Roman coin types and imitations thereof from Scandinavia presents a bewildering picture that must reflect differences in what was coveted and available. The differences were therefore conditioned by factors both in the recipient communities and in their networks. The distribution of *denarius* imitations reveals exchanges between Ukraine, Poland, Hungary, and the Baltic area, while the distribution of the fifth-century *solidus* finds from the Baltic area has no parallel in Ukraine. Gold imitations of coins based on Roman prototypes dated from the second to the fourth century seem to derive mainly from the Chernyakhiv culture in northern Ukraine. Contrary to the distribution of *denarius* imitations, the finds of gold imitations in Scandinavia concentrate on Funen. The distribution patterns of Roman gold medallions and medallion imitations hardly overlap, and neither

[58] Wigg-Wolf (2020). [59] Aspeborg (2012).
[60] Skaare (1976: 35); the mint is not indicated. [61] Horsnæs (2010); Rau (2013).

Roman medallions nor Nordic(?) imitations have been found so far in the areas of the Baltic with high numbers of fifth-century *solidi*. Indeed, in Norway gold medallions and imitations thereof almost outnumber the finds of official Roman gold coins. The different distribution patterns in Scandinavia must reflect different networks as well as changes over time. The best-known and often discussed feature is the marked difference between the Baltic area (with the Danish island of Bornholm) on one side and the remaining parts of modern Denmark (and perhaps Norway) on the other side.

Some Roman coins must have circulated outside the Empire, but it is also possible that a number of the Roman coins deposited in hoards have been assembled partly or wholly outside Scandinavia, arriving as batches. This is most likely the case with the two early imperial hoards from Denmark, the Gudme III *siliqua* hoard, and some of the gold hoards. This may be the case when a hoard contains a close-knit group of coins (chronologically or otherwise) that is not commonly found elsewhere in Barbaricum.

While some coins may have travelled as ensembles to Denmark, there are several examples of a 'topping up' of a coin hoard. This is the case when the coins were used as parts of jewellery sets in conjunction with bracteates or other locally produced pendants, beads, or other valuables. These objects could either be local or imported from other areas. Imports other than Roman coins might provide a hint as to the route for the coins, or they could be independent imports. The addition of local objects, such as Nordic bracteates, most likely happened within Scandinavia.

Though most of the loops added to the Late Roman gold coins are relatively simple and therefore difficult to relate to specific workshops or areas, more elaborate loops and mounts or rims on coins may be compared to the loops and mounts employed on other pendant types found in non-Roman Europe and thereby provide hints to connectivity over long distances. None of the loops or mounts of Roman coins found in Scandinavia were made in Roman workshops.

USE AND REUSE OF ROMAN COINS IN SCANDINAVIA

As previously mentioned, few coins have been found in closed contexts, yet these contexts provide valuable information about the circumstances of the depositions, as seen, for example, in burials from the Late Roman Iron Age (period C1b–C3, *c.* AD 210/20–400). Most coins were deposited as part of the deceased's personal belongings. Reworked coins were inserted as part of a necklace in female burials and in one case in the burial of a boy or young adult male. Coins that were not reworked have been found in a position on or at the hips, indicating that they may have been kept in a purse hanging from the belt; in a unique example from a burial at Rævekulebakke (Bornholm), the possible purse contained four coins.[62] The coins found in the Illerup weapon sacrifice were also kept in purses together with other personal belongings such as combs or strike-a-lights. By the end of period C (*c.* AD 400) burials disappear from the archaeological record in Denmark, and so too does our chance to extract information from this group.

Denarius hoards seem most often to be single type depositions, although it is possible that mixed depositions have been overlooked. The deposition date of *denarius* hoards can normally only be established as a *t.p.q.* by the end coin of the hoard. This may create a false assumption that most hoards were deposited in the early third century, while there is good evidence that at least some *denarii* were not deposited until at least the early sixth century, as seen in the example in the Gudme II Hoard, deposited in a post hole and consisting of Nordic gold bracteates, local jewellery, and a looped *denarius* from the second century. Roman gold coins from the fourth and fifth centuries were often deposited with local jewellery and/or Nordic bracteates. Here the coins were often used in a manner similar to the use of Nordic bracteates and other types of gold pendants. Reworked coins, medallions, and bracteates are found in female burials in Norway and north-west Europe, and the composition of gold hoards from the Early Germanic Iron Age in Denmark corresponds closely to the jewellery sets in rich female burials outside Denmark.[63] Whether deposited in a hoard or in a burial, gold coins, medallions, and jewellery display wealth and status.[64]

Several hoards are concentrated in sites that can also be regarded as central places with both religious and secular functions. Other hoards as well as single finds of gold have been found close to or in wetlands/streams/moors or close to natural borders in the landscape that later became administrative borders, such as those for parishes. In these cases, the depositions are most likely to be of a cult kind. There are a few cases where rescue excavations of a hoard site have revealed traces of near-contemporary buildings, but almost no other finds. In fact, there are marked differences between metal-rich central places such as Gudme and sites with building remains that have revealed few, if any, finds other than a coin hoard (for example, Tagesgård, CHRE 20018). We may speculate whether the hoard was forgotten when the site was cleared and abandoned or was an intentional votive deposition.

It has often been claimed that Roman coins were the main source of precious metal in an area without natural gold and silver resources. So far, no hard evidence for this theory has been presented. Finds of partially melted *denarii* are rare, and in most cases they derive from sites with remains of a burnt building. It is therefore argued that partly melted coins were hidden (forgotten or left on

[62] Horsnæs (2013: 60). [63] Nicolay (2014). [64] Wicker (2005).

purpose) in a building that caught fire. A few cut *solidi* have been found. The cutting of coins may be seen in relation to the finds of the hacksilver coins from the early sixth century, and one of the cut *solidi* indeed derives from the Høgsbrogård hacksilver hoard.[65] Whether the cutting of objects was made to facilitate the use of the precious metal as a means of payment (money) or as preparation for the use of raw material is difficult to say. It is, however, improbable that the hoards should be seen as a goldsmith's cache, as later evidence suggest that goldsmiths did not own precious metal. The smiths were, rather, assigned an amount of metal to produce specified objects for his master,[66] suggesting that the hacksilver and gold hoards should be seen as a part of the master's possession. Yet it is highly probable that some coins may have been melted down for reuse, but silver was probably available in higher quantities as Roman plate. However, no archaeometallurgical attempts have been made to compare the sources for locally produced objects in silver and gold in the Late Roman and Early Germanic Iron Age with the metals from Roman coins.

The distinction between hoards and single finds is useful in many ways. Less useful is the popular assumption that hoards are deliberate depositions, while single finds represent casual losses. Indeed, it may not be so. The CHRE project has decided to include single finds of gold coins, 'as their high value and archaeological behaviour merit their consideration as hoards in themselves', thus stressing both the high value (one *aureus* has the value of 25 *denarii*) and the ways in which gold may be deposited.[67] Among the single finds of Roman gold coins in Denmark the topography often hints that the coin was deposited deliberately. It is more difficult to interpret the ever-growing number of seemingly single finds of *denarii*. However, it seems unlikely that so many silver *denarii* were lost accidentally—silver being valuable. The clipping phenomenon in post-Roman Britain has been explained as a means to recover silver, and thus underlines the importance and value of silver. The majority of the more than 15,000 *siliquae* from the Hoxne hoard (CHRE 2008) were clipped. If an average of half a gram of silver was cut off each coin, approximately 7 kg of silver could have been recovered from clipping coins of the Hoxne hoard.[68] The clipping of the rims of so many coins demanded an enormous and time-consuming effort, but evidently it was worthwhile. We must therefore ask why so many second-century Roman *denarii*, originally weighing more than 3 g each, are found one by one. As mentioned, today 1,570 of the *denarii* recovered in Denmark have been interpreted as single finds. Even though they are often a bit below the ideal weight of second-century Roman *denarii*, the total weight of the find would be between 3 and 4.5 kg—a considerable fortune. As such, instead of automatically interpreting single *denarii*

[65] Feveile (2010). [66] Codine-Trécourt (2014).
[67] https://chre.ashmus.ox.ac.uk/content/about (accessed 12 April 2023). [68] Guest (2005).

as the result of casual losses, we should start to acknowledge the possibility that a single Roman silver coin would be a valuable and conscious deposition. Many single finds of *denarii* have been made in the Scandinavian central places that are normally regarded to hold cult as well as secular importance. Here they appear alongside hoards of *denarii*, gold coins, or valuables in other materials. They are normally found during metal detector surveys of disturbed plough layers, which effectively prevents a detailed analysis of their primary archaeological contexts, but their presence in these special sites may be compared to coin finds from pre-Roman sanctuaries in central and insular (Celtic) Europe.[69] If single *denarii* could be deliberately deposited within a central place, this may also be a possible interpretation for at least some of the single finds from more ordinary settlements or other types of sites.

FROM LATE ANTIQUE TO EARLY MEDIEVAL: BRIDGING A GAP

The influx of coins into Iron Age Scandinavia only took off in the third century with the import of imperial *denarii*. *When* it stopped is difficult to say; it all depends on assumptions about movements outside the Empire. As noted, the coins seem to circulate for some time. The number of gold coins is relatively stable from the first into the sixth century west of Øresund, while the situation is vastly different in the Baltic area. West of Øresund, imports derive from different areas of origin through the fourth and fifth centuries, but seem to come increasingly from north Germany, the Netherlands, and Britain from the latter part of the fourth century onwards.

The few finds of coins or coin imitations based on prototypes after *c.* AD 500 probably reflect the diminishing minting in western Europe in the transition from the Late Antique to Early Medieval periods, but this should not in itself be seen as evidence for a growing isolation of southern Scandinavia. On the contrary, there seem to have been continuous contacts towards the Frisian area and eventually to the Merovingian Franks, and after an almost 'coinless' period in the late sixth and early seventh centuries, a small trickle of *tremisses* of the Dorestad Madelinus types from the period *c.* AD 640–75 appears from the Frisian areas.[70] The majority have appeared recently through metal detecting, and *tremisses* are still rare finds in Denmark: there are fewer than ten specimens, including the first finds of two die-identical seventh-century *denarii* and a *tremissis* in a hoard at Dankirke.[71] The finds are mainly from southern Jutland, thus stressing the North Sea connections. The *tremisses* herald the next imports from the North Sea area,

[69] Webley and Haselgrove (2016).

[70] Pol (2018: 215); Pol and van der Veen (2021: 266).

[71] Feveile (2006) for interpretations.

namely the English and Frisian sceattas of the late seventh century, and the first examples of coins struck within the borders of modern Denmark, the Wotan/monster (type X) sceattas of Ribe normally dated *c.* 720–50. However, apart from the large number of sceattas found in Ribe, coin finds from the seventh and eighth centuries are quite rare in Denmark, and are normally restricted to single finds from a limited number of sites, among which are central places such as Gudme, Tissø, and Lejre. Here they may be interpreted as the result of deliberate depositions of coins with a symbolic function, as suggested above for the Roman coins. This interpretation is further strengthened by the distribution of the rare Early Medieval coin types within Tissø and the fact that these coin types are often reworked into pendants.[72] Larger numbers of coin finds only appear again in Scandinavia with the dirham imports from the later ninth and tenth centuries.[73]

REFERENCES

Anokhin, O. (n.d.). 'КАТАЛОГ ВАРВАРСКИХ ПОДРАЖАНИЙ РИМСКИМ МОНЕТАМ - Главная', http://barbarous-imitations.narod.ru/ (accessed 3 August 2022).

Aspeborg, H. (2012). 'Et sensationellt men svårtolkat myntfund', *Myntstudier* 2012.1: 20–2.

Baastrup, M. P. and Feveile, C. (2013). 'Danefæ: samarbejdet mellem finder, lokalmuseum og Nationalmuseum', *Nationalmuseets Arbejdsmark* 2013: 284–95.

Balling, J. (1966). 'De romerske møntfund fra Skåne, Halland og Blekinge', *Nordisk Numismatisk Årsskrift (Nordic Numismatic Journal)* 1966: 5–81.

Bjerg, L. M. H. (2007). *Romerske denarfund fra jyske jernalderbopladser: en arkæologisk kulegravning*. Aarhus.

Bjerg, L. M. H. (2008). 'The Ginderup hoard: a re-evaluation of the early *denarii* in Jutland', in A. Bursche, R. Ciołek, and R. Wolters (eds), *Roman Coins Outside the Empire, Ways and Phases, Contexts and Functions: Proceedings of the ESF/SCH Exploratory Workshop Radziwill Palace, Nieborów (Poland) 3–6 September 2005* (Collection Moneta 82). Wetteren, 147–57.

Bogucki, M., Dymowski, A. and Śnieżko, G. (eds) (2020). *Slivers of the Antiquity. Use of Ancient Coins in Central, Eastern and Northern Europe in the Medieval and Modern Periods / Okruchy starożytności: Użytkowanie monet antycznych w Europie Środkowej, Wschodniej i Północnej w średniowieczu i okresie nowożytnym*. Warsaw.

Breitenstein, N. (1944). 'De romerske møntfund fra Bornholm', *Nordisk Numismatisk Årsskrift (Nordic Numismatic Journal)* 1944: 1–85.

Bursche, A. (2011). *Illerup Ådal 14: Die Münzen*, Jysk Arkæologisk Selskab, Aarhus.

[72] Jørgensen (2006). [73] See Jankowiak, this volume (chapter 12).

Bursche, A. and Myzgin, K. (2015). 'Gold coins, Alexandria Troas and Goths', in R. Bland and D. Calomino (eds), *Studies in Ancient Coinage in Honour of Andrew Burnett*. London, 237–57.

Bursche, A. and Niezabitowska, B. (2018). 'Two antique gold coins from Ulów in Roztocze', in B. Niezabitowska-Wiśniewska, P. Łuczkiewicz, S. Sadowski, M. Stasiak, and M. Erdrich (eds), *Studia Barbarica. Professorowi Andrzejowi Kokowskiemu w 65 rocznicę urodzin*, Volume 2. Warsaw, 248–67.

Codine-Trécourt, F. (2014). 'Precious metalwork: Coins and objects in Merovingian and Carolingian times', in T. Abramsom (ed.), *Sifting the Evidence* (Studies in Early Medieval Coinage 3). London, 29–43.

de Bruin, J., Bakels, C., and Theuws, F. (2021). *Oegstgeest: A Riverine Settlement in the Early Medieval World System* (Merovingian Archaeology in the Low Countries no. 7). Bonn.

Degler, A. (2015). 'East Germanic imitation of an aureus of Severus Alexander with runic legend: the newest acquisition to the collection of ancient coins in the Ossolineum', Wiadomości Numizmatyczne *R. LIX, z. 1–2*/Polish Numismatic News IX: 47–65.

Dobat, A. S. and Jensen, A. T. (2016). '"Professional amateurs". Metal detecting and metal detectorists in Denmark', *Open Archaeology* 2.1: 70–84.

Dymowski, A. (2019). 'The problem of the presence of barbarian imitations of Roman Imperial denarii in the lands of present-day Poland: An attempt at balance', *Notae Numismaticae* 14: 149–74.

Fagerlie, J. M. (1967). *Late Roman and Byzantine Solidi Found in Sweden & Denmark* (Numismatic Notes and Monographs 157). New York.

Feveile, C. (2006). 'Sceattaerne fra Dankirke – skatte eller enkeltfund?', *Nordisk Numismatisk Unions Medlemsblad* 2006.1: 3–9.

Feveile, C. (2010). 'Høgsbrogård-dkatten—en brudsølvskat fra ældre germansk jernalder i Sydvestjylland', in S. Kleingärtner, S. Lützen Pedersen, and L. Matthes (eds), *Arkæologi i Slesvig/Archäologie in Schleswig* 13. Neumünster, 111–23.

Feveile, C. (2015). 'Metaldetektorproblematikken – uens regler og deres konsekvenser', in A. Pedersen and S. M. Sindbæk (eds), *Et fælles hav—Skagerrak og Kattegat i vikingetiden: Seminar på Nationalmuseet, København, 19.–20. September 2012*. Copenhagen, 120–35.

Fischer, S. (2022). 'The Late Roman and Early Byzantine solidi of Scania & the Lund University History Museum', *Journal of Archaeology and Ancient History* 30: 1–66.

Fuglesang, S. H. and Wilson, D. M. (eds) (2006). *The Hoen Hoard: A Viking Gold Treasure of the Ninth Century* (Norske Oldfunn 20). Oslo.

Grundvad, L., Schaadt, N., and Ejstrud, B. (2017). *Fæstedskatten: Danmarks største guldskat fra vikingetiden*. Aarhus.

Guest, P. (2005). *The Late Roman Gold and Silver Coins from the Hoxne Treasure*. London.

Gullbekk, S. H. (2019), 'Kildekritiske refleksioner omkring metallsøking og myntfunn. Må mynthistorien skrives om?', *Viking, Norsk Arkeologisk Årbok* 82: 173–82.

Henriksen, M. B. (2010). 'Gold deposits in the Late Roman and Migration Period landscape: A case study from the Island of Funen (Fyn), Denmark', in U. Lund Hansen, and A. Bitner-Wróblewska (eds), *Worlds Apart* 2005–2008 (Nordiske Fortidsminder, ser. C., vol. 7). Copenhagen and Warsaw, 389–432.

Holst Nielsen, R. (2019). '10 års romerske guldmønter', *Fund & Fortid* 2019.1: 15–18.

Holst Nielsen, R. (2021). *Pecuniam probant veterem et diu notam. Romerske denarskatte i Danmark, en metodisk opdatering.* Cand. Mag. thesis, Copenhagen University.

Horsnæs, H. W. (2006). 'Many coins from one site', in H. W. Horsnæs and J. C. Moesgaard (eds), *Single Finds, the Nordic Perspective*, Nordisk Numismatisk Årsskrift/Nordic Numismatic Journal (2000-2002). Copenhagen, 100–8.

Horsnæs, H. W. (2008). 'Roman coins and their contexts in Denmark', in A. Bursche, R. Ciołek, and R. Wolters (eds), *Roman Coins Outside the Empire: Ways and Phases, Contexts and Functions. Acts of the ESF/SCH Exploratory Workshop Raziwill Palace, Nieborów (Poland), 3–6 September 2005* (Collection Moneta 82). Wetteren, 135–45.

Horsnæs, H. W. (2009). 'Late Roman and Byzantine coins found in Denmark', in M. Wołoszyn (ed.), *Byzantine Coins in Central Europe between the 5th and 10th Century*, Moravia Magna vol. III. Krakow, 231–70.

Horsnæs, H. W. (2010). *Crossing Boundaries. An Analysis of Roman Coins in Danish Contexts.* Vol. 1: *Finds from Sealand, Funen and Jutland* (Publications from the National Museum, Studies in Archaeology and History 18). Copenhagen.

Horsnæs, H. W. (2011). 'Imitations in gold', in N. Holmes (ed.), *Proceedings of the XIV International Numismatic Congress, Glasgow Monday 31st August to Friday fourth September 2009.* Glasgow, 742–8.

Horsnæs, H. W. (2013). *Crossing Boundaries: An Analysis of Roman Coins in Danish Contexts.* Vol. 2: *Finds from Bornholm* (Publications from the National Museum, Studies in Archaeology and History 18). Copenhagen.

Horsnæs, H. W. (2017). 'Møntfund og danefæ – før og nu', in P. K. Madsen and I. Wass (eds), *Nationalmuseets Arbejdsmark* (Nationalmuseets Arbejdsmark 2017). Copenhagen, 172–85.

Horsnæs, H. W. (2018). 'Coin finds and metal detector archaeology. Evidence from surveys and excavations in Bornholm, Denmark', in G. Pardini, N. Parise, and F. Marani (eds), *Numismatica e archeologia. Monete, stratigrafie e contesti. Dati a confronto. Roma, 28–30 settembre 2011.* Rome, 501–10.

Horsnæs, H. W. (2021). 'En "glemt" medaljon-imitation – i Den kgl. Mønt- og Medaillesamling (Nationalmuseet, København)', *Nordisk Numismatisk Unions Medlemsblad* 2021.2: 37–44.

Horsnæs, H. W. (2023). 'Large imperial gold medallions from the fourth century: Reflections on the distribution and use of Roman medallions in Barbaricum. The medallions from the Vindelev hoard, Denmark', *Numismatic Chronicle* 183: 169–88.

Horsnæs, H. W. (forthcoming). 'Denarius finds from Denmark: 10 years after', in F. Hunter (ed.), *Acts of the Seminar Denarii beyond the Empire: Political and Cultural Perspectives on Roman Silver Coins in Barbaricum. Edinburgh 2019.*

Horsnæs, H. W. and Beck, M. (2018). 'A hoard of Republican denarii from Skellerup, Denmark: A preliminary report', *Notae Numismaticae* 13: 37–52.

Horsnæs, H. W. and Ravn, M. (2021). 'The Queen's gift. A coin-like pendant and a gold hoard from Hjarnø in a comparative perspective', in R. Ciołek and R. Chowaniec (eds), *Aleksanderia. Studies on Items, Ideas and History Dedicated to Professor Aleksander Bursche on the Occasion of his 65th Birthday*. Wiesbaden, 167–77.

Jørgensen, L. (2006). 'Tracking down the aristocracy. Distribution patterns and coin use at the Viking manor and market at Lake Tissø, Denmark', in H. W. Horsnæs and J. C. Moesgaard (eds), *6th Nordic Numismatic Symposium. Single finds: the Nordic Perspective*. Nordisk Numismatisk Årsskrift/Nordic Numismatic Journal (2000–2002): 190–204.

Klindt-Jensen, O. (1957). *Bornholm i folkevandringstiden og forudsætningerne i tidlig jernalder*. Copenhagen.

Laursen, K. O. and Ravn, M. (2022). 'Guldfundet fra Vindelev og verdens største brakteat'/'The Gold Hoard from Vindelev and the World's Largest Bracteate', in M. Ravn and C. Lindblom (eds), *Magt og guld. Vikinger i øst / Power and Gold. Vikings in the East*. Aarhus, 52–77.

Lind, L. (1981). *Roman Denarii found in Sweden: 2, Catalogue. Text* (Stockholm Studies in Classical Archaeology 11:2). Stockholm.

Lind, L. (1988). *Romerska denarer funna i Sverige*. Stockholm.

Lind, L. (2013a). *Hoards: Gotland, Fröjel par., Mulde (Roman Denarii, Hoards and Stray Finds in Sweden 2013:1)*. Stockholm Numismatic Institute, https://www.su.se/polopoly_fs/1.594922.1643640753!/menu/standard/file/Roman_Denarii_2013_1_Lasvanlig.pdf (accessed 12 April 2023).

Lind, L. (2013b). *Hoards: Gotland, Hogrän par., Djupbrunns* (*Roman Denarii, Hoards and Stray Finds in Sweden* 2013.2). Stockholm Numismatic Institute, https://www.su.se/polopoly_fs/1.594923.1643640796!/menu/standard/file/Roman_Denarii_2013_2_Lasvanlig.pdf (accessed 12 April 2023).

Lind, L. (2015). *Hoards: Gotland, Garde par., Robbenarve* (*Roman Denarii, Hoards and Stray Finds in Sweden* 2015.1). Stockholm Numismatic Institute, https://www.su.se/polopoly_fs/1.594924.1643640938!/menu/standard/file/Roman_Denarii_2015_1_Lasvanlig.pdf (accessed 12 April 2023).

Lind, L. (2018). *Imitations of Roman Denarii Found in Sweden* (*Roman Denarii, Hoards and Stray Finds in Sweden* 2018,1). Stockholm Numismatic Institute, https://www.su.se/polopoly_fs/1.594926.1643640911!/menu/standard/file/Roman_Denarii_2018_1_Lasvanlig.pdf (accessed 12 April 2023).

Lind, L. (2020). 'Hulterstad-Uggårde gruppen av romerska denarimitationer och en ny stampkoppling Öland-Ukraina', *Myntstudier* 2020.1.1: 68–71, https://www.su.se/

polopoly_fs/1.594911.1643639751!/menu/standard/file/Myntstudier2020_1.pdf (accessed 12 April 2023).

Lund Hansen, U. (1987). *Römischer Import im Norden. Warenaustausch zwischen dem Römischen Reich und dem freien Germanien* (Nordiske Fortidsminder, Serie B 10). Copenhagen.

Metcalf, D. M. (1995). 'The president's address: Viking-Age Numismatics 1. Late Roman and Byzantine gold in the northern lands', *Numismatic Chronicle* 155: 413–41.

Myzgin, K., Vida, I., and Więcek, T. (2018). 'Gold imitations of Roman coins from collection of Hungarian National Museum in Budapest', in B. Niezabitowska-Wiśniewska, P. Łuczkiewicz, S. Sadowski, M. Stasiak, and M. Erdrich (eds), *Studia Barbarica. Professorowi Andrzejowi Kokowskiemu w 65 rocznicę urodzin*, Volume 2. Warsaw, 222–47.

Nicolay, J. A. W. (2014). *The Splendour of Power: Early Medieval Kingship and the Use of Gold and Silver in the Southern North Sea Area (5th to 7th Century AD)* (Groningen Archaeological Studies). Groningen

Pesch, A. (2001). 'Uppåkra im Licht der Formular-Familien der völkerwanderungszeitlichen Goldbrakteaten', in L. Larsson and B. Hårdh (eds), *Central Places in the Migration and Merovingian Periods. Papers from the 52nd Sachsensymposium Lund, Uppåkrastudier* 6. Lund, 55–78.

Pesch, A. (2007). *Die Goldbrakteaten der Völkerwanderungszeit—Thema und Variation.* (Ergänzungsbände zum Reallexikon der Germanischen Altertumskunde 36). Berlin.

Pesch, A. (2011). 'Gold bracteates and female burials. Material culture as a medium of elite communication in the Migration Period', in D. Quast (ed.), *Weibliche Eliten in der Frühgeschichte—Female Elites in Protohistoric Europe. Internationaler Tagung vom 13. bis zum 14. Juni 2008 in RGZM im Rahmen des Forschungsschwerpunktes 'Eliten'*. Mainz, 377–97.

Pol, A. (2018). 'Journeying with Madelinus - Bergeijk, via Nijmegen, Amsterdam and Leiden, to the plains and hills of Northern Italy', in M. Kars, R. van Oosten, and M. A. Roxburgh (eds), *Rural Riches & Royal Rags? Studies on Medieval and Modern Archaeology, presented to Frans Theuws*. Zwolle, 119–25.

Pol, A. and van der Veen, B. J. (2021). 'The coins of "Oegstgeest": finds of an early medieval settlement on the Rhine', in J. de Bruin, C. C. Bakels, and F. C. W. J. Theuws (eds), *Oegstgeest. A Riverine Settlement in the Early Medieval World System*. Bonn, 262–73.

Rasmussen, A. (2014). 'Two new denarius hoards from the island of Lolland', *Danish Journal of Archaeology* 3.2: 175–86.

Rau, A. (2013). 'Where did the late empire end? Hacksilber and coins in continental and northern Barbaricum c. AD 340–500', in F. Hunter and K. Painter (eds), *Late Roman Silver*. Edinburgh, 339–58.

Skaare, K. (1976). *Coins and Coinage in Viking-Age Norway: The Establishment of a National Coinage in Norway in the XI Century, with a Survey of the Preceding Currency History*. Oslo.

Skaare, K. (1993). 'Roman gold medallions and their imitations in Scandinavia', *Rivista Italiana di Numismatica* 95: 473–86.

Stribrny, K. (2003). *Funktionsanalyse barbarisierter, barbarischer Denare mittels numismatischer und metallurgischer Methoden: zur Erforschung der sarmatisch-germanischen Kontakte im 3. Jahrhundert n. Chr.* (Studien zu Fundmünzen der Antike 18). Mainz am Rhein.

Ulriksen, J. (2013). 'Detektorarkæologi – en succeshistorie med begyndende brudflader', *Romu* 2012: 27–49.

Webley, L. and Haselgrove, C. (2016). 'Lost purses and loose change? Coin deposition on settlements in Iron Age Europe', in C. Haselgrove and S. Krmnicek (eds), *The Archaeology of Money*. Leicester, 85–113.

Wicker, N. L. (2005). 'Display of Scandinavian Migration Period bracteates and other pendant jewelry as a reflection of prestige and identity', in R. Bork (ed.), *De Re Metallica: The Use of Metal in the Middle Ages* (AVISTA Studies in the History of Medieval Technology, Science and Art). Aldershot, 49–61.

Wigg-Wolf, D. (2020). 'Constantine III and the Rhine frontier: new numismatic evidence', in J. Chameroy (ed.), *Argentum Romanorum Sive Barbarorum. Tradition und Entwicklung im Gebrauch des Silbergeldes im römischen Westen 4.-6. Jh.* Mainz, 103–16.

Helle W. Horsnæs and Rasmus Holst Nielsen, *Roman Coin Hoards from Southern Scandinavia: Reflections in Light of Recent Finds* In: *Roman Coin Hoards Across Frontiers*. Edited by: Benjamin D. R. Hellings, Marguerite Spoerri Butcher, and Chris Howgego, Oxford University Press. © Oxford University Press 2026. DOI: 10.1093/9780198986478.003.0005

6

Hoarding the *Denarius*: Thoughts on the Outflow of *Denarii* from Gaul to German Barbaricum

Jérémie Chameroy and Pierre-Marie Guihard

INTRODUCTION

The conception and understanding of single finds and hoards of Roman coins in German Barbaricum (i.e. the territory of modern Germany east of the Rhine) have been greatly influenced by two well-known statements by Tacitus (*Germania* V, 4–5): *Quamquam proximi ob usum commerciorum aurum et argentum in pretio habent formasque quasdam nostrae pecuniae adgnoscunt atque eligunt; interiores simplicius et antiquius permutatio mercium utuntur* and *Pecuniam probant ueterem et diu notam, serratos bigatosque; argentum quoque magis quam aurum sequuntur.*

Although the preference of Germanic peoples for silver coins seems to be largely confirmed by the evidence of coin finds from Barbaricum (where *denarii* make up the majority of finds), it has long been recognized that Tacitus' passage reflects the ideas the Romans had about Germanic acceptance of the coinage.[1] Above all, it stresses that the Romans thought Germanic peoples accepted Roman coins solely on their metallic content, while they had a modern conception of *pecunia numerata* based on the value guaranteed by the state. In fact, if archaeological finds provide some support for the predilection of Germanic peoples for Roman silver coins, they do not show any preference for specific Republican *denarii* (*bigati* and *serrati*).[2] Instead, there is a growing archaeological record of *denarii subaerati* at settlements in Barbaricum to suggest a Roman influence on coin use and an acceptance of the *denarii* based on their types rather than their

[1] Lund (1987–8: 49–50); Kolendo (2008: 363–4). See also the discussion of this passage by Woytek (this volume, chapter 14).

[2] This assumption has been defended by Regling (1912: 217, 220) but contested in almost all later studies, e.g. Laser (1980: 33); Wolters and Stoess (1985: 35–6); Kolendo (2008: 370).

intrinsic value.[3] Furthermore, the deposition of *denarius* hoards is not concentrated among the *proximi*, who lived near the border, but rather among the *interiores*, who lived farther away. Therefore, the diffusion of Roman *denarii* was much more widespread than described by Tacitus.

Many studies, ranging from those by Sture Bolin to those by Frank Berger, Reinhard Wolters, and the authors of *Fundmünzen der römischen Zeit in Deutschland* (*FMRD*), have stressed the patterns of *denarius* hoards found in German Barbaricum.[4] With the exception of an Augustan group, the bulk of hoards end with *denarii* issued by the Antonine dynasty until Septimius Severus. Thus, they do not differ significantly from the hoards of *denarii* found in other regions of Barbaricum.[5] After the debasement of the *denarius* by Septimius Severus in AD 194, post-reform *denarii* are very scarce and correspond at most to the tail of the hoards deposited in Barbaricum.[6] Based on Tacitus' statement, earlier scholars interpreted the scarcity of Severan *denarii* in Barbaricum as an explicit rejection of debased silver coins, given the presumed preference for Roman coins of high intrinsic value.[7] More recent assumptions have focused on the role of Septimius Severus, who had been successful in pacifying the Rhine and Danube frontiers and possibly ended payments and subsidies to Barbarians,[8] thus explaining the scarcity of Severan *denarii* across the *limes*.

Due to the lack of contextual coin finds, the chronology and evolution of coin export into Barbaricum often rest on a comparative study of hoard composition. In this sense, attempts have recently been made to classify the hoards from eastern Barbaricum (principally Poland, Ukraine, and Moldova) based only on their contents. The method implies, however, that hoards sharing a similar profile should be considered contemporaneous and that their date of burial cannot have

[3] Bursche (1996: 34–5) first drew attention to the high proportion of *denarii subaerati* among the single finds on Polish settlements. For a recent synthesis on this topic see Dymowski (2020b). No examples from German Barbaricum are known so far.

[4] The volumes published since the 1960s cover all German Länder from Bayern (*FMRD* I) to Mecklenburg-Vorpommern (*FMRD* XIV).

[5] 84% of the 230 hoards from European Barbaricum (east of the Rhine and north of the Danube up to Denmark and Romania) recorded by Lucchelli (1998: 134–5) end with coins of Marcus Aurelius to Septimius Severus.

[6] The Severan reform consisted in restoring the weight of the *denarius* to the Neronian standard (1/96 pound) and reducing its silver content from *c.* 70% to around 45%: Butcher and Ponting (1997: 26, 29; 2012: 74). Covering a wider area than Germany, Bolin's fundamental study distinguished only between hoards containing pre-Neronian and post-Neronian *denarii*: Bolin (1929: 98–9). Both groups are clearly identified in the list of 83 hoards from Germany, Poland, the Czech Republic, Slovakia, Denmark, and southern Sweden compiled by Wolters and Stoess (1985: 21), but differences appear for smaller regions, such as north-west Germany, where earlier hoards close under Trajan; see Berger (1992: 138–9).

[7] Bolin (1929: 136–7); Laser (1980: 19, 38).

[8] Voß and Wigg-Wolf (2017: 117–18) suggest that after AD 194 *denarii* were principally used for military pay, so that Septimius Severus suspended the payments of *denarii* to the northern European Barbaricum. In a similar way, according to Bursche (1993: 300–1), the increasing value of silver may have stopped the outflow of *denarii*.

been much later than the date of issue of the latest *denarius* they contain.[9] This thesis is closely related to the widespread assumption that the export of *denarii* took place over a short time (between the Marcomannic Wars and the early years of the reign of Septimius Severus), since this phenomenon is believed to have been closely related to military events or their consequences (e.g. payment of tribute to barbarians). The emerging impression is that hoards from within and outside the Empire followed broadly the same evolution. Difficulties are encountered, however, since *denarii* struck after the reform of AD 194 do not appear in great quantity beyond the *limes*. The outcome is that the composition and concealment dates of hoards from Barbaricum drifted away from each other.

As studying the composition of hoards from Barbaricum may not always be the best way to determine their *terminus post quem* (*t.p.q.*),[10] this chapter proposes a different approach by comparing hoards from German Barbaricum with those from the Gallic provinces, from where the overwhelming outflow of *denarii* to *Germania libera* is supposed to have originated. Considering that most of the exported coins were Antonine *denarii*, it is important to determine their circulation peak in Gaul before addressing the question of whether or not Septimius Severus' reign truly ended the influx of *denarii* to Germany. Having defined the period of the influx of *denarii* east of the Rhine, one must consider both the possible consequences for the hoarding of *denarii* within the Gallic provinces and the patterns of their acceptance in Barbaricum.

HOARDING THE *DENARIUS* IN GERMAN BARBARICUM

For German Barbaricum, we know of 45 hoards primarily composed of at least ten *denarii* closing between Augustus and Severus Alexander (Table 6.1).[11] Detailed content information is available for only 33 of them, yielding over 4,200 *denarii* ranging from the Republic to Severus Alexander (see Appendix 1). The majority of the hoards have been taken from the systematic inventory of the coins finds in Germany (published in the *FMRD*), to which a few recent finds have been added. Moreover, our sample can be checked with the recent inventory of *denarius* hoards from European Barbaricum published by Arkadiusz Dymowski.[12] The list of 33 hoards compiled for our study is therefore representative of the *denarii* available and concealed in German Barbaricum. As in other regions of Barbaricum, the

[9] Dymowski and Myzgin (2014: 46). Uncertainty of classification occurs concerning the type D-hoards ending with *denarii* of Septimius Severus but showing a late chronological structure with only few *denarii*, or none at all, issued after the first years of the reign of Septimius Severus; see Dymowski and Myzgin (2014: 52).

[10] In the same way, Horsnæs (2010: 134) notes that the *denarii* of the Flavian to the Severan issues may have arrived at any time in Denmark approximately 200 years after their issue.

[11] See Lucchelli (1998: 8–24) and Dymowski (2020a: 206–8) for references concerning the hoards.

[12] Dymowski (2020a) starts his inventory with *denarius* hoards from the reign of Nero onwards.

Table 6.1. Chronological distribution of *denarius* hoards (>10 *denarii*) from German Barbaricum according to their *t.p.q.*

T.P.Q.	Quantity
Augustus	7
Hadrian	2
Antoninus Pius	6
Marcus Aurelius	9
Commodus	10
Pertinax	1
Septimius Severus	5
Caracalla	3
Severus Alexander	2
Total	**45**

most frequently represented emperors are Antoninus Pius, Marcus Aurelius, Trajan (about 17% each), Hadrian (12%), and Vespasian, next to *denarii* of the Roman Republic (about 10% each) (Fig. 6.1).

The seven hoards ending with *denarii* of Augustus should be connected to campaigns in Germany from Drusus to Varus: three hoards come from the Augustan camp at Haltern or nearby findspots, while one has been found near Kalkriese, the site of the *clades variana* (Fig. 6.2). These hoards should be regarded as Roman because they occurred either in Roman contexts or in contexts related to the Roman presence in this region.[13] This seems to be confirmed by the fact that no hoards of *denarii* with a *t.p.q.* from Tiberius to Hadrian have been found in *Germania libera*. The bulk of the hoards end with *denarii* of the Antonines, as in most other regions of Barbaricum.[14] Hoards closing with Severan *denarii* are, however, rarer in Germany than in eastern European Barbaricum, Scotland, and Sweden (Fig. 6.3).[15]

Denarius hoards from Barbaricum have been assumed to have been assembled within the Empire and exported as closed ensembles, and subsequently buried outside the frontiers.[16] Complementary evidence from seven German hoards, such as their containers (mostly ceramic vessels), is too scant to be conclusive.[17]

[13] Wolters and Stoess (1985: 34); Berger (1992: 47).

[14] E.g. almost half of the *denarii* found in Denmark were struck from AD 138 to 192; Horsnæs (2010: 125).

[15] For a synoptic view of *denarius* hoards from European Barbaricum, see Dymowski (2020a).

[16] Berger (1992: 145). Some scholars, however, considered the outflow of the coins to Barbaricum and the formation of the hoards as two distinct phases, e.g. Lucchelli (1998: 139, 161–2) and Laser (1980: 23).

[17] In one instance (Nordholz: 20 *denarii*, Antoninus Pius to Commodus; Berger 1988: 224, no. 8067), the coins were contained in a cloth roll, which is strongly reminiscent of some hoards from the Roman Empire. This may indicate that the Nordholz assemblage was composed in the Empire before

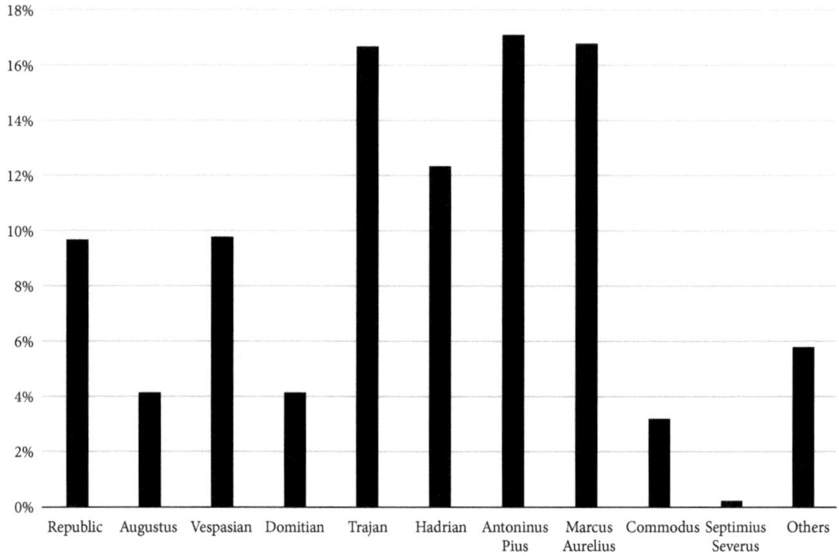

Fig. 6.1. Chronological distribution of the 4,239 *denarii* belonging to the 33 hoards found in German Barbaricum, by period and reign, expressed in percentages.

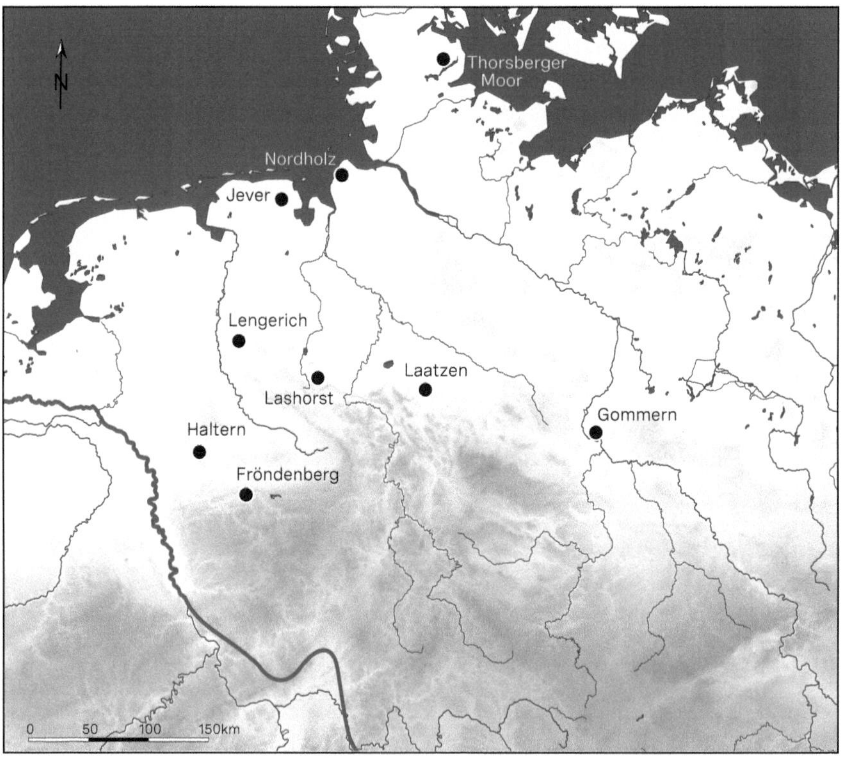

Fig. 6.2. Map of the principal hoards and burials from German Barbaricum mentioned in the text. Map: Michael Ober, LEIZA.

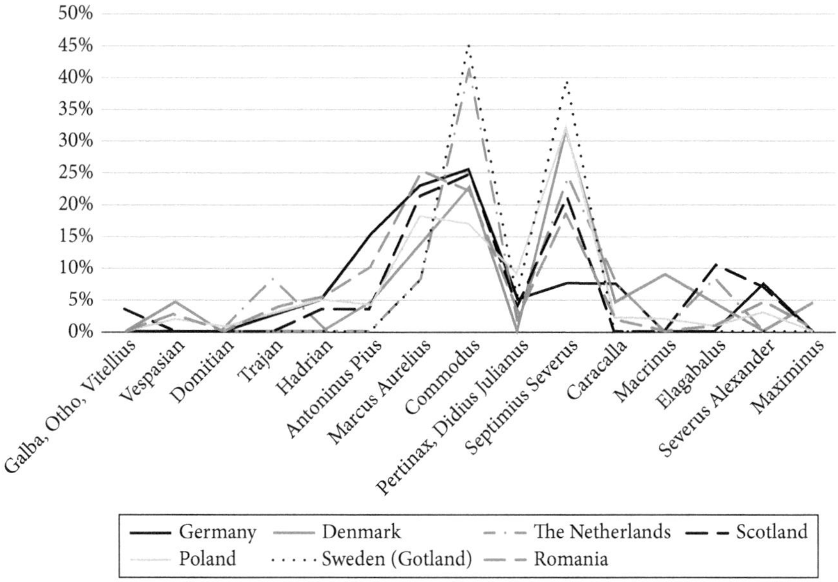

Fig. 6.3. Chronological distribution by closing reign, expressed in percentages (Germany, n = 39; Denmark, n = 22; Netherlands, n = 12; Scotland, n = 28; Poland, n = 99; Sweden, n = 35; Romania, n = 107) of *denarius* hoards from Germany and other regions in Barbaricum, after Dymowski (2020a).

Similarly, more evidence would be needed about the find contexts to comment on the function(s) of these ensembles in German Barbaricum. In the middle of the nineteenth century, many objects including 37 *denarii* were found in the moors of Thorsberg near the Danish frontier.[18] The *denarii* from Thorsberg (some of which were divided among a minimum of four purses) clearly belong to a cultural deposition within the array that is highly reminiscent of the weapon deposits of Illerup and Nydam, in Denmark.[19] The function of the other hoards from German Barbaricum (possibly a store of value) cannot be defined with certainty.

Special attention must be given to the *denarius* hoards that were mixed before deposition with other later coins in Barbaricum, such as barbarian imitations of *denarii* or fourth-century *siliquae,* as encountered with the Lashorst and Laatzen hoards. In both hoards, Volker Zedelius and subsequently Karlhorst Stribrny identified die-linked barbarian imitations, which are characterized by their blundered legends and the rough style of the busts and figures.[20]

being exported and deposited in Barbaricum. One cannot exclude the fact that Germanic peoples also occasionally adopted the practice of burying *denarii* in cloth rolls, so this may not indicate anything about where the hoard was assembled.

[18] Ceramic and wood vessels, *fibulae,* belt fittings, weapons, rings, remains of textiles and leather, wooden tools, and wheels were excavated; Komnick (1994: 118–30, no. 1082); Bursche (2011: 66–7).

[19] Jørgensen and Vang Petersen (2003); Bursche (2011); Bursche (2018).

[20] Zedelius (1974: 35–9); Stribrny (2003: 51–9).

Fig. 6.4. Barbarian imitation of the *Salus Augusti* group from the Laatzen hoard, Landesmuseum Hanover, 407–485: 1981. From: Stribrny (2003: plate 4, no. La 3), with permission of the Landesmuseum Hanover.

Stribrny called this die-link chain the *Salus Augusti* group (SAG) based on the reverse type they copy (Fig. 6.4). The occurrence of these imitations seems to be strictly limited to Barbaricum, even if their place of production remains uncertain.[21] As stressed by Stribrny, the barbarian imitations of the SAG copied obverses up to Marcus Aurelius (Faustina II), while the reverse types were copied from Antonine or Severan *denarii* up to Severus Alexander. Thus, the barbarian SAG imitations were issued around the mid-third century at the earliest—that is, about a half-century after the *t.p.q.* given by the latest official *denarii* in the Lashorst and Laatzen hoards.[22]

The 68 *denarii* (dating between Vespasian and Commodus) and the barbarian imitations of *denarii* that comprise the Laatzen hoard were mixed with three mid-fourth-century silver coins (two *miliarenses* of Constantius II and Julian Caesar, one *siliqua* of Constantius II) and one barbarian imitation of a *siliqua* of Constantius II. A further assemblage of coins from Lengerich offers obvious similarities in the association of *denarii* with later Roman coins.[23] It consists of three hoards: the first, found under a large stone, comprised over 1,147 *denarii* from Trajan to Septimius Severus (or possibly Severus Alexander). East of this first hoard, two more hoards lay under two additional large stones, one including gold jewellery and ten *solidi* of the Constantinian dynasty (*t.p.q.* AD 327), and the other more than 70 silver coins from Constantine to Magnentius. All three assemblages certainly belong to the same hoard that was deliberately deposited in different amounts and metals.

The important point to note is evident: assemblages of *denarii* up to the early third century were not necessarily deposited in Barbaricum immediately but could have been available (in circulation?) for a long time; alternatively, some came to

[21] Two additional *denarii* found in Ukraine have recently been added to the SAG and suggest that the coins belonging to this die-chain were produced there. See Dymowski (2019b: 157).

[22] Stribrny (2003: 60–1, 91).

[23] Berger and Stoess (1988: 67–88, nos 1032–5); Schmauder (1999).

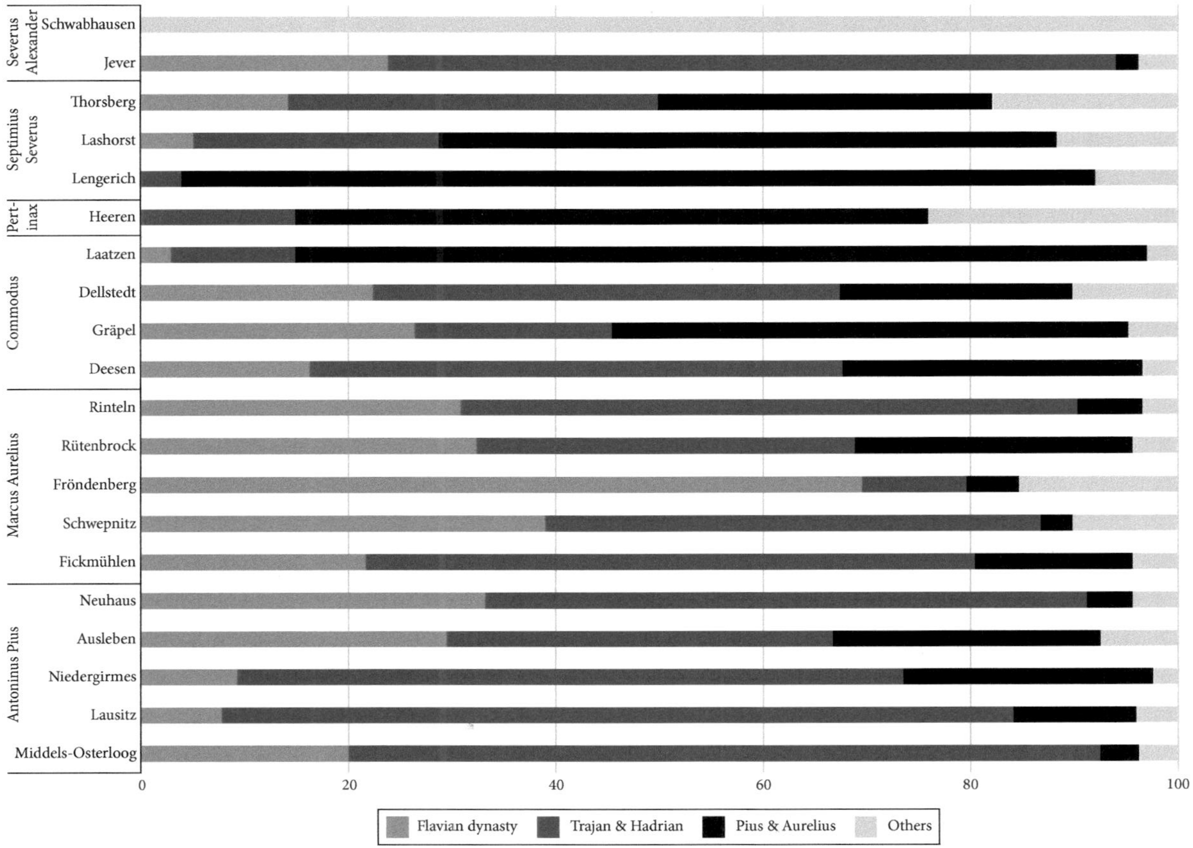

Fig. 6.5. Composition, expressed in percentages by period, of 20 hoards from German Barbaricum with a *t.p.q.* ranging from Antoninus to Severus Alexander.

Barbaricum later than indicated by the latest coin in the hoard.[24] Moreover, the occurrence of barbarian imitations of Antonine *denarii* in a hoard may point to its deposition in the AD 230s or 250s at the earliest, as in the case of the imitations belonging to the SAG. Consequently, the *t.p.q.* of the hoard from Lashorst, given by the official *denarii* of Septimius Severus, must be revised by a few decades through the presence of SAG barbarian coins.

Furthermore, one of the characteristics of the hoards from German Barbaricum is the significant number of old *denarii*. This can best be seen in the hoards ending with *denarii* of Antoninus Pius to Commodus, composed primarily of *denarii* of Trajan or Hadrian.[25] This is all the more apparent in the later Jever hoard (*t.p.q.* Septimius Severus), for which 70% of the published coins are *denarii* of Trajan and Hadrian (Fig. 6.5). The Fröndenberg hoard, closing under Marcus Aurelius, even has a significant number of *denarii* of the Flavian dynasty.[26] This similarly confirms that one cannot securely base the chronology of hoards from Barbaricum on their composition, since their 'early structure'—apparently provided by the first- and early second-century *denarii*—obviously contrasts with their late second-century *t.p.q.* The wide variety of hoard structures in Barbaricum makes it more challenging to identify the specific time span of the influx of *denarii* from Gaul to German Barbaricum.

THE EXPORT OF *DENARII* FROM GAUL: AN EXTENSIVE PHENOMENON IN THE TIME OF SEPTIMIUS SEVERUS?

For the Gallic provinces, we have assembled a sample consisting of 49 hoards with *t.p.q.*s ranging between Augustus and Gordian III. Thirty-nine of these provide quantifiable documentation consisting of over 10,800 *denarii* (see Appendix 2). The documentation is largely based on the CHRE database,[27] which relies in part on systematic regional inventories (e.g. the *Corpus des trésors monétaires antiques de la France*) and on recent finds from single publications (e.g. from the *Trésors monétaires* series). Thus, our sample should be considered to be representative of the circulation pool in Gaul. The first important point to emerge is the very high proportion of hoards ending with Antonine (25%) or Severan (29%) *denarii*, together representing more than half of the sample (Fig. 6.6). When comparing the composition of the hoards, however, the presence of first- and second-century

[24] Lucchelli (1998: 141–2).

[25] Hoards from the Netherlands (see Figs 6.10 and 6.11 below) are not considered here because their small size makes them difficult to employ in this statistical study.

[26] One hundred and seventeen *denarii* out of 257 belong to the Flavian dynasty; Regling (1912: 194).

[27] https://chre.ashmus.ox.ac.uk/ (accessed 14 April 2023).

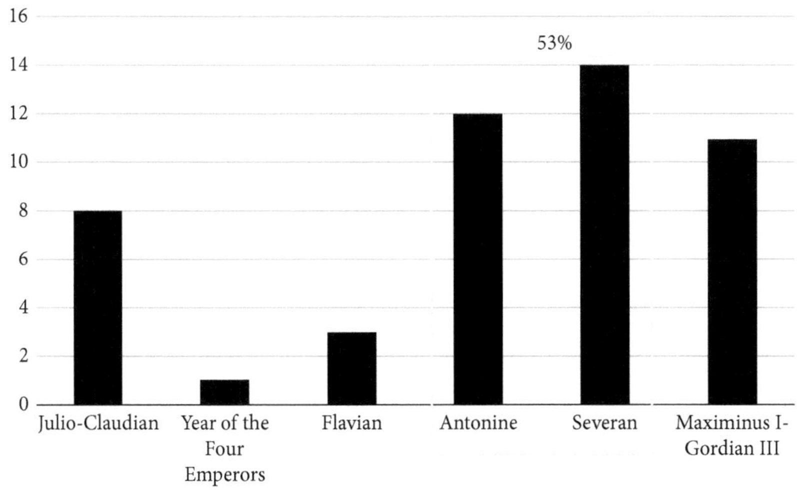

Fig. 6.6. Number of *denarius* hoards (n = 49) from Gaul according to their *t.p.q.*

denarii stands out. This is an important trend that will help clarify the influx of *denarii* east of the Rhine.

The most characteristic fact is that, among first-century *denarii*, those of the Flavian dynasty always represent a large contingent, i.e. more than 90% of coins. From Domitian onwards, indeed, the pre-Neronian-reform *denarii* tend to disappear (they still represent 53% in the Aubenton hoard) until they were withdrawn under Trajan.[28] In any case, it can be noted that Flavian *denarii* are present in hoards ending with Antonine coins. The percentages are unequal (7% to 47%) (Fig. 6.7), but the frequency of occurrence indicates a real permanence of first-century coins up to the early third century, as in the hoards of Sceaux (11%), Avezé (19%), and Morienval (5%), which closed under Septimius Severus, Elagabalus, and Gordian I, respectively.

In hoards closing after Antoninus Pius, however, first-century *denarii* only represent a small contingent of the coinage. These ensembles show a recycling of Flavian *denarii* taking place during the first half of the second century, so that Antonine coins filled the gap and formed a significant proportion of the coins (26% to 92%) (Fig. 6.8). These facts are only the forerunners of a movement which is clearly accentuated in hoards closing under Septimius Severus: *denarii* issued between Trajan and Marcus Aurelius make up the overwhelming majority (over 80%) of the silver coinage. The conditions remain unchanged up to the hoards with a *t.p.q.* under Elagabalus or Severus Alexander. These assemblages demonstrate a clear shift: second-century coins undergo a rapid and drastic

[28] West (1941: 83); Cassius Dio, 68,15.

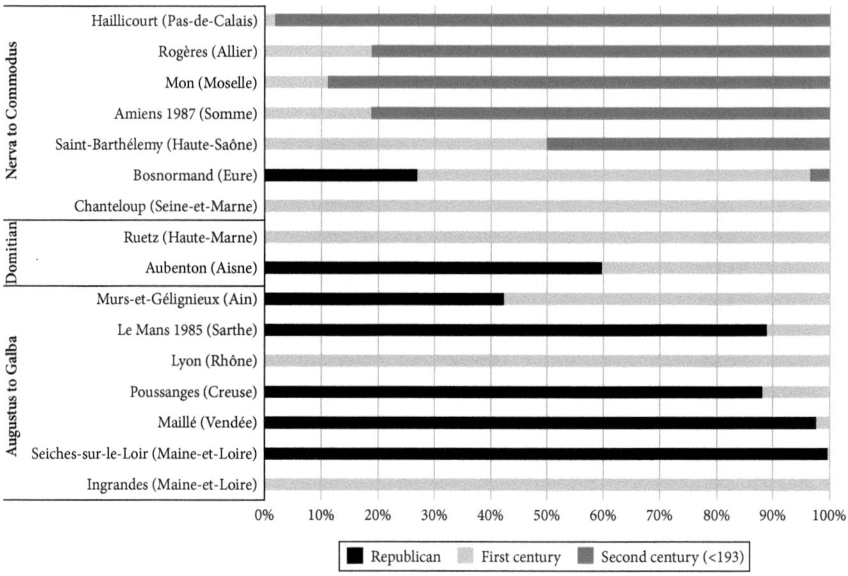

Fig. 6.7. Composition, expressed in percentages by chronological period, of 16 *denarius* hoards from Gaul, with a *t.p.q.* ranging from Augustus to Commodus.

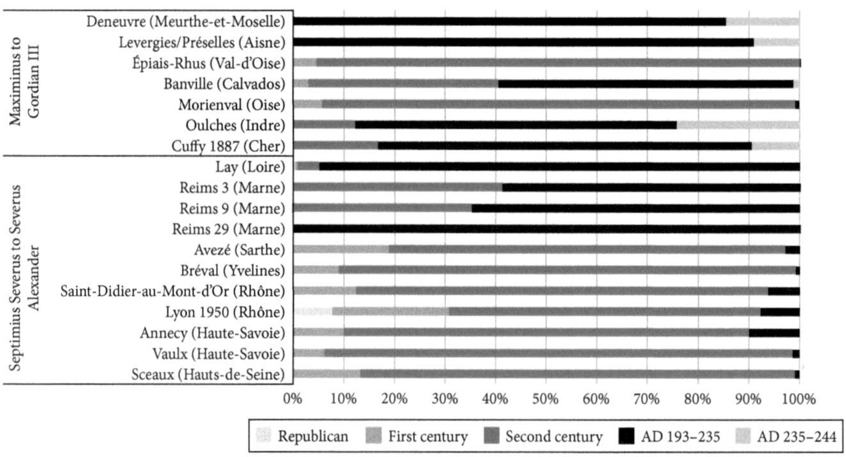

Fig. 6.8. Composition, expressed in percentage by chronological period, of 18 *denarius* hoards from Gaul, with a *t.p.q.* ranging from Septimius Severus to Gordian III.

decline overall (<5%) and are replaced by a sudden increase in Severan coins (>60% from Severus Alexander, then >80% from Gordian III) (Fig. 6.8). The Reims hoards are good examples of this new monetary situation being established. This probably corresponds to a recycling of the Antonine issues allowing the Severan *denarii* to become the major silver coinage in circulation.[29] Nevertheless, some differences emerge throughout Gaul in some coin hoards with *t.p.q.*s between Maximinus and Gordian III. In western Gaul, hoards contain slightly more second-century coins (Morienval, Banville, Épiais-Rhus). In eastern Gaul, hoards present a different picture: the replacement of second-century *denarii* with Severan coins is particularly profound (Levergies/Préselles, Deneuvre, etc.). The later hoards (Philip to Probus) bear witness to this intense renewal of the circulation pool after Severus Alexander, which consisted of Severan *denarii* and *antoniniani*.[30]

This survey of Gallic hoards demonstrates parallels with hoards from German Barbaricum: the high proportion of first-century (mostly Flavian) *denarii* in hoards with a *t.p.q.* up to Marcus Aurelius, and their decrease in hoards with a *t.p.q.* under Commodus or Septimius Severus in favour of Antonine *denarii*. Therefore, the composition of the Gallic hoards shows that Antonine *denarii* made up the most significant proportion of silver coins circulating within the Empire up to about AD 220 (see Figs 6.7 and 6.8). This seems to be largely confirmed by the almost complete absence of Septimius Severus' *denarii* observed in the coin pool circulating in the western provinces until *c.* 210,[31] and implies that the Antonine *denarii*, which make up the overwhelming majority of the hoards in German Barbaricum, could have been exported up to the first quarter of the third century.

One can only guess at the means of export. The differences in composition observed in the hoards from Barbaricum (e.g. the varying number of early *denarii*) suggest that *denarii* were not exported in bulk to German Barbaricum; otherwise one could expect to find a concentration of hoards in a particular region of German Barbaricum with the same *t.p.q.* and the same structure. This is not the case, as can be seen, for example, in hoards from German Barbaricum with a *t.p.q.* of Marcus Aurelius that differ widely in composition through varying proportions of *denarii* of Antoninus Pius, Hadrian, or Vespasian (Table 6.2). In addition, it is worth noting that most of the hoards deposited in German Barbaricum comprise a limited number of *denarii*: 42% count fewer than 50 coins, and about two-thirds of them fewer than 100 coins (Fig. 6.9). This, again, hardly seems to agree with the supposedly vast amounts of *denarii* that are said to have been exported by the Antonine emperors as subsidies and payments to make peace with the Germans—even if one accepts the idea of a redistribution of the coins among the Germans. To sum up, the finds from German Barbaricum do not provide evidence for large subsidy payments that may have been hoarded by

29 Murphy (2020: 149).
30 Callu (1969: 251); Christol (1977: 252–3); Chameroy and Guihard (2016: 249–50).
31 Reece (1987: 55); Abdy (2002: 24–5); Bland (2018: 59); Murphy (2020: 147–9).

Table 6.2. Distribution of *denarii* in hoards from German Barbaricum with a *t.p.q.* under Marcus Aurelius.

	Ausleben	Ausleben	Erfurt	Erfurt	Neuhaus	Neuhaus	Fickmühlen	Fickmühlen	Schwepnitz	Schwepnitz
Republic to Claudius		0.00%		0.00%		0.00%		0.00%		0.00%
Nero		0.00%		0.00%	2	0.58%		0.00%	4	3.31%
Galba, Otho, Vitellius	1	3.70%		0.00%	9	2.61%		0.00%	6	4.96%
Vespasian	6	22.22%		0.00%	56	16.23%	4	8.70%	32	26.45%
Titus	1	3.70%		0.00%	17	4.93%	2	4.35%	6	4.96%
Domitian	1	3.70%		0.00%	42	12.17%	4	8.70%	9	7.44%
Nerva	1	3.70%		0.00%	4	1.16%	2	4.35%	2	1.65%
Trajan	6	22.22%	3	10.34%	116	33.62%	17	36.96%	39	32.23%
Hadrian	4	14.81%	7	24.14%	84	24.35%	10	21.74%	19	15.70%
Antoninus Pius	5	18.52%	9	31.03%	11	3.19%	5	10.87%	3	2.48%
Marcus Aurelius	2	7.41%	10	34.48%	4	1.16%	2	4.35%	1	0.83%
Total	**27**		**29**		**345**		**46**		**121**	

	Fröndenberg	Fröndenberg	Rütenbrock	Rütenbrock	Rinteln	Rinteln	Deesen	Deesen
Republic to Claudius	6	2.35%		0.00%	2	0.84%		0.00%
Nero	16	6.27%	1	1.35%	1	0.42%		0.00%
Galba, Otho, Vitellius	17	6.67%	1	1.35%	4	1.69%	2	3.23%
Vespasian	153	60.00%	18	24.32%	29	12.24%	4	6.45%
Titus	22	8.63%	2	2.70%	7	2.95%	3	4.84%
Domitian	2	0.78%	4	5.41%	37	15.61%	3	4.84%
Nerva		0.00%	1	1.35%	1	0.42%		0.00%
Trajan	11	4.31%	21	28.38%	105	44.30%	23	37.10%
Hadrian	15	5.88%	6	8.11%	36	15.19%	9	14.52%
Antoninus Pius	11	4.31%	17	22.97%	10	4.22%	15	24.19%
Marcus Aurelius	2	0.78%	3	4.05%	5	2.11%	3	4.84%
Total	**255**		**74**		**237**		**62**	

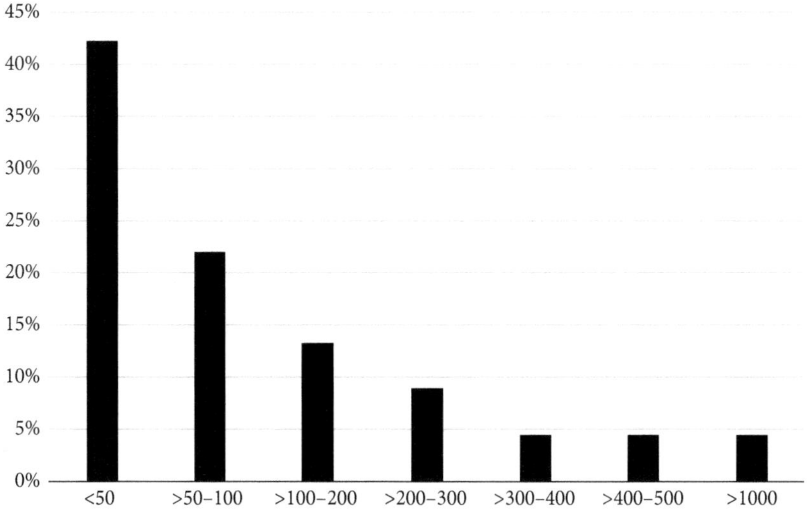

Fig. 6.9. Distribution of 45 *denarius* hoards from German Barbaricum according to size (number of coins), expressed in percentages.

Germans after receiving the coins. Rather, the frequency of small hoards and of ensembles with different structures may correspond to modest savings composed of coins commonly used in Barbaricum and made available through trade exchanges across the *limes* and possibly in Barbaricum; in that case, the influx of silver coins would have been spread out over many years.[32]

Owing to the dates of the hoards from German Barbaricum, it is worth emphasizing that 80% of the coins were deposited after the beginning of Marcus Aurelius' reign and 47% even after the beginning of Septimius Severus' reign. More precisely, about 30% (corresponding to the *denarii* from the Laatzen and Lengerich hoards) were deposited around the mid-fourth century at the earliest. Thus, a possible scenario for the export of *denarii* to German Barbaricum could be an influx beginning under Marcus Aurelius, reaching its zenith under Commodus and the early reign of Septimius Severus, and ending around the reign of Elagabalus. Considering the time needed (a few decades) for a new coinage to dominate the circulation pool (as stressed above for the *denarii* of Septimius Severus), it is not surprising that huge quantities of Antonine *denarii* still circulated in early third-century Gaul, from where they may have been exported to

[32] For alternative interpretations of the export of *denarii*, see David Wigg-Wolf in this volume (chapter 7) and note 8 above.

Germania libera.[33] By contrast, an influx starting after AD 220, as proposed by Lennart Lind, cannot be confirmed.[34] Within the Empire, in fact, most of the hoards closing after AD 220 show a significant reduction in the number of Antonine *denarii* in favour of Severan *denarii* and *antoniniani.*[35] Therefore, it seems improbable that vast quantities of Antonine *denarii* could have been exported to Barbaricum during the reign of Severus Alexander or under his successors.

In any case, the documentation gathered warns us to be cautious about considering that Septimius Severus' alleged decision to end the export of silver coins would have definitively stopped the influx of *denarii* into Barbaricum. If the stoppage indeed resulted from an imperial decision, such as an export ban, then this measure would have applied exclusively to the new Severan *denarii*, while the emperors would have allowed the Antonine *denarii* (with higher silver content) to be exported to Barbaricum at a time when the Roman state lacked silver. This interpretation seems highly doubtful because, after the debasement of the *denarius* in AD 194, it is thought that the old silver coins were recycled to supply the production with silver.[36] The second point is that the Germans not only were able to distinguish between pre- and post-reform *denarii* but also regarded the latter coins differently, i.e. as silver coins that were not worth hoarding because of their lower silver content. The rejection of post-reform *denarii* of the Severans in Barbaricum is not a new thesis, but may be explained differently from in the past.

HOARDED OR REJECTED: THE SEVERAN *DENARIUS* AS VIEWED BY THE GERMANS

Assuming that quantities of Antonine *denarii* crossed the Rhine up to AD 220, what happened to the Severan *denarii* circulating in the Empire? Mapping the *denarii* hoards of the late second and early third century allows us to recognize a

[33] Gebhart *et al.* (1956: 46–51). As a possible effect of this delay, Horsnæs (2010: 186) interestingly observed that in Denmark Antonine *denarii* became increasingly prominent the later the assemblage was deposited. However, scholars supposing a direct outflow of the *denarii* after their production did not take this delay into account. Bursche (1994: 472) assumed a massive outflow of *denarii* between the Marcomannic Wars and the beginning of the reign of Septimius Severus. Lucchelli (1998: 161) placed the influx of *denarii* between the early reign of Trajan to Antoninus Pius, ending about AD 194 or a few years later. In the same way, Regling (1912: 222–4) dated the massive export of *denarii* to the reigns of the Flavians to Antoninus Pius.

[34] Lind (1993: 292–3). In fact, his argument depends on hoards from different provinces of the Empire which must not be representative of the circulation pool of *denarii* in the early third century. His thesis was mostly rejected by scholars, e.g. Bursche (1994: 472), Lucchelli (1998: 154–7).

[35] See Murphy (2020: 149), noting a rapid decline of pre-reform *denarii* in hoards of the period AD 220–45 where they were replaced by post-reform *denarii.*

[36] Butcher and Ponting (2022: 277) stress that Severus' reform took place at a time when coin recycling seems to have restarted.

progressive concentration of the assemblages in the German provinces. This trend starts with hoards closing with *denarii* of Septimius Severus (Fig. 6.10) and becomes more apparent for hoards with a *t.p.q.* under Severus Alexander or Maximinus (Fig. 6.11); as noted above, these hoards consist of an overwhelming majority of post-reform *denarii.*[37]

Considering the significant presence of Severan *denarii* in the border provinces, it is surprising how few of these coins crossed the Rhine in the early third century, for example during Maximinus' campaign in Barbaricum. Instead, it seems probable that the Germans deliberately avoided the Severan *denarii* as much as possible. The reason for the differing acceptance of pre- and post-reform *denarii* in Barbaricum can best be approached through barbarian *denarii* and some exceptional burial finds.

As previously explained, Severan *denarii* did not serve as models for the obverses of the barbarian copies of the *Salus Augusti* group found in the German hoards from Lashorst and Laatzen, although the production of these irregular coins took place at the time of Severus Alexander at the earliest. The same observation has been made concerning other groups of barbarian copies, where only busts of pre-Severan emperors (mostly the Antonine dynasty) were copied: the *Ceres* group defined by Arkadiusz Dymowski consists of 46 *denarii* found in Ukraine, Poland, and Sweden; their portraits show prototypes of Antoninus Pius to Commodus, although the production started around the mid-third century in Ukraine.[38] A smaller group of eight barbarian *denarii* struck with obverses of the Antonine emperors share the same reverse die, copying a *Venus Victrix* type of Severus Alexander.[39] In Sweden, finally, the 66 recorded copies on Gotland and Öland have portraits of Trajan to Commodus but reverses that imitate third-century *denarii* (from the reign of Severus Alexander at the latest).[40]

A further example of the particular reception pre-reform *denarii* enjoyed in German Barbaricum is provided by the *Fürstengrab* from Gommern. In this burial, which can be dated between AD 230 and 250, an *aureus* of Trajan was deposited in the mouth of the prince, while five *denarii* of Hadrian (1), Antoninus Pius (3), and Lucius Verus (1) were found near the pelvis, most probably the contents of a purse.[41] This suggests that the *denarii* were considered *pecunia* in the same way as the Romans regarded their own coins. But a later *t.p.q.* is provided by two gold off-strikes of the same *denarius* of Severus Alexander, which served as decorative elements for the shield's handgrip. As a very special piece with silver fittings, the painted shield itself must have been made in Barbaricum, where

[37] The recycling of pre-reform *denarii* probably accelerated the circulation of the Severan *denarii*; in this sense, see the conclusions of Murphy (2020: 149).

[38] Dymowski (2019a: 179, 182).

[39] Dymowski (2019b: 157).

[40] Lind (2018: 1–2, 11).

[41] Becker (2010: 117, 347–8).

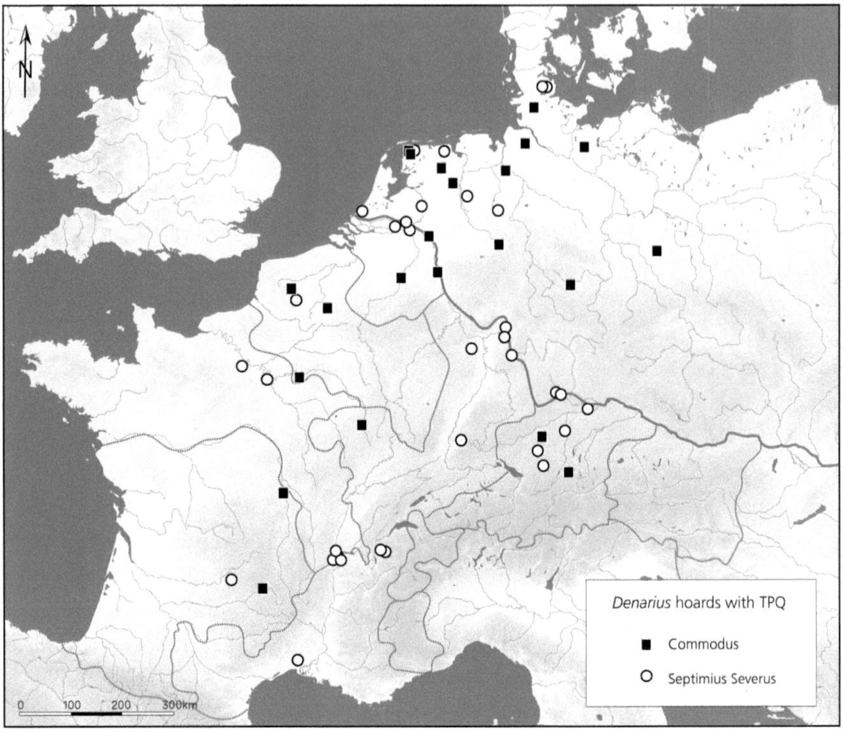

Fig. 6.10. Distribution map of *denarius* hoards with a *t.p.q.* under Commodus (AD 180–92) and Septimius Severus (AD 193–211). Map: Michael Ober, LEIZA.

comparable showpieces have been found in *Prunkgräber*. The vital point to recall is that during the early to mid-third century, late Severan *denarii* were available, but they may not always have been considered and accepted as fully equivalent to the pre-Severan *denarii* and thus were not deposited in the purse together with the Antonine *denarii*.

Another indication of the special status of the finer *denarii* in Barbaricum is suggested by the presence of hoards of pre-reform *denarii* in the German provinces up to the early third century (Fig. 6.10). The conclusion that could be drawn from the particular distribution of the finds is that the composition of these hoards could be related to the *denarius*' debasement of AD 194. Aware of the modifications introduced by Septimius Severus' reform in the metallic content of *denarii*, coin users may have sought to set aside pre-Severan *denarii* with the idea of exporting them to Barbaricum, where they were accepted at their metallic value—a hypothesis that cannot be excluded. These coin hoards should therefore be considered as possible sets intended to speculate on the 'good *denarius*', to be specifically used in Barbaricum.

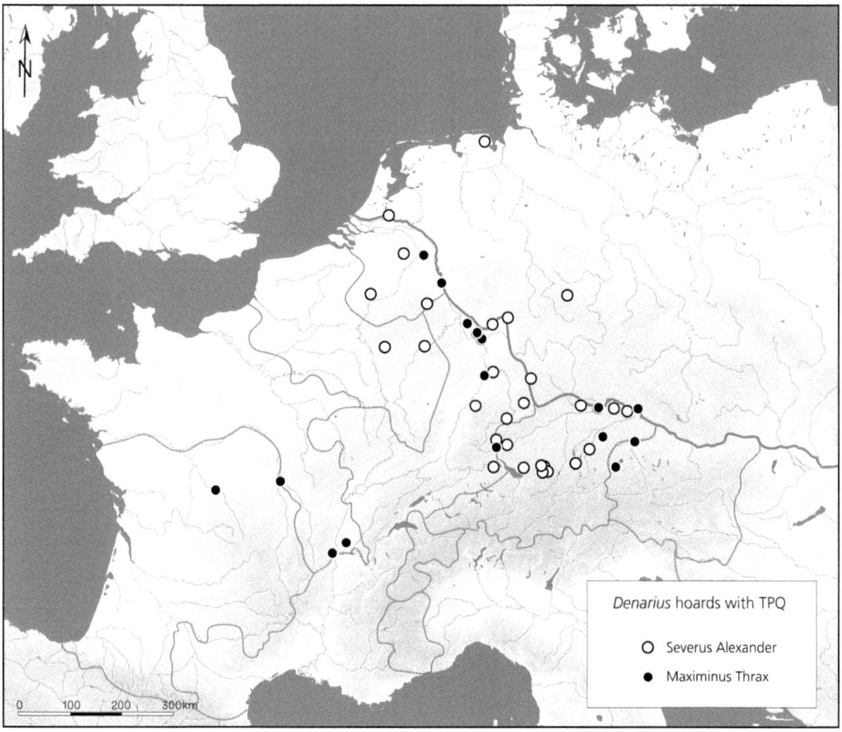

Fig. 6.11. Distribution map of *denarius* hoards with a *t.p.q.* under Severus Alexander (AD 222–35) and Maximinus Thrax (AD 235–8). Map: Michael Ober, LEIZA.

As Tacitus' statements suggest, the pre-Severan *denarii* played the role of a reference coinage for the Germans;[42] the find evidence speaks to the fact that, at least in parts of *Germania libera*, Roman coinage circulated in the same way as in the Empire.[43] Therefore, it seems very probable that Severan *denarii* were excluded due to their lower silver content. In Barbaricum, as in the Empire, the coins were first identified by their iconographic types, which, in the eyes of the Germans, were supposed to confirm the silver content. If the Germans regarded the *denarii* as small ingots, the Antonine portraits may have constituted a sufficient

[42] Tacitus, *Germania* V, 4–5, cited in the 'Introduction' section above. Stribrny (2003: 93): 'nach der severischen Zeit wurde der Qualitätsbegriff allein mit Denaren des 2. Jahrhunderts verknüpft'. Indeed, the period AD 156/7–94 is one of extreme stability of the silver content (*c.* 70%) of the *denarius*; see Butcher and Ponting (2012: 82).

[43] Berger (2008: 106–9) suggests the existence of a coin circulation in Westphalia and on the northern coast of Germany, where many single finds of *denarii* and Roman bronze coins have been recorded. On the contrary, the assumption that the principal use of *denarii* in Barbaricum was as a source of metal (Bursche 2018: 468)—implying, thus, their rapid melting down—is not supported by the presence of *denarii subaerati* in deposits like Thorsberg or Nydam (Bursche 1996: 36).

guarantee of their silver content when their use developed outside the Empire. In this sense, the Germans must not have checked the intrinsic value of each *denarius* they received, but progressively accepted them as *pecunia numerata* in the Roman *usus*.[44] Therefore, it is not surprising to also find some *denarii subaerati* in Barbaricum (Fig. 6.12).[45]

The evidence for the particular reception of the pre-Severan *denarius* may also be observed in later hoards from fourth- and fifth-century Gaul (Table 6.3). For example, the Beaurains and Berry-au-Bac assemblages have in common a high number of Antonine coins, a lack of Severan coins, and the mixture with

Fig. 6.12. *Denarius subaeratus* of Faustina II issued after AD 179 (2.59 g, 5 h). The prototype seems to correspond to the *aureus RIC* III, 671. Unknown findspot; collection of the Leibniz-Zentrum für Archäologie (LEIZA) O.27877. © LEIZA, René Müller.

Table 6.3. Distribution of *denarii* in three fourth- to fifth-century hoards from Gaul.

	Beaurains		**Berry-au-Bac**		**Childeric's grave**	
Period/Reign	**Quantity**	**%**	**Quantity**	**%**	**Quantity**	**%**
Republic					1	2.44
Nero					1	2.44
Vitellius	1	1.25				
Vespasian	7	8.64				
Nerva						
Trajan	9	11.11	1	5.88	2	4.87
Hadrian	10	12.34	2	11.79	5	12.20
Antoninus Pius	29	35.80	4	23.52	22	53.66
Marcus Aurelius	16	19.75	6	35.29	6	14.64
Commodus	9	11.11	4	23.52	2	4.87
Septimius Severus					1	2.44
Caracalla					1	2.44
TOTAL	81		17		41	

[44] Chantraine (1985: 379–80), assuming that the Germans accepted the Republican *denarii* 'nach Aussehen und Stückzahlen', as suggested by the weight differences observed among the coins and the absence of scales in early *Germania libera*.

[45] In the same sense, Dymowski (2020b: 174).

fourth-century silver coins.[46] These characteristics are strongly reminiscent of hoards from German Barbaricum and may therefore point to their owners' Germanic origin. The same applies to the silver coins from Childeric's grave, where a majority of Antonine *denarii* were associated with an *argenteus* of Constantius II.[47] The fact that these hoards are mostly made up of second-century coins again suggests that the Germans' preference for hoarding pre-Severan *denarii* was a permanent phenomenon that also had consequences for the hoarding process in late Roman and early medieval Gaul. Furthermore, the significant presence of *denarii subaerati* in the Beaurains hoard seems to confirm that the Roman custom of considering money according to its type rather than its intrinsic value remains the normal usage among the Germans.[48]

CONCLUSION

Compositional parallels have been observed in *denarii* hoards from Gaul and German Barbaricum up to the early third century. A comparison of hoard samples from both sides of the Rhine prompts the conclusion that the influx of *denarii* to German Barbaricum started in the late Antonine period at the earliest and persisted until approximately AD 220. Therefore, the reign of Septimius Severus should not be considered as the end of the influx of *denarii* but, rather, as its peak.

The fact that Severan *denarii* represent a very small part of this export raises doubt about the intervention of the emperor in this phenomenon. Indeed, a supposed ban on the export of *denarii* by Septimius Severus, ending payments and subsidies to barbarians, is hardly understandable when it could not prevent the finer, pre-Severan *denarii* from crossing the Rhine. Instead, it is probable that the debasement of the *denarius* by Septimius Severus accelerated the drain—perhaps through private initiatives—of pre-reform *denarii* to Barbaricum, since these finer silver coins were apparently undervalued within the Empire after AD 194.

The aspects discussed above stress that the Germans had an economic use and conception of the Roman silver coins through the influence of Roman *habitus*, even if their use of small change was more limited than in the Empire. Consequently, the role of the *denarius* in Barbaricum should not be limited to strictly social, political, or even religious functions.[49] The Germans also attached a genuine economic value to Roman *denarii*.

[46] Beaurains: Bastien and Metzger (1977). Berry-au-Bac: Delmaire (1997: nos 19–20).

[47] Chifflet (1655); Fischer and Lind (2015).

[48] Among the 81 *denarii* of the first and second centuries, 12 (i.e. 15%) were plated: Bastien and Metzger (1977: 47–68).

[49] This corresponds, in other words, to the definition of a limited-purpose currency, as has been proposed by various authors. See, among others, Bursche (2002), or more recently Fischer and Lind (2015).

Appendix 1: 33 hoards from German Barbaricum

Ausleben (Lkr. Oschersleben): Dymowski (2020a: 205, no. 46); *t.p.q.* Marcus Aurelius.
Barenaue-Lutterkrug (Lkr. Osnabrück): Berger (1992: 239–44); *t.p.q.* Augustus.
Bingum-Soltborg (Lkr. Leer): Berger and Stoess (1988: 123–5, no. 2008); *t.p.q.* Augustus.
Deesen (Westerwaldkr.): Dymowski (2020a: 205, no. 48); *t.p.q.* Marcus Aurelius.
Dellstedt (Kr. Norderdithmarschen): Dymowski (2020a: 205, no. 49); *t.p.q.* Commodus.
Delmenhorst-Dwoberg (Kreisfreie Stadt Delmenhorst): Dymowski (2020a: 205, no. 51); *t.p.q.* Commodus.
Dörpstedt (Kr. Schleswig): Dymowski (2020a: 205, no. 50); *t.p.q.* Antoninus Pius.
Erfurt (region of): Dymowski (2020a: 205, no. 52); *t.p.q.* Marcus Aurelius.
Fickmühlen (Lkr. Wesermünde): Dymowski (2020a: 205, no. 53); *t.p.q.* Marcus Aurelius.
Fröndenberg (Kr. Unna): Regling (1912); Dymowski (2020a: 205, no. 54); *t.p.q.* Marcus Aurelius.
Gehrden (Lkr. Hannover): Berger (1988: 54–6, no. 4031); *t.p.q.* Augustus.
Gräpel (Lkr. Stade): Dymowski (2020a: 205, no. 56); *t.p.q.* Commodus.
Haltern I (Kr. Recklinghausen): Korzus (1971: 56–7, no. 4054); *t.p.q.* Augustus.
Haltern III (Kr. Recklinghausen): Korzus (1971: 57–61, no. 4056); *t.p.q.* Augustus.
Heeren (Lkr. Stendal): Dymowski (2020a: 205, no. 59); *t.p.q.* Pertinax.
Jever (Lkr. Friesland): Dymowski (2020a: 205, no. 60); *t.p.q.* Septimius Severus.
Laatzen (Region Hannover): Zedelius (1974); Dymowski (2020a: 205, no. 62); *t.p.q.* Commodus.
Lashorst (Lkr. Lübbecke): Dymowski (2020a: 205, no. 63); *t.p.q.* Septimius Severus.
Lausitz (Lkr. Bad Liebenwerda): Dymowski (2020a: 205, no. 64); *t.p.q.* Antoninus Pius.
Lengerich I (Lkr. Lingen): Schmauder (1999); Dymowski (2020a: 206, no. 65); *t.p.q.* Septimius Severus.
Middels-Osterloog (Lkr. Aurich): Dymowski (2020a: 206, no. 66); *t.p.q.* Antoninus Pius.
Neuhaus (Lkr. Land Hadeln): Dymowski (2020a: 206, no. 68); *t.p.q.* Marcus Aurelius.
Niedergirmes (Lahn-Dill-Kr.): Dymowski (2020a: 206, no. 69); *t.p.q.* Antoninus Pius.
Niederlangen (Lkr. Aschendorf-Hümmling): Berger and Stoess (1988: 37–41, no. 1004); *t.p.q.* Augustus.
Niemegk (Lkr. Belzig): Dymowski (2020a: 206, no. 70); *t.p.q.* Hadrian.
Rinteln (Lkr. Schaumburg): Berger (1992: 248–56); Dymowski (2020a: 206, no. 74); *t.p.q.* Marcus Aurelius.
Rütenbrock (Stadt Haren, Lkr. Emsland): Dymowski (2020a: 206, no. 75); *t.p.q.* Marcus Aurelius.
Schlieben (Lkr. Guben): Dymowski (2020a: 206, no. 77); *t.p.q.* Commodus.
Schwabhausen (Lkr. Gotha): Dymowski (2020a: 206, no. 78); *t.p.q.* Severus Alexander.
Schwepnitz (Lkr. Kamenz): Dymowski (2020a: 206, no. 79); *t.p.q.* Marcus Aurelius.
Seppenrade (Lkr. Lüdinghausen): Korzus (1971: 44–6, no. 4039); *t.p.q.* Augustus.
Thorsberger Moor 1 (Kr. Schleswig): Komnick (1994: 122–7, no. 1082A); Dymowski (2020a: 206, no. 81); *t.p.q.* Septimius Severus.
Thorsberger Moor 2 (Kr. Schleswig): Komnick (1994: 127–30, no. 1082B); Dymowski (2020a: 206, no. 82); *t.p.q.* Septimius Severus.

Appendix 2: 39 hoards from Gaul

Amiens (Somme), CHRE 5240; *t.p.q.* Antoninus Pius.
Annecy (Haute-Savoie), CHRE 3139; *t.p.q.* Septimius Severus.
Aubenton (Aisne), CHRE 6240; *t.p.q.* Domitian.
Avezé (Sarthe), CHRE 5836; *t.p.q.* Elagabalus.

Bailly-en-Rivière (Seine-Maritime), CHRE 5663; *t.p.q.* Trajan.
Banville (Calvados), Guihard and Léon (2020); *t.p.q.* Balbinus and Pupienus.
Bosnormand (Eure), CHRE 5766; *t.p.q.* Trajan.
Bréval (Yvelines), CHRE 6995; *t.p.q.* Septimius Severus.
Chanteloup-en-Brie (Seine-et-Marne), CHRE 7043; *t.p.q.* Nerva.
Cuffy (Cher), CHRE 12451; *t.p.q.* Maximinus.
Deneuvre (Meurthe-et-Moselle), CHRE 12513; *t.p.q.* Gordian III.
Épiais-Rhus (Val-d'Oise), CHRE 3233; *t.p.q.* Gordian III.
Haillicourt (Pas-de-Calais), CHRE 5618; *t.p.q.* Commodus.
Ingrandes (Maine-et-Loire), CHRE 5905; *t.p.q.* Augustus.
Laharmand (Haute-Marne), CHRE 12373; *t.p.q.* Commodus.
Lay (Loire), CHRE 2967; *t.p.q.* Severus Alexander.
Le Mans 1985 (Sarthe), CHRE 5461; *t.p.q.* Tiberius.
Levergies/Préselles (Aisne), CHRE 3313; *t.p.q.* Gordian III.
Lurcy-Lévis (Allier), CHRE 7299; *t.p.q.* Elagabalus.
Lyon (Rhône), CHRE 6315; *t.p.q.* Augustus.
Lyon (Rhône), CHRE 6335; *t.p.q.* Antoninus Pius.
Lyon (Rhône), CHRE 6337; *t.p.q.* Septimius Severus.
Maillé (Vendée), CHRE 5976; *t.p.q.* Augustus.
Mont (Moselle), CHRE 6134; *t.p.q.* Antoninus Pius.
Morienval (Oise), CHRE 3344; *t.p.q.* Gordian I.
Murs-et-Gélignieux (Ain), CHRE 6216; *t.p.q.* Galba.
Oulches (Indre), CHRE 12482; *t.p.q.* Maximinus.
Poussanges (Creuse), CHRE 6091; *t.p.q.* Augustus.
Reims 3 (Marne): Doyen (2007: 220–4); *t.p.q.* Severus Alexander.
Reims 9 (Marne): Doyen (2007: 220–4); *t.p.q.* Severus Alexander.
Reims 29 (Marne): Doyen (2007 : 444–52); *t.p.q.* Elagabalus.
Rongères (Allier), CHRE 7312; *t.p.q.* Marcus Aurelius.
Ruetz (Haute-Marne), CHRE 6254; *t.p.q.* Domitian.
Saint-Barthélemy (Haute-Saône), CHRE 9717; *t.p.q.* Hadrian.
Saint-Didier-au-Mont-d'Or (Rhône), CHRE 6338; *t.p.q.* Septimius Severus.
Sainte-Consorce (Rhône), CHRE 6325; *t.p.q.* Maximinus.
Sceaux (Hauts-de-Seine), CHRE 3010; *t.p.q.* Septimius Severus.
Seiches-sur-le-Loir (Maine-et-Loire), CHRE 5913; *t.p.q.* Augustus.
Vaulx (Haute-Savoie), CHRE 3034; *t.p.q.* Septimius Severus.

ABBREVIATIONS

RIC III Mattingly, H. and Sydenham, E. (1930). *The Roman Imperial Coinage* Vol. III: *Antoninus Pius to Commodus*. London.

REFERENCES

Abdy, R. A. (2002). *Romano-British Coin Hoards*. Princes Risborough.

Bastien, P. and Metzger, C. (1977). *Le trésor de Beaurains (dit d'Arras)* (Numismatique romaine 10). Wetteren.

Becker, M. (2010). *Das Fürstengrab von Gommern* (Veröffentlichungen des Landesamtes für Denkmalpflege und Archäologie Sachsen-Anhalt—Landesmuseum für Vorgeschichte 63, 1–2). Halle.

Berger, F. (1988). *Die Fundmünzen der römischen Zeit in Deutschland* VII. *Niedersachsen und Bremen. 4–9. Hannover—Lüneburg—Braunschweig—Hildesheim—Stade—Bremen*. Berlin.

Berger, F. (1992). *Untersuchungen zu römerzeitlichen Münzfunden in Nordwestdeutschland* (Studien zu Fundmünzen der Antike 9). Berlin.

Berger, F. (2008). 'Die römischen Fundmünzen in Niedersachsen und Westfalen. Kontext und Funktionen', in Bursche, Ciołek, and Wolters (2008), 105–11.

Berger, F. and Stoess, C. (1988). *Die Fundmünzen der römischen Zeit in Deutschland* VII. *Niedersachsen und Bremen. 1–3. Osnabrück—Aurich—Oldenburg*. Berlin.

Bland, R. (2018). *Coin Hoards and Hoarding in Roman Britain AD 43–c.498* (The British Numismatic Society Special Publication 13). London.

Bolin, S. (1929). 'Die Funde römischer und byzantinischer Münzen im freien Germanien', *Berichte der Römisch-Germanischen Kommission* 19: 86–145.

Bursche, A. (1993). 'Pourquoi les *denarii* frappés après 194 étaient-ils absents dans le Barbaricum?', in T. Hackens and G. Moucharte (eds), *Proceedings of the XI*th *International Numismatic Congress (Brussels, September 8th–13th 1991)* Vol. 2. Louvain-la-Neuve, 297–303.

Bursche, A. (1994). 'Die Markomannenkriege und der Zufluß römischer Münzen in das Barbaricum', in H. Friesinger, J. Tejral, and A. Stuppner (eds), *Markomannenkriege. Ursachen und Wirkungen*. Brno, 471–85.

Bursche, A. (1996). 'Denarii subaerati from the Jakuszowice settlement in North Małopolska', *Wiadomości Numizmatyczne* 40: 31–42.

Bursche, A. (2002). 'Circulation of Roman coinage in Northern Europe in Late Antiquity', *Histoire & Mesure* 17–3.4: 1–18.

Bursche, A. (2011). *Illerup Ådal 14. Die Münzen* (Jutland Archaeological Society Publications 25). Højbjerg.

Bursche, A. (2018). 'Roman coins from Illerup Ådal (Denmark)', in G. Pardini, N. Parise, and F. Marani (eds), *Numismatica e Archeologia. Monete, stratigrafie e contesti. Dati a confronto*. Rome, 465–74.

Bursche, A., Ciołek, R., and Wolters, R. (2008). *Roman Coins outside the Empire: Ways and Phases, Contexts and Functions. Proceedings of the ESF/SCH Exploratory Workshop Radziwiłł Palace, Nieborów (Poland) 3–6 September 2005* (Collection Moneta 82). Wetteren.

Butcher, K. and Ponting, M. (1997). 'A study of the chemical composition of Roman silver coinage, A.D. 196–197', *American Journal of Numismatics* 9: 17–36.

Butcher, K. and Ponting, M. (2012). 'The beginning of the end? The denarius in the second century', *Numismatic Chronicle* 172: 63–83.

Butcher, K. and Ponting, M. (2022). 'Hoarding of denarii and the reforms of Nero and Septimius Severus', in J. Mairat, A. Wilson, and C. Howgego (eds), *Coin*

Hoards and Hoarding in the Roman World (Oxford Studies in the Roman Economy). Oxford, 273–81.

Callu, J.-P. (1969). *La politique monétaire des empereurs romains de 238 à 311* (Bibliothèque des Écoles Françaises d'Athènes et de Rome 214). Paris.

Chameroy, J. and Guihard, P.-M. (2016). '*Falsa fusio* à Trèves. Les moules monétaires du IIIe siècle de la Löwenbrauerei et la place du denier dans la circulation monétaire en Gaule du Nord', in J. Chameroy and P.-M. Guihard (eds), *Produktion und Recyceln von Münzen in der Spätantike* (RGZM Tagungen 29). Mainz, 235–63.

Chantraine, H. (1985). 'Die Bedeutung der römischen Fundmünzen in Deutschland für die frühe Wirtschaftsgeschichte', in K. Düwel, H. Jankuhn, H. Siems, and D. Timpe (eds), *Untersuchungen zu Handel und Verkehr der vor- und frühgeschichtlichen Zeit in Mittel- und Nordeuropa* 1. *Methodische Grundlagen und Darstellungen zum Handel in vorgeschichtlicher Zeit und in der Antike* (Abhandlungen der Akademie der Wissenschaften in Göttingen, Philologisch-Historische Klasse 3/143). Göttingen, 367–429.

Chifflet, J.-J. (1655). *Anastasis Childerici I, Francorum regis: sive Thesaurus sepulchralis Tornaci Neruiorum effossus, et commentario illustratus*. Antwerp.

Christol, M. (1977). 'Effort de guerre et ateliers monétaires de la périphérie au IIIe siècle après J.-C. : l'atelier de Cologne sous Valérien et Gallien', in *Armées et fiscalité dans le monde antique. Actes du colloque, Paris 14–16 octobre 1976* (Colloques internationaux du CNRS 936). Paris, 235–77.

Delmaire, R. (1997). *Corpus des trésors monétaires antiques de la France (Picardie)*, 8, 2 *(Aisne et Oise)*. Paris.

Doyen, J.-M. (2007). *Économie, monnaie et société à Reims sous l'Empire romain. Recherches sur la circulation monétaire en Gaule septentrionale intérieure* (Archéologie urbaine à Reims 7). Reims.

Dymowski, A. (2019a). 'The CERES group of barbarian imitations of Roman denarii', *Numismatic Chronicle* 179: 179–204.

Dymowski, A. (2019b). 'The problem of the presence of barbarian imitations of Roman imperial denarii in the lands of present-day Poland: An attempt at a balance', *Notae Numismaticae* 14: 149–82.

Dymowski, A. (2020a). 'Roman imperial hoards of denarii from the European Barbaricum', in C. Găzdac (ed.), *Group and Individual Tragedies in Roman Europe: The Evidence of Hoards, Epigraphic and Literary Sources* (Journal of Ancient History and Archaeology Monographic Series 1). Cluj-Napoca, 193–242.

Dymowski, A. (2020b). 'Some remarks on the problem of occurrence of denarii subaerati in Barbaricum', *Notae Numismaticae* 15: 167–77.

Dymowski, A. and Myzgin, K. (2014). 'Inflow and redistribution of Roman imperial denarii in the area of the Przeworsk, Wielbark and Chernyakhiv cultures and in the Baltic islands in the light of chronological structure of coin hoards', *Notae Numismaticae* 9: 39–58.

Fischer, S. and Lind, L. (2015). 'The coins in the grave of King Childeric', *Journal of Archaeology and Ancient History* 14: 3–36.

Gebhart, H., Kraft, K., Küthmann, H., Franke, P., and Christ, K. (1956). 'Bemerkungen zur kritischen Neuaufnahme der Fundmünzen der römischen Zeit in Deutschland', *Jahrbuch für Numismatik und Geldgeschichte* 7: 9–71.

Guihard, P.-M. and Léon, G. (2020). 'Le dépôt de Banville (Calvados, France): étude archéonumismatique de monnaies d'argent romaines (69–238 apr. J.-C.) contenues dans deux bourses en cuir', *Journal of Archaeological Numismatics* 10: 87–133.

Horsnæs, H. (2010). *Crossing Boundaries: An Analysis of Roman Coins in Danish Contexts.* Vol. 1: *Finds from Sealand, Funen and Jutland.* Copenhagen.

Jørgensen, B. and Vang Petersen, P. (2003). 'Nydam Bog–new finds and observations', in L. Jørgensen (ed.), *The Spoils of Victory: the North in the Shadow of the Roman Empire.* Copenhagen, 258–87.

Kolendo, J. (2008). 'Die Germania des Tacitus und die Funktionen römischer Münzen im *Barbaricum*', in Bursche, Ciołek, and Wolters (2008), 363–75.

Komnick, H. (1994). *Die Fundmünzen der römischen Zeit in Deutschland* VIII. *Schleswig-Holstein und Hamburg.* Berlin.

Korzus, B. (1971). *Die Fundmünzen der römischen Zeit in Deutschland* VI. *Nordrhein-Westfalen. 4. Münster.* Berlin.

Laser, R. (1980). *Die römischen und frühbyzantinischen Fundmünzen auf dem Gebiet der DDR* (Schriften zur Ur- und Frühgeschichte 28). Berlin.

Lind, L. (1993). 'The monetary reforms of Nero, Domitian and Septimius Severus and the finds of Roman denarii in Eastern and Northern Europe', in T. Hackens and G. Moucharte (eds), *Proceedings of the XIth International Numismatic Congress (Brussels, September 8th–13th 1991)* Vol. 2. Louvain-la-Neuve, 289–95.

Lind, L. (2018). *Roman Denarii: Imitations of Roman Denarii Found in Sweden.* Stockholm.

Lucchelli, T. M. (1998). *La moneta nei rapporti tra Roma e l'Europa barbarica: aspetti e problemi.* Florence.

Lund, A. A. (1987–8). 'Wie benutzten die Germanen zu Tacitus' Zeiten die römischen Münzen?', *Jahrbuch für Numismatik und Geldgeschichte* 37–8: 41–51.

Murphy, N. (2020). 'The Severan reforms of the late second century AD: A case of monetary déjà vu?', in K. Butcher (ed.), *Debasement: Manipulation of Coin Standards in Pre-Modern Monetary Systems.* Oxford, 145–50.

Reece, R. (1987). *Coinage in Roman Britain.* London.

Regling, K. (1912). 'Römischer Denarfund von Fröndenberg', *Zeitschrift für Numismatik* 29: 189–253.

Schmauder, M. (1999). 'Der Verwahrfund von Lengerich, Ldkr. Emsland: Spiegel innerrömischer Kämpfe?', *Die Kunde* 50: 91–118.

Stribrny, K. (2003). *Funktionsanalyse barbarisierter, barbarischer Denare mittels numismatischer und metallurgischer Methoden. Zur Erforschung der sarmatisch-germanischen Kontakte im 3. Jahrhundert n. Chr.* (Studien zu Fundmünzen der Antike 18). Mainz.

Voß, H.-U. and Wigg-Wolf, D. (2017). 'Romans and Roman finds in the Central European *Barbaricum*: A new view on Romano-Germanic relations?', in S. González Sánchez and A. Guglielmi (eds), *Romans and Barbarians beyond the Frontiers: Archaeology, Ideology and Identities in the North* (TRAC Themes in Roman Archaeology 1). Oxford, 105–24.

West, L. C. (1941). *Gold and Silver Coin Standards in the Roman Empire* (Numismatics Notes and Monographs 94). New York.

Wolters, R. and Stoess, C. (1985). 'Die römischen Münzschatzfunde im Westteil des Freien Germaniens - Ein Beitrag zur Beurteilung des Geldumlaufs im Gebiet zwischen Rhein, Donau und Oder während der ersten beiden Jahrhunderte n. Chr.', *Münstersche Beiträge zur antiken Handelsgeschichte* 4.2: 3–41.

Zedelius, V. (1974). *Spätkaiserzeitlich-völkerwanderungszeitliche Keramik und römische Münzen von Laatzen, Ldkr. Hannover* (Materialhefte zur Ur- und Frühgeschichte Niedersachsens 8). Hildesheim.

Jérémie Chameroy and Pierre-Marie Guihard, *Hoarding the* Denarius*: Thoughts on the Outflow of* Denarii *from Gaul to German Barbaricum* In: *Roman Coin Hoards Across Frontiers*. Edited by: Benjamin D. R. Hellings, Marguerite Spoerri Butcher, and Chris Howgego, Oxford University Press. © Oxford University Press 2026. DOI: 10.1093/9780198986478.003.0006

7

Inside–Outside: (How) Are Hoards from beyond the Empire Different? The Perspective from the Rhine Frontier

David Wigg-Wolf

INTRODUCTION

There is a very straightforward answer to the central question in the title of this chapter, for the Coin Hoards of the Roman Empire Project (CHRE) provides a large, readily accessible, and structured dataset that allows an immediate response: there are indeed very clear differences between hoards from within and without the Empire. But the secondary question of 'how?' is more complex, for it requires a closer look at the factors, filters, and mechanisms involved, not only in the actual formation of hoards but also behind how, when, and why Roman coins crossed the frontier in the first place. An important role is also played by the function of coins in societies outside the Empire and how this may differ from their use within the provinces. This chapter considers the question from the perspective of the Rhine frontier, looking in particular at hoarding from the Augustan coinage reform to the mid-third century AD. Thanks to the comprehensive inventories of coin finds provided by the various *Fundmünzen* projects (*FMRD*, *FMRL*, and *FMRN*) and the *Corpus der Römischen Funde im Europäischen Barbaricum* (*CRFB*), the differences can be analysed in considerable detail and put into the broader context of coin supply and use in the study area, in turn raising important theoretical questions.

But what are the differences? Looking first at finds of gold coins,[1] and limiting the analysis to hoards containing no more than 50 coins in order to minimize potential distortions caused by individual hoards, Figure 7.1 presents the data from France and from Belgium, the Netherlands, Luxembourg, and Germany, areas within the Empire for which a comprehensive corpus of gold coins is

[1] Single gold coins are counted as hoards.

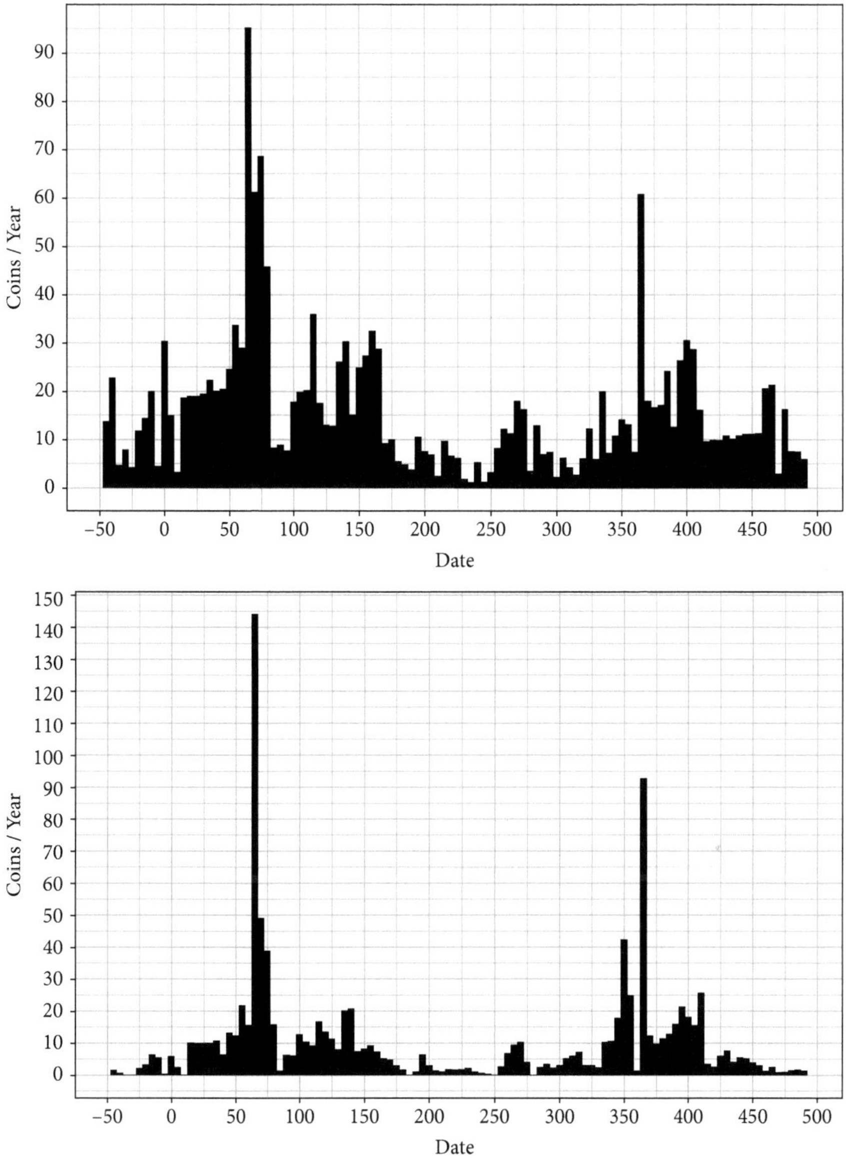

Fig. 7.1. The chronological profile of gold coins in hoards. Above: France. Below: Belgium, the Netherlands, Luxembourg, and Germany (within the Empire). Hoards containing over 50 coins are excluded in order to avoid any distortion very large hoards might cause. Source: CHRE database, https://chre.ashmus.ox.ac.uk/, accessed 3 November 2023. © David Wigg-Wolf.

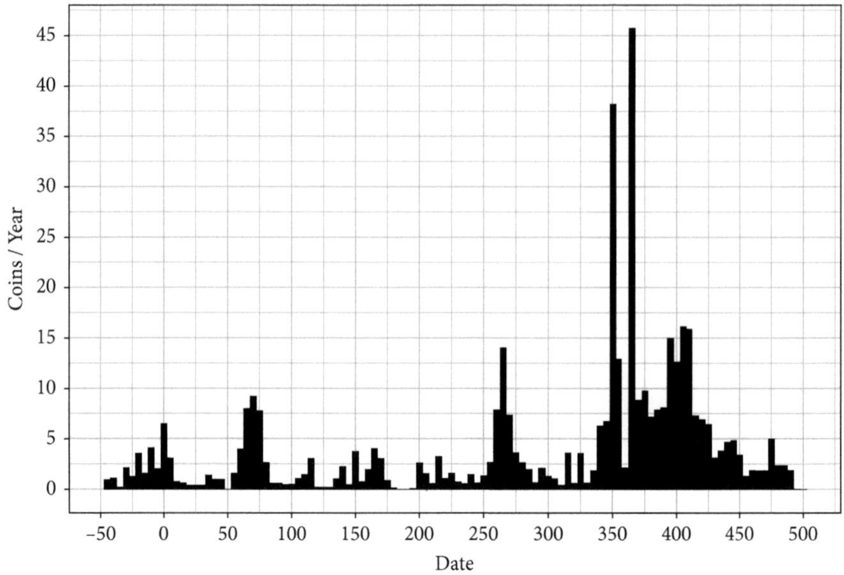

Fig. 7.2. The chronological profile of gold coins in hoards from northern German Barbaricum. Hoards containing over 50 coins are excluded in order to avoid any distortion very large hoards might cause. Source: AFE database, http://afe.dainst.org/, accessed 3 November 2023. © David Wigg-Wolf.

available thanks to the work of Callu and Loriot.[2] Overall, both bar charts present a strikingly similar picture, with two main peaks around the late Neronian/early Flavian period (the Year of the Four Emperors AD 68/69, the Batavian Revolt AD 69/70, and the Flavian reconstruction), and at the beginning of the reign of Valentinian I (ruled AD 364–75). There is also a distinct lack of gold coins of the second quarter of the third century, followed in both samples by an increase, leading to a small peak around AD 275.

Figure 7.2 presents the corresponding data for hoards from the area of modern Germany to the north-east of the Rivers Rhine and Main outside the Empire, as recorded in the AFE–RGK database of the Römisch-Germanische Kommission in Frankfurt am Main.[3] The same three peaks are visible, but differently weighted, with significantly more gold coinage of the late fourth century present in hoards outside the Empire. But there is also a further, fundamental difference: while gold of the second century AD is present in significant numbers within the Empire, beyond the frontier it is much rarer.

[2] Callu and Loriot (1990), with the supplement by Bland and Loriot (2010). The histograms were plotted using a script in RStudio that is available on Zenodo: https://doi.org/10.5281/zenodo.10182784. My thanks go to John Wigg, Angela Trentacoste, and Mario Schlapke for help with the code.

[3] http://afe.dainst.org/.

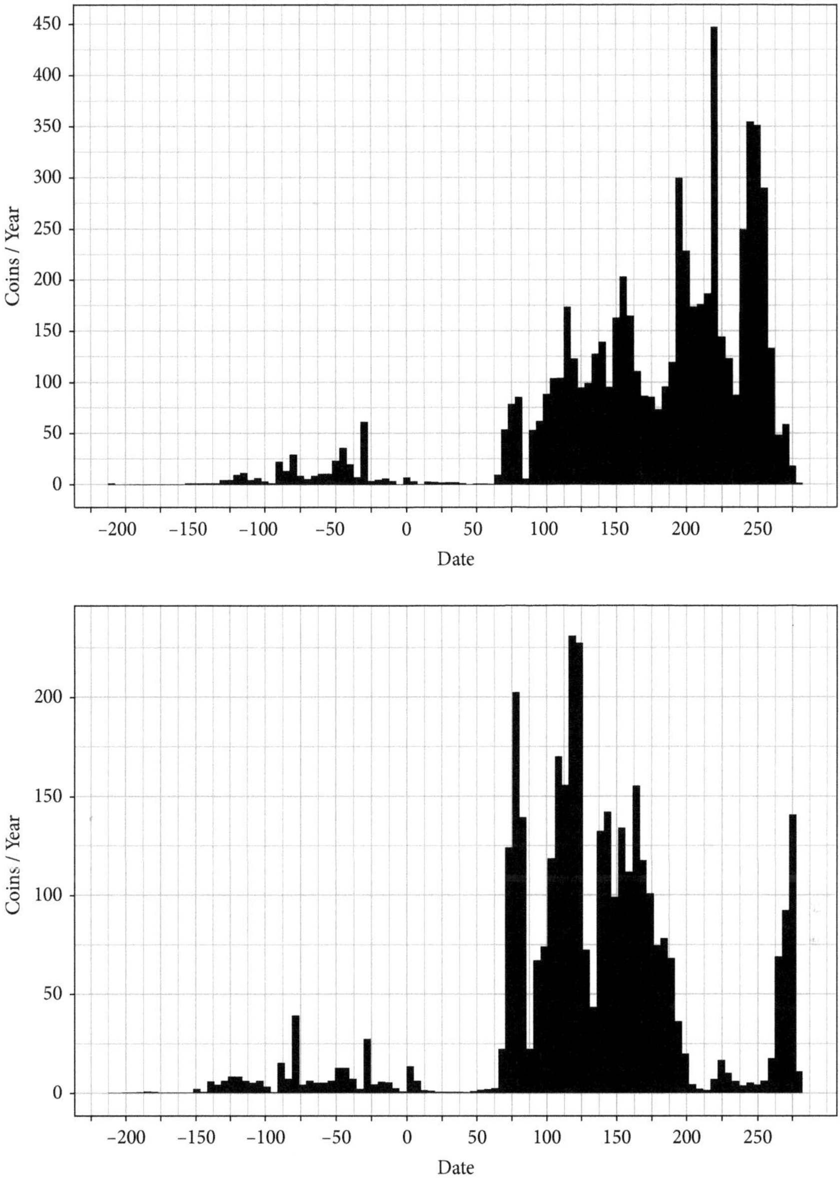

Fig. 7.3. The chronological profile of silver coins in hoards, from the introduction of the *denarius* to the fall of the Gallic Empire. Above: Belgium, the Netherlands, Luxembourg, and Germany. Below: northern German Barbaricum. Sources: above, CHRE database, https://chre.ashmus.ox.ac.uk/, accessed 3 November 2023; below, AFE database, http://afe.dainst.org/, accessed 1 November 2023. © David Wigg-Wolf.

The impression presented by the data is that while the pattern of gold coins and hoards outside the Empire to some extent reflects the pattern in the neighbouring provinces, there are nevertheless noticeable differences in hoarding behaviour between the two regions, as reflected in the occurrence of recorded finds of gold.

Turning to hoards of silver coins, differences become even more apparent (Fig. 7.3). Within the provinces the peak of hoarding comes in the third quarter of the third century AD, whereas in German Barbaricum the vast majority of silver hoards consist of issues of the late first and the second century AD. This predominance of silver outside the Empire in the second century AD contrasts strongly with the situation for gold of the same period, which, as shown above, was rarer outside the Empire. Hoards closing with coins of the third century, particularly of the third quarter, are considerably rarer outside the Empire than within the provinces.

Clearly there are differences in the patterns of hoards recorded today within and outside the Empire, for both gold and silver, and the frontier appears to play an important role in hoarding patterns.

THE LIFE OF COIN HOARDS

But what exactly do such comparisons tell us about actual hoarding in the two regions in antiquity, for there are many filters between the practices of coin use and hoarding in the ancient world and the pattern visible in the record today? In order to properly understand and interpret the figures, it is necessary first of all to consider the processes involved in the composition, burial, and non-recovery of the complexes of coins and other objects that we characterize as hoards, as well as the particular relevance of such processes when studying hoards outside the Empire. To what extent do they account for the differences observed above?

In a world without banks, the burial of coins and other valuables in the ground was absolutely normal. It did not require any particularly exceptional circumstances. This is excellently illustrated by the fable of the farmer's treasure that is attributed to Aesop:[4] on his deathbed a farmer tells his sons that a treasure lies buried among the vines; the sons then dig up the vineyard, but find no treasure; the treasure was in fact the fine harvest that they enjoyed as a result of their efforts working in the vineyard. But when hoards are studied, there has been a tendency, dating back to at least Adrien Blanchet's *Les trésors de monnaies romaines et les invasions germaniques en Gaule*, published in 1900 in the shadow of the Franco-Prussian War of 1870–1, to interpret hoards very much monocausally, as the

[4] Perry (1965: Appendix no. 42). Diogenes Laertius II 33 attributes the fable to Socrates: Rodríguez Adrados (1999: 381).

result of violent events such as Germanic invasions,[5] as if people were frantically burying hoards as the barbarians came over the hill rather than taking the money and running.[6] This attitude is still to be found in more recent works such as Heinz-Joachim Schulzki's 'Der Katastrophenhorizont der zweiten Hälfte des 3. Jahrhunderts im Raum der CCAA. Historisches Phänomen und numismatischer Befund' of 2002.[7] But what the fable of the farmer tells us is that in fact hoarding did not have to take place under exceptional circumstances but was actually a normal, even everyday, practice. For the sons it was entirely credible that their father had indeed buried his treasure in the fields. The question that is of interest is thus not so much why hoards were buried in the first place but why they were not recovered in antiquity and thus are visible in the archaeological record today. Many may indeed have not been recovered because of a catastrophe or emergency, but the role of such events has often been exaggerated in the past.

In his 1979 analysis of the taphonomy of coin finds, Hans-Christoph Noeske identified two distinct phases in the life of coin hoards: 1) Formation and concealment ('Bildung und Verbergung'); and 2) Rediscovery in the present day ('Wiederfinden in der Gegenwart').[8] Although the use of two words to describe the first phase hints at it involving two distinct processes, formation and concealment, an example from seventeenth-century England demonstrates that these processes can in fact be even more complex, with multiphase and multilocational processes, even in a situation where hoarding is triggered by a single, sudden threat. The example has been often quoted in connection with discussions of hoarding. Nevertheless, it is well worth quoting at length for the detail it provides of the events, processes, and motivations, some of them almost ludicrous, that could be involved in the formation of a hoard.[9]

In his diary for June and October 1667 Samuel Pepys recounts in detail how he acted, not when the barbarians came over the hill, but when the Dutch sailed into the Thames estuary and destroyed the English fleet anchored in the Medway.

> Thursday 13 June 1667... which put me into such a fear, that I presently resolved of my father's and wife's going into the country; and, at two hours' warning, they did go by the coach this day, with about 1300l. in gold in their night-bag... They gone, I continued in fright and fear what to do with the rest... I did, about noon, resolve to send Mr. Gibson away after my wife with another 1000 pieces... In the evening, I sent for my cousin Sarah [Gyles] and her husband, who come; and

[5] Blanchet (1900).

[6] An example of burying and not running in the face of a threat (but there was not actually anywhere to run to) is the tale of the staff of Raffles Hotel in Singapore burying the hotel silver—including the fine silver beef trolley—in the Palm Court of the hotel when the Japanese invaded in 1942. Reputedly, the Japanese invested a great deal of energy in trying to locate the silver, only to see it being dug up when the British retook Singapore: https://en.wikipedia.org/wiki/Raffles_Hotel (accessed 20 November 2023).

[7] Schulzki (2002).

[8] Noeske (2000: Beilage 30).

[9] The episode is discussed, for example, by Casey (1986: 53–5).

I did deliver them my chest of writings about Brampton, and my brother Tom's papers, and my journalls, which I value much; and did send my two silver flaggons to Kate Joyce's: that so, being scattered what I have, something might be saved. I have also made a girdle, by which, with some trouble, I do carry about me 300*l.* in gold about my body, that I may not be without something in case I should be surprised... I made my will also this day, and did give all I had equally between my father and wife, and left copies of it in each of Mr. Hater and W. Hewer's hands, who both witnessed the will, and so to supper and then to bed, and slept pretty well, but yet often waking.

Saturday 15 June 1667 Mr. Gibson... had one of his bags broke, through his breeches, and some pieces dropped out, not many, he thinks, but two, for he 'light, and took them up, and went back and could find no more. But I am not able to tell how many, which troubles me...

Wednesday 19 June 1667 I and my wife to talk, who did give me so bad an account of her and my father's method in burying of our gold, that made me mad: and she herself is not pleased with it, she believing that my sister knows of it. My father and she did it on Sunday, when they were gone to church, in open daylight, in the midst of the garden; where, for aught they knew, many eyes might see them: which put me into such trouble, that I was almost mad about it, and presently cast about, how to have it back again to secure it here, the times being a little better now... Such was my trouble at this, that I fell out with my wife, that though new come to towne, I did not sup with her, nor speak to her tonight, but to bed and sleep.

Wednesday 9 October 1667 My father and I, with a dark lantern; it being now night, into the garden with my wife... But, Lord! what a tosse I was for some time in, that they could not justly tell where it was... by poking with a spit, we found it, and then begun with a spudd to lift up the ground. But, good God! to see how sillily they did it, not half a foot under ground, and in the sight of the world from a hundred places... upon my lifting up the earth with the spudd, I did discern that I had scattered the pieces of gold round about the ground among the grass and loose earth; and... the bags were all rotten... I could not judge what was wanting, or what had been lost by Gibson in his coming down... and then, all people going to bed, W. Hewer and I did all alone, with several pails of water and basins, at last wash the dirt off of the pieces, and... by a note which I had of the value of the whole in my pocket, do find that there was short above a hundred pieces, which did make me mad; and considering that the neighbour's house was so near that we could not suppose we could speak one to another in the garden at the place where the gold lay — especially my father being deaf — but they must know what we had been doing on.[10]

[10] All passages from Pepys' diaries are taken from the Project Gutenberg version: https://www.gutenberg.org/files/4200/4200-h/4200-h.htm (accessed 20 November 2023).

circulation pool
→ selection
→ collection
→ storage
→ burial
→ non-recovery

Fig. 7.4. The processes in the life of a hoard. © David Wigg-Wolf.

Attention has often been drawn to the fact that the chaotic, bad-tempered scenes that Pepys so vividly describes resulted in the non-recovery of two complexes of coins at different sites some distance from the event that triggered his actions. However, the episode also demonstrates just how complex the processes that led to non-recovery in antiquity, and in some cases to discovery today, can be, even when some of the intricacies such as a deaf father and darkness are ignored (Fig. 7.4).

The processes start with what might be described as the circulation pool, that is, what is available to be taken to safety. First a process of selection takes place. Pepys chooses objects that are of particular value, importance, or use: not just coins but also silver vessels and his journals. This is followed by collection: in the case of the silver coins two separate collections are to be made, in the morning and at noon, the flagons and journals in the evening. The second collection of coins taken by Mr Gibson can potentially have contributed to both complexes lost, *en route* and in the garden of their house in the country, but the first collection was taken by his wife only to deposit in his garden. The next process is storage: here Pepys, as he states himself, spreads the risk, sending different things to different places, and in the case of the gold coins carries them around on his person. Such is his frame of mind that he even makes his will!

Only in the case of the coins do we know that actual burial took place, even if for the coins that Mr Gibson lost and failed to recover this was involuntary. As for non-recovery, deafness and darkness are not factors that are normally included in scholarly work on hoarding, but they are a warning as to how surprisingly mundane the processes behind hoarding and non-recovery can be. We will be returning to Pepys below.

Looking now at the case of an ancient hoard that was not recovered, we can see how using the processes just described can help us to understand its composition. In 1895 a hoard consisting of some 150,000–250,000 late Roman bronze *nummi* was discovered at Marienplatz in Cologne. Only a part of the hoard was ever analysed, so there is not absolute certainty as to its original composition, but it seems to have been composed mainly of issues of AD 320–30, with just a few coins of AD 330–4.[11] In his 1988 publication of a part of the hoard held by the National Museum of

[11] Nuber (1984: 1003 4a–n).

Wales, George C. Boon suggests that most of the hoard was assembled in or before AD 330, before being buried as a reaction to the reduction in weight of the bronze *nummus* in AD 335.[12] What Boon importantly does is to distinguish between the hoard being assembled and it being concealed. But while these two stages of the life of the hoard are identified, a third stage/event, or rather a non-event, is not addressed by Boon. In the case of Pepys' hoards, we know why the coins were never recovered (and to our knowledge have remained so), but we do not know why the coins from Cologne remained in the ground until 1895. On Boon's interpretation, the hoard was buried as a reaction to the reduction in the weight of the *nummus* because the coins were no longer useful or valid, in the hope that at a later date the coins could once again be used profitably. If this is the case, the cause of non-recovery could have been an event or circumstances (for example, the death of the owner) that took place a considerable time after assembly and burial.

A well-documented example of this kind of separation of the acts of burial and non-recovery is provided by a hoard from Neftenbach in Switzerland.[13] It has a terminal coin of Postumus dating to AD 265 and was found carefully buried in the outbuilding of a villa, but was sealed beneath a destruction level that contained a coin of Probus (!) that was probably struck in AD 277–80. Although the Neftenbach hoard was collected, and perhaps concealed, in or soon after AD 265, it would seem that its non-recovery could well have been the result of an event that took place some 11 years or more later. The events of assembly and assumed concealment on the one hand, and non-recovery on the other, were apparently separate.

This separation of the various phases in the life of hoards introduces an important aspect that plays a part in the processes of deposition and the present-day discovery of coin finds—that of intention (Fig. 7.5). In his analysis of the taphonomy of coin finds, Hans-Christoph Noeske follows the standard division of coin finds that are the basis of the various *Fundmünzen* series of *Einzelfunde*, *Schatzfunde*, *Grabfunde*, and *Votivfunde* (single finds, hoards, funerary, and votive deposits). Günther Thüry, in his 2016 volume *Die antike Münze als Fundgegenstand*, adds a further category of coin finds to the traditional division, the quasi-hoard of 'accidental nature', a concept previously developed by Bolin.[14] These are groups of coins that were unintentionally deposited at the same time, for example when a purse was lost, or when coins entered the ground as a result of a natural catastrophe, as was the case at Pompeii in AD 79. When the concealment/loss and (non-)recovery of coin finds, that is the stages that follow the final assembly and formation of the deposit, are viewed as a series of processes, then

[12] Boon (1988: 136–7). [13] von Kaenel *et al.* (1993).

[14] Bolin (1958: 81–4); Thüry (2016: 9). On the role of intention more generally in coin finds, see Wigg-Wolf (2019).

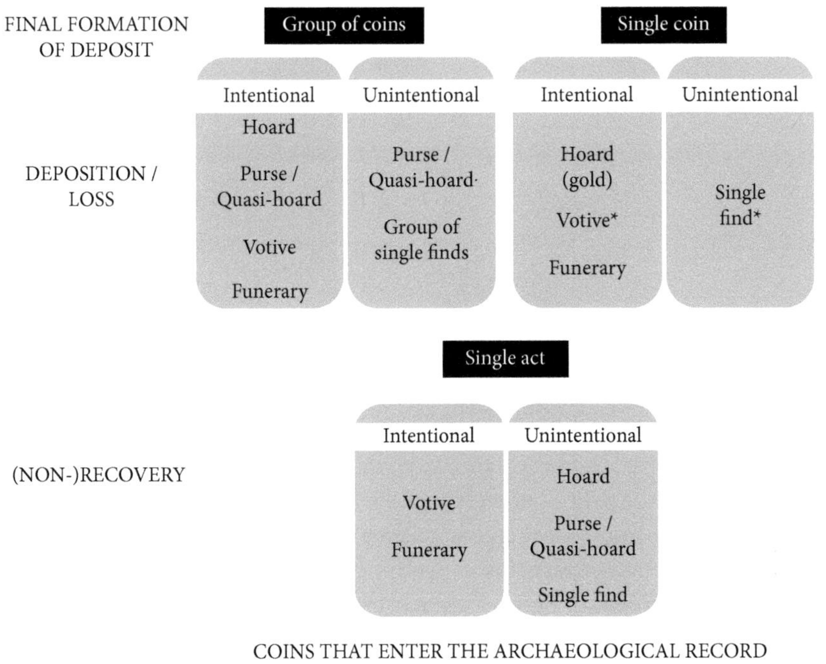

Fig. 7.5. The role of intention in the taphonomy of finds. © David Wigg-Wolf.

the different ways in which intention plays a role in the different find categories become apparent.

At a very simple level, in the phase of deposition single finds are generally assumed to consist of coins that were deposited unintentionally, i.e. were lost. On the other hand, hoards, funerary deposits, and votive deposits were deposited intentionally. But in the phase of (non-)recovery in antiquity, hoards were intended for recovery, while funerary and votive deposits were intended to stay in the ground. Thüry's quasi-hoards have their own pattern. Their 'accidental' nature distinguishes them from 'hoards proper', which were buried intentionally. Pompeii provides a good example of this. The various complexes of coins that have been recovered may include the contents of purses composed of the small change that had come together as the result of everyday coin use, without any specific choice or selection being involved; in other words, what people happened to have in their pockets.

But some of the complexes will consist of coins that were in effect 'hoards in waiting': that is, savings, stores of money that had been selected perhaps to finance a future purchase or event. Thus in Figure 7.5 quasi-hoards are represented as both intentional and unintentional at the level of deposition, but only as unintentional at the level of non-recovery.

circulation pool – empire
"transfer"
→ circulation pool – Barbaricum
→ selection
→ collection
→ storage
→ burial
→ non-recovery

Fig. 7.6. The processes in the life of a hoard outside the Empire. © David Wigg-Wolf.

Turning then to hoards outside the Empire and how the different processes of formation and factors such as intention affect them, the case of Pepys' hoards draws our attention to a component that plays a very different, but important, role when the frontier is crossed—that of distance. Pepys' hoards were deposited at two different sites at some distance from the event that triggered his actions, as well as from his house in London where the objects were available and the processes of selection and collection had taken place. With hoards from outside the Empire, there is another aspect to distance—that of distance from the provinces. The coins in the hoards in Barbaricum had crossed the frontier into a very different social, economic, and political context, and this introduces a number of new factors that affect the hoarding patterns that we see today (Fig. 7.6).

Potentially, some hoards from northern European Barbaricum will actually have been collected and assembled inside the Empire and then transferred across the frontier before being deposited there still in their original state. Such hoards were thus collected from the circulation pool within the provinces and should be no different from provincial hoards, unless a conscious and unusual selection of particular coins had been made. An apparent example of this is the *denarius* hoard of Wetzlar-Niedergirmes, discovered just some 20 km north-west of the Wetterau *limes*. The composition of the hoard is very similar to that of provincial hoards and significantly different to most contemporary *denarius* hoards from beyond the frontier in north-west Germany.[15] But most hoards from Barbaricum will have been drawn from the pool of coins and other objects available outside the Empire, so that the factor of distance, as reflected in the process of transfer across the frontier and how it could have affected the pool of coins available for hoarding, comes into play.

[15] Wigg and Wigg (1994). In a much-cited passage in his *Germania* (5, 3), Tacitus states that the *Germani* who lived close to the provinces ('*proximi*') were well acquainted with Roman gold and silver coins, actually preferring silver. But while the composition of the Niedergirmes hoard might at first sight seem to confirm his statement, Roman coins are in fact overall less common in the area around Niedergirmes than in regions more distant from the Empire, such as Mecklenburg-Vorpommern on the Baltic coast in north-east Germany.

GERMANIA UNTIL THE MID-THIRD CENTURY AD

Any analysis of hoards from beyond the frontier therefore requires first an analysis of the pool of coin that was available there and from which coins for hoards could be drawn. There were indeed quite obvious differences between the pools of coins inside and outside the Empire, as is clearly demonstrated by a comparison of the coin finds from northern German Barbaricum and the Niederrheinisches Lössgebiet, an area to the west of Cologne in the direct hinterland of the Lower Rhine frontier that is a fairly typical sample of coin series from the Rhine provinces (Fig. 7.7). The most important difference in the context of this chapter is the large numbers of *denarii* of the late first and second centuries AD in Barbaricum, coins which are significantly rarer in the Rhine provinces. The contrast is too stark for it to simply be the result of varying taphonomic circumstances applying either side of the frontier. As discussed below, very particular factors must have acted as filters to the movement of coins across the frontier and affected the pool of coin that was available for hoarding. There clearly was not simply a steady, consistent outflow of a representative cross-section from the pool in the provinces.

THE FUNCTION OF COINS OUTSIDE THE EMPIRE

This difference will certainly have had an effect on hoarding patterns. But another factor will also have been of great importance: the function of Roman coins among the *Germani*. Significant differences in the denominational structure of the coin finds from Mecklenburg-Vorpommern in north-east Germany and that of finds within the Empire indicate that coins must have been used in a very different way once they crossed the frontier. Figure 7.8 shows the proportions of individual denominations from Mecklenburg-Vorpommern, the town of *Colonia Ulpia Traiana* (Xanten), and the town's hinterland for coins of the period from the Augustan coinage reform to the mid-third century, when the Augustan system finally collapsed.

Within the Empire the smallest denomination of the coinage, the *asses*, are more common in the town than in the surrounding countryside.[16] In rural contexts, on the other hand, the proportion of larger bronze denominations and of precious metal is higher. A similar pattern was noted by Joris Aarts in his doctoral thesis on the coin finds in the Maas-Dremel-Scheldt region to the south of the Lower Rhine.[17] This is not necessarily due to the lower value coin not being available to the inhabitants of the countryside, but, rather, that they will have used, and thus lost, their *asses* in the market context of the town. Coins generally end

[16] *Semisses* and *quadrantes* are excluded, as they are extremely rare in the study area.
[17] Aarts (2000).

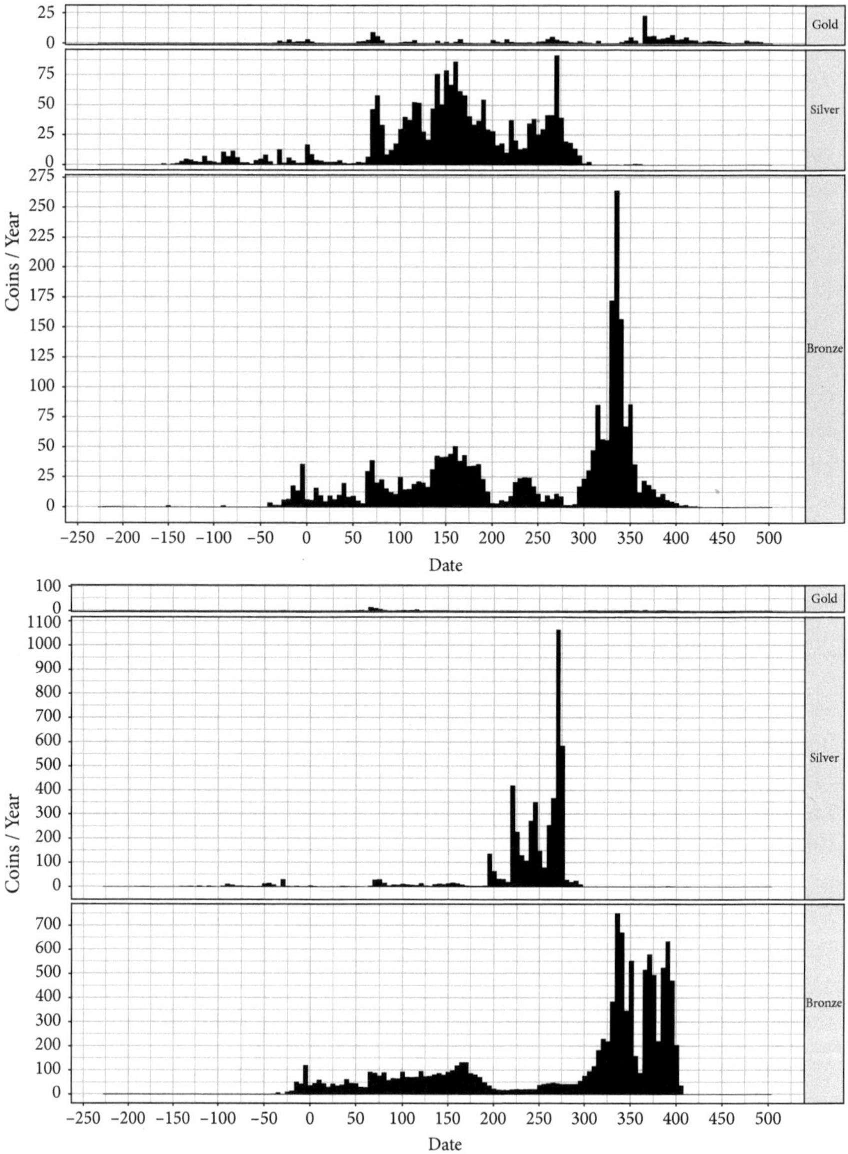

Fig. 7.7. Comparison of the presence of the main metals in single finds. Above: northern German Barbaricum. Source: AFE database, http://afe.dainst.org/, accessed 3 November 2023. Below: Niederrheinisches Lössgebiet (Otte [2024]). © David Wigg-Wolf.

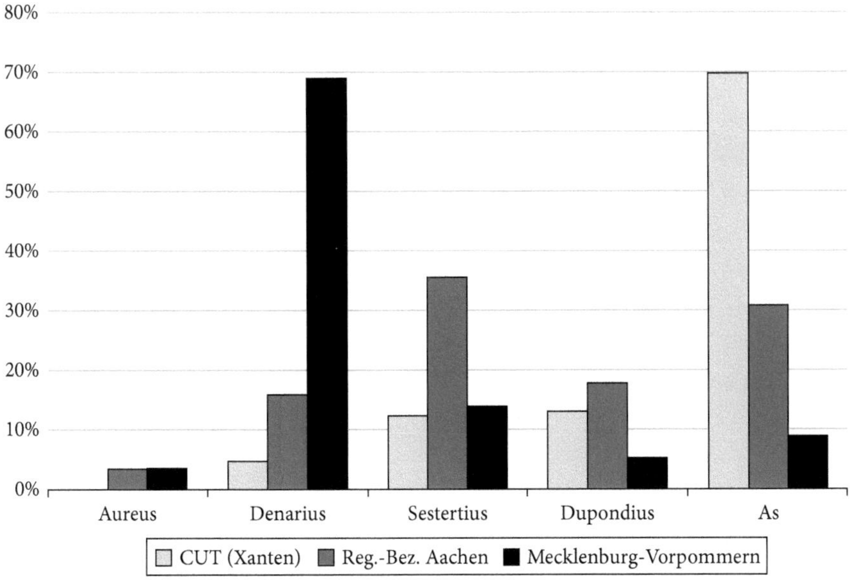

Fig. 7.8. The spectrum of coins at Colonia Ulpia Traiana (CUT [Xanten]) (Komnick [2015]); the rural hinterland of the German Lower Rhine (Reg.-Bez. Aachen) (Komnick, Heinrichs, and Päffgen [2008] and Komnick [2010]), and Mecklenburg-Vorpommern in north Germany. Source: AFE database, http://afe.daint.org, accessed 25 July 2022. © David Wigg-Wolf.

up in the ground because they are either intentionally deposited or unintentionally lost, and they are more likely to be lost when they are actively used, for example in commercial exchanges at markets, than when they are simply passively stored at home in a villa. In the countryside outside of market centres there were fewer contexts in which coins would actually be used and change hands, and therefore be lost.

In Barbaricum, the proportion of bronze coinage is significantly lower even than in the rural hinterland of the *colonia*, indicating that very different conditions must have existed for the use of coins there in comparison with the provinces. Silver *denarii* were the commonest coins. The contexts in which the *denarii* are found beyond the frontier are also important: they were preferentially hoarded. Whereas across northern German Barbaricum *denarii* already account for some 55% of the coins of 27 BC–AD 250 in the single finds, a massive 93% of the coins in the corresponding hoards are *denarii* (Fig. 7.9).

Coinage was clearly being used in a very different way outside the Empire. There were not the central settlements such as Xanten that could have supported market centres, and in the absence of a coin-using market there was clearly little need for small denominations. There was no market environment in which low-value bronze could have played a role. Silver *denarii* were suited to very different

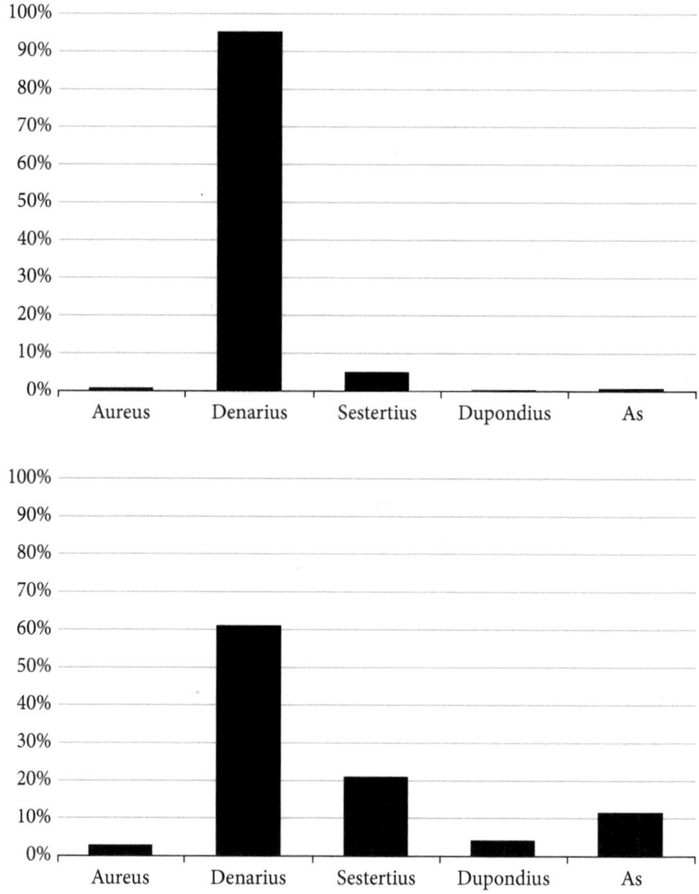

Fig. 7.9. The proportions of denominations of coins from the introduction of the *denarius* to the reintroduction of the *antoninianus* in AD 238. Above: hoards; below: single finds in northern German Barbaricum. Source: AFE database, http://afe.dainst.org/, accessed 3 November 2023. © David Wigg-Wolf.

conditions.[18] Their function is well illustrated by the coins from deposit A at Illerup-Ådal where, in the early third century AD, the weapons and equipment of a defeated Germanic warband were deposited by the victors in what was then a lake. The finds include 199 Roman coins, almost all of them silver *denarii*; only

[18] Tacitus (*Germania* 5, 3) states that the *Germani* preferred silver because it was more convenient for purchasing everyday, cheap merchandise. But while he is right in identifying a preference for silver, the reason he gives is too simplistic. Silver was not suitable for the kind of low-value exchange to be found in the market centres within the provinces. Tacitus follows the Aristotelian tradition that saw the introduction of coinage very much in the context of exchange, ignoring other uses typical of primitive or social moneys: Aristotle, *Politeia* I 1257 a–b; Seaford (2004: 5); Graeber (2010: 24).

one copper-alloy coin, a *sestertius*, was found.[19] Many of the coins were found in small groups and had apparently originally been contained in pouches or purses attached to warriors' belts. But only a relatively small number of warriors appear to have had access to and carried coins with them. Although it is estimated that the equipment of as many as 1,000 warriors was deposited, the coins were found associated with only 25 belts: one had 71 coins, others up to 20.[20] These complexes of high-value *denarii* were quite clearly not small change intended for everyday use in the marketplace, but were stores of wealth that were not available to everyone but reserved for a small number of persons. Any transactions they were used for will have been of higher value. Similarly, in her study of Roman coins from Denmark, Helle Horsnæs concludes: 'Roman coins were luxury items, found in small numbers in particular contexts.'[21]

In his analysis of the coins from Illerup-Ådal, Aleksander Bursche draws attention to the work of Karl Polanyi and the important distinction he made between general-purpose and special-purpose money.[22] The former is variously defined as serving up to five basic functions: means of exchange, method of payment, standard of value, store of wealth, and unit of account.[23] Special-purpose money serves just one or two of these, and then only within specific spheres of exchange. What is more, general purpose money allows conversion between the spheres. Within the Roman Empire it is clear that coins as money had taken on many, but not necessarily all, of the functions of general-purpose money, and that some conversion between spheres was certainly possible. But the situation within Germanic society was very different, and coins were used for a much more limited range of uses. They were very much special-purpose money, and moneys like this are sometimes referred to as 'social currencies'. They were rarely used to acquire material goods but, rather, in a very different context: for diplomatic exchange between elites, as tribute, for the payment of penalties and bride wealth/dowries, and, as the extensive hoarding of *denarii* demonstrates, for the storage of wealth.[24]

IMPERIAL POLICY AND THE OUTFLOW OF *DENARII*

As was noted above, Roman *denarii* were preferentially hoarded in Germanic society, and one of their main functions was as a storage of wealth. As a result,

[19] Bursche (2011).

[20] Deposit A contained the remains of more than 340 shields, 137 combs, and 129 strike-a-lights, as well as 150 sword blades of Roman manufacture (Ilkjaer 2002: 77–44, 100), a marked contrast to the 24 complexes of coins in purses and four individual coins. The largest single complex consisted of 71 coins (Fundkonzentration 6/60); Bursche (2011: 57).

[21] Horsnæs (2010: 75). [22] Polanyi (1957: 264–6).

[23] As Maurer (2006: 20) notes, not all five functions are always mentioned. Polanyi (1957: 264) mentions only 'payment, standard, and exchange'.

[24] See, for example, Graeber (2010: 165 and *passim*).

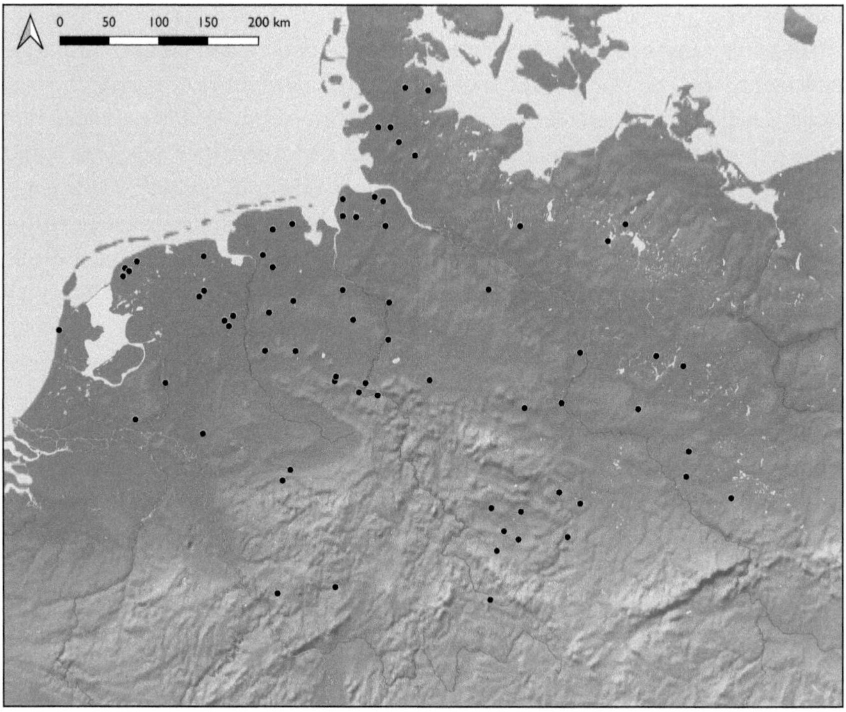

Fig. 7.10. Hoards of *denarii* with a terminal date of AD 14–238 in northern Germany and the Netherlands. Sources: Dymowski [2020] and AFE database, http://afe.dainst.org/, accessed 3 November 2023. Map: A. Wilson/D. Wigg-Wolf.

they were hoarded in large numbers across northern Barbaricum. In northern Germany and the Netherlands some 75 *denarius* hoards with terminal coins dating between the end of the Augustan campaigns in Germany and the (re)introduction of the *antoninianus* have been recorded and are particularly common in the north-west (Fig. 7.10). A notable feature of these hoards is that very few of them contain coins struck later than AD 194. A similar break-off is also visible in the single finds, although it is not so prominent (Fig. 7.11). This drop in the number of *denarii* coincides with the reduction in the silver content of the *denarius*, which Septimius Severus in AD 194 reduced from 68% to just 46%, that is by almost a third.[25] Referring to a passage in Tacitus' *Germania* that is often interpreted as indicating that the Germans preferred better-quality silver, it has been proposed that the inhabitants of northern Barbaricum rejected the reduced Severan silver because it was significantly debased.[26] Contacts, whether in the form of trade or

[25] Butcher and Ponting (2012: 77).

[26] Tacitus, *Germania* 5, 3: 'pecuniam probant veterem et diu notam, serratos bigatosque'. Cf. discussion of this passage by Woytek, chapter 14, this volume.

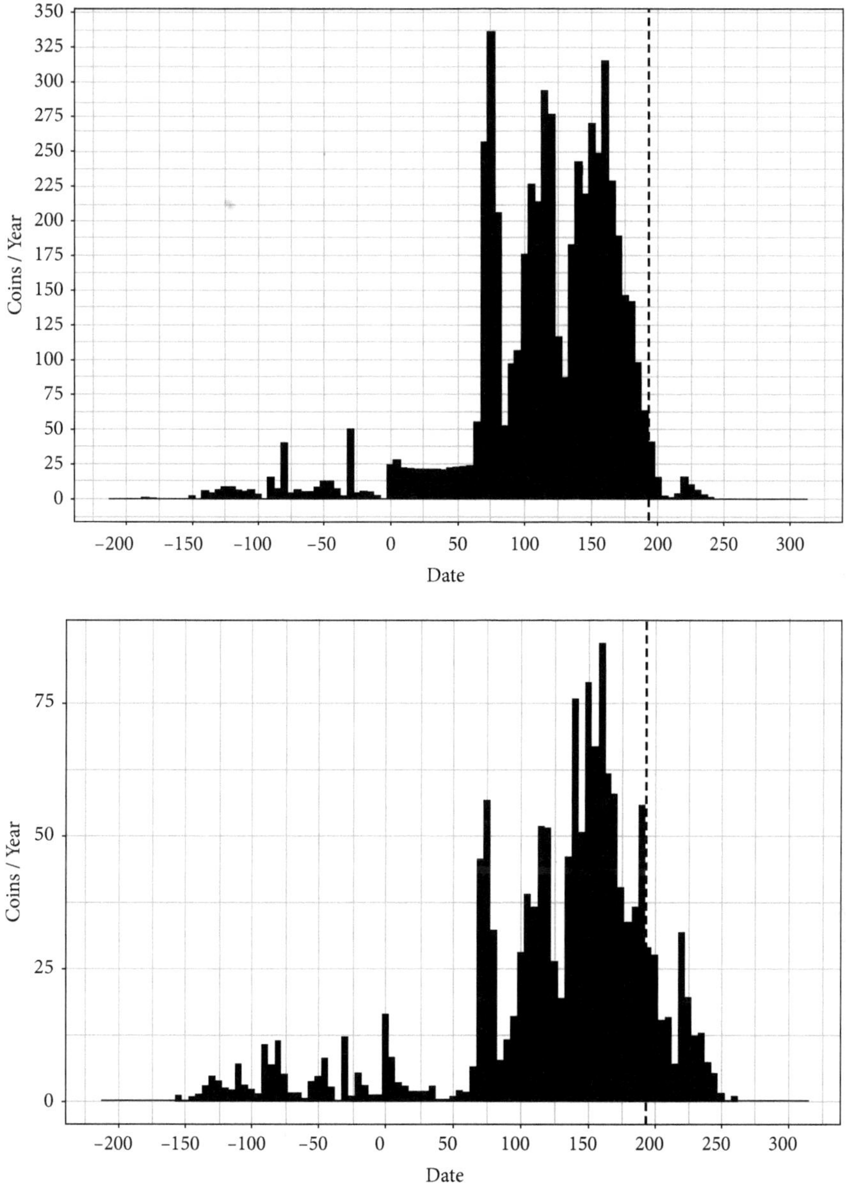

Fig. 7.11. The chronological profile of the *denarii*. Above: hoards; below: single finds in northern German Barbaricum. The vertical dashed line represents the break in AD 193/4. Source: AFE database, http://afe.dainst.org/, accessed 3 November 2023. © David Wigg-Wolf.

of a diplomatic or political nature, are presumed to have continued using the better-quality, pre-Severan *denarii* that were supposedly preferred by the Germans. However, Tacitus was writing a century before the reform of Septimius Severus, and presumably relied in part on even older sources. As discussed below, by the early third century monetary contacts between the *Germani* and the Empire had changed greatly from the situation when Tacitus was writing. Furthermore, by the late second century AD the *serrati* and *bigati* that Tacitus refers to had long since disappeared from circulation; indeed, they already had disappeared by the time Tacitus was writing.[27]

This interpretation of the lack of *denarii* struck after AD 194 is very much related to the view that *denarii* left the Empire in the course of trade connections. The suggestion is that there was a conscious choice on the part of the inhabitants of the regions north of the Empire to reject the poorer coins in commercial exchange.[28] However, the role of trade in the outflow of coin from the Empire has more recently been called into question, and diplomatic contacts have come to be seen as the main phenomenon behind the movement of coins beyond the northern frontier, in particular in the form of subsidies to friendly groupings to secure the northern frontier.[29] The role of such contacts in the transfer of Roman objects is confirmed by Tacitus' statement that the *Germani* had many silver vessels which their ambassadors and chiefs had received as gifts.[30] These contacts were clearly of an episodic nature and did not lead to a steady, consistent outflow that led to the coinage present in Barbaricum directly reflecting the circulation pool within the Rhineland provinces. The large numbers of late first- and second-century *denarii* found across northern Barbaricum have been interpreted as subsidies to friendly groupings to secure their allegiance during the Marcomannic Wars and their aftermath.[31]

The sudden drop in the number of *denarii* from AD 194 also appears in a new light when the figures for northern Germany are compared with those for the provincial capital and legionary fortress at Mainz on the Rhine (Fig. 7.12). In Mainz the numbers of *denarii* increase significantly around AD 194, when

[27] The withdrawal and disappearance of Republican *denarii* from circulation within the Empire is discussed at length by Butcher and Ponting (2014: *passim*). On Republican coins in the Eastern European Barbaricum see Dymowski (2016).

[28] Bolin (1929: 136); Guey (1955: 208, n. 1). See also Bursche (1994: 472; 1996: 123–5) for further literature.

[29] On the role of coinage in trade: Bolin (1929: 128–40); Guey (1955: 205–6). For further literature: Bursche (1994: 472; 1996: 102 n. 24); Dymowski and Myzgin (2014: 42). On trade as the main channel of contact between Rome and the peoples beyond the frontiers more generally: Eggers (1951); Wheeler (1954). That other mechanisms, such as diplomatic contacts as well as tribute, ransom, and army pay, were the main motor: Bursche (1994: 474–5; 1996: 105); Kehne (2008); Dymowski and Myzgin (2014).

[30] Tacitus, *Germania* 5, 3: 'est videre apud illos argentea vasa, legatis et principibus eorum muneri data'.

[31] Erdrich (2001: 127–8); Voß and Wigg-Wolf (2017: 117).

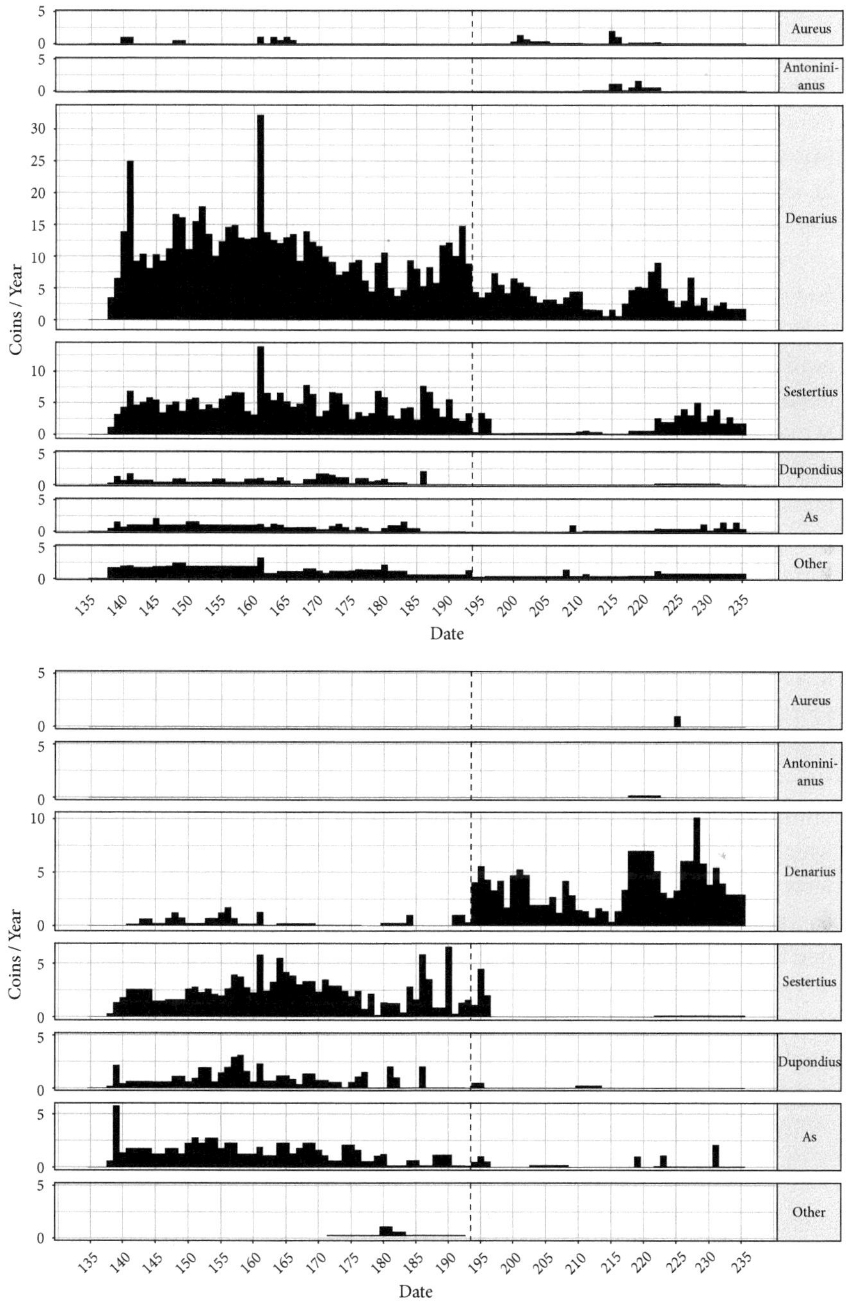

Fig. 7.12. Comparison of the presence of the main denominations in the coin series. Above: northern German Barbaricum (single finds); below: Mainz, civilian settlement. The vertical dashed line represents the break in AD 193/4. Sources: above: AFE database, http://afe.dainst.org/, accessed 3 November 2023, below: Gorecki [2006: 1258]. © David Wigg-Wolf.

Septimius Severus appears to have stopped using bronze as a component of military pay in the north-west and to have now relied on silver alone. This pattern is visible across all of the north-west provinces and is to be seen in the context of a number of fiscal policies pursued by Severus that also included raising military pay, which, given that in the north-west this was now probably supplied entirely in silver, will have greatly increased the demand for *denarii*.[32] This demand appears to have necessitated not only a significant debasement of the *denarius* but also the suspension of, or at least a significant reduction in, diplomatic payments and subsidies to the *Germani*.[33] This will have resulted in the pool of coins available for hoarding outside the Empire being very different from that which was available in the provinces, and this will have been a contributing factor in the differences in the hoarding patterns visible today within and outside the Empire (Figs 7.1–7.3).

But the break in the outflow of *denarii* across the northern frontier by no means led to a cessation in the use of silver coins in Barbaricum. On the contrary, the huge outflow in the second half of the second century would appear to have stimulated the use of silver as a special purpose money in certain spheres of Germanic society, and the reduction in the supply of silver resulted in the production of imitations of *denarii*. Their interpretation poses a number of problems, however. In the absence of datable production contexts, they are difficult to date more exactly than the *terminus post quem* of the type that they imitate—if there is indeed an identifiable prototype, which for many there is not. *Denarius* imitations have been found in huge numbers on the territory of present-day Ukraine, but unfortunately mostly under uncontrolled, even illicit, conditions by detectorists, which limits the amount of information we can deduce from them.[34] Find contexts are rarely known, but the phenomenon can be placed in the context of the Sântana de Mureş–Chernyakhiv culture that developed in the region in the second half of the third century AD and is generally associated with the Goths.

The earliest datable find context for a *denarius* imitation is provided by the bog deposit of Illerup-Ådal in Denmark (discussed above). The *terminus post quem* for the deposit is provided by a wooden shield with a dendrochronological date of AD 205, and among the 198 *denarii* were four *denarius* imitations from one purse, all struck with the same pair of dies.[35] In their work on *denarius* imitations in

[32] On the increase in military pay: Speidel (1992: 365).

[33] Voß and Wigg-Wolf (2017: 118). Berger (2008: 105) similarly proposes a deliberate suspension of payments to the *Germani* by Severus, though without relating this to the overall financial situation within the Empire.

[34] Oleg Anokhin assembled data on a huge number of *denarius* imitations from Ukraine, mainly collected from internet forums, and published them on the website http://barbarous-imitations.narod.ru/ (accessed 20 November 2023), which is sponsored by the University of Warsaw. Dymowski (2019) provides a comprehensive survey of *denarius* imitations from Poland together with a detailed bibliography of work on northern European finds.

[35] They were found in bag SAPP together with 15 official *denarii*: Bursche (2011: 19).

Ukraine, Myzgin, Dymowski, and Chemuranov place 'the production and use of Roman Imperial *denarii* imitations in the region (the area of the Chernyakhiv Culture)... at the earliest to the first half of the third century'.[36] The latest secure date for a *denarius* imitation is provided by an example with an obverse of Antoninus Pius from Ukraine that is reverse die-linked to a gold imitation with a late third-/early fourth-century Tetrarchic obverse portrait.[37]

Although this is perhaps rather scant evidence for the chronology of the imitations, it suggests that the outflow of *denarii* into northern Barbaricum in the second half of the second century led to a demand for silver coin that, following the virtual suspension of payments and subsidies by Septimius Severus about AD 194, was met by the production of imitations.[38]

The important role of silver in Germanic society, highlighted by the production of imitations, has important repercussions when it comes to analyzing and understanding *denarius* hoards outside the Empire.[39] Such was the demand for them that the *denarii* continued to be used in Germanic contexts long after they had disappeared from circulation within the Empire in the mid-third century. This is confirmed by the significant number of hoards of the fourth century and later from across the entire northern Barbaricum that contain often large quantities of *denarii*.[40] Indeed, sometimes the only coins they contain are *denarii*, accompanied by other late Roman objects. The Lengerich hoard from Lower Saxony in north-west Germany consists of three apparently related deposits: one consisting of 1,152 *denarii* with a terminal date of 194 (plus a possibly intrusive *denarius* of Severus Alexander); one with 10 *solidi* with a *terminus post quem* of AD 327–40; and one with 76 fourth-century silver coins including a *miliarensis* of Magnentius struck in AD 350–1. The gold coins had been deposited together with a number of late antique gold objects, including a crossbow fibula.[41] The Laatzen hoard from near Hanover was found in 1967 in a grey ceramic container of local fabric that is dated to the fourth/fifth century. The hoard consisted of four mid-fourth-century silver coins (one of them an imitation) with a terminal date of AD 360–3, alongside 75 *denarii*, the latest of which was struck in AD 192.[42] But one

[36] Myzgin, Dymowski, and Chemuranov (2020: 365).

[37] Anokhin (2018: 38, fig. 4).

[38] For an alternative interpretation of the lack of *denarii* of Septimius Severus in hoards outside the Empire, see the contribution by Chameroy and Guihard, chapter 6 in this volume.

[39] The focus of this chapter is on more general aspects of the differences in hoards from within and without the Empire, and in particular in the Rhineland and Germany. However, the situation within the Barbaricum itself was complex. For an excellent, detailed discussion of *denarius* hoards in northern Europe, see Dymowski and Myzgin (2014).

[40] Guey (1955: 206–9); Dymowski and Myzgin (2014: 45); Bursche and Myzgin (2025). Such hoards were the topic of a paper, '"Obsolete" hoards of *denarii*', delivered by Aleksander Bursche and the author at the conference Coin Hoarding in the Roman Empire in Oxford, in September 2016. My thanks are due to Aleksander for leading the work.

[41] Berger and Stoess (1988a: nos 1033–5); Schmauder (1999). The numbers are not exact: most of the coins are lost, so that exact details are vague, but the hoard was well recorded by Hahn (1854).

[42] Zedelius (1974); Berger and Stoess (1988b: no. 4033).

of the most remarkable examples of the longevity of *denarii* in Germanic contexts is provided by the tomb of the Frankish king Childerich, who was buried in Tournai in AD 480/1.[43] The tomb was discovered and opened in 1653, but unfortunately most of the rich objects it contained were stolen and are now lost. However, the 1655 publication of the hoard by Jean-Jacques Chifflet, which includes drawings of many of the objects, provides some details of the coins it contained. He mentions 100 gold and 200 silver coins, and describes more precisely 89 *solidi*, 41 *denarii*, and one *siliqua*, although only three of the *denarii* are illustrated.[44] In spite of the limited detail about the coins, it is clear that *denarii* were still available in Germanic contexts nearly two and a half centuries after the coins had disappeared from circulation within the Empire.

An important feature of these 'late' hoards—and there are many more examples from across northern Barbaricum—is that they almost never contain *denarii* struck later than AD 194.[45] This has important implications for the dating of *denarius* hoards from outside the Empire that close with coins of the late second century AD. They could have been deposited appreciably later than their terminal coins, in some cases even three (or more?) centuries later.

Returning to Figure 7.6 and the processes in the life of *denarius* hoards outside the Empire, for northern Barbaricum we have to add two extra factors: the virtual suspension of the transfer of coins across the frontier, and what we might perhaps term the 'fossilization' or 'stagnation' of the circulation pool that resulted from the virtual suspension of this transfer (Fig. 7.13). The two factors mean that the date of the collection and deposition of a hoard cannot normally be determined from the contents of the hoard itself, for example from the date of the youngest coin or the chronological profile of the hoard—for the circulation pool from which the coins were drawn may have been depleted but will not have changed in overall composition over time.[46] The hoard can only be dated if there is good contextual information that throws light on the date of its deposition, as is the case for the burial of Childerich, or if other datable objects are included. Archaeological context is always important, but for *denarius* hoards found outside the Empire particularly so. Unfortunately, this is often not the case, above all for the numerous hoards from the territory of the Chernyakhiv culture, coming as they so often do from undocumented, even illicit, activity.

[43] Chifflet (1655). On the coins, Martin (2004); Quast and Ament (2015: 178–9); the view of Fischer and Lind (2015) that the *denarii* remained in circulation within the Empire into late antiquity is contentious, to say the least, and was heavily criticized by one of the peer reviewers—https://journals.uu.se/jaah/article/view/145/128 (accessed 20 November 2023).

[44] Chifflet (1655: 271).

[45] Bursche and Myzgin (2025).

[46] *Contra* Dymowski and Myzgin (2014: 50–1), who suggest that the older coins will have preferentially disappeared 'as a result of the gradual wear and tear of coins'. However, as they note (2014: 45), very little coin was added to the pool in Barbaricum after the early years of Septimius Severus, and the depletion of the pool through loss and deposition should have affected all coins equally, whether old or young.

circulation pool – empire
"transfer"
(suspension)
→ circulation pool – Barbaricum
(*stagnation/fossilisation*)
→ selection
→ collection
→ storage
→ burial
→ non-recovery

Fig. 7.13. The processes in the life of the circulation pool and hoards outside the Empire. © David Wigg-Wolf.

CONCLUSIONS

Returning to the questions posed at the beginning of this chapter, now that the differences are clear, a third question should be added: 'Why?' The answer covers two main aspects. The first concerns the transfer of coins across the frontier. Clearly coins were not simply leaving the Empire as a steady, consistent outflow across all denominations and metals that effectively would have seen northern European Barbaricum become an extension of the monetary circuit of the frontier provinces. Rather, there were a number of factors and filters that affected the outflow: for example, filters such as the imperial political and strategic policies of the late second century that resulted in the huge numbers of *denarii* of the late first and early second centuries transferred to Barbaricum, and the fiscal policies of Septimius Severus that led to the cessation of payments. Such factors will have resulted in the pool of coins available for hoarding outside the Empire being very different to that which was available in the provinces, and this will have been a contributing factor to the differences in the hoarding patterns visible today.

The other aspect concerns the function of coins. Once they had left the Empire, the *denarii* entered a very different social and economic context in which they functioned differently from how they had in the provinces. In Barbaricum they will no longer have played any significant role in a market-oriented economy (except in the vicinity of the *limes* in the course of contacts with market centres along the frontier), but have functioned as special-purpose or social money. They will not have been used for everyday market exchange and transactions but for diplomatic exchange between elites, as tribute, for the payment of penalties, and bride wealth/dowries. The storage of wealth was also a function of particular importance, leading to the deposition of hoards in large numbers across northern Barbaricum. It should also be noted that it is only stores of wealth that were actually deposited in the ground but not recovered that are found today. Many other stores of wealth will have gone through the phases of selection and collection, as described in Figure 7.4, but not been deposited. Numerous complexes of coins such as those found in the burial of Childerich must have circulated in this way over the centuries, effectively circulating as hoards in waiting to which we have no access.

ABBREVIATIONS

CRFB *Corpus der römischen Funde im Europäischen Barbaricum.* Bonn, 1994–.
FMRD *Fundmünzen der Römischen Zeit in Deutschland.* Berlin/Mainz/Bonn, 1960–2015.
FMRL *Fundmünzen der Römischen Zeit im Großherzogtum Luxemburg.* Vols I–V. Berlin, 1972–96.
FMRN *Fundmünzen der Römischen Zeit in den Niederlanden.* Vols I–III. Berlin/Mainz, 1992–2002.

REFERENCES

Aarts, J. (2000). *Coins or Money? Exploring the Monetization and Functions of Roman Coinage in Belgic Gaul and Lower Germany 50 BC–AD 450.* PhD thesis, Vrije Universiteit Amsterdam.

Anokhin, O. (2018). 'Do pytannya chasu karbuvanya ta obigu varvars'kykh nasliduvan'. To the question of the coinage and circulation of the barbarous imitations', in V. Kotsur (ed.), *Aktual'ni problemy numizmatyky u systemi special'nykh galuzej istorychnoyi nauky: trezy dopovidej V Midzhnarodnoyi naukovo-praktychnoyi konferenciyi, 21–22 chervnya 2018 r.* Medzhibizh/Pereyaslav Khmel'nyc'kyi/Kropivnic'kyi/Kyiv, 35–8.

Berger, F. (2008). 'Die römischen Fundmünzen in Niedersachsen und Westfalen', in A. Bursche and R. Ciolek (eds), *Roman Coins outside the Empire. Ways and Phases, Contexts and Functions: Proceedings of the ESF/SCH Exploratory Workshop Radziwill Palace, Nieborów (Poland) 3–6 September 2005.* Wetteren, 105–11.

Berger, F. and Stoess, C. (1988a). *Die Fundmünzen der römischen Zeit in Deutschland. Abteilung VII, Band 1–3: Niedersachsen und Bremen.* Berlin.

Berger, F. and Stoess, C. (1988b). *Die Fundmünzen der römischen Zeit in Deutschland. Abteilung VII, Band 4–9: Niedersachsen und Bremen.* Berlin.

Blanchet, A. (1900). *Les trésors de monnaies romaines et les invasions germaniques en Gaule.* Paris.

Bland, R. and Loriot, X. (2010). *Roman and Early Byzantine Gold Coins found in Britain and Ireland: With an Appendix of New Finds from Gaul* (Royal Numismatic Society Special Publication 46). London.

Bolin, S. (1929). 'Die Funde römischer und byzantinischer Münzen im freien Germanien', *Bericht RGK* 19: 86–145.

Bolin, S. (1958). *State and Currency in the Roman Empire to 300 A.D.* Stockholm.

Boon, G. C. (1988). 'Ein neuer Teil des Kölner "Massenfundes" römischer Münzen von 1895', in *Schatzfunde römischer Münzen im gallisch-germanischen Raum* (Studien zu Fundmünzen der Antike 5). Berlin, 133–51.

Bursche, A. (1994). 'Die Markomannenkriege und der Zufluss römischer Münzen in das Barbaricum', in J. Tejral, A. Stuppner, and H. Friesinger (eds), *Markomannenkriege. Ursachen und Wirkungen. 6. Internationales Symposium 'Grundprobleme der frühgeschichtlichen Entwicklung im nördlichen Mitteldonaugebiet', Wien, 23.–26. November 1993*. Brno, 471–85.

Bursche, A. (1996). *Later Roman-barbarian Contacts in Central Europe, Numismatic Evidence: Spätrömische Münzfunde aus Mitteleuropa. Ein Beitrag zur Geschichte der Beziehungen zwischen Rom und dem Barbaricum im 3. und 4. Jh. n. Chr.* (Studien zu Fundmünzen der Antike 11). Berlin.

Bursche, A. (2011). *Illerup Ådal: 14. Die Münzen* (Jutland Archaeological Society publications 25). Aarhus.

Bursche, A. and Myzgin, K. (2025). 'Denarii in Late Roman and Migration period hoards', in A. Blackwell, M. Goldberg, and A. Rau (eds), *Silver Beyond the Empire: The Transition from Late Roman to Early Medieval Europe*. Leiden, 127–42.

Butcher, K. and Ponting, M. (2012). 'The Beginning of the end? The denarius in the second century', *Numismatic Chronicle* 172: 64–83.

Butcher, K. and Ponting, M. (2014). *The Metallurgy of Roman Silver Coinage: From the Reform of Nero to the Reform of Trajan*. Cambridge.

Callu, J.-P. and Loriot, X. (1990). *L'or monnayé* II: *la dispersion des aurei en Gaule romaine sous l'Empire* (Cahiers Ernest-Babelon 3). Juan-les-Pins.

Casey, J. (1986). *Understanding Ancient Coins*. London.

Chifflet, J.-J. (1655). *Anastasis Childerici I, Francorum regis: sive Thesaurus sepulchralis Tornaci Neruiorum effossus, et commentario illustratus*. Antwerp.

Dymowski, A. (2016). *Nummi serrati, bigati et alii: Coins of the Roman Republic in East-Central Europe North of the Sudetes and the Carpathians*. Warsaw.

Dymowski, A. (2019). 'The problem of the presence of Barbarian imitations of Roman Imperial denarii in the lands of present-day Poland. An attempt at a balance', *Notae Numismaticae-Zapiski Numizmatyczne* 14: 149–81.

Dymowski, A. (2020). 'Roman Imperial hoards of denarii from the European Barbaricum', in C. Găzdac (ed.), *Group and Individual Tragedies in Roman Europe: The Evidence of Hoards, Epigraphic and Literary Sources* (Journal of Ancient History and Archaeology: monographic series 1). Cluj-Napoca, 193–243.

Dymowski, A. and Myzgin, K. (2014). 'Inflow and redistribution of Roman Imperial denarii in the area of Przeworsk, Wielbark and Chernyakhiv Cultures and in the Baltic Islands in the light of chronological structure of coin hoards', *Notae Numismaticae* 9: 39–69.

Eggers, H. J. (1951). *Der römische Import im freien Germanien* (Atlas der Urgeschichte 1). Hamburg.

Erdrich, M. (2001). *Rom und die Barbaren: das Verhältnis zwischen dem Imperium Romanum und den germanischen Stämmen vor seiner Nordwestgrenze von der späten römischen Republik bis zum Gallischen Sonderreich* (Römisch-germanische Forschungen 58). Mainz.

Fischer, S. and Lind, L. (2015). 'The coins in the grave of King Childeric', *Journal of Archaeology and Ancient History* 14: 1–36.

Gorecki, J. (2006). *Die Fundmünzen der römischen Zeit in Deutschland. Abt. IV Bd. 1, Nachtrag 1: Rheinland-Pfalz Stadt Mainz* (Mainzer Archäologische Schriften 5). Mainz.

Graeber, D. (2010). *Debt: The First 5,000 Years*. Brooklyn, NY.

Guey, J. (1955). 'Trésors de monnaies romaines en Europe orientale', *Mélanges d'archéologie et d'histoire* 67: 189–216.

Hahn, F. (1854). *Der Fund von Lengerich im Königreiche Hannover: Goldschmuck und roemische Muenzen*. Hanover.

Horsnæs, H. W. (2010). *Crossing Boundaries. An Analysis of Roman Coins in Danish Contexts*. Vol. 1: *Finds from Sealand, Funen and Jutland* (Publications of the National Museum. Studies in Archaeology and History 18). Copenhagen.

Ilkjaer, J. (2002). *Illerup Ådal—ein archäologischer Zauberspiegel* (Jysk Arkaeologisk Selskabs Skrifter 25,0). Højbjerg.

Kehne, P. (2008). 'Auskünfte antiker Schriftquellen zu Umständen und Größenordnungen des Abflusses römischer Münzen ins "Barbaricum" vom 1.–5. Jahrhundert n. Chr.: eine Problemskizze', in A. Bursche and R. Ciolek (eds), *Roman Coins outside the Empire. Ways and Phases, Contexts and Functions: Proceedings of the ESF/SCH Exploratory Workshop Radziwill Palace, Nieborów (Poland) 3–6 September 2005* (Moneta 82). Wetteren, 75–88.

Komnick, H. (2010). *Die Fundmünzen der römischen Zeit in Deutschland. Abteilung VI, Band 2,2: Nordrhein-Westfalen. Reg.-Bez. Aachen (Kreisfreie Stadt Aachen, Landkreise Aachen, Monschau, Schleiden, Selfkantkreis Geilenkirchen-Heinsberg)*. Mainz.

Komnick, H. (2015). *Die Fundmünzen der römischen Zeit aus dem Bereich der Colonia Ulpia Traiana* (Xantener Berichte 29). Darmstadt.

Komnick, H., Heinrichs, J., and Päffgen, B. (2008). *Die Fundmünzen der römischen Zeit in Deutschland. Abteilung VI, Bd. 2, 1: Nordrhein-Westfalen Reg.-Bez. Aachen (Landkreis Düren, Erkelenz, Jülich)*. Mainz.

Martin, M. (2004). 'Childerichs Denare: Zum Rückstrom römischer Silbermünzen ins Merowingerreich', in H. Friesinger and A. Stuppner (eds), *Zentrum und Peripherie. Gesellschaftliche Phänomene in der Frühgeschichte. Materialien des 13. Internationalen Symposiums 'Grundprobleme der frühgeschichtlichen Entwicklung im mittleren Donauraum' Zwettl, 4.–8. Dezember 2000*. Vienna, 241–78.

Maurer, B. (2006). 'The anthropology of money', *Annual Review of Anthropology* 35: 15–36.

Myzgin, K., Dymowski, A., and Chemuranov, O. (2020). 'Typical features of a Roman denarius hoard from the Chernyakhiv Culture territory – the case of the Skypche hoard from Ukraine', in C. Găzdac (ed.), *Group and Individual Tragedies in Roman Europe. The Evidence of Hoards, Epigraphic and Literary Sources* (Journal of Ancient History and Archaeology: monographic series 1). Cluj-Napoca, 359–83.

Noeske, H.-C. (2000). *Münzfunde aus Ägypten* I: *Die Münzfunde des ägyptischen Pilgerzentrums Abu Mina und die Vergleichsfunde aus den Diocesen Aegyptus und Oriens vom 4.–8. Jh. n. Chr.: Prolegomena zu einer Geschichte des spätrömischen Münzumlaufs in Ägypten und Syrien* (Studien zu Fundmünzen der Antike 12). Berlin.

Nuber, E. (1984). *Die Fundmünzen der römischen Zeit in Deutschland. Abteilung VI, Band 1,1: Nordrhein-Westfalen Stadt Köln*. Berlin.

Otte, R. (2024). *Monetarisierung und Geldumlauf in ländlichen Siedlungen des niederrheinischen Lössgebietes* (Rheinische Ausgrabungen 86). Cologne and Bonn.

Perry, B. E. (1965) *Babrius and Phaedrus* (Loeb classical library 436). London and Cambridge, MA.

Polanyi, K. (1957). 'The economy as instituted process', in K. Polanyi, C. M. Arensberg, and H. W. Pearson (eds), *Trade and Market in the Early Empires: Economies in History and Theory*. Glencoe, 243–70.

Quast, D. and Ament, H. (eds) (2015). *Das Grab des fränkischen Königs Childerich in Tournai und die 'Anastasis Childerici' von Jean-Jacques Chifflet aus dem Jahre 1655* (Monographien des Römisch-Germanischen Zentralmuseums 129). Mainz.

Rodríguez Adrados, F. (1999) *History of the Graeco-Latin Fable*, vol. 1 (Mnemosyne, bibliotheca classica Batava. Supplementum 201). Leiden, Boston, and Cologne.

Schmauder, M. (1999). 'Der "Schatzfund" von Lengerich: Hort eines römischen Offiziers?', in M. Fansa (ed.), *Über allen Fronten: Nordwestdeutschland zwischen Augustus und Karl dem Grossen* (Archäologische Mitteilungen aus Nordwestdeutschland Beiheft 26). Oldenburg, 85–90.

Schulzki, H.-J. (2002). 'Der Katastrophenhorizont der zweiten Hälfte des 3. Jahrhunderts im Raum der CCAA. Historisches Phänomen und numismatischer Befund', *Kölner Jahrbuch* 34: 7–88.

Seaford, R. (2004). *Money and the Early Greek Mind: Homer, Philosophy, Tragedy*. Cambridge.

Speidel, M. A. (1992). 'Roman army pay scales', *Journal of Roman Studies* 82: 87–106.

Thüry, G. E. (2016). *Die antike Münze als Fundgegenstand: Kategorien numismatischer Funde und ihre Interpretation*. Oxford.

von Kaenel, H.-M., Brem, H., Elmer, J. Th., Gorecki, J., Hedinger, B., King, C. E., Klee, M., Leuthard, M., Northover, J. P., Rychener, J., and Zürcher, A. (1993). *Der Münzhort aus dem Gutshof von Neftenbach. Antoniniane und Denare von Septimius Severus bis Postumus*. Zurich.

Voß, H.-U. and Wigg-Wolf, D. (2017). 'Romans and Roman finds in the Central European Barbaricum: A new view on Romano-Germanic relations?', in S. González Sánchez and A. Guglielmi (eds), *Romans and Barbarians beyond the Frontiers: Archaeology, Ideology and Identities in the North*. Oxford, 105–24.

Wheeler, R. E. M. (1954). *Rome beyond the Imperial Frontiers*. London.

Wigg, A. and Wigg, D. G. (1994). 'Ein römerzeitlicher Münzschatzfund aus dem Lahntal bei Wetzlar', *Germania* 72.1–2: 298–313.

Wigg-Wolf, D. (2019). 'Rethinking coin finds as a process', in S. Krmnicek and J. Chameroy (eds), *Money Matters. Coin Finds and Ancient Coin Use*. Bonn, 13–20.

Zedelius, V. (1974). *Spätkaiserzeitlich-völkerwanderungszeitliche Keramik und römische Münzen von Laatzen, Ldkr. Hannover* (Materialhefte zur Ur- und Frühgeschichte Niedersachsens Heft 8). Hildesheim.

David Wigg-Wolf, *Inside–Outside: (How) Are Hoards from beyond the Empire Different? The Perspective from the Rhine Frontier* In: *Roman Coin Hoards Across Frontiers*. Edited by: Benjamin D. R. Hellings, Marguerite Spoerri Butcher, and Chris Howgego, Oxford University Press.
DOI: 10.1093/9780198986478.003.0007

8

Roman Coin Hoards in Eastern Europe

Kyrylo Myzgin

INTRODUCTION

Roman coins in the territory of eastern Europe are represented by finds of *denarii* of the period of the Roman Republic as well as by all main denominations of the Roman Empire.[1] This chapter addresses coin finds of the imperial period, including the coinage of central imperial mints, provincial and autonomous coinage, and semi-unofficial coins from barbarian territories.

AREA AND STATE OF RESEARCH

My research area is defined by the term 'eastern Europe' and is limited to the territories of present-day Belarus, Moldova, the European part of Russia, and Ukraine, or, in other words, the European part of the post-Soviet Union. In some respects, the choice of this region is due to the interrelated tendencies of its archaeological development as well as to my access to materials.[2] The Baltic region has not been included because it belongs to a different historical and archaeological area, and its inclusion would confuse the general international understanding of the evidence. Moreover, the chapter also excludes the ancient centres of the Black Sea region (the Greek cities of Olbia, Nikonion, Tyras, Chersonesus, etc.) and the cities of the Bosporan Kingdom (Panticapaeum, Theodosia, Nymphaion, etc.),[3] concentrating therefore on an area commonly referred to as 'eastern Barbaricum'.

The first general studies of Roman coin hoards from the region date back to the second half of the nineteenth and early twentieth centuries.[4] However, their

[1] On the finds of Roman Republican coins in eastern Europe, see Myzgin (2017b).

[2] This is inconsistent with, for example, the UN nomenclature of Belarus, Bulgaria, the Czech Republic, Hungary, Moldova, Poland, Romania, Russia, Slovakia, and Ukraine as part of eastern Europe.

[3] On coin circulation in the Bosporan Kingdom, see Højberg Bjerg (2014).

[4] Fundukley (1848); Antonovich (1878); Samokvasov (1884); Liaskoronskiy (1901); and others.

systematic study was not undertaken until the mid-twentieth century. A series of works by Vladislav Kropotkin presented a concept of periodization and causes of hoarding and process of hoard thesaurization in eastern Europe; he also attempted to identify stages of coin influx to Barbaricum.[5] At the same time, Mykhailo Braichevskiy was actively investigating this field.[6] Later, however, up to the beginning of the 2000s, this question was studied rather casually, mainly at the level of particular regions,[7] or when new finds of hoards were published.[8] In a doctoral dissertation of 2010 the problem of Roman coin hoards in eastern Europe was developed, proposing typologies and reasons for depositing.[9] Although since 2010 more scholars have considerably enlarged the source base and made several observations on various categories of hoards, the present chapter is the first general overview of this problem in more than half a century.

TO THE DEFINITION OF 'COIN HOARD': THE CASE OF EASTERN BARBARICUM

The Coin Hoards of the Roman Empire Project (CHRE) uses the following definition of a hoard: any group of coins that appears to have been deposited together.[10] In eastern Europe and ancient numismatics, the definition of 'coin hoard' is similar: a group of coins buried in the ground or hidden in a dwelling.[11] Nevertheless, these generally accepted definitions of a coin hoard do not include the important question of the number of coins in the deposit. Of course, for the Roman Empire, a territory where coins fulfilled all the basic functions of money, this issue is not critical: even a single find of a gold coin can be considered a hoard (as the CHRE project does). It seems that in Barbaricum, where Roman coins had yet different functions, the matter of the number of coins in a hoard is significant. For example, in eastern European numismatics, there is a particular tradition of considering several dozens of coins a hoard, whereas smaller deposits, i.e. fewer than 10–20 specimens, are usually called 'wallets' or 'pouches' (even in the case of ancient coins, although this term is more typical for the Middle Ages and Modern period), and are not considered hoards by either professional or amateur

[5] Kropotkin (1951; 1961; 1967). [6] Braichevskiy (1959: 71–83).

[7] For example, for Moldova: Nudelman (1982); Ciobanu (1999); Popa and Ciobanu (2003); for the northern Pontic region: Stoliarik (1989); for the Bukovina region: Pivovarov (2002); for Volhynia: Kozak (1995); for south-west Russia: Radiush (2008); etc.

[8] For example: Magomedov and Karoieva (1988); Gluschenko (1989); Shilin (2003); and others.

[9] Myzgin (2010).

[10] https://chre.ashmus.ox.ac.uk/content/about (accessed 6 April 2023). See also the history of the discussion around this definition in ancient numismatics: Aitchison (1988: 270–4).

[11] Cf. Kropotkin (1961: 14). According to a very correct observation by Bland (2018: 9), finding an object/coin in the ground is not a prerequisite for defining it as hoard.

Fig. 8.1. Finds of soldered *denarii* ('small hoards') from the Ukraine. 1) Poltava region (B.183); 2) Vinnytsia region (B.223); 3) Cherkassy region (B.138); 4) Ukraine (unlocated) (B.212). © K. Myzgin.

numismatists.[12] In this regard, a good example can be the finding of coins that have been fused together, for example, due to exposure to high temperatures (Fig. 8.1). At least 35 cases from Ukraine are known, though not yet published. In six cases, three coins were connected, in seven cases four coins, in one case five coins, in three cases six coins, and in two cases seven coins. Can we call these a hoard? Surely they are 'small hoards'. In 2010, it was proposed to define a coin hoard as 'a discovered assemblage of more than five compactly arranged coins, which were buried in the ground or hidden on the surface'.[13] Now it seems that the quantitative bar can be lowered to three coins found together. If a hoard is a 'closed group' of associated artefacts,[14] I consider a coin hoard to be 'three or more coins hidden

[12] So far only two hoards with fewer than ten coins have been published: the hoard of nine *sestertii* from the second and third centuries from Perehinka (central Ukraine)—Nadvirnyak and Pohorilets (2019)—and a hoard of four coins minted by Trapezus from the Arabat Spit—Myzgin (2020). Of the 132 hoards reported by treasure hunters, only six contain data on hoards containing fewer than ten coins. Obviously, there are more such hoards, but because they are not perceived as hoards, they are most often reported as 'a few single finds', so they are almost impossible to record.

[13] Myzgin (2010: 79–80).

[14] Aitchison (1988: 271).

in ancient times, subsequently discovered together or concentrated in a small area (at least three per square metre)'.

ARCHAEOLOGICAL BACKGROUND: A SHORT OVERVIEW

During the Roman period, the archaeological situation in the eastern Barbaricum was complex and dynamically changing. This applies above all to the southern and south-western parts of eastern Europe: here, the character of ethnocultural development in early Roman and late Roman times differed considerably.

In the early Roman period (first to early third centuries), south-eastern Europe was shaped by the disappearance or significant transformation of the La Tène period cultures. On a considerable part of the territory of modern Ukraine, in the basins of the southern Bug, Pripyat, Desna, Dnieper, and Seversky Donets, from the middle of the first century to the late second or early third century, there were sites of the post-Zarubyntsi horizon, which combined Zarubyntsi and autochthonic features but also had a Sarmatian component.[15] In western Ukraine, in the Middle and Upper Dniester area, from the beginning of the first to the early third century, the Lipitsa culture was located, which is associated with the Dacian tribes, possibly with the participation of the Przeworsk and Zarubyntsi population.[16] In the area between the Dnieper and the Western Bug rivers, some Przeworsk sites also appeared, connected with the insignificant migration of the central European population to the east.[17] In the Middle Dniester and Pripyat basins area, the Zubrytsia culture appeared, probably due to interaction between the post-Zarubyntsi, Przeworsk, and part of the Lypytsia populations.[18] The Sarmatian tribes occupied the steppe region of the northern Pontic.[19] In Crimea, in the first and second centuries, the sites of the Crimean Scythia still existed but were in their final stage, while the Sarmatian population emerged, which continued to exist here in late Roman times and the Great Migration period.[20] In the more northern and eastern regions, namely in the forest zone of eastern Europe, several cultures of Baltic and Finno-Ugric origin (Brushed Pottery culture, Dnieper-Dvina culture, Dyakovo culture, Gorodetskaya culture, culture of the Ryazan-Oka burial grounds, and others) existed.[21]

In the late second and early/mid-third centuries, significant changes took place in the forest-steppe and steppe zones of eastern Europe, connected primarily with

[15] Bashkatov and Terpilovskiy (2010: 36–53); Voroniatov (2014: 132–8); Liubichev (2019: 119–28); Beliavets (2016).

[16] Vakulenko (1989: 22–34); Kozak (1990: 43–56).

[17] Kokowski (2003: 115, fig. 17); Andrzejowski (2010: 70, fig. 9); Tkach (2013: 95).

[18] Kozak (2008: 14, fig. 2; 225–301).

[19] Istvánovits and Kulcsár (2017: 158–60).

[20] Khrapunov (1995: 71–2); Aybabin and Khayredinova (2017: 26–148).

[21] Shmidt (1992); Mironov (1995: 68–89); Yegoreichenko (2006); Akhmedov, Belotserkovskaya, and Rumiantseva (2007: 133–275); Krenke (2011).

the migration of East Germanic tribes (Goths) to this region from Polish Pomerania. Probably in the middle of the third century, their presence in the upper course of the Dniester Basin forced the local (early Slavic?) population to move to the left bank of the Dnieper: here, in the middle of the third and early fourth centuries, the existence of the so-called Boromlya horizon is associated with them.[22] In the late second and early third centuries, a part of the post-Zarubyntsi horizon groups formed the basis of the Kyiv culture, which existed till the fifth century and occupied, according to various estimates, the areas from the Middle Dnieper and Desna basin to the Dvina basin.[23] Undoubtedly the driver of ethnocultural development in eastern Europe in the late Roman period was the Chernyakhiv culture. It emerged in the middle of the third century in the region between the upper reaches of the Southern Bug and the middle Dniester because of the occupation of this territory by the Goths. The formation of the culture saw close contact of the population with the Roman provinces, such as during the Gothic Wars in the third century. The material complex of the Chernyakhiv culture illustrates strong Roman provincial influences, which can be seen in the techniques of land cultivation, production of pottery, jewellery, glassware, etc. By the mid-fourth century, by the time of the flourishing of the Chernyakhiv culture, it had covered a vast territory, from the Seim River in the east to the Western Bug in the north-west and Muntenia in the south-west, and from the Middle Dnieper to the northern Black Sea coast. Ethnically speaking, the Goths were undoubtedly the core of this culture, but it also included Late Sarmatian, Late Scythian, Thracian, and Early Slavic populations.[24] The Goths' migration also affected Crimean territory: here, they appeared in the middle of the third century and settled in the south-western part of the peninsula.[25] The cities of the Bosporan Kingdom continued to exist here, as did other major ancient centres, such as Chersonesus. In the Carpathian area and the north of Moldova, there was a culture of the Carpathian barrow, lately associated with the Typhalian tribes and strongly influenced by the province of the Roman Empire.[26] At the same time, new cultural groups, for example the Moschino culture,[27] emerged in the forest zone of eastern Europe alongside the existing Baltic cultures. Many of the forest cultures of the Late Roman period were influenced by the Chernyakhiv culture. At the end of the fourth century cardinal changes in eastern Europe, especially in its southern part, were brought about by the Huns. At least, their activity in the region is usually associated with the final stage of the Chernyakhiv culture, the subsequent processes of internal migrations, and the appearance of post-Chernyakhiv archaeological horizons.[28]

[22] Liubichev (2019: 182–4). [23] Oblomskiy (2007). [24] Magomedov (2001: 134–43).
[25] Kazanski (2006: 26–41). [26] Vakulenko (2010). [27] Vorontsov (2013).
[28] Cf. Magomedov (2001: 143–7). Although the situation here does not look so clear-cut either: cf. Petrauskas (2021: 26); Liubichev (2019: 187–90).

This greatly simplified picture of ethnocultural processes in eastern Europe in Roman times helps to show that the territories in question in this chapter were subject to highly complex archaeological processes, which means that the process of hoarding and hoards' deposition may have differed significantly in different periods and different areas.

DYNAMICS OF GATHERING INFORMATION

Information about finds of Roman coins in eastern Europe, including hoards, has been systematically accumulated since the early nineteenth century. Figure 8.2, which represents the dynamics of this process, shows at least four periods of activity in the discovery of coins that are associated with different stages of the development of archaeology in eastern Europe. The first period, from the 1860s to the 1900s, is connected to the activities of the Russian Imperial Archaeological Commission, whose work was aimed at registering, studying, and publishing antiquities discovered within the Russian Empire.[29] The next period covers the 1920s and 1930s, related to the interwar period (after a succession of revolutions and the civil war), when researchers were able to return to constant research. The third period in recording finds of Roman coins, which falls in the 1950s and 1970s, is associated with significant activity by Soviet numismatists and archaeologists after World War II, coinciding with numerous financially supported archaeological studies along with active publication of sources.[30] All these periods of activity do

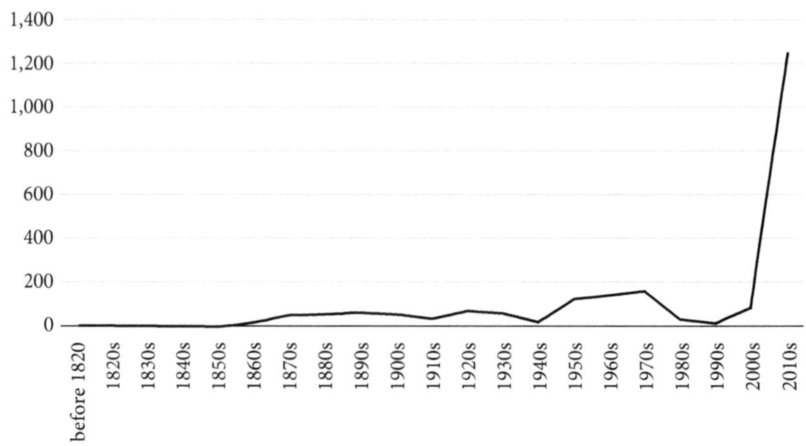

Fig. 8.2. Number of Roman coin finds (hoards and single finds) in eastern Europe by decade of discovery; after Myzgin (2010).

[29] Cf. Bursche (1996: 46–7).

[30] Myzgin (2010: 12–20); Myzgin (2013: 218).

not compare with the dynamics of information accumulation in eastern Europe in the last two decades. This is due to several factors: the widespread and largely uncontrolled use of metal detectors in the amateur environment, the extensive use of online communication, and the significant expansion and increasing commercialization of treasure hunting. Until the early 2000s, information about hoards of Roman coins was based almost exclusively on chance finds, especially finds made during construction or agricultural work, in ravines, in road gullies, or on the banks of rivers. There is almost no information from chance finds any longer, as the main search tool has become a metal detector. Moreover, amateurs do not stick to a single period or area of searching but search for new and atypical sites.[31]

The reliability and quality of data about hoards are a complex matter. In the pre-detector era, information from finders was mainly based on those who could accurately state the location and circumstances of the find but often could not precisely state the conditions of its occurrence. The coins themselves, however, were often added to museum collections and thus came into the possession of researchers. In the era of the metal detector, researchers now have access to pictures of coins and more precise information about the condition of the hoards, but this has come at a cost. With the commercialization of treasure hunting, amateurs prefer to conceal the specific location of their finds, and coins become less available to researchers or enter museum collections. Collecting information about these newer finds is a difficult task, as a diverse number of sources need to be consulted: treasure hunters' online forums, social networks, information from police, museums, archaeologists, or private people, media, or personal contacts. In eastern Europe, the primary way to find information is on the treasure hunters' online forums, where pictures of coins and sometimes a short description of the find conditions are published. When information about a find's location is provided, this needs to be validated through communication with the treasure hunter personally. In most cases, the finders report the administrative region of the find, such as the region or district, and only in rare cases do they indicate a specific locality. The information presented here can therefore only reflect the a limited level of completeness but nevertheless is an important step forward, making this information available to the wider academic community.

GENERAL STATISTICS

As of early May 2022, data on at least 301 hoards of Roman coins have been validated and collected. These hoards comprise at least 63,264 coins, including 228

[31] As an example, a hoard near Khmelivka, Ukraine, was found in the forest, in a hard-to-reach place where no archaeological research has ever been carried out: Myzgin and Petrauskas (2021).

Table 8.1. Quantitative distribution of Roman coin hoards by type of coinage.

Type of coinage	Number of hoards		Number of coins	
Roman imperial *denarii*	228	75.75%	57,447	90.81%
Cast copies of *denarii*	2	0.66%	20	0.03%
Sestertii, 1st–3rd c. AD	6	1.99%	138	0.22%
Antoniniani	18	5.98%	1,548	2.45%
Aurei, 1st–3rd c. AD	3	1.00%	33	0.05%
Barbarian gold imitations	1	0.33%	6	0.01%
Roman provincial coins, 1st–3rd c. AD	2	0.66%	25	0.04%
Siliquae	11	3.65%	889	1.41%
Late Roman bronze coins	20	6.64%	2,697	4.26%
Solidi and *multipla*	10	3.32%	461	0.73%
Total	301		63,264	

Table 8.2. Number of detector and chance finds in eastern Europe (hoards only).

			Chance finds		Detector finds	
Country/Region	Cases	Coins	Hoards	Coins	Hoards	Coins
Belarus	16	4,679	4	2,880	12	1,799
Moldova	28	2,562	26	2,386	2	176
West and South-West Russia	25	2,393	7	997	18	1,396
Crimea	25	3,030	11	913	14	2,117
Ukraine	207	*c.* 50,600	82	*c.* 23,000	125	*c.* 27,600
Total	**301**	***c.* 63,264**	**130**	***c.* 30,176**	**171**	***c.* 33,088**

hoards of Roman imperial *denarii* (75.75%), two hoards(?) of copies of *denarii* (0.66%), six hoards of *sestertii* (1.99%), 18 hoards of *antoniniani* (some including *denarii*) (5.98%), three hoards(?) of *aurei* (1.0%), one hoard of gold-plated imitations (0.33%), two hoards of Roman provincial coins (0.66%), 11 hoards of *siliquae* (3.65%), 20 hoards of late Roman bronze coins (6.64%), and ten hoards of *solidi* or late Roman gold medallions (3.32%) (Table 8.1). The largest number of hoards of Roman coins was found in Ukraine (207 hoards, 68.77%), then in the Republic of Moldova (28 hoards, 9.3%), in western and south-western Russia (25 hoards, 8.31%), in Crimea (25 hoards, 8.31%), and in Belarus (16 hoards, 5.32%) (Table 8.2). Of this number, 130 hoards (43.19%) are chance finds, while 171 hoards (56.81%) have been discovered using a metal detector. Moreover, in over 200 years of research into hoards of Roman coins in the region, only four deposits have been studied archaeologically: the hoards of *denarii* from Khmelivka[32] and Hlyn'ske,[33]

[32] Myzgin and Petrauskas (2021).

[33] Magomedov and Karoieva (1988).

and the hoards of late Roman bronze coins from Lucăşeuca (Appendix, list H, no. 9, or in short H.9) and Rozhdestvenno (H.15).

The hoards of Roman coins in eastern Europe are still insufficiently studied, with at least 31% of the deposits awaiting detailed and thorough research and publication, accounting for more than 10,000 coins. The most poorly studied are the hoards of *sestertii*, although a significant number of *denarius* and *antoninianus* hoards also lack complete identification and publication.

HOARDS OF *SESTERTII* (APPENDIX, LIST A)

Hoards of *sestertii* are the least studied category of finds in eastern Europe. Of the six deposits known to me, only four have been published to varying degrees: two hoards from Koporje in north-western Russia (A.1, A.2), Trubchevsk in western Russia (A.6), and Perehinka in western Ukraine (A.4). Two more hoards—a deposit from the vicinity of Rokytne in the Middle Dnieper region (A.5) and a hoard found in the vicinity of Myrhogorod on the left bank of the Dnieper (A.3)—have not yet been published. Chronologically the hoards from Koporje, Rokytne, Trubchevsk, and Myrhorod form a compact group: all of them include *sestertii* from the early imperial period only. The hoard from Perehinka, however, has a later chronological structure, combining coins of the second half of the second century and the first half of the third century.

The four coin hoards also contained other items. The second hoard from Koporje contained a fragment of a bronze bracelet, part of a brooch of Almgren 55 type, and a fragment of a bronze torque dating to the end of the first to the middle of the second century.[34] The hoard from Rokytne contains four brooches of Almgren 61 type, dating to the second half of the second century. Two hoards belong to the horizon of champlevé enamels: Trubchevsk, which included two horseshoe-shaped brooches with enamel of the Gorokhovsky 1 type of the Baltic-Dnipro-Oka series and a bronze bell dating to the second half of the third century;[35] and the unpublished hoard from Myrhorod, which comprised a T-shaped fibula with enamel remains, two bracelets, and fragments of a chain dating from the late second to mid-third century (Fig. 8.3). As we will see, in contrast to the hoards of *denarii* with accompanying items, artefacts from *sestertii* hoards are generally contemporary with the coins.

Small denominations of the Roman coinage system on the territory of Barbaricum can be regarded as relatively rare. The western Baltic region forms an exception, where *sestertii* are the dominant denomination encountered, but their

[34] Sharov, Palaguta, and Khavrin (2010: 338–9). The hoard also included a *denarius* of Antoninus Pius (for Diva Faustina I).

[35] Voroniatov and Stoliarova (2020: 76); Voroniatov and Shinakov (2020: 84; 106).

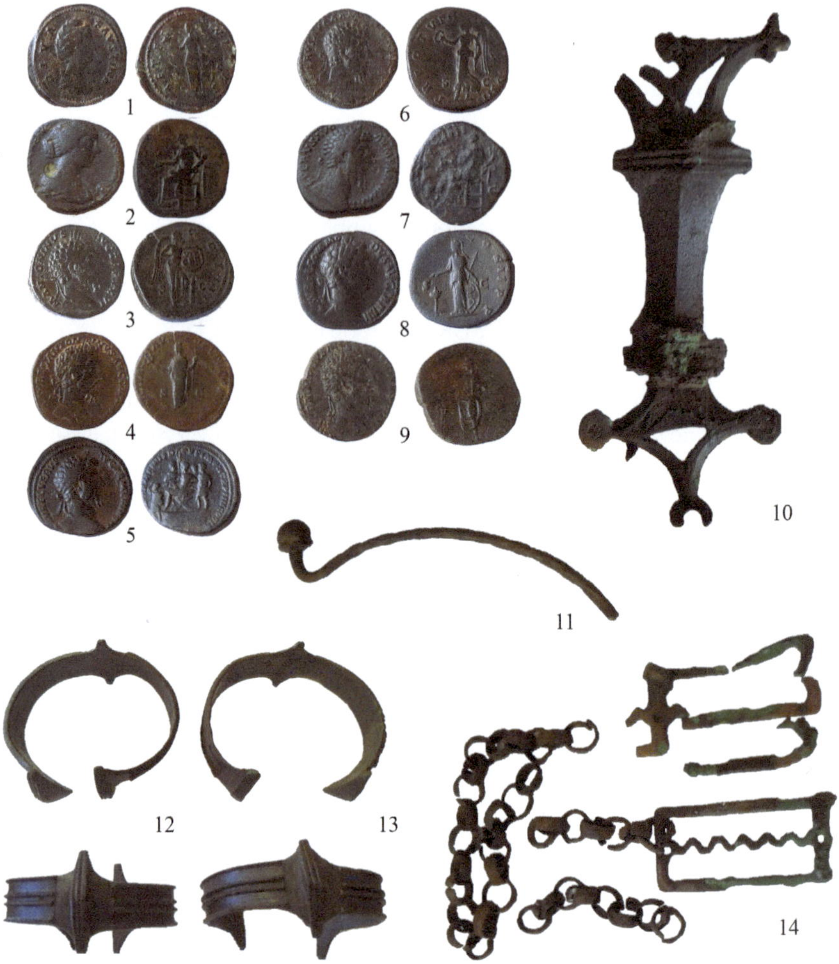

Fig. 8.3. Hoard comprising second-century *sestertii* and ornaments made in the champlevé enamel style from Myrhorod, Poltava region, Ukraine (A.3). © K. Myzgin, M. Filatova, and D. Filatov.

arrival had particular circumstances.[36] The inflow of *aes* (*sestertii* form the majority, while *asses* and *dupondii* are less frequent) into eastern Europe took place before the mass spread of *denarii*, or, in other words, before the Chernyakhiv culture period. The accompanying items from the hoards of *sestertii* provide the evidence: hoards from Rokytne, Trubchevsk, and Myrgorod contain ornaments, which are typical for the pre-Chernyakhiv period, with objects of the post-Zarubyntsi horizon and the early Kyiv culture. I believe the population of the Kyiv

[36] For details, see Zapolska (2013: 108–12).

culture was the primary recipient of early Roman imperial bronze coins. The origin of these coins is an important consideration. It is possible that the high concentration of coins within the west Baltic cultural area in the early Roman period suggests that the flow of coins to the Kyiv culture came from the Baltic area,[37] but it is also plausible that some of the coins came to eastern Barbaricum from the Roman Empire.

The Perehinka hoard stands out because it is distinguished by the area it was found in and by its chronological structure. The exact cultural context of the hoard is unknown,[38] but we can reliably say that it is related to the Chernyakhiv culture. *Antoniniani* hoards have also been found in the same site.[39] Finds of *sestertii* are rare in the Chernyakhiv culture, though when found they date to the same period as finds of Roman provincial coins (see below). It is possible that the arrival of coins from Perehinka could relate to the influx of Roman provincial coins into eastern Europe, for reasons such as the Gothic Wars of the third century.

The relative scarcity of finds of early imperial *aes* in eastern Europe does not indicate that their deposition into hoards was somehow connected with local coin circulation. The second hoard from Koporje gives us a hint in determining the reasons for the hoard's deposition: the chemical analysis of the coins and objects found together shows significant similarities, meaning that the coins may have been used as raw material for ornaments. Unfortunately, there is no possibility of similar analyses for the Rokytne, Trubchevsk, and Myrhorod hoards. Coins could have been a significant, if not the only, source of bronze for the Chernyakhiv culture. If this were to be the case, these hoards should be regarded as 'jewellers' deposits'. The reasons for the deposit of the Perehinka hoard are less clear if we consider that the metal smiths in Chernyakhiv had access to Roman bronze objects,[40] including provincial Roman coins; the *sestertii* from Perehinka should then not be regarded as a material for jewellery.[41]

HOARDS OF ROMAN IMPERIAL *DENARII* (APPENDIX, LIST B)

In the entire Barbaricum, including eastern Barbaricum except for the west Baltic region, Roman *denarii* from the period after the reform of Nero (AD 64) until the early years of Septimius Severus dominate among the finds of Roman coins.

[37] In the case of finds of such coins from Belarus, this is particularly pointed out by Sidarovich (2022: 85). The same also applies to the influx of bronze coins into the Izhora Plateau (hoards from Koporje).

[38] The settlement where it was found has not been studied archaeologically, and the hoard itself does not contain additional objects.

[39] Nadvirniak, Pohorelec, and Nadvirniak (Jr.) (2017).

[40] Magomedov (2001: 95–6).

[41] The results of the chemical analysis of the coins from the hoard are published in Nadvirnyak and Pohorilets (2020).

Nevertheless, the *denarius* hoards are still concentrated mainly in the forest-steppe zone of eastern Europe—in the area occupied in late Roman times and at the beginning of the Great Migration period by the population of the Chernyakhiv culture. A particular concentration, however, can also be identified in western Belarus, which at the time was part of the area of the Wielbark culture.

Although *denarius* hoards from eastern Europe consist exclusively of *denarii* (in exceptional cases including other, mostly late, denominations such as *antoniniani* or *siliquae*), their chronological structure cannot be called standardized. In 2014, Arkadiusz Dymowski and I published the results of a study of the chronological structure of *denarius* hoards from northern, central, and eastern Europe, identifying six types of hoards, some of which have subtypes.[42] Their chronological profiles are characterized by relatively constant proportions between subsets of coins of each issue of each ruler. In the hoard types A and B, the closing coins are *denarii* issued between the reigns of Hadrian and Antoninus Pius and Marcus Aurelius; in type C, the closing coins are those from the early reign of Septimius Severus; the chronological structure of the type BC has features of the types B (especially their part up to Antoninus Pius) and C (especially their part from Marcus Aurelius). Types A, B, C, and BC are more typical for central and northern Europe, while they are known in a few cases in eastern Europe.[43] Hoards of type D are essentially a development of type C and BC, resulting from their 'ageing' and minor reformation. Unlike the earlier types of hoards, the coins are heavily worn. These hoards often also contain accompanying items of a very late chronology. These deposits are the product of modification by barbarians. This type of hoard is widespread in eastern Europe, as well as in central and northern Europe.[44] The nature of type E hoards, with closing coins issued after Septimius Severus, is not yet completely clear.[45]

The typology proposed is an attempt not only to systematize a massive group of material but also to facilitate a better understanding behind the circumstances of the influx of *denarii* into the territory of eastern Europe. The question of the timing of the influx of *denarii* into eastern Barbaricum has been debated for a long time; for more than half a century after the discovery of the first sites of the Chernyakhiv culture, Roman *denarii* were the main argument in favour of the dating of its emergence in the first or second century. In the late 1960s and 1970s, however, several researchers concluded that the Chernyakhiv culture should not be dated earlier than the early third century.[46] Roman *denarii* were regarded as anachronistic, so researchers assumed that they arrived with some pre-Chernyakhiv population (possibly with the tribes of the post-Zarubyntsi horizon or Kyiv

[42] Dymowski and Myzgin (2014: table 1).

[43] Dymowski and Myzgin (2014: 48–50).

[44] Dymowski and Myzgin (2014: 50–2).

[45] Dymowski and Myzgin (2014: 52).

[46] Cf. Magomedov (2001: 15).

culture).[47] The archaeological evidence has now disproved this: Roman *denarii* are known almost exclusively from sites of the Chernyakhiv culture. Therefore, in 1987, Boris Magomedov suggested that these coins still came to the Chernyakhiv population, but in the middle of the third century, either as booty or as payments during the Gothic Wars.[48] This hypothesis remained mainstream until the early 2010s. The problem, however, is that Magomedov's hypothesis contradicted the conclusions that Roman *denarii* had almost completely gone out of circulation in the Empire by the AD 230s–40s. It is therefore improbable that the Goths could have obtained such vast volumes of Roman silver at the time of the Gothic Wars because there was none circulating in the Roman provinces.[49] In 2013 I drew attention to this impossibility and to the similarity of the structure of *denarius* deposits from the territory of the Przeworsk, Wielbark, and Chernyakhiv cultures. Because of the chronology of the Chernyakhiv culture and its doubtless connexion with the migration of the Welbark populations from Polish Pomerania to the south-east in the early third century, it was hypothesized that these *denarii* did not come from the Empire directly but from Central Europe, where they had arrived at some point earlier, probably as a result of the Marcomannic wars.[50] The evolution of hoards from type C and BC to type D, according to the classification by Dymowski and me, and their distribution pattern, are two strong reasons in favour of the argument that *denarii* were brought to the territory of modern Ukraine by the Gothic migrants in the first half or middle of the third century.[51] Moreover, the assembling of the coins in these deposits could have occurred in central and eastern Europe; they could have come as a finished or partly finished group.[52] On the territory of the Chernyakhiv culture, some assembling could also have taken place, as evidenced by such finds in hoards of coins of local production (see below). This, however, appears to have been only a possible scenario for deposits consisting of several dozen or even hundreds of coins. Smaller hoards of 3–10 *denarii* are to be interpreted as short-term hoards, inadvertently lost or hidden in a dwelling.

While the process of hoarding so far seems relatively straightforward, it is more difficult to understand the timing and reasons for the concealment of hoards. Deposits with other objects bring some clarity to this matter. Among the hoards of eastern Europe, hoards with additional material constitute a relatively small number (10.3%), but they are typically of average or large size (up to 200–800 coins) and can be divided into several categories: hoards containing metal,

[47] Tikhanova (1973: 71–2); Schukin (1976: 303–17); Romanova (1995: 122–4).
[48] Magomedov (1987: 79); Magomedov and Karoieva (1988: 84–6).
[49] For example, Reece (2008: 65); for more see Myzgin (2013).
[50] Myzgin (2013: 221–3); see also Myzgin (2019: 213–14).
[51] The earliest Chernyakhiv graves have distinctly Wielbark culture features; cf. Bursche and Myzgin (2020: 203–11).
[52] Dymowski and Myzgin (2014: 54).

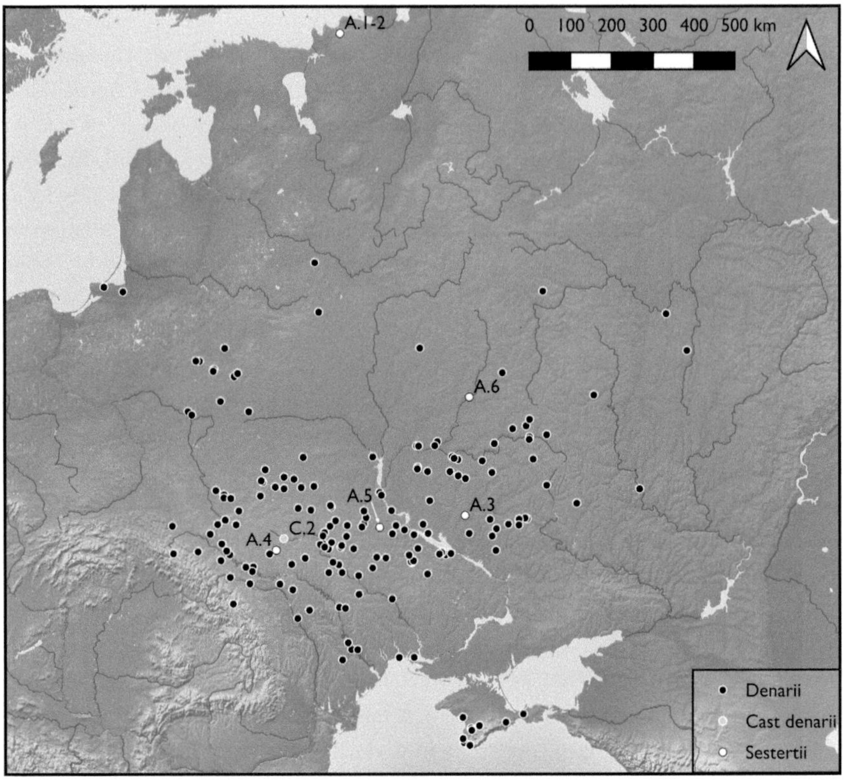

Fig. 8.4. Distribution map of hoards of Roman imperial *denarii*, cast *denarii*, and *sestertii*. Map: A. Wilson/K. Myzgin.

primarily silver vessels (three hoards); hoards containing items of everyday use (household items, three hoards); hoards containing silver or gold ingots (four hoards), and hoards containing jewellery, brooches, belt sets, and buckles (21 hoards) (Fig. 8.4). The objects in the hoards—especially pottery, jewellery, and clothing items—are excellent chronological indicators. At least seven of the hoards contained items dating back to the fourth century and the beginning of the fifth century (phases C3 and C3/D1 of the central European chronological system); the other eight had objects dating to the end of the fourth century and the first half of the fifth century (phases D1, D1/D2). This chronology demonstrates that there were at least 100 to 150 years between the time of the hoards' formation in the Chernyakhiv culture and the time of their deposition. It is hard to determine whether this signals that these deposits were actively involved in the economic life of the barbarian population for several generations or just passively stored and occasionally supplemented by new coins.

The problem of why the owners did not return for their hoards is critical to assess. It is traditionally believed that one of the reasons for the decline of the

Chernyakhiv culture was the Hun invasion at the end of the fourth century.[53] Most of the items in the *denarii* hoards also date to the possible Hunnic invasion of the late fourth century, and it is therefore tempting to connect the concealment of these hoards with the arrival of the Huns in the region. Recent studies of the Chernyakhiv culture, however, indicate that in the territory of the Ukrainian forest-steppe (where the *denarius* hoards are found), mass traces of the Hunnic invasion are not encountered.[54] In that case, what could have been the main reason for the horizon of the hoards? What event or series of events prevented the owners of the Roman silver deposits from retrieving them from the ground? An internal political struggle that did not fall into the orbit of the written sources? Or an environmental disaster that caused mass deaths and hasty evacuation? The possibility of answering these questions still rests on our incomplete understanding of the function of hoards of Roman coins in barbarian society. Was it only economic, or was it also cultic? Were the hoards solely individual property or clan or community property?[55] Could they also be votive, meaning they were a 'gift not to be returned'? Or did they have all these functions?

The steppe region of Ukraine can possibly provide insight here. Most traces of Hunnic presence are recorded in this region, so this is where it is logical to expect the most *denarius* hoards to be found. However, there are almost no finds of *denarius* hoards (except for two: B.142; B.156), although there are well-known single finds of *denarii*.[56] The absence of *denarius* hoards in the steppe area of the Chernyakhiv culture is improbable to be connected with the state of research, since the region has a relatively long history of archaeological research and treasure hunters are no less active than in other regions. It is also improbable that it could relate to any local tradition characterized by a lack of coin hoarding and depositing (considering the considerable presence here of the Late Sarmatian and Late Scythian population). It is possible that hoards were successfully taken away by their owners during the evacuation from the region during the Hunnic invasion, highlighting the difference between the steppe and forest-steppe.

The occurrence of hoards outside the Chernyakhiv culture also needs to be discussed (Fig. 8.5). Hoards from south-west Belarus should be connected to the Wielbark culture, but it is more complicated with hoards from the north-west of Belarus, in the Neman River basin. It is possible that Germanic migrants may have left these hoards at the beginning of the Great Migration period, but it is also plausible that, as Vital Sidarovich has suggested, these hoards may have come to the local Balt population after intensive contact with the eastern Germanic peoples.[57] The appearance of the Roman *denarii* (as well as their hoards) further to the east,

[53] Cf. Magomedov (2001: 143–7). [54] Liubichev (2019: 188); Petrauskas (2021: 25–6).

[55] The presence in the hoards of a set of items characteristic of a single costume (one or two brooches and/or buckles, jewellery), or household items, still testifies instead to the fact that these hoards were in individual possession. My thanks to Maxim Levada for this valuable observation.

[56] Petrauskas (2021: 16, fig. 1). [57] Sidorovich (2021: 39).

Fig. 8.5. Hoards of Roman imperial *denarii* with accompanying artefacts. 1) Ukraine (unlocated) (B.210); 2) Karachev, Bryansk region, Russia (Zaytsev 2020: fig. 1); 3) Cherkasy region, Ukraine (B.136); 4) Buzhany, Volyn region, Ukraine (B.132). © K. Myzgin.

in the Don and Oka basins, and even in the western part of the Middle Volga region, can probably be associated with contacts with the population of the Chernyakhiv culture.[58] Some of the Roman hoards of the forest area (to the north of the Chernyakhiv culture), however, might be connected with the migration of Goths in the Great Migration period. A good illustration of this is the hoard of *denarii* found near the town of Karachev in the Bryansk Region in Russia.[59]

[58] Cf. Akhmedov (2010: 33–4); Akhmedov, Gavrilov, and Choref (2018: 449–50).
[59] Zaytsev (2020).

It comprises items typical of early fifth-century Germanic style (a silver buckle and gold earrings) and three barbarian *denarius* imitations, two of which belong to the CERES group. The vast majority of imitations of the CERES group were found in central and western Ukraine, where they most probably were produced.[60] The finds of two such imitations together with the objects of Germanic style so deep in the forest zone of eastern Europe can be regarded as demonstration of migration processes from the territory of the Chernyakhiv culture. We can see that the hoards with the later items (from the late fourth and the first half of the fifth century) are situated closer to the outskirts of the Chernyakhiv culture, which probably can be explained by the migration processes of the Chernyakhiv population in the early fifth century. The direction of this migration was not only south-west (towards the Danube and the Carpathian Basins), as traditionally assumed,[61] but also north-west (to the territory of Poland and Scandinavia),[62] north-east (to the Seim River basin and further),[63] and, possibly, north (Neman River basin).[64]

In eastern Europe, the Crimean *denarius* hoards represent a unique group. Some of these deposits are unambiguously connected with ancient cities, such as Panticapaeum or Chersonesus, and were probably deposited by their inhabitants (B.148, B.177, B.186, B.190, and, possibly, B.194). The precise findspot of the other hoards from south-west Crimea is less clear (B.143, B.170, B.193, and, probably, B.192). They may, however, still be associated with the local barbarian population that had established close contacts with the nearby ancient centres.[65] On the other hand, their chronological structure differs from the Chernyakhiv hoards: in all these deposits, the closing coins are issues of the first quarter of the third century (which is somewhat characteristic of Dymowski and Myzgin's hoard type E). Whether these deposits were left by the local Sarmatian population, appearing together with the arrival of the Germanic people in the Crimea in the middle of the third century, or are hoards connected with the Roman presence in the Crimea, remains an open question.[66]

This brief overview of *denarius* hoards in eastern Europe has focused on official *denarii*. It is also necessary to pay attention to the presence of barbarian *denarius* imitations within these hoards. This problem has been recently specially studied by the Polish–German project *Imagines Maiestatis:* Barbarian Coins, Elite Identities and the Birth of Europe (IMAGMA). At least 22 hoards (7.3%) contained barbarian *denarius* imitations, imitating imperial *denarii*.[67] All barbarian *denarius* imitations

[60] Dymowski (2019a: 180, map 1). [61] Cf. Magomedov (2001: 147).
[62] For example, the finds of Chernyakhiv items in the Hanged Man Cave in southern Poland: Mączyńska (2020: 459).
[63] Cf. Radiush (2018: 586). [64] Sidorovich (2021: 39).
[65] Cf. Choref (2013: 200–2). [66] Cf. Sidorenko (2009: 542–3, 545).
[67] For the IMAGMA project, barbarian imitations of Roman coins were defined as coins or coin-like objects modelled on Roman imperial or provincial coins or inspired by them, made by barbarians (continental Europe), excluding post-Roman minting activity; see Dymowski and Myzgin (2021: 200).

recorded in the hoards were made of silver, but with two different production techniques (striking or casting). It is believed that their production took place on the territory of the Chernyakhiv culture, where most of their finds in Barbaricum are concentrated, and that the beginning of this production should be dated to the middle or the second half of the third century.[68]

Dymowski and I noticed that *denarius* hoards containing barbarian imitations have a very late chronological pattern (type D according to our typology)—an observation that has proven to be a rule. Moreover, such hoards often contain other artefacts (most often brooches, various parts of belt sets, and/or jewellery) dating back to the end of the Chernyakhiv culture (late fourth and first half of the fifth century).[69] All of this therefore suggests a rather prolonged use of imitations in barbarian societies up to the Great Migration period. It is quite significant that the imitations from some of the hoards from Barbaricum are die-linked. At least four die-link chains have been published: the SALVS AVGVSTI Group,[70] the Hulterstad-Uggårda Group,[71] the CERES Group,[72] and the VENVS VICTRIX Group.[73] All this is evidence of widespread circulation of silver coins in the vast Barbaricum area between the Danube and Scandinavia and between the Rhine and the Black Sea.

The phenomenon of *denarius* hoards with silver imitations and late-dated items in modern Ukraine, Poland, Sweden (Gotland), and Denmark (Öland and Bornholm) aligns perfectly with the Chernyakhiv-Przeworsk-Wielbark-Baltic zone of Roman coinage arrival and redistribution.[74] As in the case of the hoard from Karachev, the hoards with imitations in central and northern Europe may be evidence of migration in Barbaricum during the Great Migration, such as from the territory of the Chernyakhiv culture to the Danubian area (Hungarian plain) or north-westwards (to Poland and Scandinavia).[75] In this respect, the absence of 'Chernyakhiv' types of barbarian *denarius* imitations among single finds and in 'barbarian' hoards of Roman coins in Crimea is interesting.[76] This again confirms that at the beginning of the Great Migration period the territory of the Crimean Peninsula was not touched by the mass migration processes from the area of the Chernyakhiv culture: at this time came the Huns, and probably the Goths seized power in the Bosporus.[77]

[68] Dymowski and Myzgin (2021: 205). [69] Dymowski and Myzgin (2021: 205–7).
[70] Stribrny (2003: 51–67). [71] Lind (1988: 117–18); Lind (2007: 53–7).
[72] Dymowski (2019a: 187–200). [73] Dymowski (2019b: 157, fig. 1).
[74] Dymowski and Myzgin (2014: 42–56); Dymowski and Myzgin (2021: 208).
[75] Dymowski and Myzgin (2021: 208).
[76] Although, judging by the finds from burial grounds, there was quite close contact between the barbarian (Gothic and Alanian) population of the Crimea and the Chernyakhiv culture; cf. Aybabin and Khayredinova (2017: 33–59).
[77] Kazanski (2006: 26–41); Kazanski (2020: 145).

HOARDS(?) OF CAST COPIES OF *DENARII* (APPENDIX, LIST C)

In contrast to barbarian *denarius* imitations, *denarius* copies in Barbaricum are a recent topic for research.[78] Within this find category, at least two types should be distinguished: *subaerati* (or silver-plated coins) and copies made by casting from metal alloys. Copies may also have been made by striking.[79] Despite many finds of *subaerati* in central and eastern Europe, traces of their manufacture have not yet been found.[80] Nevertheless, silver-plated copies were common in the area of the Chernyakhiv culture, which could indicate the possibility of their production here. *Subaerati*, however, have not yet been found as single type hoards and are only encountered as single coins within a hoard of official *denarii*.[81]

The remains of at least six workshops for the production of cast copies, with both the production waste and the products themselves, have been found in the territory of the Chernyakhiv culture.[82] Moreover, there are at least two coin deposits containing exclusively cast copies of *denarii*: from an unspecified location in Ukraine (C.1) and, possibly, from the Khmelnytskyi region (C.2).[83] Unfortunately, neither the context nor the conditions of these finds is well known. It is also possible that the finds represent remains of another workshop rather than a hoard. A reliable hoard find of *denarius* copies would allow us to better determine the function of Roman coins in the Chernyakhiv culture, because the concealment of such a group would imply that these items had value as a means of accumulating wealth, testifying to the circulation of copies as monetary objects.

HOARDS OF *ANTONINIANI* (APPENDIX, LIST D)

Eighteen hoards of *antoniniani* are located in the south and south-west of eastern Europe, which consists of the territory of forest-steppe and steppe Ukraine, Lower Dniester Moldova, and south-western and eastern Crimea.[84] All but two of the deposits in eastern Crimea (the territory of the Bosporan Kingdom) are

[78] Dymowski (2021: 111). These products were the subject of a study within the framework of the 'Barbarian Fakers. Manufacturing and use of counterfeit Roman Imperial denarii in East-Central Europe in antiquity' project financed by Poland's National Science Centre (2018/31/B/HS3/00137) and implemented at the Faculty of Archaeology, University of Warsaw (Principal Investigator: Dr hab. A. Dymowski). During these studies, I proposed the use of a new term for such products: *denarii flati*.

[79] Dymowski (2021: 112–14).

[80] Dymowski (2021: 113–14).

[81] The hoard from Shilovo contained the most coins of unofficial production, mainly of *subaerati* (A.190).

[82] Nadvirnyak and Pohorilets (2019: 32–5).

[83] Interestingly, both hoards contain coin pairs made from the same 'dies'.

[84] I also classify in this category hoards that contain *denarii* from the second half of the second and early third centuries, but with *antoniniani* absolutely predominating.

connected with barbarian contexts. Most barbarian *antoninianus* hoards close with coins minted between AD 238 and 251, belonging to the reigns of Gordian III (D.3, D.14), Philip I (D.13, D.15), and Decius (D.1, D.7, D.18). Three hoards ended with coins from the time of Trebonianus Gallus and/or Volusian (D.2, D.11, D.16), one from the time of Valerian (D.10), two for Gallienus (D.8, D.12), and two from the time of Claudius II (D.5, D.9).

At least three waves of *antoniniani* into the eastern part of Barbaricum can be distinguished.[85] The first wave reflects hoards with closing coins issued during the reigns of Gordian III, Philip I, Decius, and Trebonianus Gallus/Volusian (73.3% of all hoards). The most numerous coins in these hoards are issues of Gordian III,[86] while a sharp decrease is observed for the time of Decius, Trebonianus Gallus/ Volusian.[87] Bursche has correctly identified that this influx of *antoniniani* in Barbaricum is connected to the victory of the barbarians at Abritus in the summer of AD 251, the consequence of which was the payment of contributions by Trebonianus Gallus.[88] The connection between the population of the Chernyakhiv culture and the victory at Abritus is irrefutable (see below for more concerning *aurei*). *Antoniniani* of the first half and the middle of the third century still contained a relatively high percentage of silver, and it is for this reason that barbarians accepted them. The good state of preservation of the coins indicates they were deposited shortly after being struck or did not circulate long or widely. It is necessary to pay close attention to the similarity between the chronological structure of the *antoniniani* hoards from the first half and the middle of the third century in eastern Europe and those found in the Balkan provinces of the Roman Empire, where they were buried as a consequence of the invasions of barbarian tribes during the Gothic Wars of the third century.[89]

The second wave of influx is dated to the reigns of Valerian and Gallienus. Most of the coins in these hoards belong to the time of the joint reign of these two emperors (AD 253–60), and since these joint-reign *antoniniani* appear together with other earlier ones, the hoards still contain a relatively large quantity of silver. The arrival of this group is probably connected with the military and political activity of the barbarians in the late AD 250s and 260s. At that time, barbarian groups were actively recruited to serve under the Empire, as well as for its enemies (the usurpers), and could be paid both in silver (*antoniniani*) and gold (*aurei*; see below).[90] As an example, Aleksander Bursche has attributed the influx of *antoniniani* issued between AD 248/9 and AD 259 in the territory of the Luboszyca culture

[85] Myzgin and Perederey (2021: 317); I had previously highlighted two waves: Myzgin (2017c: 152).
[86] This is undoubtedly due to the considerable volume of *antoniniani* coinage struck during this emperor's reign; cf. Bland (2012: 517, fig. 28.52).
[87] Myzgin (2017c: 152).
[88] Bursche (1996: 97, 127); Myzgin (2017c: 150–1); Myzgin and Perederey (2021: 317).
[89] Cf. Varbanov (2012: 289, 301); Minkova (2015: 34).
[90] Myzgin and Perederey (2021: 317).

(north-western Poland) to the payments for possible military service of some of the local population in the Raetia province or on the Rhine border.[91]

In the case of eastern Europe, these hoards could have formed as a continuation of the first wave of the influx of *antoniniani*, where contributions from Trebonianus Gallus were joined by deposits received as payment in the AD 260s.[92] Judging by the limited number of hoards, however, it was a question not of the mass involvement of Gothic units but only of a few individual cases.

Hoards with later coins, of Claudius II, are clearly connected with the final stage of the *antoniniani* influx. These hoards contain issues from the late reign of Gallienus and Claudius II's reign. The hoards no longer represent stores of silver but billon and,[93] similarly to the previous wave, are not encountered frequently, representing isolated cases of individuals who participated in the events of the late AD 260s and early 270s in the Empire, whereby billon coins were received as payment and brought back to their home territory. At present, there is no reason to connect the arrival of these coins to specific historical events.

It is noteworthy that in the 'mainland' (outside Crimea), finds of *antoniniani* hoards are located along the Dniester River basin. The distribution of these hoards is probably the result of conditions of research rather than any specific historical pattern, but one cannot easily ignore the proximity of these areas and finds to the Roman *limes*.

HOARDS OF ROMAN PROVINCIAL COINS (APPENDIX, LIST E)

There are four hoards of Roman provincial coins in eastern Europe:[94] a hoard of Alexandrian tetradrachms from the village of Turec in western Belarus (E.2); a hoard from the Obolon district in Kyiv, containing some third-century bronzes from Antioch in Pisidia;[95] a small hoard of Trapezus coins from the Arabat Spit in Crimea (E.1); and a small hoard of Prusa coins from Khmelnytskyi oblast.[96] Unfortunately, all these deposits have varying degrees of credibility. It was only recently established that the Obolon hoard is most probably an unreliable find,[97] based not only on the circumstances of its discovery and entry into the museum

[91] Bursche (1996: 97, 127).

[92] Cf. Choref and Yakushechkin (2016: 585–6).

[93] Cf. Bland (2012: 530).

[94] This chapter does not consider the hoards of Bosporan coins from eastern Europe, although they are traditionally included in the catalogues of Roman provincial coinage. Outside the Bosporus, only one such hoard is known, from Ksizovo, Lipetsk region, Russia: Beidin and Myzgin (2015). See the most up-to-date overview of Bosporan coinage and monetary circulation: Højberg Bjerg (2014).

[95] Antonovich (1878).

[96] Unpublished find. Information based on: https://forum.violity.com/viewtopic.php?t=1874108 (accessed 12 June 2019).

[97] Myzgin (2020).

but, above all, on its composition. The composition is particularly bizarre, with 44 bronze coins minted at Antioch of Pisidia in the time from Gordian III to Gallienus together with 13 late Roman bronze coins minted between Maximian and Procopius. The influx of these two groups of coins into Barbaricum had very different chronologies and circumstances (see below); moreover, it is improbable that a hoard of long accumulations consisting only of bronze coins existed. The other hoards of Roman provincial coins were discovered by treasure hunters using a metal detector. Unfortunately, the discovery from the Khmelnytskyi has not yet been authenticated or verified, with coins minted at Prusa dating between Macrinus and Gordian III. Although finds of second- and third-century Bithynian coins are well known in this region,[98] it remains difficult to assert the veracity of this hoard. Only two deposits are verified and relatively reliable: the hoard of Alexandrian tetradrachms from Turets and the small hoard of Trapezus coins from Arabat Spit (Fig. 8.6).

The hoard from Turec comprised 21 Alexandrian billon tetradrachms issued between the reigns of Probus and Maximian (AD 278–95).[99] In addition to this hoard, several other single finds of Alexandrian tetradrachms are known in eastern Europe.[100] There are several opinions about the influx of these coins: as booty from the Danubian provinces of Rome during the Gothic Wars, where the coins could have reached the Roman armies from Alexandria of Egypt;[101] as payment for the participation of barbarians in the Roman army as mercenaries (*auxilia*);[102]

Fig. 8.6. Hoard of Roman provincial coins minted in Trapezus from Arabat Spit, Crimea, Ukraine (E.1). From Myzgin (2020: 150). © K. Myzgin.

[98] Myzgin (2016: 165). [99] Sidarovich (2013: 173).
[100] See Sidarovich (2013: 177 and n. 6). [101] Kunisz (1973: 36–9); Bursche (1983: 59).
[102] Bursche (2002: 222); Magomedov (2008: 173).

or as the result of Roman and barbarian trade relations.[103] In the case of the Turec hoard, none of these hypotheses seems to be satisfactory because the find's cultural context is not entirely clear (the owner could have come from the Brushed Pottery culture or from the Wielbark culture).[104] It is improbable that 'Alexandrian' merchants were active in such deep woodland regions of Barbaricum, especially as this is not yet supported by other finds of Roman imports here. It also seems improbable that the local population was recruited into the Roman army. Considering the mixed circulation in the Danubian provinces, the possibility of a 'pure' hoard of Alexandrian tetradrachms (without coins from other cities) arriving also seems doubtful. Therefore, the circumstances of the arrival of the Alexandrian coins to western Belarus and the reasons for their deposition cannot be determined for now.

There is greater clarity for the Arabat Spit hoard (Fig. 8.6). It is necessary to provide a few general remarks about Roman provincial and autonomous coin finds from eastern Barbaricum. Over the past ten years one can note a tenfold increase in the recording of these types of coins.[105] On the territory of eastern Europe, these coin finds are concentrated predominantly within the area of the Chernyakhiv culture. There is a certain noteworthy pattern in their distribution: in the regions west of the Dnieper, one finds coins minted at mints of the Balkan provinces (these coins are in the majority) as well as coins from western and north-western cities of Asia Minor. In the regions to the east of the Dnieper, coins minted in northern and central Asia Minor are prevalent. These patterns reflect the military activity of different barbarian groups during the Gothic Wars of the third century.[106] Therefore, the finds of provincial and autonomous coins, encountered to the west of the Dnieper (and further to the territory of Belarus and Poland) can be associated with the participation of Goths in the incursions of the AD 230s and 240s directed to the Balkan provinces of the Roman Empire (Lower Moesia, Thrace, and Macedonia), and, in the AD 260s, on the north-western and western regions of Asia Minor (primarily Bithynia).[107] Another example of this phenomenon is finds from Nicaea, which were in circulation both in north-west Asia Minor and in the Balkans. It is noteworthy that their distribution concentrates to the west of the Dnieper, and there is an almost complete absence on the opposite side of that river.[108] To the east of the Dnieper, the coins of one city, Trapezus, were prevalent. Zosimus' *Historia nova* and one of the epistles (*Epistula Canonica*) of Gregory Thaumaturgus mention several references to the tribe of the Borani/Borans, who managed to establish control over the Bosporan Kingdom and from there launched a campaign against Trapezus.[109]

[103] Vakulenko (2010: 182); Milutinović (2017: 173).
[104] Cf. Sidarovich (2013: 180).
[105] Cf. Myzgin (2018: 88–9); Sidarovich (2014).
[106] Myzgin (2016: 166); Myzgin (2018: 95).
[107] Myzgin (2016: 163–4).
[108] See Myzgin and Sidarovich (2020).
[109] *Zos.* I.32–3; *Greg. Thaumat.* Epist. Can., V.

This campaign led to looting along the Black Sea's south-eastern coast and probably the destruction of Trapezus. It is probable that the participants in this campaign later settled east of the Dnieper, as evidenced by the finds of Trapezus coins there.[110] The hoard from the Arabat Spit may mark the path of their advancement from the Bosporan Kingdom to the north.[111]

Finds of Roman provincial hoards in eastern Barbaricum are exceptional and should be regarded as isolated instances of small batches of coins obtained somewhere in the Empire and then subsequently brought to Barbaricum. The number of provincial coins in the hands of barbarians was not as significant as silver or billon *antoniniani*, and thus could not form much of the circulation or hoarding pool (Fig. 8.7). This may stem from the fact that they had a lesser

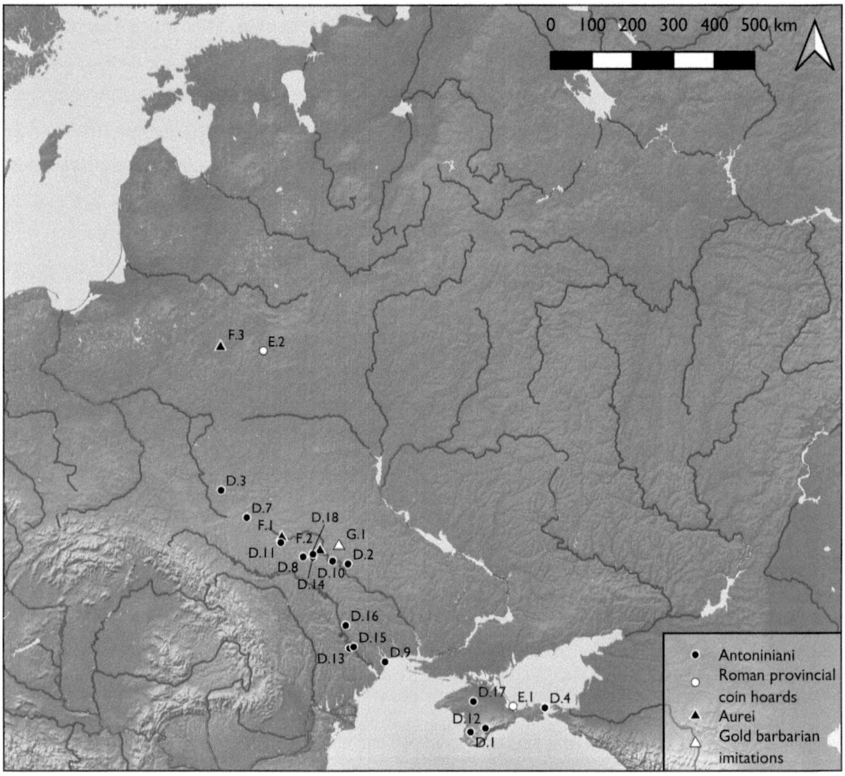

Fig. 8.7. Distribution map of hoards of *antoniniani*, provincial issues, *aurei*, and gold-plated barbarian imitations. Map: A. Wilson/K. Myzgin.

[110] One can go further and make the assumption that in the second half of the third century the areas between the Dnieper and the Dniester corresponded to the Goths, and those between the Dnieper and the Seversky Donets to the Borans: Myzgin and Didenko (2021: 324–5).
[111] Cf. Myzgin (2020: 149).

value than *denarii* or *antoniniani*, or that they generally served as keepsakes of participants in the campaigns of the Gothic Wars, or were saved to be repurposed for jewellery.

HOARDS(?) OF *AUREI* (APPENDIX, LIST F)

There are no finds of *aureus* hoards in eastern Europe, given the definition of 'hoard' applied to other coin categories. Therefore, *aureus* finds are limited to single finds and small groups of gold coins in a funerary deposit. The Coin Hoards of the Roman Empire Project treats single finds and funerary deposits of *aurei* as hoards. It is difficult to dispute the idea that this approach is sensible for finds within the Roman Empire, where gold coins were indeed of the greatest value and were used as an element of monetary circulation and as a storage of wealth. This was not always the case in Barbaricum, where, alongside their obvious economic functions, *aurei* may also have played a symbolic or religious/votive role.

The study of *aureus* finds has intensified in recent years due to a significant increase in the number of reported finds. In the early 2000s no more than ten *aurei* dating from the first to the third centuries were known in eastern Europe,[112] but by 2017 314 *aurei* were known,[113] and by the time of this publication they could possibly number more than 800. Most of these *aurei* were found by amateurs, so only minimal information is known about their context and precise find location. More than a third of the finds date from the reigns of Gordian III, Philip I, and especially Decius.[114] The most convincing explanation of this phenomenon has been provided by Aleksander Bursche, who connected the influx of these coins with the victory of the Goths over the army of Decius at Abritus in AD 251, resulting in the imperial treasury (*aurarium*) falling into barbarian hands.[115] In eastern Europe, *aureus* finds of Gordian III, Philip I, and Decius are concentrated in central and western Ukraine, between the middle reaches of the Dnieper and the middle Dniester, probably marking the areas of resettlement of the participants of these events.[116] It should also be noted that the vast majority of *aurei* were pierced, most often above the image of the emperor's head, which emphasizes the symbolic role of these coins for their owners.[117]

[112] Kropotkin (1951: 262, no. 164); Kropotkin (1961: 50, no. 164; 70, no. 748; 110, no. 1705, 1707); Kropotkin (2000: 31, no. 1862; 38, no. 2003; 40, no. 2042; 44, no. 2133).

[113] Myzgin (2017a: 37–8).

[114] Bursche and Myzgin (2020: 213; 215, fig. 9).

[115] Bursche (2013: 163–4).

[116] Cf. Bursche and Myzgin (2020: 213, map 4). It is interesting that in Crimea the finds of third-century *aurei* are unknown, which, in my opinion, can only mean one thing: the groups of the Germanic population who appeared there in the middle of the third century did not participate actively in the events near Abritus in AD 251, and there was no tradition among them of wearing this type of prestige symbol.

[117] Bursche and Myzgin (2020: 215–20).

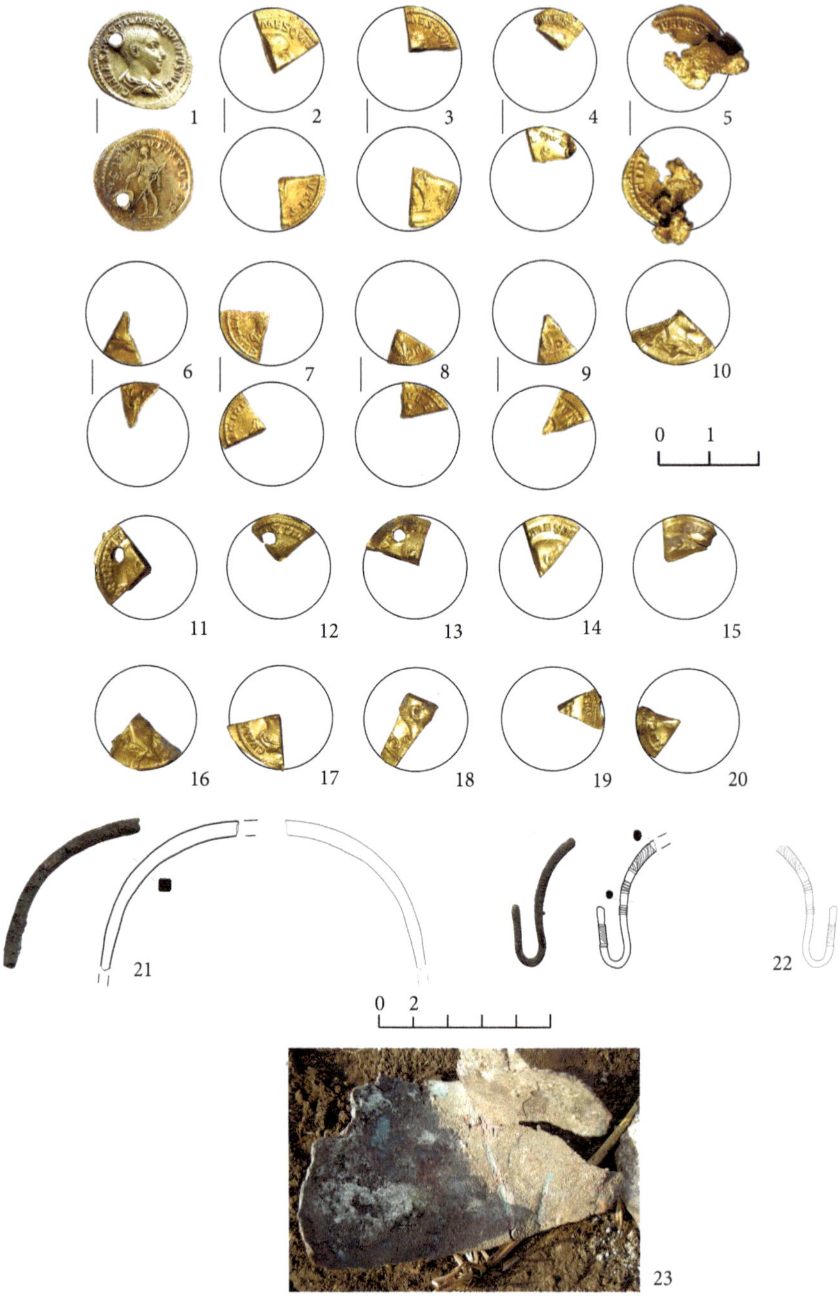

Fig. 8.8. 'Assemblage 2' of the Selysche burial ground in Vinnytsia Region, Ukraine (F.2). From: Bursche and Myzgin (2020: fig. 4). © K. Myzgin.

In eastern Europe, *aureus* finds are also known from graves, such as an *aureus* of Philip I with a portrait of Otacilia Severa, found in grave 265 of the Cherneliv-Rus'ky cemetery.[118] This grave, judging by its pieces of armour, most probably belonged to a member of the local military elite.[119] In 2014, treasure hunters in the Khmelnytskyi region discovered eight *aurei* from the time of Decius along with fragments of Roman bronze cauldrons (F.1). In the vicinity of Shchuchin in Belarus, five coins, also minted during the reign of Decius, were found together (F.3).[120] No precise contextual information is known, but judging by traces of their being in a fire, we can conclude that they were involved with cremation.

At least three assemblages with cut *aurei* in the east Germanic cultural environment are known. Two of them are on the territory of the Wielbark culture—that is, outside the focus area of this chapter—near Stara Wieś in one of the graves of the Ulów burial ground, in the territory of Poland.[121] The other assemblage of cut *aurei* was found in grave 2 of the Selische cremation burial ground in central Ukraine, where one whole *aureus* and 19 fragments of *aurei* from the time of Decius were found, together with a fragment of a Roman bronze cauldron (F.2) (Fig. 8.8).[122] The custom of cutting *aurei* may be connected with the Germanic custom of destroying (spoiling, breaking, cutting) things before putting them into votive contexts.[123]

HOARDS OF GOLD BARBARIAN IMITATIONS (APPENDIX, LIST G)

There is only one single small hoard of gold-plated barbarian imitations. A treasure hunter discovered it in 2017 in the vicinity of Lipovets in the Vinnytsia region of Ukraine (G.1) (Fig. 8.9).[124] All six coins of the hoard were minted with the same dies, imitating an *aureus* of Severus Alexander issued in AD 232 at Rome (*RIC* IV 245). Mass production of gold or gold-plated barbarian imitations occurred here from the 260s,[125] and this particular *RIC* IV 245 imitation is common throughout central and western Ukraine.[126] Presumably, the reason for their mass production came as a result of a decrease in the flow of original gold coins to Barbaricum from the mid-250s, but with continued local demand, possibly

[118] Gereta (2013: 81–3). [119] Madyda-Legutko (2021: 269).

[120] Probably like all other melted or partially melted *aurei* found in eastern Europe; cf. Bursche and Myzgin (2020: 217–19).

[121] Bursche (2013: 151–2; Bursche and Niezabitowska-Wiśniewska (2018: 249–61).

[122] Bursche and Myzgin (2020: 206). [123] In more detail: Bursche and Myzgin (2020: 219).

[124] Bursche and Więcek (2018: 79–80).

[125] By 2015, 288 finds of such coins from the territory of Ukraine and Moldova were known; cf. Anokhin (2015). By early 2023, their known number had tripled.

[126] Bursche and Więcek (2018: 79).

Fig. 8.9. Hoard of gold-plated barbarian imitations from Lipovets', Vinnytsia region (G.1); after Bursche and Więcek (2018: fig. 3). Images from http://barbarous-imitations.narod.ru/. © University of Warsaw, K. Myzgin.

spurred by the victory at Abritus.[127] The Lipovets hoard gives the impression, on the basis of the coins' similarity and relatively well-preserved condition, that it was a fresh batch of coins from a barbarian workshop that were to be sold but were either lost or hidden (by the master or the new owner).[128]

HOARDS OF LATE ROMAN BRONZE COINS (APPENDIX, LIST H)

Until the 2010s, hoards of late Roman bronze coins were known mainly to the west of the Dniester River (H.2, H.5, H.9, and beyond in Romania) and in southern, south-western, and north-western Crimea (H.1, H.3, H.4, H.6, H.7, H.8, H.11, H.13, H.17, H.19). Finds of such hoards are also known from the middle course of the Dnieper (G.12) and in the Seim River basin (H.18). Five new hoards found

[127] Myzgin, Vida, and Więcek (2018: 224, 227).

[128] The assemblage is believed to be dated towards the end of the third century.

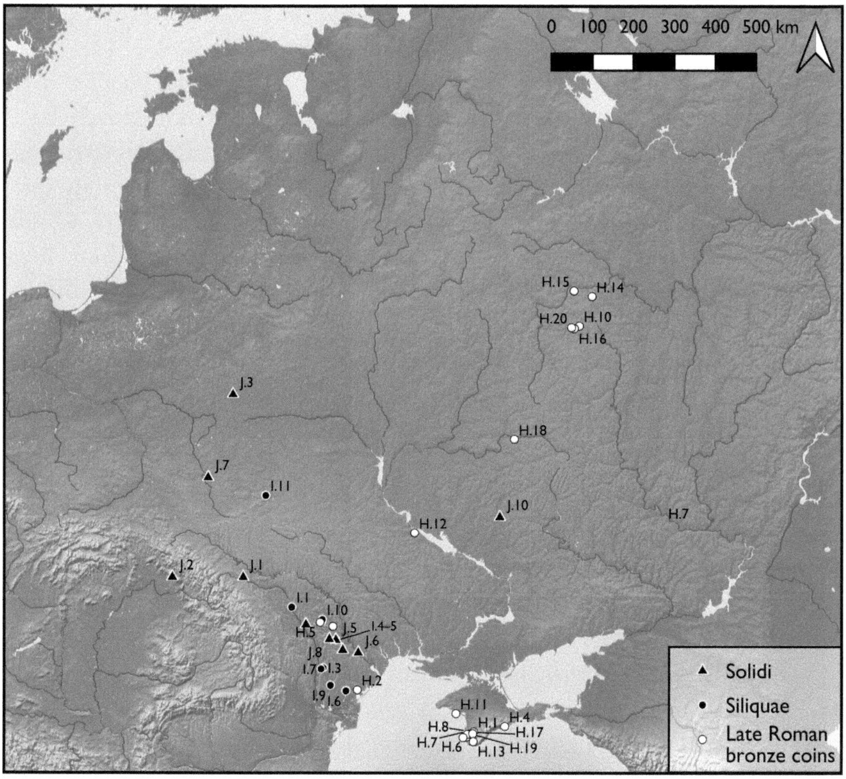

Fig. 8.10. Distribution map of hoards of *solidi*, *siliquae*, and late Roman bronze coins. Map: A. Wilson/K. Myzgin.

between 2019 and 2022 can be added to the existing inventory from the upper Oka River basin in the Tula region in Russia (H.10, H.14, H.15, H.16, H.29) (Fig. 8.10).

The times and circumstances of hoard formation and deposition in different parts of eastern Barbaricum may have varied considerably. In the late Roman and early Byzantine periods, the southern and south-western Crimean territories, including Chersonesus and the Bosporan Kingdom, were in the zone of regular circulation of late Roman coins. This is perfectly illustrated by the hoards from this area, which, along with the late Roman bronze coins that are primarily of very late date, also include local coins from the Bosporan Kingdom (H.4) or Chersonesus (H.7, H.13). At the same time, such hoards usually contain several hundred coins (H.13: 214 coins; H.8: 389 coins; H.6: 450 coins).

Hoards from north-western Crimea (H.1, H.11) belong to the 'barbarian' deposits, distinguished by much more modest volumes (a few dozen coins, except for H.11: 291 and H.15: 140 coins). The hoards from north-western Crimea and the 'Dniester' series are characterized by relatively early coin dates. The coins from the Bakhchisarai hoard (H.1), for example, date only to the period of the

Tetrarchy, though there may have been later issues. The remaining three deposits, however, date mainly from the Constantinian dynasty (H.2, H. 9, H.11). These hoards can be attributed to the involvement of the local barbarian population in trade with nearby Roman provinces.[129] This is supported by the relatively large number of single finds of late Roman bronze coins found in barbarian territories to the west of the Dniester River. These hoards, rather than the single finds, may represent private savings of their owners: the hoard from Lucăşeuca (H.9) was found at a settlement, as well as possibly the hoard from Borysivka (H.2). These could also have been deposits of former *foederati* of the Roman army returning home from service (see below). There is a particular temptation to connect these hoards with certain well-known historical events, such as the expedition of the emperor Valens against the Goths to the Lower Danube in AD 369.[130] It does appear, however, that such a possibility is too hypothetical. Indeed, there is no archaeological evidence that the emperor's campaign was successful, which could have prevented the local tribes from retrieving their deposits. And, of course, there can be many reasons why the owners did not return for their hoards, including epidemics or internal military conflicts.

The other hoards from the more inland areas of eastern Barbaricum have a much broader chronology (except for a few coins from the Sugrovo hoard: H.18), consisting of issues from the Constantinian, Valentinian, and Theodosian dynasties. It is challenging to connect these hoards to trade because the sites of their finds are hundreds of kilometres away from the *limes*. It is more plausible to regard them as deposits of former *foederati*;[131] since the early fourth century the Germanic tribes were quite active enlisting into the Roman army, entering into a multi-year contract (*foedus*).[132] Inhabitants of eastern Europe were most actively recruited for service in the eastern part of the Roman Empire, which is also confirmed by the absolute predominance by eastern mints in the hoards. Although hoards from Moshny and Sugrovo are undoubtedly connected with the area of the Chernyakhiv culture (the area where the *foederati* may have lived after their return), what does the concentration of hoards in the area of the upper Oka River, which is far outside the Chernyakhiv area, indicate? Together with Alexey Vorontsov, I suggest that the finds of late Roman coins here (both single coins and hoards) may reflect migration processes in the Hunnic period (towards the end of the Chernyakhiv culture). These coins would therefore have been brought by groups of the Chernyakhiv population (including former *foederati*) from the Seim River basin. The archaeological evidence from the Upper Oka region supports this because late Roman coins were found on the Krivoluchye-type sites, where a number of items are also connected to Chernyakhiv culture.[133] The latest coins in

[129] Myzgin (2013: 227, 229). [130] Dzigovskiy (2020: 361–6).
[131] Cf. Bursche (1996: 117–19); Alekseenko and Levada (2011: 382).
[132] Bursche (1996: 117). [133] Vorontsov and Myzgin (2019: 255–7).

these hoards (Theodosius II) indirectly suggest the approximate chronology of these processes and the general time of deposition.

HOARDS OF *SILIQUAE* (APPENDIX, LIST I)

Hoards of *siliquae* are known almost exclusively to the west of the Dniester (I.1–I.10). The exception is Verkhiv (I.11), but in this case, all five *siliquae* were used as parts for ornaments. Most of the coins in the *siliquae* hoards date from the time of Constantius II, with only two deposits comprising later coins: Procopius (Lărguța, I.7) and Valens (Taraclia, I.9) (Fig. 8.10).

In 2021, Lilia Dergaciova conducted a comprehensive study of *siliquae* finds from the Dniester–Prut interfluvial region, producing a catalogue of ten hoards and 108 single finds.[134] Dergaciova was able to find die links among the coins in the region's hoards and shows very convincingly that these deposits originated from one large batch of *siliquae* probably imported in the 360s. In the light of written sources, Dergaciova makes a very interesting suggestion that the *siliquae* were delivered to the Dniester–Prut region as payment to the Gothic mercenaries hired by the usurper Procopius to fight against Valens.[135] The good preservation of the coins in the hoards certainly helps support the argument, since the *siliquae* were most probably deposited shortly after being struck and reaching eastern Barbaricum. The time of the production of imitations of Constantius II's *siliquae*, which form part of some of the hoards (I.2, I.6), could provide more clarity. This question requires a separate study, although it is clear that they were produced somewhat later than their original prototypes.

Increasing single finds of *siliquae* and their imitations found by amateurs east of the Dniester in western and central Ukraine (between the middle reaches of the Dniester and the Dnieper) have been recorded since 2008. This material has not yet been published, but the finds are predominantly coins from Constantius II. The lack of hoards of *siliquae* in this area indicates that only a small group of such coins reached this region (along with the Gothic mercenaries or migrants from the Dniester–Prut interfluvial area?). This group of finds probably should be associated with the *siliquae* from the Verkhiv hoard (I.11).[136]

HOARDS OF LATE ROMAN GOLD COINS (APPENDIX, LIST J)

The finds of hoards and single finds of late Roman gold coins in eastern Europe can be divided into coins of the first to third quarter of the fourth century and

[134] Dergaciova (2021: 119–43).
[135] Dergaciova (2021: 155–6).
[136] Myzgin (2019: 35).

coins of the last quarter of the fourth century to first half of the fifth century. The sources and circumstances of these two chronological groups and the circumstances of hoarding and their deposition differ.

For the first periodization of late Roman gold, in the three hoards as well as among the single finds,[137] the absolute majority belong to the period of the dynasty of Constantine. Each of these finds is a particular case. Almost a quarter of the hoard from Brestiv (Ormód) (J.2) comprises of coins issued before Constantine I; it contained two second-century *aurei*, and three *aurei* and a *quinarius* of the Tetrarchic period. The lack of archaeological context makes it virtually impossible to determine how and when this hoard was formed. It is known that the Carpathian area in Roman times and the Great Migration period was an arena of active ethnic mixing and a kind of 'corridor of peoples' through which migrations of different population groups passed.[138] In the past, others have connected this hoard with Sarmatians (Quadi),[139] Hepidians,[140] and northern Thracians,[141] who may have received coins as payment, gifts (*donativa*), or annual payments (*annonae*).[142] More attention should be paid to the presence of second- and third-century pierced *aurei*, which are quite typical for finds from the neighbouring territory of the Chernyakhiv culture. In the Chernyakhiv culture the custom of adding loops to the gold coins (starting en masse with *aurei* of Aurelian) was widely spread at the end of the third century, persisting into the fourth century.[143] This situation may point to the possibility that some coins could have come to the trans-Carpathian region from the Chernyakhiv culture, possibly as a result of migrations or internal exchange, although we should place greater weight on coins coming directly from the Roman Empire. What is unclear is why the hoard was concealed; this could have been caused by Hunnic invasions,[144] or some internal political events at that time.[145] The Bronnaja Hara (J.2) hoard is very similar to the Brestiv hoard (Fig. 8.11). Here, all seven *solidi* were minted during the Constantinian dynasty, are looped, and probably formed part of a single necklace. The hoard was found in an area occupied by the Wielbark culture in the late Roman period.[146]

An extraordinary find is a hoard of seven looped gold medallions from the Constantinian period, discovered at the village of Laskiv (J.7), which also probably formed part of a necklace.[147] It is well known that Roman emperors, with the help of gifts such as medallions, sought to win favour or neutrality from elite barbarians. According to Aleksander Bursche, the owners of the Laskiv hoard may

[137] In 2017, information was available to me about 29 single coin finds from the Constantinian and Valentinian dynasties in Ukraine: Myzgin (2017a: 38). However, this number has now at least doubled.
[138] Vakulenko (2009: 44–5). [139] Prohászka (2007: 36–7). [140] Bóna (1991: 157).
[141] Kotigoroshko (1993: 132, 134).
[142] Cf. Bursche (1996: 110–17); Prohászka (2003: 59–62).
[143] Bursche and Myzgin (2020: 217). [144] Bóna (1991: 157). [145] Prohászka (2007: 37).
[146] Sidarovich (2019: 189–90). [147] Bursche (1998: 167).

Fig. 8.11. Hoard of late Roman *solidi* from Bronnaja Hara, Brest region, Belarus. From Sidarovich (2019). © V. Sidarovich.

have been 'princes' who were in direct contact with Roman administration,[148] but the hoard was only deposited much later in the early Hunnic period (the late fourth century or the first half of the fifth century).[149] In the case of the Laskiv and Bronnaja Hara hoards, from the most eastern parts of the Wielbark culture, we do not know with any certainty that their deposition was connected with an external threat, which may have come from a Hun invasion, because the region probably did not have direct contact with them (see above). Rather, the hoards may testify to an internal political struggle. Whatever the case, we cannot but notice that all three deposits described shared a common custom of placing gold coins as part of necklaces—adornment that should be regarded as a method to emphasize the wealth, prestige, or power of its owners.[150]

The hoards belonging to the second periodization of late Roman gold coins include coins from Theodosius I and later. These deposits differ significantly from the previous group in several ways. First, nearly all these hoards (except for the deposit from Rublivka, J.10) were found to the west of the Dniester, and their distribution does not overlap with *solidi* hoards of the first to the third quarter of the fourth century. Second, these hoards contained considerably more coins than the previous group, which can be deduced from the Chirileni (J.4) and Rublivka hoards (J.10). Third, the coins from these hoards present no traces of secondary use, such as holes or loops, indicating that their function was different from that of the earlier *solidi*. They did not necessarily serve as a display of prestige and power but, rather, served an economic purpose. Igor Gavritukhin rightly believes that these coins record the last inflows to eastern Barbaricum from the Empire's territory; in other words, they mark the final military and political significance of

[148] Bursche (1998: 41). [149] Bursche (1998: 68). [150] Cf. Bursche (1998: 41).

the population.[151] The sources of these coins could have been trade or diplomatic gifts,[152] but the reasons behind their deposition remain unclear.

It is generally believed that the topography of the hoards of late Roman *solidi* indicates a gradual shift of the centres of barbarian power to the west in the early Hunnic period.[153] Nevertheless, there are known rich graves of the Hunnic period (of chieftaincy or princely status), including those with gold items but without gold coins, to the east of the Dnieper.[154] There are several possible reasons why these local power centres stopped receiving gold coins, just as was the case, for example, in the fourth century. I believe the most significant reason may have been the remoteness of these areas from the *limes*, i.e. the lack of physical ability to trade with the Roman provinces. If these deposits were diplomatic gifts, they could have been paid out by the Roman administration to the 'nearest' barbarians. However, there are exceptions, such as the Rublivka hoard in eastern Ukraine, where it is possible that it could be connected with a particular post-Chernyakhiv early Germanic 'kingdom' which existed in the Vorskla River basin.[155]

CLOSING REMARKS

Just as the ethnocultural history of the territory of eastern Europe during the Roman and Great Migration periods was complex and multidimensional, so were the sources, reasons, and circumstances of the influx of the various categories of Roman coins. When studying the processes of hoarding and deposition of Roman coin in Barbaricum, the completeness and reliability of the information, the proximity of places of finds to the frontiers of the Roman Empire, the dynamics and character of archaeological development of areas in which coins are found, the character and chronology of accompanying items, the presence and character of unofficial coins, and other aspects should be considered together and as a whole. Unfortunately, not all the components are always known.

Another important factor is the recent enormous increase in information about new Roman coin finds in eastern Europe, including hoards, primarily as a consequence of the 'era of the metal detector'. This has radically changed views on the quantity and nature of almost all categories of coins in Barbaricum. Only recently have hoards of deposits of *sestertii*, provincial Roman coins, gold-plated barbarian imitations, and probable assemblages of *aurei* from the first/third centuries and copies of Roman imperial *denarii* become known in eastern

[151] Gavritukhin (2005: 236). [152] Cf. Myzgin (2013: 230).
[153] Cf. Gavritukhin (2005: 236–7); Lyubichev and Myzgin (2020: 767).
[154] Radiush (2014: 234–51). [155] Kazanski (1997: 24–6); Gavritukhin (2005: 237).

Barbaricum. Moreover, the distribution of *antoniniani* and late Roman bronze hoards has fundamentally changed. Due to new finds, the areas of deposits of late Roman *solidi* and *siliquae* have expanded significantly. The ideas about the character of the largest category of finds—hoards of *denarii*—have evolved considerably due to the study of barbarian imitations in their composition and accompanying items in these hoards. This has made it possible to recast ideas about the scale of circulation of Roman silver in Barbaricum and the directions of migrations in the early Hunnic era.

The study of practically all categories of the hoards of Roman coins in eastern Europe (except for the early Roman *sestertii*) has once again demonstrated that the Chernyakhiv culture was the facilitator of the ethnocultural development of this region in late Roman times and during the Great Migration period. Most Roman coins come from this culture, and impulses for a partial redistribution of them in Barbaricum derived from it. Since this culture was under strong Roman provincial influences, the dynamics of the influx of Roman coins in the third-fifth centuries depended entirely on the nature and rhythms of Roman–barbarian relations.

After more than two centuries of research, the study of hoards of Roman coins in eastern Europe is still in its infancy. On the one hand, the reason for this is the tremendous number of new finds which have yet to be fully published. On the other hand, the knowledge base for many finds is still limited: many 'old' hoards need thorough verification or even republishing, and most of the 'new' hoards lack information that would allow them to be used in the future. This chapter is a preliminary, but important, presentation of the problems and the evidence. Creating a fuller picture is a matter for the future and may not be so far away.

ACKNOWLEDGEMENTS

I prepared this chapter as part of the Coins and Barbarians between Southern Scandinavia and the Black Sea Region in the Late Roman Period project, which I carried out in 2021–3 at the Centre for Baltic and Scandinavian Archaeology (Schleswig, Germany) as part of the Alexander von Humboldt Foundation fellowship. Parts of this chapter are the result of research undertaken for The Neural Network of Solidi: Contacts between Romano-Byzantine and Barbarian Worlds in the Light of Die-linked Gold Coins Found in Europe and Central Asia project, conducted at the Faculty of Archaeology, University of Warsaw, and funded by National Centre of Science Poland (2020/39/B/HS3/01513).

I express my sincere gratitude to all colleagues who helped me with support, advice, and guidance during the preparation of this chapter, including Aleksander Bursche, Arkadiusz Dymowski, Cristian Găzdac, Benjamin Hellings, Maxim Levada, Marjanko Pilekić, Marguerite Spoerri Butcher, Vital Sidarovich, and others.

Appendix: Lists of Roman coin hoards from eastern Europe

LIST A. HOARDS OF *SESTERTII*

1. ***Koporje 1, Leningrad Region*** (RUS), 30 coins, Trajan–Antoninus Pius (Sharov, Palaguta, and Khavrin 2010: 337–8)
2. ***Koporje 2, Leningrad Region*** (RUS), 13 coins (12 *sestertii* and one *denarius*), Titus–Antoninus Pius (Sharov, Palaguta, and Khavrin 2010: 338–9)
3. ***Myrhorod, Poltava Region*** (UA), 12 coins, Antoninus Pius–Commodus (not published)
4. ***Perehinka, Khmelnyts'kyi Region*** (UA), 9 coins, Marcus Aurelius–Gordian III (Nadvirnyak, Pohorilets, and Nadvirnyak 2016)
5. ***Rokytne, Kyiv Region*** (UA), 60 coins, Trajan–Marcus Aurelius (not published)
6. ***Trubchevsk, Briansk Region*** (RUS), 14 coins, Trajan–Septimius Severus (Voroniatov and Stoliarova 2020: 75, fig. 14; 76; Riabchevskiy 2020: 149, no. 34).

LIST B. HOARDS OF ROMAN IMPERIAL *DENARII*

1–127. Nine hoards from Belarus, 9 hoards from Moldova, 15 hoards from the Russian Federation, 94 hoards from Ukraine (listed in Dymowski *et al.* 2020: 204–5, nos 2–10; 210–11, nos 105–13; 226–9, nos 342–54; 234–43, nos 443–537)

128. ***Baykivka, Vinnytsia Region*** (UA), at least 160 coins, 1st–2nd c. (not published)
129. ***Bilopillia (environs), Sumy region*** (UA), 180 coins, Trajan–Septimius Severus (not published)
130. ***Borderland of Ternopil' and Ivano-Frankivs'k Region*** (UA), *c.* 500 coins, Nero–Antoninus Pius (not published)
131. ***Buryakove, Kharkiv Region*** (UA), 52 coins, Trajan–Septimius Severus (Kodatskiy and Myzgin 2020: 465–78)
132. ***Buzhany, Volyn Region*** (UA), 265 coins, Domitian–Septimius Severus (Royko and Kal'kov 2018: 70–1)
133. ***Central Ukraine (Cherkassy Region?)*** (UA), 21 coins, Domitian–Commodus (not published)
134. ***Charniauka, Hrodna Region*** (BY), 87 coins (15 survived), Trajan–Commodus (Sidarovich 2021: 178–9)
135. ***Cherkassy Region*** (UA), at least 259 *denarii*, 1st–2nd c. (not published)
136. ***Cherkassy Region*** (UA), *c.* 400 coins, 1st–2nd c. (not published)
137. ***Cherkasy Region*** (UA), 161 coins, Vespasian–Commodus (not published)
138. ***Cherkasy Region*** (UA), 6 coins (soldered), 2nd c. (not published)
139. ***Chernivtsi Region*** (UA), 111 coins, Vespasian–Antoninus Pius (not published)
140. ***Chernivtsi Region*** (UA), *c.* 500 coins, 1st–2nd c. (not published)
141. ***Chyhyryn (environs), Cherkassy Region*** (UA), 32 coins, Trajan–Commodus (not published)
142. ***Dmytrivka, Mykolayiv Region*** (UA), 10 coins, Nero–Marcus Aurelius (Stolba and Peter 2021: 223–32)
143. ***Dorozhnoe, Crimea*** (UA), 150 coins, Titus–Elagabal (Kropotkin 1961: 63, no. 573)
144. ***Fastiv (environs), Kyiv Region*** (UA), *c.* 70 coins (soldered, partly melted), 1st–2nd c. (not published)

145. ***Goshcha (environs), Rivne Region*** (UA), 220 coins, Hadrian–Septimius Severus (not published)
146. ***Havryshivka, Vinnytsia Region*** (UA), at least 50 coins, Vespasian–Commodus (not published)
147. ***Ivano-Frankivs'k (environs), Ivano-Frankivs'k Region*** (UA), 385 coins, Nero–Marcus Aurelius (not published)
148. ***Kadykovka-Balaklava, Crimea*** (UA), 57 coins, Vitellius–Severus Alexander (Filippenko and Alekseenko 2000: 167–75)
149. ***Kapitanivka, Kirovohrad Region*** (UA), 28 coins, Trajan–Septimius Severus (not published)
150. ***Kharkiv Region*** (UA), 31 coins, Trajan–Commodus (not published)
151. ***Khmelivka, Zhytomyr Region*** (UA), 63 coins, Vespasian–Septimius Severus (Myzgin and Petrauskas 2021: 255–69)
152. ***Khmelnyts'kyi or Vinnytsia Region*** (UA), 30 coins, Trajan–Septimius Severus (not published)
153. ***Khmelnyts'kyi or Vinnytsia Region*** (UA), 88 coins, 1st–2nd c. (not published)
154. ***Khmelnyts'kyi Region*** (UA), 15 coins, Vespasian–Commodus (not published)
155. ***Khmelnyts'kyi Region*** (UA), 3 coins (soldered), 2nd c. (not published)
156. ***Koblevo, Mykolayiv Region*** (UA), 86 coins, Vespasian–Commodus (not published)
157. ***Kolomyia, Ivano-Frankivs'k Region*** (UA), 28 coins, Vespasian–Antoninus Pius (not published)
158. ***Konotop (environs), Sumy Region*** (UA), 25 coins, Hadrian–Septimius Severus (not published)
159. ***Kurchoucy, Hrodna Region*** (BY), at least 5 coins, Hadrian–Marcus Aurelius (Sidarovich 2021: 179)
160. ***Kyiv Region (?)*** (UA), 6 coins, 2nd c. (not published)
161. ***Kyiv Region*** (UA), 138 coins, Galba–Antoninus Pius (not published)
162. ***Kyiv Region*** (UA), 291 coins (incl. 4 imitations), Hadrian–Commodus (not published)
163. ***L'viv Region (?)*** (UA), 6 coins, Vitellius–Hadrian (not published)
164. ***L'viv Region*** (UA), 114 coins, Hadrian–Septimius Severus (not published)
165. ***L'viv Region*** (UA), 47 coins, Vespasian–Antoninus Pius (not published)
166. ***L'viv Region*** (UA), 757 coins, 1st–2nd c. (not published)
167. ***L'viv Region*** (UA), at least 125 *denarii*, at least Hadrian–Septimius Severus (not published)
168. ***Lisovychi, L'viv Region*** (UA), 40 coins, Trajan–Caracalla (not published)
169. ***Lozovata, Vinnytsia Region*** (UA), *c.* 160 coins, 1st–2nd c. (not published)
170. ***Lugovoe, Crimea*** (UA), 22 coins, Nero–Caracalla (Kropotkin 1961: 64–5, no. 609)
171. ***Matysiv, Cherkassy Region*** (UA), 286 coins, Trajan–Septimius Severus (not published)
172. ***Merva, Volyn Region*** (UA), 80 coins, Vespasian–Commodus (not published)
173. ***Myronivka (environs), Kyiv Region*** (UA), 310 coins, Trajan–Commodus (not published)
174. ***Mytky 1, Vinnytsia Region*** (UA), 10 coins, Hadrian–Commodus (Bakalets' 2019: 12)
175. ***Mytky 2, Vinnytsia Region*** (UA), 7 coins (incl. 1 imitation), Vespasianus or Titus–Commodus (Bakalets' 2019: 12)
176. ***Orativ, Vinnytsia Region*** (UA), *c.* 300 coins, at least Nerva–Septimius Severus (not published)
177. ***Orlinoe, Crimea*** (UA), 22 coins (10 survived), Trajan–Marcus Aurelius (Isaenko and Sukhoruchenko 2017: 7)

178. ***Piaschanka, Hrodna Region*** (BY), at least 6 coins, Hadrian–Commodus (Sidarovich 2021: 179)
179. ***Pohrebyshche, Vinnytsia Region*** (UA), *c.* 30 coins, 1st–2nd c., and perhaps *solidus* of Constantius II (not published)
180. ***Polonne (environs), Khmelnyts'kyi Region***(UA), 60 coins (incl. 2 imitations), Vespasian–Commodus (not published)
181. ***Poltava Region (?)*** (UA), 10 coins, Hadrian–Commodus (not published)
182. ***Poltava Region (?)*** (UA), 12 coins, Trajan–Commodus (not published)
183. ***Poltava Region*** (UA), 11 coins (soldered and partly melted), 1st–2nd c. (not published)
184. ***Poltava Region*** (UA), 120 coins, Trajan–Septimius Severus (not published)
185. ***Poltava Region*** (UA), 125 coins, Hadrian–Septimius Severus (not published)
186. ***Pribrezhnoe, Crimea*** (UA), at least 57 coins, Republican *denarius* of P. Clodius, Augustus–Titus (Kropotkin 1961: 65, no. 617)
187. ***Pysarivka*** (or ***Hrushkivtsi***), ***Vinnytsia Region*** (UA), at least 20 coins, Trajan–Commodus (not published)
188. ***Repino, Crimea*** (UA), at least 38 coins, Antoninus Pius–Elagabal (Sidorenko 2009: 534–49)
189. ***Rivne Region*** (UA), 6 coins, Vespasian–Hadrian (not published)
190. ***Sevastopol', Crimea*** (UA), 17 coins (12 survived), Trajan–Commodus (Isaenko and Sukhoruchenko 2017: 6–7)
191. ***Shilovo, Riazan' Region*** (RUS), 61 coins, Vespasian–Commodus (Akhmedov, Gavrilov, and Choref 2018: 436–57)
192. ***Simferopol' (Scythian Neapolis), Crimea*** (UA), 130 coins (incl. 2 Greek coins), Nero–Macrinus (Kropotkin 1961: 65, no. 622)
193. ***South-West Crimea*** (UA), at least 18 coins, Marcus Aurelius–Severus Alexander (Sidorenko 2009: 543–4)
194. ***Staryi Krym, Crimea*** (UA), at least 30 coins (11 survived), Vespasian–Hadrian (Isaenko and Sukhoruchenko 2017: 6)
195. ***Sumy Region*** (UA), 12 coins, Trajan–Septimius Severus (not published)
196. ***Sumy Region*** (UA), 243 coins (incl. 2 imitations), Trajan–Didius Julianus (not published)
197. ***Turbiv, Vinnytsia Region*** (UA), *c.* 1,200 coins, Trajan–Didius Julianus (not published)
198. ***Ukraine 1*** (UA), 48 coins, 1st–2nd c. (not published)
199. ***Ukraine 2*** (UA), 111 coins, 1st–2nd c. (not published)
200. ***Ukraine 3*** (UA), 63 coins, Hadrian–Commodus (not published)
201. ***Ukraine 4, Kyiv or Cherkassy Region?*** (UA), 12 coins, Antoninus Pius–Commodus (not published)
202. ***Ukraine 5*** (UA), 88 coins, Vespasian–Septimius Severus (not published)
203. ***Ukraine 6*** (UA), 10 coins, Vespasian–Antoninus Pius (not published)
204. ***Ukraine 7, Crimea?*** (UA), 11 (or 13?) coins, Trajan–Septimius Severus (or Maximinus I?) (not published)
205. ***Ukraine 8*** (UA), 20 coins, Trajan–Septimius Severus (not published)
206. ***Ukraine 9*** (UA), 157 coins, 1st–2nd c. (not published)
207. ***Ukraine 10*** (UA), 13 coins, 1st–2nd c. (not published)
208. ***Ukraine 11*** (?) (UA), at least 72 coins, 1st–2nd c. (not published)
209. ***Ukraine 12*** (UA), 6 coins, Hadrian–Septimius Severus (not published)

210. ***Ukraine 13, Zhytomyr Region?*** (UA), *c.* 50 coins, at least Trajan–Commodus (not published)
211. ***Ukraine 14*** (UA), at least 15 coins (soldered and melted), 1st–2nd c. (not published)
212. ***Ukraine 15*** (UA), 7 coins (soldered), 1st–2nd c. (not published)
213. ***Ukraine 16*** (UA), *c.* 25 coins (soldered and melted), 1st–2nd c. (not published)
214. ***Ukraine 17*** (UA), 3 coins (soldered), 2nd c. (not published)
215. ***Ukraine 18*** (UA), 4 coins (soldered), 1st–2nd c. (not published)
216. ***Ukraine 19*** (UA), 4 coins (soldered), 1st–2nd c. (not published)
217. ***Ukraine 20*** (UA), 3 coins (soldered), 2nd c. (not published)
218. ***Uman' (environs), Cherkassy Region*** (UA), 126 coins, Trajan–Septimius Severus (not published)
219. ***Varanki, Hrodna Region*** (BY), 111 coins, (Sidarovich 2021: 178)
220. ***Vinnytsia, Vinnytsia Region*** (UA), *c.* 280 coins, 1st–2nd c. (not published)
221. ***Vinnytsia Region*** (UA), 102 coins, Otho–Caracalla (not published)
222. ***Vinnytsia Region*** (UA), 4 coins (soldered), Trajan–Hadrian (not published)
223. ***Vinnytsia Region*** (UA), 6 coins (soldered), 1st–2nd c. (not published)
224. ***Vinnytsia Region*** (UA), 6 coins, (soldered), 1st–2nd c. (?) (not published)
225. ***Vinnytsia Region*** (UA), at least 15 coins (soldered and melted), 1st–2nd c. (not published)
226. ***Volhynia (?)*** (UA), 116 coins, 1st–2nd c. (not published)
227. ***Volhynia*** (UA), 54 coins, Hadrian–Septimius Severus (not published)
228. ***West (?) Ukraine*** (UA), 4 coins, Trajan–Commodus (not published)

LIST C. HOARDS (?) OF CAST ROMAN IMPERIAL *DENARII*

1. ***Ukraine*** (UA), 7 coins, Antoninus Pius–Commodus (not published)
2. ***Khmelnyts'kyi Region (?)*** (UA), 13 coins, Hadrian–Marcus Aurelius (not published)

LIST D. HOARDS OF *ANTONINIANI*

1. ***Dolinnoe, Crimea*** (UA), 120 coins (*denarii, antoniniani*), Caracalla–Trajan Decius (Pioro and Gertsen 1974: 81–90)
2. ***Haisyn, Vinnytsia Region*** (UA), 32 coins (8 *denarii*, 24 *antoniniani*), Caracalla–Gallus/Volusian (Kodatskiy and Myzgin 2017)
3. ***Horokhiv, Volyn Region*** (UA), *c.* 500 coins (*denarii, antoniniani*), Septimius Severus–Gordian III (not published; short information: Myzgin and Perederey 2021: 316).
4. ***Kerch, Crimea*** (UA), 71 coins (*denarii, antoniniani*), Septimius Severus–Valerian I (Kunina 1962: 329–42)
5. ***Khmelnyts'kyi Region*** (UA), 81 coins (*antoniniani*), Gallienus–Claudius II (not published)
6. ***Khmelnyts'kyi Region*** (UA), 167 coins (*denarii*?, *antoniniani*), no information about rulers (not published)
7. ***Myshkivtsi, Ternopil Region*** (UA), at least 7 coins (1 *denarius*, 6 *antoniniani*), Severus Alexander–Decius (Bursche 1996: 154, no. 56)
8. ***Mytky, Vinnytsia Region*** (UA), 6 coins (3 *denarius*, 3 *antoniniani*), Septimius Severus–Gallienus (Bakalets' 2019: 12)

9. ***Odessa, Odessa Region*** (UA), 44 coins (*antoniniani*), Gallienus–Claudius II (unpublished; short information: Myzgin and Perederey 2021: 316)
10. ***Ostapkivtsi, Khmelnyts'kyi Region*** (UA), *c.* 300 coins of which 167 survived (16 *denarii*, 151 *antoniniani*), Septimius Severus–Valerian I (Myzgin and Perederey 2021: 314)
11. ***Perehinka, Khmelnyts'kyi Region*** (UA), 41 coins (*antoniniani*), Gordian III–Gallus/ Volusian (Nadvirniak, Pohorelec, and Nadvirniak (Jr.) 2017)
12. ***Pereval'noe, Crimea*** (UA), 34 coins (4 *denarii* and 30 *antoniniani*), Antoninus Pius–Gallienus (Choref and Yakushechkin 2016)
13. ***Protiagaylovka, municipality of Bender (Tighina)*** (MD), at least 12 coins (2 *denarii*, 10 *antoniniani*), Severus Alexander–Philip I (Rozumenko 1982: 136)
14. ***Stanislavchyk, Vinnytsia Region*** (UA), *c.* 80 coins (*denarii*?, *antoniniani*), including Gordian III (not published)
15. ***Tiraspol, municipality of Tiraspol*** (MD), *c.* 400 coins, 11 coins survived (1 *denarius*, 10 *antoniniani*), Severus Alexander–Philip I (Rozumenko 1982: 136)
16. ***Vasil'evka, municipality of Dubosary*** (MD), at least 11 coins (2 *denarii*, 9 *antoniniani*), Severus Alexander–Gallus (Rozumenko 1982: 135).
17. ***Vojkove, Crimea*** (UA), at least 7 coins (*antoniniani*), Caracalla–Valerian I (Abramzon and Frolova 2008: 385–6).
18. ***Zhmerynka, Vinnytsia Region*** (UA), at least 9 coins (1 *denarius*, 8 *antoniniani*), Septimius Severus–Decius (not published)

LIST E. HOARDS OF ROMAN PROVINCIAL COINS

1. ***Arabat Spit, Crimea*** (UA), 4 coins (3 coins minted in Trapezus, one coin minted in Caesarea in Cappadocia) (Myzgin 2020: 150)
2. ***Turec, Hrodna Region*** (BY), 21 coins (Alexandrian tetradrachms), Probus–Maximian (Sidarovich 2013)

LIST F. HOARDS (?) OF *AUREI*

1. ***Khmelnyts'kyi Region*** (UA), 8 coins (in cremation; all pierced), Decius (Bursche and Myzgin 2020: 217)
2. ***Selyshche, Vinnytsia Region*** (UA), 20 coins (1 pierced and 19 cut), Decius (Bursche and Myzgin 2020: 206)
3. ***Shchuchyn, Hrodna Region*** (BY), 5 coins (in cremation?; all pierced), Decius (Shtalenkov 2017: 68)

LIST G. HOARD OF GOLD BARBARIAN IMITATIONS

1. ***Lipovets', Vinnytsia Region*** (UA), 6 coins (all pierced), prototype: *aureus* of Severus Alexander, 232 AD, *RIC* IV 245 (Bursche and Więcek 2018: 79–80).

LIST H. LATE ROMAN BRONZE COINS

1. ***Bakhchisaray, Crimea*** (UA), at least 5 coins, Diocletian–Licinius (Choref 2013: 209–10)

2. ***Borysivka, Odessa Region*** (UA), at least 9 coins, Constantine dynasty (Kropotkin 1961: 71, no. 774)
3. ***Crimea (unlocated)*** (UA), *c.* 400 coins, Theodosius I–Valentinian III (Isaenko and Sukhoruchenko: 2020)
4. ***Dachnoe, Crimea*** (UA), 517 late Bosporan coins and 65 late Roman coins, Maximian–Constantine I (Kropotkin 1961: 63–4, no. 578)
5. ***Hirişeni, Teleneşti District*** (MD), at least 107 coins, 4th c. (not published)
6. ***Inkerman, Crimea*** (UA), 450 coins, Maximian–Honorius (Korshenko 2011: 114–18)
7. ***Kaponiry, Crimea*** (UA), 242 coins, coins of Chersonesus mint and Roman coins, Diocletian–Honorius (Korshenko 2012: 21–3)
8. ***Krasnozorenskoe, Crimea*** (UA), 389 coins, Gratian–Honorius (Korshenko 2011: 110–14)
9. ***Lucăşeuca, Orhei District*** (MD), 43 coins, Constans–Julian II (Popa and Ciobanu 2003: 60)
10. ***Malaya Strekalovka, Tula Region*** (RUS), 11 coins, Constantine and Valentinian dynasties (Vorontsov and Myzgin 2019: 257–8; Vorontsov 2023: 400)
11. ***Molochnoe, Crimea*** (UA), 297 coins, Constantine I–Constantius II (Kovalenko 2011: 89–107)
12. ***Moshny, Cherkassy Region*** (UA), 71 coins, Constantius II–Theodosius I (Alekseenko and Levada 2011: 373–95)
13. ***Novobobrovka, Crimea*** (UA), 214 coins, coins of Chersonesus and Roman coins: Licinius–Anastasius (Korshenko 2013: 31–2)
14. ***Pavlovskoe, Tula Region*** (RUS), 19 coins, Kushan–Sasanid (?) coin, Constantine I–Theodosius II (Vorontsov 2023: 392)
15. ***Rozhdestvenno, Tula Region*** (RUS), 140 coins, Constantine I–Theodosius II (Vorontsov 2023: 392–4)
16. ***Samokhvalovka, Tula Region*** (RUS), 13 coins, Constantius II–Theodosius II (Vorontsov 2023: 392)
17. ***Streleckaya Buchta, Crimea*** (UA), 178 coins, Valerian–Justinian I (Kropotkin 1961: 65, no. 627)
18. ***Sugrovo, Kursk Region*** (RUS), at least 9 coins, Constantine dynasty (Radiush 2008: 142, no. 15)
19. ***Verkhnesadovoe, Crimea*** (UA), at least 15 coins, Constantine I–Theodosius I (Dem'ianchuk 2008: 419–24)
20. ***Vozdremo, Tula Region*** (RUS), 20 coins, 4th–early 5th c. (Vorontsov 2023: 394)

LIST I. HOARDS OF *SILIQUAE*

1. ***Branişte, Rîşcani District*** (MD), dozens of coins, 1 coin survived, Constantius II (Dergaciova 2021: 121)
2. ***Budăi, Teleneşti District*** (MD), 126 coins (incl. 1 imitation), Constantius II (Dergaciova 2021: 119–21)
3. ***Capaclia, Cantemir District*** (MD), *c.* 100 coins, 1 coin survived, Constantius II (Dergaciova 2021: 121)
4. ***Chişinău*** (MD), at least 250 coins, 21 coins survived, Constantius II (Dergaciova 2021: 121–2)
5. ***Chişinău*** (MD), *c.* 200 coins, Constantius II (Dergaciova 2021: 122)
6. ***Holms'ke, Odessa Region*** (UA), 93 coins (incl. 1 imitation), Constantius II (Dergaciova 2021: 123–7)
7. ***Lărguţa, Cantemir District*** (MD), 86 coins, Constantius II–Procopius (Dergaciova 2021: 127–8)

8. ***Moldova*** (so called 'Chişinău, the airport'), at least 6 coins, Constantius II (Dergaciova 2021: 122–3)
9. ***Taraclia, Taraclia District*** (MD), a few dozen, 4 coins survived, Constantius II–Valens (Dergaciova 2021: 128–9)
10. ***Teleneşti (environs), Teleneşti District*** (MD), at least 26 coins, Constantius II (Dergaciova 2021: 129–31)
11. ***Verkhiv, Rivne Region*** (UA), 5 coins (as part of pendants), Constantius II (partly published in Myzgin 2019: 34, fig. 1; 35)

LIST J. HOARDS OF LATE ROMAN GOLD COINS

1. ***Beleluya, Ivano-Frankivs'k Region*** (UA), 3 coins survived (*solidi*), Theodosius I–Honorius (Kropotkin 1961: 74–5, no. 872)
2. ***Brestiv (Ormód), Zakarpattia Region*** (UA), 25 coins (5 *aurei*, 1 *quinarius*, 19 *solidi*; 3 pierced coins, 10 with suspension loops), Trajan (Sabina)–Valens (Prohászka 2009: 485, no. 4; Eremić 2014: 124–9)
3. ***Bronnaja Hara, Brest Region*** (BY), 7 coins (*solidi*; all with suspension loops), Constantine I–Constantius II (Sidarovich 2019: 185–6)
4. ***Chirileni, Ungheni District*** (MD), 213 coins, 13 coins survived (*solidi*), Gratian–Honorius (Popa and Ciobanu 2003: 46–7)
5. ***Chişinău*** (MD), 1 coin survived (*solidus*), Theodosius II (Popa and Ciobanu 2003: 53)
6. ***Cremenciug, Soroca District*** (MD), 2 coins survived (*solidi*), Theodosius I (Popa and Ciobanu 2003: 64)
7. ***Laskiv, Volyn Region*** (UA), 7 coins (medallions; all with suspension loops), 2 coins survived, Constantius II–Constans (Bursche 1998: 66–9, 234–5)
8. ***Malkoci, Ialoveni District*** (MD), 1 coin survived (*solidus*), Theodosius II (Popa and Ciobanu 2003: 52)
9. ***Ochiul Roş, Anenii Noi District*** (MD), 1 coin survived (*solidus*), Marcian (Ciobanu 1999: 118)
10. ***Rublivka, Poltava Region*** (UA), 201 coins (*solidi*), Valentinian II–Marcian (Kropotkin 1961: 72, no. 813)

ABBREVIATIONS

RIC IV Mattingly, H., Sydenham, E. A., and Sutherland, C. H. V. (1930). *The Roman Imperial Coinage*. Volume IV, part II: *Macrinus–Pupienus (217–238)*. London.

REFERENCES

Abramzon, M. G. and Frolova, N. A. (2008). *Korpus bosporskih kladov antichnyh monet,* tom 1: *1834–2005 gg*. Simferopol and Kerch.

Aitchison, N. B. (1988). 'Roman wealth, native ritual: Coin hoards within and beyond Roman Britain', *World Archaeology* 20.2: 270–84.

Akhmedov, I. R. (2010). '«Svev» iz Mordovii. K izucheniyu kul'turnyh kontaktov povolzhskih finnov v III v. n.e.', *Rossijskaya arheologiya* 1: 26–37.

Akhmedov, I. R., Belotserkovskaya I. V., and Rumiantseva, O. S. (2007). 'Glava 3. Kul'tura ryazano-okskih mogil'nikov', in I. O. Gavritukhin and A. M. Oblomskiy (eds), *Vostochnaya Evropa v seredine I tys. n.e. Arheologiya slavyan i ih sosedej* (Ranneslavyanskij mir 9). Moscow, 133–275.

Akhmedov, I. R., Gavrilov, A. P., and Choref, M. M. (2018). 'Klad rimskih monet I–II vv. iz Srednego Pooch'ya', *Materialy po arheologii i istorii antichnogo i srednevekovogo Prichernomor'ya* 10: 436–57.

Alekseenko, N. A. and Levada, M. Ye. (2011). 'Klad u sela Moshny', *Stratum plus* 4: 373–95.

Andrzejowski, J. (2010). 'Przeworsk Culture. A brief story (for the foreigners)', in U. Lund Hansen and A. Bitner-Wróblewska (eds), *Worlds Apart? Contacts across the Baltic Sea in the Iron Age. Network Denmark-Poland, 2005-2008*. Copenhagen and Warsaw, 59–110.

Anokhin, O. V. (2015). *Fal'shyvomonetnichestvo u varvarskikh plemion na territorii sovremennoj Ukrainy i Moldovy. Katalog varvarskikh podrazhanij*. Dniptopetrovs'k.

Antonovich, V. B. (1878). 'Opisanie Kievskogo klada, soderzhashchego rimskie monety III–IV v.v.', *Drevnosti* VI: 241–4.

Aybabin, A. I. and Khayredinova, E. A. (2017). *Krymskie goty strany Dori (seredina III–VII v.)*. Simferopol.

Bakalets', O. (2019). 'Znakhidky rymskykh monet na poselenniakh cherniakhivskoi kultury II-IV st.', *Numizmatyka i falerystyka* 3: 10–15.

Bashkatov, Yu. Yu. and Terpilovskiy, R. V. (2010). 'Pozdnezarubineckie pamyatniki Srednego Podneprov'ya', in A. M. Oblomskiy (ed.), *Pozdnezarubineckie pamyatniki na territorii Ukrainy (vtoraya polovina I—II v. n.e.)* (Ranneslavyanskij mir 12). Moscow, 36–44.

Beliavets, V. G. (2016). 'Stan i aktualnyia prablemy vyvuchennia pomnikaŭ postzarubinetskaha haryzontu ŭ Belaruskim Palessi', in O. N. Levko and V. H. Belevets (eds), *Slaviane na terrytorii Belarusy v dogosudarstvennyj period*, vol. 1. Minsk, 334–83.

Bland, R. (2012). 'From Gordian III to the Gallic Empire (AD 238–274)', in W. Metcalf (ed.), *The Oxford Handbook of Greek and Roman Coinage*. New York, 514–37.

Bland, R. (2018). *Coin Hoards and Hoarding in Roman Britain AD 43–c.498*. London.

Bóna, I. (1991). *Das Hunnenreich*. Budapest.

Braichevskiy, M. Yu. (1959). *Rymska moneta ta terytorii Ukrainy*. Kyiv.

Bursche, A. (1983). 'Moneta i kruszec w kulturze wielbarskiej w okresie późnorzymskim', *Przegląd Archeologiczny* 31: 59.

Bursche, A. (1996). *Later Roman-Barbarian Contacts in Central Europe* (Studien zu Fundmünzen der Antike 11). Berlin.

Bursche, A. (1998). *Złote medaliony rzymskie w Barbaricum. Symbolika prestiżu i władzy społeczeństw barbarzyńskich u schyłku starożytności* (Światowit Supplement, Series A: Antiquity 2). Warsaw.

Bursche, A. (2002). 'Circulation of Roman coinage in Northern Europe in Late Antiquity', *Histoire & Mesure* 17.3–4: 121–44.

Bursche, A. (2013). 'The battle of Abritus, the Imperial treasury and *aurei* in Barbaricum', *Numismatic Chronicle* 173: 151–69.

Bursche, A. and Myzgin, K. (2020). 'Mid-3rd century Gothic invasions: Coins and archaeology in Barbaricum', *Journal of Roman Archaeology* 33: 195–229.

Bursche, A. and Niezabitowska-Wiśniewska, B. (2018). 'Two antique gold coins from Ulów in Roztocze', in B. Niezabitowska-Wiśniewska, P. Łuczkiewicz, S. Sadowski, M. Stasiak-Cyran, and M. Erdrich (eds), *Studia barbarica. Profesorowi Andrzejowi Kokowskiemu w 65. rocznicę urodzin*, vol. 2. Lublin, 248–67.

Bursche, A. and Więcek, T. (2018). 'Novye dannye k izucheniyu varvarskih podrazhanij na territorii Vostochnoj Evropy', in M. V. Liubichev and K. V. Myzgin (eds), *Khronologiya i monetnye nahodki pozdnerimskogo vremeni i epohi Velikogo pereseleniya narodov. Aktual'nye arheologicheskie issledovaniya v Central'noj i Vostochnoj Evrope (materialy polevogo seminara na baze ekspedicii vozle s. Vojtenki 15–17 sentyabrya 2016 g.)* (Ostrogothica-Serie: Hefte 3). Kharkiv, 56–75.

Choref, M. M. (2013). 'K voprosu o periodizacii denezhnogo obrashcheniya Tavriki v epohu rimskogo gospodstva', *Stratum plus* 4: 191–215.

Choref, M. M. and Yakushechkin, A. V. (2016). 'Klad rimskih monet, najdennyj bliz c. Pereval'nogo (Krym)', *Materialy po arheologii i istorii antichnogo i srednevekovogo Kryma* 8: 579–91.

Ciobanu, L. (1999). 'Les découvertes monétaires romaines dans la zone Pruto-Nistraine en Moldavie', in G. Gomolka-Fuchs (ed.), *Die Sîntana de Mureș-Černjachov-Kultur. Akten des Internationalen Kolloquiums in Caputh vom 20. bis 24. Oktober 1995.* Bonn, 115–28.

Dem'ianchuk, S. G. (2008). 'Klad pozdneantichnyh monet iz okrestnostej sela Verhnesadovoe', *Sugdejskij sbornik* III: 419–24.

Dergaciova, L. (2021). 'The siliqua coin finds in the region between Dniester and Prut: A case study', in V. Varbanov and N. Rusev (eds), *Coin Hoards in Southeastern Europe (1st–6th century AD)* (Proceedings of the Rousse Regional Museum of History, vol. 24). Rousse, 118–86.

Dymowski A. (2019a). 'The CERES group of Barbarian imitations of Roman denarii', *Numismatic Chronicle* 179: 179–204.

Dymowski, A. (2019b). 'The problem of the presence of Barbarian imitations of Roman denarii in the lands of present-day Poland: An attempt at a balance', *Notae Numismaticae-Zapiski Numizmatyczne* XIV: 149–82.

Dymowski, A. (2021). 'Barbarian copies of Roman Imperial denarii', in R. Ciołek and R. Chowaniec (eds), *Aleksanderia. Studies on Items, Ideas and History Dedicated to ProfessorAleksander Bursche on the Occasion of his 65th Birthday*. Wiesbaden, 111–16.

Dymowski, A., in collaboration with Bliujienė, A., Horsnæs, H., Nielsen, R. H., Hunter, F., Lind, L., Militký, J., Munteanu, L., Myzgin, K., Pelsdonk, J., Sidarovich, V., Stoklas, B., Vida, I., Vojvoda, V., Wigg-Wolf, D., and Woytek, B. (2020). 'Roman Imperial hoards of denarii in the European Barbaricum', in C. Găzdac (ed.), *Group and Individual Tragedies in Roman Europe: The Evidence of Hoards, Epigraphic and*

Literary Sources (Journal of Ancient History and Archaeology: monographic series, 1). Cluj-Napoca, 193–243.

Dymowski, A. and Myzgin, K. (2014). 'Inflow and redistribution of Roman Imperial denarii in the area of Przeworsk, Wielbark and Chernyakhiv cultures and in the Baltic islands in the light of chronological structure of coin hoards', *Notae Numizmaticae-Zapiski Numizmatyczne* 9: 39–69.

Dymowski, A. and Myzgin, K. (2021). '"Wspólna waluta" Barbarzyńców? Barbarzyńskie naśladownictwa denarów rzymskich z okresu Cesarstwa w skarbach znalezionych w Europie Środkowej, Wschodniej i Północnej', in E. Droberjar and B. Komoróczy (eds), *Příspěvky k poznání barbarských komunit* (Archeologie barbarů 2016 a 2018). Brno, 195–217.

Dzigovskiy A. N. (2020). 'Nekotorye zamechaniya otnositel'no sobytij tret'ej chetverti IV v. n. e. v Budzhake', in M. V. Liubichev and K. V. Myzgin (eds), *Inter Orientem et Occidentem. Sbornik statej k 65-letiyu doktora Erdmute SHul'tce i 20-letiyu Germano-Slavyanskoj arheologicheskoj ekspedicii* (Ostrogothica-Serie: Band 3). Kharkiv, 361–7.

Eremić, D. (2014). 'Coin finds beyond the Danube: functions of fourth century gold coins within barbarian societies', in C. Rowan and A. Bokern (eds), *Embodying Value: The Transformation of Objects in and from the Ancient World* (BAR International 2592). Oxford: 121–30.

Filippenko, A. A. and Alekseenko, N. A. (2000). 'Der römische Münzschatzfund von Balaklava', in T. Sarnowski and O. Ja. Savelja (eds), *Balaklava. Römische Militärstation und Heiligtum des Jupiter Dolichenus*. Warsaw, 167–75.

Fundukley, I. I. (1848). *Obozrenie mogil, valov i gorodishch Kievskoj gubernii*. Kyiv.

Gavritukhin, I. O. (2005). 'Nekotorye perspektivy izucheniya finala chernyahovskoj kul'tury', *Trudy Gosudarstvennogo istoricheskogo muzeya* 145: 231–40.

Gereta, I. P. (2013). *Chernelevo-Ruskyi mohylnyk* (Oium 3). Kyiv and Ternopil.

Gluschenko, V. P. (1989). 'Klad rimskih denariev iz s. Lukishchina', *Numizmatika i epigrafika* XV: 19–52.

Højberg Bjerg M.-B. (2014). *Money, Power and Communication. Coin circulation in the Bosporan Kingdom in the Roman Period* (Collection Moneta 168). Wetteren.

Isaenko, O. and Sukhoruchenko, S. (2017). *Tri novyh klada rimskih monet iz Kryma. K voprosu ob obrashchenii rimskoj monety v Tavrike v I-II vv. n.e.* Simferopol.

Isaenko, O. and Sukhoruchenko, S. (2020). *Novyj klad pozdnerimskih monet iz Kryma*. Simferopol.

Istvánovits, E. and Kulcsár, V. (2017). *Sarmatians: History and Archaeology of a Forgotten People* (Römisch-Germanisches Zentralmuseum: Monographien 123). Mainz am Rhein.

Kazanski, M. M. (1997). 'Ostrogotskie korolevstva v gunnskuyu epohu: rasskaz Iordana i arheologicheskie dannye', *Stratum plus Peterburgskij arheologicheskij vestnik* 1: 181–93.

Kazanski, M. M. (2006). 'Germancy v Yugo-Zapadnom Krymu v pozdnerimskoe vremya', in R. V. Terpilovskiy (ed.), *Goty i Rim*. Kyiv, 26–41.

Kazanski, M. M. (2020). 'Goty na Bospore Kimmerijskom v nachale epohi Velikogo pereseleniya narodov', *Bosporskie issledovaniya* 40: 140–57.

Khrapunov, I. N. (1995). *Ocherki etnicheskoj istorii Kryma v rannem zheleznom veka. Tavry. Skify. Sarmaty*. Simferopol.

Kodatskiy, S. V. and Myzgin, K. V. (2017). 'Klad denariev i antoninianov III v. iz Vinnickoj oblasti', *Zapiski otdela numizmatiki i torevtiki Odesskogo arheologicheskogo muzeya* III, 72–83.

Kodatskiy, S. V. and Myzgin, K. V. (2020). 'Ot Trayana do Septimiya Severa: novyj klad rimskih denariev iz okrestnostej sela Buryakovoe v Khar'kovskoj oblasti', in M. V. Liubichev and K. V. Myzgin (eds), *Inter Orientem et Occidentem. Sbornik statej k 65-letiyu doktora Erdmute SHul'tce i 20-letiyu Germano-Slavyanskoj arheologicheskoj ekspedicii* (Ostrogothica-Serie: Bände, Band 3). Kharkiv, 465–78.

Kokowski, A. (2003). 'Die Przeworsk-Kultur. Ein Völkerverband zwischen 200 vor Chr. und 375 nach Chr.', in L. Christian, B. Nicole, and A. Kokowski (eds), *Die Vandalen. Die Könige, die Eliten, die Krieger, die Handwerker*. Nordstemmen, 77–183.

Korshenko, A. N. (2011). 'Krymskie klady pozdnerimskih mednyh monet', *Numizmatika i epigrafika* 18: 108–35.

Korshenko, A. N. (2012). 'Klad monet iz Bajdarskoj doliny 2011 g.', in N. A. Aleekseenko (ed.), *PriPONTijskij menyala: den'gi mestnogo rynka». II Mezhdunarodnyj Numizmaticheskij Simpozium. Teizsy dokladov i soobshchenij*. Sevastopol, 21–3.

Korshenko, A. N. (2013). 'Novyj klad pozdnerimskih monet iz yugo-zapadnogo Kryma', in A. I. Aybabin (ed.), *ΧΕΡΣΩΝΟΣ ΘΕΜΑΤΑ: «imperiya» i «polis». Tezisy dokladov i soobshchenij V Mezhdunarodnogo Vizantijskogo Seminara, Sevastopol 27–31.05.2013*. Sevastopol, 31–2.

Kotigoroshko, V. G. (1993). 'Rimskie importy i vydeleniya ekonomicheskih rajonov v Verhnem Potis'e', *Vestnik drevnej istorii* 3: 121–36.

Kovalenko, S. A. (2011). 'Klad pozdnerimskih monet iz Severo-Zapadnogo Kryma', *Numizmatika i epigrafika* 18: 89–107.

Kozak, D. N. (1990). 'Osoblyvosti kulturohenezu na terytorii Pivnichno-Zakhidnoi Ukrainy u pershii polovyni I tys. n. e. (za materialamy pamiatok lypytskoho typu)', *Arkheolohiia* 4: 43–56.

Kozak, D. N. (1995). 'Kulturno-istorychna interpretatsiia skarbiv Volyni rubezhu IV–V st.', *Arkheolohiia* 4: 50–65.

Kozak, D. N. (2008). *Venedy*. Kyiv.

Krenke, N. A. (2011). *D'yakovo gorodishche: Kul'tura naseleniya bassejna Moskvy-reki v I tys. do n.e. – I tys. n.e.* Moscow.

Kropotkin, V. V. (1951). 'Klady rimskih monet v Vostochnoj Evrope', *Vestnik drevnej istorii* 4: 241–81.

Kropotkin, V. V. (1961). *Klady rimskih monet na territorii SSSR* (Svod arheologicheskih istochnikov G 4–4). Moscow.

Kropotkin, V. V. (1967). *Ekonomicheskie svyazi Vostochnoj Evropy v I tysyacheletii nashej ery*. Moscow.

Kropotkin, V. V. (2000). 'Dopolnenie k spisku nahodok rimskih monet', *Stratum plus* 6: 20–117.

Kunina, N. Z. (1962). 'Kerchenskiy klad serebrianykh rimskikh monet', *Arkheologiya i istoriya Bospora*, vol. II: 329–42.

Kunisz, A. (1973). 'East and central European finds of autonomous coins from the Roman Empire Period', *Wiadomości Numizmatyczne* 17: 36–39.

Liaskoronskiy, V. G. (1901). 'Nahodki rimskih monet v bassejne Srednego Pridneprov'ya', in P. S. Uvarova and S. S. Sluckij (eds), *Trudy XI Arheologicheskogo S'ezda*, vol. 1. Moscow, 458–64.

Lind, L. (1988). *Romerska denarer funna i Sverige*. Stockholm.

Lind, L. (2007). 'A group of barbarous Roman denarii represented in Sweden and Hungary (and Germany and Britain?)', in M. Andersen, H. W. Horsnæs, and C. Moesgaard (eds), *Magister Monetae. Studies in Honour of Jörgen Steen Jensen*. Copenhagen, 53–8.

Liubichev, M. V. (2019). *Rannyaya istoriya dnepro-doneckoj lesostepi I–V vekov* (Ostrogothica-Serie: Bände, 2:1). Kharkiv.

Lyubichev, M. and Myzgin, K. (2020). 'Migration-Period Culture and Changes in the East European Forest-Steppe Zone', in A. Bursche, J. Hines, and A. Zapolska (eds), *Migration Period between the Odra and the Vistula*, vol. 2. Leiden and Boston, 731–70.

Mączyńska M. (2020). 'Chapter 12: Southern and Central Poland', in A. Bursche, J. Hines, and A. Zapolska (eds), *Migration Period between the Odra and the Vistula*, vol. 2. Leiden and Boston, 455–70.

Madyda-Legutko, R. (2021). 'Among the eastern, central, and north European Barbaricum', in R. Ciołek and R. Chowaniec (eds), *Aleksanderia. Studies on Items, Ideas and History Dedicated to Professor Aleksander Bursche on the Occasion of his 65th Birthday*. Wiesbaden, 263–72.

Magomedov, B. V. (1987). *Chernyahovskaya kul'tura Severo-Zapadnogo Prichernomor'ya*. Kyiv.

Magomedov, B. V. (2001). *Chernyahovskaya kul'tura. Problema etnosa*. Lublin.

Magomedov, B. (2008). 'Coins as a source of insight on Chernyakhiv tribes', in A. Bursche, R. Ciolek, and R. Wolters (eds), *Roman Coins Outside the Empire: Ways and Phases, Contexts and Functions* (Collection Moneta 82). Wetteren, 171–8.

Magomedov, B. V. and Karoieva, L. R. (1988). 'Skarb denariiv poblyzu s. Hlynsk Vinnytskoi obl.', *Arkheolohiia* 62: 82–6.

Milutinović, D. (2017). 'Monety prowincjonalnorzymskie aleksandryjskie w Barbaricum Środkowoeuropejskim', *Folia Numismatica* 31.2: 159–84.

Minkova, M. (2015). 'Klad antoninianov i denariev II–III w. iz derevno Gledachevo, oblast Stara Zagora', in I. V. Shyryakov (ed.), *XVIII Vserossijskaya numizmaticheskaya konferencyja. Tezisy dokladov i soobscheniy*. Moscow, 34–6.

Mironov, V. G. (1995). 'Gorodetskaya kul'tura: sostoyanie problemy i perspektivy izucheniya', in V. P. Chelyapov (ed.), *Arheologicheskie pamyatniki Srednego Pooch'ya*. Ryazan, 68–89.

Myzgin, K. V. (2010). *Antichnye monety na pamyatnikah chernyahovskoj kul'tury*. PhD thesis, Institute of Archaeology of National Academy of Science of Ukraine.

Myzgin, K. V. (2013). 'Rimskie monety v areale chernyahovskoj kul'tury: problema istochnikov postuplenniya', *Stratum plus* 4: 217–33.

Myzgin, K. V. (2016). 'Gotskie vojny, rimskie monety i chernyahovskaya kul'tura', *Stratum plus* 4: 153–71.

Myzgin, K. V. (2017a). 'O hronologii postupleniya zolotyh rimskih monet na territoriyu Yugo-Vostochnogo Barbarikuma', in Ye.V. Zaharov (ed.), *Numizmaticheskie chteniya Otdela numizmatiki Gosudarstvennogo istoricheskogo muzeya 2017 goda. Materialy dokladov i soobshchenij*. Moscow, 35–40.

Myzgin, K. (2017b). *Roman Republican Coins and their Imitations from the Territory of Ukraine and Belarus*. Warsaw.

Myzgin, K. (2017c). 'Trzeciowieczne monety rzymskie we wschodnim Barbaricum: antoniniany', *Folia Numismatica* 31.2: 147–58.

Myzgin, K. (2018). 'Finds of Roman provincial coins on the territory of eastern Europe: Balkan cities mintage', in V. Ivanišević, B. Borić-Brešković, and M. Vojvoda (eds), *Proceedings of the International Numismatic Symposium "Circulation of the antique coins in Southeastern Europe", Viminacium, Serbia, September 15th to 17th, 2017*. Belgrade, 87–103.

Myzgin, K. V. (2019). 'Rimskie monety pervyh vekov nashej ery na territorii Central'noj i Vostochnoj Evropy: obshchaya i sravnitel'naya harakteristika (po materialam kladov)', in I. O. Gavritukhin and A. M. Vorontsov (eds), *Lesnaya i lesostepnaya zony Vostochnoj Evropy v epohi rimskih vliyanij i Velikogo pereseleniya narodov. Konferenciya 4*, vol. 2. Tula, 210–25.

Myzgin, K. (2020). 'Provincial'no-rimskie monety s Arabatskoj Strelki', in N. A. Alekseenko (ed.), *PriPONTijskij menyala: den'gi mestnogo rynka. VII Mezhdunarodnyj Numizmaticheskij Simpozium (Sudak, 21–25.09. 2020 g.). Materialy nauchnoj konferencii*. Simferopol, 147–52.

Myzgin, K. and Beidin, G. (2015). 'Klad pozdnebosporskikh mednykh staterov iz Ksizovo' in A. M. Oblomskij (ed.), *Ostraja Luka Dona w drevnosti. Arkheologicheskij kompleks pamiatnikov gynnskogo vremeni u s. Ksizovo (konec IV—V vv.)* (Ranneslavyanskij mir, 16). Moscow, 165–80.

Myzgin, K. and Didenko, S. (2021). 'Borany Zosima, Bosporskoe carstvo i pohod na Trapezund', in M. Matera and R. Karasiewicz-Szczypiorski (eds), *Pontica et Caucasica II: Interdisciplinary research on the antiquity of the Black Sea* (Światowit Supplement Series C: Pontica et Caucasica, II). Warsaw, 311–36.

Myzgin, K. and Perederey, A. (2021). 'A hoard of third century coins (denarii and antoniniani) from Ostapkivtsi (Ukraine)', in V. Varbanov and N. Rusev (eds), *Coin Hoards in Southeastern Europe (1st–6th century AD)* (Proceedings of the Rousse Regional Museum of History, vol. 24). Rousse, 314–44.

Myzgin, K. V. and Petrauskas, A. V. (2021). 'Klad rimskih denariev iz s. Khmelevka, Zhitomirskaya oblast' (Ukraina)', *Stratum plus* 4, 255–69.

Myzgin, K. and Sidarovich, V. (2020). 'Znaleziska prowincjonalnych monet miast Bitynii na terenach Białorusi', *Wiadomości Numizmatyczne* 64.208: 187–12.

Myzgin, K., Vida, I., and Więcek, T. (2018). 'Gold imitations of Roman coins from collection of Hungarian National Museum in Budapest', in B. Niezabitowska-Wiśniewska, P. Łuczkiewicz, S. Sadowski, M. Stasiak-Cyran, and M. Erdrich (eds), *Studia barbarica. Profesorowi Andrzejowi Kokowskiemu w 65. rocznicę urodzin*, vol. 2. Lublin, 222–47.

Nadvirnyak, O. and Pohorilets, O. (2019). '«Falshyvomonetnytstvo», «neofitsiini imitatsii» chy «neofitsiine monetne vyrobnytstvo»? Do pytannia prysutnosti «lytykh» denariiv I-III stolittia n.e na «varvarskykh» terytoriiakh Pivdenno-Skhidnoi Evropy (za materialamy mezhyrichchia Serednoho Dnistra i Pivdennoho Buhu)', *Ukrainskyi numizmatychnyi shchorichnyk* 3: 28–41.

Nadvirnyak, O. and Pohorilets, O. (2020). 'Osoblyvosti elementnoho skladu metalu kompleksu sestertsiiv z obiektu piznorymskoho chasu Perehinka (Balakyri) 2', in M. V. Liubichev and K. V. Myzgin (eds), *Inter Orientem et Occidentem. Sbornik statej k 65-letiyu doktora Erdmute SHul'tce i 20-letiyu Germano-Slavyanskoj arheologicheskoj ekspedicii* (Ostrogothica-Serie Bände: Band 3). Kharkiv, 302–11.

Nadvirnyak, O., Pohorilets, O., and Nadvirnyak, O. (2016). 'Kompleks sestertsiiv z obiektu piznorymskoho chasu Perehinka (Balakyri) 2', in V. P. Kotsur (ed.), *Aktualni problemy numizmatyky u systemi spetsialnykh haluzei istorychnoi nauky. Tezy dopovidei IV Mizhnarodnoi naukovo-praktychnoi konferentsii*. Kyiv, 21–3.

Nadvirniak, O., Pohorelec, O., and Nadvirniak, O. (Jr.) (2017). 'An assemblage of antoniniani from the Late Roman site of Pereginka (Balakiri) 2', *Notae Numismaticae/ Zapiski Numizmatyczne* 11: 199–214.

Nudelman, A. A. (1982). 'Rimskaya moneta v mezhdurech'e Dnestra, Pruta i Dunaya', in V. L. Yanin (ed.), *Numizmatika antichnogo Prichernomor'ya*. Kyiv,125–33.

Oblomskiy, A. M. (ed.) (2007). *Pamyatniki kievskoj kul'tury v lesostepnoj zone Rossii (III–nachalo V v. n. e.)* (Ranneslavyanskij mir 10). Moscow.

Oblomskiy, A. M. (ed.) (2012). *Pozdnezarubineckie pamyatniki na territorii Ukrainy (vtoraya polovina I–II vv. n.e.)* (Ranneslavyanskij mir 12). Moscow.

Petrauskas, O. V. (2021). 'Cherniakhivska kultura ta huny (za materialamy arkheolohichnykh pamiatok Ukrainy), *Arkheolohiia* 2: 15–32.

Pioro, I. S. and Gertsen, A. G. (1974). 'Klad antoninianov iz s. Dolinnoe Krymskoj oblasti', *Numizmatika i sfragistyika* 5: 81–90.

Pivovarov, S. V. (2002). *Numizmatychni pamiatky Bukovyny (antychnyi i serednovichnyi chas)*. Chernivtsi.

Popa, A. and Ciobanu, L. (2003). *Moneda romana in Basarabia (Ghid metodic)*. Chişinău.

Prohászka, P. (2003). 'Angaben zur Archäologie und Geschichte des Wallsystems in der grossen ungarischen Tiefebene', in É. Garam, P. Patay, and S. Soproni (eds), *Sarmatisches Wallsystem im Karpatenbecken* (Régészeti Füzetek 2/23). Budapest, 79–89.

Prohászka, P. (2007). 'Der spätrömische Schatzfund von Szűgy (1837). Ein Beitrag zum Umlauf spätrömischer Goldmünzen im Karpatenbecken', *Numismatický sborník* 22: 31–8.

Prohászka, P. (2009). 'Die römischen Goldmünzen der Spätkaiserzeit aus dem Barbaricum des Karpatenbeckens. Von der Tetrarchie bis zum Ende der Herrschaft von Theodosius I', in S. Bíró (ed.), *"Ex officina...". Studia in honorem Dénes Gabler*. Győr, 471–90.

Radiush, O. A. (2008). 'Nahodki rimskih monet s territorii Kurskoj oblasti', in V. V. Yenukov (ed.), *Slavyano-russkie drevnosti Dneprovskogo Levoberezh'ya*. Kursk, 140–5.

Radiush, O. A. (2014). '«Knyazheskie» i «vozhdeskie» pogrebeniya nachala V veka v Verhnem Podneprov'e: novye issledovaniya i nahodki', *Kratkie soobshcheniya Instituta Arheologii RAN* 234: 234–51.

Radiush, O. A. (2018). 'L'govsko-Fatezhskaya gruppa pamyatnikov finala chernyahovskoj kul'tury v verhov'yah r. Sejm (Kurskaya oblast', Rossiya)', in B. Niezabitowska-Wiśniewska, P. Luczkiewicz, S. Sadowski, M. Stasiak-Cyran, and M. Erdrich (eds), *Studia Barbarica. Professorowi Andrzejowi Kokowskiemu w 65. rocznicę urodzin*, vol. 1. Lublin, 570–91.

Reece, R. (2008). 'Roman silver goes abroad', in A. Bursche, R. Ciolek, and R. Wolters (eds), *Roman Coins outside the Empire: Ways and Phases, Contexts and Functions* (Collection Moneta 82). Wetteren, 59–73.

Riabchevskiy, N. G. (2020). 'Nahodki vostochnoevropejskih vyemchatyh emalej na territorii Bryanskoj oblasti (materialy k svodu)', *Germania-Sarmatia* 3: 128–53.

Romanova, G. A. (1995). 'O topografii kladov rimskih monet na Levoberezh'e Dnepra', in O. P. Motsia (ed.), *Arkheolohichni starozhytnosti Podesennia*. Chernihiv, 122–4.

Royko, O. and Kal'kov A. (2018). 'Znakhidka skarbu davnorymskykh denariiv I-III st. v s. Buzhany Horokhivskoho raionu', *Volynskyi kolektsioner* 1: 70–4.

Rozumenko, Yu. G. (1982). 'Klad antoninianov iz Bolgradskogo raiona', in V. L. Yanin (ed.), *Numizmatuka antichnogo Prochernomorya*. Kyiv, 135–6.

Samokvasov, D. Ya. (1884). *Istoriya russkogo prava*, vol. 2: *Proiskhozhdenie Slavyan*. Warsaw.

Schukin, M. B. (1976). 'O nachal'noj date chernyahovskoj kul'tury', *Prace Arheologiczne* 422.22: 303–17.

Sharov, O. V., Palaguta, I. V., and Khavrin, S. V. (2010). 'Nahodki kladov rimskih monet v rajone Kopor'ya', *Rossijskij arheologicheskij ezhegodnik* 1: 335–59.

Shilin, Yu. (2003). 'Nova informatsiia pro cherniakhivske poselennia bilia s. Hlynsk Vinnytskoi oblasti', *Podilska starovyna* 1: 58–65.

Shmidt, E. A. (1992). *Plemena verhov'ev Dnepra do obrazovaniya Drevnerusskogo gosudarstva. Dnepro-dvinskie plemena (VIII v. do n. e. – III v. n. e.)*. Moscow.

Shtalenkov, I. (2017). 'Novye nahodki antichnyh monet v Belarusi', *Bankaŭski vesnik* 2.643: 67–71.

Sidarovich, V. (2013). 'A hoard of Alexandrian tetradrachms from the last quarter of the 3rd century AD found in the Upper Neman Region', *Notae Numismaticae/Zapiski Numizmatyczne* 8: 173–81.

Sidarovich, V. (2014). 'The finds of Greek and Roman provincial coins in Belarus', *Notae Numismaticae/Zapiski Numizmatyczne* 9: 71–91.

Sidarovich, V. (2019). 'New find of gold Roman coin-pendants in the South-West of Belarus', *Notae Numismaticae/Zapiski Numizmatyczne* 14: 183–91.

Sidarovich, V. (2021). 'Novi dani pro skarby rymskykh monet iz Hrodnenskoi oblasti Respubliky Bilorus', *Ukrainskyi numizmatychnyi shchorichnyk* 5: 174–87.

Sidarovich, V. (2022). 'Miednyja maniety Rymskaj Impieryi ŭ Hrodzienskim Paniamońni', in A. U. Cichamiraŭ (ed.), *Labor Omnia Vincit. Praca zaŭsiody pieramahaje: Materyjalnaja kultura ŭ histaryčnym kantekście Prablemy vyvučeńnia i zachavańnia*. Hrodna, 83–95.

Sidorenko, V. A. (2009). 'Klad rimskih denariev iz okrainy s. Repino Bahchisarajskogo r-na', *Materialy po arheologii, istorii i etnografii Tavrii* 15: 534–49.

Sidorovich, V. M. (2021). 'Monetno-veshchevye depozity IV–V vv. s territorii Belorussii', in P. G. Gajdukov (ed.), *Dvadcat' pervaya Vserossijskaya numizmaticheskaya konferenciya (Tver', 24-29 maya 2021 g.). Tezisy dokladov i soobshchenij*. Tver, 38–9.

Stolba, V. F. and Peter, U. (2021). 'Klad rimskih denariev iz okrestnostej Ol'vii', in N. A. Alekseenko (ed.), *«PriPONTijskij menyala: den'gi mestnogo rynka». VIII Mezhdunarodnyj Numizmaticheskij Simpozium (Kerch', 2-6 oktyabrya 2021 g.). Materialy nauchnoj konferencii*. Simferopol, 223–32.

Stoliarik, E. S. (1989). 'Rimskaya moneta v Severo-Zapadnom Prichernomor'e', in T. L. Samojlova (ed.), *Arheologicheskie pamyatniki stepej Podnestrov'ya i Podunav'ya*. Kyiv, 45–52.

Stribrny, K. (2003). *Funktionsanalyse barbarisierter, barbarischer Denare mittels numismatischer und metallurgischer Methoden. Zur Erforschung der sarmatisch-germanischen Kontakte im 3. Jahrhundert n. Chr.* (Studien zu Fundmünzen der Antike 18). Mainz am Rhein.

Tikhanova, M. A. (1973). 'K voprosu ob obmene i torgovle v epohu chernyahovskoj kul'tury', *Kratkie soobshcheniya Instituta arheologii SSSR* 138: 66–73.

Tkach, Ye. (2013). 'Kostoboki v markomanskih voynah', *Revista Arheologică (serie nouă)* 9.2: 85–103.

Vakulenko, L. V. (1989). 'Etnokul'turnaya situaciya v Verhnem Podnestrov'e v I-II vv. n.e. (po materialam mogil'nikov)', in P. P. Tolochko (ed.), *Drevnie slavyane i Kievskaya Rus'*. Kyiv, 22–34.

Vakulenko, L. V. (2009). 'Etnokul'turnaya situaciya v Verhnem Podnestrov'e v I-II vv. n.e. v pozdnerimskoe vremya', *Rossijskaya arheologiya* 1: 36–46.

Vakulenko, L. V. (2010). *Ukrainski Karpaty v piznorymskyi chas (etnokulturni ta sotsialno-ekonomichni protsesy)*. Kyiv.

Varbanov, V. (2012). 'Barbarian invasions in the Roman provinces of Lower Moesia and Thrace in the mid-3rd century and the coin hoards from that period', in L. F. Vagalinski (ed.), *The Lower Danube Roman Limes (1st–6th c. AD)*. Sofia, 289–310.

Voroniatov, S. V. (2014). 'Postzarubineckie hronologicheskie gorizonty (postanovka voprosa)', *Zapiski Instituta istorii material'noj kul'tury RAN* 9: 132–40.

Voroniatov, S. V. and Shinakov, E. A. (2020). 'Otdel'nye nahodki i klady kruga «varvarskih emalej» v Bryanskom Podesen'e', *Germania-Sarmatia* 3: 80–115.

Voroniatov, S. V. and Stoliarova, T. V. (2020). 'Glazhevskaya kollekciya: istoriya izucheniya i analiz sostava', *Germania-Sarmatia* 3: 64–79.

Vorontsov, A. M. (2013). *Kul'turno-hronologicheskie gorizonty pamyatnikov II–V vekov na territorii Oksko-Donskogo vodourazdela*. Tula.

Vorontsov, A. M. (2023). 'Tul'skiy fenomen: novye nakhodki pozdnerimskikh bronzovykh monet s pravoberezh'ya verkhney Oki', *Stratum plus* 4: 387–408.

Vorontsov, A. M. and Myzgin, K. V. (2019). '*Ultima Thule*? O nahodkah pozdnerimskih monet na territorii Tuly', in Petrauskas, O. V. Hopkalo, and S. A. Gorbanenko (eds), *Starozhytnosti varvarskykh plemen u pershii polovyni I tys. n. e.: do 90-richchia V. D. Barana* (Oium 6). Kyiv, 244–61.

Yegoreichenko, A. A. (2006). *Kul'tury shtrihovannoj keramiki*. Minsk.

Zapolska, A. (2013). 'The influx of Roman coins to the West Balt culture environment', *Notae Numismaticae/Zapiski Numizmatyczne* 8: 105–22.

Zaytsev, V. V. (2020). 'O datirovke Karachevskogo monetno-veshchevogo klada s rimskimi imperatorskimi denariyami', in N. A. Alekseenko (ed.), *PriPONTijskij menyala: den'gi mestnogo rynka». VII Mezhdunarodnyj Numizmaticheskij Simpozium. Materialy nauchnoj konferencii*. Simferopol, 75–82.

Kyrylo Myzgin, *Roman Coin Hoards in Eastern Europe* In: *Roman Coin Hoards Across Frontiers*.
Edited by: Benjamin D. R. Hellings, Marguerite Spoerri Butcher, and Chris Howgego, Oxford University Press.
 DOI: 10.1093/9780198986478.003.0008

PART III

EVIDENCE AND INTERPRETATIONS: THE EAST

9

Crossing Frontiers in the East: Hoarding of Roman Coinages from Pontus to Mesopotamia

Marguerite Spoerri Butcher

The aim of this chapter is to provide a broad overview of hoarding patterns in the eastern part of the Roman Empire and its adjacent regions, with the exclusion of Armenia and Caucasian Iberia, which are the subject of a separate chapter in this volume by Anahide Kéfélian (chapter 10).[1]

While the chronological focus is on the first three centuries AD, some of the evidence reviewed in this chapter comes from sites that were destroyed in the mid-third century AD, which incidentally explains the non-retrieval of the hoards discussed here. While this provides valuable evidence on hoarding for that period, these same sites are much less informative for prior centuries.

The first three centuries AD were a time when cities and local communities produced their own coinages throughout the east of the Empire. These coinages are commonly referred to as 'Roman provincial'. This has direct implications for hoarding practices, as imperial issues, especially *aes*, but to some extent also silver, were predominantly supplied to the western part of the Empire and did not necessarily constitute the main currency in the east. This plurality of currencies resulted in the creation of local and regional circulation pools, the establishment of *de facto* internal 'frontiers' for currency within the Empire, and the movement of coins across these internal frontiers, raising the question of the acceptance (or non-acceptance) of non-local coins elsewhere.

[1] Data for this chapter were compiled by the author, partly drawing on information provided by the Coin Hoards of the Roman Empire Project (CHRE) (https://chre.ashmus.ox.ac.uk, last accessed 30 May 2023). Subsequently, any additional data discussed here, especially for modern-day Iraq, have been ingested into the CHRE database in order to reflect the full geographical coverage of this contribution. Credit to individual contributors of the CHRE project can be found in the credit line of each hoard. This includes (in alphabetical order) the author of the present chapter, Matthew Ball, Rob Bennett, Cristian Găzdac, and Anahide Kéfélian, as well as William E. Metcalf, who provided the CHRE project with an unpublished dataset of 180 *denarius* hoards including coin-level information. A general presentation of the coin circulation in the east of the Roman Empire has been provided by Yalçin (2017), based on excavation reports, hoards, but also holdings of eastern Turkish museums. For a detailed discussion of circulation models and coin use in Roman Syria, see Butcher (2004: 143–95).

The main focus of this chapter is, however, the movement of coins across the external frontiers of the Empire and their subsequent hoarding and deposition. The frontiers included the sea on the northern shores of Asia Minor (the Black Sea), though no shipwreck hoards are attested there. Political frontiers existed in the Caucasus with Colchis and the kingdoms of Iberia and Armenia. In the east, across the Syrian Desert and its various oases, Rome bordered the Persian Empire, ruled by the Parthians and, from AD 224 onwards, by the Sasanians. These rivalled Rome for the control of the region in a succession of wars that led to a constant shift of frontiers. Far from being a well-delimited physical border system, much of the Roman frontier system from the Black Sea to the Red Sea consisted therefore of a zone serving as a surveillance and defence line with changing spheres of influence and open to trade.[2]

THE NORTHERN PONTIC COAST: A SEA FRONTIER?

At least two third-century hoards deposited along the shores of the Black Sea provide evidence for the predominantly local circulation of bronze coins (Fig. 9.1). The first hoard was found in Sinop in 2015 (CHRE 18896), during the excavations of a Roman villa.[3] It consisted of 162 provincial bronzes, ranging from Antoninus Pius to the joint reign of Valerian and Gallienus. Though not all coins were legible enough to be identified, 134 were produced by Sinope itself (which represents 82% of the total amount or 99% of all legible specimens), and only one single 'foreign' specimen, minted in the name of Gordian III, belonged to a different mint, Trapezus.

The second hoard, of smaller size, was found at an unknown location near Trabzon, ancient Trapezus (CHRE 18663), and was seen in commerce shortly before 1971. It may therefore not have been recorded in its entirety, but its 19 bronzes, ranging from Geta to Philip I, consisted of 18 specimens from Trapezus and a single specimen from Caesarea in Cappadocia, in the name of Severus Alexander.[4]

Unfortunately, no full account is available for the large number of coins of Tium and Heraclea Pontica unearthed in Filyos (ancient Tium), further west on the Pontic coast, during the building works of industrial plants between 1944 and 1954. These coins (or at least some of them) were later published as part of the collection of Hans von Aulock, where 131 specimens for Tium and 92 for Heraclea Pontica are recorded as originating 'mostly' from these finds.[5] The absence of proper documentation prevents us from asserting whether these finds—which might be regarded as groups of single finds or one or several hoards—reflect only a

[2] Whittaker (1994).
[3] Oyarçin and Girgin (2021).
[4] Price (1971: 124–5).
[5] See the introduction to *SNG* vAulock.

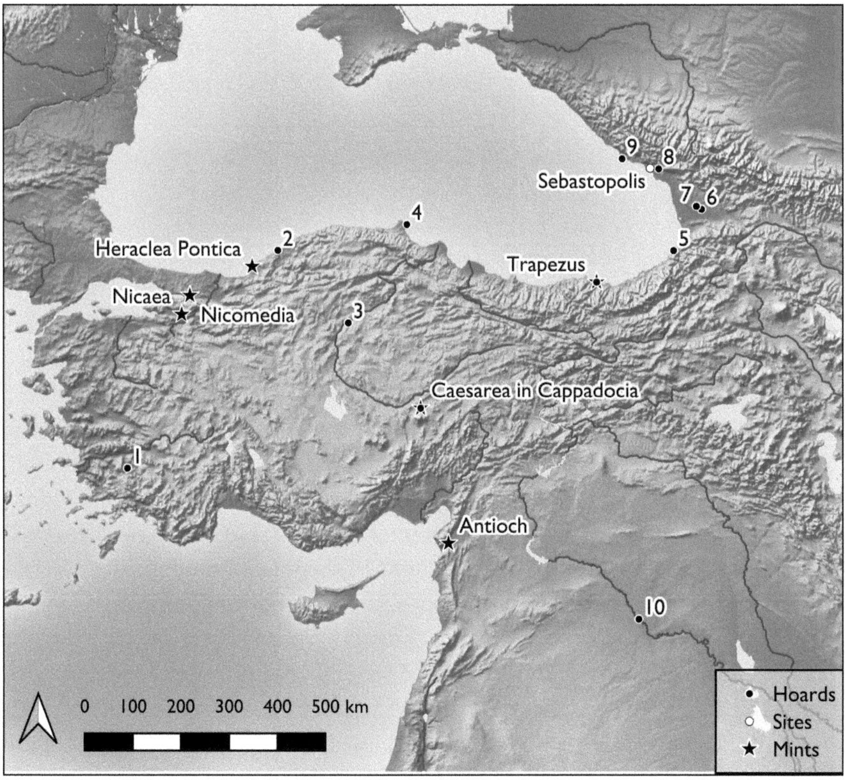

Fig. 9.1. Northern Pontic coast and western Caucasus. Map of the hoards discussed (excluding the smaller hoards from Colchis), with main sites or mints mentioned in the text. Numbers refer to the following hoards: 1. Haydere; 2. Filyos (Tium); 3. Sulakyurt; 4. Sinop; 5. Gonio (Apsaros); 6. Sepieti; 7. Eki; 8. Gerzeul; 9. Pitsunda (Pityus); 10. Dura-Europos. Map: A. Wilson/M. Spoerri Butcher.

local circulation pool, restricted to the two neighbouring cities of Tium and Heraclea Pontica, or whether coins from more distant places were also included.

A similar picture emerges from a series of local finds from western Bithynia in which coins of the two main mints of the region, Nicaea and Nicomedia, dominated by far. While some of these finds are poorly documented, the so-called 'Fundkomplex' now at the Institut für Altertumskunde, Universität zu Köln (its findspot is unknown), shows a regional circulation pool with 387 or 399 coins ranging from the time of Septimius Severus to Gallienus, comprising predominantly issues of Nicaea (228 or 233 specimens) and Nicomedia (151 or 150 specimens), associated with a few coins from other cities, all located in Bithynia.[6]

[6] The best account of these finds can be found in Johnston (2007: 166–8). Apart from the Cologne 'Fundkomplex', these include an undocumented large number of coins from the construction site of a paper factory in İzmit (ancient Nicomedia), of which some are now in the Istanbul museum and

Finds made along the northern coast within the borders of modern Turkey therefore suggest an absence of movement of coinage along or, even, across the sea, though one could argue that this might be due to the paucity of the evidence available.[7]

AT THE FRINGES OF THE EMPIRE: THE WESTERN CAUCASUS REGION

The eastern coast of the Black Sea, a region known in antiquity as Colchis (part of modern-day Georgia), became an administrative dependency of the Roman Empire after the annexation of the Pontic Kingdom, ruled by the client king Polemon II (AD 38–64). A series of forts (*castella*) was subsequently established on the coastline, as early as the Flavian period for Apsaros and Sebastopolis (formerly Dioscurias) and under Hadrian for Pityus. At the same time, Roman control extended only loosely to the hinterland, inhabited by Transcaucasian tribes, while the more mountainous regions in the west of modern-day Georgia were home to the kingdom of Iberia, bordering the kingdom of Armenia.[8] Hoarding and coin circulation in these three geographical areas, comprising the Roman forts, their immediate hinterland, and Iberia, differ quite significantly from each other and diverge also from what can be observed in neighbouring Armenia.[9] In what follows, the main emphasis is placed on the coastal regions comprising the Roman forts and their immediate hinterland (Fig. 9.1).[10]

others possibly published in the von Aulock collection, as well as 148 coins of Nicaea and Nicomedia now in the Yapı Kredi collection, said to probably come from a single hoard; see Tekin (1994: 228).

[7] For movements of provincial coins across the sea to the kingdom of the Bosporus on the northern shores of the Black Sea and more generally the influx of Roman coinages, see Højberg Bjerg (2014: 146–65), noting, however, that provincial coins constitute only a small fraction among all coin finds within the kingdom; see Spoerri Butcher (2019), documenting two large-sized third-century bronzes of Heraclea Pontica, found within a funerary context in Kertch.

[8] Vitale (2013); Braund (1994).

[9] On hoarding patterns from Armenia compared to Iberia and Colchis, see Kéfélian's contribution in this volume (chapter 10). On coin circulation in Iberia in the first three centuries AD, see Sherozia (2008: 238–40), but also Fabian (2017), applying network analysis to coin find data from across the Caucasus, especially Iberia and Albania.

[10] For a brief overview on the subject, see Dundua (2008). Some of the hoards discussed here have never been published in detail, and their analysis is constrained by this limitation. In some cases, divergent information is available on their exact content (breakdown by reign), which is the reason we have opted for a broad chronological analysis instead of a finer examination by date of issue. Other data, notably from the Apsaros fort, are currently awaiting publication, and a more in-depth analysis of the coin circulation at the fort is being prepared by Jaworski. Any conclusions drawn here should therefore be considered provisional.

The Roman forts

Three hoards, the contents of which are summarized in Table 9.1, have been discovered so far in two of the Roman forts, Apsaros (modern Gonio) and Pityus (modern Pitsunda).[11]

Despite their different end dates, size, and composition, all three hoards contain Cappadocian silver, represented mostly by drachms and occasional didrachms and hemidrachms dating primarily from the time of Hadrian (AD 117–38) and the Severans (AD 193–222). The absence of earlier Cappadocian silver is noteworthy, especially as several specimens from Tiberius and Nero have been reported in two foundation deposits from the Apsaros fort.[12] Silver production ceased at Caesarea between AD 217 and 240, which explains the absence of any later Cappadocian silver for the Gonio 2018 hoard. However, the Pitsunda 1958 hoard, with a *t.p.q.* of AD 244/5, did not include any of the Cappadocian silver minted in abundance under Gordian III, between AD 240 and 242, of which at least some made its way into single finds both at Apsaros and Pityus.[13] Given that the chronological range of Cappadocian silver extended from Hadrian to the Severans in all three hoards, the relatively low numbers seen for the Antonine period (AD 138–92) are perhaps the more surprising feature. According to a first chronological overview by metal of all coins found in Apsaros given by Piotr Jaworski, this phenomenon corresponds to a more general dip in the influx of coins at that time.[14]

Only the Gonio 1998 hoard included silver coins from mints other than Cappadocia. These are drachms of the Pontic king Polemon II (AD 38–62) and Roman *denarii* ranging from Tiberius to Caracalla. Because of the low number of specimens involved (four Pontic drachms and 15 *denarii*, compared to 22 Cappadocian silver coins), a chronological evaluation by period of issue makes little sense, though the presence of Pontic drachms and two first-century *denarii* (one of Tiberius and another of Vespasian) are noteworthy. The survival of early first-century silver until the time of Caracalla might seem surprising, but is

[11] See also Fig. 9.5 below. Data for the hoards from Apsaros are based on Jaworski (2021: table 2), with the same information also published in Jaworski, Karasiewics-Szczypiorski, and Mamuladze (2021: 300, table 3). For Pitsunda, see Golenko (1964: 75, no. 45) with reference to a report by Kapanadze in 1961 (*non vidi*), Kapanadze (1966), Lorkipanize and Dundua (1995: 34), Kropotkin and Depeyrot (2005: 263, no. 1646), and Tsotselia (2010: 102, no. 597). No full publication has yet been given for this hoard, which explains inconsistencies between the lists provided by these various authors.

[12] Jaworski, Karasiewics-Szczypiorski, and Mamuladze (2021: 295, table 2).

[13] Apsaros: one didrachm of Gordian's year 5 (AD 242); see Jaworski, Karasiewics-Szczypiorski, and Mamuladze (2021: 301, fig. 9.2); Jaworski (2021: Plate 3, B). Pityus: one drachm of Gordian III; see Golenko (1964: 63–4, no. 14) and Kropotkin and Depeyrot (2005: 263, no. 1919).

[14] Jaworski, Karasiewics-Szczypiorski, and Mamuladze (2021: 292, fig. 2); Jaworski (2021: Plate 1, Chart 2).

Table 9.1. Colchis. Hoards found at the Roman forts of Apsaros (modern Gonio) and Pityus (modern Pitsunda), after Jaworski (2021: 300) for the two Gonio hoards, and after Kropotkin and Depeyrot (2005: 263, no. 1646) for Pitsunda.

Hoard	Content	*t.p.q.*
Gonio 1998 (CHRE 16080)	42 silver coins: 4 Pontic drachms (Polemon II), 15 *denarii* (Tiberius to Caracalla), 23 silver coins from Caesarea in Cappadocia (Hadrian to Caracalla).	AD 211–17
Gonio 2018 (CHRE 20923)	14 coins: 8 silver coins from Caesarea in Cappadocia (Hadrian to Caracalla), 6 bronze coins from Trapezus (Trajan to Severus Alexander).	AD 222–35
Pitsunda 1958 (CHRE 16062)	149 coins: 10 silver coins from Caesarea in Cappadocia (Hadrian to Caracalla), 139 bronze coins from Trapezus (Commodus or Septimius Severus to Philip I).	AD 244/5

attested by a few rare examples from within the Empire. One of them is a hoard from eastern Turkey (CHRE 4843), with a *t.p.q.* of AD 249–51, comprising *c.* 2,626 *denarii* ranging, beside one Republican specimen, from Augustus to Gordian III, 78 *antoniniani*, and five provincial silver coins (two hemidrachms from Caesarea minted by Vespasian and Hadrian, as well as three Lycian drachms issued by Trajan).[15] Jaworski also comments on the fact that the Pontic drachms are in pristine condition, unlike the *denarius* of Tiberius, which seems to indicate that they circulated little before being thesaurized.[16]

While the mixture of provincial and imperial silver currencies is not unknown elsewhere, as attested, for example, by the large find of approximately 2,000 silver coins from Caesarea in Cappadocia made near Kayseri that also included *c.* 100 *denarii* (CHRE 8772),[17] the association of provincial silver with provincial bronze, as seen in the Gonio 2018 and Pitsunda 1958 hoards, is far more unusual. Both hoards contained, in addition to Cappadocian silver, provincial bronze coins minted in Trapezus (Pontus). Although only few Trapezuntine issues are present in Gonio 2018 (six, compared to eight silver specimens, i.e. 43%), they constitute an overwhelming majority in the Pitsunda 1958 hoard (139, compared to only ten silver coins, i.e. 93%). For Pitsunda, most of them date from the Severan period, with the reigns of Septimius Severus, Caracalla, and Elagabalus totalling

[15] Bendall (1966). [16] Jaworski (2021: 127).

[17] The hoard is reported as having been found close to Kayseri (ancient Caesarea in Cappadocia) and was dispersed in the art trade soon after its discovery in 1980. Only part of it was documented, with a large portion published by Metcalf (1996) and another one by Weiser (1984); see Metcalf (1996: 2) for a breakdown of coins documented by these two publications, ranging from Tiberius to Commodus. Additional coins were recorded in Paris; see Amandry and Burnett (2015: 376, no. 4).

92 specimens, while Gordian III's reign is still represented by 17 coins and that of Philip I by four coins. These coins belong to the last issue produced by Trapezus in AD 244/5, after which the mint stopped its activity. The breakdown of the hoard by reign seems to show a gap for Severus Alexander, though this might be due to misidentifying some of the admittedly badly preserved coins (26 are uncertain), rather than reflecting a real gap in availability.[18]

Bronze coins of Trapezus are known elsewhere from single finds at Pitsunda, Sebastopolis/Dioscurias (modern-day Sukhumi), and Apsaros,[19] confirming their availability at these forts, not only as hoarded currency. Interestingly, their presence in Colchis seems restricted to these Roman forts, as none have been found in hoards or single finds in the hinterland.

The hinterland

Hoarding in the hinterland of the forts, which were only loosely under Roman control, is mainly documented by three large hoards (Gerzeul, Eki, and Sepieti), totalling more than 1,700 coins between them and composed almost exclusively of silver currencies (Table 9.2).

The Gerzeul hoard (Fig. 9.2) is comprised of Cappadocian didrachms, drachms, and hemidrachms, ranging from Nero to Marcus Aurelius and Lucius Verus, with large numbers of coins for Trajan, Hadrian, and Antoninus Pius.[20] Its concealment has been linked with the Roman–Parthian Wars of Lucius Verus in Armenia (AD 161–6).[21] The hoard also contained two non-Cappadocian coins: an imitation of a gold stater of Lysimachus, as well as a *denarius* of Augustus of the Gaius and Lucius type.[22] Beyond that single specimen, no further Roman *denarii* have been recorded for Gerzeul.

[18] Furthermore, no detailed publication of this hoard exists, which has resulted in a number of discrepancies between authors who have attempted to give a breakdown of the composition of the hoard by emperor; see n. 11, above, for the relevant bibliography.

[19] Pitsunda: 32 bronzes, from Lucius Verus to Gordian III, see Kropotkin and Depeyrot (2005: 263–4, no. 1919), based on Golenko (1964: 74, no. 44). Sukhumi: 8+ bronzes, from Commodus to Orbiana, wife of Severus Alexander, see Kropotkin and Depeyrot (2005: 266, no. 1923), based on Golenko (1964: 75–6, nos 46–8). Apsaros: Jaworski, Karasiewics-Szczypiorski, and Mamuladze (2021: 297, fig. 7); Jaworski (2021: Plate 1, Chart 2).

[20] Ivaschenko (1931), mentioning 467 coins, but only describing 259 in detail. A further list was given by Zograf (1945: 78–9, no. 179), in which he combined coins of Antoninus Pius and Marcus Aurelius, given that he had not been able to see the coins. Finally, 91 coins in the Abkhazian State Museum were published by Abramzon (2003).

[21] See Abramzon (2003: 247–8), with references to previous Russian bibliography.

[22] On the Gaius and Lucius *denarii*, occurring frequently in Caucasian Iberia, in the east of modern-day Georgia, where imitations of them were also produced, see Sherozia (2008: 238–9) and the account given by Kéfélian in the current volume (chapter 10). For the Lysimachus imitations, see Frolova (2009); Fabian (2019: 42–5).

Table 9.2. Colchis. Hoards from the hinterland, after Zograf (1945) for Gerzeul, and after Dundua (1979) for Eki and Sepieti.

Hoard	Content	*t.p.q.*
Gerzeul (CHRE 5478)	467+? silver coins of Caesarea in Cappadocia (Nero to Marcus Aurelius), 1 *denarius* of Augustus, 1 imitation of a gold stater of Lysimachus. Found in a ceramic vessel.	AD 161–9
Eki (CHRE 5334)	907 silver coins: 1 Parthian drachm (Orodes I), 771 didrachms (Nerva to Lucius Verus) and 3 drachms (Julia Domna to Caracalla) of Caesarea in Cappadocia, 131 *denarii* (Commodus to Severus Alexander), and 1 drachm of Petra (Caracalla). Found in a clay pot.	AD 222–35
Sepieti (CHRE 5333)	377 (or more?) silver coins: 365 *denarii* (Trajan to Severus Alexander) and 12 Cappadocian drachms (Hadrian?; Septimius Severus to Caracalla). Found in a ceramic vessel.	AD 222–35

The absence of other *denarii* in the Gerzeul hoard is noteworthy and is certainly linked to the overall predominance of Cappadocian silver in finds from the hinterland until the end of the second half of the second century AD, as attested by smaller hoards or groups of single finds, some of which were made in graves. As is the case for the Gerzeul hoard, these finds comprised almost exclusively silver currencies and some very rare gold coins, with no bronze reported at all. Silver consisted of early Roman *denarii* (up to Augustus), Pontic drachms of Polemon II (these coins were mostly issued in the AD 50s), Cappadocian silver up to the Severans, and some Severan *denarii*.[23]

The influx of coinage changes towards the end of the second century, though the absence of hoard or small finds evidence from that period makes it difficult to trace the evolution in any detail. Evidence for the first half of the third century is provided by two large hoards ending with coins issued during the reign of Severus Alexander: Eki and Sepieti. Both contained a mixture of Cappadocian silver and *denarii*, though in variable proportions.

[23] The finds are: Nazodelavo (CHRE 16046: 23 Republican *denarii*, one *denarius* of Augustus of the Gaius and Lucius type, and one drachm of Archelaus of Cappadocia), Pakhulani (CHRE 18828: ten drachms of Polemon II), Samurzakan (CHRE 18754: 60–70 drachms of Polemon II), Takhulani (CHRE 16068: 8+? didrachms and drachms of Trajan and Hadrian), Tsebelda (CHRE 18182: six didrachms of Caesarea, from Nerva to Antoninus Pius, all found in a grave), Nosiri (CHRE 16059: 18 didrachms, drachms, and hemidrachms of Caesarea, from Vespasian to Antoninus Pius), Tsebelda (CHRE 18182: six Cappadocian silver coins, from Nerva to Antoninus Pius, found in a grave), Nobakevi (CHRE 16079)/Otobaya (CHRE 16060)—the two hoards being possibly identical (12 didrachms and one drachm, of Hadrian, Septimius Severus, and other emperors), Ureki 1942 (CHRE 16070: four drachms of Hadrian, one *denarius* of Septimius Severus, one *aureus* of Tacitus, and one unidentified barbarous gold imitation, all found in a grave).

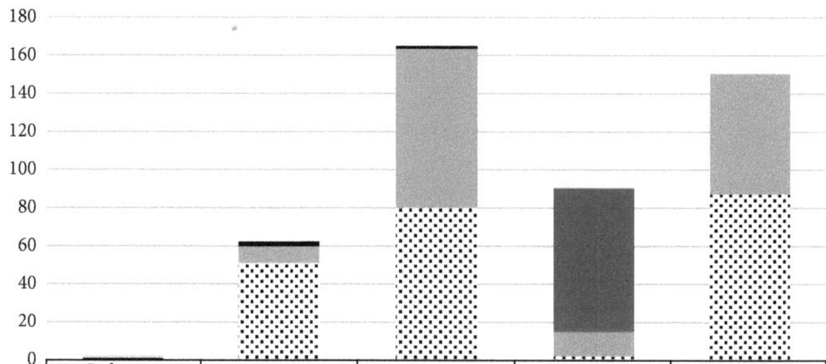

	Before 14	14–98	98–117	117–38	138–92
Other	1				
Roman denarius	1				
Cappadocian hemidrachms		2	1	73	
Cappadocian drachms		9	84	13	63
Cappadocian didrachms		51	80	2	87

Fig. 9.2. Composition of the Gerzeul hoard, in number of coins by chronological period and type of coinage, including denominations; after Zograf (1945).

The composition of the Eki hoard (Fig. 9.3) is peculiar, as it comprised a very large number of didrachms of Hadrian (AD 117–38) from Caesarea (712 specimens, totalling 78% of the content of the hoard), 55 didrachms (6%) minted under Antoninus Pius (AD 138–61), followed by 110 *denarii* (12%) from the reign of Septimius Severus (AD 193–211).[24] The few remaining specimens fall on either side of these peaks, and the hoard closes with six *denarii* of Severus Alexander (AD 222–35). The Eki hoard therefore consisted of two disconnected peaks of currencies: a first one under Hadrian and Antoninus Pius with Cappadocian didrachms, followed by a second one under the Severans with imperial *denarii*, a majority of which had been minted in eastern mints (83% for Septimius Severus alone).[25] Mixed up with these were a few drachms minted in Caesarea for Julia Domna and Caracalla, as well as a single drachm minted for Caracalla in Petra (Jordan).[26] These two groups of coins might correspond to two periods of hoarding, possibly reflecting two different periods of arrival of silver in the region, given that it seems unlikely that the group of 712 didrachms of Caesarea from Hadrian would have remained unmixed with other coins over a period of more than 60 years at least. The coins were contained in a clay pot that broke when it was found, and the disposition of the coins within their container was not recorded. This certainly excludes the possibility of two unconnected deposits, though one could still envisage two different depositions within the same container at different moments in time. The coins of Hadrian and the Antoninus Pius both show signs of wear, suggesting that they had circulated before being deposited. Whether they

[24] Dundua (1979). [25] Dundua (1979: 15).

[26] Dundua (1979: 105, no. 901, ill. pl. 23), where identified as a drachm of Elagabalus from Caesarea. On these coins, see Butcher (1989: 169–71). The Eki specimen therefore adds an eastern findspot to these drachms.

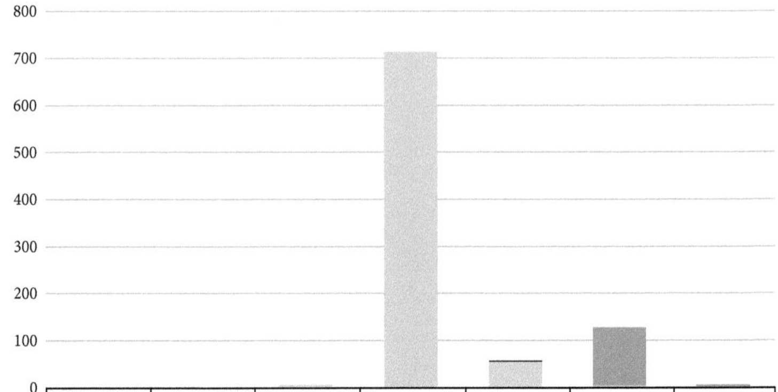

	Before 14	14–98	98–117	117–38	138–92	193–222	222–35
■ Parthian drachm	1						
■ Roman denarius					1	124	6
■ Cappadocian silver		1	2	712	56	3	
■ Other provincial silver						1	

Fig. 9.3. Composition of the Eki hoard, in number of coins by chronological period and type of coinage; after Dundua (1979).

circulated within the Empire, or in the region where they were found, will remain a matter of conjecture. On the other hand, the *denarii* definitely show fewer signs of wear, so it is to be assumed that they had circulated less.

The last hoard, Sepieti (Fig. 9.4), found in the same general area as Eki, also ends under Severus Alexander, but presents yet another picture. In contrast to Eki, its content consisted almost exclusively of *denarii* (365 or 407 specimens),[27] with only a few Cappadocian silver coins. The latter are all drachms minted under Septimius Severus *et sui*, ending with a drachm minted in year 3 of Geta (now dated to AD 211).[28] The switch of denomination (didrachm to drachm) is explained by the fact that Caesarea did not issue any didrachms at that time, although tridrachms were produced, but these do not seem to have found their way into Colchis. While the *denarii* range broadly from Trajan to Severus Alexander, most were, as in the case of Eki, issued under Septimius Severus (*c.* 255 *denarii*), with again a large contingent of eastern mints (80% for Septimius Severus).[29] Also noteworthy is a contingent of 33 *denarii* from the time of Commodus.

[27] Two different accounts of its composition exist, with Dundua (1979) cataloguing 377 specimens (365 *denarii* and 12 Cappadocian drachms), while Zograf (1945: 74–5, no. 158; 80–1, no. 184) gives a list by reign of 407 *denarii* and only ten Cappadocian drachms.

[28] Dundua (1979: 164, no. 318), where dated to AD 213. We follow here the chronology adopted for volume V.3 of the *RPC* series (forthcoming at https://rpc.ashmus.ox.ac.uk).

[29] Dundua (1979: 17, table 2).

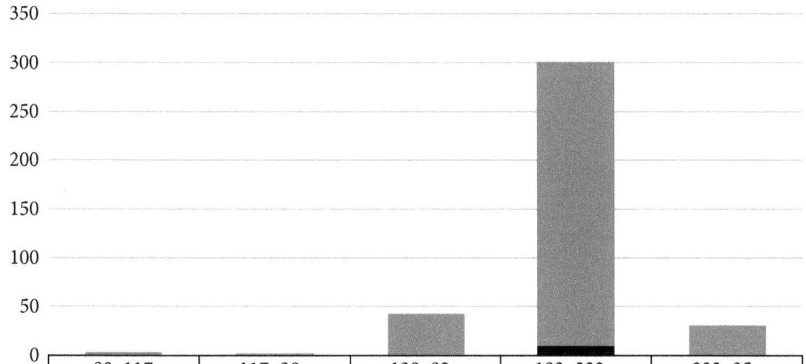

	98–117	117–38	138–92	193–222	222–35
Roman denarius	2		43	289	31
Cappadocian silver		1		11	

Fig. 9.4. Composition of the Sepieti hoard, in number of coins by chronological period and type of coinage; after Dundua (1979).

The similarity in composition between the Sepieti and Eki hoards regarding the Severan *denarii* needs to be emphasized, especially as the two findspots are relatively close to each other. It is also noteworthy that, in contrast with Cappadocian silver, Roman Severan *denarii* are only rarely found in smaller ensembles in the hinterland, with only one grave find attested so far at Ureki, comprising four Cappadocian drachms of Hadrian, one *denarius* of Septimius Severus, one *aureus* of Tacitus, and one uncertain gold imitation.[30] This absence further highlights the exceptional nature of the Eki and Sepieti hoards.

Comparative hoard evidence from within the Empire, including such a large proportion of Severan eastern *denarii,* is rare according to the data entered on the CHRE website in 2023, to the extent that the ones found in these two hoards from Colchis constitute the largest sample documented so far in hoards from the eastern Mediterranean (excluding the Balkans).

Eastern finds with more than ten eastern *denarii* each are indeed limited to a few hoards from Turkey (Haydere, CHRE 3711; Sulakyurt, CHRE 3120) or Syria (Dura-Europos Hoards 3 and 4, CHRE 9800). The Haydere hoard in western Turkey (2,330 *denarii* and *antoniniani* recorded out of a total of 5,578, *t.p.q.* AD 264, though the *denarii* it contained have been considered as a separate lot ending under Elagabalus in AD 217–22) had only 15 eastern specimens out of the 366 minted under Septimius Severus (4%).[31] As for Sulakyurt, in north-central Turkey (428 *denarii* and one Cappadocian drachm, *t.p.q.* AD 236–8), only 16 out of the 168 *denarii* minted under Septimius Severus came from eastern mints (9.5%).[32] The proportion is slightly higher for the Dura-Europos Hoards 3 and 4

[30] Ureki 1942 (CHRE 16070). [31] Bland and Aydemir (1991). [32] Kızılkaya (1991).

(402 silver coins, *t.p.q.* AD 217–18).[33] This hoard also contained, next to 31 Syrian tetradrachms ranging from Marcus Aurelius to Macrinus and one Antiochene tridrachm of Trajan, 370 *denarii* ranging from Nero to Caracalla. Of these, 135 specimens were issued during the reign of Septimius Severus, including 62 eastern *denarii*. Finds of silver of various currencies are generally associated at Dura with payments to soldiers, given that a Roman camp was established within the northern sector of the site in the earlier third century AD. In this instance, however, the greater wear of earlier coins suggests that this assemblage was withdrawn from normal circulation at some time around AD 218, and the fact that the two jars containing the hoard were deposited in a priest's house beside the temple of Artemis and Atargatis makes a military explanation much less probable. The 370 *denarii* of Dura Hoards 3 and 4 comprised quite a high proportion of pre-Severan specimens (61%), which is to be expected at a site like Dura. This contrasts sharply with the significantly lower proportion of pre-Severan *denarii* in Eki (5%) and Sepieti (11%), indicating that these coins did not penetrate into Colchis in any numbers.

Therefore, if eastern *denarii* were obviously mixed up in circulation with other non-eastern issues prior to their deposition within the eastern part of the Empire, this does not really appear to have been the case in Colchis, suggesting a possible bulk import of these coins followed by an extremely limited use, once there. Their deposition might have occurred more or less directly for Sepieti, while in the case of Eki they were added to coinages from a different origin, assembled more than 50 years earlier.

Phases and purpose(s) of 'import'

Looking at the hoard evidence collected here, including smaller deposits for the hinterland,[34] several phases of influx can be differentiated (Figs 9.5 and 9.6).[35]

Material prior to AD 14 is present in the hinterland predominantly in the form of Republican *denarii*, deposited at the earliest in the time of Augustus. Two hoards from the hinterland comprised exclusively Pontic drachms of Polemon II, produced locally in the AD 50s. These Pontic drachms are still present in early third-century hoard material in the Roman forts (Gonio 1998). As they do not occur in any later hoards in the hinterland, this seems to suggest that they had stopped being in use or certainly were not mixed with new influxes of coinage.

[33] Bellinger (1949: 167–9). Coins were contained in two jars, hence the label 'Hoards 3 and 4', though it was recognized that they constituted a single hoard.

[34] See above, n. 23.

[35] For evidence provided by single finds or foundation deposits not discussed here, notably for Apsaros, see Jaworski, Karasiewics-Szczypiorski, and Mamuladze (2021: 296–7). This includes first-century AD bronzes minted in Syria and Judaea, but also *cistophori* of Hadrian, which all show yet a different type of monetary influx. An extensive discussion of the coin circulation in Colchis has been offered by Golenko (1964).

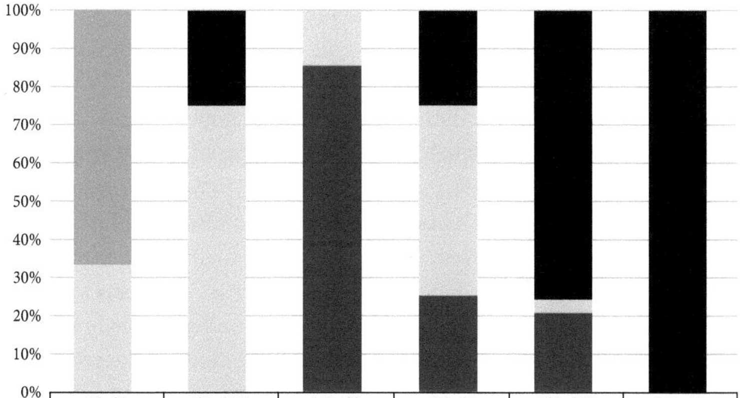

	14–98	98–117	117–38	138–92	193–222	222–45
■ Trapezus (AE)		1		2	94	22
■ Pontic drachm	4					
■ Roman denarius	2	3	2	4	4	
■ Cappadocian silver			12	2	26	

Fig. 9.5. Colchis. Content of the hoards found at Apsaros and Pityus (n = 204), in relative proportions by chronological period, excluding 26 uncertain coins. After Jaworski (2021: 142, table 2) for the Gonio 1998 and 2018 hoards. For Pitsunda 1958, coins from Trapezus are listed following Kropotkin and Depeyrot (2005), upon consultation of Kapanadze (1966). The eight coins itemized as belonging to either Commodus or Septimius Severus are excluded here.

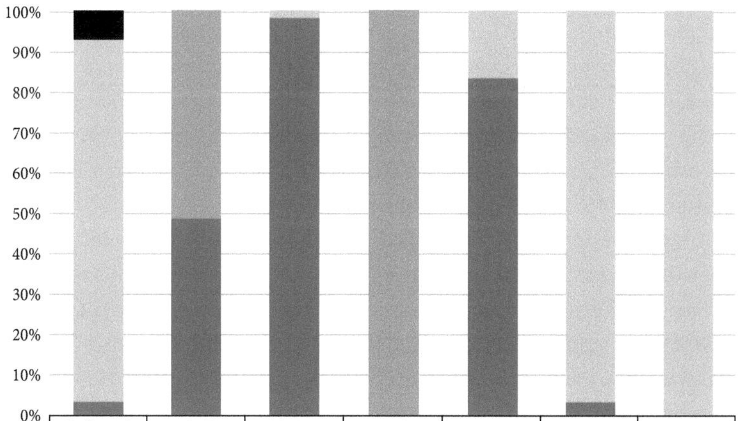

	Before 14	14–98	98–117	117–38	138–92	193–222	222–45
■ Other	2						
■ Pontic drachm		70					
■ Roman denarius	25		2		42	456	38
■ Cappadocian silver	1	66	178	819	209	15	

Fig. 9.6. Colchis. Content of all hoards found in the hinterland (n = 1,946), in relative proportions by chronological period, excluding 23 uncertain coins. Data downloaded from CHRE for all smaller hoards (accessed 22 March 2023), and after Zograf (1945) for Gerzeul and Dundua (1979) for Eki and Sepieti.

In what follows until the end of the Antonine period, the picture slightly changes between the Roman forts and the hinterland, though it needs to be stressed that hoard data from the forts are extremely limited for this period and may not be fully representative. Nevertheless, they seem to show at times (AD 98–117 and 138–92) a higher proportion of *denarii* for the reigns of Trajan and Hadrian compared to the hinterland, almost entirely dominated by Cappadocian silver until the end of the Antonine period.[36] Admittedly, all Roman *denarii* were found in one single hoard (Gonio 1998), which may distort the evidence. Compared to the *denarius*, Cappadocian silver is well represented in the forts under Hadrian (AD 117–38) and then also later under the Severans (AD 193–222), at a time when the influx in the hinterland had heavily shifted towards *denarii*.

Cappadocian silver was produced in a range of denominations comprising mainly didrachms, drachms, and hemidrachms, though not all were minted at all times. Both in the Roman forts and the hinterland, didrachms dominate for the reign of Hadrian (AD 117–38), and also in the Antonine period (AD 138–92) for the hinterland. For the latter region, the picture is admittedly heavily distorted by the very large Eki hoard, consisting almost entirely of didrachms (771, compared to only 5 drachms), of which the overwhelming majority were minted under Hadrian (712 specimens), with a further 55 minted under Antoninus Pius. On the other hand, the Gerzeul hoard also contained, next to a majority of didrachms, a fair contingent of drachms and even hemidrachms (Fig. 9.2). Under the Severans (AD 193–222), only drachms occur because didrachms were no longer minted.

The influx of Cappadocian silver stops with Caracalla. Published hoards with detailed coin level data indicate an end of 'supply' early in his reign well before Caesarea interrupted its silver production in AD 217, but more detailed evidence is needed to confirm this.[37] In any case, a few single finds show the presence of some Cappadocian silver produced for Gordian III between AD 240 and 242, as mentioned above, reminding us that hoards do not necessarily reflect the full picture of coin supply in a region.

Under the Severans, at the same time as Cappadocian silver subsided, Roman *denarii* are imported in larger numbers, predominantly from eastern mints. These *denarii* are attested in small numbers in the Roman fort of Apsaros (Gonio 2018 hoard), but appear predominantly in the hinterland. In this regard, the small number of Roman *denarii* reported for Roman forts for AD 193–222 compared to Cappadocian silver (4 *denarii* vs 24 drachms and two of undocumented denominations, i.e. 13.3%) contrasts curiously with data from the hinterland, where these proportions are reversed (456 *denarii* vs 15 drachms, i.e. 96.8%), further underlining the exceptional nature of the Eki and Sepieti hoards. The import of imperial

[36] See Abramzon (2003: 247) for large numbers of single finds of Cappadocian silver in present-day Abkhazia in the north of Georgia.

[37] The last Caesarean drachm from Sepieti belongs to year 3 of Geta (AD 211); see Dundua (1979: 164, no. 318), where dated to AD 213, and n. 28 above.

denarii remains short-lived and stops with Severus Alexander, after which no further Roman imperial coins are found in hoards, nor in any significant numbers as single finds, before the reforms of Diocletian. No *antoninianus* has so far been recorded for any hoard in the region, nor in the wider Caucasus region at all, though some are attested among single finds at the Roman fort of Pityus.[38] This lack of influx of imperial coinage in the later third century might be connected, for Colchis, with the incursions of the Boranoi, who, in the AD 250s, raided the eastern shores of the Black Sea, taking Pityus and plundering even Trapezus. The fort at Apsaros too shows traces of destruction and subsequent abandonment in the third century, to be rebuilt only in Byzantine times.[39]

One last category of coins to penetrate the coastal region, but not the hinterland, were civic provincial bronze coins minted by Trapezus until AD 244/5, represented in the Gonio 2018 (Apsaros) and Pitsunda 1958 (Pityus) hoards. Their presence in Apsaros is hardly surprising, given the relative geographical proximity of the sites, but Pityus is located much further north. If the Gonio 2018 hoard reveals an early specimen from the reign of Trajan (AD 98–117), most of them date from the time of the Severans. This coincides with an increased production of the mint, under Septimius Severus, but also Severus Alexander.[40] Trapezuntine bronzes are also attested among single finds at Pityus and Sebastopolis/Dioscurias (modern Sukhumi), next to some rare specimens from other provincial mints.[41]

Several explanations have been advanced in order to account for the presence of these coins in Colchis. It is generally admitted that both the Cappadocian silver and the Roman *denarii* penetrated into the hinterland through the Roman forts on the coast, given that these currencies are mostly absent from Caucasian Iberia and Armenia.

One assumption is that the Roman garrisons were paid in these currencies, especially the Cappadocian silver.[42] Confirmation that legionaries stationed at Apsaros were paid in coins comes from a passage of the *Periplus Maris Euxini* 6.ii, written by the Greek historian Arrian, governor of Cappadocia under Hadrian, where it is stated:

> *Καὶ ἤλθομεν πρὸ τῆς μεσημβρίας σταδίους πλείονας ἢ πεντ[ήκοντα καὶ δι]ακοσίους εἰς Ἄψαρον, ἵναπερ αἱ πέντε σπεῖραί εἰσιν ἱδρυμέναι.* Καὶ τὴν μισθοφορὰν τῇ

[38] Dundua (2008: 310).

[39] Jaworski, Karasiewics-Szczypiorski, and Mamuladze (2021: 297–300).

[40] Wojan (2006: 219).

[41] The catalogue established by Golenko (1964: 72–6, nos 36–48) comprises bronzes of Caesarea in Cappadocia, Laodicea, Antioch, Amastris, and Trapezus, most of which were found at Pitsunda and Sukhumi. Except for Trapezus, numbers remain very low. Bronzes minted in Neocaesarea, Sinope, Amisus, and Nicomedia are listed by Dundua (2008: 310, table 1) at Pityus. For single finds of coins of Trapezus, see above, n. 19.

[42] Golenko (1964: 24–8); Bland (1996: 66; 2023: 481); Jaworski (2021: 131).

> στρατιᾷ ἔδωκα [emphasize added] *καὶ τὰ ὅπλα εἶδον καὶ τὸ τεῖχος καὶ τὴν τάφρον καὶ τοὺς κάμνοντας καὶ τοῦ σίτου τὴν παρασκευὴν τὴν ἐνοῦσαν.*
>
> And before midday we came more than [2]50 stades to Apsaros, where five cohorts are stationed. *I gave the army its pay* [emphasis added] and inspected its weapons, the walls, the trench, the sick, and the food supplies that were there.[43]

Variation in the supply of silver to the Roman forts has also been put into direct relationship with military activities on the Pontic frontier, suggesting an active part played by the forts or at least a more intense occupation by Roman units during times of conflict under Trajan, Hadrian, Septimius Severus, and Caracalla, resulting in an enhanced supply in silver coinage.[44] Another view links the presence of Cappadocian silver with the activities of merchants and connects the presence of bronze to military pay.[45] This hypothesis seems less convincing, at least for the silver, given that at least two hoards from the hinterland show a concentrated 'import' of coins that is unlikely to be the result of regular trade exchanges.

Foreign bronzes, including the provincial issues from Trapezus, all absent from the hinterland, are considered to have been imported in order to meet the soldiers' daily needs for small change, given the limited access to coins in the region.[46] An alternative view could be that these coins had become part of or possibly replaced silver as military pay by the third century AD. This is not necessarily to say that they were minted for this specific purpose, but, given their production in abundant numbers, they could have been available for such a use. Their appearance in the Roman forts is difficult to date, though they certainly did not come in any significant numbers before the Severan period, judging from the hoard evidence. This raises the question of what coinage fulfilled the role of 'small change' before that time. No hoard evidence exists, but single finds at Apsaros have revealed the presence of relatively important numbers of heavily worn and countermarked Antiochene SC and Judaean bronzes, dating to the periods AD 54–68 and 69–79. It is thought that these coins travelled north in connection with troop movements associated with Trajan's Parthian Wars.[47]

Interestingly, the two hoards found at Apsaros, both of relatively small size, were unearthed beyond the perimeter of the Roman fort, in an area belonging to a *vicus*, hinting at a possible monetary use of coinage outside a strictly Roman environment.[48]

[43] Translation by Liddle (2003).

[44] For Apsaros, see Jaworski (2021: 128–32 and 141, table 1). More generally for Colchis and the hinterland, see Abramzon (2003: 247–8) with previous bibliography.

[45] Dundua (2008: 311–12).

[46] Jaworski, Karasiewics-Szczypiorski, and Mamuladze (2021: 297); Jaworski (2021: 132).

[47] Jaworski (2021: 128–30).

[48] Jaworski, Karasiewics-Szczypiorski, and Mamuladze (2021: 301).

A monetary use should not necessarily be assumed for coins in the hinterland, where finds are characterized by an absence of bronze coins, a high frequency of Cappadocian silver from the second half of the first century until the end of the second century, succeeded by an influx of eastern *denarii* under Septimius Severus. The three large hoards of Gerzeul, Eki, and Sepieti point towards the deliberate hoarding of large numbers of silver coins, possibly imported in bulk. They have been connected to various military events, with the Sepieti hoard, for example, interpreted as part of the treasury of a Roman detachment.[49] For smaller finds, context information is largely unavailable, though some finds come from graves, which informs us little about their use prior to a funerary context.[50] In the absence of any textual sources, it is in the end impossible to ascertain whether these silver coins of varying size and weight (didrachms, drachms, hemidrachms, and later *denarii*) represented specific units of value for the tribes of the Colchian hinterland within a possibly monetized economy. It therefore remains to be seen whether these coins were used, rather, as prestige objects and/or store of wealth, or why they were deposited in such large assemblages.

CROSSING (INTERNAL) FRONTIERS ON THE EUPHRATES: ZEUGMA AND DURA-EUROPOS

The sites of Zeugma (Turkey) and Dura-Europos (Syria) are both located on the Euphrates and share a number of similarities in terms of occupation, history, and military role (Fig. 9.7). Both were founded by Seleukos I in the early third century BC. Dura-Europos (often referred to as Dura given that the compound name Dura-Europos is a modern creation) was at times under Parthian domination, before being occupied first by Trajan and then reintegrated into the Roman Empire after AD 165. More importantly, both cities were sacked by the Sasanian king Shapur I in the mid-250s, which led to the complete destruction and subsequent abandonment of Dura. Zeugma was later partially rebuilt. Both sites have also been extensively excavated, Dura mainly from 1928 to 1937 and Zeugma in the late 1990s and 2000, with further excavations resumed since 2005. Extensive publications were devoted to coin finds from both sites.[51] As both sites were subjected to an approximately contemporary destruction, the numismatic material retrieved from the destruction deposits belongs to a similar time horizon and can therefore be meaningfully compared with one another. One difference, however, lies in the fact that Zeugma issued its own bronze coinage during the Roman period, whereas Dura-Europos did not.

[49] Abramzon (2003: 247), with previous Russian bibliography.

[50] See Fabian (2019: 41), highlighting the long-standing tradition of the mortuary use of coins in Colchis since the fifth century BC, which later spread to Caucasian Iberia.

[51] Zeugma: Butcher (2013); Frascone (2013); Toumpan (2015; 2020). Dura-Europos: Bellinger (1949).

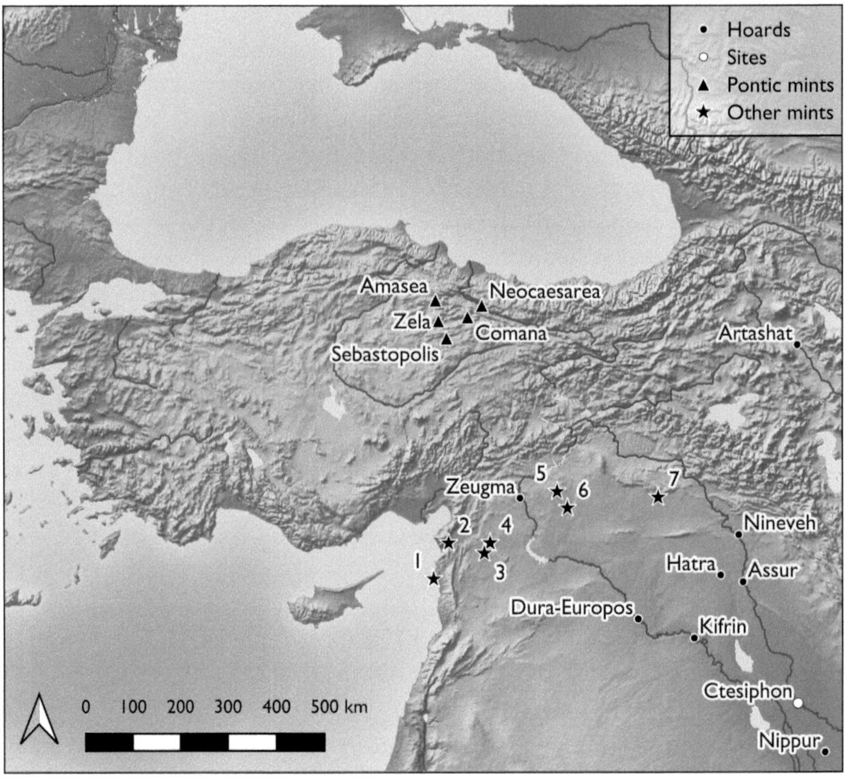

Fig. 9.7. Zeugma, Dura-Europos, and Mesopotamia. Map of the hoards discussed, with main sites and mints mentioned in the text. Numbers refer to the following mints: 1. Laodicea ad Mare; 2. Antioch; 3. Chalcis; 4. Beroea; 5. Edessa; 6. Carrhae; 7. Nisibis. Map: A. Wilson/M. Spoerri Butcher.

It should also be noted that while Dura was subject to Parthian rule before AD 165, very few coins were retrieved from contexts dating to this period, and little can in the end be said on the subject of the use of Roman coins during that time.[52] Similarly, Parthian and later Sasanian coinage occurs only in modest quantities in later contexts, and there seem to have been few exports of these currencies into the Roman Empire.[53]

Various aspects of regional and local coin circulation have been explored, suggesting the existence of a 'network of coin circulation' along the Euphrates consisting of Antiochene, Mesopotamian, Pontic, and Peloponnesian coins.[54] The presence of Pontic and Peloponnesian issues, all made under Septimius Severus, might surprise at first sight but has long been recognized as an integral part of the

[52] Pollard (2004). [53] See below, n. 88. [54] Butcher (2013: 7–8).

coin assemblages found not only at Dura and now Zeugma but also at other sites of Mesopotamia along the Euphrates.[55]

The Peloponnesian coins all belonged to a large issue produced by a variety of mints between AD 202 and 205. As for the Pontic coins, these were produced between AD 205 and 207 in Amasea, and also in Neocaesarea, Zela, and Comana.[56] Both groups of coins were taken out of their normal circulation regions no later than Caracalla's reign and are therefore likely to be associated with Caracalla's eastern campaigns in AD 214–15. The Pontic coins were, admittedly, part of a more regular movement of coins along the eastern *limes*, as earlier or even later issues are also found at Dura. As detailed by Howgego, neither group of coinage is likely to have been specifically produced for 'export', and the reason these coins were issued is ultimately unlikely to be connected with the final use of some of them in Syria and Mesopotamia. Having travelled a long distance from their original place of issue and crossed multiple regional boundaries, these coins were nonetheless accepted alongside other more 'local' bronze issues, as attested by single finds across the wider Mesopotamian region.

In Dura, Pontic coins were also found in six hoards (Table 9.3), mixed with other provincial bronze coins of mostly later date given that the hoards all end between the reigns of Gordian III (AD 238–44) and Trebonianus Gallus (AD 251–3).[57]

All six hoards cover a large chronological span, ranging for the bulk of the coins from Septimius Severus to their respective end dates, and can therefore be analysed together. The content of these hoards has been summarized in Table 9.4, listed by chronological period and geographical provenance of all 3,717 coins. Most of the coins belong to the reigns of Gordian III (32%), Severus Alexander (25%), and Septimius Severus (21%). The peak under Gordian III is particularly noteworthy and may well be connected to his campaign against the Persians, in AD 242–4.

Given that Dura-Europos never produced any coinage during the Roman period, all coins in use in the city were imported. Unsurprisingly, Mesopotamian issues, produced predominantly in Edessa and Nisibis, are extremely well represented for most periods and constitute 61% of the total number of coins of these six hoards. Syrian coins, minted chiefly in Antioch, are also present, but in lesser numbers. Their absence under Gordian III is due to the fact that Antioch and other northern Syrian mints did not produce any bronze coins during that period. More surprising perhaps is the geographical origin of the coins issued under

[55] See the discussion given for both groups of coins by Howgego (1985: 25–8) and more recently Frascone (2005). For the presence of Peloponnesian coins in Syria, see more specifically Seyrig (1936; 1957). Seyrig (1957: 256–9) includes a list of 43 such coins with a local provenance documented by the author across wider Syria. For two Peloponnesian coins from Kifrin (Iraq), see Butcher (2021: 63, nos 59 and 60).

[56] For a discussion of the circulation of Amasea's coinage, see Dalaison (2008: 185–8).

[57] Bellinger (1949).

Table 9.3. Dura-Europos. Bronze hoards containing Pontic and Peloponnesian coins, after Bellinger (1949). Data downloaded from CHRE (accessed 2 June 2023).

Hoard	Content	*t.p.q.*
Hoard 22 (CHRE 9827)	21 provincial bronzes (Septimius Severus to Gordian III; Amasea: 5, Neocaesarea: 1).	AD 238–44
Hoard 15 (CHRE 9819)	232 provincial bronzes, some illegible (Septimius Severus to Philip I; Amasea: 37, Comana: 1, Neocaesarea: 10).	AD 244–9
Hoard 16 (CHRE 9820)	107 provincial bronzes, some illegible (Nerva to Philip I; Amasea: 20, Neocaesarea: 4).	AD 244–9
Hoards 8 and 9 (CHRE 9828)[a]	2,832 coins, including 2 Hellenistic coins, 2 *denarii* (Severus Alexander), 2,817 provincial bronzes (Domitian to Decius; Amasea: 515, Comana: 13, Neocaesarea: 49, Zela: 17, Peloponnesian mints: 11), and 11 illegible coins.	AD 249–51
Hoard 14 (CHRE 9818)	265 provincial bronzes, some illegible (Trajan to Decius; Amasea: 52, Neocaesarea: 10).	AD 249–51
Hoard 12 (CHRE 9817)	260 provincial bronzes (Domitian to Gallus; Amasea: 7, Comana: 4, Neocaesarea: 6, Zela: 2).	AD 251–3

[a] Hoards 8 and 9 were found under the floor of the same room and treated as one deposit; see Bellinger (1939; 1949: 172–5).

Septimius Severus. Indeed, these consist almost solely in issues produced by Pontic mints (96%), the vast majority being issued by Amasea (636 specimens, issued in AD 205/6 and 206/7), followed by Neocaesarea (80 specimens, issued in AD 205/6), Zela (19 specimens, issued in AD 205/6 and 206/7), Comana (18 specimens, issued in AD 205/6), and Sebastopolis (one specimen, issued in AD 205/6). Peloponnesian mints are also represented, but in very small numbers (11 coins, i.e. 1.4%), as are Mesopotamian issues (12 coins from Edessa, i.e. 1.5%). It is perhaps not so much the presence of Pontic coins in itself that is surprising but, rather, their overwhelming dominance and the simultaneous absence of any more locally produced bronze coinage, including the Edessan issues made in abundant numbers for Septimius Severus and king Abgar VIII.

Any attempt to explain this absence needs to take into account the fact that similar proportions were noted in Zeugma in regard to single finds for the time of Septimius Severus, together with a more general scarcity of Severan coinage from Mesopotamia.[58] As suggested by Kevin Butcher, one could envisage, for example,

[58] Butcher (2013: 8, with table 4). There is, however, no such scarcity for the time of Severus Alexander at Dura-Europos.

Table 9.4. Number of coins by geographical origin and reign in the Dura-Europos hoards 8, 9, 12, 14, 15, 16, and 22, after Bellinger (1949). Not included are 180 completely illegible coins. Data downloaded from CHRE (accessed 2 June 2023).

Period	Peloponnesus	Pontus	Syria	Mesopotamia	Other	Total
Pre-Severan			24	1	5	30
Septimius Severus	11	754	1	12	2	780
Caracalla - Macrinus			17	4	6	27
Elagabalus			142	44	1	187
Severus Alexander			89	846	5	940
Gordian III				1,200		1,200
Philip I			203	149		352
Decius—Gallus			5	16		21
Total	11	754	481	2,272	19	3,537

that such coins were no longer present in circulation by the mid-third century AD at the time of the Persian destruction of the site, given that all deposits were dated from that time, while Pontic and Peloponnesian coins remained for some reason available. Mesopotamian coins from Severus Alexander are admittedly present in the Dura hoards, though we do not know how and when these hoards were formed.

In any case, one could certainly envisage that the Pontic coins were deliberately 'imported', in order to cover a larger than usual need or to compensate for the unavailability of other regional bronze coinages. It is noticeable that all Pontic issues were large modules (27 to 31 mm), whereas contemporary Mesopotamian coinage was of smaller size. Why these coinages were specifically chosen remains a matter of conjecture, but the enormous output of the Pontic cities, especially Amasea (in AD 205/6 and 206/7) and Neocaesarea (in AD 205/6), certainly contributed to this currency being widely available. No later or earlier coins were part of the same transfer, for the simple reason that production only resumed in these cities at a much later date, under Elagabalus in AD 218/19, and no previous coinage had been issued by them since at least the reign of Commodus.

Another case of 'crossing frontiers', but of a different nature, is provided by hoards that fall outside the normal range of coins one would expect to find at either site. This is the case with two hoards from Zeugma: Zeugma 2000 Hoard 1 (462 coins, *t.p.q.* AD 243/4) and Zeugma 2006 (46 coins, *t.p.q.* AD 249–51).[59] Though of different sizes, both hoards comprised a range of unexpected coinages that differ from the profile of coin circulation at Zeugma given by single finds.

[59] Zeugma 2000 Hoard 1 (CHRE 4751): Butcher (2013: 10–14 and 45–86, with figure 5 for a distribution map of all mints represented in the hoard); Zeugma 2006 (CHRE 20075): Toumpan (2015: 82–94 and 129–32; 2020: 195).

The oddity of these deposits resides in the complete absence or scarcity of the kind of bronze coinage that is otherwise common in Zeugma among single finds, namely coins of Zeugma itself (none in either hoard) and issues of Edessa or Carrhae (one or possibly two in Zeugma 2000 Hoard 1; one in Zeugma 2006). Instead, one finds a quite bewildering range of distinct components, corresponding to separate circulation areas withing the Roman Empire (Table 9.5). Both hoards comprised a substantial number of imperial *aes* coinages (*sestertii*, *dupondii*, *asses*, and *semisses*) representing 28% (130 specimens) and 41% (19 specimens) of their respective content, whereas imperial *aes* is excessively rare among single finds.[60] Provincial coinages from the Balkans and Asia Minor more generally constitute another large element, with a group of 150 bronzes (i.e. 32%) from Caesarea in Cappadocia (Commodus to Gordian III) being specifically noticeable in the Zeugma 2000 Hoard 1. The presence of coins produced by more than 20 mints located in Moesia Inferior, Thrace, and western Asia Minor, with each mint only represented by very few specimens, is certainly an oddity.

Given the absence of overlap between currencies common among single finds and coinages common in the Zeugma 2000 Hoard 1, Butcher argued that the coins in that hoard had been assembled precisely because they were *not* in general

Table 9.5. Composition of the Zeugma 2000 Hoard 1 and Zeugma 2006 hoards, after Butcher (2013) and Toumpan (2015).

Content	Zeugma 2000 Hoard 1 (CHRE 4751)		Zeugma 2006 (CHRE 20075)	
Imperial *aes*	130	28.0%	19	41.0%
Imperial silver	2	0.5%	1	2.0%
Caesarea in Cappadocia	150	32.5%	1	2.0%
Balkans and Asia Minor	65	14.0%	12	26.0%
Northern Syrian mints	20	4.5%	2	4.5%
Southern Syrian mints	14	3.0%	2	4.5%
Mesopotamia	2? (Edessa)	0.5%	5 (Edessa, Nisibis, Rhesaena)	11.0%
Provincial silver		0.0%	2 (Antioch, Alexandria in Egypt)	4.5%
Other	1 (Seleucid coin)	0.5%		0.0%
Worn or uncertain	78	16.5%	2	4.5%
Total	**462**		**46**	

[60] Butcher (2013: 9) recorded one specimen, Frascone (2013: 280) four specimens, and Toumpan (2020: 194) five specimens.

use in Zeugma.[61] Different degrees of wear between the individual groups of coins further suggests that these were constituted at various times, possibly in various places, and perhaps only assembled together in Zeugma. The facts that the hoard ends with coins of Gordian III minted in Caesarea in Cappadocia in AD 243/4 and that it includes coins from mints in the Balkans and western Asia Minor might indicate that some of its components were collected by individuals or groups of individuals travelling eastwards through the Empire. This suggests a possible connection for some of its content with Gordian III's campaign against the Persians in AD 242–4.[62] According to Butcher, the content of this hoard would therefore provide us with a good example of what was regarded as 'foreign' in Zeugma in the 240s and 250s, challenging at the same time a number of assumptions relating to the way we traditionally regard hoards as representing coin circulation at a given place. The discovery of a second hoard with a similar content (though with a slightly different chronological frame, as it ends with coins of Trajan Decius, AD 249–51) ought not necessarily to question this interpretation, as the coins from the Zeugma 2006 hoard could very well have also been put aside or collected precisely because many of them were foreign (the coins were found in the destruction layer of a house, next to broken sherds of a pot).[63] The inclusion of some medallion-sized coins (37+ mm) among the specimens of western Asia Minor (Mytilene and Pergamum for Zeugma 2000 Hoard 1; Themisonium for Zeugma 2006) speaks further against the hypothesis that these coins might have had monetary use in Zeugma, as these modules are far larger than the norm for the coinages of Zeugma and Edessa.

A final word ought to be said about Dura-Europos Hoards 8 and 9, already mentioned above in the discussion of the presence of Pontic issues. This assemblage too was composed of coinages from a multitude of cities, stretching across Greece, Asia Minor (including four specimens from western Asia Minor—one from Peltae and three from Antioch in Pisidia), Syria, and Mesopotamia. As such, it has been cited as a parallel for the two hoards from Zeugma, with the reservation that it actually contained numerous coins that were also attested at the site as single finds, and which cannot therefore be characterized as 'foreign'.[64]

BEYOND THE EUPHRATES

The region beyond the Euphrates witnessed only intermittent Roman occupation, serving mainly as a stronghold of the Parthian and then Sasanian realm, though

[61] Butcher (2013: 12–14); Butcher (2019a).

[62] The bulk of the coins from the Balkans and western Asia Minor seem to date from the reigns of Septimius Severus and Elagabalus, so a succession of several 'voyages' could also be envisaged.

[63] In some ways, these two hoards resemble the 'Periplous hoards' discussed by Ariel in the present volume (chapter 3).

[64] Butcher (2013: 12).

at times independent kingdoms like Hatra (Iraq) had close ties with Rome.[65] If Trajan conquered Mesopotamia in the wake of his Parthian War in AD 115, pushing across the Tigris into Adiabene and even reaching the Persian Gulf the following year, the newly established provinces of Mesopotamia and Assyria were short-lived and abandoned under Hadrian in AD 117.[66] Lucius Verus, in his Parthian campaigns, also successfully raided southern Mesopotamia and sacked Ctesiphon (AD 164/5). A more permanent province of Mesopotamia, in the north of the region was then re-established by Septimius Severus, who, emulating Trajan, sacked Ctesiphon (Iraq) in AD 198.[67] Probably also under the Severans, the Euphrates *limes* was extended further down the Euphrates, south of Dura-Europos. During Caracalla's Parthian War, the Romans crossed the Tigris again and re-entered Adiabene in AD 216, taking Arbela, but were then defeated, under Caracalla's successor Macrinus, at the Battle of Nisibis in AD 217. Hostilities were resumed under Severus Alexander, but this time by the Sasanians, who by then had taken over from the Parthians and pursued a more offensive strategy. Events culminated in the 240s with the Sasanian capture of Hatra, Gordian III's subsequent *Expeditio Orientalis* (AD 242–4), and the defeat of Valerian, who was taken prisoner by the Sasanian king Shapur at the Battle of Edessa between AD 258 and 260 and died in captivity.

Against this backdrop of shifting political control and military incursions, a few sites have yielded coin finds that allow us to examine the phenomenon of movements of currencies across the Euphrates border (Fig. 9.7). As shall be seen, these 'movements' pertained to a range of coinages and took a variety of forms.

The site for which coin finds are specifically well documented is Assur (Iraq), an old Assyrian city located on the Tigris that was revived under the Parthians and became an administrative centre of Parthian-ruled north Mesopotamia. The excavations conducted there by the Deutsche Orient-Gesellschaft between 1903 and 1913 encompassed 320 single finds belonging to the first three centuries AD, as well as five hoards.[68] A few other sites from Arsacid-controlled northern and middle Mesopotamia also yielded Roman-period finds, with most including hoards alongside some single gold coins. These sites are the caravan city of Hatra (three hoards), the ancient city of Nineveh (modern-day Mosul) on the Tigris (two hoards; one single gold coin), the fortified settlement of Kifrin on the eastern bank of the Euphrates south of Dura-Europos (one hoard), the Sumerian site of Sippar on the Euphrates, *c.* 30 km south-west of modern-day Baghdad (a few single finds), and the Sumerian city of Nippur, 200 km south of Baghdad (one

[65] On Hatra, see Luther (2014: 501–3).
[66] Millar (1993: 99–105). For a broad historical narrative, see Edwell (2021).
[67] On Septimius Severus' Parthian Wars, see, for example, Hartmann (2009).
[68] Butcher (2017). A preliminary list was given by Heidemann and Miglus (1996: 354).

single gold coin). Hoard data from Mesopotamia, including records of single gold coins, are summarized in Tables 9.7 and 9.8.

Except for a hoard of 154 Parthian tetradrachms ranging down to 24/23 BC, and a group of 14 tetradrachms of Vologaeses IV (*c.* AD 147–91) that may have constituted a hoard, very little Arsacid coinage is present on the site of Assur.[69] In contrast, single finds show a substantial import of Roman provincial bronze coins, comprising a large group of SC coins from Antioch in Syria, next to issues produced by a few other Syrian (Beroea, Hierapolis, Laodicea ad Mare) or Mesopotamian (Edessa, Carrhae) cities. The SC coins range in date from Augustus to Commodus, with 71 recorded as single finds and some present in hoard material (Assur, Hoard 5 and Hoard 9). A similar chronological range applies to the Syrian mints, whereas the few coins from Edessa and Carrhae were produced in the early third century AD (Elagabalus and Severus Alexander).

Though perhaps unexpected at first sight, the presence of first- and early second-century AD Antiochene SC bronzes among site finds in Parthian Mesopotamia is not unusual and seems to indicate a common pool of circulation specific to northern Mesopotamia. Some specimens also occurred in Kifrin (on the eastern bank of the Euphrates, south of Dura-Europos), Sippar (on the Euphrates, *c.* 60 km north of Baghdad), or even Seleucia on the Tigris (on the western bank of the Tigris, facing Ctesiphon).[70] The reasons for the presence of these coins in Mesopotamia are unclear, as they could reflect commercial relations, be a deliberate import by local authorities, or be the result of movements of Roman troops. According to Kevin Butcher, a deliberate import could be favoured based on the fact that some provincial coins minted under Trajan and Antoninus Pius, especially at Laodicea ad Mare, were deliberately selected in order to be overstruck by some local imitative SC coinages.[71]

These imitative SC coinages display on the reverse the letters SC, though inverted or reversed compared to the Antiochene originals. Several classes can be distinguished. The ones depicting the sun god Shamash on the obverse coupled with an eagle on the reverse have been attributed to Hatra (Fig. 9.8). Others, showing the moon god Sin, a blank obverse, or Assur-Bel with, on the reverse, a crescent, could well have been produced in Assur itself.[72] A possible model could consist in the import of Antiochene SC bronzes between the late first and the late second centuries, succeeded by a local production of imitative coinages during

[69] Hoard of 154 Parthian tetradrachms: Schultz (1982) and Butcher (2017: 44, Hoard 1); hoard of 14 tetradrachms of Vologaeses IV: Butcher (2017: 28, nos 56–69). See also Hoard 2, Butcher (2017: 45), consisting of two further tetradrachms of the same ruler found in a tomb, though the coins could have been residual.

[70] Kifrin: Butcher (2021); Sippar: Butcher (2015); Seleucia on the Tigris: Le Rider (1998: 103, nos 1–3).

[71] Butcher (2015: 186–7; 2017: 12–13, 16–17). The overstrikes all belong to the so-called 'Class 2' category of coins, quite carelessly made and produced at Hatra.

[72] See Butcher (2017: 14–21; 2022) for the most recent overviews on these imitative coinages.

Fig. 9.8. Hatra, imitative SC coinage, bronze, 12.75 g. © Bibliothèque nationale de France, département Monnaies, médailles et antiques, Luynes 3459. Image from https://gallica.bnf.fr/ark:/12148/btv1b11318564z (accessed 15 November 2023).

the second century AD. The import of Antiochene SC bronzes and the subsequent production of SC imitations are clearly related and might be connected with the rise in importance of Hatra. A religious use as 'temple coins' has been envisaged for issues made at Hatra, though according to Butcher this is an unnecessary restriction of their use given that they are also found over a wide geographical area in Mesopotamia and even beyond, often associated with provincial coins in hoards or even sometimes cut in half like other provincial issues.[73]

Provincial coins and imitative SC coinages occur in a number of hoards or groups of coins that may have been hoards, from both Assur and Hatra (Table 9.6). If Assur Hoard 5 is composed exclusively of Roman provincial coins from a variety of north Syrian mints, including four specimens produced in Laodicea ad Mare, such diversity is not seen in the other deposits, which consist of imitative coinages sometimes associated with SC bronze from Antioch. In this respect, Assur Hoard 9, found in a pot but without any archaeological context recorded, illustrates the simultaneous hoarding of Antioch SC coins and imitative coinages, a sign that both types of coin were certainly used for the same purpose(s), at least at Assur. Other hoards, such as Hatra 1951, found in one of the buildings at Hatra, may have consisted solely of imitation issues.[74]

Next to provincial bronze coinage, Roman imperial coins also penetrated into Mesopotamia (Tables 9.7 and 9.8). Hoard material consists solely of *aurei* (Assur, with also single gold finds recorded for Assur, Nineveh, Nippur, and Northern Iraq) and *denarii* (Kifrin, Nineveh).

[73] Butcher (2015: 25). For a religious use of the Hatra issues, see Slocum (1977: 44–5) and Gaslain (2009: 26–7). Other categories of SC imitations include crudely made cast specimens; see Slocum (1977: 41–2), where labelled as 'Series 3', and Butcher (2017: 14). These occur in Mesopotamia, but also in Armenia, where a hoard of them was found at Artashat (CHRE 20937); see Vardanyan (2009). It is still not entirely certain where these were produced, as explained in Kéfélian's contribution in this volume (chapter 10). For further SC imitations that could be linked with Mesopotamia, see Butcher (2004: 133; 2017: 13–14) for the Flavian period, and Butcher (2019b) for Augustus.

[74] Safar (1952: 11–12); Slocum (1977: 38, n. 7).

Table 9.6. Mesopotamia. Hoards containing Roman provincial coinages and imitative SC issues. The numbering of hoards follows Butcher (2017). For the Hatra 1951 hoard, see Safar (1952: 11–12). The Hoards 3 and 4 from Hatra (marked with an asterisk [*]) were acquired from locals and could be groups of single finds rather than proper hoards.

Hoard	Provincial coins	Chronological range of Provincial coins	Imitative issues
Assur, Hoard 5 (CHRE 20607)	9 (Antioch 1, Beroea 2, Chalcis 1, Laodicea ad Mare 4, uncertain 1)	Trajan 4, Antoninus Pius 4, uncertain 1	0
Assur, Hoard 6 (CHRE 20617)	?		23 (Assur)
Assur, Hoard 9 ('Lühl') (CHRE 20615)	15 (Antioch)	Nerva 3, Trajan 2, Hadrian 4, Antoninus Pius 6	4 (Hatra 2, Assur 2)
Hatra, Hoard 3 (CHRE 20614)*	1 (Antioch)	Claudius	3 (Hatra)
Hatra, Hoard 4 (CHRE 20618)*	0		14 (Hatra)
Hatra 1951 (CHRE 20616)	0		47 (Hatra, some specimens halved)

The Assur excavations yielded the largest number of gold finds (Table 9.7), with a hoard of 15 *aurei* (Hoard 7), two single finds (one *aureus* of Vespasian, one *aureus* of Pertinax), as well as one *aureus* of Nero found together with ten unidentified copper alloy coins in a ceramic vessel (Hoard 8). Hoard 7, ending in AD 215, has been associated with Caracalla's campaign in Adiabene in AD 216 and could therefore be directly connected with a physical Roman presence in the region.[75] As for the two first-century gold coins, these circulated for a prolonged period of time and could have arrived at Assur at any time, though the *aureus* of Vespasian finds an interesting parallel in another *aureus* of the same emperor from an undocumented findspot in northern Iraq.

Further single gold coins are documented for funerary contexts. For Nineveh, an *aureus* of Tiberius was found in 1852 at Kouyunjik in a burial believed to be that of a woman.[76] It consisted of a sarcophagus that also contained a large assemblage of gold jewellery, golden face and eye covers, as well as four gold-leaf impressions of a bronze coin of Trajan, part of an issue struck in Rome for

[75] Herzfeld (1907: 116); Maricq (1957: 302, n. 2).

[76] Northern Iraq: the British Museum online collection database, Coins and Medals 1854,0505.23, https://www.britishmuseum.org/collection/object/C_1854-0405-23 (accessed 25 August 2023); Nineveh: Curtis (1976: 63, no. 21).

Table 9.7. Mesopotamia. Single gold finds and hoards containing Roman *aurei*, after Butcher (2017) for Assur, Hilprecht (1903: 504–8) for Nippur, Curtis (1976: 63, no. 21) for Nineveh, and https://www.britishmuseum.org/collection/object/C_1854-0405-23 (accessed 25 August 2023) for northern Iraq.

Hoard	Type of find	Content	*t.p.q.*
Nineveh 1852 (CHRE 20619)	Single find, burial	1 *aureus*, Tiberius	AD 14–37, but the burial dates to at least AD 116
Nippur (CHRE 20722)	Single find, burial	1 *aureus*, Tiberius	AD 14–37
Assur, Hoard 8 (CHRE 20604)	Hoard	1 *aureus* (Nero), 10 copper alloy coins (no identification available)	AD 66–7, with a later deposition date likely
Northern Iraq (CHRE 20621)	Single find	1 *aureus*, Vespasian	AD 72–3
Assur (CHRE 20606)	Single find	1 *aureus*, Vespasian	AD 73
Assur (CHRE 20608)	Single find	1 *aureus*, Pertinax	AD 193
Assur, Hoard 7 (CHRE 20603)	Hoard	15 *aurei*, Marcus Aurelius to Caracalla	AD 215

circulation in the east and dated to AD 116.[77] The date of AD 116 is relevant insofar as this corresponds to the conquest of Adiabene by Trajan and its transformation into the Roman province of Assyria. As mentioned above, this conquest was short-lived and the region reverted to being a Parthian client kingdom under Hadrian in AD 117. Roman coins could well have been imported during the annexation, even if there is no necessity to establish a direct connection between these events and this burial. More generally, the inclusion of a Roman *aureus* in a funerary context next to other golden objects testifies to a specific mortuary practice, in which the incorruptible nature of the metal was certainly relevant.[78]

The inclusion of another *aureus* of Tiberius in a funerary context is known from the tomb of two Parthian officers at Nippur, an ancient Sumerian city that at the time had become a Parthian citadel, located between the Euphrates and the Tigris approximately 200 km south of modern-day Baghdad.[79] A striking parallel with Nineveh is the use of gold, as all ornaments that had adorned the garment

[77] *RPC* III, 3671, 3672, or 3676.

[78] Curtis (1976: 60–1), also highlighting possible trade contacts with the Roman Empire and alluding to the Hellenistic custom of the obol payable to Charon, the ferryman to the underworld. On the subject of 'funerary archaeology' applied to the study of coins, see Doyen, Duchemin, and Iossif (2019), though with a focus on the western Mediterranean, Greece, and western Asia Minor.

[79] Hilprecht (1903: 504–8).

Table 9.8. Mesopotamia. Hoards containing Roman silver coins, after Butcher (2021) for Kifrin, Layard (1853: 479) for Nineveh 1849–51, and Hill (1931) for Nineveh 1929.

Hoard	Content	*t.p.q.*
Kifrin 1983 (CHRE 20613)	3 *denarii* (Trajan 1, Septimius Severus 2)	AD 194
Nineveh 1849–51 (CHRE 20620)	89 *denarii* (Vespasian to Septimius Severus)	AD 201
Nineveh 1929 (CHRE 4849)	1 SC bronze coin and 386 silver coins: 121 posthumous Philip Philadelphus tetradrachms (31–18 BC), 29 Syrian tetradrachms (Nero to Septimius Severus), 3 Arabian didrachms (Trajan), 141 *denarii* (Galba to Septimius Severus, AD 207), and 92 Parthian drachms (up to Artabanus IV, AD 213–27)	AD 213–27

and the sandals of the deceased men were made of that precious metal, including two sheets of beaten gold and a ring. The Roman *aureus*, placed next to the head of one of the skeletons, had certainly again been selected to be part of this set of golden funerary objects, as a symbol of status and wealth in the afterlife.

As for silver, three hoards of varying content and sizes could be traced (Table 9.8). One, comprising only three *denarii*, was found in the fortified settlement of Kifrin, on the Euphrates south of Dura-Europos, and probably dates from the time when the Roman *limes* was briefly extended to that area, under the Severan emperors.[80] The two other hoards were found much further east, on the Tigris at Nineveh.[81]

Of these, the Nineveh 1849–51 hoard comprised only *denarii*, ranging from Vespasian to Septimius Severus. Though its composition is currently only known through a list of emperors represented, without a clear breakdown in terms of quantities, this group of coins shows obvious similarities with the 141 *denarii* belonging to the much larger Nineveh 1929 hoard, ranging, as far as the *denarii* are concerned, from Galba to Septimius Severus (AD 207).[82] The majority of these coins were issued under the reign of Septimius Severus (103 *denarii*), and the more recent ones were described as being 'in mint state', which indicates that they circulated little before being deposited.[83] How and why these two groups of chronologically similar *denarii* arrived at Nineveh escapes us today, especially as there is no direct connection with military events in this case.

[80] Butcher (2021: 52 and 64).

[81] On Graeco-Parthian Nineveh, see Reade (1998), but also Le Rider (1967: 14–17), with references to coin finds and the two hoards discussed here.

[82] Nineveh 1849–51: Layard (1853: 479); Nineveh 1929: Hill (1931).

[83] Hill (1931: 170).

The Nineveh 1929 hoard is additionally interesting as it included, besides the Roman *denarii*, several different types of other silver coinages from various periods, comprising posthumous Philip Philadelphus tetradrachms, Syrian tetradrachms, Trajanic Arabian didrachms, and Parthian drachms. *Denarii* were therefore hoarded alongside similar-sized coins (Parthian drachms) but also larger denominations (didrachms and tetradrachms). From a chronological perspective, four clusters emerge, with the first one, by numerical size, comprising Severan *denarii* and tetradrachms, the second late Republican and early imperial posthumous Philip Philadelphus tetradrachms, the third mid-first-century AD Parthian drachms, and the last one, a much smaller group, second-century AD *denarii*. Given this chronological breakdown, it could be envisaged that these groups were assembled at different times, though coin wear speaks against this hypothesis, with earlier issues clearly more worn than coins from the Severan period.[84] The Nineveh 1929 deposit is therefore clearly a Severan hoard that contained a significant number of earlier issues that seemed still to have been in circulation.

The presence of posthumous Philip Philadelphus tetradrachms is more specifically of interest, as these coins are attested in other late second- and third-century AD deposits from Mesopotamia, whereas they had disappeared from circulation in Syria by the second century AD.[85] This is the case for a hoard found at Hatra, associating 96 of them with 1,214 Parthian tetradrachms (up to AD 191).[86] This is also the case for the Dura-Europos Hoard 5 (CHRE 9792), associating 15 of them with six first- and second-century *denarii* (up to Commodus) and seven first-century Syrian tetradrachms, as well as one *antoninianus* of Valerian.[87] Even if this last coin may represent a later addition to the hoard, this hoard was lost during the Sasanian sack of Dura-Europos in the mid-250s, implying that these coins were at least still kept, possibly as a store of wealth. How and when these coins arrived in Mesopotamia is less clear, given that they are exclusively found in third-century deposits. According to Butcher, they could have been exported *en bloc* or possibly preferred for trade.

While some of the examples reviewed here seem to establish a link between the presence of Roman imperial coins and movements of the army, especially for gold deposits (Nineveh 1852 and Assur Hoard 7), others are less easy to explain given the absence of any direct chronological association with military events. This is notably the case for the two silver deposits from Nineveh (Nineveh 1849–51 and Nineveh 1929). Harl assumed that the Parthian rulers deliberately imported

[84] Hill (1931) does not provide illustrations of the coins, but a large number of them were accessioned by the British Museum, and 149 of them are now available online at https://www.britishmuseum.org/collection (accessed 12 September 2023), with a direct link to the search at https://www.britishmuseum.org/collection/search?keyword=nineveh&keyword=coin&keyword=1930).

[85] See Butcher (2017: 11–12) on the continued presence of posthumous Philips in Mesopotamia.

[86] Al-Salihi (1974); *CH* 3, no. 92.

[87] Newell (1933); Bellinger (1949: 169–70).

Roman silver coins in order to 'sustain their own silver coinage'. The same author also suggests that Roman coins were then returned to the Empire, rather than Parthian coins being imported into the Empire, which would explain the scarcity of Parthian finds within the eastern Roman provinces.[88] A case for an import of Roman coins, both provincial and imperial, can certainly be made, whether through trade, movements of people, or deliberate political or administrative decisions. The reuse of single Roman gold coins in funerary contexts further testifies to specific mortuary practices, but ultimately does not give any indication about how and why these coins reached Mesopotamia.

CONCLUSION

This discussion of hoarding on some of the eastern fringes of the Roman Empire has demonstrated a number of movements of coinages during the time frame covered here, both within the Empire and across its borders.

The picture that emerges seems to indicate some intentional transfers of coins within the Empire to where they were needed. This is the case for long-distance movements of provincial bronzes minted in the Pontus and also the Peloponnese issued under the Severans that 'travelled' to Zeugma, Dura-Europos, and other sites along the Euphrates. A higher than usual need, combined with a lack of availability of local coins, could explain this large-scale import of Pontic coinages, possibly in connection with troop movements associated with Caracalla's Parthian War. Similarly, Cappadocian silver was exported to the Roman forts along the eastern shore of the Black sea in Colchis until the early third-century AD, possibly serving as pay for the military units stationed there.[89] Part of a similar type of circuit were provincial bronzes issued by the Pontic city of Trapezus, found in hoards at the Roman forts of Apsaros and Pityus. In the absence of any local coinages in Colchis, these might have fulfilled a role of small change or partly even served as military pay, given that most of them were issued between the reigns of Septimius Severus and Philip, after the influx of Cappadocian silver had stopped.

[88] Harl (1996: 301). The CHRE database (consulted 13 September 2023) only records two such Parthian hoards with a *t.p.q.* after 27 BC. One (CHRE 7820, comprising 57 tetradrachms of Vologases IV, *t.p.q.* AD 171/2) was allegedly found on Arados—see Simonetta (1971)—while the other (CHRE 8007, 29+ tetradrachms ranging from Artabanus II to Vologases I, *t.p.q.* AD 76/7) was found in the Lebanese mountains at Akura (east of Byblos); see Sawaya (2002).

[89] For an alternative view that imperial coinages minted in the west were the main currencies for military pay in the east of the Roman Empire, see van Heesch (2014), admittedly focusing on Asia Minor, Roman Syria, and Palestine, but not Colchis.

Acceptance of 'foreign' provincial currencies, minted in silver or bronze, did not seem to be a problem for Roman military units, possibly because what mattered was the presence of imperial portraits on these coins. At Dura-Europos, Pontic bronzes were accepted alongside more local coinages and certainly hoarded together with them. The acceptance of 'foreign' bronzes as a rule is, however, questioned through two hoards found at Zeugma that assembled coins that are otherwise unattested among single finds at the site. These coins surely show movement(s) of people across the Balkans and large areas of Asia Minor, but might have been hoarded or deposited together precisely because they were considered to be foreign.

Movements beyond frontiers were restricted to silver in the case of Colchis, with Cappadocian provincial silver in the first and second century AD replaced by eastern Roman *denarii* under the Severans. The reasons for the formation and subsequent deposition of large silver hoards like Gerzeul, Eki, or Sepieti escape us today, though these coins were evidently intentionally hoarded. These coins could be the result of possible bulk imports and may have partly belonged to the treasury of Roman military units. The absence of any bronze coins is noteworthy, but could simply indicate a preference for silver, whatever its use in the Colchian hinterland may have been.

The influx of coins into Arsacid-controlled Mesopotamia was of a more complex nature, pertaining to a larger range of currencies. The region witnessed the import of first- and second-century AD provincial bronzes, among which the SC bronzes produced in Antioch constituted the main group. The mechanisms of import are unclear, but these coins certainly fulfilled a specific purpose and were considered desirable, given that SC bronzes were imitated locally in Hatra and perhaps also Assur. In parallel to provincial bronzes, imperial gold and silver also penetrated into Mesopotamia. Some of the gold finds of *aurei* (notably at Assur and perhaps Nineveh) could be associated with Roman military campaigns and therefore were brought in by the armies, though this does not seem to be the case with either of the two larger silver hoards found at Nineveh. Silver circulated in the region in the form of Arsacid drachms and tetradrachms, so Roman *denarii* might have been imported or used to supplement local currency. Equally, the survival of posthumous Philip Philadelphus tetradrachms in late second- or third-century AD contexts is certainly remarkable, though again it remains unclear whether these coins were imported (or exported, depending on the point of view) *en bloc* or simply preferred for trade in Mesopotamia. If Roman bronze and silver could have been a component of the wider monetary economy of Mesopotamia, one wonders about the role of the gold. Some Roman *aurei* were found in funerary contexts, pointing to their role as prestige objects, symbols of status and eternal afterlife. This is quite similar to some graves in Colchis, except that in that case Cappadocian silver was used as grave goods.

ABBREVIATIONS

CH 3	Price, M. J. (ed.) (1977). *Coin Hoards* III. London.
CHRE	Coin Hoards of the Roman Empire Project (https://chre.ashmus.ox.ac.uk).
RPC	*Roman Provincial Coinage.*
RPC III	see Amandry and Burnett (2015).
RRCH	Crawford, M. H. (1969). *Roman Republican Coin Hoards* (Royal Numismatic Society Special Publication 4). London.
SNG vAulock	*Sylloge Nummorum Graecorum Deutschland. Sammlung von Aulock* (Berlin, 1957–81).

REFERENCES

Abramzon, M. G. (2003). 'The Gerzeul hoard of coins of Caesarea of Cappadocia (in the Museum of Abkhazia)', *Revue Numismatique* 159: 243–56.

Al-Salihi, W. (1974). 'The excavation coins from Hatra 1971–1972', *Sumer* 30: 155–62 (in Arabic).

Amandry, M. and Burnett, A. (2015), in collaboration with J. Mairat. *Roman Provincial Coinage* III: *Nerva, Trajan and Hadrian (AD 96–138).* London and Paris.

Bellinger, A. (1939). *The Eighth and Ninth Dura Hoards* (Numismatic Notes and Monographs 85). New York.

Bellinger, A. (1949). *Excavations at Dura-Europos, Final Report* VI: *The Coins.* New Haven.

Bendall, S. (1966). 'An Eastern hoard of Roman imperial silver', *Numismatic Chronicle* 6: 165–70.

Bland, R. (1996). 'The bronze coinage of Gordian III from Caesarea in Cappadocia', in R. Ashton (ed.), *Studies in Ancient Coinage from Turkey.* Ankara, 49–96.

Bland, R. (2023). *The Coinage of Gordian III from the Mints of Antioch and Caesarea* (Royal Numismatic Society Special Publication 60). London.

Bland, R. and Aydemir, P. (1991). 'The Haydere hoard and other hoards of the mid-third century from Turkey', in C. S. Lightfoot (ed.), *Recent Turkish Coin Hoards and Numismatic Studies* (Oxbow Monograph 7 and British Institute of Archaeology at Ankara Monograph Series 12). Oxford, 91–180.

Braund, D. C. (1994). *Georgia in Antiquity: A History of Colchis and Transcaucasian Iberia, 550 BC–AD 562.* Oxford.

Butcher, K. (1989). 'Two notes on Syrian silver of the third century AD', *Numismatic Chronicle* 149: 160–72.

Butcher, K. (2004). *Coinage in Roman Syria: Northern Syria, 64 BC–AD 253.* London.

Butcher, K. (2013). 'Coins and hoards', in W. Aylward (ed.), *Excavations at Zeugma Conducted by Oxford Archaeology* III. Los Altos, 1–92.

Butcher, K. (2015). 'Coins from Sippar', *Journal of the Oriental Society of Australia* 47: 182–9.

Butcher, K. (2017). 'From the Achaemenids to the Arsacids', in S. Heidemann and K. Butcher. *Regional History and the Coin Finds from Assur. From the Achaemenids to the Nineteenth Century. Regionale Geschichte und Münzfunde aus Assur. Von der Zeit des Achämeniden bis zum neunzehnten Jahrhundert* (Wissenschaftliche Veröffentlichungen der Deutschen Orient-Gesellschaft 148). Wiesbaden, 7–81.

Butcher, K. (2019a). 'Hoards, single finds and monetary circulation', in S. Frey-Kupper, C. Stannard, and N. Wolfe-Jacot (eds), *Contexts and the Contextualization of Coin Finds: Proceedings of the Sixth International Colloquium of the Swiss Group for the Study of Coin Finds (Geneva, March 5–7 2010)*. Lausanne, 47–58.

Butcher, K. (2019b). 'CRS Antioch 60 and the coinage of Parthian Mesopotamia', in C. Schinzel (ed.), *Benedictum sit... Festschrift für Benedikt Zäch zum 60. Geburtstag* (Schweizer Studien zur Numismatik 5). Winterthur, 45–8.

Butcher, K. (2021). 'Small change of the edge of Empire: The coin finds from Kifrin', *Mesopotamia* 55: 51–70.

Butcher, K. (2022). 'Bigger stuff beyond Palmyra: The coinage of the Hatrans and Assyrians', in R. Raja (ed.), *The Small Stuff of the Palmyrenes: Coins and Tesserae from Palmyra* (Studies in Palmyrene Archaeology and History 5). Turnhout, 163–74.

Curtis, J. (1976). 'Parthian gold from Nineveh', *British Museum Yearbook* 1: 47–66.

Dalaison, J. (2008). *L'atelier d'Amaseia du Pont. Recherches historiques et numismatiques* (Numismatica Anatolica 2). Bordeaux.

Doyen, J.-M., Duchemin, J.-P., and Iossif, P. P. (2019). *Proceedings of the International Conference, A Coin for the Dead, Coins for Living. Charon's Obol: The End of a Myth?/ Une monnaie pour le mort, des monnaies pour les vivants. L'obole à Charon : la fin d'un mythe ?* (The Journal of Archaeological Numismatics 9). Brussels.

Dundua, G. F. (1979). *Coins Hoards of Georgia: Coins from the Roman Period from the Villages of Eki and Sepieti*. Tbilisi (in Georgian, with a Russian translation of the introduction).

Dundua, T. (2008). 'Influx of Roman coins in Georgia', in A. Bursche, R. Ciołek, and R. Wolters (eds), *Roman Coins outside the Empire: Ways and Phases, Contexts and Functions. Proceedings of the ESF/SCH Exploratory Workshop Radziwill Palace, Nieborów (Poland) 3–6 September 2005*. Wetteren, 309–17.

Edwell, P. M. (2021). *Rome and Persia and War: Imperial Competition and Contact, 193 to 363 AD*. London and New York.

Fabian, L. (2017). 'Numismatic communities in the northern South Caucasus 300 BCE–300 CE: A geospatial analysis of coin finds from Caucasian Iberia and Caucasian Albania', in H. F. Teigen and E. H. Seland (eds), *Sinews of Empire: Networks in the Roman Near East and Beyond*. Oxford and Philadelphia, 37–69.

Fabian, L. (2019). 'The meanings of coins in the ancient Caucasus', *Historische Anthropologie* 27.1: 32–51.

Frascone, D. (2005). 'Des monnaies du Pont et du Péloponnèse à Zeugma', *Anatolia Antiqua/Eski Anadolu* 13: 263–70.

Frascone, D. (2013). *Zeugma* IV. *Les monnaies* (Travaux de la Maison de l'Orient et de la Méditerranée 63). Lyon.

Frolova, N. (2009). 'Caucasian imitations of Alexander and Lysimachus' golden stater (from the State Historical Museum and the State Hermitage Collections)', in S. Drougou *et al.* (eds), *ΚΕΡΜΑΤΙΑ ΦΙΛΙΑΣ. Τιμητικός τόμος για τον Ιωάννη Τουράτσογλου*. Athens, 127–33.

Gaslain, J. (2009). 'Le monnayage hatréen', *Dossier d'archéologie* 334: 24–7.

Golenko, K. V. (1964). *Денежное обращение Колхиды и Римское время* [*Monetary Circulation in Colchis during the Roman Period*]. Leningrad.

Harl, K. (1996). *Coinage in the Roman Economy, 300 B.C. to A.D. 700*. Baltimore.

Hartmann, U. (2009). 'Ein Arsakide im Heer des Septimius Severus. Überlegungen zu den Hintergründen des zweiten Partherkrieges', *Electrum* 15: 249–66.

Heidemann, S. and Miglus, P. A. (1996). 'Fundmünzen aus Assur und Lokalgeschichte in islamischer Zeit', in P. A. Miglus (ed.), *Das Wohngebiet von Assur. Stratigraphie und Architektur*. Berlin, 353–76.

Herzfeld, E. (1907). 'Untersuchungen über die historische Topographie der Landschaft am Tigris, kleinen Zâb und Gebel Hamrîn', *Memnon* 1: 89–143 and 217–38.

Hill, G. F. (1931). 'A hoard of coins from Nineveh', *Numismatic Chronicle* 11: 160–70.

Hilprecht, H. V. (1903). *Exploration in Bible Lands during the 19th Century*. Philadelphia.

Højberg Bjerg, M.-B. (2014). *Money, Power and Communication: Coin circulation in the Bosporan Kingdom in the Roman Period* (Collection Moneta 168). Wetteren.

Howgego, C. J. (1985). *Greek Imperial Countermarks: Studies in the Provincial Coinage of the Roman Empire* (Royal Numismatic Society Special Publication 17). London.

Ivaschenko, M. M. (1931). 'Герцеульский клад монет [*The Gerzeul hoard of coins*]', *Известия Государственной Академии Истории Материалбной Культуры* [*Proceedings of the State Academy of the History of Material Culture*] 7, 1–19 (*non vidi*).

Jaworski, P. (2021). 'Reading the history of the Roman fort in Apsaros (autonomous Republic of Adjara, Georgia) from a numismatic perspective', *Notae Numismaticae/Zapiski Numizmatyczne* 16: 125–42.

Jaworski, P., Karasiewics-Szczypiorski, R., and Mamuladze, Sh. (2021). 'The rise and fall of the Roman fort in Apsaros: recent numismatic evidence', *Polish Archaeology in the Mediterranean* 30.2: 289–306.

Johnston, A. (2007). *Greek Imperial Denominations, ca 200–275. A Study of the Roman Provincial Bronze Coinages of Asia Minor* (Royal Numismatic Society Special Publication 43). London.

Kapanadze, D. G. (1966). 'Нумизматические находки Пистундской археологической экспедиции за 1953–1959 гг. [Numismatic finds of the Pitsunda Archaeological Expedition, 1953–1959]', *Вестник Древней Истории* [*Journal of Ancient History*] 4: 173–9.

Kızılkaya, A. (1991). 'The Sulakyurt hoard', in C. S. Lightfoot (ed.), *Recent Turkish Coin Hoards and Numismatic Studies* (Oxbow Monograph 7 and British Institute of Archaeology at Ankara Monograph Series 12). Oxford, 213–17.

Kropotkin, V. V. and Depeyrot, G. (2005). *Les trouvailles de monnaies romaines en U.R.S.S.* (Collection Moneta 49). Wetteren.

Layard, A. H. (1853). *Discoveries among the Ruins of Nineveh and Babylon; with Travels in Armenia, Kurdistan and the Desert: being the Result of a Second Expedition undertaken for the Trustees of the British Museum*. New York.

Le Rider, G. (1967). 'Un trésor de petites monnaies de bronze trouvé à Ninive', *Iranica Antiqua* 7: 4–20.

Le Rider, G. (1998). *Séleucie du Tigre. Les monnaies séleucides et parthes*. Florence.

Liddle, A. (2003). *Arrian. Periplus Ponti Euxini. Edited with Introduction, Translation and Commentary*. Bristol.

Lorkipanize, G. and Dundua, G. (1995). 'Das numismatische Material von Pityunt (2. Jh. v. Chr. – 5. Jh. n. Chr.)', *Georgica. Zeitschrift für Kultur, Sprache und Geschichte Georgiens und Kaukasiens* 18: 32–8.

Luther, A. (2014). 'Völker und Staaten an den Grenzen der Römischen Welt. 4.2 Nordmesopotamien', in K.-P. Johne (ed.), *Die Zeit der Soldatenkaiser: Krise und Transformation des Römischen Reiches im 3. Jahrhundert n. Chr. (235–284)*. Berlin, 501–9.

Maricq, A. (1957). 'Classica et Orientalia 2. La chronologie des dernières années de Caracalla', *Syria* 34: 297–302.

Metcalf, W. E. (1996). *The Silver Coinage of Cappadocia, Vespasian–Commodus* (Numismatic Notes and Monographs 166). New York.

Millar, F. (1993). *The Roman Near East: 31 BC—AD 337*. Cambridge, MA.

Newell, E. T. (1933). *The Fifth Dura Hoard* (Numismatic Notes and Monographs 58). New York.

Oyarçin, K. and Girgin, A. (2021). 'A Roman provincial coin hoard from Sinope', *Numismatic Chronicle* 181: 381–403.

Pollard, N. (2004). 'Roman material culture across imperial frontiers? Three case studies from Parthian Dura-Europos', in S. Colvin (ed.), *The Greco-Roman East: Politics, Culture, Society*. Cambridge, 119–44.

Price, M. J. (1971). 'Greek imperial coins. Some recent acquisitions by the British Museum', *Numismatic Chronicle* 11: 121–34.

Reade, J. E. (1998). 'Greco-Parthian Nineveh', *Iraq* 6: 3–16.

Safar, F. (1952) 'Hatra and the first season of excavations, 1951: Part 1', *Sumer* 8: 3–16.

Sawaya, Z. (2002). 'The Akura hoard of Parthian coins, 1994 (CH 9.591)', in A. Meadows and U. Wartenberg (eds), *Coin Hoards* IX: *Greek Hoards* (Royal Numismatic Society Special Publication 35). London, 292.

Schultz, S. (1982). 'Ein Fund parthischer Tetradrachmen aus der Zeit des Praates IV.', *Forschungen und Berichte* 22: 117–26.

Seyrig, H. (1936). 'Antiquités syriennes 18. Les trouvailles de monnaies péloponnésiennes et la guerre parthique de Caracalla', *Syria* 17: 174–6.

Seyrig, H. (1957). 'Antiquités syriennes 65. Les trouvailles de monnaies péloponnésiennes en Syrie', *Syria* 34: 249–59.

Sherozia, M. (2008). 'Monetary circulation in Iberia in the 1st century B. C.–1st century A. D.', in A. Furtwängler, I. Gagoshidze, H. Löhr, and N. Ludwig (eds), *Iberia and Rome: The Excavations of the Palace at Dedoplis Gora and the Roman Influence in the Caucasian Kingdom of Iberia* (Schriften des Zentrums für Archäologie und Kulturgeschichte des Schwarzmeerraumes). Langenweißbach, 235–52.

Simonetta, B. (1971). 'Un interessante tesoretto di tetradrammi di Vologeses III', *Rivista italiana di numismatica e scienze affini* 19: 57–62.

Slocum, J. J. (1977). 'Another look at the coins of Hatra', *Museum Notes. The American Numismatic Society*, 22: 37–47.

Spoerri Butcher, M. (2019). 'De Kertch à Winterthur: une monnaie d'un type "inédit" d'Héraclée du Pont et son usage en contexte funéraire', in C. Schinzel (ed.), *Benedictum sit... Festschrift für Benedikt Zäch zum 60. Geburtstag* (Schweizer Studien zur Numismatik 5). Winterthur, 59–68.

Tekin, O. (1994). *Grek ve Roma sikkeleri: Yapı Kredi koleksiyonu/Greek and Roman Coins: The Yapı Kredi Collection*. Istanbul.

Toumpan, F. (2015). *Zeugma Kazı Sikkeleri: 2005–2012*. MA thesis, Ankara University.

Toumpan, F. (2020). 'Coin finds from the recent excavations at Zeugma: A preliminary report', *Berytus* 59–60: 193–8.

Tsotselia, M. (2010) with the cooperation of G. Depeyrot. *Coin Finds in Georgia (6th Century BC–15th Century AD)* (Collection Moneta 112). Wetteren.

van Heesch, J. (2014). 'Paying the Roman soldiers in the East (1st–2nd century AD)', in M. Reddé (ed.), *De l'or pour les braves! Soldes, armées et circulation monétaires dans le monde romain*. Bordeaux, 139–59.

Vardanyan, R. (2009). 'A hoard of copper coins from Artashat archaeological excavations', *Handes Amsorya* 1.12): 32–68 (in Armenian).

Vitale, M. (2013). 'Kolchis in der hohen Kaiserzeit: Römische Eparchie oder nördlicher Aussenposten des limes Ponticus?', *Historia. Zeitschrift für alte Geschichte* 62.2: 241–58.

Weiser, W. (1984). 'Ein Teil eines umfangreichen Fundes kappadokischer Silbermünzen der römischen Kaiserzeit', *Epigraphica Anatolica* 3: 109–32.

Whittaker, C. R. (1994). *Frontiers of the Roman Empire: A Social and Economic Study*. Baltimore and London.

Wojan, F. (2006). 'Trapézonte du Pont sous l'Empire romain: étude historique et corpus monétaire', *Revue numismatique* 162: 181–229.

Yalçin, D. Ö. (2017). *Numismatik Veriler Işığında Roma İmparatorluğu Doğu Sınırı Sikke Sirkülasyonu*. Unpublished PhD thesis, Ankara University, https://tezarsivi.com/numismatik-veriler-isiginda-roma-imparatorlugu-dogu-siniri-sikke-sirkulasyonu (accessed 15 November 2023).

Zograf, A. N. (1945). 'Находки античных монет на Кавказе [Finds of Ancient Coins in the Caucasus]', *Труды отдела нумизматики Государственного Эрмитажа* [*Proceedings of the Numismatics Department of the State Hermitage*] 1: 29–85.

Marguerite Spoerri Butcher, *Crossing Frontiers in the East: Hoarding of Roman Coinages from Pontus to Mesopotamia* In: *Roman Coin Hoards Across Frontiers*. Edited by: Benjamin D. R. Hellings, Marguerite Spoerri Butcher, and Chris Howgego, Oxford University Press. © Oxford University Press 2026. DOI: 10.1093/9780198986478.003.0009

10

Hoards of Roman Coins from Ancient Armenia and their Regional Contextualization

Anahide Kéfélian

This chapter is based on a dataset of 1,548 coins collected during the Marie Skłodowska-Curie project Roman Coin Circulation in Ancient Armenia (RoCCAA).[1] The dataset includes Roman coins as well as other contemporary coinages, such as Armenian, Parthian, and Sasanian, with the aim of studying coin circulation in the Greater Armenian Kingdom from 95 BC to AD 428.[2] Data already published were used to update the CHRE online database (https://chre.ashmus.ox.ac.uk) for the region.[3]

The study of the mechanisms involved in the deposition of coinage and monetary circulation within the Greater Armenian Kingdom provides valuable insights that broaden our understanding of a region that has been studied predominantly from Greco-Roman literature.[4] It provides an alternative approach to the study of

[1] The RoCCAA project has received funding from the European Union's Horizon 2020 research and innovation programme under the Marie Skłodowska-Curie grant agreement No. 892180. The analysis presented here is based on the dataset collected as of December 2022. For Armenian transliteration, I have adhered to the traditional HMB system (for reference, see *Revue des Études Arméniennes* transliteration guidelines). Conversely, the modern names of scholars have been transliterated using the Library of Congress convention.

[2] The catalogue is based as much as possible on the consultation of the coins in Armenian museums (History Museum of Armenia, History Museum of Gyumri, Ełegnajor Regional Museum; Museum of Erebuni), as well as scientific publications, including excavation reports, corpora, monographs, academic publications, and PhD theses.

[3] In addition to the data compiled by the author, we should highlight the contributions of Cristian Găzdac and Marguerite Spoerri Butcher for the online CHRE database.

[4] The study refers to the Greater Armenian Kingdom, which will be referred to as the 'Armenian Kingdom' or 'ancient Armenia' in the chapter. It should not be confused with the Kingdom of Armenia Minor, an independent kingdom, which was later allied with Rome and annexed to the Roman Empire under Vespasian. The Greater Kingdom of Armenia is situated in the south Caucasus region. Its borders are defined by the Euphrates to the west, while the Kura marks the northern boundary with Caucasian Iberia and Albania. The eastern part of the Kingdom is partially bounded by the Caspian Sea, while the southern boundary is less distinct and follows the Tigris, before reaching Lake Matiane (Urmia) and finally the Caspian Sea; see Strabo, *Geography* (11.14.1–3). The surface area of this territory fluctuated until the fall of the Armenian branch of the Arsacid dynasty in AD 428.

past interactions, correcting an existing imbalance caused by the scarcity of Armenian and Parthian literary sources.

The Kingdom of Armenia offers a very interesting case study in an environment where Armenian, Roman, and also Parthian and Sasanian coins are found together. The question therefore arises as to the acceptance of these coinages within the territory of the Greater Armenian Kingdom. Neither part of the Roman Empire, except for a few years, nor completely outside Roman control, the Kingdom of Armenia offers a good case study in the movement of Roman coins beyond the borders of the Roman Empire.

The Kingdom of Armenia was an area of contention for the Roman, Parthian, and later Sasanian Empires for over five centuries. As a result, the Kingdom was at the centre of diplomatic and military conflicts since the first half of the first century BC.[5] Despite some failed attempts to stabilize the situation in ancient Armenia during the first half of the first century AD, an unprecedented agreement between Rome and Parthia, known as the Treaty of Rhandeia, was finally reached in AD 63. This treaty stipulated that the Romans were entitled to the right of investiture of the Armenian throne, while a branch dynasty of the Parthian Arsacids was allowed to sit on the Armenian throne. However, the rise of the Sasanians in AD 224 marked a turning point, as the Romans and Parthians ruling over ancient Armenia were forced into a closer military alliance to counter this new threat. It is within this complex political landscape that Roman coins spread and circulated.

The first section of this chapter examines the hoards discovered in ancient Armenia. In order to ascertain whether the Armenian monetary pattern was in any way unique, the second section compares the Armenian hoards with those of other kingdoms in the southern Caucasus, namely Iberia and Colchis. The third section aims to provide a broader perspective by adding a consideration of the single finds.

The study of the movement of coins in the Greater Armenian Kingdom faces several challenges owing to the various parameters that affect the data-recording process. Despite the research undertaken so far, the current data provide only an initial understanding of the depositional process and a first step towards a comprehensive study of the monetary circulation. It is important to consider both the modern and the ancient factors that influence the number of finds collected for study.[6] Modern factors, such as the state of research, authorization to access and publish the material, and the level of publication by modern country, as well as the geopolitical instabilities and ideological narratives, act as a brake on research.[7]

[5] The reign of Trajan also marks the beginning of the expansion of regional conflicts into Upper Mesopotamia. The Armenian question remained a bone of contention until the end of the fourth century. See Chaumont (1976) for a study on Roman and Armenian relationships.

[6] Howgego (1994).

[7] The territory of the Greater Armenian Kingdom now spreads across several modern-day countries. See Kohl (1998); Kohl and Tsetskhladze (1995); Lindsay and Smith (2006) for the regional context and ideological narratives.

Similarly, the inaccessibility of the Armenian royal residences of Vałaršapat (under the Holy See of the Armenian Apostolic Church) and Dvin (whose later archaeological layers prevent access to the older layers) greatly limits our understanding and knowledge of monetary circulation and deposition from the latter half of the second century AD.[8] The absence of archaeological contextualization owing to factors such as looting, the lack of stratigraphy, and incomplete excavation reports (depending on the country and date of publication) also presents a significant obstacle. These factors hinder scholars from conducting anthropological studies of these coins, including practices that have led to their deposition.

Further, bias may result from the lower loss rate of precious metal coinage and the possibility that it may have been melted down. The deposits available to be excavated today inevitably exclude ancient hoards recovered in antiquity. Certain parameters, such as the changes over the centuries in the borders of the Greater Armenian Kingdom, are not always well known. Additionally, it is difficult to follow the changes in political and administrative divisions.

As this is the first systematic overview of the material from the areas discussed here, more space is given to setting out the evidence than is required for better-published regions. Further, the relative scarcity of data and of well-published contexts means that interpretations must inevitably be tentative. But one has to start somewhere. *Caveat lector.*

Despite the limitations of the dataset, it is still possible to offer something new. In particular, the corpus includes evidence from the Araxes Plain, where the main royal residences of the Greater Armenian Kingdom—Artašat, Vałaršapat, and Dvin—were located.[9]

ROMAN DEPOSITS FROM ANCIENT ARMENIA

The categorization of the data follows the terminology used by the Coin Hoards of the Roman Empire Project (CHRE).[10] Accordingly, the dataset of the RoCCAA project consists of 18 deposits, or, more precisely, eight hoards, two possible hoards, and eight groups of single finds.[11] Among those, Romans coins are contained in

[8] Donabédian (2010); Kalantarian (2010).

[9] Artašat is also known as Artaxata, while Vałaršapat is known in Greco-Roman literature as Kainepolis. Donabédian (2010).

[10] The classification of the deposits follows the wide definition of 'hoard' used by CHRE, which aims to collect 'any group of coins which appears to have been deposited together'; https://chre.ashmus.ox.ac.uk/content/about (accessed 6 April 2022).

[11] According to the internal guidelines for the collaborators of the project established for the CHRE project, a group of single finds refers to 'coins found in the proximity to each other which, on the basis of circumstances of discovery or of archaeological context, are likely to have been deposited or lost at the same time but which do not constitute a hoard under the generally accepted meaning'.

four hoards and five groups of single finds. Furthermore, ten out of 11 single gold finds are also Roman.[12]

Single gold finds

Gold finds are very rare in Armenia, with only ten Roman single gold finds and a local imitation of a stater of Lysimachus from the northern part of the south Caucasus (Fig. 10.1). They account for only 1% of the Roman coins catalogued in the RoCCAA database and 0.5% of the total number of coins collected. The gold coins are single finds and do not seem to have been mixed with other metals or coins.[13]

The Roman gold single finds can be divided into two groups: the first relates to the first century AD and the second to the end of the fourth and the fifth century. Of the four coins belonging to the first century, three *aurei* were issued before the reform of AD 64: one is dated from the reign of Tiberius and two from the reign of

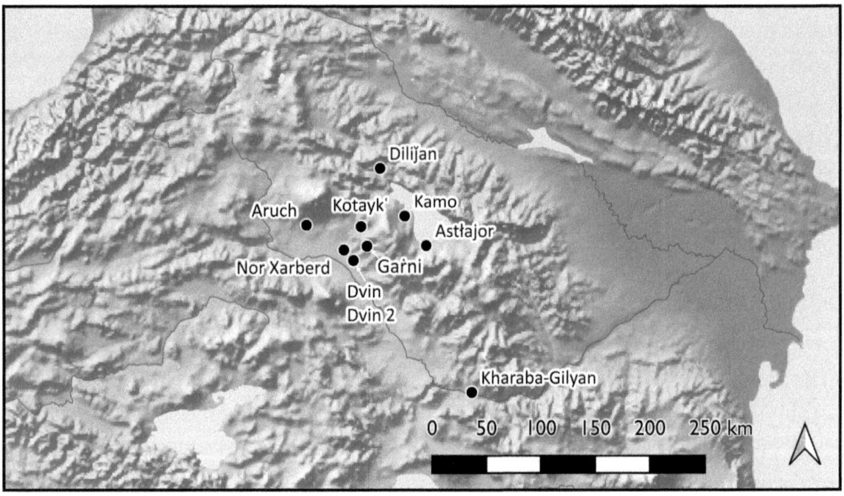

Fig. 10.1. Distribution map of gold coins in the Greater Armenian Kingdom. Source: CHRE database (accessed 22 December 2023). Map: A. Wilson/A. Kéfélian.

[12] CHRE aims to enter single gold finds into the database for their 'their high value and archaeological behaviour [which] merit their consideration as hoards in themselves'; https://chre.ashmus.ox.ac.uk/content/about (accessed 6 April 2022).

[13] The only exception is a gold coin found in a tomb in Sisian. It is a local imitation of a Lysimachus stater from the north Caucasus. However, the tomb had been robbed and the coins were only recovered later. It is therefore impossible to determine whether single gold coins were deposited with the other silver coins, or whether the gold coin was placed separately in the tomb; Vardanyan (2011a).

Nero.[14] The fourth single gold coin of the first century AD is a post-Neronian reform *aureus*, dated from AD 65–6.[15]

The second group of gold coins covers the end of the fourth century AD and the fifth century AD, with a *solidus* of Honorius, three *solidi* of Theodosius II, and two *solidi* of Leo I.[16] The absence of finds from the second century may result from the inaccessibility of the relevant archaeological layers of the royal residences of Vałaršapat and Dvin, owing to modern urbanization for the former and the overlying medieval archaeological stratigraphy for the latter.

There is currently no discernible pattern in the distribution of single gold coins. The *aurei* dating to the first century were found in the Araxes Plain, which includes several royal residences, and in the royal summer residence of Gaṙni.[17] In addition, two coins were found on the south-western shore of Lake Sevan. As for the late fourth-century and early fifth-century coins, some were discovered at the royal residence of Dvin and along an axis running northwards from the Araxes Plain along a section of Lake Sevan. On the other hand, the *solidus* of Honorius was unearthed in the south of the Armenian Kingdom.

The limited presence of gold coins in ancient Armenia is in part to be explained by the fact that neither the Armenians nor their neighbours, the Parthians, struck gold coins.[18] Moreover, at least during the chronological limits of the present study, the Sasanian gold coins minted by Ardashir I (AD 224–41) did not spread to ancient Armenia.[19] Elsewhere in the Roman east, gold coins were minted in Asia Minor during the reign of Augustus, particularly in Ephesus and Pergamum.[20] This suggests that they must have played a role at least during the Early Empire. Recent research on Roman provincial coins has also confirmed the minting of gold coins in Syria during the reign of Vespasian, and later during the reigns of Pescennius Niger and Septimius Severus, but the phenomenon remains rare in the region.[21] However, the lack of evidence for the circulation of gold coins in Syria is noted by Kevin Butcher, who states that they are 'virtually absent from site

[14] The coins followed by the designation HMA are kept in the History Museum of Armenia. HMA 13658 (CHRE 17479) refers to the Tiberian *aureus* and HMA 19107 (CHRE 17480) and HMA 19558 to the Neronian *aurei*. The coin HMA 19558 is so far unpublished. See Table 10.4 as well.

[15] HMA 19714. The coin is so far unpublished as well.

[16] The location where the coin of Honorius (CHRE 18109) is kept is uncertain, but it was mentioned by Paxomov (1926–59 [1938: 15, no. 354]) and Kropotkin (1961: no. 1539). The three coins of Theodosius II are kept in the History Museum of Armenia under the inventory numbers HMA 17797; HMA 14520; HMA 14459 (CHRE 18805, 18807, 18808). The two coins of Leo I are registered under CHRE 20027 for the Aruč find, and under CHRE 18112 for the Dvin discovery. Both are kept in the History Museum of Armenia. I was unable to verify the accuracy of the data for the two Leo I coins because my project cut off date is AD 428.

[17] The use of the term 'capital' does not align with the political structure of ancient Armenia because the king often moved from place to place; therefore the term 'royal residences' is more appropriate.

[18] Sinisi (2012: 276).

[19] Khurshudyan and Zohrabyan (2002).

[20] Giard (1976: 42–4, 144–5, 147, 151–3).

[21] Burnett, Amandry, and Ripollès (1992: 26–7); Burnett, Amandry, and Carradice (1999: 8–9); Amandry (2002: 141–2); Butcher (2004: 195); van Heesch (2014: 145) provides a broader overview of gold coinage in the east.

finds and hoards'.[22] Furthermore, these eastern *aurei* and *denarii* are recorded almost exclusively in the western part of the Roman Empire, and more specifically in Britain and Germany.[23]

The first-century AD gold coins are relevant to determining Armenia's uniqueness in relation to the surrounding regions. We can propose two main hypotheses: the coins could have been introduced from the beginning of the first century AD or only much later, towards the end of the first century or during the second century. In the first case, the pattern of gold coins seen in Armenia would be exceptional, but not inexplicable. Gold coins could have been introduced by the military movements that occurred frequently during the reigns of Augustus (Tiberius, Gaius), Tiberius (Germanicus), and Nero (Corbulo, Paetus), or possibly later during military expeditions in the Flavian period.[24] For instance, the *aureus* of Tiberius, found in Gaṙni, represents the later PONTIF MAXIM type featuring decorated legs on the chair.[25] Therefore, the introduction of the coins with the arrival of Germanicus in AD 18 can be disregarded.[26] The coin could have been introduced during Claudius' reign, when a garrison in the fortress of Gaṙni is attested by Tacitus, or under Nero during the war of AD 58–63 between Rome and the Arsacids in ancient Armenia.[27] In the case of the two pre-reform Neronian *aurei*, it is possible that they reflect an early supply of these gold coins in Armenia, possibly during the war of AD 58–63.[28] In contrast, the fourth coin, the post-Neronian *aureus*, could have arrived under the Flavians or much later, as other regions attest to the long circulation of post-Neronian reform *aurei* up to the Severan period.[29]

The lack of evidence for the circulation of gold coins in Syria before the late first or early second century AD, coupled with the composition of hoards, warrants consideration of alternative explanations.[30] The circulation of gold coins in Syria is associated with the production of *aurei* and *denarii* in Antioch during the

[22] Butcher (2004: 180; 2012: 469).

[23] See Howgego (2015) for Vespasianic *aurei* discovered in Britain and Germany, and Howgego (1996; 2002) for *denarii* issued by Septimus Severus. Duncan-Jones (2001; 2002) attributes the presence of these coins in Britain as a result of Gresham's Law, in a response to Howgego's hypothesis that suggested that their presence resulted from supply (see also Hellings 2016 for Septimius Severus *denarii* in Germany). Hellings (2020) further nuanced Howgego's argument that the presence of these specific eastern imperial coins can be explained by a regional pattern rather than Gresham's Law as argued by Duncan-Jones.

[24] Chaumont (1976: 73–129).

[25] *RIC* I^2, nos 25, 27, 29 for *aurei* types. They were minted during Tiberius (14 to 37 AD).

[26] I am grateful to Chris Howgego for the evidence he provided for the dating of the issue according to the style of the chair.

[27] Tacitus, *Annals*, 2, 56, 2. See also *RPC* I, nos 3629–30. For the Roman garrison at Gaṙni, see Tacitus, *Annals*, 12, 45.

[28] Chaumont (1976: 101–16).

[29] Hellings (2022: 283–6) for a case study for north-west Europe, and see below for the Neronian *aurei* in Syria.

[30] Butcher (2004: 192; 2012: 469); van Heesch (2014: 148–9).

reign of Vespasian (AD 69–79).[31] However, there is currently no evidence of *aurei* appearing in hoards before the middle of the second century.[32] The Kuşakkaya hoard, whose *terminus post quem (t.p.q.)* is dated to the reign of Antoninus Pius on the basis of the 45 coins recorded out of *c.* 1,400, contained at least 17 *aurei* issued under Nero.[33] Similarly, the Akko-Ptolemais 1980 hoard, featuring coins from Nero to Lucius Verus, included three *aurei* of Nero.[34] The hoard of Turkey 1972 B, discovered on the border between Syria and Turkey, consisted of over 200 coins from Nero to Commodus, including at least one *aureus* of Nero.[35] However, the lack of precise dating on these Neronian coins makes it difficult to ascertain whether they are pre- or post-reform *aurei*. It is not possible to determine accurately the date of introduction or the longevity of the gold coins in circulation in Syria, although the presence of *aurei* in Syria in the second half of the second century is certain.

It is likely therefore that some gold coins, especially the *aurei* predating the Neronian reform, were introduced in an earlier phase of the Roman military offensives during the first half of the first century AD, but it is also possible that some other gold coins were distributed much later, following the Syrian pattern.

The presence of individual gold coins from the late Roman period can be attributed to a number of factors. The increasing importance of the gold *solidus* and its subdivisions within the monetary system was witnessed not solely in the Greater Armenian Kingdom but also in the Roman Empire itself after the monetary reform implemented by Constantine.[36] This trend is evidenced by the large number of late gold coin entries in the CHRE database for the period AD 311–478, with 26,188 coins for all regions combined.[37] Geopolitical factors could also have contributed to the dissemination of Roman gold. The geopolitical context of the Armenian Kingdom underwent significant changes in the third century.[38] In *c.* AD 390, the country was divided between the Roman and Persian Empires. The Arsacid dynasty from Armenia made an unsuccessful attempt to establish its dominance over the Persian area. Following the downfall of the Arsacid dynasty in Armenia in AD 428,[39] gold coins could have been a product of diplomatic gifts or subsidies to the Sasanian Empire, as observed in other regions such as central Europe.[40]

[31] Amandry (2002: 141–3); Burnett, Amandry, and Carradice (1999: 8–9).
[32] Butcher (2004: 192 and 274, nos 33c–34).
[33] CHRE 5438: Ergeç (1996: 37–9); Butcher (2004: 274, no. 33c).
[34] Also known as the Acre hoard (CHRE 7909): *CH* VII: 157–9, no. 243; Butcher (2004: 274, no. 34). Within this region, see also the Caesarea hoard (CHRE 9012): Kindler (1969) and the hoard of Naḥal Shalwa (CHRE 7617).
[35] CHRE 5494: *CH* II: no. 236; *CH* III: no. 156; Hurter (2005); Yalçın (2017: 104–5).
[36] Moorhead (2012).
[37] Dataset accessed on 12 December 2023.
[38] Dédéyan (2008: 163–71); Hewsen and Salvatico (2001: 71).
[39] Traina (2009).
[40] Kéfélian (2025); Bursche (1996: 105); Kehne (2008); Moisil (2002).

The predominance of silver hoard evidence in ancient Armenia

So far, eight hoards (Aşvan, Artašat 1972, Artašat 1971, Saṙnakunk‘, Qaradonlu, Artašat 2005, Gaṙni, and Erevan) have been recovered from the Greater Armenian Kingdom (Fig. 10.2), and only four of these are composed, at least in part, of Roman coins: Saṙnakunk‘, Artašat 2005, Gaṙni, and Erevan. Roman silver coins are predominantly found in three of them (Saṙnakunk‘,[41] Gaṙni 1955,[42] and Erevan),[43] while the fourth is composed entirely of bronze coins (Artašat 2005).[44] Two hoards from the Kingdom of Caucasian Albania (Tazakend and Chukhur Gabala) complement the hoard dataset from the region.[45] Supplementing the hoards, three groups of single finds of Roman coins have been discovered in funerary contexts, alongside Parthian and Armenian coins in Tavuš, P‘arak‘ar, and Sisian.[46]

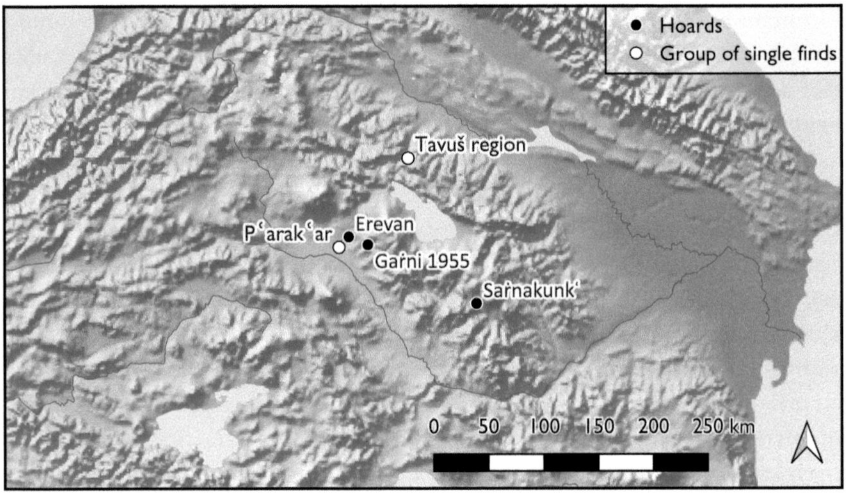

Fig. 10.2. Distribution map of silver deposits in the Greater Armenian Kingdom. Source: CHRE database (accessed 22 December 2023). Map: A. Wilson/A. Kéfélian.

[41] Paxomov (1926–59 [1954: 10–25, no. 1536]); Kropotkin (1961: 104–5, no. 1558); Musheghian (1973); Mousheghian†, Mousheghian, and Depeyrot (2000: 169–73); Vardanyan (2011b) for the Roman coins.

[42] Kropotkin (1961: 104, no. 1549); Golenko (1964: no. 65); Mousheghian†, Mousheghian and Depeyrot (2000: 169–73). See CHRE 17473.

[43] Paxomov (1926–59 [1926: 42, no. 51]); Zograph (1945: 77–9, no. 159); Kropotkin (1961: 104, no. 1552); Mousheghian†, Mousheghian, and Depeyrot (2000: 175). See CHRE 4511.

[44] Vardanyan (2009).

[45] See CHRE 18189 for Tazakend and CHRE 4008 for Chukhur Gabala. It is also known by the appellations Çuxur Qəbələ and Chukhurkabala.

[46] Groups of single finds from Tavuš, P‘arak‘ar, and possibly Mingəçevir 1947 1 (CHRE 20079). The latter is on the border with the Kingdom of Albania. The lack of precise location does not allow us to understand on which riverbank the hoard was found. Moreover, the borders fluctuated over time. See Mousheghian†, Mousheghian, and Depeyrot (2000, 139–40) for the Tavuš group of single

The hoards fall into two categories: those containing a single currency, such as Aşvan comprised of 48 Cappadocian coins (*t.p.q.* 64 BC),[47] Artašat 1971 composed of 28 Armenian coins (*t.p.q.* 58 BC),[48] Gaṙni 1955 consisting of 48 Roman *denarii* (*t.p.q.* AD 191),[49] or Qaradonlu containing 47 Parthian coins (*t.p.q.* 2 BC);[50] and those which demonstrate some co-circulation of different coinages, like Artašat 1972 and Saṙnakunk‘ (*t.p.q.* 32 BC).[51] If we consider groups of single finds resulting from funerary contexts, other evidence of the mixing of currencies can be found in Tavuš, P‘arak‘ar, and Sisian.[52]

It is worth looking at these hoards in more detail and with reference to their archaeological and wider contexts. Among the hoards composed of only one currency, the Aşvan hoard was found close to the Euphrates which constituted the border between the kingdoms of Cappadocia and Armenia. In contrast, the Gaṙni hoard was found at the summer residence of kings situated on a naturally fortified rock promontory.

The royal complex at Gaṙni encompasses various structures such as a 'palace', a bath complex, a Roman architectural temple, a 'military cantonment', and uncertain buildings to the north of the fortress,[53] all located in the fortified site.[54] At first glance, a hoard consisting entirely of Roman coins in this location may seem unexpected, given that this enclosed fortress was used to gather the royal court during the summer. However, owing to the function of the site and the location of the discovery, votive deposition should be disregarded. The hoard was found not within the palace and 'temple complex' but, rather, in a room adjoining the eastern wall fortification, near the north area of the fortress thought to be a 'military containment' from the third and fourth centuries.[55] The fortress served not only as a royal residence throughout its history but also as a Roman garrison during Claudius' reign, as recounted by Tacitus.[56] One possible explanation for the

finds, Mousheghian†, Mousheghian, and Depeyrot (2000, 101–2) for the P‘arak‘ar group of single finds, and Vardanyan (2011a: 67–70).

[47] *IGCH* 1741. [48] Musheghyan (1978).

[49] Arakeljan (1957: 52–4, pl. XX–I); Mousheghian†, Mousheghian, and Depeyrot (2000: 168–73).

[50] Paxomov (1926–59 [1926: 40, no. 30]); Golenko and Radžabli (1975: 88, no. 21); Fabian (2018: 435, no. 12).

[51] For Artašat 1972, see Arakeljan (1957: 52–4, pl. XX–I), and, regarding the Saṙnakunk‘ hoard, see Musheghyan (1973).

[52] Mousheghian†, Mousheghian, and Depeyrot (2000, 139–40) for the Tavuš group of single finds, Mousheghian†, Mousheghian, and Depeyrot (2000, 101–2) for the P‘arak‘ar group of single finds, and Vardanyan (2011a: 67–70).

[53] The 'military cantonment' is mentioned on the tourist map of Gaṙni fortress, as well as in the publication from AMAP (Armenian Monuments Awareness Project [ՀՀԾԾ]), which states that soldiers were stationed on the right side after the entrance to the fortress during the third and fourth centuries AD. However, it seems that no academic publication has resulted from the study or excavation of these remaining buildings. Therefore, caution is required, since this thesis does not appear to have been founded on comprehensive research.

[54] Kéfélian (2021b); Arakeljan (1957); Magarditchian (2018).

[55] Arakeljan (1957: 82–5). Unfortunately, none of this research seems to have been published, and we do not know the argument on which the theory is based.

[56] Tacitus, *Annals*, 12, 45.

deposition of the hoard here may be connected with the later use of the site by a Roman garrison, either at the end of the second century or more likely in the first half of the third century. Despite the ongoing warfare in Armenia until the end of the fourth century and beginning of the fifth century, the state of research, and the lack of archaeological and literary sources from the end of the second century do not allow us to understand fully the military activity in the Greater Armenian Kingdom from the third century AD. The last epigraphic evidence for Roman legions in Armenia comes from the royal residences of Vałaršapat during the reigns of Marcus Aurelius and Commodus.[57]

The Gaṙni 1955 hoard consists of 48 Roman *denarii* dating between the reigns of Vespasian and Commodus. A *t.p.q.* of Commodus is a common pattern in hoard evidence and is consistent with 2,030 other silver hoards in the CHRE online dataset.[58] These coins predate the Severan debasement of AD 194. However, Kevin Butcher and Matthew Ponting stressed that this pattern should be analysed carefully, as other examples, such as Pompeii, have shown that the last coin deposited can give a 'false impression of the date of concealment' and that hoards closing with coins of Commodus may have been deposited 'under the Severans or later'.[59] The hoard is primarily composed of Vespasianic coins, with the highest ratio of coins by reign, followed by coins from Hadrian and Antoninus Pius (Fig. 10.3).

The hoard's composition is broadly comparable to other hoards from the Roman Empire that ended with Commodus, but with some distinct oddities (Fig. 10.4). It stands out from the hoards of Gualdo Tadino, Hallicourt, or Synton because of the high number of Vespasianic *denarii* and the significant proportion of *denarii* from Hadrian. Vespasianic coins constitute 17% of the Gaṙni hoard, by contrast with the Gualdo Tadino, Haillicourt, and Synton hoards, which contain less than 1% Vespasianic coins.[60] In the hoard of Parava 1937 from north-western Europe that closed with coins from the reign of Commodus, Vespasianic *denarii* account for about 8.5% of the coins found.[61] When comparing the composition of hoards deposited between Marcus Aurelius and Macrinus from Turkey and Syria, the percentage of Vespasianic coins ranges from 6% to 8.5%, (Table 10.1), while the Gaṙni hoard stands out with 17%.

A putative high level of supply of Vespasianic coins to the region may explain this distortion. However, it is unclear whether the extra supply occurred during the Flavian era, when the *Legio XII Fulminata* was present in various locations in

[57] Kéfélian (2020: 90–1).

[58] 2,031 hoards have been catalogued in the CHRE online database (last accessed 20 December 2023).

[59] Butcher and Ponting (2022: 279).

[60] In addition to these eight Vespasian *denarii*, the list should also include the coin of Titus, struck to honour Divus Vespasian.

[61] Hellings (2022: 291, fig. 13.7).

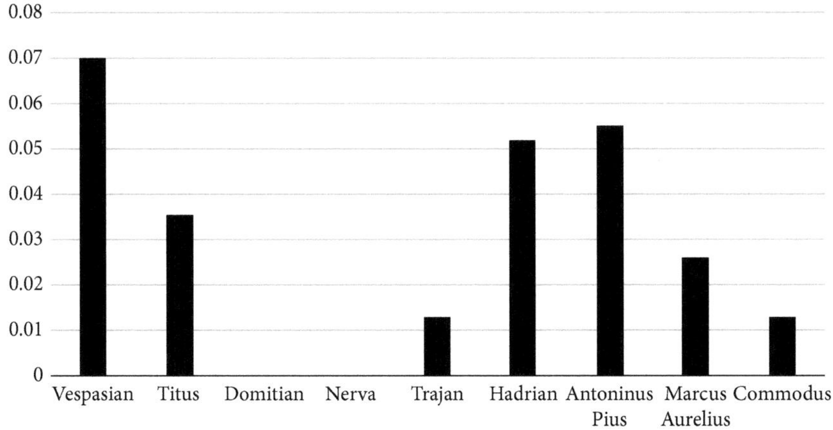

Fig. 10.3. Gaṙni 1955 hoard: number of coins per months of reign.

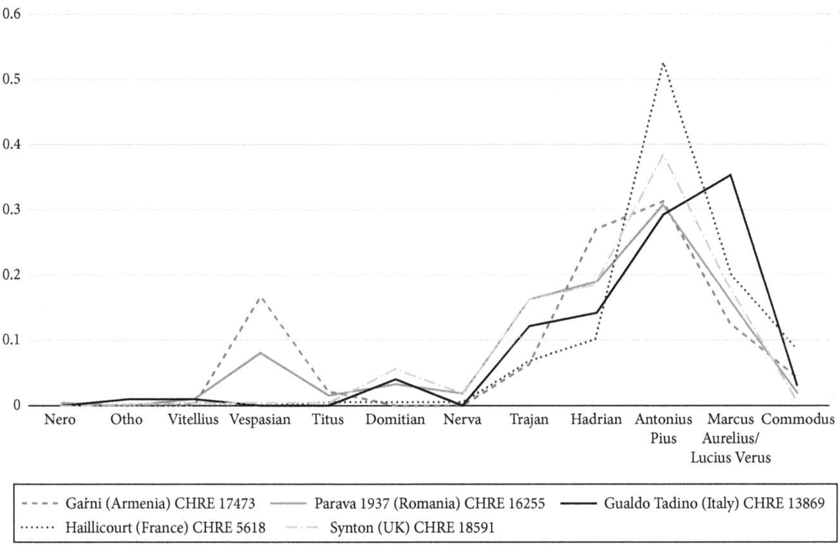

Fig. 10.4. Percentage of coins from a selection of silver hoards closing under Commodus, by reign. Source: CHRE database (accessed 22 February 2024).

the Caucasus, including Albania, Iberia, and Armenia, or later in the second century.[62] By contrast, the Colchian hoard of Gonio 1998 contained only a single Vespasianic *denarius* according to modern Georgian documentation. The average weight of the coins of Vespasian is approximately 2.9 g, and the worn aspect of the coins suggests a prolonged circulation, which would seem to

[62] See below and Kéfélian (2020, 2021a, and 2025).

Table 10.1. Percentage of coins (*denarii*, all denominations) minted in Vespasian's reign in hoards from Turkey and Syria. Source: CHRE database (accessed 22 February 2024).

Hoard	*t.p.q.*	*Denarii*	All denominations
Antioch (Pisidia) (CHRE 12944)	81–96	?	?
Kuşakkaya (CHRE 5438)	143–4	?	?
Manyas (CHRE 5474)	145–60	0.24?	?
Latakia 1966 (CHRE 9736)	169–80	8.00	47.60
Dura Europos 21 (CHRE 9826)	183	5.60	5.60
Syria 1923—unknown findspot (CHRE 15419)	214	7.60	7.60
Dura Europos 3 and 4 (CHRE 9800)	217–18	5.70	5.70
Dura Europos 19 (CHRE 9824)	218–22	0	0
Denarius hoard (Erimtan collection) (CHRE 8878)	218–22	1.60	1.60
Gindaros (CHRE 20581)	222–35	0.80	0.80

exclude different phases of deposition. Furthermore, various hoards such as Londonthorpe,[63] Grocka,[64] Nemenikuće,[65] Bella Reka,[66] Radalj,[67] Llíria 1999,[68] Zadar,[69] and Kamenica provide evidence for the existence of Vespasian coins weighing 2.90 g in hoards whose *t.p.q.* date from AD 153–61 to 235–8.[70]

The percentage of Hadrianic coins found in the hoards of Hailicourt, Parava 1937, Synton, and Gualdo Tadino ranges from 10% to 19%. The average rate for all hoards recorded in the CHRE database is 17.7%.[71] In contrast, the Gaṙni hoard contains a higher percentage of Hadrianic coins (27%). It is as yet unclear how this can be explained.

In contrast to the single-currency hoards, the Saṙnakunk' hoard shows evidence of a mixed currency consisting of at least 373 coins (perhaps originally more; Table 10.2).[72] The hoard was discovered by villagers in 1945 and subsequently divided among themselves before being reconstituted more than two decades later.

Two hypotheses can be made regarding the introduction and deposition of the Roman Republican coins. The first theory dates the deposit fairly close to the *terminus post quem* of 32 BC, based on the latest coins depicting Mark Antony

[63] CHRE 1264. [64] CHRE 2781. [65] CHRE 2782.
[66] CHRE 2806. [67] CHRE 16736. [68] CHRE 12824. [69] CHRE 3045.
[70] CHRE 16612. Only the hoards of Bare (CHRE 16027 *t.p.q.* 81) and Hastings 1989 silver (CHRE 5230 *t.p.q.* 121–3) were excluded.
[71] The percentage has been calculated on the basis of hoards with a closing period dating to Commodus that contain *denarii* of Hadrian. All uncertain data have been removed.
[72] Musheghyan (1973); Vardanyan (2011b) for the Roman Republican *denarii*. Mousheghian†, Mousheghian, and Depeyrot (2000: 103–17).

Table 10.2. Sařnakunk' hoard. Source: RoCCAA project, based on autopsy of the coins.

Coinage	Number of coins	Denominations
Roman Republican	225	210 *denarii* and *denarii serrati* 7 *cistophori* (*RPC* I, no. 2201) 8 tetradrachms (*RPC* I, nos 4094–5)
Asia Minor	8	6 *cistophori* from Pergamum 2 *cistophori* from Ephesus
Seleucid	58	tetradrachms
Phoenician	39	tetradrachms
Parthian	22	drachms
Armenian	10	7 drachms 3 tetradrachms
Cappadocian	8	drachms
Alexander the Great	2	1 tetradrachm 1 drachm
Pontus	1	tetradrachm
Total	**373**	

and Cleopatra associated with the Armenian tiara and the legend ANTONI ARMENIA DEVICTA.[73] The second hypothesis points to a later introduction, as Republican coins are attested in hoards until the end of the first century AD, before starting to be recycled from Domitian to Trajan. However, Republican coins are still attested in circulation on the periphery of the Roman Empire until the second part of the second century AD.[74] Despite the attestation of the long circulation of Republican coins, several parameters suggest an early deposition of the Sařnakunk' hoard in 32 BC or shortly thereafter.[75] The latest coins are in a very good state of preservation, and the average weight of *denarii* in the hoard is around 3.86 g. The correspondence analysis of this hoard shows a very modern profile in comparison with contemporaneous hoards, with almost 62.2% of the Roman coins minted between 49 and 32 BC.[76] However, the Sařnakunk' hoard also differs from the later contemporary hoards in the absence of legionary *denarii* of Mark Antony, which are already attested in some hoards with a *t.p.q.* of 32–31 BC, and become more common from the reign of Augustus.[77] The hoard also contains eight well-preserved tetradrachms bearing portraits of Antony and Cleopatra[78], and seven *cistophori* struck on the initiative of Mark Antony.[79] All of these factors argue against a late deposition and make a deposition close to the

[73] HMA 15143; HMA 16116; 17824/173 for *RRC* 543/1 dates from 32 BC, see Kéfélian (forthcoming).
[74] Butcher and Ponting (2014: 190, 226, 235–7, 276–7); Woytek (2022: 245–6).
[75] See Kéfélian (forthcoming) for a detailed cased study of Sařnakunk hoard.
[76] Lockyear (2007: 134–9).
[77] Lockyear (2007: 138 and 183).
[78] *RPC* I, nos 4094–6.
[79] *RPC* I, no. 2201.

date of the latest coins more likely. Therefore, the Sarnakunk' hoard is a rare testimony to an early introduction of *denarii* in the Roman east and beyond.

The hoard of Chukhur Gabala, discovered in the Kingdom of Albania, constitutes a second example of a mixed currency hoard.[80] It is composed of *c.* 200 Parthian, Roman, and Sasanian silver coins, ranging from so-called 'Gotarzes II Parthian drachms' (AD 12–81) to Wahram II Sasanian drachms (AD 274–91).[81] The hoard also contains an uncertain number of Roman *denarii* of Otho, Vespasian, Trajan, and Hadrian, which were deposited at the end of the third century.

The third hoard available is the Erevan hoard. It offers a rare perspective on fourth- to fifth-century Roman material in Armenia. Current knowledge suggests that about 50 *siliquae* were initially discovered, of which 30 were added to the Evgenij Paxomov collection. It is highly probable that the National Museum of History of Azerbaijan houses these 30 coins, consisting of *siliquae* from Theodosius I, Honorius, and Valentinian III dating between AD 379–95 and 425–55. This hoard is interesting given the geopolitical situation of Armenia at this time, which was under Sasanian authority, and three years later witnessed the downfall of the Arsacid dynasty, but limited information prohibits any more detailed interpretation.

The dataset as a whole confirms the predominant role of Roman imperial coins in the coin supply of the Greater Armenian Kingdom, where only a few Armenian issues were struck after the collapse of the Artaxiad dynasty at the beginning of the first century AD. The scant evidence of Parthian coins minted during the first and second centuries attested in ancient Armenia corroborates this picture.

Bronze deposits

Bronze hoards are very scarce, with only one confirmed hoard containing Roman coins and imitations of Roman coins (Artašat 2005). Two potential Parthian hoards might have been discovered at Art'ik and Vardenut,[82] but there are doubts whether these were actual hoards or, rather, individual finds brought together as a set to the Historical Museum of Armenia.

The 2005 discovery of the Artašat bronze hoard during excavations opens new perspectives for the entire region. The hoard contained 56 bronze coins, including two provincial coins of Antoninus Pius from Laodicea ad Mare and Corinth, 53 cast imitations of SC Antiochene coins, designated as 'Slocum 3 series' (see below),

[80] CHRE 4008.

[81] The so-called 'Gotarzes II drachms', according to Sellwood (1980), range from Artabanus II (12–38/41), Gotarzes II (43/4–51), to Artabanus III (79/80–1).

[82] Regarding the Roman hoard Artašat 2005, see Vardanyan (2009). The Parthian hoards of Art'ik and Vardenut have been published in Mousheghian†, Mousheghian, and Depeyrot (2000: 99–100 for Art'ik and 141–2 for Vardenut).

and one illegible coin.[83] This discovery provides new data on the circulation and mint location of these imitative SC Antiochene coins. In addition to the 53 imitative specimens found in this hoard, three recent site finds in Artašat now provide a total of 56 SC cast imitations compared to the nine specimens previously published.[84]

Prior to this discovery, imitations were restricted to Upper Mesopotamia and Syria,[85] but now the Artašat hoard and the site finds demonstrate that SC imitations were also present in the Greater Armenian Kingdom. The provenances of 71 SC cast imitations are now known: 56 from the Greater Armenian Kingdom, 11 from the Mesopotamian region, and four from Levantine merchants (without a precise location of discovery) (Table 10.3).

These cast imitations are called 'series 3' by John J. Slocum in his analysis of the coinage of Hatra.[86] Slocum concluded that the coins were cast in Hatra during the first half of the third century, based on two specimens discovered there during archaeological excavations.[87] Kevin Butcher has recently questioned this interpretation, arguing that the location of the casting cannot be determined at present, and that these coins could be of an earlier date.[88] Despite the 56 specimens added to the corpus of SC imitations, the limited number of known findspots still

Table 10.3. Finds of SC cast imitations.

Discovery location	Number of coins	References
Hatra	2	Aṣ-Ṣāliḥī (1974: pl. 2, nos. 20–1; Slocum (1977: 42)
Specimens from Levantine dealers	4	Slocum (1977: 42)
Sippar	1	Butcher (2004: 169 (2); 2015: 184, no. 6 and fig. 6 (1); 2017a: 14 (1))
Tel Sheh Hamad	1	Oettel (2005: 178, no. 78)
Nisibis?	6	Vardanyan (2009: 54), kept in History Museum of Armenia
Artašat	56	Vardanyan (2009), 53 specimens; 3 site finds discovered during RoCCAA research
Assur	1	Butcher (2017a: 14, 35, no. 225)

[83] Vardanyan (2009; 2018: 28) (CHRE 20937). The History Museum of Armenia houses a further six coins from Nisibis in its collections (Table 10.3). Vardanyan (2009: 54). See the chapter by Spoerri Butcher (chapter 9) for a Mesopotamian contextualization.

[84] Walker (1958); Slocum (1977); Butcher (2004; 2015; 2017a; 2017b; 2021a; 2021b; 2022).

[85] I thank Kevin Butcher for our exchange about the SC cast imitations.

[86] Slocum (1977: 41–2).

[87] Slocum (1977: 44).

[88] See Butcher (2021b: 45; 2022: 168–9).

precludes making conclusive assertions about any mint location. However, the presence of a Laodicean coin from Syria in the Artašat 2005 hoard would support the argument for a production in Upper Mesopotamia or Syria. Currently, there is no evidence for the presence of Laodicean coins in the Artašat plain.[89] Furthermore, these Laodicean coins, minted in Syria and attested in Upper Mesopotamia, were used to overstrike the SC imitations from Hatra known as 'Class 2'.[90] While it remains possible that the casts originated in Armenia or Syria, a more compelling argument is that they were made in Upper Mesopotamia, although not necessarily in Hatra.[91]

Slocum suggested that the SC cast imitation series dated to the first half of the third century, in contrast to the two preceding series produced in Hatra (which date from the latter half of the second century AD), owing to their crude quality and debased alloy.[92] Butcher has refined Slocum's dating, suggesting that the series may possibly belong to an earlier date than previously assumed,[93] based on metrological data that align with SC Antiochene coins from the late first century to the mid-second century AD. The Artašat 2005 hoard provides evidence supporting a date in the mid- or second half of the second century AD. Slocum dates 'series 1 and 2' to the mid- or late second century based on the evidence that they were overstruck on coins of Laodicea belonging to the reigns of Trajan, Hadrian, and Antoninus Pius.[94] Nonetheless, the Artašat 2005 hoard included a coin from Laodicea that is typically used for overstrikes of 'Slocum series 1 and 2'. It is therefore possible that the 'Slocum 3 series' was manufactured prior to the 'Slocum series 1 and 2', or contemporaneously but in a different location.

Both the cast and struck imitations, as well as the numerous genuine specimens found in ancient Armenia and Upper Mesopotamia, suggest that the SC cast imitations were not limited to local circulation but instead played a role in macro-regional coin circulation.

The question arising from this overview is whether Armenia stands alone, based on the data we have collected, or whether regional hoarding preferences can be observed when compared to neighbouring regions. A comparison with the kingdoms of Iberia and Colchis is therefore presented in the second part of this study.[95]

[89] Caution must be exercised, as data on the royal residence of Vałaršapat are not available.

[90] Slocum (1977: nos 12, 15, 17); Butcher (2017a: 16–7; 36, nos 238–50).

[91] Vardanyan (2009) questioned the theory of its local production in Artašat, but he exercised prudence.

[92] Slocum (1977: 44).

[93] Butcher (2022: 168).

[94] Slocum (1977: 38–41 and 44); Butcher (2017a: 14–21) for an updated classification of these different struck imitations of SC Antiochene coins; Butcher (2022).

[95] Unfortunately, data are too scarce for establishing a comparison with the Albanian evidence. These data rely on the CHRE database (last accessed 21 December 2023). Preliminary sets of information have been completed, updated, and added through my work as a John Fell Fund fellow on 'Roman Hoards from Georgia' (1 September 2021 to 31 January 2022). The entries stem from the Soviet

CONTEXTUALIZATION OF ANCIENT ARMENIAN COIN DEPOSITION: THE CASE OF THE IBERIAN AND COLCHIS KINGDOMS

The significance of gold coin circulation in the Iberian kingdom in funerary contexts

Gold coins recorded in Iberia and Colchis are much more widespread than in ancient Armenia (Fig. 10.5).[96] Ancient Armenia has only 11 records of single gold coin finds, whereas Georgia, which includes the kingdoms of Iberia and Colchis, has 122 coins gathered from 49 hoards or single finds.[97] The data show a much higher number of gold coins in Iberia from the first to the end of the fourth century AD (Table 10.4). At the beginning of the fifth century AD, the gap between Armenia and Iberia narrows. The more consistent Georgian dataset arises from a state of research where sites and cemeteries were excavated over a prolonged period and followed by regular publications.

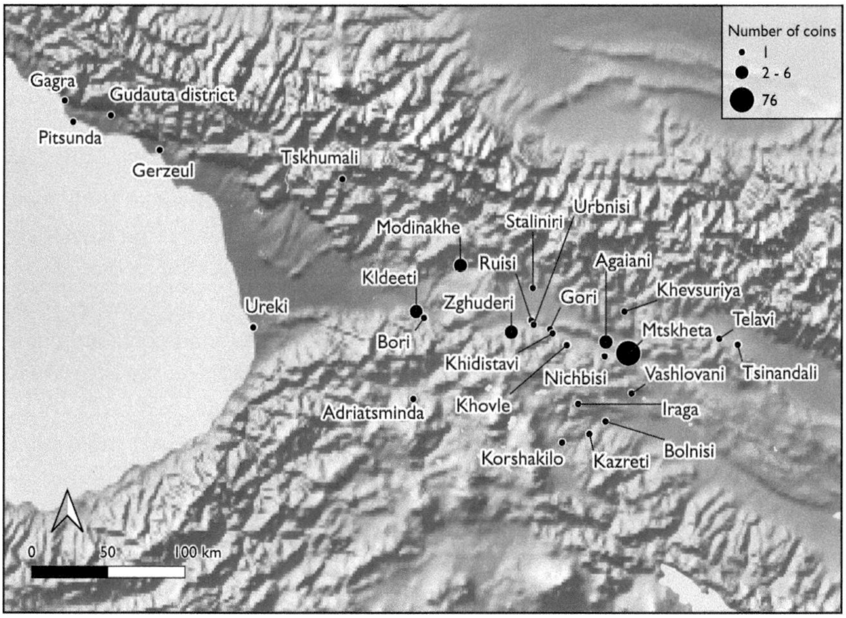

Fig. 10.5. Distribution map of gold coins from the Kingdoms of Iberia and Colchis, nowadays in the territory of Georgia. Source: CHRE database (accessed 22 December 2023). Map: M. Spoerri Butcher/A. Kéfélian.

Corpora's hoard inventory and research by scholars like Paxomov, Zograph, Kropotkin, Golenko, and Kapanadze, as well as the edited volume in the Moneta collection and other publications.

96 Kapanadze (1949).

97 Source: CHRE database (accessed 21 December 2023).

Table 10.4. Number of gold coins in Iberia and Colchis until Leo I (AD 457–71) compared to Greater Armenia.

Period	Iberia and Colchis	Greater Armenia
BC[a]	25	1
First century AD	29	4
Second century AD	24	
Third century AD	22	
Fourth century AD	8	0
Fourth or fifth century AD	0	1
Fifth century AD	13	5
Uncertain	1	
Total	**122**	**11**

[a] This line includes specimens of Alexander III staters, Colchian gold coins, and, notably, local imitations of Lysimachus gold coins.

Although the results are clearly unbalanced, other factors suggest that gold coins may have played a more important role in Iberia and Colchis. In addition to Roman gold, the Georgian dataset offers a range of other gold coins, including the minting of local gold imitation staters of Alexander and Lysimachus. The earliest ones, termed 'Aka staters', were produced in Colchis from the first quarter of the second century BC.[98] Then, imitation staters of Lysimachus started to be produced at the same time until the last quarter of the first century BC. They were followed by imitations of staters of Alexander issued from the first century BC to the first century AD.[99] Later, gold imitations of Roman coins were also minted, starting from the second half of the third century AD.[100]

A third difference in the Armenian hoard evidence is that gold coinage from Iberia and Colchis is mostly found in groups consisting of gold coins only or a combination of gold and silver coins.[101] The latter is observed in the—Mtskheta Samtavro 1985 find, discovered in a sarcophagus, which consisted of 34 coins, including three *aurei*, 12 *denarii*, 16 Parthian drachms, one Caesarean hemidrachm from Cappadocia, and two unidentified silver coins.[102] Iberian and Colchis hoards may contain exclusively Roman coins,[103] or Roman combined with Parthian and coins from other local mints.[104]

[98] http://geonumismatics.tsu.ge/public/en/catalogue/types?type=15 (accessed 17 March 2022). Dundua and Dundua (2013: 210–1); Golenko (1964: 10–18); Fabian (2019: 43–6).

[99] http://geonumismatics.tsu.ge/public/en/catalogue/types?type=7 and http://geonumismatics.tsu.ge/public/en/catalogue/types?type=15 (accessed 17 March 2022). Zograph (1936: 178–92); Golenko (1964: 11, 13, 15); Dundua and Dundua (2013: 211–25); Fabian (2019: 44–5).

[100] http://geonumismatics.tsu.ge/public/en/catalogue/types?type=28 (accessed 18 March 2022).

[101] The only exception for Armenia is the group of single finds found in Sisian.

[102] Apakidze and Nikolaishvili (1994): CHRE 16032.

[103] See notably the hoard of Mtskheta—Armazi 1941 2: CHRE 16037.

[104] See Mtskheta 1951: CHRE 16043.

The fourth main disparity between the gold dataset from ancient Armenia and the one from the kingdoms of Iberia and Colchis involves the depositional context. In Georgia, 79% of the recorded coins in the CHRE database originate from funerary contexts, concentrated mainly in Iberia, while 21% are unidentified archaeological contexts. Lara Fabian confirms the tendency to deposit gold coins in funerary contexts in Iberia thanks to her comprehensive personal database, where just 3.2% of the gold coins in her overall database account for 11% of all coins in funerary contexts.[105] Their high frequency in funerary contexts suggests that they may have served as 'Charon's obol'.[106] In contrast, only 12.5% of the Armenian gold coins were deposited in funerary contexts, whereas 87.5% come from uncertain contexts.

Additional differences are also observed in the Georgian data, such as the presence of pierced coins or coins mounted in jewellery, indicating that the coins were more often used here for the purposes of adornment.[107] The Georgian circulation of gold coinage therefore appears to share similarities with the systems observed in the Zarubintsy and Chernyakhiv cultures, located in the north-western part of the Black Sea, while contrasting with the patterns found in Armenia.[108] The possible influence on the circulation of gold of the nomadic Scythians—who migrated from the central Asian steppes to the modern territory of southern Russia and Ukraine—should be further investigated.[109]

Silver Roman imperial coins versus silver Roman provincial coins

The Georgian deposits contain a wider range of silver denominations than those found in Armenia and are characterized by four times the number of silver coins.[110] As has already been noted in the case of gold coins, there were different circulation pools of silver coins between the kingdoms of Iberia and Colchis (Fig. 10.6), which need to be addressed separately.

Unlike ancient Armenia, the Kingdom of Iberia shows a variety of silver deposition practices. Based on the current data in the CHRE database, Roman silver coins in Iberia have been almost exclusively discovered in funerary contexts. However, it is challenging to determine to what degree the extensive excavations

[105] Fabian's database (2017: 52) contains information on all ancient coinages with an associated findspot, but she excluded two Hellenistic hoards.

[106] Fabian (2018: 41).

[107] See also Fabian (2019: 49–50).

[108] Kéfélian (2025). Moisil (2002: paragraphs 18, 22, 49, 50).

[109] On *aurei* in Ukraine, see also Myzgin's contribution in the current volume (chapter 8).

[110] For Georgia, 2,351 coins were entered in CHRE database compared to only 633 for Armenia (data accessed 21 December 2023).

of the ancient cemeteries from the nineteenth century, namely Samtavro, Armaziskhevi, and Bagineti, may have influenced this outcome.[111]

Besides funerary deposits, only three hoards illuminate the circulation of silver coins within the Iberian Kingdom, and two of these comprise exclusively Sasanian coins.[112] The third hoard discovered at Mtskheta-Bagineti in 1944 comprised 22 *denarii* of Augustus. No further description is available, but it is probable that these were *denarii* of Gaius and Lucius. The coins were found scattered within a single archaeological layer and thus judged to constitute a hoard.[113]

For Iberia, the CHRE database contains numerous entries attesting that Roman imperial coins, local imitations, and Parthian coins were deposited together in graves, and could be a mixture of gold and silver. One example is the Mtskheta 1951 group of single finds consisting of four Roman *aurei*, five stater imitations, three Augustus *denarii*, 51 Parthian drachms, and a gold bracelet.[114]

Another difference between the Iberian and the ancient Armenian deposits relates to long-term circulation patterns. Unlike Armenia, where the contextualization and burial dates remain unclear, the information from Georgia provides valuable insights into the circulation duration. A clear example is the Khovle funerary deposit, which demonstrates that *denarii* of Augustus could be deposited until at least the first half of the third century.[115] This particular deposit consists of two *denarii* of Augustus, two drachms of the 'so-called' Gotarzes drachms, and an *aureus* of Elagabalus.

It is worth noting the scarcity of Roman Republican *denarii* in Iberia, with only 24 coins, and that no Republican coins were hoarded. Of these, eight Republican coins were found as single finds and 16 in funerary contexts (Fig. 10.7), where they appear to be more prevalent.[116] Like Roman gold in funerary contexts, Republican *denarii* served various purposes, including being used as ornaments. For example, the Republican *denarius* issued from 118 BC, found in Burial 39 in Nastagisi, was mounted as jewellery.[117]

[111] Samtavro is a very important cemetery with *c.* 3,000 graves discovered to date. It has been excavated since the second part of the nineteenth century, and excavations are still continuing. Armaziskhevi and Bagineti have also been excavated from the nineteenth century and comprise more than 425 graves. See Gamkrelidze *et al.* (2013: 350–63) for Mtskheta and Samtavro, and Gamkrelidze *et al.* (2013: 46–54) for Armazi. Apakidze, Gobedzhishvili, Kalandadze, and Lomtatidze (1955); Ivashenko (1980); Kalandadze (1980; 1981; 1982); Apakidze (1985); Sagona *et al.* (2010).

[112] Tsotselia and Depeyrot (2010: 124, nos 657 and 660).

[113] CHRE 18190. Kropotkin (1961: 107, no. 1622).

[114] CHRE 16043. Paxomov VII (1926–59 [1957: 24, no. 1738]); Kropotkin (1961: 107, no. 1633).

[115] CHRE 16078. Tsotselia and Depeyrot (2010: 88, no. 537).

[116] It is difficult to assess the extent to which the long excavations of cemeteries in the vicinity of Mtskheta may be skewing the data from Colchis and ancient Armenia; updated on dataset from 20 December 2023. The Nazodelavu hoard contains 23 Republican coins, a *denarius* of Augustus, and a drachm of Archelaus IV of Cappadocia; CHRE 16046; Dundua (1987: 133–5). For the discoveries including single finds, Sherozia (2008: 236–8) gathered in Iberia 24 coins. See also Fabian (2019: 47) for Roman Republican coins from Colchis.

[117] Sherozia (2008: 249; 1. *Denarius*, 118 BC. GNM CGC 25378).

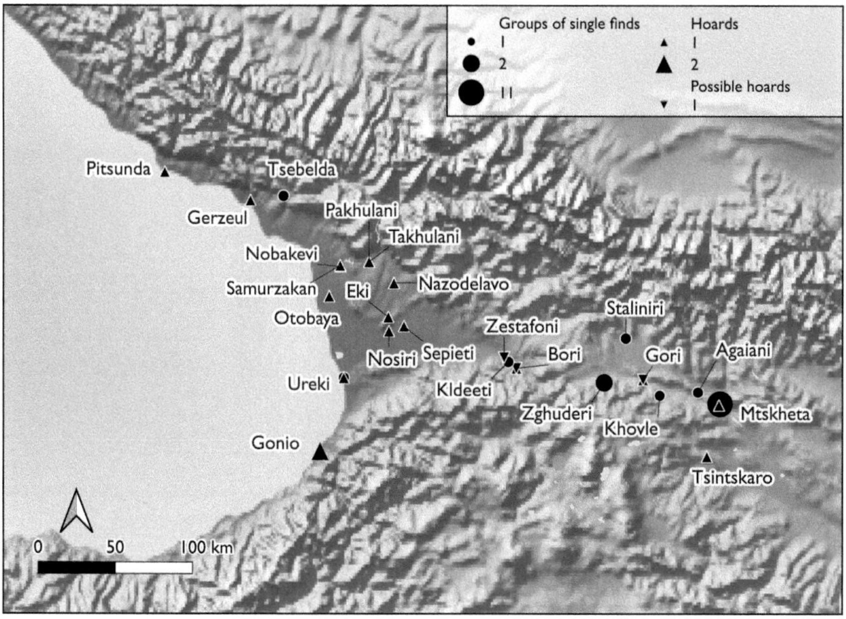

Fig. 10.6. Distribution map of silver deposits in the Kingdoms of Iberia and Colchis, nowadays in the territory of Georgia. Source: CHRE database (accessed 22 December 2023). Map: M. Spoerri Butcher/A. Kéfélian.

Finds in Colchis include 33 Roman Republican coins, 23 of which were deposited in the same hoard (Fig. 10.7).[118] According to Fabian, ten additional coins were discovered and appear to be divided between two single finds and eight coins from groups of single finds.[119] The level of finds observed in Iberia and Colchis appears to differ greatly from the Armenian record of 251 coins, although this is heavily distorted by the significant Sar̄nakunk‘ hoard, which contained 225 Republican coins on its own.[120]

The quantity of Roman gold coins discovered in Iberia (117 coins) and Colchis (5 coins) is nearly equivalent to that of Roman imperial silver coins discovered in that same area (81 coins).[121] While gold coins were distributed continuously between the reigns of Augustus and Constantius II, and later during the reign of Theodosius II, imperial silver coins were almost exclusively limited to the reign of Augustus. Medea Sherozia recorded 350 specimens of Gaius and Lucius *denarii* attributed between the years 2 BC and AD 4, taking into account both hoards and

[118] See the chapter by Spoerri Butcher in the current volume (chapter 9).
[119] Fabian (2019: 47, n. 78).
[120] See above for the contextualization of Republican finds in the hoard of Sar̄nakunk‘.
[121] Refer to Table 10.5 for the number of Roman imperial silver coins. The number of gold coins refers to the gold coins entered in the CHRE database (Table 10.4).

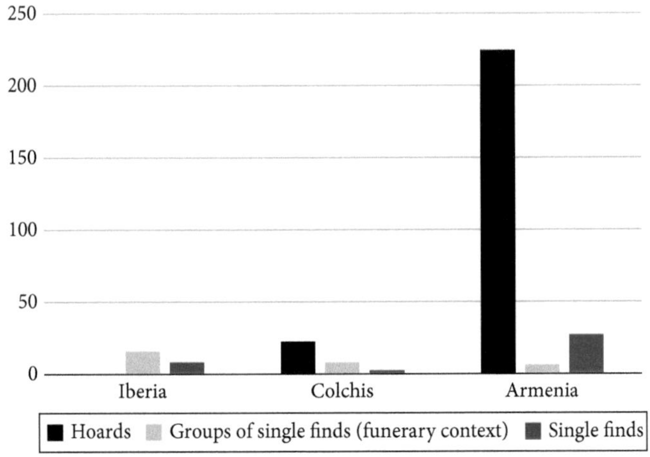

Fig. 10.7. Number of Republican *denarii* across the southern Caucasus kingdoms, by find type. Source: CHRE database (accessed 22 December 2023) for Armenia and Colchis; Sherozia (2008) for Iberian data; Fabian (2019) for Colchis; and RoCCAA project for Armenia.

individual finds.[122] The number of Gaius and Lucius coins found in hoards from Colchis is significantly lower than in Iberia (Table 10.5). As for ancient Armenia, no specimens of Gaius and Lucius coins have been found in any hoards, but a total of 76 single finds have been recorded in the corpus.[123] This inconsistency may stem from a bias in the research, as few hoards have been recorded for Armenia.

Apart from the cluster of Augustan coins and a *denarius* of Tiberius, there is a small cluster of *denarii* between the reigns of Trajan and Marcus Aurelius. The trend of a considerable increase in coins between Hadrian and Antoninus Pius and a decline from Marcus Aurelius and Commodus is also observed in Armenia in the hoard of Gaṙni, and indeed widely in other hoards of the Roman Empire, tracking patterns of coin production.[124] In contrast to Colchis, provincial coins are rare in Iberia, with only one instance of provincial coins dating from the reign of Hadrian.[125]

The Colchis dataset indicates a distinctive pool of circulation compared to the Iberian and Greater Armenian Kingdoms. While Iberian data (Table 10.5) come mainly from funerary contexts, except for the probable hoard of Mtskheta-Bagineti 1944 (CHRE 18190), the Colchis dataset includes numerous hoards. Three main components are evident from the dataset: the coins of Pontus, the

[122] Sherozia (2002). [123] See below for Gaius and Lucius coins in single finds.

[124] See Figs 10.3 and 10.4 for a comparison with various hoards with a closing period of Commodus.

[125] See Mtskheta-Samtavro 1985 (CHRE 16032).

provincial coins of Caesarea of Cappadocia, and later *denarii* from the late Antonine and Severan periods.

Across the Black Sea, Colchis was in close proximity to the Roman coast of Asia Minor. As a result, coins from the Kingdom of Pontus are numerous there, especially those issued by Polemon II, which are attested by 74 specimens (Table 10.6). The hoard of Pakhulani consists of ten drachms of Polemon II, while Samurzakan consists of at least 60 such coins.[126] The presence of coins of Polemon II can also be explained by the fact that he ruled over Colchis from AD 38 to 41.[127] However, because these hoards consist of a single currency and lack a recorded archaeological context, it is not possible to narrow the date of their deposition.

The second main pattern is the widespread circulation of Roman provincial silver coins originating from Caesarea in Cappadocia—especially didrachms, drachms, and hemidrachms—from the reigns of Nero to Septimius Severus (Tables 10.5 and 10.6).[128] Coins from Caesarea in Cappadocia are known from 15 hoards out of the 17 entries of silver coins in the Colchis dataset. Coins from Caesarea in Cappadocia were deposited from the beginning of the second century AD. However, they are more commonly encountered in hoards deposited after the reign of Septimius Severus.[129] The Gerzeul hoard, for example, consisted of 469 silver coins struck at Caesarea in Cappadocia dating from Nero to Lucius Verus.[130] This same hoard also had a *denarius* of Augustus, a probable coin of Gaius and Lucius, and an imitation stater of Lysimachus. The Gerzeul hoard therefore provides evidence for the prolonged circulation of Gaius and Lucius coins beyond the mid-second and early third centuries AD, when they seem to have become less common. This later scarcity led to the production of imitations of Gaius and Lucius coins in Iberia in the second half of the third century.[131] Konstantin Golenko dates the introduction of the Cappadocian coins to the second half of the first century AD following the establishment of Roman garrisons in Apsaros (Gonio), Phasis, Dioscuria/Sebastopolis (Sukhumi), and Pityus (Pitsunda), considered to be part of the *exercitus Cappadocicus*.[132] In the absence

[126] Pakhulani (CHRE 18826): Paxomov (1926–59 [1940: 28, no. 771]); Zograph (1945: 78, no. 175); Kropotkin (1961: 108, no. 1660); Golenko (1964: 63, no. 12) and Samurzakan (CHRE 18754): Paxomov (1926–59 [1926: 39, no. 27]); Zograph (1945: 78, no. 174); Kropotkin (1961: 105, no. 1576); Golenko (1964: 63, no. 11).

[127] Braund (1994).

[128] For a detailed study of hoards from Colchis, see Spoerri Butcher's contribution in the current volume (chapter 9).

[129] See hoards Pitsunda 1958 (CHRE 16062); Otobaya (CHRE 16060); Novabeki (CHRE 16079); Gonio 1998 (CHRE 16080); Gonio 2018 (CHRE 20923); group of single finds of Ureki 1942 (CHRE 16070).

[130] CHRE 5478. See notably Paxomov (1926–59 [1938: 13, no. 346]); Zograph (1945: 70, no. 133; 78–9, no. 179); Kropotkin (1961: 105, no. 1577); Golenko (1964: 65–6; 17–17a; 81, no. 62); Abramzon (2003; 2005).

[131] http://geonumismatics.tsu.ge/en/catalogue/types?type=27 (accessed 15 June 2022).

[132] Pliny, *Natural History*, 6.1. Golenko (1964: 28–43); Braund (1994: 171–204); Bennett (2006); Speidel (2009: 601–2); Fabian (2019: 48).

Table 10.5. Number of imperial and provincial silver coins from hoards across the southern Caucasus kingdoms, by reign (Iberia, n = 82; Colchis, n = 1908; Armenia, n = 100). Source: CHRE database and RoCCAA (last updated 22 December 2023).

	Kingdom of Iberia		**Kingdom of Colchis**		**Greater Armenian Kingdom**
Reign	**Imperial silver**	**Provincial silver**	**Imperial silver**	**Provincial silver**	**Imperial silver**
Augustus	73		2		
Tiberius	1		1		
Gaius				1	
Nero				1	
Galba					
Vespasian			1	31	8
Titus	0				1
Domitian				10	
Nerva				24	
Trajan	2		5	178	3
Hadrian	1	1	2	830	13
Antoninus Pius	1		3	122	15
Antoninus Pius or Marcus Aurelius			2	59	
Marcus Aurelius	1		6	30	6
Marcus Aurelius or Commodus	1		1	28	
Commodus			35		2
Pertinax			6		
Septimius Severus	1		381	19	
Septimius Severus or Caracalla			58	8	
Pescennius Niger			2		
Clodius Albinus			17		
Caracalla				2	
Elagabalus			5		
Severus Alexander			38		
Theodosius I -Valentian III					50
Total	**81**	**1**	**565**	**1,343**	**98**
	82		**1,908**		**98**

Table 10.6. Hoards from Colchis containing Roman provincial silver coins of Caesarea in Cappadocia and Polemon II, by *t.p.q*. Source: CHRE database (accessed 23 December 2025).

Hoard	Caesarea in Cappadocia (*t.p.q.*)	Polemon II (*t.p.q.*)
Pakhulani (CHRE 18828)		X (AD 38–74)
Gonio 2015 (CHRE 21289)	X (AD 54–68)	
Gonio 2019 (CHRE 21290)	X (AD 54–68)	X (AD 54–68)
Samurzakan (CHRE 18754)		X (AD 49–63)
Takhulani (CHRE 16068)	X (AD 117–38)	
Nosiri (CHRE 16059)	X (AD 131–61)	
Tsebelda (CHRE 18182)	X (AD 139)	
Gerzeul (CHRE 5478)	X (AD 161–9)	
Novabeki (CHRE 16079)	X (AD 193–211)	
Gonio 1998 (CHRE 16080)	X (AD 193–211)	X (AD 193–211)
Otobaya (CHRE 16060)?	X (AD 193–211)	
Gonio 2018 (CHRE 20923)	X (AD 222–35)	
Sepieti (CHRE 5333)	X (AD 222–35)	
Eki (CHRE 5334)	X (AD 222–35)	
Pitsunda 1958 (CHRE 16062)	X (AD 244–5)	
Ureki 1942 (CHRE 16070)	X (AD 275–6)	
Ureki 1948 (CHRE 16071)	X (uncertain)	

of archaeological context, it is not possible to determine whether Vespasianic coinage was introduced in the second half of the first century or during the second century AD. Some of these coins are commonly found in military settings within a fortress or in a funerary context in the vicinity of a fortress. The increase in coins discovered could also be associated with the relocation of troops involving vexillations of *Legio XII Fulminata* and *Legio XV Apollinaris*, as well as auxiliaries with four *alae* and ten cohorts, along with allied contingents from Colchis and Armenia who had faced the Alans in AD 134–5.[133] Some of the coins of Caesarea in Cappadocia minted in the second century AD remained in circulation until the latter half of the third century, when they were deposited alongside coins from Trapezus, as detailed below.

The third pattern can be observed through the Eki and Sepieti hoards (Table 10.5), with their high number of *denarii*.[134] Their *t.p.q.* is the reign of Severus Alexander. The proportion of imperial coins in these two hoards is much higher compared to other hoards, with 15% in the Eki hoard and between 86% and 96% in the Sepieti hoard (depending on the list from Zograph or coins kept in the National Museum of Georgia). Additionally, these hoards were found inland, which contrasts with the previously studied hoards.

133 Speidel (2009: 620–3); Lalanne (2014: 74).

134 CHRE 5334 for Eki and CHRE 5333 for Sepieti. For a detailed analysis of these hoards, see the chapter by Spoerri Butcher in this volume (chapter 9).

The regional circulation of bronze coinage in Colchis

Although the Roman bronze hoard dataset from Armenia is limited to only two Roman provincial coins associated with 53 SC cast imitations, the Colchis dataset presents a distinct pattern that is linked to its geographical location. It includes several significant hoards that contain bronze coins deposited from the mid-third century onwards (Fig. 10.8).[135] There are two main features that emerge from a precise geopolitical and military context and that stand out from the dataset observed in ancient Armenia.[136]

The first feature, evidenced by the discovery of two hoards in the vicinity of Roman military forts, is the hoarding of Trapezus bronze coins alongside silver coins from Caesarea in Cappadocia. The Pitsunda 1958 hoard, unearthed on the northern Black Sea coast in the former city and fortress of Pityus, comprised 149 Roman provincial coins, including ten silver coins from Caesarea in Cappadocia dating from Hadrian to Septimius Severus and 139 bronze coins from Trapezus dating from Commodus/Septimius Severus to Philip I.[137] The second hoard, Gonio 2018, was found in the vicinity of the Roman fort of Apsaros. It consisted

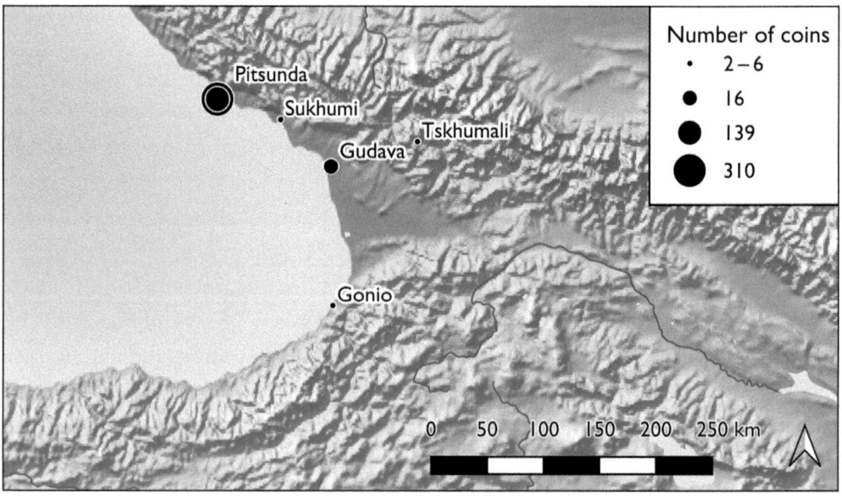

Fig. 10.8. Distribution map of hoards containing bronze coins from Colchis. Source: CHRE database (accessed 15 December 2022). Map: A. Wilson/A. Kéfélian.

[135] Pitsunda 1958 (CHRE 16062); Pitsunda 1961 (CHRE 16063); Sukhumi (CHRE 16067); Gudava (CHRE 16085); Gonio (CHRE 20923). See also Spoerri Butcher's contribution in the current volume (chapter 9) for a more detailed examination of the third-century hoards.

[136] See notably Abramzon (2003; 2005); Fabian (2019: 48).

[137] CHRE 16062.

of 14 burned coins: eight coins of Caesarea of Cappadocia dating from Hadrian to Caracalla and six bronzes of Trapezus dating from Marcus Aurelius to Severus Alexander.[138]

The coins were buried during the tumultuous situation around the Black Sea in the second half of the third century. As reported by Zosimus, the Boranoi infiltrated the Black Sea coast in the 250s and, after several attempts, captured the fortress of Pityus before reaching other places along the coast of the Black Sea.[139] On the basis of recent archaeological excavations and numismatic studies of stray finds, tomb finds, and hoards, including the Gonio 2018 hoard, it is suggested that the fortress of Apsaros may have been abandoned due to the frequent raids.[140]

The closure of the mints at Trapezus during the reign of Philip I,[141] and at Caesarea in Cappadocia under Gordian III, had an impact on supplies and consequently on the coinage available in the region.[142]

The second feature observed with bronze hoards is the arrival of *nummi* deposited in three Roman fort sites: Pitsunda,[143] Sukhumi,[144] and Gudava.[145] These coins range from the late Tetrarchy to the mid-fourth century. As far as we can tell from the evidence we have, these coins were concentrated in the vicinity of, and in, Roman forts.[146] Consequently, Golenko attributes the *nummi* to the presence of Roman garrisons.[147] These hoards may be associated with the tumultuous context of Goths and Huns settling in the north of the Black Sea.

The *nummi* represented in these three hoards (Table 10.7) are dominated by coins from Antioch (86 coins), followed by Nicomedia (53 coins), Cyzicus (31 coins), and Constantinople (18 coins). The Pitsunda hoard 1961 contains coins from various other mints, with, in addition to the mints mentioned above, ten coins from Alexandria, five from Siscia, one from Heraclea, and one from Rome. In contrast, the Sukhumi hoard consists of only three coins, two minted at Nicomedia, and a coin from Antioch. The third hoard from Gudava is more problematic, as only two of the 16 coins in the hoard have been identified. These two coins originated from Heraclea and Nicomedia.

[138] CHRE 20923. For Apsaros, see notably Speidel (1986); Karasiewicz (2016); Karasiewicz-Szczypiorski, Mamuladze, Jaworski, and Wagner (2016); Jaworski, Karasiewicz-Szczypiorski, and Mamuladze (2021). On coins from Apsaros see Varshalomidze (2009). See also the chapter by Spoerri Butcher in the current volume (chapter 9).

[139] Zosimus, *Historia Nova* I. XXXII, 1–4. Apakidze (1975–7); Lavrov (1995); Bolgov (2004); Jaworski, Karasiewicz-Szczypiorski, and Mamuladze (2021: 298–9).

[140] Kakhidze (2008: 305); Jaworski, Karasiewicz-Szczypiorski, and Mamuladze (2021: 299).

[141] Wojan (2006). [142] Bland (2001).

[143] Arkeologiuri gatkhrebi apkhazetshi (1975–8).

[144] Formerly Dioscurias/Sebastopolis. Trapš (1955: 206–27); Shervashidze and Solov'ev (1960: 171–9); Lekvinadze (1966: 203–10); Brašinskij (1968: 114–15); Inadze (1968); Lordkipanidze (1970).

[145] Kassab *et al.* (2007: 197–8).

[146] Golenko (1964: 34). [147] Golenko (1964: 33).

Table 10.7. Number of coins per mint in hoards of *nummi* from Colchis. Source: CHRE database (accessed 16 December 2023).

Mint	Pitsunda 1961 (CHRE 16063)	Sukhumi (CHRE 16067)	Gudava (CHRE 16085)
Rome	1		
Siscia	5		
Heraclea			1
Nicomedia	50	2	1
Thessalonica	2		
Cyzicus	31		
Constantinople	18		
Antioch	85	1	
Alexandria	10		
Uncertain	108		14

The comparison with Iberia and Colchis helps to contextualize and highlight the uniqueness of Greater Armenia. The Georgian dataset also demonstrates the longevity of circulation of coinage in the region and the need to be cautious in interpreting dates of deposition. The absence of regular coin issues in the region and the function played by Roman coin may have affected the duration of coins in circulation. Roman coins had a significant impact in Iberia and Colchis beyond their monetary value. The presence of large quantities of imperial gold coins in funerary contexts highlights their probable function as Charon's obol. Additionally, Roman imperial coins were used for adornment, as seen notably in the case of a Republican *denarius* that was mounted as jewellery.

CONTEXTUALIZATION OF THE HOARD DATASET WITH SINGLE FINDS FROM THE GREATER ARMENIAN KINGDOM

In order to assess monetary circulation properly, hoards and single finds must be considered together. Small change (bronze, copper, and orichalcum coins) represents 30% of the coins recorded in the RoCCAA corpus, which includes not only the Roman but also the Armenian, Parthian, and other coins. Hoards typically consist of the highest value coins and are biased against small change. Likewise, single finds typically reflect the presence of lower-value coins. The higher-value coins are less likely to be lost due to their intrinsic value and the owner's willingness to look carefully in the case of loss.

The diversity of Roman Republican coins in single finds

The Armenian dataset, in which 265 Republican coins are recorded (including those from Sar̄nakunk' hoard), contrasts with what was observed in Georgia, with 57 coins for Iberia and Colchis combined (Fig. 10.7). Republican *denarii* represent 69% of all Roman coins from hoards in ancient Armenia, owing to the large numbers present in the Sar̄nakunk' hoard.[148] By contrast, they represent only 4% of the single finds specimens catalogued for the RoCCAA project.

Roman Republican *denarii* also appear in funerary contexts, where they are associated with coins of Tigranes II (95–55 BC) and Orodes II (57–38 BC). This is particularly evident in the case of the grave of P'arak'ar, which comprises three Roman *denarii* (78–42 BC), three Armenian coins of Tigranes II (83 to 69 BC), and a drachm of Orodes II. The proportion of Armenian and Roman coins varies, but the presence of Parthian coins is less significant or absent in all three cases. The Tavuš grave contains eight coins, including two Roman *denarii* from 63 to 31 BC, five coins of Tigranes II (61–59 BC), and a drachm of Orodes II.[149] The Mingechaur 1949 2 grave, whose attribution to the Greater Armenian Kingdom remains uncertain, contains two coins of Tigranes II and four Roman Republican *denarii* dating from 62 to 47 BC.[150]

Additionally, Roman Republican coins have been identified in 29 single finds (Table 10.8). Amongst the coins, 15 are silver *denarii*. The majority of the silver Republican coins were minted in Rome or produced during the campaigns of Julius Caesar and Mark Antony in the Roman east, via itinerant mints. The remaining 14 are bronze coins, predominantly civic coins minted in Antioch. Those civic coins from Antioch were all discovered in the royal residency of Artašat or in close proximity, with the exception of one coin discovered in the modern village of Nšavan and one from Aygezard.[151] It is probable that these Antiochene civic coins were introduced in ancient Armenia at a later date, along with the SC coins from Antioch.[152] It is also noteworthy to mention the presence of a Republican coin, with a Janus' head, which was discovered in the royal residency of Artašat.[153]

[148] See above.

[149] The list of coins varies. I follow the acquisition records of the museum, while Mousheghian†, Mousheghian, and Depeyrot (2000: 101–2, 139–40) base their list on that of Khach'atur Musheghyan. A potential ninth Roman coin (47/46 BC) may be associated with the same context, according to Ṛuben Vardanyan. See HMA 17869. *SNA*, p. 60–1, no. 300.

[150] The uncertainty regarding the attribution to the Greater Armenian Kingdom arises from the lack of knowledge about the bank of the river where the grave was discovered and the fluctuations of the border across centuries. See Paxomov (1926–59 [1954: 28–9 no. 1548]); Fabian (2018: 433, no. 8).

[151] Eleven (or possibly 12) civic coins from Antioch have been registered in the coin corpus. From Artašat: HMA 19878/23-24; 19992/104,106,109; 20088/27; 20093/7-8; 20095/7; 20105/10. Kéfélian (2025, 279). See HMA 20019/16 for the Antioch civic coin from Nšavan and HMA 19981 for Aygezard.

[152] Kéfélian (2025).

[153] HMA 20093/6.

Table 10.8. Republican coins in ancient Armenia collected during the RoCCAA project (based on dataset from December 2022).

Metal	Denomination	Mint location	Date range	Number of coins
AR	*Denarii*	Rome	124–42 BC	8[a]
		Itinerant mints	49–31 BC	6[b]
		Africa	47–46 BC	1[c]
AE	*As*	Rome	206–190 BC	1[d]
	Civic coins	Antioch	92–38 BC	10[e]
		Apamea (Phrygia)	88–40 BC	1[f]
		Prusa ad Olympum (Bithynia)	59–58 BC	1[g]
Total				**28**

[a] HMA 7645 in *SNA*, n. 371, HMA 17334 in *SNA*, n. 135, HMA 17342 in *SNA*, n. 74, HMA 13475 in *SNA*, n. 361, HMA 13476 in *SNA*, n. 35, HMA 19979/11 in *SNA*, n. 146, HMA 20142/1, HMA 20178/3.

[b] HMA 17433 in *SNA*, n. 258, HMA 18255 in *SNA*, n. 407, HMA 18547 in *SNA*, n. 261, HMA 19992/84 in *SNA*, n. 437 & HMA 19992/85 in *SNA*, n. 432, HMA 20029/5.

[c] HMA 17869 in *SNA*, n. 300.

[d] HMA 20093/6 in *SNA*, n. 3a.

[e] HMA 19878/23-24,19992/104& 106, 20088/27, 20093/7-8, 20095/7, 20105/10, 20019/16.

[f] HMA 19992/121.

[g] HMA 19992/120.

The regional circulation of gaius and lucius coins

The second significant difference between hoards and single finds pertains to the Gaius and Lucius coins. These coins are currently absent from ancient Armenian hoards.[154] Their only hoard attestation in the region comes from Tazakənd in the Kingdom of Albania, with four specimens as part of a larger hoard of 12 coins.[155] Unfortunately, the hoard is incomplete and difficult to interpret because 75% of the coins were burned in the modern-day fire at the Oren-Kala archaeological base in Beylagan. The near absence of these coins in hoards contrasts sharply with the 76 single finds recorded so far in ancient Armenia, and it is very likely that this number will increase as recording and publication practices improve.[156]

[154] Kéfélian (2025).

[155] Paxomov (1926–59 [1957, 7, no. 1737]); Kropotkin (1961: 251 no. 1538); CHRE 18189.

[156] The large number of these coins in Armenia led some researchers to believe that they were minted locally in Armenia. See Kéfélian (2025 and forthcoming) for a paper questioning the hypothesis of a local mint in ancient Armenia. See Musheghian (1997: 24 in Armenian and 112 in English); Mousheghian and Depeyrot (1999: 63–72); Depeyrot (2019) for the hypothesis of a local minting.

Sherozia collected evidence that highlights the wide circulation of Gaius and Lucius *denarii* in the Kingdom of Iberia and, to a lesser extent, Colchis.[157] Although it is difficult to estimate their period of circulation in ancient Armenia, since they are chance finds, several corroborating pieces of evidence attest to their circulation until the first half of the third century AD in Georgia, which coincides with the start of production of Gaius and Lucius imitations, possibly as a result of continued demand and the decreasing presence of official coins.[158]

The scarcity of silver Roman provincial coins

The preponderance of imperial silver coins contrasts significantly with the scarcity of provincial silver coinage, which is limited to eight specimens.[159] The vast majority of the silver provincial coins (drachms, didrachms, and tetradrachms) date from the reign of Nero to Trajan and originate from Caesarea of Cappadocia. They belong to a period of several significant changes in military strategy towards the Greater Armenian Kingdom.[160] The restructuring of Anatolia facilitated the establishment of an enduring legionary presence in Cappadocia, especially the *Legio XII Fulminata*, and an uncertain legion, which were later replaced by the *Legio XV Apollinaris*.[161] Several inscriptions, as well as testimony from the Armenian author Movsēs Xorenac'i in his *History of Armenia*, affirm military movements, and especially of the *Legio XII Fulminata* in the south Caucasus during the Flavian era.[162] During Trajan's campaign in Armenia, Cassius Dio provides details of the itinerary of Trajan and the legions to invade the Kingdom of Armenia.[163] Trajan bypassed the usual route (from Melitene to Artašat). Instead, he departed from the city of Antioch and proceeded to the fort of Satala, where a safer second itinerary (Satala-Artašat) was chosen.[164] It is probable that the six coins discovered in the royal residence of Artašat reflect military troop movement from Cappadocia. They may have arrived during Trajan's invasion from the

[157] Sherozia (2002).

[158] See notably the Khovle deposit (CHRE 16078), https://geonumismatics.tsu.ge/public/en/catalogue/types?type=27 [14 May 2022]. Dundua (2005: Plate 2; 2014); Kéfélian (2025 and forthcoming). See also Kapanadze (1962).

[159] Among the specimens is a *cistophorus* dated to the reign of Augustus (HMA 19877/8) and a tetradrachm from Antioch dated to the reign of Elagabalus (HMA 19993/5). Regarding coins of Caesarea in Cappadocia, there are one coin from Nero (HMA 19948/4), three coins from Vespasian (HMA 19992/94; HMA 19992/93; HMA 19877/12), and two from Trajan (HMA 198777/1; HMA 19877/2). There are also three bronze coins from Caesarea of Cappadocia. See below and Table 10.10.

[160] Kéfélian (2021a). [161] Kéfélian (2021a: 139–42).

[162] Kéfélian (2020: 95–6). Regarding the mention of Movsēs Xorenac'i, see *History of Armenia*, II, 54. For a French translation, see Khoren, Mahé, and Mahé (1993) and for an English version, see Khorenatsi and Thomson (1978).

[163] Dio Cassius, *Roman History*, LXVIII, 19 (Loeb edition). Traina and Kéfélian (2020)

[164] Manandyan (1965: 80–1); Kéfélian (2021a: 135–9).

Cappadocian *limes*.[165] Their presence in the royal residence of Artašat indicates that they probably arrived prior to the relocation of the royal residence to Vałaršapat in the second half of the second century AD. These coins may have been transported to ancient Armenia on multiple occasions from the Flavian period or/and as a lot during Trajan's invasion from the Cappadocian *limes*.[166] An alternative explanation for the coins of Caesarea discovered in Artašat might lie in the presence of Armenian allied troops, referred to as *summakhoi*, in Colchis during the reign of Hadrian.[167] As previously noted, the silver provincial coins of Caesarea in Cappadocia largely circulated in the Colchis region during this period. For now, our understanding is restricted by the absence of archaeological context. Moreover, the inaccessibility of the new royal residence, where Roman garrisons were stationed from the second half of the second century, makes it impossible to determine for now the extent to which Roman silver provincial coins continued to circulate.

The diversity of bronze coinage discovered in ancient Armenia

Single finds of bronze coins amount so far to a total of 361 specimens. Of these, at least 44% are Armenian bronze coins and 35% are Roman provincial coins.[168] The number of Parthian bronze coins is comparatively low, representing only 8% of the total number of bronze coins in the corpus. In addition to the aforementioned categories, the corpus comprises 5% of Nabatean coins, 3% of Pontic coins, 2% of Judean coins (including those from the First Revolt), and 2% of Bosporan coins. The remaining coins comprise less than 1% of Adiabene and Commagene coins, as well as SC Antiochene cast imitations and bronze coin imitations (with the exception of those found in the Artašat 2005 hoard).[169]

As might be expected, Armenian coins account for almost half of the total. This figure is likely to be an underestimate, given the numerous Armenian coins that are currently in the possession of public and private collections. However, the corpus only includes Armenian coins that have a known discovery location. The majority of these are coins minted under the rule of Tigranes II. Notwithstanding

[165] Kéfélian (2021a: 139–42). [166] Kéfélian (2021a: 139–42).

[167] Braund (1994: 176); Speidel (2009: 620–1); Lalanne (2014) mentions Armenians from Asia Minor, but it is more likely that they were from Greater Armenia. Inscriptions and historical accounts (notably *Historia Augusta*) from the time attest to the presence of Armenians among Roman military troops.

[168] Based on the corpus of the RoCCAA project (December 2022). The corpus of single bronze coins is still in progress. Around 50 coins are still to be studied in the HMA Museum. The analysis excludes coins of uncertain provenance and those from Tigranakert, given the lack of clarity surrounding their origin. This is due to the existence of various hypotheses regarding its location.

[169] Total based on the corpus dated December 2022. This does not include the coins from Tigranakert/Tigranocerta. See note to Table 10.10 for an explanation.

recent discoveries and reattributions, Armenian numismatics continues to confront significant challenges in identifying the issuers, mint locations, and dating of issues.[170] At present, there is no research available that provides insight into the duration of circulation of these Armenian bronze coins. Following the decline of the Artaxiad dynasty, the production of Armenian coins became episodic. This is one of the reasons that may explain the high incidence of foreign bronze coins in Armenia, which were reinforced by the numerous issues from Syria and Cappadocia from the first century BC.

While there are 97 Parthian silver coins, Parthian bronze is less common, with 31 specimens. There appears to be a correlation between the number of silver Parthian coins by reign and the number of bronze coins found: the more silver coins from a Parthian king that are found, the more bronze coins of the same ruler are also attested.[171] The first century BC is the most abundant in terms of both silver and bronze coins, with 71 silver coins and 24 bronze coins (Table 10.9). The most represented coins date from the reign of Orodes II (57–37 BC), followed by the reign of Mithradates II (124–91 BC), and Phraates IV (37–2 BC). It is unclear when the Parthian coins of Orodes II and Phraates IV were introduced into Armenia and how long they circulated before being demonetized or deposited. The shortage of Parthian hoards within the boundaries of the Greater Armenian Kingdom adds to the uncertainty. The only confirmed Parthian hoard is the silver hoard of Qaradonlu, which included at least 47 silver coins, consisting of two drachms of Mithradates II (124–91 BC) and 45 drachms of Phraates IV (37–2 BC).[172] Two uncertain hoards from Vardenut and Art'tik consisted entirely of bronze Parthian coins.[173] The Art'tik hoard contained bronze Parthian coins dating from 124–91 BC to AD 40–5, while the Vardenut hoard contained coins dating from 57–54 BC to 37–2 BC. The wide range of coins from Art'tik made Kh. Musheghyan doubt about its identification as a hoard. It is possible that the coins were simply brought together as a single lot to the Historical Museum of Armenia.

During the first century AD, the number of Parthian coins decreased significantly, with a preponderance of Gotarzes II (AD 40–51) coins. The scarcity of

[170] See Nercessian (1984; 1995; 2000a; 2000b); Bedoukian (1978; 1987); Musheghian (1997) and Vardanyan (2003; 2007; 2008; 2018). More recently, Nurpetlian (2008–9) and Kovacs (2016) provides a new catalogue of Armenian numismatics. Some attributions remain very uncertain and some of the attributions of Kovacs remains very uncertain. Despite the few issues attributed to the first century AD (Kovacs (2016) for the more recent catalogue; Zohrabyan and Vardanyan (2018)), issues of civic coins from Artašat whose dating remains uncertain (Amandry (2002); Kovacs (2016); Nurpetlian (2007); Zohrabyan and Vardanyan (2018)), as well as the hypothetical issue of a Roman provincial coin in Armenia (*RPC* III, no. 6554), the production of bronze coins in Armenia from the first century AD is very limited (Kéfélian (2025), fig. 1).

[171] The Parthian silver coins discovered in ancient Armenia are almost exclusively drachms, with the exception of two tetradrachms. See Table 10.9. The Parthian bronzes discovered are mainly *chalkoi*, followed by few a specimens of dichalkoi and tetrachalkoi.

[172] Paxomov (1926–59 [1926: 40, no. 30]); Golenko and Radžabli (1975: 88, no. 21); Fabian (2018: 435, no. 12).

[173] Mousheghian†, Mousheghian, and Depeyrot (2000: 99–100 for Art'ik, and 141–2 for Vardenut).

Table 10.9. Parthian coins discovered in ancient Armenia by century and their best-represented reigns from each period.

Period		Best-represented reigns	Silver coins	Bronze coins
First century BC	*Total*		*71*	*24*
		Mithradates II	13	3
		Orodes II	28	11
		Phraates IV	11	3
First century AD	*Total*		*15*	*5*
		Gotarzes II	6	1
Second century AD	*Total*		*9*	*2*
		Vologaeses III	5	2

coins increases in the second century AD, and they are mainly represented by Vologaeses III (AD 110–47) coins. While one might have expected an increase in Parthian bronze coins due to the installation of the Parthian Arsacids on the throne of Armenia under the authority of Rome (AD 63), this does not appear to have been the case. In fact, the decrease of Parthian coins can be explained by the debasement of the drachms from the mid-first century BC. This was followed by the decline of the imperial series in favour of local coinages.[174]

While Parthian bronze coins are rare but attested, Sasanian copper and lead coins seem not to have circulated in Armenia, at least during the period under study. This is in contrast to silver coins, attested by 41 specimens from AD 224 to 428.

With regard to the mint origin of Roman bronze and orichalcum coins, the majority are represented by provincial coins, representing 89% of the total. These findings contrast with those of Republican bronze coins, which represent less than 1% of the total, and imperial coins, which account for 3.2%. Only four imperial bronze and orichalcum coins issued from Trajan to Septimius Severus (two *sestertii*, one *dupondius*, and one *as*) have been discovered in Armenia.[175] Additionally, a particularly scarce example of a Republican *as*, dating from between 206 and 190 BC, has been identified, featuring a laureate head of Janus and a prow.[176] The remaining 7.8% of the collection comprises civic coins from Antioch, Prusa ad Olympum, Apamea, and late bronze coins.

Roman bronze provincial single finds are the most prevalent, with notable examples from Syria, Cappadocia, and Galatia (Table 10.10). These coins represent three-quarters of the total of Roman provincial coins. The proportion of Roman provincial coins in circulation in ancient Armenia that were minted in

[174] Sinisi (2018: 481–3).

[175] Trajan coins are HMA 13893 (*RIC* II, no. 636) and HMA 18326 (*RIC* II, no. 484); the Hadrian coin is HMA 8612 (*RIC* II, no. 84 = *RIC* II/3, no. 220); and the Septimius Severus coin dedicated to Julia Domna is HMA 8842 (*RIC* IV/2, no. 877).

[176] HMA 20093/6. *RRC*, nos 110–32; *SNA* I, no. 3a.

Syria was 53.8%. The majority of Syrian mints are represented by Antiochene coins, which account for 76% of the total. In addition to Roman provincial coins, 11 or possibly 12 civic coins from Antioch need to be added. Among the various Roman provincial bronze coins from Antioch, the genuine SC coins form a substantial part (representing 90% of the coins minted at Antioch).[177] In terms of mint issues, Antioch bronze coins from the first century AD amount to 76%.[178] The absence of the city name on these coins may have facilitated the wide circulation of this type.[179] The long period of circulation of these genuine SC coins is attested by the wear of the coins and numerous countermarks (Roman and Edessenian), the presence of an uncertain countermark applied only to SC coins in eight specimens from ancient Armenia (*GIC* no. 503), and the casting of SC imitations. All this points to the importance of SC Antiochene coins in Syria, Armenia, and Upper Mesopotamia. SC Antiochene coins may have had different roles to play in those regions. Initially, they may have been introduced to ancient Armenia by military movement.[180] Howgego emphasizes that the early minting of SC bronze coins may have resulted from a military need for payment.[181] Later countermarks associated with legions, especially of the *Legio XII Fulminata* and *Legio XV Apollinaris*, attest that the coins circulated within the military sphere.[182] Regarding the SC coins found in Mesopotamia, Butcher suggests that they may have been introduced from the late first century to the end of the second century, possibly during the Parthian War under Lucius Verus.[183] Additionally, SC Antiochene coins may have played a role in trade exchange in the region and/or may have been deliberately imported, as Butcher suggests.[184]

The Cappadocian region accounts for 8% of the total finds including issues from Caesarea of Cappadocia, Tyana, and Amasea, which was brought under the province of Galatia-Cappadocia for Trajan's war in ancient Armenia.[185] In addition, there is possibly a group of five coins of Nicopolis ad Lycum that were minted in AD 112–13 of which four were discovered at Artašat and one has an unknown findspot. If the discovery location is confirmed, it is probable that these coins were distributed throughout ancient Armenia during Trajan military's campaign from Satala to Artašat in the spring of AD 114.[186] Another group consists

[177] It is possible that an additional six coins, on account of their metrological characteristics, could be included in the total number of coins, but their condition has excluded them at this time. Butcher (2012: 476).

[178] 59% for the first half and 17% for the second half. The proportion of coins decreases to 17% for the second century and then 13% for the third century.

[179] Butcher (2004: 29). See Kéfélian (2025) which examines the place of SC coins in the regional circulation pattern.

[180] Kéfélian (2025).

[181] Brunk (1980); Howgego (1982); *GIC* nos 26i, 26ii, 695; Butcher (2004: 187–8); van Heesch (2014: 146).

[182] Kéfélian (2025). See also Brunk hoard (CHRE 9638) in Brunk (1980).

[183] Butcher (2017a: 12).

[184] Butcher (2015: 186; 2017a: 11–3).

[185] Sartre (1995: 174); Kéfélian (2021a).

[186] Kéfélian (2021a: 139–42).

Table 10.10. Distribution of Roman provincial bronze coins found in the Greater Kingdom of Armenia by province. Source: RoCCAA (accessed 18 December 2022).

Province	Mint	Number of coins	Percentage
Syria	Antioch	41	53.8%
	Laodicea	2	
	Tyre	2	
	Aradus	1	
	Gabala	1	
	Hierapolis	1	
	Tripolis	1	
	Uncertain CA mint coinage	5	
Cappadocia	Caesarea	5	8.0%
	Tyana	2	
	Amasea	1	
Galatia	Ancyra	6	6.8%
	Koinon of Galatia	1	
Galatia-Cappadocia	Nicopolis ad Lycum	5 + 1?	6.9%
	Amasea	1	
Achaea	Corinth	1	3.9%
	Larissa	1	
	Gytheion	2	
Commagene	Zeugma	2	3.9%
	Uncertain mint	2	
Judaea	Jerusalem	4[a]	3.9%
Mesopotamia	Nisibis	2	2.9%
	Carrhae	1	
Asia	Uncertain CA mint	1	1.0%
Bithynia and Pontus	Prusias ad Hypium	1	1.0%
Macedonia	Amphipolis	1	1.0%
Uncertain province	Uncertain mint[b]	7	6.9%
Total		**101**	

Notes: Coins from Tigranocerta are excluded here. Several hypotheses have been suggested for the location of Tigranocerta, including both the left and right banks of the Euphrates. However, the Euphrates River defined the boundaries of the Greater Armenian Kingdom. In addition, it is impossible to determine the exact location from which the coins were found. Therefore, it is more reasonable to exclude them from the table.

[a] Four more coins from the First Revolt have since been added to the dataset.

[b] This category includes coins minted from an unknown mint, coins published in reports with insufficient details to determine their type, and illegible coins (such as the three possible SC coins from Antioch).

mainly of coins from Caesarea in Cappadocia. The silver coins from Caesarea range from Nero to Trajan, while the five bronze coins were minted later, from the end of the second century.[187] In terms of geographical distribution, five coins were discovered around the Araxes Plain, at Artašat and Vałaršapat. The coin at Vałaršapat is among the few coins discovered in the royal residence from the third quarter of the second century AD. Although the available evidence is limited, the discovery of 27 or 28 Cappadocian silver and bronze coins supports the hypothesis of an increase in coin supply from Cappadocia connected to a major change in the military strategy of invading Armenia from Cappadocia for greater security.[188] This shift was reflected not merely in a modification of tactics to invade the Greater Kingdom of Armenia but also in the sustained presence of Cappadocian legions. This change in military strategy appears from the Flavian period and was fully implemented from the reign of Trajan. It aligns with coins from Cappadocia collected from ancient Armenia, which date from the second century.[189] However, the scarcity of data from Cappadocia may be attributed to the lack of numismatic evidence from the newly established royal residence in the mid-second century, namely Vałaršapat, and a gap in numismatic data from the western part of the Greater Armenian Kingdom.

The third main group consists of coins from Galatia, which make up 6.8% of the total provincial bronze coins gathered for RoCCAA project. These coins originated from Ancyra, with six coins, and one from an uncertain Galatian mint.[190] The coin from the Koinon of Galatia was minted during the reign of Tiberius or Caligula. The six other coins were minted between the reigns of Nerva (two minted AD 96–8) and Trajan (four minted AD 98–100). These coins may have circulated in Armenia during Trajan's offensive against Armenia, as was the case with other bronze coins. In addition to the coin of Nerva found in Gaṙni and the Tiberius–Caligula specimen discovered in Marmašen, one of the remaining six coins was discovered in the royal residence of Artašat. However, special attention should be paid to one of Trajan's coins (HMA 19878/45), as it bears two countermarks: a six-rayed star (*GIC* no. 452a), which is also found on another coin from Galatia, and a probable LXF countermark of the *Legio X Fretensis* (*GIC* no. 733). This countermark was applied in Sebastea or Jerusalem between AD 84–5 and

[187] These three coins of Caesarea in Cappadocia are composed of an uncertain second-century coin (HMA 12067) and two coins of Marcus Aurelius (HMA 20113/4 and 20131/5).

[188] Kéfélian (2021a: 139–42). These coins do not reflect the entire numbers of Cappadocian coins which circulated. New finds are to be expected. There is a particular gap in knowledge from the western part of the Greater Armenian Kingdom nowadays in Turkey, as well as coins in Vałaršapat.

[189] See above for the eight silver coins of Cappadocia and also the eight bronze coins below. Altogether they form 21, or possibly 22, coins.

[190] Ancyra coins (HMA 17593/3,19992/122, 19992/123, 19878/45, 19878/5, 20130/1), and a Koinon of Galatia coin (HMA 18678/2).

the reign of Trajan. If the countermark *Legio X Fretensis* is confirmed, it would indicate that the coin from Ancyra circulated in Judaea before entering into ancient Armenia.

In total, three-quarters of the Roman bronze coins collected in the RoCCAA database are Syrian, Cappadocian, and Galatian. While SC Antiochene coins are known to have to have circulated widely, previously there was little evidence of Cappadocian coins circulating beyond their region. The discovery of these coins in Armenia represents a significant shift.

CONCLUSIONS

The dataset gathered during the RoCCAA project highlights the peculiarities of Armenia in comparison to the kingdoms of Iberia and Colchis, which had distinctive patterns of circulation. Specifically, the Greater Kingdom of Armenia had a clear preponderance of Republican and imperial silver coins, in stark contrast to the paucity of gold coinage. The Armenian hoard evidence for silver coins also differs from the circulation in Anatolia and Syria owing to the limited presence of Roman provincial silver. The bronze coins, mainly studied on the basis of single finds, included a great variety of provincial coins, as well as Roman coin imitations.

The study also highlights some notable regional circulation patterns, including the circulation of silver coins of Gaius and Lucius in Armenia and Iberia, as well as the circulation of both genuine and imitation bronze SC coins between Syria, Armenia, and Upper Mesopotamia.

The Roman numismatic dataset from the Greater Armenian Kingdom has here been predominantly explained through the lens of military presence, particularly in the case of hoards containing Roman coins. This does indeed seem to make sense of much of the evidence. However, it is likely that other mechanisms of Roman coin supply, such as trade and diplomacy, also played a part.[191] This is especially the case for late gold coins, which may be attributed to diplomatic exchanges, although it is also worth noting the role of Artašat as one of the three official trading hubs between the Roman and Sasanian Empires during the Late Empire. It remains difficult to define criteria by which the roles of diplomacy and trade may be established. Understanding the significance of other such causes of the movement of coin remains a crucial area for further investigation.[192]

[191] Howgego (1992).

[192] In the meantime, see Fabian (2023: 484–8).

ACKNOWLEDGEMENTS

This work has been supported by the research and innovation programme of the European Union's Horizon 2020. The RoCCAA project received funding under the Marie Skłodowska-Curie grant agreement No 892180 and has been hosted by Oxford University.

I would also like to express my gratitude to the successive directors of the History Museum of Armenia—Anelka Grigoryan, Grigor Grigoryan, and Davit Poghosyan—as well as the Deputy Scientific Director, Nzhdeh Yeranyan, the Head Keeper of the Coin Room, Ṛuben Vardanyan, and his colleagues Hasmik Hovhannisyan and Armine Zohrabyan for providing me with access to study the coins.

I am grateful to Marguerite Spoerri Butcher and Chris Howgego for supporting me during the RoCCAA project, and for offering me the opportunity to contribute a chapter to this volume.

I would like to thank Benjamin Hellings, Chris Howgego, Marguerite Spoerri Butcher, and Andrew Wilson for their advice.

Finally, I thank Kevin Butcher for our correspondence on the data from Syria and Mesopotamia.

ABBREVIATIONS

CH II	Price, M. J. (1976). *Coin Hoards* I. London.
CH III	Price, M. J. (1977). *Coin Hoards* III. London.
CH VII	Price, M. J. (1985). *Coin Hoards* VII. London.
CHRE	Coin Hoards of the Roman Empire database (https://chre.ashmus.ox.ac.uk/).
GIC	see Howgego (1985).
HMA	History Museum of Armenia.
IGCH	Thompson, M., Mørkholm, O., Kraay, C. M., Noe, S. P., and Sydney P. (1973). *An Inventory of Greek Coin Hoards*. New York.
RIC II	Mattingly, H. and Sydenham, E. A. (1926). *The Roman Imperial Coinage*, vol. II: *Vespasian to Hadrian (AD 96–138)*. London.
RIC II/3	Abdy, R. A. and Mittag, P. F. (2019). *Roman Imperial Coinage*, vol. II.3: *From AD 117 to AD 138: Hadrian*. London.
RIC IV/2	Mattingly, H., Sydenham, E. A., and Sutherland, C. H. V. (1938). *The Roman Imperial Coinage*, vol. IV.2: *Macrinus—Pupienus (AD 217–238)*. London.
RPC I	see Burnett, Amandry, and Ripollès (1992).
RPC II	see Burnett, Amandry, and Carradice (1999).
RPC III	Burnett, A. and Amandry, M. (2015). *Roman Provincial Coinage* III: *From Nerva to Hadrian (AD 96–138)*. London and Paris.
RRC	Crawford, M. H. (1974). *Roman Republican Coinage*. London.
SNA	see Vardanyan (2011b).

REFERENCES

Abramzon, M. G. (2003). 'The Gerzeul hoard of coins of Caesarea of Cappadocia (in the Museum of Abkhazia)', *Revue numismatique* 159: 243–56.

Amandry, M. (2002). 'La politique monétaire des Flaviens en Syrie de 69 à 73', in C. Augé and F. Duyrat (eds), *Les monnayages syriens: quel apport pour l'histoire du Proche-Orient hellénistique et romain? Actes de la table ronde de Damas 10–12 novembre 1999*. Beirut, 141–4.

Ambrazon, M. G. (2005). 'Serebrjanye monety Kesarii Kappadokijskoj iz Gerzeul'skogo klada' ['Silver coins of Cappadocian Caesarea from the Gerzeul hoard (Collection of the State Museum of Abkhazia)'], *Numizmatika i èpigrafika [Numismatique et épigraphie]* 17: 190–202 (in Russian).

Apakidze, A. (ed.) (1975–7). *Velikij Pitiunt* I–III [*The Great Pitiunt I–III*]. Tbilisi (in Georgian).

Apakidze, A. (ed.) (1985). *Mtstketa* VII. *Archeologiuri kvleva dziebis shedegebi: didi mtskhetis adrerkinis, antikuri da adrefeodaluri xanis arqeologiuri dzeglebi* [*Mtstketa* VII. *The Results of Archeological Investigations: The Archaeological Sites of Great Mtskheta Early Iron, Classical and Medieval period*]. Tbilisi (in Georgian).

Apakidze, A., Gobedzhishvili, G., Kalandaze, A., and Lomtatidze, G. (1955). *Mtskheta* I. *Archeologiuri -kvleva dziebis shedegebi: armaziskhevis arqeologiuri dzegelebi 1937–1946 ww. Gatxrebis mixedvit* [*Mtskheta* I. *The Results of Archaeological Investigations: The Sites of Armaziskhevi, Based on the Excavations 1937–1946*]. Tbilisi (in Georgian).

Apakidze, A. and Nikolaishvili, V. (1994). 'An aristocratic tomb of the Roman period from Mtskheta, Georgia', *Antiquaries journal* 74: 16–54.

Arakeljan, B. N. (1957). *Arxeologičeskie raskopki v Armenii, no. 3.* Гарни I [*Archaeological Excavations in Armenia, no. 3. Garni 1*]: *Rezul'taty rabot garnijskoj arxeologičeskoj èkspedicii 1951–1955 gg. (antičnyj period)* [*Results of the Garni Archaeological Expedition of 1951–1955 (ancient Period)*]. Erevan (in Russian).

Arkeologiuri gatkhrebi apkhazetshi (1975–8). *Didi p'it'iunt'i: arkeologiuri gatkhrebi bich'vintashi: t'omi* I–III [*Great Pitiunt: Archaeological excavations*]. Tbilisi (in Georgian).

Aṣ-Ṣāliḥī, W. (1974). 'Al-Ḥadr: an-nuqūd al-muktašafa ẖilāl tanqībat (1971–1972)' ['Hatra Excavations in Group of Tombs of 1971–1972'], *Sūmir: mağallaẗ baḥṯ fī āṯār al-ʿIrāq al-qadīm* [*Sumer: a journal of Archaeology and History in Arab World*] 30: 155–62 (in Arabic).

Bedoukian, P. Z. (1978). *Coinage of the Artaxiads of Armenia*. London.

Bedoukian, P. Z. (1987). *Armenian Coin Hoards*. Los Angeles.

Bennett, J. (2006). 'The origins and early history of the Pontic-Cappadocian frontier', *Anatolian Studies* 56: 77–93.

Bland, R. (2001). 'The last coinage of Caesarea of Cappadocia', in R. Martini and N. Vismara (eds), *Ermanno A. Arslan Studia Dicata I.* Milan, 213–52.

Bolgov, N. (2004). 'Meždu imperiej i varvarami: final Antičnosti na Bospore Kimmerijskom' ['Between the Empire and barbarians: The end of antiquity on the Cimmerian Bosporus']. *Ukraïna v Central'no-Shìdnìj Êvropì* 4: 39–76 (in Russian).

Brašinskij, I. B. (1968). 'Recherches soviétiques sur les monuments antiques des régions de la Mer Noire', *Eirene* 7: 114–15.

Braund, D. C. (1994). *Georgia in Antiquity: A History of Colchis and Transcaucasian Iberia, 550 BC–AD 562.* Oxford.

Brunk, G. A. (1980). 'A hoard from Syria countermarked by the Roman legions', *Museum Notes* 25: 63–76.

Burnett, A., Amandry, M., and Carradice, I. (1999). *Roman Provincial Coinage* II: *From Vespasian to Domitian (AD 69–96).* London and Paris.

Burnett, A., Amandry, M., and Ripollès, P. P. (1992). *Roman Provincial Coinage* I: *From the Death of Caesar to the Death of Vitellius (44 BC–AD 69).* London and Paris.

Bursche, A. (1996). *Later Roman-barbarian Contacts in Central Europe, Numismatic Evidence. Spätrömische Münzfunde aus Mitteleuropa: Ein Beitrag zur Geschichte der Beziehungen zwischen Rom und dem Barbaricum im 3. und 4. Jh. n. Chr.* Berlin.

Butcher, K. (2004). *Coinage in Roman Syria. Northern Syria, 64 BC—AD 253* (Royal Numismatic Society Special Publication 34). London.

Butcher, K. (2012). 'Syria in the Roman period, 64 BC - AD 260', in W. E. Metcalf (ed.), *The Oxford Handbook of Greek and Roman Coinage.* Oxford, 468–84.

Butcher, K. (2015). 'Coins from Sippar', *Journal of the Oriental Society of Australia* 47: 182–9.

Butcher, K. (2017a). 'From the Achaemenids to the Arsacids', in S. Heidemann and K. Butcher, *Regional History and the Coin Finds from Assur. From the Achaemenids to the Nineteenth Century. Regionale Geschichte und Münzfunde aus Assur. Von der Zeit des Achämeniden bis zum neunzehnten Jahrhundert* (Wissenschaftliche Veröffentlichungen der Deutschen Orient-Gesellschaft 148). Wiesbaden, 7–48.

Butcher, K. (2017b). 'Some Flavian coins of Laodicea ad Mare in Syria', in L. Bricault, A. Burnett, V. Drost, and A. Suspène (eds), *Rome et les provinces. Monnayage et histoire. Mélanges offerts à Michel Amandry.* Bordeaux, 189–93.

Butcher, K. (2021a). 'Small change of the Edge of Empire: The coin finds from Kifrin', *Mesopotamia* 55: 51–70.

Butcher, K. (2021b). 'Eastern imitations and the beginning of the Antiochene SC coinage', in R. Ciolek and R. Chowaniec (eds), *Aleksanderia—Studies on Items, Ideas and History. Dedicated to Professor Aleksander Bursche on the Occasion of his 65th birthday.* Wiesbaden, 45–50.

Butcher, K. (2022). 'Bigger stuff beyond Palmyra: The coinage of the Hatrans and Assyrian', in R. Raja (ed.), *The Small Stuff of the Palmyrenes: Coins and Tesserae from Palmyra*. Turnhout, 163–74.

Butcher, K. and Ponting, M. (2014). *The Metallurgy of Roman Silver Coinage: From the Reform of Nero to the Reform of Trajan*. Cambridge.

Butcher, K. and Ponting, M. (2022). 'Hoarding of denarii and the reforms of Nero and Septimius Severus', in Mairat, Wilson, and Howgego (2022), 271–81.

Chaumont, M.-L. (1976). 'L'Arménie entre Rome et l'Iran, 1. De l'avènement d'Auguste à l'avènement de Dioclétien', in *Aufstieg und Niedergang der römischen Welt* II. 9.1. Berlin, 71–194.

Dédéyan, G. (ed.) (2008). *Histoire du peuple arménien*. Paris.

Depeyrot, G. (2019). '4. La monnaie dans le sud du Caucase', in M. Espagne, H. Isaxanli, and S. Mutafayev (eds), *La Montagne des langues et des peuples: Imbrications et transferts culturels dans l'espace du Caucase*. Paris, 119–42, https://doi.org/10.4000/books.demopolis.3267 (accessed 25 June 2022).

Donabédian, P. (2010). 'Vagharshapat : de la capitale royale à la capitale religieuse', in P. Donabédian, C. Mutafian, and E. Van Lauwe (eds), *Les douze capitales de l'Arménie*. Paris and Marseille, 111–21.

Duncan-Jones, R. (2001). 'The *denarii* of Septimius Severus and the mobility of Roman coin', *Numismatic Chronicle* 161: 75–89.

Duncan-Jones, R. (2002). 'The *denarii* of Septimius Severus and the mobility of Roman coin: Further comment', *Numismatic Chronicle* 162: 342–5.

Dundua, T. (2005). *Influx of the Roman Coins in Georgia*. Tbilisi.

Dundua, T. (2014). 'Online English-Georgian Catalogue of Georgian Numismatics', http://geonumismatics.tsu.ge/en/catalogue (accessed 14 May 2022).

Dundua, T. and Dundua, G. F. (2013). *Kartuli numizmat'ik'is k'at'alogi. I nats'ili: puli adreant'ik'ur da elinist'ur khanashi. Samonet'o sakme da samonet'o mimoktseva k'olkhetsa da iberiashi* [*Catalogue of Georgian Numismatics: Part One: Money in Classical and Hellenistic Periods. Coin Issues and Monetary Circulation in Colchis and Iberia*]. Tbilisi.

Ergeç, A. (1996). 'The Kuşakkaya hoard of *aurei*', in R. Ashton (ed.), *Studies in Ancient Coinage from Turkey*. London, 37–9.

Fabian, L. (2017). 'Numismatic communities of the northern South Caucasus 300 BCE–300 CE: A geospatial analysis of coin finds from Caucasian Iberia and Caucasian Albania', in H. F. Teigen and E. H. Seland (eds), *Sinews of Empire: Networks in the Roman Near East and Beyond*. Oxford, 29–63.

Fabian, L. (2018). *Examining the Archaeology of 'Antik'-quity The Eastern Caucasus beyond Rome and Parthia*. PhD thesis, University of Pennsylvania.

Fabian, L. (2019). 'The meanings of coins in the Ancient Caucasus', *Historische Anthropologie* 27.1: 32–51.

Fabian, L. (2023). 'Multifaceted Highlands: The economy of Armenia and its South Caucasus context', in S. von Reden (ed.), *Handbook of Ancient Afro-Eurasian Economies:* Vol. III. Berlin and Boston, 441–504.

Gamkrelidze, G., Mindorashvili, D., Bragvadze, Z., and Kvachadze, M. (2013). *Kartlis tskhovrebis t'op'oarkeologiuri leksik'oni* [*Toparchaeological Dictionary of Kartli Life*]. 1st edition, Tbilisi (in Georgian).

Giard, J.-B. (1976). *Catalogue des monnaies de l'Empire romain:* I. *Auguste*. Paris.

Golenko, K. V. (1964). *Denežnoe obraščenie kolxidy v rimskoe vremja* [*Monetary circulation of Colchis in Roman period*]. Leningrad (in Russian).

Golenko, K. V. and Radžabli, A. M. (1975). 'Ali-Bajramlinskij klad i nekotorye voposy obraščenija parfjanskix monet v Zakavkaz'e'['The Ali-Bairamli Hoard and the Circulation of Parthian Coins in Transcaucasia'], *Vestnik drevnej istorii* [*Journal of Ancient History*] 132.2: 71–93.

Hellings, B. D. R. (2016). 'The *denarii* of Septimius Severus and the mobility of Roman coin: the case of Roman Germany', *Numismatic Chronicle* 176: 171–81.

Hellings, B. D. R. (2020). 'Financing Germanic military campaigns with eastern *denarii*', *Journal of Ancient History and Archaeology* 7: 289–99.

Hellings, B. D. R. (2022). 'Coin supply and longevity of circulation: Three case studies from hoards in North-West Europe', in Mairat, Wilson, and Howgego (2022), 281–93.

Hewsen, R. H. and Salvatico, C. C. (2001). *Armenia: A Historical Atlas*. Chicago.

Howgego, C. (1982). 'Coinage and military finance: the Imperial bronze coinage of the Augustan East', *Numismatic Chronicle* 142: 1–20.

Howgego, C. (1985). *Greek Imperial Countermarks: Studies in the Provincial Coinage of the Roman Empire*. London.

Howgego, C. (1992). 'The supply and use of money in the Roman World 200 BC–AD 300', *Journal of Roman Studies* 82: 1–31.

Howgego, C. (1994). 'Coin circulation and the integration of the Roman economy', *Journal of Roman Archaeology* 7: 5–21.

Howgego, C. (1996). 'The circulation of silver coins, models of the Roman economy, and crisis in the third century A.D.: some numismatic evidence', in C. E. King and D. Wigg (eds), *Coin Finds and Coin Use in the Roman World*. Berlin, 219–36.

Howgego, C. (2002). 'The *denarii* of Septimius Severus and the mobility of Roman coin: A reply', *Numismatic Chronicle* 162: 16–9.

Howgego, C. (2015). 'The circulation of the gold coinage of Vespasian struck in the East', in R. Bland and D. Calomino (eds), *Studies in Ancient Coinage in Honour of Andrew Burnett*. London, 121–37.

Hurter, S. M. (2005). 'Some gold issues of Commodus' sole rule in the light of an unpublished hoard', *Numismatica e antichità classiche. Quaderni ticinesi* 34: 273–80.

Inadze, M. P. (1968). *Prichernomorskie goroda drevnei Kolkhidy* [*The coastal cities of ancient Colchis*]. Tbilisi (in Georgian).

Ivashenko, M. (1980). *Mtskheta* III. *Resultati Arkheologicheskikh Isledovanie: Samtavrskie Pogrebenie I–III v.v.* [*The Results of Archaeological Investigation Burials of I–III Centuries*]. Tbilisi (in Russian).

Jaworski, P., Karasiewicz-Szczypiorski, R., and Mamuladze, S. (2021). 'The rise and fall of the Roman fort in Apsaros: Recent numismatic evidence', *Polish Archaeology in the Mediterranean* 30.2: 289–306.

Kakhidze, E. (2008). 'Apsaros: A Roman fort in southwestern Georgia', in P. G. Bilde and J. H. Petersen (eds), *Meetings of Cultures in the Black Sea Region: Between Conflict and Coexistence*. Aarhus, 303–32.

Kalandadze, A. (1980). *Mtskheta* IV. *Archeologiuri -kvleva dziebis shedegebi: Samtavros tsina antikuri xanis arqeologiuri dzegelebi* [*Mtskheta* IV. *The Results of Archaeological Investigations: Samtavro Sites of before Classical Period*]. Tbilisi (in Georgian).

Kalandadze, A. (1981). *Mtskheta* V. *Archeologiuri -kvleva dziebis shedegebi: I Samtavros samarovnis tsina antikuri xanis arqeologiuri dzegelebi, II Mtskheta 1977–78 tslebis savele—arqeologiuri kvleva-dziebis shedegebi* [*Mtskheta V. The Results of Archaeological Investigations: I Samtavro Sites of Before Classical Period, II Mtskheta. The Results of Archaeological Investigations of 1977–8*]. Tbilisi (in Georgian).

Kalandadze, A. (1982). *Mtskheta* VI. *Archeologiuri–kvleva dziebis shedegebi: I Samtavros samarovnis tsina antikuri xanis arqeologiuri dzegelebi, II Mtskheta 1976–79 tslebis savele—arqeologiuri kvleva-dziebis shedegebi* [*Mtskheta* VI. *The Results of Archaeological Investigations: I Samtavro sites of before Classical Period, II Mtskheta. The Results of Archaeological Investigations of 1976–9*]. Tbilisi (in Georgian).

Kalantarian, A. (2010). 'Dvin, capitale administrative et siège patriarcal', in P. Donabédian, C. Mutafian, and E. Van Lauwe (eds), *Les douze capitales de l'Arménie*. Paris and Marseille, 124–37.

Kapanadze, D. G. (1949). 'O drevnejšix zolotyx monetax Gruzii' ['About Ancient the gold coins of Georgia'], *Vestnik drevnej istorii* [*Journal of Ancient History*] 3 (n° 29): 156–69 (in Russian).

Kapanadze, D. G. (1962). 'Oprodolžitel'nosti obraščenija denariev Avgusta i draxmy Gotarza v drevnej Iberii' ['The Duration of the Circulation of the *Denarii* of Augustus and the Drachma of Gotarzes in Ancient Iberia'], *Sovetskaja Arxeologija* [*Soviet Archaeology*] 4: 59–65 (in Russian).

Karasiewicz-Szczypiorski, R. (2016). 'Apsaros. Early Headquarters Building (Principia). New Localization?', *Pro Georgia* 26: 53–63.

Karasiewicz-Szczypiorski, R., Mamuladze, S., Jaworski, P., and Wagner, M. (2016). 'Gonio (Apsaros) in Adjara: Excavation of a Roman fort. Interim report on the first season of the Polish–Georgian archaeological expedition', *Polish Archaeology in the Mediterranean* 25: 521–32.

Kassab T. D., Kebuladze, N., Lomitashvili, D., and Zamtaradze, M. (2007). 'Les sites de Gudava et d'Ilori (Colchide): amphores de Sinope et amphores locales de l'époque romaine', *Anatolia Antiqua* 15: 197–214.

Kéfélian, A. (2020). 'Les inscriptions romaines d'Arménie', in J. P. Vallat, R. Gonzales Villaescusa, and G. Traina (eds), *Les mondes romains*. Paris, 89–99.

Kéfélian, A. (2021a). 'Interactions entre l'Anatolie et le Royaume de Grande Arménie aux Ier et IIe siècles après J.-C.', in *Dialogues d'histoire ancienne. Supplément* 22: *L'Anatolie de l'époque archaïque à Byzance*: 125–53.

Kéfélian, A. (2021b). 'Regards croisés de voyageurs occidentaux sur le site de Gaṙni', in A. Ferrari, S. Haroutyunian, and P. Lucca (eds), *Il viaggio in Armenia Dall''antichità ai nostri giorni*. Venice, 63–89.

Kéfélian, A. (2025). 'First insights of Roman monetary circulation in ancient Armenia', in J. Bodzek, A. Bursche, and A. Zapolska (eds), *Proceedings of the XVI International Numismatic Congress, 11-16.09.2022, Warsaw*. Volume II: *Roman Numismatics*. Turnhout, 723–33.

Kéfélian, A. (forthcoming). 'Circulation de la monnaie romaine ad fines Imperii Romani: le cas du Royaume de Grande Arménie', in P. M. Guihard and J. Chameroy (eds), *Les voyages de la monnaie dans l'Antiquité romaine*. Rennes.

Kehne, P. (2008). 'Auskünfte antiker Schriftquellen zu Umständen und Größenordnungen des Abflusses römischer Münzen ins "Barbaricum" vom 1.–5. Jahrhundert n. Chr. – Eine Problemskizze', in A. Bursche, R. Ciołek and, R. Wolters (eds), *Roman Coins Outside the Empire: Ways and Phases, Contexts and Functions*. Wetteren, 75–88.

Khoren, M., Mahé, J. P., and Mahé, M. (1993). *Histoire de l'Arménie*. Paris.

Khorenatsi, M. and Thomson, R. W. (1978). *History of the Armenians*. Cambridge.

Khurshudyan, E. and Zohrabyan, A. (2002). *Sassanian Coins of Armenia*. Erevan.

Kindler, A. (1969). 'Hoard of Roman gold coins from the first and second century [*sic*] CE (in Hebrew)', *Alon: Internal Quarterly of the Israel Numismatic Society* 3.3: 69–78.

Kohl, P. L. and Tsetskhladze, G. R. (1995). 'Nationalism, politics, and the practice of archaeology in the Caucasus', in P. L. Kohl and C. Fawcett (eds), *Nationalism, Politics, and the Practice of Archaeology*. Cambridge, 149–74.

Kohl, P. L. (1998). 'Nationalism and archaeology: On the constructions of nations and the reconstructions of the remote past'. *Annual Review of Anthropology* 27: 223–46.

Kovacs, F. L. (2016). *Armenian Coinage in the Classical Period*. London.

Kropotkin, V. V. (1961). *Klady rimskix monet na territorii SSSR* [*Hoards of Roman coins on the territory of the USSR*]. Moscow (in Russian).

Lalanne, S. (2014). 'Ordre de bataille contre les Alains', in A. Hostein and S. Lalanne (eds), *Le monde d'Arrien de Nicomédie, Actes de la journée d'étude organisée le 7 décembre 2012, Ktèma* 39: 74–85, https://hal.science/hal-01981694v1.

Lavrov, V. V. (1995). 'Goty i Bospor v III v. n. è. [Goths and Bosporus in the 3rd c. AD]', in È. D. Frolov (ed.), *Antičnyj polis: problemy social'no-političeskoj organizacii i ideologii antičnogo obŝestva*. St Petersburg, 112–22 (in Russian).

Lekvinadze, V. A. (1966). 'Oboronitel'nye sooruzheniia Sebastopolisa' [fortifications of Sebastopolis], *Sovetskaja arxeologija* 1 [Soviet archaeology]: 203–10 (in Russian).

Lindsay, I. and Smith, A. T. (2006). 'A history of archaeology in the Republic of Armenia', *Journal of Field Archaeology* 31(2): 165–84.

Lockyear, K. (2007). *Patterns and Process in Late Roman Republican Coin Hoards, 157–2 BC*. BAR International Series, 1733. Oxford.

Lordkipanidze, G. A. (1970). *K istorii drevnei Kolkhidy* [On the history of ancient Colchis]. Tbilissi (in Russian and Georgian).

Magarditchian, A. (2018). *Le temple de Garni—The temple of Garni—Gaṙnii Tačarə*. Geneva.

Mairat, J., Wilson, A., and Howgego, C. (eds) (2022). *Coin Hoards and Hoarding in the Roman World* (Oxford Studies on the Roman Economy). Oxford.

Manandyan, H. (1965). *The Trade and Cities of Armenia in Relation to Ancient World Trade*. Lisbon.

Mattingly, H., Sydenham, E. A., and Sutherland, C. H. V. (1938). *The Roman Imperial Coinage: 4.2. Macrinus—Pupienus (AD 217–238)*. London.

Moisil, D. (2002). 'The Danube "Limes" and the "Barbaricum" (294–498 A.D.). A study in coin circulation', *Histoire & Mesure* 17.3/4: 79–120.

Moorhead, S. (2012). 'The Coinage of the Later Roman Empire, 364–498', in W. E. Metcalf (ed.), *The Oxford Handbook of Greek and Roman Coinage*. Oxford, 601–32.

Mousheghian, A. and Depeyrot, G. (1999). *Hellenistic and Roman Armenian Coinage (1st c. BC–1st c. AD)*. Wetteren.

Mousheghian, K.†, Mousheghian, A., and Depeyrot, G. (2000). *History and Coin Finds in Armenia: Antiquity*. Wetteren.

Musheghyan/Mousheghian, Kh. (1973). *Hayastani dramakan ganjerə* 1 [*The hoards of coins from Armenia*]. Erevan (in Armenian).

Musheghyan/Mousheghian, Kh. (1978). 'Artašati haykakan ganjerə' ['Armenian hoard from Artašat'], *Armenian Numismatic Journal* 4: 105–27 (in Armenian).

Musheghyan/Mousheghian, Kh. (1997). *Hayoc patmut'yun dramagitakan//Istorija Numizmatiki Armenii* [*History of coins from Armenia*]. Erevan (in Armenian, Russian).

Nercessian, Y. T. (1984). *Armenian Numismatic Bibliography and Literature*. Los Angeles.

Nercessian, Y. T. (1995). *Armenian Coins and their Values*. Los Angeles.

Nercessian, Y. T. (2000a). *Selected Armenian Numismatic Bibliography of Ancient and Medieval Periods, 1981–2000*. Los Angeles.

Nercessian, Y. T. (2000b). *Armenian Numismatic Studies*. Pico Rivera.

Nurpetlian, J. (2008–9). 'Ancient Armenian coins: The Artaxiad dynasty (189 B. C.–A. D. 6)', *Berytus* 51.2: 117–67.

Oettel, A. (2005). 'Die antiken Münzen aus Tall Šēḫ Ḥamad: Die Funde der Grabungskampagnen 1978 bis 2000', in H. Kühne (ed.), *Magdalu/Magdala: Tall Šēḫ Ḥamad von der postassyrischen Zeit bis zur römischen Kaiserzeit*. Berlin, 161–86.

Paxomov, A. I. (1926–59). *Monetnye klady Azerbajdžana i drugix respublik, kraev i oblastej Kavkaza* vols 1–8 [*Coin Hoards of Azerbaijan and other Republics, Territories and Regions of the Caucasus*]. Baku (in Russian).

Sagona, A., Nikolaishvili, V., Sagona, C., Ogleby, C., Pilbrow, V., Giunashvili, G., and Manegaladze, G. (2010). 'Excavations at Samtavro 2008-2009: An interim report', *Ancient Near Eastern Studies* 47: 1–136.

Sartre, M. (1995). *L'Asie Mineure et l'Anatolie : d'Alexandre à Dioclétien (IVe s. av. J.-C./ IIIe s. ap. J.-C.)*. Paris.

Sellwood, D. (1980). *The Coinage of Parthia*. 2nd edition. London.

Sherozia, M. (2002). 'Spreading of *denarii* of Octavianus Augustus and so-called Gotarzes on the territory of Kartli Kingdom', *Bulletin du Cercle d'Études Numismatiques* 39.1: 173–80.

Sherozia, M. (2008). 'Monetary circulation in Iberia in the 1st century B. C. – 1st century A. D.', in A. Furtwängler, I. Gagoshidze, H. Löhr, and N. Ludwig (eds), *Iberia and Rome. The Excavations of the Palace at Dedoplis Gora and the Roman Influence in the Caucasian Kingdom of Iberia*. Langenweißbach, 235–52.

Shervashidze, L. A. and Solov'ev, L. N. (1960). 'Issledovanie drevnego Sebastopolisa' ['Notes on excavations from ancient Sebastopolis'], *Sovetskaja arxeologija* 3 [*Soviet archaeology*]: 171–9 (in Russian).

Sinisi, F. (2012). 'The coinage of the Parthians', in W. E. Metcalf (ed.), *The Oxford Handbook of Greek and Roman Coinage*. Oxford, 275–94.

Sinisi, F. (2018). 'Some remarks on the Patterns of Coin Production in the Parthian Empire', in R. J. van der Spek and B. van Leeuwen (eds), *Money, Currency and Crisis. In Search of Trust, 2000 BC to AD 2000*. London, 473–96.

Slocum, J. J. (1977). 'Another look at the coins of Hatra', *Museum Notes* 22 (American Numismatic Society): 37–47.

Speidel, M. A. (1986). 'The Caucasus frontier. Second century garrisons at Apsarus, Petra and Phasis', in C. Unz (ed.), *Studien zu den Militärgrenzen Roms* III, 13. *Internationaler Limeskongress*. Stuttgart, 657–8.

Speidel, M. A. (2009). 'The development of the Roman forces in Northeastern Anatolia. New evidence for the history of the exercitus Cappadocicus', in M. A. Speidel, *Heer und Herrschaft im Römischen Reich der Hohen Kaiserzeit*. Stuttgart, 595–631.

Traina, G. (2009). *428. Une année ordinaire à la fin de la fin de l'Empire romain*, trans. (from Italian) Gérard Marino. Paris.

Traina, G. and Kéfélian, A. (2020). 'Trajan et Parthamasiris à Elégeia', in A. Gonzales and M. T. Schettino (eds), *Peuples et États à l'épreuve de la diplomatie. Entrevues, ambassades, négociations: les sons de la diplomatie ancienne, Actes du colloque, Besançon, 26–27 mars 2015*. Besançon, 69–91.

Trapš, M. (1955). 'Nekotorye itogi arkheologicheskogo issledovaniia Sukhumi v 1951–1953 gg.' ['Some results of research conducted at Sukhumi in 1951–1953'], *Sovetskaâ arheologiâ [Soviet Archaeology]* 23: 206–27 (in Russian).

Tsotselia, M. and Depeyrot, G. (2010). *Coin Finds in Georgia (6th Century BC–15th Century AD)*. Wetteren.

van Heesch, J. (2014). 'Paying the Roman soldiers in the East (1st–2nd century AD)', in M. Reddé (ed.), *De l'or pour les braves ! Soldes, armées et circulation monétaire dans le monde romain*. Bordeaux, 139–59.

Vardanyan, Ṛ. (2003). 'Nouveaux regards sur la numismatique de l'Arménie ancienne', *Electrum* 7: 111–30.

Vardanyan, Ṛ. (2007). 'Regarding civic bronzes struck in Armenia in AD 1–4', *Armenian Numismatic Journal* 33.3: 69–76.

Vardanyan, Ṛ. (2008). 'Newly-found groups of Artaxiad copper coins', *Armenian Numismatic Journal* 34: 77–94.

Vardanyan, Ṛ. (2009). 'Płnjē Dramneri Ganjʿ Artašati Hnagitakan Pełumeneric' ['A hoard of bronze coins from Artašat Archaeological Excavations'], *Handēs Amsorya* 1–12: 31–68.

Vardanyan, Ṛ. (2011a). 'Coins', in Z. Khachatryan, 'The tomb of Sisian (second half of the 1st century BC)', *Parthica* 13: 67–72.

Vardanyan, Ṛ. (2011b). *Sylloge Nummorum Romanorum. Armenia.* Vol. I. *Roman Republic*. Erevan, 8–31 (in English and Armenian).

Vardanyan, Ṛ. (2018). 'Otarerkrya dramnerə Hayastanoum' ['Foreign coins in Armenia'], in A. Zohrabyan and Ṛ. Vardanyan (eds), *Hayastani dramašrǰanaṙutʿyan patmutʿyunə* [*The history of monetary circulation in Armenia*]. Erevan, 8–31.

Varshalomidze, I. (2009). *Monetebi Gonio-apsarosidan* [*Coins from Gonio-Apsaros*]. Batumi (in Georgian).

Walker, J. (1958). 'The coins of Hatra', *Numismatic Chronicle* 18: 167–72.

Wojan, F. (2006). 'Trapézonte du Pont sous l'Empire romain: étude historique et corpus monétaire', *Revue numismatique* 162: 181–229.

Woytek, B. E. (2022). 'The Imperial afterlife of Roman Republican coins and the phenomenon of the restored denarii', in Mairat, Wilson, and Howgego (2022), 237–72.

Yalçın, D. Ö. (2017). *Numismatik Veriler Işığında Roma İmparatorluğu Doğu Sınırı Sikke Sirkülasyonu* [*Monetary Circulation Amongst the Eastern Frontier of the Roman Empire in Light of Numismatic Data*], DPhil thesis, University of Ankara.

Zograph, A. N. (1936). 'Antičnye zolotye monety Kavkaza' ['Ancient gold coins of the Caucasus'], *Izvestija Gosudarstvennoj akademii istorii material'noj kul'tury* [*Reports of the State Academy of the History of Material Culture*] 110: 178–92.

Zograph, A. N. (1945). 'Naxodki antičnyx monet na Kavkaze' ['Finds of ancient coins in the Caucasus'], *Труды отдела нумизматики Государственного Эрмитажа* [*Proceedings of the Numismatics Department of the State Hermitage*], 29–85 (in Russian).

Zohrabyan, A. and Vardanyan, Ṛ. (eds) (2018). *Hayastani dramašrǰanaṙut'yan patmut'yunə*. Erevan (in Armenian).

Anahide Kéfélian, *Hoards of Roman Coins from Ancient Armenia and their Regional Contextualization* In: *Roman Coin Hoards Across Frontiers*. Edited by: Benjamin D. R. Hellings, Marguerite Spoerri Butcher, and Chris Howgego, Oxford University Press. © Oxford University Press 2026. DOI: 10.1093/9780198986478.003.0010

11

Hoards of Roman Coins and Imitations in India

Emilia Smagur

INTRODUCTION

Roman coins constitute the most abundant category of Mediterranean imports found in India. They have attracted the attention of scholars and collectors for over two hundred years because they offer evidence for Indian Ocean trade and an insight into the economic, social, and religious lives of ancient Indian societies.[1]

The focus of this chapter are hoards of *denarii* and *aurei* recorded from the territories located south and east of the Kushan Empire. A particular feature of this part of India is that it participated directly in the Indian Ocean trade, which was distinct from the northern, overland trade. For the sake of clarity, the area studied has been divided into four regions: Tamilakam, confined within the modern states of Tamil Nadu and Kerala, as well as southern parts of Andhra Pradesh and Karnataka, and politically comprising the chiefdoms of the Cholas, the Pandyas, and the Cheras; Deccan, which in the first centuries AD was ruled by the Satavahanas, who flourished at the same time as the period of extensive Roman interactions with India;[2] the territories north-west of the Satavahanas, including the main area of Western Kshatrapas in the modern state of Gujarat; and Kalinga, the eastern coastal region of the modern state of Odisha, broadly speaking, which became essentially autonomous between the Mauryan and Gupta periods.[3] The Indo-Roman contacts that started with Augustus' conquest of Ptolemaic Egypt in 30 BC fall mostly within the Indian Early Historic period (*c.* 500 BC to *c.* AD 500),[4] although the latest Indian finds of *solidi* date to the mid-seventh century.[5]

[1] The earliest reference to Byzantine coin finds from the subcontinent comes from Sir Thomas Browne (1684: 210), while the information about the hoard from Nellore, found in 1786, is the earliest published mention pertaining to finds of *aurei*; Turner (2023: 169).

[2] The Satavahana dynasty collapsed by the late third century. In the eastern Krishna river valley they were replaced by the Ikshvaku dynasty.

[3] See Tomber (2008: 117–43); Darley (2013: 346–51).

[4] The imprecise chronology of the Early Historic and medieval periods in India is one of the main problems faced by researchers; see Kennet (2013: 331). For Rome and the Indian Ocean trade, see Cobb (2018).

[5] Darley (2013: 53–4).

This study is based on the analysis of a dataset which contains information from multiple sources. These include the well-known book by Paula Turner supplemented by information provided by Sethuraman Suresh, the archives of the Indian Numismatic, Historical, and Cultural Research Foundation (INHCRF) in Nashik, as well as the archive of Peter Berghaus, currently stored in the Department of Numismatics and Monetary History at the University of Vienna, and supplemental data collected by the author.[6]

HOARDS OF *DENARII* AND THEIR IMITATIONS

The total number of *denarii* found in India is difficult to establish since not all hoards were properly registered and published. This is particularly the case for finds recovered in the nineteenth century, such as the Karur hoard discovered in 1856 with, possibly, thousands of *denarii* deposited in a pot.[7] Better documented finds amount to *c.* 6,364 *denarii* or imitations of *denarii* spread over 68 different findspots. Those finds can be grouped into hoards (24), all of which were discovered by chance, single settlement finds unearthed during excavations (11), grave chance finds (2), and single chance finds without context (31). The vast majority of them (over 6,264 specimens) were recovered from hoards (Table 11.1 and Appendix 1, with Fig. 11.7).

Indian finds of *denarii* are virtually limited to specimens struck in fine-quality silver before the currency reform of Nero in AD 64, especially *denarii* minted under Augustus and Tiberius. Finds of *denarii* issued by Caligula, Claudius, and Nero (of the eight *denarii* of Nero, all but one predate the reform) are admittedly quite scarce in the subcontinent but appear in hoards alongside earlier issues, whereas post-Neronian *denarii* are represented by only two examples, both stray finds (Figs 11.1a and 11.1b).[8] Two types are most common among finds: the C L

Table 11.1. Number of *denarii* (genuine coins and imitations), by find categories.

Find category	Quantity	Number of coins
Hoard	24	6,264
Single settlement find	11	33
Grave find	2	2
Single finds without context	31	65

[6] Turner (1989); Suresh (2004).

[7] Turner (1989: 59). As far as most of the hoards are concerned, references are given only to Turner's book, which still constitutes the most comprehensive catalogue of finds that has been published.

[8] A stray find *denarius* of Marcus Aurelius from Junagadh (INHCRF archives) and a *denarius* of Hadrian registered together with the Thrissur Taluka/Laccadive Island hoard but considered to be an intruder (Turner 1989: 90).

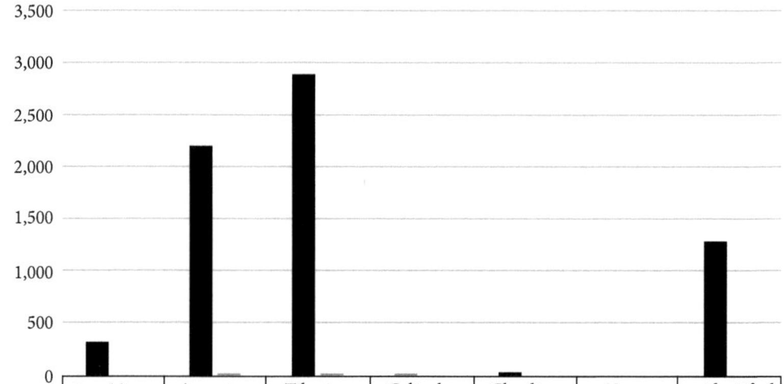

	Republican	Augustus	Tiberius	Caligula	Claudius	Nero	unidentified
■ genuine coins	328	2,190	2,884	16	45	8	1,302
■ imitations		25	32				

Fig. 11.1a. Hoards of *denarii*: chronological structure of their content (genuine *denarii* and imitations), by reign.

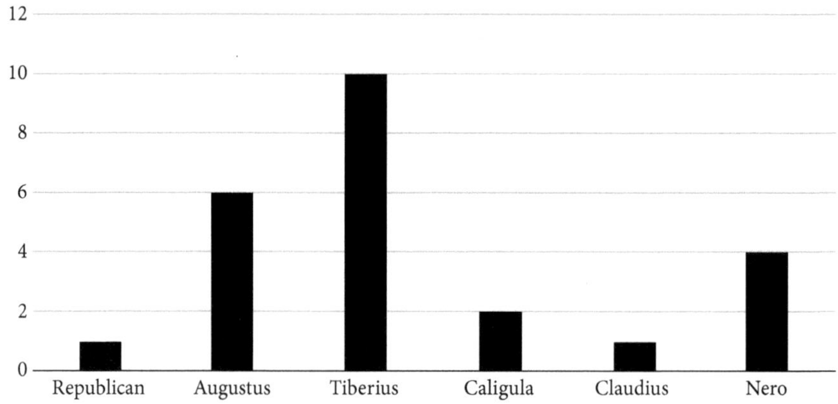

Fig. 11.1b. Hoards of *denarii*: number of hoards, by end reign (n = 24).

CAESARES Gaius and Lucius type of Augustus (2 BC–AD 4, Lugdunum mint) and the PONTIF MAXIM seated 'Livia' type of Tiberius (AD 14–37, Lugdunum mint).[9] The reason for the predominance of these two types might have been twofold: first, their high output; second, their fineness. It is probable that Indian traders had a good knowledge of the debasement of *denarii*. Therefore, those two distinctive reverse types were specifically selected by merchants for trade with

[9] *RIC* I[2] Augustus 207–8, 210–4; *RIC* I[2] Tiberius 26–8, 30; see also Turner (1989: 20–4); Berghaus (1992); Johrden and Wolters (2008).

India, where they were recognized and desired as pre-reform issues and did not need to be tested.[10]

Since the publication of Paula Turner's book, two new hoards (Nedumkandam and Uthamapuram) were reported and one (Thrissur Taluka/Laccadive Island) was revised. In general the new finds support previous suppositions as to the spatial and chronological distribution of *denarii* from India. Nevertheless, one of them allows a more detailed discussion regarding the date of the beginning of their influx to the subcontinent.

Two finds from the Idduki district in Kerala, most probably belonging to the Nedumkandam hoard, were reconstructed by Kathrin Johrden and Reinhard Wolters.[11] They consisted of Republican and Augustan *denarii* dated between 138 BC and AD 5. There are significant features to be noted about these finds. First, they include a diversity of Augustan types, from various mints of the Roman Empire, contrasting with an absence of the Tiberian Livia coin types. The latter constitute a significant share (over 53%) of *denarii* found in India. The finds consist mainly of specimens dated to the Civil War period and the reign of Augustus, with a particularly high proportion of Gaius and Lucius type coins (27%). The high proportion of Republican *denarii* (40 out of 126) also contributes to the exceptional composition of these two hoards. Therefore, these finds, which differ significantly from other hoards from India, are evidence of the beginning of the Roman coin inflow to the subcontinent that must have started before Nero's reign and were formed before the mass of Livia-type *denarii* entered India. Moreover, as in the case of other hoards, legionary *denarii* of Mark Antony are absent from those finds, which constitutes a further argument in favour of the deliberate selection of types of better quality for export to India.

Those discoveries shed new light on the question of when the *denarii* started to reach the subcontinent, a debate surrounded by a substantial degree of controversy.[12] According to Bolin, *denarii* were sent to India directly from the mint after being struck.[13] David W. MacDowall is of the opinion that those coins were exported as bullion after the AD 64 reform.[14] The discovery of a countermark of Vespasian on a *denarius* minted under Augustus in the Budinatham hoard proves that this very coin arrived in India long after it was struck.[15] Nevertheless, the single instance of this type, though still significant, cannot be sufficient to support the theory of a post-reform influx only, as it might have been added later, in India, to *denarii* amassed earlier.[16] Turner interprets *denarius* finds as evidence

[10] Turner (1989: 23, 43); MacDowall (1990: 66; 1991: 147; 2008: 332); Meyer (2007).

[11] Johrden and Wolters (2015).

[12] An overview of this issue may be found in Cobb (2015).

[13] Bolin (1958: 73).

[14] MacDowall (1991: 149–50; 2004); see also Burnett (1998).

[15] Turner (1989: 50); MacDowall (2008: 332); Sridhar, Suresh, and Sundararajan (2011).

[16] See also Romanowski (2021: 22).

for a major thrust of Indo-Roman trade that should be dated to the early first century.[17] Moreover, Kathrin Johrden and Reinhard Wolters, based on their analysis of the chronological and type distribution in the Nedumkandam hoard, rightly suggest a continuous influx of *denarii* to India that started in the early first century AD and lasted at least up to the Flavian period.[18]

The majority of hoards were discovered in Indian spherical earthenware pots called *lotas*;[19] only one of these containers, however, associated with the HAL Airport find, has ever been published with a photo.[20] The same is true for hoards of *aurei*. This is certainly due to the fact that all *denarii* hoards are chance finds and none were discovered during excavation works.

The bulk of hoards originate from Tamilakam and only three of them (Akenpalle, Belgaum area, and Nasthullapur) were discovered outside of that area (Fig. 11.2). In the Coimbatore district (Tamil Nadu) their concentration is far greater than in any other part of India, most probably because of proximity to the port of Muziris and to Palghat Gap, through which the passage from the west coast to the Coromandel region was possible, as well as the region's connection to the beryl mines and the large pepper and cardamom plantations. Those products were regularly exported to the Roman Empire, as they were in great demand in the Mediterranean.[21] The deposition of these hoards has been explained in various ways. According to Mortimer Wheeler, they might have been lost or hidden by travellers threatened by bandits operating in the area.[22] They have also been interpreted as bullion deposits or potential markers of status and prestige in a local economy characterized by other forms of exchange, such as reciprocity, redistribution, as well as presentation and gifts.[23]

Occasionally *denarii* were hoarded alongside other objects. In five cases (Eyyal, Mambalam, Nedumkandam, Nasthullapur, and Pennar) they were deposited together with Indian silver punch-marked coins.[24] According to Parmeshwari Lal Gupta, the association of these two types of coinages in hoards suggests a monetary function for Roman *denarii* in India, since punch-marked issues constitute a native currency to which Roman coins could have been approximated 'in the same manner as the Spanish Dollars brought by the European merchants were exchanged in India during recent centuries'.[25] The special relationship between punch-marked issues and *denarii* is also suggested by specimens originating from the Navalai hoard containing 335 silver punch-marked issues and five copper

[17] Turner (1989: 43). [18] Johrden and Wolters (2008; 2015). [19] Suresh (2004: 26).
[20] A long-necked jar, Seshadri (1966: 247). [21] Turner (1989: 5); Suresh (2004: 31–2).
[22] Wheeler (1954: 172–3).
[23] Turner (1989: 16); Suresh (2004: 37); Thapar (2012: 569); see also Gurukkal (2013).
[24] The punch-marked coins were struck in the subcontinent for several hundred years up to the mid-second century BC and were in circulation at least up to the second century AD (Gupta and Hardaker 2014). The punch-marked coins from the Eyyal hoard are discussed by Unnithan (1963) and Gupta (1965: 56–7). The Nasthullapur hoard is described by Gupta (1957).
[25] Indian silver punch-marked coins issued throughout the Magadha-Nanda-Maurya period lay within the range 3.3–3.5 g, indicating the existence of an accurate system of weighing; Gupta and Hardaker (2014: 32). See also Gupta (1957: 4).

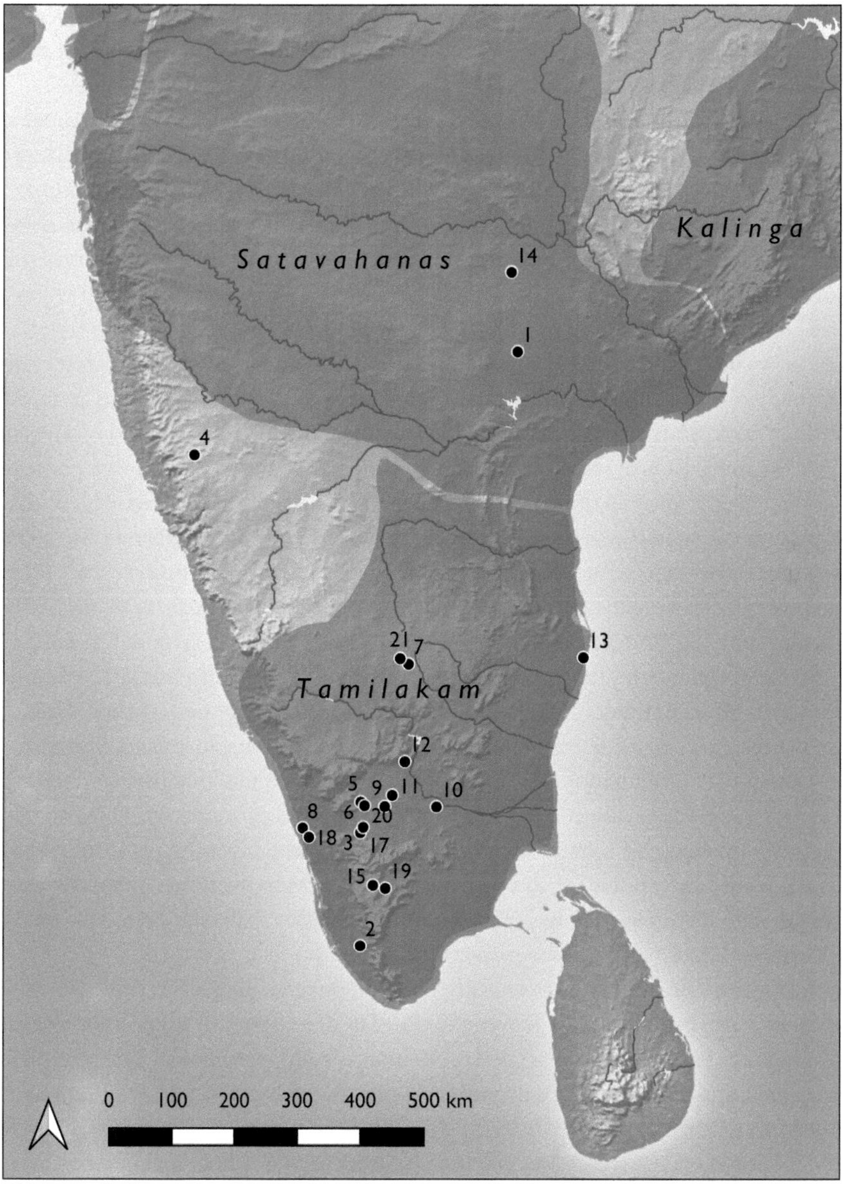

Fig. 11.2. Distribution map of hoards of *denarii* and imitations (numbers refer to Appendix 1). Map: A. Wilson/E. Smagur.

objects.[26] Two of the latter bear silver-plated impressions of fragments of *denarii* in the shape of a quarter of a coin. It seems that during their production Roman *denarii* of Augustus and Tiberius were utilized as dies and pressed onto a copper blank covered with molten silver. Due to their uniqueness it is not possible to

[26] Unfortunately, the whole hoard was never published; see Krishnamurthy (2016).

interpret them; however, most probably the person who made them wanted to produce an object in the shape of a local coin (rectangular) that at the same time resembles a *denarius*.

In several cases *denarii* occurred in hoards together with objects of valuable metals. The Vellalore find contained 23 mysterious 'unstruck blanks', and three coin hoards contained jewellery (Akenpalle, Koneripatty, and Uthamapuram).[27] So far only one hoard (Eyyal) consisted of both *denarii* and *aurei*. Those two coinages maintained their own identities and must have had different meanings and functions.[28]

In contrast to the finds from Tamilakam, hoards deposited on the territories ruled by the Satavahanas (Akenpalle, Belgaum area, and Nasthullapur) contained slashed coins. Slash marks constitute one of the peculiar characteristics of many Roman coin finds from India. They were almost always applied to the obverse over the imperial bust with a chisel or a knife. Some of the coins bear two or more marks, usually intersecting each other. This phenomenon has been widely discussed in the literature and, according to the most common explanations, those modifications were either economic or political markers.[29] However, this issue has not been resolved yet. The Akenpalle hoard, which had the largest number of slashed coins (1,505) also contained deliberately fragmented *denarii*.[30] A similar practice of deliberate fragmentation is confirmed by finds of *aurei* and *solidi* as well as their imitations.[31] The careful cutting of coins may suggest that some of their users considered them as bullion and cut them to enable lower-value transaction. On the other hand, we cannot rule out the possibility that they might have been prepared to be used as a goldsmith's handy stock of scrap metal. However, no partly melted and halved *denarii* have been recorded from the ancient silversmith workshops in the territory of India to date. Moreover, the Akenpalle find contained broken pieces of ornaments and some strips of silver; therefore, it might be assumed that those items were hoarded as bullion ready for reuse.[32]

Only two hoards (Akenpalle and Nasthullapur) yielded silver imitations of *denarii* deposited alongside genuine issues. The function of Indian imitations of Roman coins is not yet fully understood; however, the presence of a double piercing or loops on many of them points to ornamental and amuletic functions.[33] Silver imitations might have also constituted a form of investment along with saving for emergencies, which is confirmed by their presence in hoards.

The analysis of collected data reveals that *denarii* discovered in India started arriving in the subcontinent in the early first century AD, and their continued arrival influx lasted at least up to the Flavian period. Most of them were recovered from hoards, the bulk of which originate from the Tamilakam. Their concentration

[27] This Vellalore hoard was found in 1931; Turner (1989: 83). [28] See Berghaus (1991: 126).
[29] For the discussion, see Darley (2019: 73–4). [30] Suresh (2004: 40–52).
[31] Kudavelli, Pudukottai, and Veepangandla. [32] See also Darley (2019: 78).
[33] Smagur (2018); Brancaccio (2005). For Roman coin jewellery in India, see also, e.g., Suresh (2004: 77–81) and Darley (2013: 258–67).

in the southern part of the subcontinent was most probably connected to the port of Muziris, the Palghat Gap, as well as beryl mines and pepper and cardamon plantations, the origin of products regularly exported to the Roman Empire. These finds are limited to specimens issued before the coin reform of Nero in AD 64. Among them two types (the C L CAESARES type of Augustus and the PONTIF MAXIM type of Tiberius) predominate, probably because of their high output and their fineness of pre-reform issues. Hoards of *denarii* occasionally contain other objects such as local silver punch-marked coins, jewellery, or unstruck blanks. Slashed or deliberately fragmented examples as well as imitations of *denarii* are known only from hoards recorded from Deccan.

HOARDS OF *AUREI* AND THEIR IMITATIONS

Unlike *denarii*, the total number of Indian finds of *aurei* is difficult to establish, but we have reliable information on at least 1,979 registered *aurei* and their imitations originating from 88 findspots. These can be grouped into hoards (34), all but one of which were discovered by chance, single settlements finds unearthed during excavations (13), single chance finds without context (40), and stupa deposits discovered during excavations (one); however, the largest number of specimens (over 1,896) is recorded from hoards (Table 11.2 and Appendix 2, with Fig. 11.8).

Since Turner's publication in 1989, nine new hoards of *aurei* have been registered (Calicut District, Daramvaripalem, Kumbalam, Mattadakere, Nagavarappadu, Nosagere, Penuganchiprolu, Surapattu, and Tirukoilur). Additionally, the Valuvally hoard has now been fully published. Those new findings allow a more detailed discussion on the chronology of the influx of *aurei* to India that may be divided into three phases (Figs 11.3a and 11.3b).[34] The first phase lasted until near the end of Nero's reign. The composition of this group of coins is different from simultaneous *denarii* imports, as finds of Claudius and Nero are more numerous, probably

Table 11.2. Number of *aurei* (genuine coins and imitations), by find categories.

Find category	Quantity	Number of coins
Hoards	34	1,896
Single settlement finds	13	20
Single finds without context	40	61
Stupa deposits	1	2

[34] The dates of the influx of specific coin pools to India and their composition are the subject of discussion; see, e.g., Berghaus (1991: 108–21); MacDowall (2008: 331–40); Johrden and Wolters (2008: 341–54). The data presented here come from the research conducted within the framework of the author's project on Roman gold coins in India; see also Romanowski (2021).

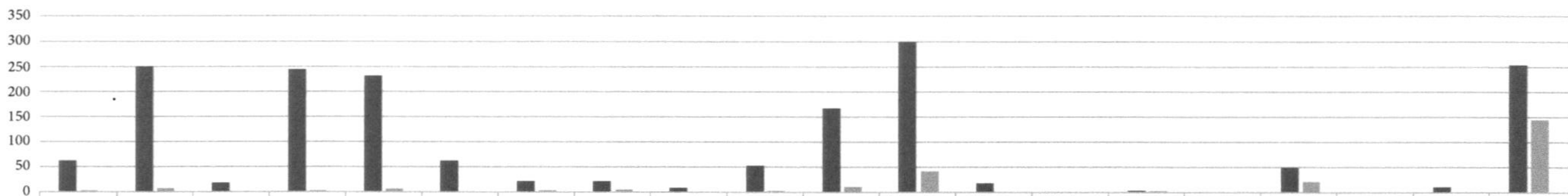

	Augustus	Tiberius	Caligula	Claudius	Nero	Vespasian	Titus	Domitian	Nerva	Trajan	Hadrian	Antoninus Pius	Marcus Aurelius	Lucius Verus	Commodus	Pertinax	Septimius Severus	Geta	Caracalla	unidentified
genuine coins	63	251	18	244	231	58	22	22	8	53	167	298	17	1	3	1	48		11	253
imitations	2	7		3	6	1	2	5		2	11	42	1	1	2		22	1	1	145

Fig. 11.3a. Hoards of *aurei*: chronological structure of their content (genuine *aurei* and imitations), by reign.

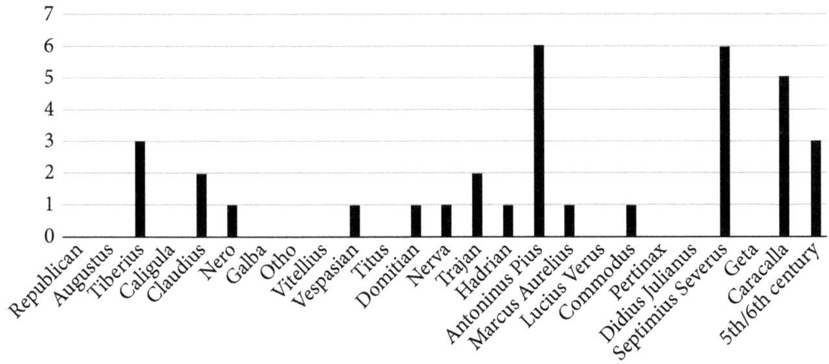

Fig. 11.3b. Hoards of *aurei*: number of hoards, by end reign (n = 34).

because no special types were preferred. The second phase extended from Vespasian to the Antonine period, with an increased amount of coins struck during Hadrian and Antoninus Pius. Coins of the second phase were most probably imported from the Roman Empire during the reign of Commodus. It is also possible to distinguish a third phase, comprising mainly *aurei* of Septimius Severus and Caracalla and witnessing the inflow of coins leaving the Empire most probably in the 220s.[35] The other types of coin finds (stray, stupa deposits) reflect the chronological distribution that can be seen in the hoards.

The geographical distribution of gold hoards is much wider than that of *denarii*, with two zones of concentration (Fig. 11.4)—in Tamilakam and the Krishna river valley—reflecting change in the trade pattern. The latter are connected with the proliferation of trade activities and trade guilds in the coastal Andhra, the eastern region of the state Andhra Pradesh, by the end of the first century. Second-century foreign traders approached the urban centres of the east coast more often than in the first century, when mainly ports of the western coast were visited by traders from the west, as evidenced by the *Periplus Maris Erythraei*.[36] The Satavahana polity also expanded over time to the east and south, reaching its maximum extent in the second century and including the territories of the modern-day state of Andhra Pradesh and the northern part of Karnataka. The second half of the third century witnessed the beginning of the decline of the Satavahana realm and its fragmentation into smaller political units.[37] In Andhra the Satavahanas were replaced by the Ikshvaku dynasty, who established their capital at Vijayapuri (modern Nagarjunakonda) and ruled the region until the early fourth century.[38]

[35] In her book, Turner (1989: 27) writes about the second-century hoards that 'it is not yet clear whether they will be able to be grouped into early second century and Severan hoards'.

[36] Suresh (2004: 34).

[37] Thapar (2002: 226–7); Tomber (2008: 130–1); Avari (2011: 149–50).

[38] Shimada (2021: 136–7).

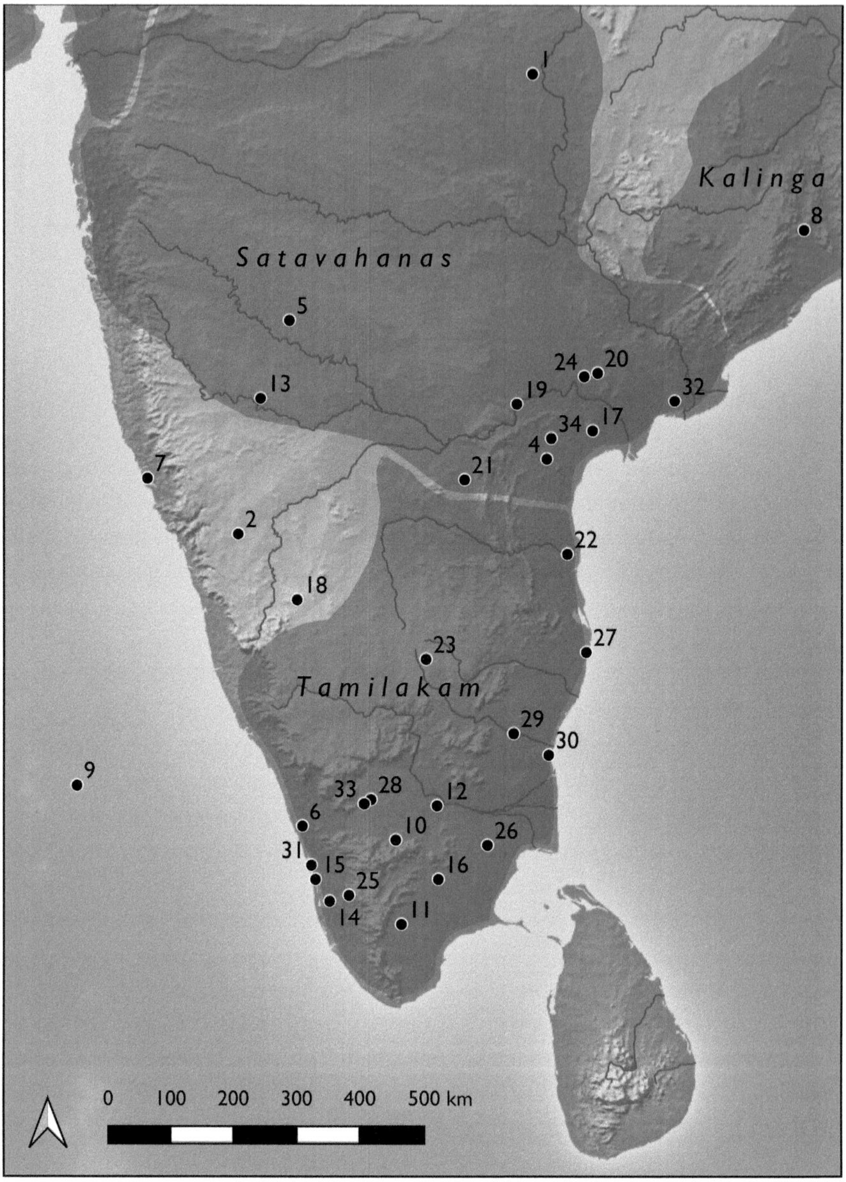

Fig. 11.4. Distribution map of hoards of *aurei* and imitations (numbers refer to Appendix 2). Map: A. Wilson/E. Smagur.

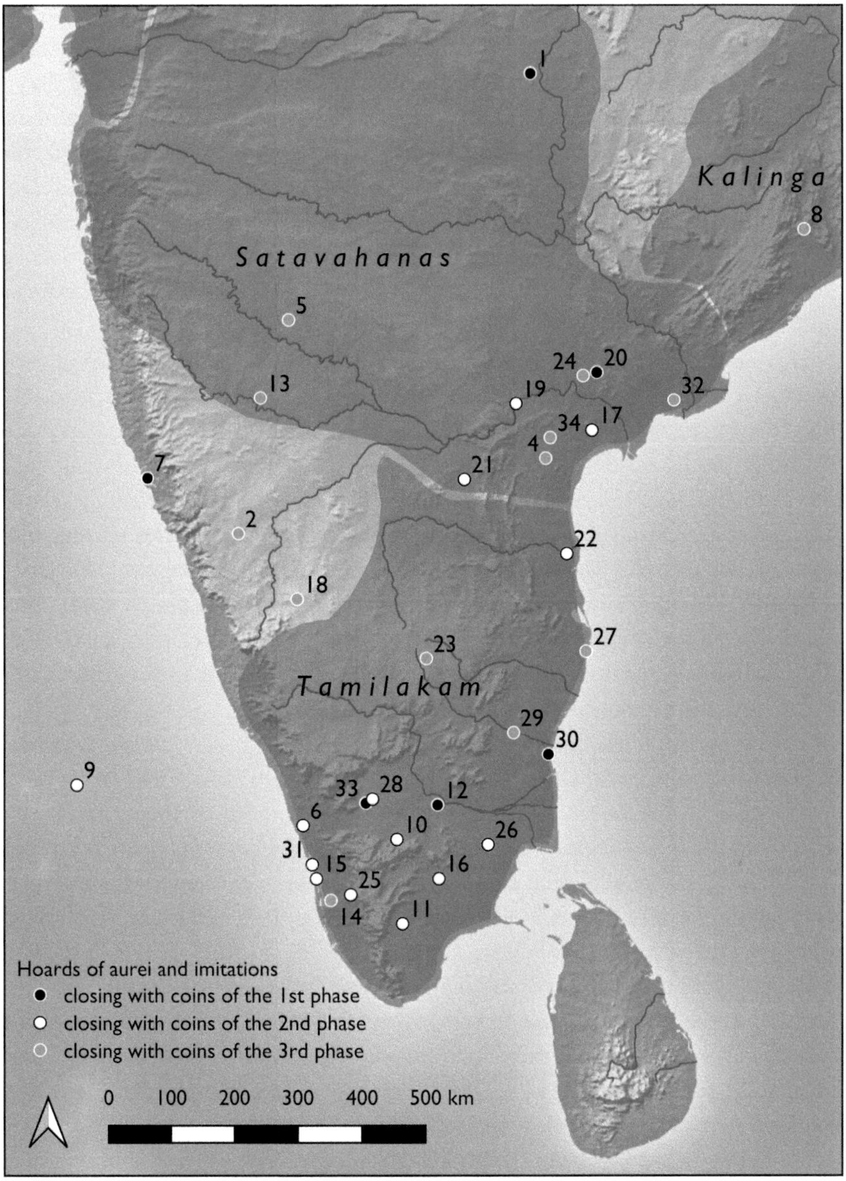

Fig. 11.5. Distribution map of hoards of *aurei* and imitations, by phase of arrival (numbers refer to Appendix 2). Map: A. Wilson/E. Smagur.

A number of observations can be made regarding the distribution of hoards containing coins arriving during specific phases (Fig. 11.5).[39] Only five hoards out of 34 (Adam, Karur, Nagavarappadu, Tondamanatham, and Vellalore) included exclusively *aurei* which had arrived during the first phase of the inflow. Some of them were found in the vicinity of places which also yielded finds of *denarii*. This is true of Adam, where Roman *denarii* and their imitations were unearthed during excavations of the Early Historic settlement, as well as Karur and Vellalore, from where hoards of *denarii* are recorded.[40] It is probable that this group of *aurei* arrived together with some of the *denarii*, as suggested by the composition of the Eyyal find, a bimetallic hoard, as well as their geographical distribution.

Hoards that close with coins arriving during the second phase of influx or their imitations are being found mostly in the southern Tamilakam (Eyyal, Kaliyampattur, Karivalamvandanallur, Kumbalam, Madurai Hills, Poonjar, Pudukottai, Sulur, and Valuvally), and, less often, in the eastern Deccan (Mallayapalem, Nagarjunakonda, Nandyal, and Nellore). Additionally, one of them was found on Kadmat Island. This contrasts sharply with the geographical distribution of hoards closing with *aurei* arriving during the third phase (Calicut Dt., Daramvaripalem, Dharpul, Kottayam, Mattadakere, Nosagere, Penuganchiprolu, Surapattu, Tirukoilur, Veeravasaram, and Vinukonda), sometimes deposited together with *solidi* (Akki Alur and Katryal) or their imitations (Gumada). The latter are much more evenly distributed and are not concentrated in the Tamilakam.

Hoards containing issues that arrived during all three phases (Daramvaripalem, Penuganchiprolu, Surapattu, Tirukoilur, Veeravasaram, and Vinukonda) were found only in the eastern part of the subcontinent. All of them, except for Vinukonda, also included imitations. The question is whether coins deposited in these hoards were circulating simultaneously or were collected by their owners over a long period of time. Finds from Penuganchiprolu, Surapattu, Tirukoilur, and Vinukonda provide data helping to solve this problem. They all contained issues subjected to all types of modifications specific to India, such as countermarking, slashing, and plugging, among others, proving that prior to the hoarding their life trajectories altered dramatically. Before their deposition those coins must have been used for a long period of time and had different functions instead of being drawn from circulation and hoarded soon after their arrival. Moreover, while the earliest coins from the hoards are very worn, a gradual improvement in the condition of the later coins can be observed. The date of deposition of those hoards is presumably close to the dates of their latest coins. Hybrid imitations whose obverse and reverse prototypes derive from two different groups of coins arriving during different phases constitute evidence of mixing those groups during circulation.[41]

[39] The following considerations regard hoards with identified coins, available for such analysis.
[40] For finds from Adam, see Nath (1995; 2016: 819–20).
[41] E.g. stray finds from Belgaum and Goottiparthy, imitations from the Tirukoilur hoard.

Additional evidence of mixing coin groups comes from Nagarjunakonda, which yielded finds of both genuine *aurei* of Antoninus Pius and Hadrian as well as imitations corresponding to the period of Ikshvaku rule.[42] Nagarjunakonda is the only site to reveal imitations of *aurei* in the form of double-pierced, bracteate-style pieces discovered in a reliquary deposited in a stupa, a Buddhist dome-shaped structure usually containing relics.[43] Both of them depict male portraits derived from coins of Augustus and Tiberius. The other finds include a gold imitation of an *aureus* of Tiberius found in a monastery, proving that first-century *aurei* must have been available to the imitation makers in the third century. The plugged *aureus* of Antoninus Pius comes from a hoard also containing a pierced, gold bracteate-style object that imitates the obverse of a Roman coin, beads, and earrings, and it was discovered in one of the residential buildings outside the citadel.[44] This find constitutes the only example of a hoard discovered during excavations of the ancient Indian settlement.

The analysis of hoards of *aurei*, categorized by their terminal reigns, suggests that certain decades can probably be identified as periods of increased hoard deposition (Fig. 11.3b). These hoards include examples ending with *aurei* or their imitations from the reigns of Antoninus Pius (e.g. Mallayapalem, Nagarjunakonda, Nellore, Poonjar, Sulur, Valuvally), Septimius Severus (e.g. Calicut District, Daramvaripalem, Dharpul, Goa, Nosagere, Penuganchiprolu), and Caracalla (e.g. Kottayam, Mattadakere, Surupattu, Tirukoilur, Vinukonda). They were most probably deposited during or after the third century. While the second half of the third century coincides with the decline of the Satavahana dynasty, the distribution of these hoards is notably widespread, with half of the known findspots located in Tamilakam. As a result, the underlying reasons for this hoarding pattern remain uncertain.

Just like *denarii*, *aurei* were sometimes hoarded alongside jewellery items (Dharamvaripalem, Karivalamvandanallur, Nagarjunakonda, Nagavarappadu, Nosagere, Sulur, Tirukoilur, and Vellalore). The Karivalamvandanallur hoard contained, in addition to *aurei* and jewellery pieces, a gold medallion imitating a gold stater of the Ptolemaic queen Arsinoe II (316 to *c.* 270–260 BC), with her portrait on the obverse and two cornucopiae on the reverse. Only two hoards contained silver punch-marked coins (Eyyal and Tondamanathan).

Specimens that were subjected to various modifications are also encountered in hoards. Finds containing slashed *aurei* and/or their imitations are known from Kalinga (Gumada), the Deccan (Adam, Nagavarappadu, Nandyal, Penuganchiprolu, and Vinukonda), and Tamilakam (Eyall, Kaliyampatur, Madurai Hills, Pudukottai, Surapattu, and Tondamanatham). Countermarked

[42] For a single find of a Hadrianic *aureus* see Gupta (1965: 61). Some of the coins and their imitations from Nagarjunakonda can be found in the database of the Museums of India: National Portal & Digital Repository, http://www.museumsofindia.gov.in/repository/home (accessed 23 January 2020).

[43] Longhurst (1938: 21–2); Sarma (1992: 41).

[44] Sarma (1994: 68); Sarkar and Misra (2006: 20–1).

specimens have been recorded from hoards unearthed in the Deccan (Daramvaripalem, Nagavarappadu, and Penuganchiprolu) and Tamilakam (Pudukottai, Tirukoilur, and Valuvally). Looped or pierced specimens were discovered in hoards from Tamilakam (Nellore, Nosagere, Surapattu, and Tirukoilur), the Deccan (Dharpul, Penuganchiprolu, and Vinukonda), and Kalinga (Gumada), while coins with refilled perforations made for ornamental purposes are known from only two hoards (Penuganchiprolu and Tirukoilur). These last specimens constitute examples of a practice aimed at restoring their original appearance and, most probably, their monetary function. One of the *aurei* from the Tirukoilur hoard has two refilled holes and a tubular loop that indicates that, at least twice, it was converted into jewellery.[45]

Plugged *aurei* and their imitations form another category of modified Roman coins from India and have been recorded from six hoards discovered on the territory of Kalinga (Gumada), the Deccan (Akki Alur, Nagarjunakonda, Penuganchiprolu, and Vinukonda), and Tamilakam (Tirukoilur). Those specimens have a characteristic and distinct feature: a big gold plug attached behind the head of an emperor. The purpose of plugging was to adjust those objects to the desired weight, and the plug was often countermarked, most probably in order to confirm that the coin was regulated by a trustworthy person. It seems that their point of reference for weight was Nero's pre-reform *aureus*. The Indian merchants must have been aware that the weight of Roman *aurei* had decreased since the Neronian reform; therefore, a greater amount of gold was needed to plug later Roman coins that arrived to India, in order to ensure that they adhered better to the pre-Neronian standard. These plugged coins prove that Roman coins and their imitations, at least at some point or in some regions of India, were considered to be money.[46]

Bent coins are known from at least three hoards recorded from the Deccan (Dharpul, Nandyal, and Penuganchiprolu), but the purpose of this practice has not been explained yet.[47] All those examples demonstrate that before their final deposition in hoards *aurei* must have had various functions and most probably different individuals were involved at different stages of their use.

Local imitations form a significant share (13%) of the hoards' content. Finds of Indian imitations of *aurei* (at least 282 coins) come from at least 26 findspots, 11 of which yielded hoards (254 coins). The latter were discovered in the Tamilakam (Calicut Dt., Nosagere, Surapattu, Tirukoilur, and Valuvally) as well as in the eastern Andhra (Daramvaripalem, Nagarjunakonda, Nagavarappadu, Penuganchiprolu, and Veeravasaram) and Kalinga (Gumada). As in the case of the genuine coins,

[45] Berghaus (2000: 499, fig. 1); Borell (2014: 28).

[46] The weights of plugged coins ranges from 6.2 to 8.4 g, the weights of specimens with countermarked plugs ranges from 7.8 to 8.3 g: Smagur (2020).

[47] See Turner (1989: 11).

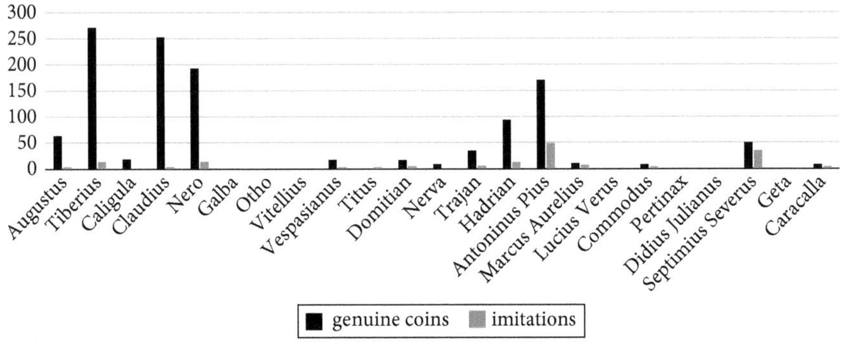

Fig. 11.6. Finds of *aurei* and their imitations, hoards and single finds combined: chronological structure, by reign.

their chronological distribution falls into three primary groups, though the proportion of imitations compared to genuine coins increases over time (Fig. 11.6). It might be assumed that the demand for those objects grew during the second century.[48]

Most of the described hoards contained coins arriving during the third phase of the influx; therefore, they must have been deposited in the third century or later. Also, half of the hoards including imitations contained coins belonging to all three groups. The majority of imitations discovered in hoards are gold pieces of a weight similar to the weight of their prototypes. Only one hoard (Nosagere) exclusively contained imitations, being also the only find including bracteate-style pieces, while gold-plated, base-metal imitations are known only from settlements. The Gumada hoard, in addition to imitations of the second-century *aurei,* contained also two imitations of *solidi* of the weight of an *aureus.*[49]

Some hoards shed light on the production process of imitations. Mould links or imitations coming from the same workshop were discovered in five hoards (Calicut Dt., Dharamvaripalem, Gumada, Nosagere, and Tirukoilur). Examples from the Gumada hoard demonstrate that a new mould was employed when the previous one had become worn out.[50] Additionally, the incidence of mould links within hoards may suggest that imitations were the product of a local workshop. Berghaus suggests that the hoard from Tirukoilur could have been the property or the stock of a goldsmith of that town, who produced imitations for sale as souvenirs or as ornaments to the pilgrims, visiting this old place of pilgrimage.[51] Imitations from the Calicut Dt. hoard show more than 50% of mould duplicates, while eight out of 18 imitations from the Gumada hoard are also mould-linked.[52]

[48] For Indian imitations of *aurei,* see Smagur (2022).
[49] Weighing 7.04 g and 6.70 g.
[50] Turner (1989: 54, 115, pl. I, nos 162–7, pl. II, nos 168–84).
[51] Berghaus (2004: 53; 2006: 18).
[52] For the Calicut Dt. hoard, see Berghaus (2004: 53).

This suggests that those objects might have been produced in the vicinity of the place of their final deposition.

Most Indian finds of *aurei*, just as in case of *denarii*, come from hoards. Their distribution is, however, wider than that of the *denarii*, with two main concentrations of finds (in the Tamilakam and the Krishna River valley) reflecting changes in trade patterns. Their influx to India that started in the first century AD and lasted until the 220s can be divided into three phases. They were sometimes deposited alongside other objects, such as jewellery or silver punch-marked coins. Slashed, countermarked, looped, pierced, bent, and plugged *aurei* or their imitations are also known from hoards.

CONCLUSION

The vast majority of *denarius* and *aureus* hoards have been recorded from Tamilakam and Deccan, where their density is far greater than in other parts of India. Such a distribution is partially connected with the location of Indian ports, as well as inland regional and local trade networks and patterns. It can be observed that coins arriving during the first and second centuries were hoarded mainly by people inhabiting the Chera, Chola, and Pandya territories, while specimens arriving in the first half of the third century were mostly hoarded by societies occupying the eastern Deccan plateau. Some of the latter most probably correspond to the post-Satavahana period. This distribution differs from that of finds occurring in types of contexts other than hoards (Figs 11.7 and 11.8).

In Tamilakam finds of *aurei* and *denarii*, as well as their imitations, are absent from excavation areas, while the settlement finds are attested from Deccan and Kalinga.[53] The rare grave finds come from Megalithic burials from the southern part of the peninsula.[54] They are linked with the iron-using Megalithic communities which in the early centuries AD participated in regional exchange networks and interacted with the Early Historic communities that traded with the westerners.[55] The only find of a stupa deposit of imitations of *aurei* is registered from the Ikshvaku site in the Deccan, and so far no Roman *denarii* or their imitations have been discovered in a reliquary.[56] This is in sharp contrast to the north-western part of the subcontinent ruled by the Kushans, where Roman coins purposely deposited in stupas have been discovered.[57]

[53] For *denarii*, see Adam, Peddabankur, Chandravalli, Vadagaon Madhavapur, and Malhar; for *aurei*, see Alluru, Kondapur, Nagarjunakonda, Peddabankur, Phanigiri, Yeleswaram, Nevasa, and Sisupalgarh.

[54] Coimbatore Dt., Chandravalli. Other finds are poorly recorded; e.g. Hough (1829: 84) writes that 'tumuli, or cairns...are scattered throughout the southern Ghauts, from which many coins, unquestionably Roman, have been taken'.

[55] Ray (1993).

[56] A stupa deposit is known from Nagarjunakonda.

[57] Ahin Posh (Aghanistan), Manikyala (Pakistan), and Taxila (Pakistan); see Turner (1989: 46, 66, 78).

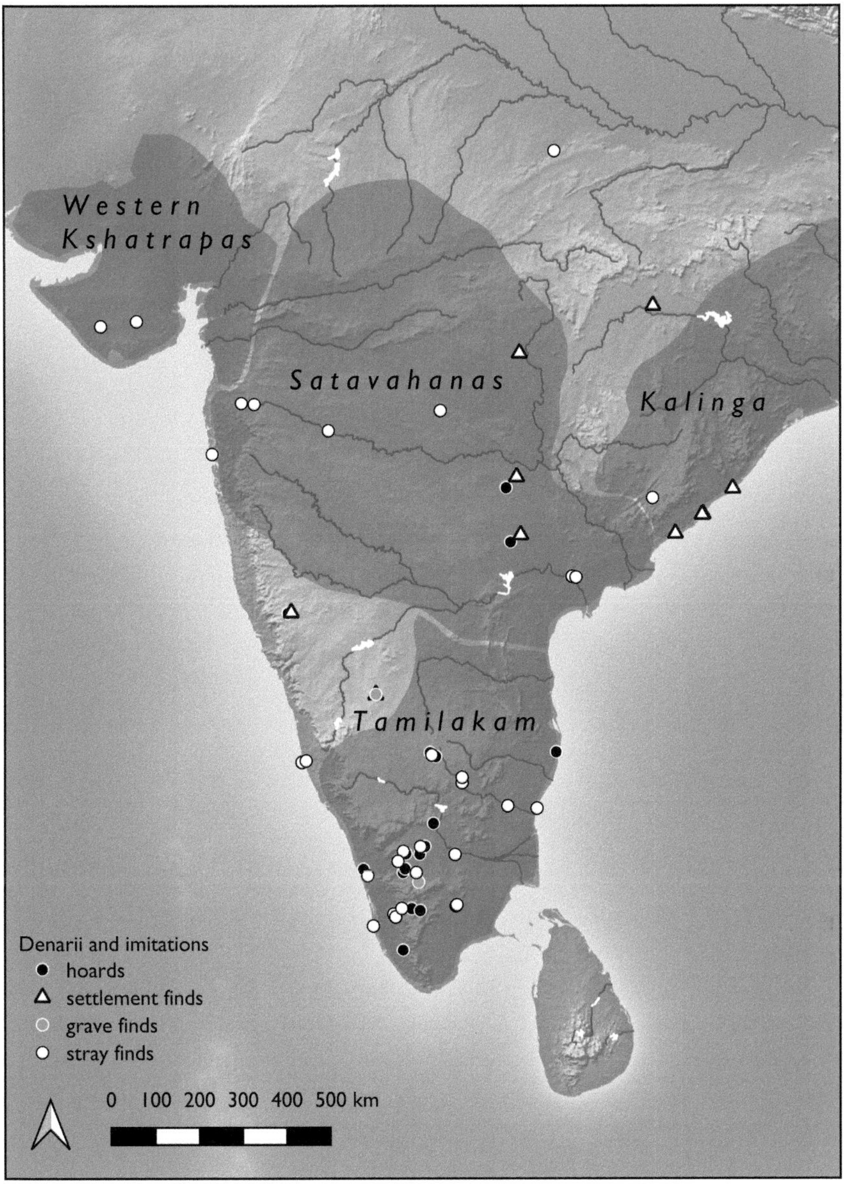

Fig. 11.7. Distribution map of *denarii* and imitations, by find categories. Map: A. Wilson/E. Smagur.

Although finds of pierced and looped *denarii* as well as their imitations are known from India, they do not occur in hoards, unlike *aurei* and their imitations.[58] *Denarii* used as ornaments and amulets are registered only from outside the territories ruled by the Cheras, the Cholas, and the Pandyas, while pierced *aurei*

[58] E.g. Adam, Kondapur, and Banavasi.

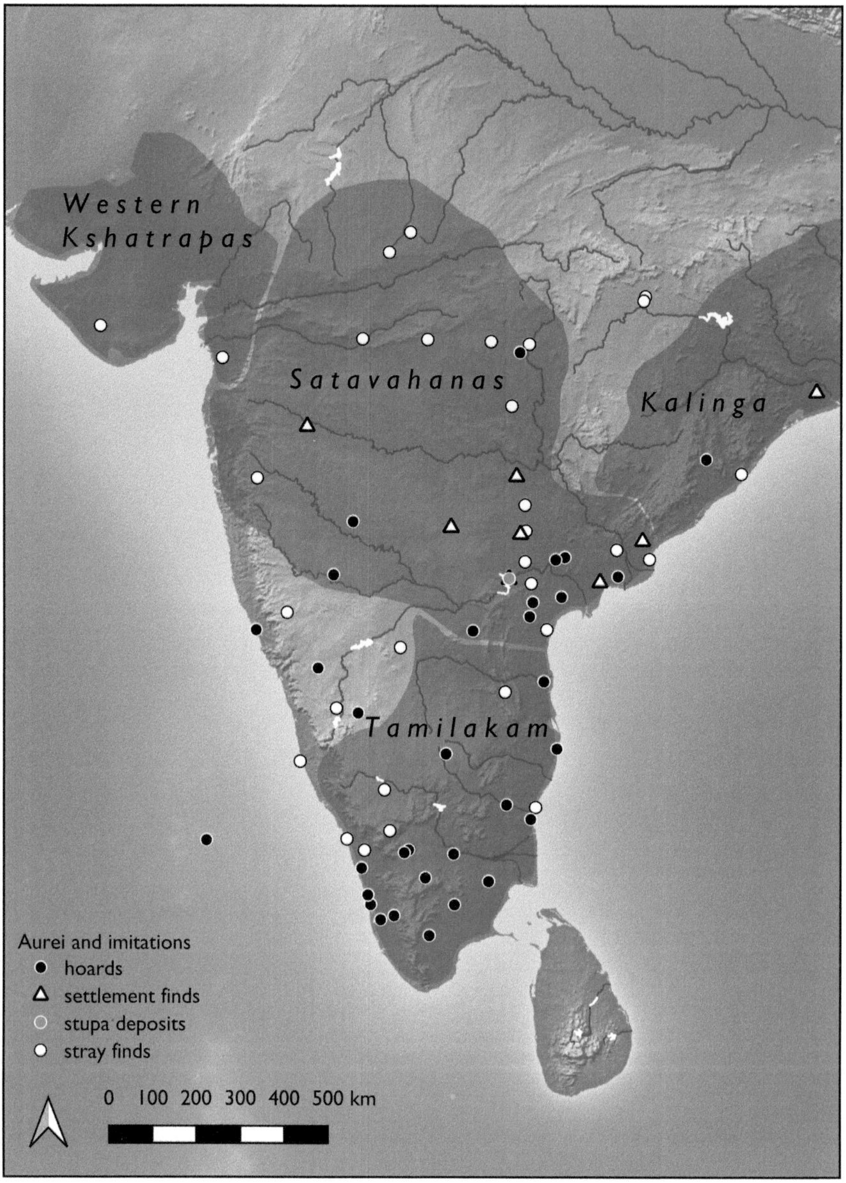

Fig. 11.8. Distribution map of *aurei* and imitations, by find categories. Map: A. Wilson/E. Smagur.

are recorded from Kalinga, the Deccan, and Tamilakam.[59] Stray and settlement finds of Indian silver and silver-plated imitations of *denarii* are specific to the Deccan, yet this region yielded only two hoards containing such objects. The distribution of hoards containing imitations of *aurei* is much wider than the

[59] E.g. Tirukoilur.

distribution of their stray and settlement finds, which come exclusively from the Deccan and Kalinga.

The lack of finds of hoards from the territory ruled by the Western Kshatrapas is striking. The author of the *Periplus Maris Erythraei*, a handbook for eastern trade written in the middle of the first century AD, states that gold and silver money imported to Barygaza could be exchanged there with much profit against the local currency.[60] However, the finds of Roman coins are rather scarce in the territory of Gujarat; all of them are stray finds, and so far there has been no strong evidence of hoarding. This paucity of finds might have been caused by the practice of Kshatrapa rulers melting them down to strike their own silver issues. The metallurgical analysis undertaken by Paula Turner showed that coins of Nahapana have a high silver content (96–9%), which is unmatched by any other Kshatrapa issues analysed. However, the Nahapana coins are similar in silver content to *denarii* of Augustus and Tiberius from the Lugdunum mint.[61] This means that in the first century AD in the Kshatrapa realm *denarii* were valued due to their silver content, with no desire to possess them as prestigious items or status symbols. Nevertheless, Kshatrapa rulers never issued gold coinage, so they did not need to melt down *aurei* for this purpose. It cannot be excluded that some finds were melted down in modern times. In 1852 Captain Drury, while reporting the discovery of the Kottayam hoard, noticed that 'the purity of the gold especially attracted the notice of the jewellers and the wealthier natives, who purchased them for the purpose of having them melted down for trinkets and ornaments'.[62] The second possible explanation is that some of those coins were distributed further from the ports to the territories where they were more desired. Finds of Roman coins are also scarce in western Deccan, where many ports and urban settlements recorded in the *Periplus* were located. The limited number of finds from the north-eastern part of the subcontinent might be the result of the indirect nature of Roman trade with that region, where amphorae finds are also absent.[63] The lack of finds of Roman coins from the Early Historic port sites is striking and has not yet been explained.

For the purpose of this chapter, specimens discovered from the Early Historic Buddhist sites located along the trade routes of Kalinga and Deccan are considered single settlement finds.[64] Due to the quality of the publications, it is only possible to be precise about the exact context of discovery for three of those findspots: Bavikonda, Thotlakonda, and Phanigiri.[65] Those coins were found in

[60] *Periplus* 49.

[61] The analysis covered 174 coins. The initial attempt to produce coins by Kshatrapas with a fairly high silver content was not maintained. Although the highest limits remain high (*c.* 95%), the lowest values drop to 63%: Turner (1984: 95, 131, 242–7, 258).

[62] Drury (1852: 371–87).

[63] Tomber (2013: 92–4).

[64] Bavikonda, Lingarajupalem, Dhulikatta, Thotlakonda, Phanigiri, and Salihundam.

[65] Two *denarii* of Tiberius and one of Augustus were unearthed at Bavikonda, of which one was found in the Vihara I, at the entrance of the thirteenth cell. Another two were discovered in Vihara II in the seventh cell; Prasad (1994: 27, 62–3, plates LXI–LXII A, B, C). Five *denarii* of Tiberius were found at Thotlakonda. One of them was discovered in the corner of the verandah of Vihara VII, and

monastic compounds, such as residential buildings (viharas), not in stupas, most probably being ritual offerings of traders or pilgrims (not necessarily of foreign origin) to the Buddhist centres, which might have been later reused to provide monks with everyday needs as well as to finance constructions and adornment of the temples. While the intention of the donor was to earn merit, the gifts to the sangha were meant to be reused. The use of Roman coins as offerings confirms their perception as ritual objects which at the same time retained their economic function.[66] Therefore, those finds may also represent stores of value in a similar way to hoards. Moreover, Rebecca Darley suggests a possible association between the Gottiparthy find, consisting of three Roman *denarii*, and Buddhist sites at Phanigiri and Gujalabanda.[67] She also points to the proximity of Kudavelli to the Chalukyan Sangameswara temple and of Peddabankur to the Buddhist site of Dhulikkata.[68] According to her, they 'may indicate the role major religious and political sites had in providing a gravitational hub for wealth and moveable goods'.[69] In the western Deccan religious donations made by Yavanas ('foreigners' or 'westerners') to the Buddhist communities are mentioned in the inscriptions,[70] but there are no finds of Roman coins from Buddhist sites in that territory.

Therefore, it was mainly in the Deccan that Roman coins might have had a number of different functions, used not only as media of payment and as a store of wealth but also in more diverse ways than their primary purpose, which was economic, as they were put to a variety of non-monetary uses. This differentiation was most probably associated with the variety of meanings these objects had within the subcontinent and reflects vital differences between the societies inhabiting Early Historic India. After the decline of the Satavahanas, a similar approach to Roman coins was exhibited by people inhabiting the Ikshvaku territory, as confirmed by finds from Nagarjunakonda and Phanigiri as well as by some of the hoards closing with coins that arrived during the third phase of the influx.

A more general observation is the problem of a relatively low number of finds of Roman coins in relation to the size of the territory and the importance of its role in Indian Ocean contacts, proving that coins were only one of the elements in the Indo-Roman trade and certainly not a crucial one in consideration of the figures quoted by Pliny the Elder.[71] Therefore, the perception of finds of Roman

the rest in Vihara IX. Two came to light inside the eleventh cell and another two in the twelfth cell; Krishna Sastry, Subrahmanyam, and Rama Krishna Rao (1992: 43, 46, 82–4, plates XLI–XLII). Two *aurei* of Nerva and Antoninus Pius were excavated from the cells of Vihara Zone 1; Visalatchy (2021: 100). One *denarius* of Augustus from Phanigiri is displayed in the Andhra Pradesh State Museum in Hyderabad; https://nmma.nic.in/nmma/antiqDetail.do?refId=142510 (accessed 9 February 2024).

[66] Fussman (1987). [67] Darley (2019: 71–2).

[68] In Kudavelli two imitations of Byzantine coins were found during the excavations. At Peddabankur five *denarii* of Augustus and Tiberius and four gold-plated lead imitations were discovered.

[69] Darley (2019: 72). [70] Ray (1986: 314–15).

[71] According to Pliny, the trade between the Roman world and India resulted in an annual outflow of at least 50 million sesterces (*N.H.* 6.101), while the trade with India, China, and the Arabian Peninsula 100 million sesterces a year (12.84). See also the contribution by Woytek in the present

coins as trade indicators as well as their role in reconstructing trade intensity and networks should be reconsidered.[72] They constitute a significant source for understanding the value and agency of imported objects in Early Historic India instead.

Appendix 1. Places that yielded hoards of *denarii* and their imitations (Fig. 11.2)

1. Akenpalle (Karimnagar Dt., Telangana); *c.* 1,476 *denarii* (Augustus–Nero) and 55 imitations (Augustus–Tiberius) deposited with broken pieces of silver ornaments and stripes.[73]
2. Akhilandapuram (Thoothukudi Dt., Tamil Nadu); *c.* 30 *denarii*, five of which are described (Augustus–Tiberius).[74]
3. Anaimalai (Coimbatore Dt., Tamil Nadu); unknown number of Tiberius *denarii.*[75]
4. Belgaum area (Belgaum Dt, Karnataka); *c.* 30 *denarii* (Tiberius).[76]
5. Budinatham (Coimbatore Dt., Tamil Nadu); 1,398 *denarii* (Augustus–Tiberius).[77]
6. Coimbatore area (Coimbatore Dt., Tamil Nadu); 73 *denarii* (Augustus–Caligula).[78]
7. HAL Airport (Bangalore city, Bangalore Dt., Karnataka); 256 *denarii* (Augustus–Tiberius).[79]
8. Eyyal (Thrissur Dt., Kerala); 12 *aurei* (Tiberius–Trajan), 71 *denarii* (Republican–Nero), and 34 Indian punch-marked coins.[80]
9. Kallakinar (Tiruppur Dt., Tamil Nadu); at least two *denarii* (Republican), found together with other unidentified silver and gold coins.[81]
10. Karur (Karur Dt., Tamil Nadu); at least two hoards of *denarii*. The first hoard (found in *c.* 1856) contained hundreds, maybe thousands of *denarii*, mainly Augustan. The second (found in 1878) consisted of *c.* 500 *denarii*, of which 117 were recorded (Augustus–Tiberius).[82]
11. Kathanganni (Tiruppur Dt., Tamil Nadu); 233 *denarii* (Augustus–Tiberius).[83]

volume (chapter 14). Despite considering the challenges related to preservation and documentation of coin finds from India, including the impact of remelting in ancient and modern times, the overall quantity of surviving evidence remains relatively low. For comparison, the number of extant second-century *denarii* discovered in the central and northern European Barbaricum is estimated to be approximately 140,000, far surpassing all finds from India; see Bursche (2002: 122).

[72] See also Nappo (2018) and Romanowski (2021: 62–3).
[73] Turner (1989: 47).
[74] Turner (1989: 47–8).
[75] Kandaswamy (1984: 42); Turner (1989: 48); INHCRF archives.
[76] Turner (1989: 90); Suresh (2004: 172).
[77] Turner (1989: 50); Sridhar, Suresh, and Sundararajan (2011).
[78] INHCRF archives.
[79] Turner (1989: 54).
[80] Turner (1989: 55–6); Satyamurthy (2011: 13–4, 21–2, 26), see also Appendix 2.
[81] Turner (1989: 57).
[82] Turner (1989: 59–60).
[83] Turner (1989: 60).

12. Koneripatty (Namakkal Dt., Tamil Nadu); 35 *denarii* (Tiberius) deposited together with two gold ornaments.[84]
13. Mambalam (Chennai city, Chennai Dt., Tamil Nadu); one *denarius* (Augustus) found together with 770 Indian punch-marked coins.[85]
14. Nasthullapur (Karimnagar Dt., Telangana); 27 *denarii* (Augustus–Tiberius), two imitations (Augustus–Tiberius), and eight Indian punch-marked coins.[86]
15. Nedumkandam (Idukki Dt., Kerala); at least 128 *denarii* (Republican–Augustus) deposited together with at least two Indian punch-marked coins.[87]
16. Pennar (Coimbatore Dt., Tamil Nadu)—the place cannot be identified but most probably was somewhere along the Pennar river; one *denarius* (Augustus) deposited together with an unknown number of Indian punch-marked coins.[88]
17. Pollachi (Coimbatore Dt., Tamil Nadu); unknown number of *denarii* (Augustus–Tiberius).
18. Thrissur Tk. (Thrissur Dt., Kerala); 34 *denarii* (Republican–Augustus) most probably belonging to the same hoard as the one recorded by Turner as coming from the Laccadive Islands and consisting of at least 554 *denarii* (Republican–Caligula). The hoard included also one *denarius* of the Numidian king Juba I (60–46 BC).[89]
19. Uthamapuram (Cumbum city, Theni Dt., Tamil Nadu); ten *denarii* (Augustus) found together with lead ornaments and pieces of lead.[90]
20. Vellalore (Coimbatore Dt., Tamil Nadu); three hoards of *denarii*. The first hoard was discovered in 1841 and contained 522 *denarii*, 210 of which (Augustus–Nero) were described. The second hoard (found in 1891) consisted of 547 *denarii* (Augustus–Nero), and the third (found in 1931) was composed of 121 *denarii* (Augustus) and 23 'unstruck blanks'.
21. Yeswanthpur (Bangalore city, Bangalore Dt., Karnataka); 163 *denarii* (Augustus–Claudius).[91]

Appendix 2. Places that yielded hoards of *aurei* and their imitations (Fig. 11.4)

1. Adam (Nagpur Dt., Maharashtra); 11 *aurei* (Augustus–Tiberius).[92]
2. Akki Alur (Haveri Dt., Karnataka); 3 *aurei* (Septimius Severus–Caracalla), 41 *solidi* (Theodosius II–Justin I), and two imitations of *solidi*.[93]

[84] Turner (1989: 61). [85] Turner (1989: 65). [86] Turner (1989: 70–1).
[87] Satyamurthy (1996); Berghaus (1998: 120); Johrden and Wolters (2015).
[88] Turner (1989: 73).
[89] Turner (1989: 90); Berghaus (1998: 122, 125). A coin of Hadrian sold with the second batch of coins from this hoard must have been an intruder.
[90] Santhalingam (1997). [91] Turner (1989: 86–7). [92] Turner (1989: 46).
[93] Turner (1989: 48); Darley (2012: 1–24).

3. Calicut Dt. (Kerala); two *aurei* (unidentified) and 23 or 25 imitations (Lucius Verus–Septimius Severus).[94]
4. Daramvaripalem (Prakasam Dt., Andhra Pradesh); 3 *aurei* (Tiberius, Nero and Domitian) and 21 imitations (Nero–Septimius Severus) found together with jewellery.[95]
5. Dharpul (Solapur Dt., Maharashtra); 18 *aurei* (Antoninus Pius–Septimius Severus).[96]
6. Eyyal (Thrissur Dt., Kerala); 12 *aurei* (Tiberius-Trajan), 71 *denarii* (Republican–Nero), and 34 Indian punch-marked coins.[97]
7. Goa; 13 *aurei*, only one described (Septimus Severus).[98]
8. Gumada (Vizianagaram Dt., Andhra Pradesh); 23 coins, 20 of which were published, including two *aurei* (Septimius Severus) and 18 imitations (of Septimius Severus and other second-century *aurei* as well as of two *solidi*, of which the direct prototypes cannot be determined).[99]
9. Kadmat Island (Lakshadweep); 15 *aurei* (Vespasian–Commodus).[100]
10. Kaliyampattur (Dindigul Dt., Tamil Nadu); 63 *aurei* (Tiberius–Nerva).[101]
11. Karivalamvandanallur (Tirunelveli Dt., Tamil Nadu); six *aurei* (Nero–Hadrian) found together with rings, a chain, beads, and a medallion imitating a coin of Ptolemy II Philadelphus.[102]
12. Karur (Karur Dt., Tamil Nadu); five *aurei* (Augustus–Claudius).[103]
13. Katryal (Bijapur Dt., Karnataka); 48 gold coins, including at least two *aurei* (unidentified) and four *solidi* (Theodosius II–Leo).[104]
14. Kottayam (Kottayam Dt., Kerala); hundreds of *aurei*, of which 74 were described (Augustus–Caracalla).[105]
15. Kumbalam (Ernakulam Dt., Kerala); nine *aurei* (Hadrian–Marcus Aurelius).[106]
16. Madurai Hills (Madurai Dt., Tamil Nadu); 11 *aurei* (Claudius–Domitian).[107]
17. Mallayapalem (Guntur Dt., Andhra Pradesh); four *aurei* (Nero–Antoninus Pius).[108]
18. Mattadakere (Chikmagalur Dt., Karnataka); 21 *aurei* (Antoninus Pius–Caracalla).[109]

[94] Berghaus (1992: 237; 2006: 18).
[95] Krishna Sastry (1992: 17–23), see also Smagur (2022: 169).
[96] Turner (1989: 53).
[97] Turner (1989: 55–6); Satyamurthy (2011: 13–4, 21–2, 26), see also Appendix 1.
[98] Turner (1989: 53).
[99] Turner (1989: 54); Smagur (2022: 169).
[100] Turner (1989: 57).
[101] Turner (1989: 58).
[102] Balakrishna Nayar (1978); Turner (1989: 58).
[103] Turner (1989: 59).
[104] Turner (1989: 60); INHCRF archives.
[105] Turner (1989: 62–3).
[106] Berghaus (1993a).
[107] Turner (1989: 64–5).
[108] Turner (1989: 65).
[109] Girijapathy and Khandoba Rao (2010).

19. Nagarjunakoda (Guntur Dt., Andhra Pradesh); one *aureus* (Antoninus Pius) deposited together with an imitation of an *aureus* (Tiberius?), beads, and earrings.[110]
20. Nagavarappadu (Khamman Dt., Andhra Pradesh); at least 54 *aurei* (Augustus–Nero) and three imitations (Augustus, Claudius) found together with beads and lead.[111]
21. Nandyal (Kurnool Dt., Andhra Pradesh); at least 161 *aurei*, 52 of which were described (Augustus–Trajan).[112]
22. Nellore (Nellore Dt., Andhra Pradesh); *c.* 40 *aurei* (including Trajan–Antoninus Pius).[113]
23. Nosagere (Kolar Dt., Karnataka); 3 imitations (Septimius Severus) deposited together with gold ornaments.[114]
24. Penuganchiprolu (Krishna Dt., Andhra Pradesh); 35 *aurei* (Augustus–Septimius Severus) and 24 imitations (Tiberius–Septimius Severus).[115]
25. Poonjar (Kottayam Dr., Kerala); 66 *aurei* (Augustus–Antoninus Pius).[116]
26. Pudukkottai (Pudukkottai Dt., Tamil Nadu); *c.* 501 *aurei* (Augustus–Vespasian).[117]
27. Surapattu (Villupuram Dt., Tamil Nadu); over 193 *aurei* (Tiberius–Caracalla) and an unknown number of imitations.[118] It cannot be ruled out that this hoard is identical to the one published under the name Tirukoilur (no. 29).
28. Sulur (Coimbatore Dt., Tamil Nadu); two *aurei* (Antoninus Pius) deposited together with a finger ring.[119]
29. Tirukoilur (Kallakurichi Dt., Tamil Nadu); at least 28 *aurei* and 163 imitations (Tiberius–Caracalla) deposited together with a gem-studded gold ring and four coin loops. The hoard was never fully published.[120]
30. Tondamanatham (Cuddalore Dt., Tamil Nadu); six *aurei* (Augustus–Claudius) deposited together with 27 Indian punch-marked coins.[121]
31. Valuvally (Ernakulam Dt., Kerala); at least 250 *aurei* (Nero–Antoninus Pius) and two imitations (Antoninus Pius).[122]
32. Veeravasaram (West Godavari Dt., Andhra Pradesh); one *aureus* (Tiberius) and 14 imitations of second century emperors.[123]
33. Vellalore (Coimbatore Dt., Tamil Nadu); an unknown number of *aurei* (Tiberius) deposited together with gold jewellery.[124]
34. Vinukonda (Guntur Dt., Andhra Pradesh); 15 *aurei* (Tiberius–Caracalla).[125]

110 Sarma (1994: 68); Sarkar and Misra (2006: 20–1).
111 Krishna Sastry 1992 (4–16, 25, 29); Berghaus (1993b: 307; 1994: 35, 38 pl. IX.6, 8; 40).
112 Turner (1989: 69–70).
113 Turner (1989: 71).
114 Gopala (1995).
115 Subrahmanyam, Rama Krishna Rao, and Brahma Chary (2008); Smagur and Romanowski (2020).
116 Turner (1989: 74).
117 Turner (1989: 74–6).
118 Suresh (2004: 163).
119 INHCRF archives.
120 Krishnamurthy (1998); Santhi (1998); Berghaus (2006).
121 Turner (1989: 79–9).
122 Turner (1989: 79); Satyamurthy (2011).
123 Turner (1989: 80–1).
124 Devasahayam (1985); Turner (1989: 84); Suresh (2004: 146–7).
125 Turner (1989: 84–5).

ACKNOWLEDGEMENTS

My warm thanks go to Chris Howgego and Andrew Wilson for the invitation to contribute to the conference and publication. I should like to express my gratitude to Kamal Maheshwari and the Indian Numismatic, Historical, and Cultural Research Foundation for their hospitality during my visits in India and for allowing me to study the Foundation's archives. I am also grateful to Reinhard Wolters for providing me with the access to Peter Berghaus' archive in Vienna, fruitful discussions, and inspiration. This work was supported by the National Science Centre in Poland under grant no. 2017/24/C/HS3/00120.

ABBREVIATIONS

RIC I² Sutherland, C.H.V. (1984). *The Roman Imperial Coinage* I. *From 31 BC to AD 69* (2nd rev. ed.). London.

REFERENCES

Ahuja, N. P. (ed.) (2021). *Phanigiri: Interpreting an Ancient Buddhist Site in Telengana*. Mumbai.

Avari, B. (2011). *Starożytne Indie*. Krakow.

Balakrishna Nayar, T. (1978). 'A Ptolemaic gold stater of Arsinoe II Philadelphos, from Tinneveli district', in R. Nagaswamy (ed.), *South Indian Studies*. Chennai, 105–8.

Berghaus, P. (1991). 'Roman coins from India and their imitations', in Jha (1991), 108–21.

Berghaus, P. (1992). 'Zu den römischen Fundmünzen aus Indien', *Schweizerische Numismatische Rundschau* 71: 226–47.

Berghaus, P. (1993a). 'Roman aurei from Kumbalam, Ernakulam district, Kerala', *Studies in South Indian Coins* 3: 29–42.

Berghaus, P. (1993b). 'Indian imitations of Roman coins', T. Hackens and Gh. Moucharte (eds), *Actes du XIe Congrès international de numismatique : organisé à l'occasion du 150e anniversaire de la Société royale de numismatique de Belgique : Bruxelles, 8-13 septembre 1991*. Brussels, 305–10.

Berghaus, P. (1994). 'Two imitations of the Valuvally Hoard of Roman Aurei (Kerala) 1983', *Studies in South Indian Coins* 4: 33–42.

Berghaus, P. (1998). 'Republican and early Roman Imperial denarii from India', in Jha and Garg (1998), 119–27.

Berghaus, P. (2000). 'Gestopfte Löcher auf römischen Goldmünzen aus indischen Funden', in B. Kluge and B. Weisser (eds), *Akten-Proceedings-Actes, XII. Internationaler Numismatischer Kongress, Berlin 1997*. Berlin, 499–502.

Berghaus, P. (2004). 'Evidence of die-links of Roman coins and their Indian imitations found in India', in MacDowall and Jha (2004), 53–4.

Berghaus, P. (2006). 'Strange mould links out of the Tirukkoilur Hoard', in R. Nagaswamy (ed.), *Sangam: Numismatic and Cultural History-Essays in Honour of Dr. R. Krishnamurthy*. Chennai, 11–20.

Bolin, S. (1958). *State and Currency in the Roman Empire to 300 A.D.* Stockholm.

Borell, B. (2014). 'The power of images. Coin portraits of Roman emperors on jewellery pendants in early Southeast Asia', *Zeitschrift für Archäologie außereuropäischer Kulturen* 6: 7–43.

Brancaccio, P. (2005). 'Satavahana Terracottas: Connection with the Hellenistic tradition', *East and West* 55.1–4: 55–69.

Browne, T. (1684). *Certain Miscellany Tracts*. London.

Burnett, A. (1998). 'Roman coins from India and Sri Lanka', in O. Bopearachchi and D. P. M. Weerakody (eds), *Origin, Evolution and Circulation of Foreign Coins in the Indian Ocean*. New Delhi, 179–89.

Bursche, A. (2002). 'Circulation of Roman coinage in Northern Europe in Late Antiquity', *Histoire & mesure* 17.3/4: 121–41.

Bursche, A., Ciołek R., and Wolters, R. (eds) (2008). *Roman Coins Outside the Empire. Ways and Phases, Contexts and Functions. Proceedings of the ESF/SCG Exploratory Workshop, Radziwiłł Palace, Nieborów (Poland), 3–6 September 2005* (Collection Moneta 82). Wetteren.

Cobb, M. A. (2015). 'The chronology of Roman trade in the Indian Ocean from Augustus to early third century AD', *Journal of the Economic and Social History of the Orient* 58.3: 362–418.

Cobb, M. A. (2018). *Rome and the Indian Ocean Trade: from Augustus to the Early Third Century CE*. Leiden and Boston.

Darley, R. (published as Day, R.) (2012). 'Tale of "four" hoards (or unpicking Akki Alur)', *Journal of the Oriental Numismatic Society* 211: 211–17.

Darley, R. (2013). *Indo-Byzantine Exchange, 4th to 7th Centuries: A Global History*. PhD thesis, University of Birmingham.

Darley, R. (2019). 'Worth and value: Roman and Byzantine coins in the culture and economy of ancient Telangana', in S. Ganvir, H. Dalavi, and H. Wirkud (eds), *Telangana through Ages: Perspectives from Early and Medieval Periods (Proceedings of the Second International Seminar, Hyderabad, 19–20 January 2018*. Hyderabad, 64–82.

Devasahayam, N. (1985). 'Roman jewellery from Vellalore site during the Sangam period', *Lalit Kala* 21: 53.

Drury, Capt. H. (1852). 'Remarks on some lately discovered Roman gold coins', *Journal of the Asiatic Society of Bengal* 20: 371–87.

Fussman, G. (1987). 'Coin deposits in north-western Indian stupas and their meaning for the archaeologists', in P. L. Gupta and A. Kumar Jha (eds), *Numismatics and Archaeology: 2nd International Colloquium*. Nashik, 11–15.

Girijapathy, M. and Khandoba Rao, H. K. (2010). 'A Roman coin hoard from Mattadakere', *Numismatic Digest* 34–35: 49–62.

Gopala, R. (1995). 'Roman gold coins from Nosagere, Karnataka', *Studies in South Indian Coins* 5: 63–5.

Gupta, P. L. (1957). 'Nasthulapur Hoard of silver Roman and punch-marked coins', *Journal of the Numismatic Society of India* 19: 1–4.

Gupta, P. L. (1965). *The Early Coins from Kerala*. Trivandrum.

Gupta, P. L. and Hardaker, T. (2014). *Punchmarked Coinage of the Indian Subcontinent: Magadha-Mauryan Series* (rev. edition). Mumbai.

Gurukkal, R. (2013). 'Classical Indo-Roman trade: A misnomer in political economy', *Economic and Political Weekly* 48.26: 67–78.

Hough, J. (1829). *Letters on the Climate, Inhabitants, Productions &c. &c. of the Neilgherries, or Blue Mountains of Coimbatoor, South India*. London.

Jha, A. K. (ed.) (1991). *Coinage, Trade and Economy: January 8th–11th, 1991, 3rd International Colloquium*. Bombay.

Jha, A. K. and Garg, S. (eds) (1998). *Ex Moneta. Essays on Numismatics, History and Archaeology in honour of Dr. David W. MacDowall*, vols 1 and 2. New Delhi.

Johrden, K. and Wolters, R. (2008). 'Die römischen Fundmünzen in Indien', in Bursche, Ciołek, and Wolters (2008), 341–54.

Johrden, K. and Wolters, R. (2015). 'Ein Hort republikanischer und augusteischer Denare aus Kerala: Ein Zeugnis für den Beginn des römischen Indienhandels', in W. Szaivert, N. Schindel, M. Beckers, and K. Vondrovec (eds), *TOYTO APECH TH XWPA: Festschrift für Wolfgang Hahn zum 70. Geburtstag*. Vienna, 119–39.

Kandaswamy, S. P. (1984). 'The Kongu and the Roman coins', *Journal of the Numismatic Society of India* 46: 39–44.

Kennet, D. (2013). 'Reconsidering the decline of urbanism in late Early Historic and Early Medieval South Asia', in C. J. Robin and J. Schiettecatte (eds), *Les préludes de l'Islam: Ruptures et continuités des civilisations du Proche-Orient, de l'Afrique orientale, de l'Arabie et de l'Inde à la veille de l'Islam*. Paris, 331–53.

Krishnamurthy, R. (1998). 'Imitation Roman gold coins from Tirukoilur hoard, Tamilnadu', in Jha and Garg (1998), 145–51.

Krishnamurthy, R. (2016). 'Navalai coin hoard: a fresh study', in *Sangam Age Tamil Coins and Ancient Foreign Coins found in Tamilnadu. A Collecion of Articles Published by Dr. R. Krishnamurthy, M.A., F.R.N.S.* Chennai, 260–6.

Krishna Sastry, V. V. (1992). *Roman Gold Coins: Recent Discoveries in Andhra Pradesh*. Hyderabad.

Krishna Sastry, V. V., Subrahmanyam, B., and Rama Krishna Rao, N. (1992). *Thotlakonda (A Buddhist site in Andhra Pradesh)*. Hyderabad.

Longhurst, A. H. (1938). *The Buddhist Antiquities of Nagarjunakonda, Madras Presidency* (Memoirs of the Archaeological Survey of India No. 54). New Delhi.

MacDowall, D. (1990). 'Finds of Roman coins in South Asia: Problems of interpretation', *Ancient Ceylon* 9: 49–74.

MacDowall, D. W. (1991). 'Indian imports of Roman silver coinage', in Jha (1991), 145–63.

MacDowall, D. W. (2004). 'The Indo-Roman Metal Trade', in MacDowall and Jha (2004), 39–44.

MacDowall, D. (2008). 'The context and function of the Roman coins found in India', in Bursche, Ciołek, and Wolters (2008), 331–40.

MacDowall, D. W. and Jha, A. (eds) (2004). *Foreign Coins Found in the Indian Sub-Continent*. Nasik.

Meyer, J. C. (2007). 'Roman coins as a source for Roman trading activities in the Indian Ocean', in E. H. Seland (ed.), *The Indian Ocean in the Ancient Period: Definite Places and Translocal Exchange*. Oxford, 59–67.

Nappo, D. (2018). 'Money and flows of coinage in the Red Sea trade', in A. Wilson and A. Bowman (eds), *Trade, Commerce, and the State in the Roman World* (Oxford Studies on the Roman Economy). Oxford, 557–78.

Nath, A. (1995). 'Roman coins and bullae from Adam', in D. Handa (ed.), *Oriental Numismatic Studies*, vol. 1. New Delhi, 91–7.

Nath, A. (2016). *Excavations at Adam (1988–1992), a City of Asika Janapada*. New Delhi.

Prasad, N. R. V. (1994). *Bavikonda: A Buddhist Site in North Coastal Andhra Pradesh*. Hyderabad.

Ray, H. P. (1986). *Monastery and Guild: Commerce under the Satavahanas*. Delhi and New York.

Ray, H. P. (1993). 'A resurvey of Roman contacts with the East', *Topoi* 3.2: 479–91.

Romanowski, A. (2021). 'Roman coins in Andhra in the Early Historical period', *Wiadomości Numizmatyczne* 65: 15–76.

Santhalingam, C. (1997). 'Roman coins from Kambam Valley in Tamilnadu', *Studies in South Indian Coins* 7: 57–9.

Santhi, R. (1998). 'Consecration coins of Faustina I from Tirukkoilur hoard', *Studies in South Indian Coins* 8: 40–3.

Sarkar, H. and Misra, B. N. (2006). *Nagarjunakonda*. New Delhi.

Sarma I. K. (1992). 'Roman coins from Andhra Pradesh: Their contexts, chronology and cultural significance', *Studies in South Indian Coins* 2: 35–50.

Sarma I. K. (1994). 'A critical study of the numismatic evidences from Nagarjunakonda excavations', *Studies in South Indian Coins* 4: 79–86.

Satyamurthy, T. (1996). 'Nedumkandam hoard of Roman denarii', *Studies in South Indian Coins* 6: 31–41.

Satyamurthy, T. (2011). *Catalogue of Roman Gold Coins (in the Collections of the Department of Archaeology, Kerala)*. Thiruvananthapuram.

Seshadri, M. (1966). 'Roman contacts with South India', *Archaeology* 19.4: 244–7.

Shimada, A. (2021). 'Phanigiri in the Buddhist Landscape of the Ikshvaku Era', in N. P. Ahuja (ed.), *Phanigiri: Interpreting an Ancient Buddhist Site in Telangana*. Telangana, 131–51.

Smagur, E. (2018). 'From coin to bulla: a cultural response to the influx of Roman denarii to India', *Numismatic Digest* 42: 63–78.

Smagur, E. (2020). 'Regulated Roman coins and their imitations from India; did Roman coins circulate as money in the subcontinent?', *Notae Numismaticae-Zapiski Numizmatyczne* 15: 179–210.

Smagur, E. (2022). 'Indian imitations of Roman aurei reconsidered', *Numismatic Chronicle* 182: 153–78.

Smagur, E. and Romanowski, A. (2020). 'Review: B. Subrahmanyan, G.V. Rama Krishna Rao and p. Brahma Chary; (ed.) p. Chenna Reddy, Roman Gold Coins. "A Treasure Trove from Penuganchiprolu", Museum Series No. 31, Hyderabad (Department of Archaeology and Museums, Government of Andhra Pradesh), 2008, pp. 36 (plus front matter not paginated). ISBN 978-81-920727-1-5', *Numismatic Chronicle* 18: 484–90.

Sridhar, T. S., Suresh, S., and Sundararajan, N. (2011). *Roman Coins in the Government Museum, Chennai with a Detailed Catalogue of the Denarii Hoard from Budinatham (Tamil Nadu)*. Chennai.

Subrahmanyam, B., Rama Krishna Rao, G.V., and Brahma Chary, P. (2008). *Roman Gold Coins: A Treasure Trove from Penuganchiprolu*. Hyderabad.

Suresh, S. (2004). *Symbols of Trade: Roman and Pseudo-Roman Objects Found in India*. New Delhi.

Thapar, R. (2002). *The Penguin History of Early India from the Origins to* AD *1300*. London.

Thapar, R. (2012). 'Black gold: South Asia and the Roman maritime trade', in R. Thapar (ed.) *Cultural Pasts: Essays in Early Indian History*. New Delhi, 556–88.

Tomber, R. (2008). *Indo-Roman Trade: From Pots to Pepper*, London.

Tomber, R. (2013). 'Pots, coins and trinkets in Rome's trade with the East', in P. S. Wells (ed.), *Rome Beyond its Frontiers: Imports, Attitudes and Practices* (JRA Supplement 94). Portsmouth, RI, 87–104.

Turner, P. (1984). *Roman and Indigenous Silver Coins in Central and Southern India in the First to Third Centuries AD*. PhD thesis, University of London.

Turner, P. (1989). *Roman Coins from India*. London.

Turner, P. (2023). 'Speculation is futile: Reflections on 30 years of studies of Roman coins found in India', in H. Wang and R. Bracey (eds), *Look at the Coins! Papers in Honour of Joe Cribb on his 75th Birthday*. Oxford, 169–73.

Unnithan, N. G. (1963). 'Eyyal hoard of silver punch-marked and Roman coins', *Journal of the Numismatic Society of India* 25.1: 22–8.

Visalatchy, N. R. (2021). 'Phanigiri's archaeological labyrinth: A guide to the site', in Ahuja (2021), 92–129.

Wheeler, M. (1954). *Rome Beyond the Imperial Frontiers*. London.

Emilia Smagur, *Hoards of Roman Coins and Imitations in India* In: *Roman Coin Hoards Across Frontiers*. Edited by: Benjamin D. R. Hellings, Marguerite Spoerri Butcher, and Chris Howgego, Oxford University Press.
 DOI: 10.1093/9780198986478.003.0011

PART IV

EXPANDING EXPLANATORY FRAMEWORKS

12

Viking Age Dirham Hoards in Northern Europe: Why So Many?

Marek Jankowiak

If we imagined—by analogy to the physical notion of work, a product of force and distance—a measurement that would quantify the displacement of a quantity of precious metal over a given distance, and included a measure of time, the early medieval dirham hoards from northern Europe would have, among other pre-modern episodes of large-scale movement of specie, a good claim to pre-eminence. The aim of this chapter is, however, not to establish such a ranking but, more modestly, to speculate why so many dirhams—around 400,000 according to two independent calculations—have been unearthed in the last two to three centuries in northern Europe.[1] Any attempt to answer this question will have to account not only for the remarkable scale and longevity of their inflow from the Islamic world to northern Europe in the ninth and tenth centuries but also, equally importantly, for the failure, or perhaps unwillingness, of the owners of the dirham hoards to recover them from the ground. These questions have not often been considered from a quantitative perspective, although assumptions on the quantities involved, even if they remain implicit, strongly colour the interpretations of the dirham hoards.[2] That any quantification is inherently uncertain does not reduce the utility of this approach, as long as excessive precision is avoided; on the contrary, such thought experiments allow us to envisage scenarios invisible to the naked eye and thus lead to a fuller appreciation of the complex nature of hoarding.

THE HOARDS

The overwhelming majority of the roughly 400,000 dirhams recorded by numismatists in the last two or three centuries come from *c.* 1,700 hoards that

[1] Kovalev and Kaelin (2007: 564) list 353,094 coins and 1,255 hoards for the area defined below, on the basis of an unpublished catalogue of hoards started by Thomas S. Noonan. My independent calculation—*c.* 400,000 coins and 1,700 hoards—includes in addition more recent finds and hoards on which there is little specific information. It will appear as an appendix to my forthcoming monograph on the 'dirhams for slaves' trade system.

[2] One exception is Noonan (2000–1: 194–211), on whose estimates see below.

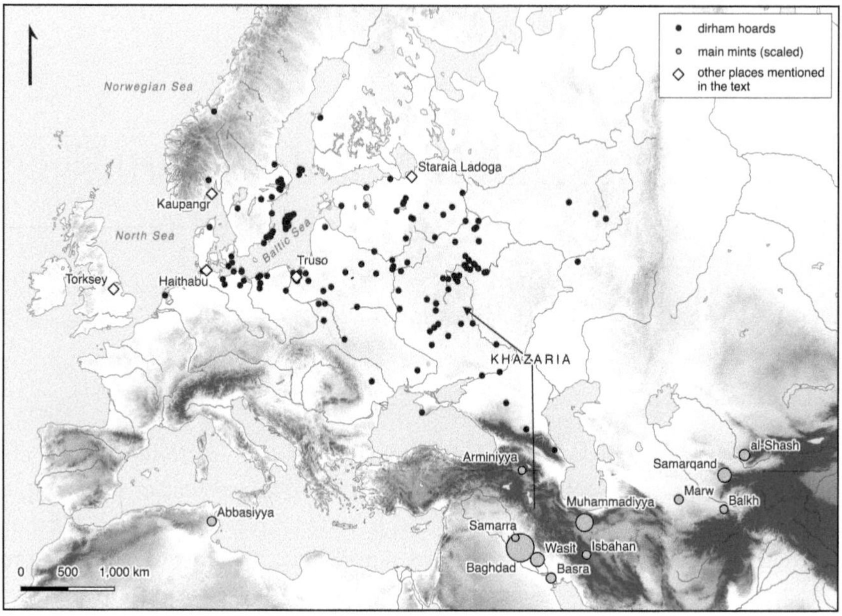

Fig. 12.1. Dirham trade in the ninth century. Only hoards with >50% dirhams are plotted. © M. Jankowiak.

were found in a broad zone stretching from modern European Russia, through the Baltic area, Scandinavia, and central Europe, to the coasts of the North Sea and the British Isles (Figs 12.1 and 12.2). Single finds are not unknown, but they are strongly concentrated in *emporia,* Viking Age trading places; even there, however, dirhams, or more commonly their tiny fragments, are only counted in the hundreds.[3] As coins are usually less fragmented in the hoards, an average hoard of 200–300 dirhams thus contains more silver than was found in even the most active *emporia.*[4] Few hoards reach sizes in the thousands of dirhams, and only three exceed ten thousand coins, including the largest hoard to have ever been mentioned, found in 1809 or 1810 under an uprooted tree near Staraia Ladoga (northern Russia) and said to have weighed *c.* 110 kg, or the equivalent of almost 40,000 dirhams. Regrettably, it ended in the crucible before it was recorded in any detail.[5]

[3] Overview in Blackburn (2008). To give a handful of examples, Kaupangr (near Oslo) yielded *c.* 125 dirhams (Rispling, Blackburn, and K. Jonsson 2008), Haithabu (near Kiel, northern Germany) 67 dirhams (Hilberg 2011: 206), and Truso (near Elbląg, northern Poland) 996 dirhams weighing in total 472 g (*FMP* V A.19A–B).

[4] Data collected by Kovalev and Kaelin (2007) result in an average of 281 dirhams per hoard; my calculations give 235 dirhams per hoard, or 196 dirhams per hoard if we exclude the three largest hoards.

[5] Rispling (2005: 218–19, no. 314); original report in Fraehn (1842: 331). The other two hoards are Spillings (Gotland, >14,000 coins, *t.p.q.* AD 870), see Pettersson (2009); and Murom (central Russia, >13,000 coins, *t.p.q.* AD 939), see Rispling (2005: 215, n. 229) and Gomzin (2013: 208–9, no. 3).

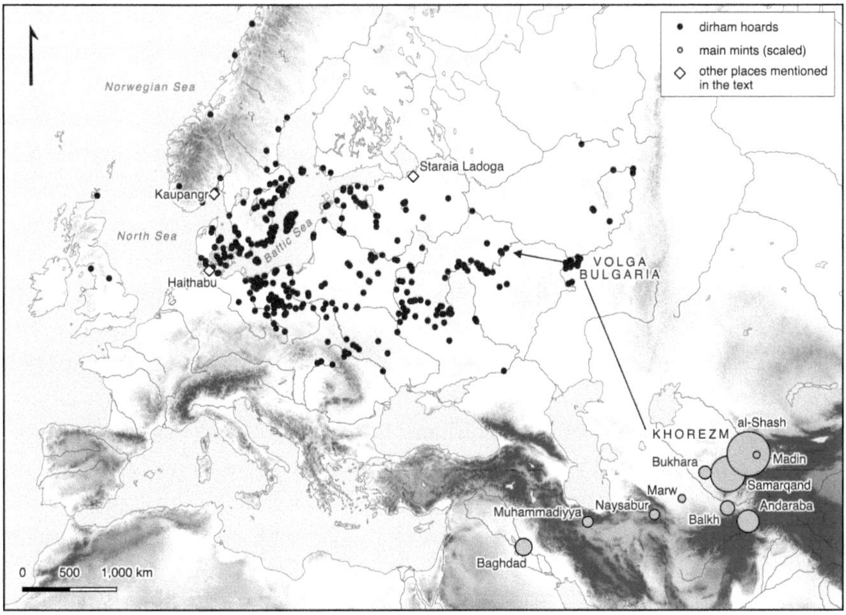

Fig. 12.2. Dirham trade in the tenth century. Only hoards with >50% dirhams are plotted. © M. Jankowiak.

More recently found hoards are not melted down for raw metal any more, but they often still remain outside academic circulation, to a large extent due to the criminalization of metal detecting in many European countries.[6] This is not the only difficulty hampering the research on dirham hoards. Many hoards remain unpublished, including those kept in coin cabinets, which comprise the two largest in terms of collections of dirhams, in Stockholm and St Petersburg.[7] No comprehensive catalogue of hoards covering the whole of northern Europe is available. In these circumstances, one must rely on national catalogues where such have been compiled (this is the case for Poland, Estonia, Finland, and roughly one-third of the Swedish material) or,[8] otherwise, on lists of hoards,[9] publications of individual finds in journals and Festschrifts,[10] and unpublished coin lists of museum collections.[11]

[6] See, e.g., Östergren (2015).

[7] This situation is currently changing with the digitization of the collection of the Ekonomiska museet—Kungliga myntkabinettet in Stockholm, available at https://samlingar.shm.se/ (accessed 26 March 2023).

[8] *FMP*; Leimus (2007); Granberg (1966); Talvio (2002); *CNS*. See also Markov (1910) for a high quality, even if antiquated, catalogue of finds from imperial Russia.

[9] Brather (1995–6); Rispling (2005: 208–19); and, particularly useful for Gotland, Gruszczyński (2019: 308–46).

[10] See, e.g., Kovalev (2001) for a list of studies by Thomas S. Noonan. *VNK*; Kuleshov (2019); and Lebedev (2021) are good starting points for the scattered publications of finds from Russia.

[11] I thank particularly warmly colleagues from the Numismatic Institute and the Royal Coin Cabinet in Stockholm, in the first place Kenneth Jonsson and Gert Rispling, for giving me access to their archives.

The wealth of data that can be collected repays this effort. At the coin level, detailed data on up to *c.* 200,000 dirhams are available. Even if this is a far cry from the almost 7,000,000 coins in the Coin Hoards of the Roman Empire database,[12] this is probably still the largest body of numismatic data available for early medieval western Eurasia. Lower quantity is, however, to some extent compensated for by the higher precision of the data since, unlike Roman, Germanic, or Byzantine coins, each dirham carries exact information on the year and place of its minting. This enables high-precision statistical analysis,[13] even if the application of statistical methods is, in some cases, limited by the fragmentation of the coins: dirhams found in Poland, for instance, are exceptionally fragmented, with the result that full information on the date and place of minting is known for only 7% of the 52,000 recorded coins.

In some respects, the inflow of dirhams is not dissimilar to that of other types of silver coins hoarded around the Baltic and North Seas in antiquity and the early Middle Ages. Their quantity is, at first sight, similar to those of Antonine and Severan *denarii* or German coins of the eleventh century, also found in northern Europe in the hundreds of thousands.[14] Of the former, around 150,000 specimens from a little over 500 hoards are currently known. The average size of a hoard (300 *denarii*), their geographical distribution (most coins come from the area between the Baltic and Black Seas, and from the Baltic islands), the fact that Roman coins were imitated, the use of the *denarii* for prestige rather than purely monetary purposes, and even the identity of their owners (Germanic tribes gradually spreading from the Baltic area towards the south-east) make this hoarding episode highly comparable to dirham hoards, even though the coins seem to have remained in circulation for a century or two longer than the dirhams.[15] As for the eleventh-century German coins, the circumstances of their inflow remain insufficiently known, but they too are found all around the Baltic in hoards of several hundred coins.[16]

However, the picture changes when it is corrected for the weight of the dirhams (around 3 g, as opposed to 1–1.5 g for most western medieval coins)—in Sweden or in Poland, for instance, they account for one-third of Viking Age coin finds by quantity, but more than a half by weight[17]—their exceptionally high

[12] https://chre.ashmus.ox.ac.uk (accessed 26 March 2023). [13] E.g. Jankowiak (2019).

[14] The quantities are much smaller for gold: I am aware of two dozen golden dinars from Viking Age hoards around the Baltic, whereas the Coin Hoards of the Roman Empire database currently records 1,666 late antique *solidi* from Denmark, Poland, and Sweden (https://chre.ashmus.ox.ac.uk, accessed 26 March 2023).

[15] See the summary article of Bursche, Dymowski, and Myzgin (2025), and the list of finds in Dymowski (2020). The figures quoted above exclude finds from the UK.

[16] Data on German coins are found in Hatz (1974), *FMP*, and *CNS*.

[17] Dirhams (and coins imported with them such as the imitations, Sasanian coins, etc.) account for 35% of recorded and identified coins in Sweden (87,074 out of 249,171) and 29% in Poland (52,201 out of 178,497); see K. Jonsson (2015: 54, table III) and the tables at the end of each volume of *FMP*. In both cases, their share by weight amounts to *c.* 45–55%.

fineness, the distances that they travelled, the longevity of their inflow (almost two centuries, compared to a century or less for German and Roman coins), and, as this chapter is going to argue, their singular propensity to remain hoarded in the ground. This raises questions not only about their handling in the north but also about their seemingly unlimited supply. In order to understand why so many dirhams ended up in northern Europe, we first need, thus, to have a closer look at the mechanisms of their inflow.

THE INFLOW

The exportation of large quantities of silver coins from the Islamic world northwards was noticed and commented on by contemporary Muslim authors, firstly by the so-called geographers. The ninth and above all the tenth century AD saw the emergence and flourishing of a literary genre unknown to the classical world: increasingly ambitious descriptions of the Muslim world focused on what André Miquel called 'la géographie humaine', of which, as opposed to what we understand by 'geography', human activity is the centrepiece.[18] In this undertaking, the surrounding world played a role insofar as it contributed to the understanding of the Muslim community. This is perhaps why north-eastern Europe, the place of origin of people and things familiar to any contemporary reader of the geographers, occupies in their works much more space than, for instance, the self-contained and disconnected worlds of western Europe or China.

These people and things were Saqaliba—that is, Slavic—slaves and furs of the animals of the taiga and tundra. Their faraway origins stimulated the curiosity of such Muslim writers as the early tenth-century geographer Ibn Rusta:

> The Rus... raid the Saqaliba, sailing in their ships until they come upon them. They take them captive and sell them in Khazaria and Bulgar. They have no cultivated fields and they live by pillaging the land of the Saqaliba.... They earn their living by trading in sable, grey squirrel and other furs. They sell them for silver coins which they set in belts and wear round their waists.... They treat their slaves well and dress them suitably, because for them they are an article of trade.[19]

Other authors interviewed the Saqaliba or travelled to the markets where they were acquired.[20] The travelogues of Ibn Fadlan, a diplomat from Baghdad who

[18] Miquel (1967–88), esp. vol. 1, pp. x–xi, for the definition of 'human geography'.

[19] Ibn Rusta, in Lunde and Stone (2012: 126), with minor modifications.

[20] Interview: al-Jahiz in Hārūn (1966–9: IV, 109); Lewicki (1956: 169). For travellers, see below. Many other useful texts are translated in Lunde and Stone (2012).

visited Volga Bulgaria (south of modern Kazan) in AD 922, and Ibrahim ibn Yaʿqub, a Jew from Muslim Spain who reached Prague four decades later, corroborate Ibn Rusta's account, not least with regard to the involvement of the Rus (that is, the Scandinavians) in the trade in Slavic slaves.[21] The interest of Muslim intellectuals in the Saqaliba coincides not only with the inflow of dirhams to northern Europe but also with frequent mentions of the Saqaliba in all manner of texts from the Islamic world,[22] with an unusual prominence of themes of captivity, slavery, and long-distance trade in northern European chronicles, and finally with staggering levels of violence revealed by the archaeology of central Europe.[23] The overarching framework of a large-scale slave trade, such as that described by the Muslim geographers and travellers, provides the best fit for this evidence and the context necessary to understand the inflow of dirhams to northern Europe.

Judging from the chronology of the hoards, dirhams first appeared in Russia and Ukraine *c.* AD 800 and soon reached the Baltic.[24] The first phase of their inflow reached its peak *c.* AD 860–70 and ended abruptly *c.* AD 875, possibly as a result of a widening gap between the decreasing Islamic demand for slaves (caused, in turn, by instability at the Abbasid court in the 860s) and the increasing Scandinavian demand for silver. The sudden resurgence of trading a quarter-century later, *c.* AD 900, was triggered by the renewed availability of large quantities of high-quality silver coin, produced since AD 893 by the Samanid rulers of central Asia. Their dirhams appeared in northern Europe almost instantly and literally flooded Scandinavia and Rus in the first half of the tenth century. Then history repeated itself: the demand for silver grew while its availability decreased. This time, however, the decline was gradual, and it took several decades for the trade to grind to a halt *c.* AD 980. Small-scale attempts to revive it were made until AD 1013, the date of the latest dirhams found in northern Europe, but by then Scandinavia and central Europe had already reoriented themselves to silver from closer sources, such as Germany and Anglo-Saxon England.

The clear division of the exchanges between northern Europe and the Islamic world into two phases (roughly AD 800–75 and 900–80) corresponds to a marked shift in their geography (Figs 12.1 and 12.2). In the first phase, dirhams imported to the north were mostly struck in the administrative centres of the Abbasid heartlands such as Baghdad or Muhammadiyya (near Tehran) and were deposited along the major waterways connecting the Black and Caspian Seas with the Baltic and on the coasts of the latter. Tenth-century hoards, by contrast, are dominated by central Asian issues, and are disseminated over much of northern Europe, with particularly significant clusters emerging in areas where state

[21] For Ibn Fadlan, see Shepard and Treadwell (2023); for Ibrahim b. Yaʿqub, Ducène (2018: 163–94).
[22] Mishin (2002). [23] Biermann and Jankowiak (2021).
[24] What follows summarizes Jankowiak (2021a).

structures—such as Denmark, Sweden, Poland, or Kievan Rus—were forming. This shift from Iraq to central Asia was mirrored by the replacement of the Khazar Khaganate (on the Lower Volga) by Volga Bulgaria (on the Middle Volga) as the main meeting point for Scandinavian and Muslim merchants.

In tenth-century central Europe, access to dirhams and political consolidation went hand in hand. Dirhams were earned through trade with the Islamic world, in practice through the sale of captives. Their enslavement required an increasingly sophisticated military organization as targeted tribes consolidated or retreated inland. When the inflow of dirhams stopped, these groups of warriors had to learn how to extract a more sustainable surplus from the populations they came to control. Political consolidation was thus hardly conceivable without slave trade. The reverse is, however, not true: access to silver did not necessarily lead to state formation, as illustrated by the Baltic islands of Gotland, Bornholm, and Öland, or the equally stateless coast of Estonia, all homes to significant clusters of hoards.[25] If there was a common denominator to the area of dirham hoarding, it was less the underlying political or economic structures than a cultural idiom diffused by Scandinavian settlers, traders, and raiders well beyond Scandinavia itself, an idiom that gave unusual prominence to silver as a store of value, marker of status, and enabler for social transactions; not, however, as a means of exchange, as shown by the scarcity of single finds, a clear indication of the absence of a monetary economy in ninth- and tenth-century northern Europe. The connection between culturally defined uses of silver and dirham hoards can also be seen in the absence of the latter from the Carolingian Empire, Byzantium, and the southern part of central Europe, in particular Bohemia and Hungary.

THE QUANTITIES

The importance of 'having' silver rather than 'spending' it thus correlates with the exceptionally high density of dirham hoards in northern Europe. Is it within our reach to estimate the proportion of imported dirhams that survived and are known to us, or, alternatively, the size of the inflow of the Islamic silver to the north? Several recent studies on northern hoards and on Islamic monetary production now make it possible to envisage such approximations.

The island of Gotland (Sweden), the largest known concentration of dirham hoards, is a good starting point.[26] Out of around 800–900 finds of precious metal dating to the Viking Age, *c.* 350 are hoards composed mostly of coins.[27] Their

[25] For Bornholm, where, differently from Sweden, archaeologists work closely with metal detectorists, see the recent update by Ingvardson (2021).

[26] See the studies collected in Gruszczyński, Jankowiak, and Shepard (2021).

[27] Gruszczyński (2019: 25–6).

spatial distribution corresponds closely with that of the farmsteads, and, as we will see, at least some of them were found in or near dwellings. The precise context of most hoards is, however, uncertain due not only to the usually haphazard circumstances of their discovery but also to the relative archaeological invisibility of Viking Age layers.[28] Nonetheless, Gotland's settlement structure in the ninth and tenth centuries can be extrapolated from, on the one hand, the dense network of stone foundations of Iron Age houses inhabited between the first and sixth centuries AD and, on the other, seventeenth-century cadastral maps. These two datasets coincide remarkably: they suggest that the island accommodated around 1,500–2,000 farmsteads, that these were similarly sized, and that their geographical distribution evolved little in the millennium that separates the stone houses from the maps.[29] This picture of a relatively unstratified society can be cautiously extrapolated onto the Viking Age, and is supported by the emergence in the thirteenth century of a dense network of a hundred similarly undifferentiated parish churches.[30]

There may thus be some truth in the stereotypical notion of Gotland as a 'peasant republic'.[31] Wealth appears to have been distributed relatively uniformly across the island, and every farmstead seemingly had access to imported silver. As we will see, every farmstead also needed it. It thus makes sense to compare the total number of farmsteads on the island with that of the findspots of the hoards (in the range of 250–300, to take into account hoards found close to each other). It turns out that silver was found in roughly every sixth Gotlandic farmstead.[32] That such an extraordinarily high ratio is not beyond the realm of possibility is corroborated by recent finds on Bornholm (Denmark), another Baltic island rich in hoards. Thanks to a more liberal approach to metal detecting, the number of known hoards increased from two dozen to a hundred in the last few decades.[33] Even if it is more difficult than in Gotland to estimate the number of farmsteads, it is clear that the inhabitants of Bornholm had a similarly broad access to silver as the Gotlanders and a similar propensity to bury it in the ground.

Gotland and Bornholm are, however, exceptions due to their decentralized social structures and, quite simply, their insularity. In order to get a more global impression of the proportion of the total inflow of dirhams to northern Europe that have survived in the archaeological record, we need to look elsewhere.

[28] Widerström (2021). [29] Svedjemo (2014).
[30] Svedjemo (2021); Wienberg (2004). [31] Siltberg (2012).
[32] Other estimates of the number of hoards originally buried in the Viking Age in Gotland range between 2,000 and 8,000; see Burström (1993: 33). According to Gruszczyński (2021: 193), hoards were found in one-quarter of the 180 archaeologically identified settlements.
[33] Ingvardson and Nielsen (2015); Ingvardson (2021); most hoards from Bornholm date from the eleventh century. See E. Jonsson (2021) on recent finds from Gotland (23 new hoards in 2005–17).

A promising avenue has been opened by recent studies on dirham imitations, the third most common coin type in dirham hoards, surpassed only by the coinage of the Abbasids and the Samanids. They have all the characteristics of the official dirhams, including the weight standard and a high silver content, but their blundered or outright illiterate inscriptions were manifestly engraved outside the official mints of the Islamic world, mostly at the two main markets where Scandinavian and Muslim merchants met to trade, Khazaria and Volga Bulgaria.[34] In conjunction with the absence of finds of imitations in the Islamic world, this suggests that their main, if not sole, purpose was to pay the Scandinavian merchants for their goods.

Thanks to the exhaustive die study of dirham imitations by Gert Rispling from the Coin Cabinet in Stockholm, it is now possible to gauge the level of their production.[35] Rispling's study includes around 10,000 coins that he attributed to *c.* 3,600 dies. Most dies are known from single specimens and seem to have been engraved and used *ad hoc*. These are less useful for our purpose. But around one-fifth can be connected into die chains, some of them impressively long. The size of the longest, K101, at present 139 dies and 1,813 coins (and still growing), indicates a stable workshop operating in the fashion of the mints of the Islamic world (Fig. 12.3). We can situate it in Volga Bulgaria and date its peak activity to *c.* AD 935–45.[36] Some of the dies of the chain K101 are known from remarkable quantities of coins: the best represented die K101/R12 (Fig. 12.4), which appears to have been engraved in *c.* AD 939, is currently known to me from almost 300 specimens. Remarkably, these die-identical coins come from over 100 finds, with no single find containing more than 13 specimens (Fig. 12.5). A similarly wide dissemination is displayed also by the three other dies of the chain K101 known to me from more than 200 coins.[37] The implication is that these coins were added to the monetary stock circulating at the market of Volga Bulgaria before they were disbursed to the Scandinavians; otherwise we would see in the northern hoards clusters of die-identical imitations, and this is exceedingly rare.[38] The survival ratio of the imitations thus provides a good proxy for the global survival ratio of the dirhams imported to the north.

[34] Jankowiak (2021b).

[35] Gert Rispling's die catalogue of dirham imitations is being prepared for publication by Luke Treadwell and myself.

[36] Jankowiak (2023).

[37] In addition to K101/R12 (296 coins, 108 finds), these are dies K4/R01 (266 coins, 96 finds), K101/R45 (212 coins, 75 finds), K101/R13 (208 coins, 74 finds). All data are provisional; finds do not include systematic collections. Eight other imitative dies are currently known to me from more than 100 specimens.

[38] The only examples of hoards with significant clusters of die-identical imitations known to me are Bertby (Åland Islands, *t.p.q.* AD 890/1); see Jankowiak (2021a: 116 and 127, n. 47), and the closely related hoards of 'Máramaros' (found in Zakarpattia, western Ukraine) and Bezliudovka (near Kharkiv, eastern Ukraine; both *t.p.q.* AD 935/6), on which see Rispling *et al.* (in preparation).

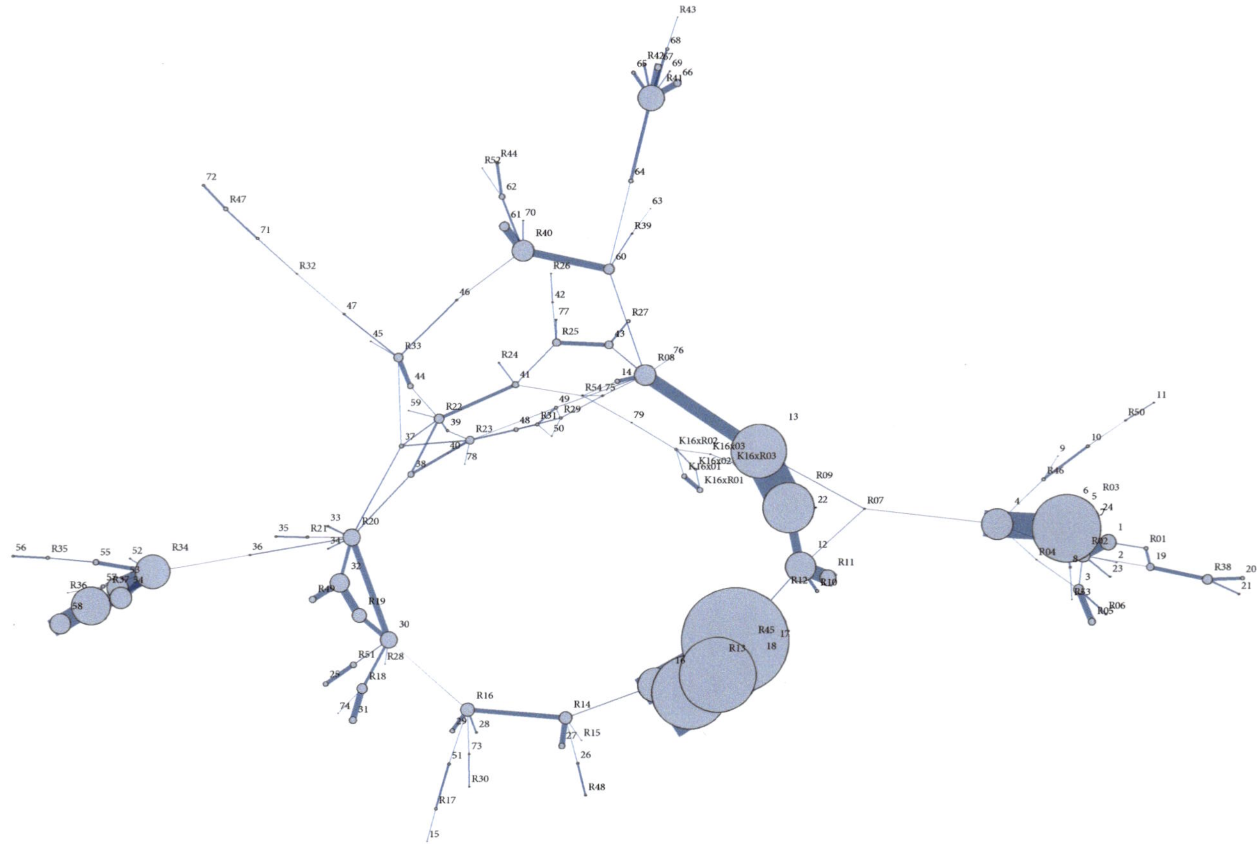

Fig. 12.3. Die chain K101. Circles represent individual dies and lines individual die links, both scaled to represent the number of extant coins or connections (max. 295 coins for R12 and 203 coins for die link R13/R45). © M. Jankowiak.

Fig. 12.4. Dirham imitation K101/R12 (right) and the obverse die K101/18 (left), with which it is often associated; 27 mm, 2.80 g. © Ekonomiska museet—Kungliga myntkabinettet, Stockholm, systematic collection. CC BY 4.0.

For dies known from 200–300 extant coins, we can assume—depending on the estimated productivity of a die—that we still have as much as *c.* 5–10% of their original production.[39] This is an unusually high ratio. But even if we look at the averages for the entire die chain K101, the number of extant coins per die, although ten times lower, is still very substantial: 22 coins for an obverse and 32 for a reverse die (on average, 26 coins per die). This implies that at least *c.* 0.5–1% of the original production survived until this day. If we now apply this ratio to the entire stream of dirhams flowing northwards (*c.* 400,000 extant dirhams), we arrive at an original inflow in the order of 40–80 million coins, or 120–240 t of silver (at 3 g per dirham).

This seems to be a very high estimate. In order to get a better sense of what it represents, let us focus on the peak period of the inflow of dirhams to the north, *c.* AD 900–50, which saw the arrival of roughly 60% of the extant dirhams, or *c.* 250,000 coins.[40] Following the logic set out above, this represents a total inflow of 25–50 million dirhams, or 0.5–1 million coins per year (or 1.5–3 t of silver per year). Such annual flows still sound very high, not least in comparison with the likely price of a slave—in the order of several dozen or perhaps a hundred dirhams. But what matters more than the precise figures is the overall logic of the model: if we set the survival ratio too low, we end up with unrealistically high annual flows of dirhams. This excludes ratios much lower than, say, 1%, such as the ratio of 0.2% borrowed by Thomas Noonan, with some modifications, from Roman numismatics.[41]

[39] I assume a productivity of *c.* 3,000–6,000 coins for an imitative die and *c.* 10,000 coins for an official die. Such a conservative assumption is meant to increase the robustness of my estimates, and takes into account the *ad hoc* nature of the production of imitations, as well as the probable lower quality of imitative dies.

[40] This ratio is based on a rough assessment of the dates of the coins and is likely to be underestimated. Using a different methodology, Noonan (2000–1: 195–204) arrived at a similar estimate—248,000 coins 'imported from Central Asia into northern Europe during the Samanid era'.

[41] Noonan (2000–1: 205–6).

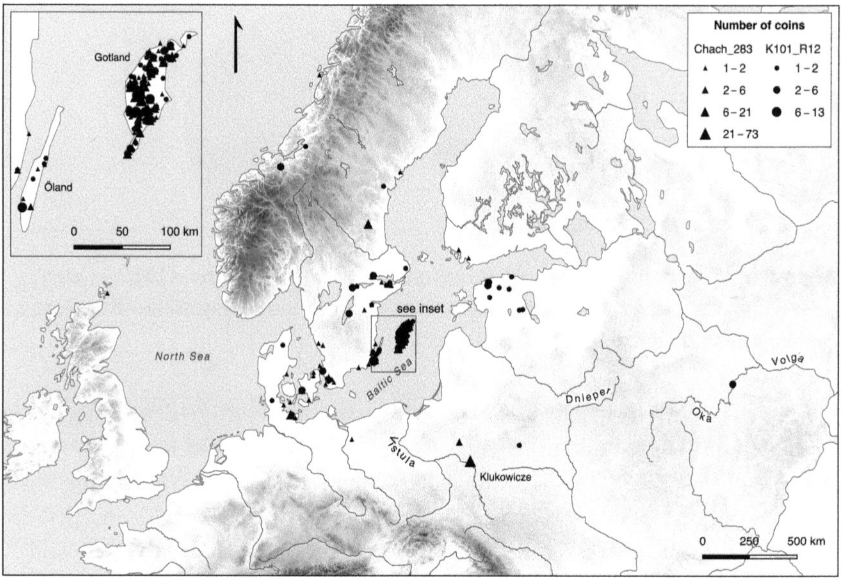

Fig. 12.5. Distribution of finds with dirham imitation K101/R12 and dirhams struck in Chach in AH 283 (AD 896/7). © M. Jankowiak.

Indeed, Noonan's estimate of the size of the dirham inflow to northern Europe—125 million dirhams over the course of the tenth century—leads to impossibly high volumes of trade.[42] Noonan converted it into annual flows of 1,250,000 coins (or 3.75 t of silver), the equivalent, for him, of half a million 'pelts of good quality fur' or, one could add, at least 12,500 captives.[43] Given the very low intensity of trade in the second half of the tenth century, Noonan's total estimate should be divided by fifty, and not one hundred, years, with the result that we would have to assume yearly sales of half a million pelts *and* over ten thousand captives by the Scandinavians visiting Volga Bulgaria. Such an industrial scale of trading is outside the realm of probability.[44] Noonan assumed too low a survival ratio, which led him to significantly overestimate the total flow of dirhams northwards. A more likely estimate would fall within the range of 1–2%, which translates into annual flows of *c.* 250–500 thousand dirhams.

Another reality check of such estimates consists in confronting them with what we can surmise about the size of the monetary stock in the Islamic world. Such an

[42] Noonan (2000–1: 206), based on the estimated number of surviving Samanid dirhams, 248,500, and the survival ratio of 0.2% mentioned above; a similar estimate also earlier in Noonan (1990).

[43] Using the value of a marten pelt given by Ibn Rusta, 2½ dirhams, see Lunde and Stone (2012: 121), and assuming the price of a slave of *c.* 100 dirhams.

[44] *Pace* Kovalev and Kaelin (2007: 568).

Fig. 12.6. Samanid dirham struck in Chach (modern Tashkent) in AH 283 (AD 896/7): Stockholm Numismatic Institute, NFG 96: 142, 2.82 g. © Stockholm Numismatic Institute.

exercise can be attempted for the Samanid coinage, once again thanks to the die studies of Gert Rispling.[45] To give an example of his results, the issue of Chach AH 283 (AD 896/7, Fig. 12.6), particularly plentiful in northern hoards, was known to him from 729 dirhams, of which he identified the dies of *c.* 500 coins (the difference is mostly due to the unavailability of photographs for some of the coins). He recognized 55 obverse and 57 reverse dies, which corresponds to an average of 9 coins per identified die. We are in the same order of magnitude as for the equivalent average for the Volga Bulgar die chain K101, 26 coins per die. This latter ratio gives an indication not only of the percentage of the original production of K101 that is still extant today but also—given that, as posited earlier, the entirety of its output was exported to the north—of how much of the original flow of silver coins from Volga Bulgaria to northern Europe has survived until today. Consequently, if out of the total quantity of imitations struck with a K101 die there survive 26 coins, then—assuming that other things, including die productivity, were equal—the survival of 9 coins per die for Chach AH 283 implies that *c.* 35% (= 9/26) of the original production of this issue was exported from Volga Bulgaria to the north (Table 12.1).

In reality, other things were not perfectly equal: the ratio of 35% would need to be adjusted downwards to account for the likely higher productivity of official dies and for the dies that are not represented in northern hoards,[46] but also upwards to compensate for the limited coverage of the dataset for Chach (based mostly on the Stockholm collection, as opposed to the broader coverage of the

[45] His die studies of Samanid coinage are mostly unpublished, but some of this material was used by Treadwell (2011: 31–6, 103–8). In the case of Chach, Treadwell (2011: 33, n. 62) excluded the reverse dies because they 'were sometimes re-used in the years subsequent to their manufacture'. The data I am using suggest that the scale of this problem is minimal. I have therefore included them in the figures presented in Table 12.2 that also differ slightly from Treadwell's data because they include more recent identifications by Rispling.

[46] The total number of dies used by a mint can be extrapolated with the formulae proposed by Esty (2006): they give, in this case, 65 obverse and 62 reverse dies, suggesting that few dies are unrepresented in the sample used by Rispling; a similar result in Treadwell (2011: 104). For die productivity, see above, n. 39; for the amended formula of Esty (2011), see below, n. 55.

Table 12.1 Estimation of the likely percentage of coins exported to the north.

Issue	Percentage exported to the north	Extant coins per die
K101	100%	26
Chach 283	x	9

Calculation: $x * 26 = 100\% * 9 \Rightarrow x = 9/26 * 100\% \approx 35\%$

data for the imitations; cf. Fig. 12.5). But the conclusion stands: a sizeable proportion of the production of the mint of Chach was used for trade with the North.

The issue of Chach AH 283 is not an outlier. Similar results emerge from other issues studied by Rispling (Table 12.2). Overall, a significant part of the Samanid monetary production appears to have been exported northwards, at least in the first two decades following its inception in AD 893: as much as half for some years in Chach (with a decreasing trend over time), *c.* 20–40% for Samarqand, and *c.* 10–20% for the more distant mints of Andaraba and Balkh. On average, as much as a quarter of Samanid silver coinage seems to have been spent on the luxuries offered by the Scandinavians. And these are conservative estimates: they ignore the central Asian silver exported to northern Europe and recast there into dirham imitations, jewellery, and early local coinages. In terms of weight, these items certainly amounted to no less than a quarter, or perhaps a half, or even more, of the weight of the extant dirhams. Given that this share cannot at present be more precisely estimated, I leave them out from my calculations, but it is apparent that the above ratios should be significantly increased, if not doubled.

This is, at first sight, an unexpected result. Samanid dirhams seem to have circulated widely within central Asia and the broader Islamic world.[47] But we are not particularly well informed of the monetary conditions within their realm, in particular of the respective functions of coinage in the three metals. In his description of the Samanid capital of Bukhara, Ibn Fadlan paid particular attention to the use of copper, rather than silver, coins:

> I saw different kinds of dirhams in Bukhara, some called *ghitrīfī* dirhams, made of copper, brass and bronze. They are counted out, without being weighed, a hundred to a silver dirham. This is the way they settle the dowry of their women: so-and-so, the son of so-and-so, marries so-and-so, the daughter of so-and-so,

[47] See, e.g., Lowick and Nisbet (1968) for a hoard of mostly Samanid dirhams from Ra's al-Khaimah in the UAE (*t.p.q.* AD 980/1).

Table 12.2 Die estimates for the main Samanid mints (after G. Rispling).

Mint and year (1)	Known coins (2)	Coins identified (3)	Dies identified (4)	Coins/die (5)=(3)/(4)	Approx. share exported to the north (6)=(5)/26
Chach AH 281 (AD 894/5)	254	200	19	10.8	42%
Chach AH 282 (AD 895/6)	453	335	26	13.1	51%
Chach AH 283 (AD 896/7)	729	507	56	9.1	35%
Chach AH 284 (AD 897/8)	433	328	25	13.1	50%
Chach AH 285 (AD 898/9)	436	301	20	15.1	58%
Chach AH 297 (AD 909/10)	543	225	39	5.8	22%
Chach AH 298 (AD 910/1)	569	259	45	5.8	22%
Chach AH 299 (AD 911/2)	435	213	35	6.2	24%
Chach AH 316 (AD 928/9)	262	117	37	3.2	12%
Samarqand AH 298 (AD 910/1)	192	81	14	6.0	23%
Samarqand AH 299 (AD 911/2)	265	104	19	5.4	21%
Samarqand AH 300 (AD 912/3)	299	139	14	10.3	39%
Samarqand AH 301 (AD 913/4)	240	174	16	11.2	43%
Andaraba AH 294 (AD 906/7)	175	101	32	3.2	12%
Andaraba AH 299 (AD 911/2)	155	129	28	4.6	18%
Andaraba AH 300 (AD 912/3)	142	110	24	4.6	18%
Andaraba AH 301 (AD 913/4)	252	194	34	5.8	22%
Balkh AH 293 (AD 905/6)	158	115	27	4.2	16%
Balkh AH 312 (AD 924/5)	154	121	29	4.2	16%

Notes: Coins and dies identified are averages for obverses and reverses; the approximate share exported to the north results from the division of coins/die by 26 (the average number of coins/die for the Volga Bulgar imitative die chain K101). Only years with particularly robust data have been selected.

> for so many thousands of *ghitrīfī* dirhams. This is how property and slaves are sold as well. They don't use any other type of dirhams for these purposes. They also have another type of bronze dirham, of which forty make up a *dānaq*. They also have a type of bronze dirham known as *samarqandī*, six of which are worth a *dānaq*.[48]

Ibn Fadlan's surprise is perceptible: differently from in Iraq, in Bukhara, and also in Khorezm,[49] silver coins were not used in everyday transactions, and not even in transactions as large as marriage contracts or the purchase of real estate or slaves. The mid-tenth-century history of Bukhara by Narshakhi claims that it was the inhabitants of Bukhara who insisted, in the early ninth century, that

[48] Ibn Fadlan in Lunde and Stone (2012: 6).

[49] Ibn Fadlan in Lunde and Stone (2012: 7): 'I noticed that the dirhams of Khwārazm are false, adulterated with lead or bronze.'

coins circulating in their city be not made of silver: 'The coins should be (such) that no one would take them from us nor out of the city, so we can carry on trading among ourselves with (this) money.' They were, accordingly, 'struck of six things: gold, silver, brass, tin, iron, and copper'.[50] We do not need to take this final information at face value, but the awareness of the elite of Bukhara that in an open economy—such as that of Sogdiana, still a major commercial hub despite the decline of the Silk Road[51]—silver coin would inevitably be taken 'out of the city' is remarkable. This attitude explains perhaps why, among the largest cities of the Samanid realm, Bukhara resisted producing silver dirhams for half a century, until the reign of Nuh ibn Nasr (AD 941–54),[52] and still preferred bronze coins to silver dirhams in the AD 960s.[53] The connection between silver coinage and external trade is further supported by the location of the main mints producing dirhams in merchant cities (e.g. Samarqand, Balkh, Chach) or in the vicinity of the main silver mines (e.g. Andaraba, also Chach). This does not imply that the production of silver coinage was decentralized: a degree of central oversight is clear from the very similar design of the dies in all the mints. But it was essentially a private enterprise taxed by the state,[54] with the result that the silver coin was not central to the functioning of the Samanid state, and that its use was limited to specific contexts, one of which, perhaps the main, was long-distance trade.

It remains for us to verify whether our hypothesis that a high proportion of the Samanid silver was exported to the north is consistent with the scale of their monetary production. This is now possible, again thanks to Rispling's die studies. As data from Table 12.2 show, he identified around 30 obverse and reverse dies each per year for the main Samanid mints (slightly fewer for Samarqand, slightly more for Chach). Some dies are certainly not represented in the northern hoards, but the formulae proposed by Warren Esty to estimate the original number of dies used by a mint suggest that these were not numerous: in most cases, they give results higher by only 5–20% than the numbers observed by Rispling. This is due to the low number of dies represented by only one coin, or, in Esty's terminology, the very high 'coverage' of the sample studied by Rispling. It is thus unlikely that our almost exclusive reliance on the northern material radically skews our perspective on Samanid silver coinage.[55]

[50] Narshakhi in Frye (1954: 36). [51] On which see Jankowiak (2024).

[52] The only earlier issue known to me is the isolated issue of AH 294 (AD 906/7).

[53] Ibn Hawqal in Kramers and Wiet (1964: 470). [54] See al-Hamdani in Dunlop (1957: 41).

[55] Similar results in Treadwell (2011: 104–5), based on formulae proposed in Esty (2006). These results apply, however, only to the years with the most robust data. The modified formula proposed in Esty (2011) has minimal bearing on these results given the high average number of coins per die in the samples; cf. Esty (2011: 44): 'If the mean number of coins per observed die is high enough, all the individual die-frequency probabilities are low, including the chance there remains an unobserved die.'

It seems safe, therefore, to assume that each of the five main Samanid mints (those listed in Table 12.2 plus Nishapur) used no more than *c.* 35–50 dies per year.[56] If we add another couple of dozen dies for minor mints, we arrive at a total of 200–300 dies per year for the entire Samanid realm. Assuming die productivity of 10,000 coins, this translates into *c.* 2–3 million dirhams per year. This is consistent with the output of an exceptionally rich silver mine in Yemen, reputed to provide the equivalent of one million dirhams per year.[57] The Samanids, who were supplied by several productive mines (the geographers list in the first place those of the Panjshir valley and the Ilaq, near Chach),[58] and probably reminted some of the coinage in circulation, could certainly afford to strike a couple million coins each year. Narshakhi's indication that 'the tax of Bukhara in olden times was 200,000 silver dirhams, or a little less' similarly locates the revenues of the Samanid state in the order of millions of dirhams.[59] But not tens of millions, despite the optimistic evaluation of the fiscal revenue of the Samanid state in the AD 960s by the geographer Ibn Hawqal, whose figure—40 million dirhams per year—should be taken to illustrate his glowing description of central Asia under the Samanids rather than to represent a realistic assessment of their budget.[60]

If we now return to our earlier proposition that as much as a quarter of the Samanid output was exported northwards, the range resulting from our assessment of their monetary production, *c.* 500–750 thousand coins per year, coincides rather well with the range estimated above on a different basis, that of the number of surviving coins per die. But even if it is reassuring to see the above back-of-the-envelope calculations converge, we should not press these figures too closely. They are only meant to give a sense of the orders of magnitude involved in the northern trade: hundreds of thousands dirhams of annual flows in the best years, a high survival ratio in excess of 1%, and the depletion of at least a quarter of the Samanid monetary stock. This final point—of which at least the inhabitants of Bukhara would have been acutely aware—probably explains the steady decline in the number of exported dirhams after AH 300 (AD 912/3), a decline only temporarily stemmed by the reminting of Volga Bulgar silver reserves as dirham imitations. Trade ground to a halt once these were exhausted, around the mid-tenth century. The decline in trade with the north thus precedes the debasement of the Samanid dirhams, which

[56] Similar, even if slightly lower, estimates in Treadwell (2011: 32–4).

[57] Al-Hamdani in Dunlop (1957: 41–2).

[58] Ibn Hawqal in Kramers and Wiet (1964: 447, 487); Dunlop (1957: 40–1).

[59] Narshakhi in Frye (1954: 36). The examples of tributes collected by the Ghaznavids, the successors of the Samanids in central Asia, in the early eleventh century listed in Noonan (2000–1: 207–9) also mostly fall in the order of hundreds of thousands or low millions of dirhams.

[60] Ibn Hawqal in Kramers and Wiet (1964: 451).

maintained a fineness of over 90% until the AH 320s (AD 930s) and over 75% until the AH 360s (AD 970s).[61]

Even if it is difficult to imagine that trade with the north did not bring profits to central Asian merchants, they do not seem to have actively fostered it. The Samanid demand for the slaves and furs acquired from the Scandinavians must have played a secondary role: these luxury goods could be dispensed with, or at least easily substituted with furs from other parts of the taiga and tundra, and slaves from other parts of the surrounding world, in particular, in the case of the Samanids, from the Turkic tribes of the steppe.[62] What could not be substituted, from the perspective of Scandinavian and Slavic elites, was the Samanid silver. The decision of Isma'il b. Ahmad to start minting large quantities of dirhams in AD 893, no doubt justified in part by his willingness to broadcast a legitimacy freshly granted to him by the Abbasid caliph, thus opened a window of opportunity that the Scandinavians were quick to exploit.[63] It is to their seemingly unlimited appetite for silver that we now need to turn.

WHY SO MANY?

Even if silver is mentioned, in various forms and functions, in a number of early medieval texts from northern Europe, it is the finds themselves that are the main, and still largely untapped, source of information about its use and purpose. As we have seen, the quasi-totality of dirhams comes from hoards, with other finds from the *emporia*, settlements, winter camps,[64] and funerary contexts accounting for *c.* 1% of the total. This pattern, although affected by modern legislation on metal detecting, particularly restrictive in Sweden, less so in Russia and Poland, and even less in Denmark and England, is unlikely to be radically distorted.

What can we, then, learn from the hoarding patterns? When information on the circumstances of their discovery is available, hoards appear to have usually been stored in receptacles such as clay pots, wooden boxes, textile wrappings, or leather pouches, that were in turn usually placed in or near dwellings, or next to prominent landmarks such as free-standing stones or significant burials. They

[61] Based on data published in Ilisch *et al.* (2003).

[62] See, e.g., the autobiographical account of Sebüktegin, the founder of the Ghaznavid dynasty, in Nazim (1933).

[63] Noonan (2000–1: 156–7).

[64] See Hadley and Richards (2016: 43) for finds from the winter camp at Torksey (Lincolnshire, England), which, among 350 coins, included 124 dirhams. For the quantities of dirhams from the *emporia*, see above, n. 3.

were thus meant to be protected from the elements and, in the vast majority of cases, to be retrieved.[65]

The case of Gotland is again instructive. The academic debate concentrated here on the relation between the hoards and the farmsteads, a matter complicated, as we have seen, by the low visibility of the latter.[66] Such excavations as were carried out at the findspots of the hoards revealed, in roughly half of the cases, post holes, hearths, or other traces of buildings; the remainder, where no significant context was detected, is difficult to interpret due to the usually very restricted area of the excavations.[67] This image is now confirmed by the more systematically excavated island of Bornholm, where the connection between hoards and habitations seems to be the norm.[68] Even if no general rule will describe the diversity of individual situations, it is at least manifest that coin deposits that were not meant to be recovered—such as coins scattered in moors or in other contexts interpreted as 'ritual'—are a marginal phenomenon.

That most Gotlandic hoards were seemingly stored in pots and kept in houses is not unrelated to the long chronological spans of many of them, suggesting that they were accumulated over several generations.[69] Such finds make one think not so much of merchants ploughing the seas on business as of expeditions undertaken once in a generation with the purpose of acquiring wealth specifically in the form of silver coins. We can extrapolate from the broader logic of the dirham trade that these expeditions consisted in acquiring captives somewhere on the southern or eastern shore of the Baltic, transporting them to Volga Bulgaria or one of the emerging urban centres in Rus, and selling them for dirhams.

So why did the Gotlanders, and no doubt other Scandinavians living on the Baltic Sea, undertake such journeys? And why did they store the wealth acquired overseas instead of using it in ways that would seem more rational to us? A study of the 231 instances of the use of the word 'silver' (*silfr*) in the sagas of Icelanders (*Íslendingasögur*) suggested to its authors that 'silver had internal, socio-strategic functions that exceeded its function as payment for goods or services. This entailed legal contexts where silver circulated as weregeld and other expenses, all within the context of the blood feud'.[70] Indeed, mentions of silver referring to wergild, the blood money customarily paid at an assembly (*thing*) as compensatory damages for killing someone, or other fines and penalties,

[65] See Gruszczyński (2019: 68–73, 132–5, 183–8) for data on Gotland, Pomerania, and Svealand; I do not follow him, however, in interpreting the hoards for which no data are available as containerless.

[66] See papers in Gruszczyński, Jankowiak, and Shepard (2021); the foundational study is Östergren (1989).

[67] Gruszczyński (2019: 38–42); Östergren (2021).

[68] Ingvardson and Nielsen (2015: 29–30); Ingvardson (2021).

[69] Odebäck (2009).

[70] Ekengren and Domeij Lundborg (2015: 25).

outnumber by far those related to payments or different forms in which silver was stored (hoards, jewellery, or other objects). Even if this picture needs to be corrected for the late date of the composition of the sagas and the near absence of finds of coins in Viking Age Iceland,[71] it is consistent with the emphasis of the Gotlandic customary law, the *Guta lag*, compiled probably in the early thirteenth century, on the monetary value of the penalties, from the wergild to the penalty for drinking more than three toasts to the in-laws at a wedding.[72] It also fits with the Icelandic sagas that the largest concentration of stray coins and weights was found on the site of the Gotlandic *thing* in Roma in the centre of the island.[73]

But the framework of socially significant transactions needs to be expanded by one that tends to remain below the radar of the texts despite—or because of—its prevalence: marriage. The importance of the dowry brought by the bride and of the bride price paid to her by the groom is confirmed by the elaborate regulations of the *Guta lag* on the property of married women—or, more precisely, the property of her family brought by her into the marriage—and its inheritance.[74] Transactions related to marriage, as well as the separation of the property of the two families maintained after it, must have encouraged the development of a standardized form of portable wealth that could be easily brought into, and withdrawn from, family alliances. Keeping in mind that silver also served a number of other purposes, such as display of status or paying off younger siblings, but less so land transactions given the regulations of the *Guta lag* discouraging the alienation or division of farmsteads,[75] it can be seen how it came to play an essential social function as soon as it became available in sufficient quantities.

It is not necessary, then, to draw a sharp distinction between 'monetary' and 'non-monetary' uses of silver. Evidence for a monetary economy in tenth-century northern Europe is scarce outside the *emporia* and winter camps: coins do not seem to have been used in everyday transactions, and the debates whether they were weighed or counted—the latter often being interpreted as an indication of a monetary economy—have not led to clear conclusions.[76] But silver became an essential tool for certain types of transactions in which its quantity mattered,

[71] Mehler and Gardiner (2021); see also Gullbekk (2011).

[72] See the excellent translation and commentary of the *Guta lag* in Peel (2009), in particular pp. xxxvi–xl (date), 19–20 (wergild), 56 (toasts), and 201–14 (summary of monetary penalties).

[73] Östergren and Gustafsson (2018) speak of 285 coins and 429 weights.

[74] Kilger (2021: 248–50), with reference to Peel (2009: 26–30, 113–24); earlier also Burström (1993).

[75] Peel (2009: 27, 113) on younger siblings, and (2009: 41–3, 148–52) on restrictions on the alienation of land.

[76] See, e.g., Jonsson (2011) for the view that tenth-century Sweden was evolving towards a monetary economy, and, *a contrario*, Blomkvist (2005: 235) for the view that 'one reason for hoarding so much silver in the Viking Age . . . could have been that there was little else one could do with it'.

whether it was weighed or counted, in a similar fashion to the inhabitants of Bukhara insisting, much to Ibn Fadlan's surprise, on using copper-alloy coins in preference to dirhams.

Such patterns, deduced from the exceptionally dense concentrations of dirham hoards on the Baltic islands, do not exhaustively describe the reasons for the accumulation and hoarding of the Islamic silver. Some hoards were lost—no doubt often in dramatic circumstances—on their way northwards; they throw a particularly helpful light on the composition of the flow of dirhams. Others reflect the growing concentration of wealth in the hands of emerging warrior elites that were establishing territorial control over areas that were soon to crystallize into early state structures. But even there some of the patterns described above can often be recognized.

This is the case with the third largest cluster of dirham hoards after Gotland and Bornholm: the core area of the future Polish state in Greater Poland. A recent catalogue lists 75 hoards that contained dirhams, of which around 50–60 can be attributed to the tenth century.[77] Uncertainty is due to the unusually high degree of fragmentation of the coins, probably resulting from Greater Poland's position at the very end of the trade routes; by the same token, however, the same area can be recognized as the supplier of the main commodity monetized for dirhams, slaves.[78] This was a violent business; it correlates with a much greater militarization of society than in Gotland and with the emergence of a hierarchy of fortified sites—ranging from central places to small garrisons—that characterizes the settlement structure of Greater Poland. It is within the radius of several kilometres from such sites, but rarely inside them, that the most prominent hoards were found, often among traces of buildings, indicating perhaps the location of elite dwellings just outside the fortifications.[79] Similarly to Gotland, due to the usually limited scope of excavations of the findspots, the absence of a clear archaeological context can only exceptionally be taken as an indication of their burial outside settlements. Despite a different social structure, the patterns of hoarding in Greater Poland are thus reminiscent of those of the Baltic islands: dirhams were used by jars not by units, were kept in receptacles clearly with the intention of retrieval, and were probably stored in houses. The implication that they were also used for similar purposes is confirmed by the account of the Spanish traveller Ibrahim ibn Ya'qub, who visited central Europe in the AD 960s:

> As for the country of [the Polish duke] Mieszko, it is the most extensive of their countries.... His taxes are levied in *mathaqil al-marqatiyya*,[80] and they are used to pay the monthly salaries of his men, each of whom receives a fixed number.

[77] *FMP* I, summary tables at pp. 810–19. [78] Jankowiak (2019).

[79] See Andrałojć *et al.* (2011) for archaeological contexts of the finds.

[80] The meaning of this is controversial, but hacksilver is probably meant.

> He has 3,000 shield-bearers.... The men are given clothing and horses and weapons and everything they require. If one of them has a child, he is immediately assigned an allowance, whether it is male or female. When it grows up, if it is male, he provides for its marriage and gives a dowry to the father of the girl. If it is female, he has congress with her and gives a donation to her father. Dowries are very important to the Saqaliba, and their customs concerning them are like those of the Berbers.[81]

In addition to dowries, dirhams were thus used to pay the military following (*druzhina*) of the ruler, taking on a more political role than on the Baltic islands. But despite the increasingly diversified use of silver in northern Europe, it still had a common origin, the trade in slaves and furs, and eventually a common fate—abandonment in the soil.

Why, then, were the silver hoards not retrieved? The answer is relatively straightforward for Greater Poland: the abrupt collapse of the first Polish state around AD 1034–9, the result of lost wars with neighbours and of the deportation of the surviving elite by the Czech duke Břetislav,[82] sealed them in the ground. The drastic decrease in population, now confirmed by palaeoenvironmental data,[83] meant that in many cases no one was left to recover the buried wealth. As no such traumatic event is recorded in Gotland, the non-recovery of the hoards there is due to more drawn-out processes. Hoarding, now mostly of German and Anglo-Saxon coins, continued on the island throughout the eleventh century and gradually stopped in the early twelfth. This change did not coincide with any perceptible political or social evolution, nor with the development of a monetary economy. Quite the opposite: finds of silver become so rare as to suggest that it lost its relevance, and the old reserves deposited in the basements of the Gotlandic farmsteads fell into oblivion. Several factors may explain why the Gotlandic farmers shunned silver. Large-scale slave trading in the Baltic, still attested in the early twelfth century,[84] appears to have come to an end with the emergence of the merchant network centred on Lübeck that later developed into the Hanse and was driven by a different logic. In a related development, Christianization affected the attitudes not only towards slavery but also, more broadly, towards marriage, inheritance, and conflict resolution, limiting the need for dowries and wergild. Finally, increasing political centralization resulted in an increased control by newly formed states over monetary circulation.[85] How precisely these evolutions affected the use of silver remains, however, a matter for future research.

[81] Ibrahim ibn Yaʿqub in Lunde and Stone (2012: 165–6).
[82] Described in the chronicle of Cosmas of Prague, ii.2–5, in Wolverton (2009: 111–20).
[83] Izdebski, Czerwiński, and Jankowiak (2025).
[84] See, e.g., Gallus Anonymus, ii.35, in Knoll and Schaer (2003: 183).
[85] See Blomkvist (2005) on many of these processes.

CONCLUSION

The image sketched above cannot pretend to cover the full range of attitudes towards silver in an area as vast as that of dirham hoarding. But it may perhaps go some way towards explaining not only the extraordinary lengths to which the Scandinavians went to obtain silver but also the reasons why so much of it remained apparently 'unused' in the ground. It also allows a couple of general observations. It was, in the last resort, a favourable conjunction of circumstances such as the availability of silver and political stability in the Islamic world, the absence of significant movements of nomads in the steppe, and the Scandinavian settlement in Rus that created the conditions for the inflow of dirhams to northern Europe in the ninth and tenth centuries. Similar episodes spanned most of the first millennium AD: whenever they were available in larger quantities, silver and, to a smaller extent, gold coins were brought back to the north by warriors raiding the Roman Empire, mercenaries serving the late antique emperors, or slave hunters trading with the Islamic world. Once back home, they used them to compete for brides, status, and power. It was only the advent of Christianity that decisively changed the parameters of this competition. This is no doubt why so many dirhams, the bulk of the final wave of silver coins to reach northern Europe, remained in the ground.

ABBREVIATIONS

CNS *Corpus nummorum saeculorum IX–XI qui in Suecia reperti sunt.* (9 vols, 1975–2010). Stockholm.

FMP Bogucki, M., Ilisch, P., and Suchodolski, S. (eds). *Frühmittelalterliche Münzfunde aus Polen. Inventar.* (5 vols, 2013–17). Warsaw.

VNK *Vserossiiskaia numizmaticheskaia konfenrentsiia.* (21 vols to date, 1993–).

REFERENCES

Andrałojć, M., Andrałojć, M., Silska, P., and Szyngiera, P. (2011). *Odkrycia skarbów wczesnośredniowiecznych z terenu Wielkopolski. Kontekst archeologiczny znalezisk.* Poznań.

Biermann, F. and Jankowiak, M. (eds) (2021). *The Archaeology of Slavery in Early Medieval Northern Europe: The Invisible Commodity.* Cham.

Blackburn, M. (2008). 'The coin-finds', in D. Skre (ed.), *Means of Exchange: Dealing with Silver in the Viking Age.* Aarhus, 29–74.

Blomkvist, N. (2005). *The Discovery of the Baltic: The Reception of a Catholic World-System in the European North (AD 1075–1225)*. Leiden.

Brather, S. (1995–6). 'Frühmittelalterliche Dirham-Schatzfunde in Europa. Probleme ihrer wirtschaftsgeschichtlichen Interpretation aus archäologischer Perspektive', *Zeitschrift für Archäologie des Mittelalters* 23–4: 73–153.

Bursche, A., Dymowski, A., and Myzgin, K. (2025). 'Roman imperial silver coins, their imitations and copies in Barbaricum', in F. Hunter, A. Dymowski, and D. Dzierzbicka (eds), *Denarii beyond the Empire: Political and Cultural Perspectives on Roman Silver Coins in Barbaricum*. Turnhout, 19–50.

Burström, M. (1993). 'Silver as bridewealth: An interpretation of Viking Age silver hoards on Gotland', *Current Swedish Archaeology* 1: 33–7.

Ducène, J. (2018). *L'Europe et les géographes arabes du Moyen Âge (IXe–XVe siècle)*. Paris.

Dunlop, D. M. (1957). 'Sources of gold and silver in Islam according to al-Hamdānī (10th century A. D.)', *Studia Islamica* 8: 29–49.

Dymowski, A. (2020). 'Roman imperial hoards of denarii from Barbaricum', *Journal of Ancient History and Archaeology* 7.1: 193–243.

Ekengren, F. and Domeij Lundborg, M. (2015). 'The social weight of silver in the Íslendingasögur and the Viking Age hoards', in L. Larsson, F. Ekengren, B. Helgesson, and B. Söderberg (eds), *Small Things—Wide Horizons: Studies in Honour of Birgitta Hårdh*. Oxford, 20–6.

Esty, W. W. (2006). 'How to estimate the original number of dies and the coverage of a sample', *Numismatic Chronicle* 166: 359–64.

Esty, W. W. (2011). 'The geometric model for estimating the number of dies', in F. de Callataÿ (ed.), *Quantifying Monetary Supplies in Greco-Roman Times* (Pragmateiai 19). Bari, 43–58.

Fraehn, C. M. (1842). 'Topographische Uebersicht der Ausgrabungen von altem Arabischen Gelde in Rußland, nebst chronologischer und geographischer Bestimmung des Inhalts der verschiedenen Funde', *Bulletin scientifique publié par l'Académie impériale des sciences de Saint-Pétersbourg* 9: 301–32.

Frye, R. N. (1954). *The History of Bukhara. Translated from a Persian Abridgment of the Arabic Original by Narshakhī*. Cambridge, MA.

Gomzin, A. A. (2013). *Vostochnoe monetnoe serebro IX—nachala XI v. v Srednem i Nizhnem Pooch'e*. PhD thesis, Institute of Archaeology, Russian Academy of Sciences.

Granberg, B. (1966). *Förteckning över kufiska myntfynd i Finland*. Helsinki.

Gruszczyński, J. (2019). *Silver, Hoards and Containers: The Archaeological and Historical Context of Silver Deposits in the Baltic c. 800–1050*. Abingdon.

Gruszczyński, J. (2021). 'Hoards, silver, context and the Gotlandic alternative', in Gruszczyński, Jankowiak, and Shepard (2021), 187–207.

Gruszczyński, J., Jankowiak, M., and Shepard, J. (eds) (2021). *Viking Age Trade: Silver, Slaves and Gotland*. Abingdon.

Gullbekk, S. E. (2011), 'Money and its use in the Saga society: Silver, coins and commodity money', in S. Sigmundsson (ed.), *Viking Settlements and Viking Society*. Reykjavik, 176–88.

Hadley, D. M. and Richards, J. D. (2016). 'The winter camp of the Viking Great Army, AD 872–3, Torksey, Lincolnshire', *Antiquaries Journal* 96: 23–67.

Hārūn, ʿAbd al-Salām Muḥammad (ed.) (1966–9). *Al-Jāḥiẓ, Kitab al-hayawan*. Misr.

Hatz, G. (1974). *Handel und Verkehr zwischen dem deutschen Reich und Schweden in der späten Wikingerzeit : die deutschen Münzen des 10. und 11. Jahrhunderts in Schweden*. Stockholm.

Hilberg, V. (2011). 'Silver economies of the ninth and tenth centuries AD in Hedeby', in J. Graham-Campbell, S. Sindbæk, and G. Williams (eds), *Silver Economies, Monetisation and Society in Scandinavia, AD 800–1100*. Aarhus, 203–25.

Ilisch, L., Lorenz, S., Stern, W. B., and Steuer, H. (2003). *Dirham und Rappenpfennig: mittelalterliche Münzprägung in Bergbauregionen*. Bonn.

Ingvardson, G. T. (2021). 'Silver hoarding in the Danish island of Bornholm and in Gotland: Hoards as windows onto Viking Age life', in Gruszczyński, Jankowiak, and Shepard (2021), 358–76.

Ingvardson, G. T. and Nielsen, F. O. S. (2015). '100 Viking Age hoards of Bornholm: Status, challenges and perspectives', in L. Larsson, F. Ekengren, B. Helgesson, and B. Söderberg (eds), *Small Things—Wide Horizons: Studies in Honour of Birgitta Hårdh*. Oxford: 27–34.

Izdebski, A., Czerwiński, S., Jankowiak, M. *et al.* (2025). 'Unbalanced social-ecological acceleration led to state formation failure in early medieval Poland', *Proceedings of the National Academy of Sciences U.S.A.* 122 (18) e2409056122.

Jankowiak, M. (2019). 'Silver fragmentation: reinterpreting the evidence of the hoards', in J. Kershaw and G. Williams (eds), *Silver, Butter, Cloth: Monetary and Social Economies in the Viking Age*. Oxford, 15–31.

Jankowiak, M. (2021a). 'Dirham flows into northern and eastern Europe and the rhythms of the slave trade with the Islamic world', in Gruszczyński, Jankowiak, and Shepard (2021), 105–31.

Jankowiak, M. (2021b). 'Classifying and interpreting Viking Age dirham imitations', *Nordisk numismatisk årsskrift* ny serie 2: 53–76.

Jankowiak, M. (2023). 'Volga Bulgar imitative coinage', in Shepard and Treadwell (2023), 315–57.

Jankowiak, M. (2024). 'Replacing the Silk Road? Central Asian merchants between China and Scandinavia, 840–1000 CE', in J. Henderson, S. Morgan, and M. Salonia (eds), *Reimagining the Silk Roads: Interactions and Perceptions Across Eurasia*. London, 199–210.

Jonsson, E. (2021). 'Metalldetektering och de nya vikingatida myntskatterna i Sverige åren 2005-2017 - en översikt', *Svensk Numismatisk Tidskrift* 2021.5: 109–13.

Jonsson, K. (2011). 'Sweden in the tenth century: A monetary economy?', in J. Graham-Campbell, S. Sindbaek, and G. Williams (eds), *Silver Economies, Monetisation and Society in Scandinavia, AD 800–1100*. Aarhus, 245–57.

Jonsson, K. (2015). 'Viking Age coins found in Sweden', in L. Larsson, F. Ekengren, B. Helgesson, and B. Söderberg (eds), *Small Things—Wide Horizons: Studies in Honour of Birgitta Hårdh*. Oxford, 51–7.

Kilger, C. (2021). 'Silver hoards and society on Viking Age Gotland: Some thoughts on the relationship between silver, long-distance trade and local communities', in Gruszczyński, Jankowiak, and Shepard (2021), 242–54.

Knoll, P. W. and Schaer, F. (2003). *Gesta principum Polonorum: The Deeds of the Princes of the Poles*. Budapest.

Kovalev, R. K. (2001). 'Bibliography of Thomas S. Noonan', *Russian History/Histoire russe* 28: 7–16.

Kovalev, R. K. and Kaelin, A. C. (2007). 'Circulation of Arab silver in medieval Afro-Eurasia: Preliminary observations', *History Compass* 5: 560–80.

Kramers, J. H. and Wiet, G. (1964). *Ibn Hauqal. Configuration de la terre (Kitab surat al-ard)*. (2 vols). Paris.

Kuleshov, V. S. (2019). *Pis'mennye i numizmaticheskie istochniki po istorii denezhnogo obrashcheniia v Vostochnoi Evrope v IX–XI vv*. PhD thesis, Russian State University for the Humanities, Moscow.

Lebedev, V. P. (2021). 'Hoards with tenth-century dirhams found or published in eastern Europe in 1990–2014', *Rus' · Lithuania · Horde. Journal of numismatics and sigillography* 9: 14–42.

Leimus, I. (2007). *Sylloge of Islamic Coins: Estonian Public Collections*. Tallinn.

Lewicki, T. (1956). *Źródła arabskie do dziejów Słowiańszczyzny*, vol. 1. Wrocław and Krakow.

Lowick, N. M. and Nisbet, J. D. F. (1968). 'A hoard of dirhems from Ra's al-Khaimah', *Numismatic Chronicle* 8: 231–40.

Lunde, P. and Stone, C. (2012). *Ibn Fadlān and the Land of Darkness: Arab Travellers in the Far North*. London.

Markov, A. K. (1910). *Topografiia kladov vostochnykh monet, sasanidskikh i kuficheskikh*. St Petersburg.

Mehler, N. and Gardiner, M. (2021). 'Coinless exchange and foreign merchants in medieval Iceland (AD 900–1600)', in L. Rahmstorf, G. Barjamovic, and N. Ialongo (eds), *Merchants, Measures and Money: Understanding Technologies of Early Trade in a Comparative Perspective*. Göttingen, 35–54.

Miquel, A. (1967–88). *La géographie humaine du monde musulman jusqu'au milieu du 11e siècle*. (4 vols). Paris.

Mishin, D. E. (2002). *Sakaliba (slaviane) v islamskom mire v rannee srednevekov'e*. Moscow.

Nazim, M. (1933). 'The *Pand-Nāmah* of Subuktigīn', *Journal of the Royal Asiatic Society of Great Britain and Ireland* 1933.3: 605–28.

Noonan, T. S. (1990). 'Dirham exports to the Baltic in the Viking Age: some preliminary observations', in K. Jonsson and B. Malmer (eds), *Sigtuna Papers: Proceedings of the Sigtuna Symposium on Viking Age Coinage*. London, 251–7.

Noonan, T. S. (2000–1). 'Volga Bulghāria's tenth-century trade with Sāmānid Central Asia', *Archivum Eurasiae medii aevi* 11: 140–218.

Odebäck, K. (2009), 'Familje- och släktskatter under äldre vikingatid', *Myntstudier* 2009.2: 9–25.

Östergren, M. (1989). *Mellan stengrund och stenhus: Gotlands vikingatida silverskatter som boplatsindikation*. Stockholm.

Östergren, M. (2015). 'An unlikely story – About looting, trials and Viking Age silver treasures on Gotland', in T. Talvio and M. Wijk (eds), *Myntstudier. Festskrift till Kenneth Jonsson*. Stockholm, 26–38.

Östergren, M. (2021). 'Hoards and their archaeological context: Three case studies from Gotland', in Gruszczyński, Jankowiak, and Shepard (2021), 208–24.

Östergren, M. and Gustafsson, N. B. (2018). 'Landets hjärta – Gutnaltinget i Roma. Nytt ljus över Gutnaltinget', *Gotländskt arkiv* 90: 60–75.

Peel, C. (2009). *Guta Lag: The Law of the Gotlanders*. London.

Pettersson, A.-M. (ed.) (2009). *The Spillings Hoard: Gotland's Role in Viking Age World Trade*. Visby.

Rispling, G. (2005). 'Osteuropäische Nachahmungen islamischer Münzen', in T. Mayer (ed.), *Sylloge der Münzen des Kaukasus und Osteuropas im Orientalischen Münzkabinett Jena*. Wiesbaden, 172–225.

Rispling, G., Blackburn, M., and Jonsson, K. (2008). 'Catalogue of the coins', in D. Skre (ed.), *Means of Exchange: Dealing with Silver in the Viking Age*. Aarhus, 75–93.

Rispling, G., Jankowiak, M., and Treadwell, L. (in preparation), *Catalogue of Dirham Imitations from Northern European Viking Age Finds*. Stockholm.

Shepard, J. and Treadwell, L. (eds) (2023). *Muslims on the Volga in the Viking Age: Diplomacy and Islam in the World of Ibn Fadlan*. London.

Siltberg, T. (2012). 'The conception of an egalitarian Gotlandic peasant society', in M. Scholz, R. Bohn, and C. Johansson (eds), *The Image of the Baltic: A Festschrift for Nils Blomkvist*. Visby, 302–27.

Svedjemo, G. (2014). *Landscape Dynamics: Spatial Analyses of Villages and Farms on Gotland AD 200–1700*. Uppsala.

Svedjemo, G. (2021). 'Social structures and landscape. Gotland's silver hoards in the context of settlements', in Gruszczyński, Jankowiak, and Shepard (2021), 291–310.

Talvio, T. (2002). *Coins and Coin Finds in Finland, AD 800–1200*. Helsinki.

Treadwell, L. (2011). *Craftsmen and Coins: Signed Dies in the Iranian World (Third to the Fifth Centuries AH)* (Denkschriften. Österreichische Akademie der Wissenschaften. Philosophisch-Historische Klasse 423). Vienna.

Widerström, P. (2021). 'Was there life before death? The Viking settlements on Gotland', in Gruszczyński, Jankowiak, and Shepard (2021), 271–90.

Wienberg, J. (2004). 'Medieval Gotland: Churches, chronologies and crusades', in J. Staecker (ed.), *The European Frontier: Clashes and Compromises in the Middle Ages*. Lund, 285–98.

Wolverton, L. (2009). *Cosmas of Prague, The Chronicle of the Czechs*. Washington, DC.

Marek Jankowiak, *Viking Age Dirham Hoards in Northern Europe: Why So Many?* In: *Roman Coin Hoards Across Frontiers*. Edited by: Benjamin D. R. Hellings, Marguerite Spoerri Butcher, and Chris Howgego, Oxford University Press.
 DOI: 10.1093/9780198986478.003.0012

13

Chemical Evidence for the Recycling of Roman Gold in the Kushan Empire

George A. Green

INTRODUCTION

The most straightforward evidence for Roman coins crossing the frontiers of the empire is the presence of Roman coins in non-Roman contexts. The greater the number of these finds, the stronger the positive case that can be made for the flow of coinage across Rome's borders into the economies of its neighbours. Does the relative absence of such evidence in certain regions, however, necessarily provide evidence for the absence of any significant flow of Roman coins to these areas? The further away from the Roman Empire, the more reasonable this assumption becomes. But when we are dealing with regions much closer to Rome, where contact and trade are almost certainly occurring, this assumption becomes much riskier. The idea that Roman coin finds are rare, not because they were never circulating there but because they were being melted down and recycled into local objects, becomes much more attractive. Such remelting and recycling will be essentially invisible in the material record but may be able to be detected in the chemical composition of these objects. It has long been claimed that finds of Roman gold are rare in the Kushan Empire because they were melted down to strike local coins. The chemical evidence for this will be investigated here.

The Kushan Empire—at its height covering large swathes of modern-day Uzbekistan, Tajikistan, Turkmenistan, Afghanistan, Pakistan, and northern India—produced its first gold coinages under Wima Kadphises, who reigned from *c.* AD 113 to 127.[1] These gold coins were initially struck under Wima Kadphises at a very high purity and a weight standard that was similar to the contemporary Roman *aureus*, which explains why it is has been thought worth investigating links with Rome. Indeed, we have good evidence for peer-polity interactions and 'numismatic contact' between the Roman and Kushan Empires.

[1] Benjamin (2018: 176–7); Jongeward, Cribb, and Donovan (2015). All dates and attributions for Kushan coins follow this work. Typologies follow Göbl (1984).

Bronze issues produced by Kajula Kadphises (*c.* AD 50–90) seem to have 'Augustus-like' portraits on the obverse;[2] graves in the burial mounds at Tillya-Tepe in Afghanistan contained an *aureus* of Tiberius alongside an obol struck under Kajula Kadphises,[3] with some 20,000 other gold, silver, bronze, iron, and ivory objects that displayed a range of artistic influences from the Greco-Roman, Chinese, Bactrian, and Indian 'worlds';[4] a *sestertius* of Nero was found alongside coins of Wima Kadphises at the Khairabad-tepe site in Uzbekistan;[5] *aurei* struck under Domitian, Trajan, and Hadrian were found alongside gold coins of Wima Kadphises, Kanishka I, and Huvishka at the Ahin Posh Buddhist monastery site near Jalalabad in Afghanistan;[6] the influence of Roman art on Gandharan art under the Kushan Empire is well established;[7] and the Begram treasure, found in storerooms in the 'New Royal City' site, contained Roman glassware and bronzes, alongside Indian ivories and Chinese silks.[8]

It is understandable, then, why an early hypothesis for the source of Kushan gold was the use of recycled Roman *aurei*.[9] However, we must also agree with Robert Bracey that some of the contemporary impetus behind this hypothesis came from a place of 'orientalism' or 'eurocentrism':[10] one must have relatively low expectations of the Kushan Empire to assume that they were incapable of exploiting local gold sources. More recently, it has been shown that the concentration of platinum in Kushan gold coinages so greatly exceeds that of Julio-Claudian *aurei* that it is impossible for them to be the *exclusive* source of Kushan gold.[11] One stresses 'exclusive' here as these results should not be used by numismatists to argue that there is 'scientific proof' that there was *no* use of recycled Roman gold at all. While we must avoid the 'orientalism' of the past, there is surely also a degree of 'low expectations' in happily assuming that the Kushan metal supply network did not make use of the complex trading connections it had expended so much effort in building and maintaining. As such, a mixture of recycled Roman and locally exploited gold is a plausible hypothesis. With all this in mind, the intention here is to investigate the hypothesis that Roman gold, while not the exclusive or even dominant source of gold, was recycled in appreciable quantities to strike Kushan gold coins.

Two chemical datasets are used to investigate this claim. In both cases the chemical data were collected by the author using the same laser ablation inductively coupled plasma mass spectrometry (LA-ICP-MS) and handheld X-ray fluorescence (XRF) equipment. The Roman dataset was collected as part of the Gold Coinage in the Roman World project, a collaboration between the Ashmolean

[2] Jongeward, Cribb, and Donovan (2015: nos 103–8).
[3] Bracey (2017: 28); Errington (2017: 213).
[4] Sarianidi (1980).
[5] Azarpay (1970); Rtveladze (1994: 252).
[6] Errington (2017).
[7] Rosenfield (1967); Zwalf (1996); Jongeward (2003); Behrendt (2007: 11–14, 36, 48).
[8] Benjamin (2018: 201).
[9] Göbl (1960: 79); Thorley (1979: 185).
[10] Bracey (2017: 28).
[11] Blet-Lemarquand (2006).

Museum in Oxford and the University of Warwick.[12] Here the data from 159 Roman *aurei* dating between AD 50 and 227 from the Ashmolean Museum are presented. The Kushan dataset was collected as part of the Determining the Flow of Gold across Ancient Asia, Africa, and Europe project at the Ashmolean Museum.[13] Here the data from 37 Kushan gold coins from the reigns of Wima Kadphises (*c.* AD 113–27) to Vasishka (*c.* AD 247–65) held by the Ashmolean Museum are presented.

Three things will be shown here. First, the finding of Maryse Blet-Lemarquand that Roman gold was not the exclusive source of Kushan gold still holds when Kushan gold is compared with *aurei* from AD 50 to 227.[14] Second, that at its inception Kushan gold seems to have been almost exclusively minted from 'local'—or at least 'non-western'—sources, although some recycling of Roman material can perhaps be detected. Third, that from Huvishka onwards (*c.* AD 151–90) Kushan gold appears to be significantly 'diluted' by metal that has a low platinum-to-palladium ratio (Pt:Pd), with the presence/absence of other elements suggesting that the recycling of Roman gold is the most plausible explanation for this.

LA-ICP-MS METHODOLOGY

The LA-ICP-MS measurements were conducted on a Perkin Elmer NexION quadrupole mass spectrometer coupled to a New Wave Research UP213 Nd:YAG laser at the University of Oxford's Department of Earth Sciences. This technique ablates an almost imperceptibly small quantity of metal from the edge of the coin using a laser, and the resulting aerosol is pulled through a plasma torch—which ionizes the atoms in the sample—and is then accelerated through a mass spectrometer. The quadrupole filters the ions by their mass-to-charge ratio, their intensities are recorded when they hit the detector, and plotting the two against each other produces a mass spectrum from which the relative abundances of the various elements in the sample can be calculated. This allows for part per million levels of precision (1 ppm = 0.0001%).[15]

The Roman and Kushan data were collected under the same protocol as outlined in Green and Smythe,[16] using a NIST 610 glass standard as the primary calibration standard. It is necessary to check the efficacy of this calibration due to the

[12] Green (2021); Green and Smythe (2021). This project was funded through the Arts and Humanities Research Council (AHRC) Collaborative Doctoral Partnership Scheme.

[13] https://www.ashmolean.org/determining-flow-of-gold (accessed 27 March 2023). This project was funded through a Leverhulme Trust Early Career Fellowship (ECF-2020-211).

[14] Blet-Lemarquand (2006).

[15] A fuller methodological description can be found in Green and Smythe (2021).

[16] Green and Smythe (2021).

potential for matrix effects—the ablation, and how trace elements respond to that ablation, will be different in silicates and gold—and the fact that the concentration of elements in NIST 610 is orders of magnitude greater or lesser than the 'unknowns' seen in ancient gold coinages.[17] To do this, two gold certified reference materials (CMRs) distributed by the London Bullion Market Association under the names AuRM4 and AuRM5 have been used.[18] These standards are pure gold blocks doped with known quantities of various trace elements commonly seen in gold, at concentrations that generally match those found in ancient gold coinages. Furthermore, two 'in-house reference materials' were used to check the efficacy of the platinum and palladium calibrations. The first is a gold fragment analysed by LA-ICP-MC-MS at the Centre National de la Recherche Scientifique, Orléans, France;[19] and the second is an *aureus* of Domitian that has been destructively sampled and analysed by flow injection-ICP-MS at Oxford's Department of Earth Sciences.[20] Measuring these allows for the detection of systematic quantification errors. Six elements are used to advance the argument: platinum (Pt), palladium (Pd), nickel (Ni), iron (Fe), tellurium (Te), and antimony (Sb). While iron was calibrated using the NIST 610 standard for the Kushan and Roman coins, the lack of appropriate gold reference material means the iron concentrations should be considered semi-quantitative. For the other five elements, a combination of the NIST and gold standards has produced precise and accurate results. The measurements of the gold standards and reference materials have an uncertainty (expressed here as the relative standard deviation) of *c.* 5–10% and are 85–95% accurate within one standard deviation (Table 13.1). The concentrations of Pt, Pd, Ni, Te, and Sb in these materials are broadly representative of the concentrations seen in Roman and Kushan gold coinage. The trace element concentrations for each coin presented here are the mean of three independent measurements.

The Kushan gold analysed ranged from *c.* 85% to 99% pure, whereas the Roman gold clusters around 99% pure. As such, all the chemical data presented have been 'scaled for Au', which essentially means a 50% pure coin would have the concentration of element X doubled in order to make a like-for-like comparison with a pure gold coin. The inherent assumption here is that the trace element of interest is almost entirely carried in with the gold source rather than any other alloying metals. In some cases, this is evidently not a safe assumption. Silver is the main alloying metal in the Kushan coinages presented here, and we know that both lead and bismuth are regularly associated with silver,[21] meaning neither of these elements can safely be used to indicate changes in the gold source. Copper

[17] Resano, García-Ruiz, and Vanhaecke (2010: 67–70).
[18] https://www.lbma.org.uk/good-delivery/reference-materials (accessed 27 March 2023).
[19] The author is grateful to Maryse Blet-Lemarquand for this.
[20] The author is grateful to Phil Holdship and Bernie Wood for this.
[21] McKerrell and Stevenson (1972); Pernicka and Bachman (1983); Butcher *et al.* (2014: 102–5).

Table 13.1. Results obtained for key elements from a variety of secondary gold standards and reference materials. The relative standard deviation indicates the spread of the data returned. The accompanying column indicates the proportion of values that were no greater or less than one standard deviation away from an acceptable result.

Element	Reference material	Acceptable range (ppm)	Measured mean	Relative standard deviation	% of measurements within 1 S.D. of acceptable range
Ni	AuRM 4	11.0–11.8	11.1	9%	90%
Ni	AuRM 5	31.5–33.3	33.2	4%	85%
Sb	AuRM 5	21.4–23.4	22.4	4%	95%
Te	AuRM 5	11.6–14.0	12.8	8%	97%
Pd	LA-ICP-MC-MS CNRS Gold fragment	6.9–8.9	7.6	18%	91%
Pd	Flow injection ICP-MS Coin sample	22.0–25.0	24.0	11%	85%
Pt	LA-ICP-MC-MS CNRS Gold fragment	184.0–234.0	197.0	10%	91%
Pt	Flow injection ICP-MS coin Sample	16.0–18.0	18.0	11%	96%

is the secondary alloying metal, only reaching a few per cent under Vasishka, and is commonly associated with chromium, cobalt, and nickel,[22] with Roman copper containing appreciable concentrations of antimony.[23] Given the low concentrations of copper in the coins analysed, it is unlikely to have a major effect on the overall chemical profile of the object. However, it is worth checking that there is not an obvious relationship between 'spikes' in the above elements and an increase in the concentration of copper in the coins analysed.

The Roman data are presented in Table 13.2 and the Kushan data in Table 13.3, both in the appendices. These are the actual quantifications returned from the coins, i.e. before being 'scaled' for gold content.

[22] Butcher *et al.* (2014: 104–5).

[23] Butcher and Ponting (2015: 31–4); Pollard *et al.* (2015).

ROMAN GOLD CANNOT BE THE *EXCLUSIVE* SOURCE OF KUSHAN GOLD

In the first and second centuries AD the most important gold extraction sites for the Roman Empire were most probably the plethora of gold mines on the Iberian Peninsula,[24] in central Bosnia (province of Dalmatia),[25] and in Romania (province of Dacia),[26] with sites in Austria (province of Noricum),[27] and Wales (Dolaucothi)[28] having significant activity as well.[29] These 'European' sources all produce gold that generally contains under 100 ppm of platinum and has a Pt:Pd ratio of 1:1 to 4:1 (Fig. 13.1). The platinum group elements (PGEs) are a useful geological indicator as the refining and parting processes used to purify gold in the ancient world struggles to remove PGE inclusions.[30] This means that a gold coin made entirely from source X should have very similar relative concentrations of platinum and palladium to those in source X.

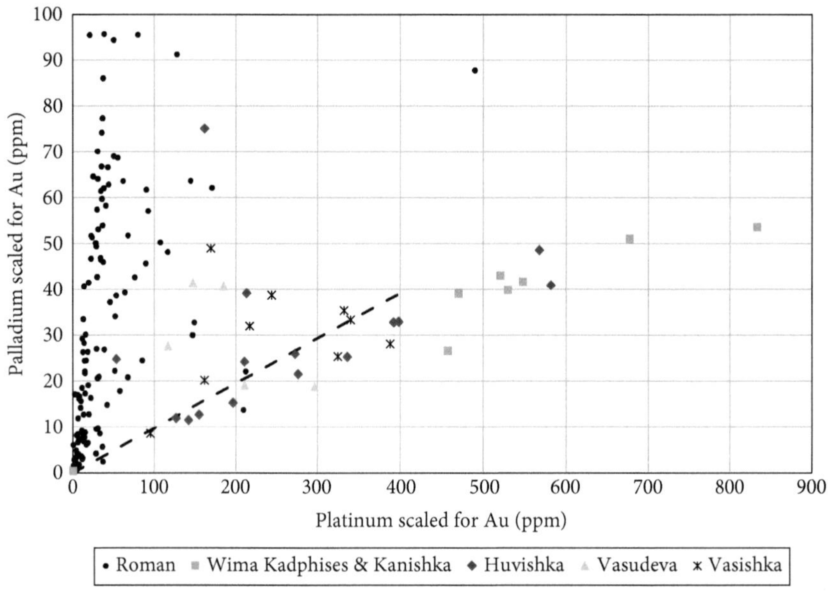

Fig. 13.1. The platinum and palladium concentrations of Roman *aurei* (AD 50–227) and Kushan gold (Wima Kadphises to Vasishka, AD 113–265). The platinum-to-palladium ratio of a hypothetical gold alloy made from 50% Roman *aurei* and 50% Wima Kadphises'/Kanishka I's gold (AD 113–51) is plotted using a dashed line.

[24] Sánchez-Palencia *et al.* (1990); Wahl (1993); Redentor (2010); Redondo Vega *et al.* (2015); Sánchez-Palencia, Romero, and Beltrán (2018).

[25] Bojanovski (1982); Glicksman (2018); Green and Smythe (2021).

[26] Cauuet and Tamas (2012); Cauuet (2014); Lim (2018); Green and Smythe (2021).

[27] Cech *et al.* (2013); Gostenčnik (2016).

[28] Burnham and Burnham (2004).

[29] On gold-mining under the Roman Empire in general, see Domergue (2008); Hirt (2010; 2020).

[30] Blet-Lemarquand *et al.* (2017).

With this in mind, when we consider the platinum and palladium concentrations in Kushan gold coinage (Fig. 13.1), it is without doubt that Roman *aurei* were not the exclusive source of the Kushan coins. Thirty-three of the 37 coins presented here have a Pt:Pd ratio of *c.* 6.5:1 or greater; 32 of the 37 contain greater than 100 ppm of platinum; the median Pt:Pd ratio is 17:1; and the median concentration of platinum is *c.* 209 ppm. Roman *aurei*—with a median Pt:Pd ratio of *c.* 1.7:1 and a median platinum concentration of *c.* 21 ppm—simply cannot have been the exclusive source of these coins. This is plainly evident from the degree of separation between the 'Roman' and 'Kushan' areas in Figure 13.1.

EARLY KUSHAN GOLD

Eight gold issues produced under Wima Kadphises (*c.* AD 113–27) and Kanishka I (*c.* AD 127–51) are presented here. These are marked by squares on Figure 13.1, with seven of the coins forming a cluster towards the right-hand side of the graph. These coins are characterized by very high Pt:Pd ratios (*c.* 34:1 to 67:1) and high concentrations of platinum (*c.* 370–660 ppm). Out of all the Kushan material, the PGE profile of this early Kushan gold diverges the most from the Roman, 'European' signature. It is quite clear, then, that the impetus behind the inception of Kushan gold coinage does not need to be connected to the potential availability of Roman *aurei*. We must, again, agree with Bracey that it is best to view these objects as made by local artists, for local reasons, using local prototypes, and—given the evidence here—most probably using local gold sources.[31]

While Roman material was clearly not an important source of early Kushan gold, we can still detect some evidence for the influx of 'European' gold into the Kushan metal supply network at this early stage. In the bottom left-hand corner of the graph (Fig. 13.1), there is a square in the cluster of Roman material. This is a 'quarter-dinar' of Wima Kadphises weighing 2.12 g (Table 13.3, no. 258; Fig. 13.2), with a Pt:Pd ratio of *c.* 3:1 and a platinum concentration of *c.* 0.4 ppm. This coin is made from a completely different geological source compared to all the other analysed coins of Wima Kadphises and Kanishka I. A Roman provenance for this gold is logical, with this idea given more credence by the purity of the coin. Gold coins of Wima Kadphises are generally of very high purity: the five others in the Ashmolean collection have an average purity of 98.85%,[32] and the two analysed by Blet-Lemarquand were recorded as 99.1% and 98.7% pure.[33] While of high quality, this is not quite as pure as Roman *aurei* from the first century AD, which, apart from those produced in the Civil Wars of AD 68/9 and their aftermath,[34]

[31] Bracey (2017: 28).
[32] Two were unavailable for trace element analysis at this time.
[33] Blet-Lemarquand (2006).
[34] Bocciarelli, Blet-Lemarquand, and Suspène (2017); Green *et al.* (2022).

Fig. 13.2. The 'quarter-dinar' of Wima Kadphises (AD 113–27), Table 13.3, no. 258, potentially made from recycled Roman *aurei*. See Jongeward, Cribb, and Donovan (2015: 272). Held at the Ashmolean Museum, University of Oxford: HCR83558, 12.5 mm, 1.90 g. © Ashmolean Museum. Photograph: George A. Green.

are consistently produced at above 99% pure. The 'quarter-dinar' of Wima Kadphises in question, however, has a purity of 99.24%, meaning that it has not only a 'Roman' PGE profile but a 'Roman' purity as well: of the 39 coins analysed by the author and the 61 analysed by Blet-Lemarquand,[35] this 'quarter-dinar' has the third-highest purity. Providing this coin is genuine, it appears that Wima Kadphises was making use of small quantities of recycled Roman gold.

SOURCE MIXING UNDER HUVISHKA, VASUDEVA I, AND VASISHKA

Under Kanishka I's successors, there is a clear chronological shift in the PGE profile of Kushan gold. From Huvishka to Vasishka (*c.* AD 151–247), Kushan gold generally contains a few hundred ppm of platinum and has a Pt:Pd ratio of from *c.* 5:1 to 30:1, with a median of *c.* 16:1. This is quite a radical reduction in both the concentration of platinum and the Pt:Pd ratio compared to early Kushan gold, and the separation can be seen quite clearly (Fig. 13.1). Two coins of Huvishka (Table 13.3, nos 156 and 162) continue to have the same PGE profile as the gold issued under Wima Kadphises and Kanishka I, with some high platinum, high Pt:Pd ratio issues of Huvishka and Vasishka potentially occupying the 'edge' of the early Kushan gold 'cluster'. Therefore, there appears to be some continuation in the exploitation of the original Kushan gold source. Beyond this handful of coins, however, the vast majority of this later gold appears to be much closer to the Roman material.

A plausible explanation is that the original Kushan gold source was now being mixed with recycled Roman gold. If we were to take the median PGE profile of those seven early Kushan gold issues and the median PGE profile of the Roman material, and create a hypothetical 50%-Kushan, 50%-Roman alloy, it would

[35] Blet-Lemarquand (2006).

result in gold that contained *c.* 208 ppm of platinum with a Pt:Pd ratio of *c.* 19:1. This ratio, up to *c.* 208 ppm of platinum, has been plotted with a dashed line (Fig. 13.1). Approximately half the material from Huvishka to Vasishka is either on or to the 'Roman side' of this line, with a few issues being almost on top of the Roman 'cluster'. Interestingly, the other half of this material does not sit neatly with the coins of Wima Kadphises and Kanishka I. Some coins occupy a 'higher palladium, lower platinum' cluster to the left of the early material, while others are closer to the Roman material yet have Pt:Pd ratios of 20:1 to 30:1. All of this cannot be explained solely by the use of recycled Roman gold. For the first 'cluster' the inclusion of a small proportion of Roman gold may well have shifted palladium 'up' and platinum 'down', but a source change could also be the cause of this. For the second group beneath the Roman 'mixing line' the platinum concentration is appropriately diluted, but the Pt:Pd ratio is still quite high. It is more probable here that a new 'local' gold source began to be exploited under Huvishka that was moderately rich in platinum—a few hundred ppm—but contained very little palladium, giving it a high Pt:Pd ratio. Further investigation of potential Kushan gold sources is needed on this front.

Regardless, the PGE profile of the later Kushan material is clearly being dragged, to varying degrees, towards the 'Roman side' of Figure 13.1. The use of recycled Roman material is the most plausible explanation for this, but a reasonable objection remains that this could actually be a result of the exploitation of local sources that happen to have this PGE profile. To eliminate this doubt, we must go beyond the PGE profile of the gold—which is perhaps best at highlighting broad geological differences—and investigate other trace elements that can be used to 'fingerprint' Roman gold. If the Kushan gold that has a 'more Roman' PGE profile really is a product of a mixture of Roman and local sources, then we would expect it to contain relatively more of the elements Roman gold is relatively high in, and relatively less of the elements that Roman gold is relatively low in. If the Kushan material on the 'Roman side' of the dashed line follows the Roman chemical pattern, then we can be much more confident in proposing that the change in the PGE profile of the gold is caused by the recycling of *aurei*.

Across the first and second centuries, Roman gold is generally low in nickel containing, on average, approximately <5 ppm (Fig. 13.3a). The gold of Huvishka, Vasudeva, and Vasiskha splits into relatively higher- and relatively lower-nickel groups; these have been ringed on Figure 13.3a.[36] If the relatively lower nickel content in these coins was caused by low-nickel Roman gold 'diluting' higher-nickel local gold, then these coins should have a much more 'Roman' PGE profile. The platinum and palladium content of these low-nickel coins is presented

[36] For Huvishka and Vasudeva coins that clustered on or below the Roman moving average were chosen (Table 13.3, nos 152–5, 157–8, 160–1, 163–4, and 167). For Vasishka, given the overall higher nickel content, the lowest concentration cluster was chosen (Table 13.3, nos 169, 171, 173, 175).

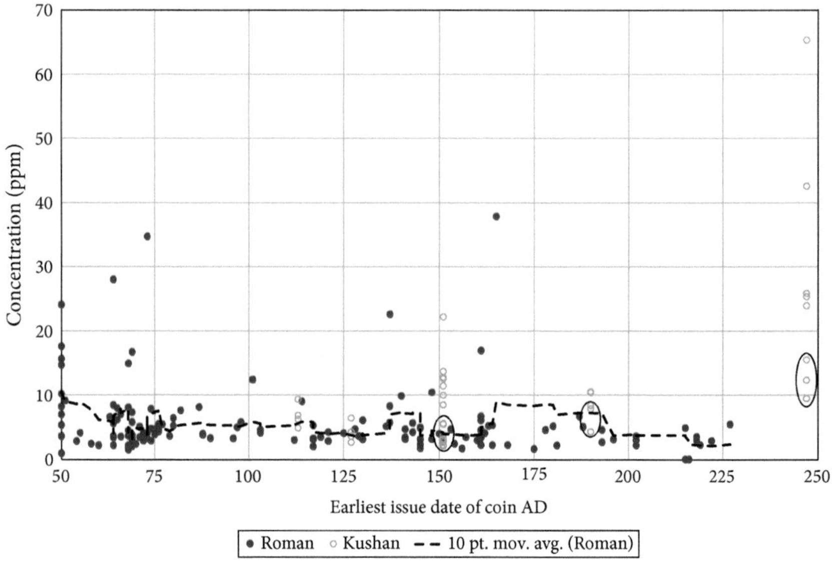

Fig. 13.3a. The concentration of nickel in Roman and Kushan gold. Relatively low-nickel Kushan gold is ringed and plotted in Figure 13.3b. A ten-point moving average is provided for the Roman data.

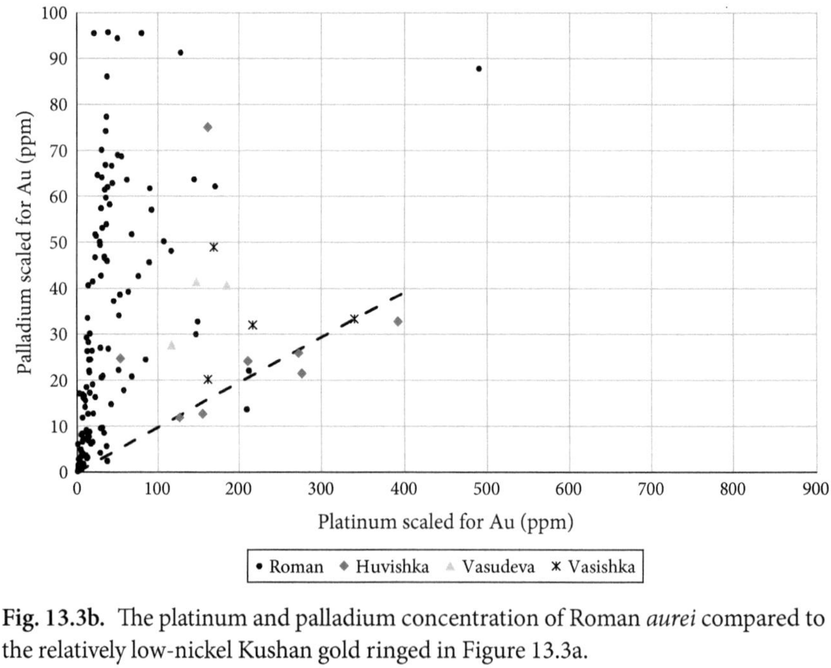

Fig. 13.3b. The platinum and palladium concentration of Roman *aurei* compared to the relatively low-nickel Kushan gold ringed in Figure 13.3a.

in Figure 13.3b, and the vast majority occupy the 'Roman area' of the graph: the median platinum concentration is *c.* 130 ppm and the median Pt:Pd ratio is *c.* 10:1.

While low in nickel, Roman gold is rich in iron across the first and second centuries. Between AD 50 and 100, the average concentration of iron increases from *c.* 400 ppm to *c.* 800 ppm; across the first half of the second century, it spikes from *c.* 1000–2500 ppm before dropping to *c.* 400–600 ppm in the latter half of the second century (Fig. 13.4a). Early Kushan gold, on the other hand, only contains *c.* 100–350 ppm of iron. If recycled Roman gold was used, in part, to make Kushan gold under Huvishka, Vasudeva I, and Vasishka, then we would expect significant concentrations of iron to have been carried in. Since Roman gold consistently averaged in excess of 400 ppm of iron, we would expect Kushan gold with a similar iron content to have a 'more Roman' PGE profile, if they really were made using some recycled *aurei.* The platinum and palladium content of Kushan gold containing greater than 400 ppm of iron is plotted in Figure 13.4b.[37] Again, most of these coins have a 'more Roman' PGE profile: the median platinum concentration is *c.* 143 ppm and the median Pt:Pd ratio is *c.* 10:1.

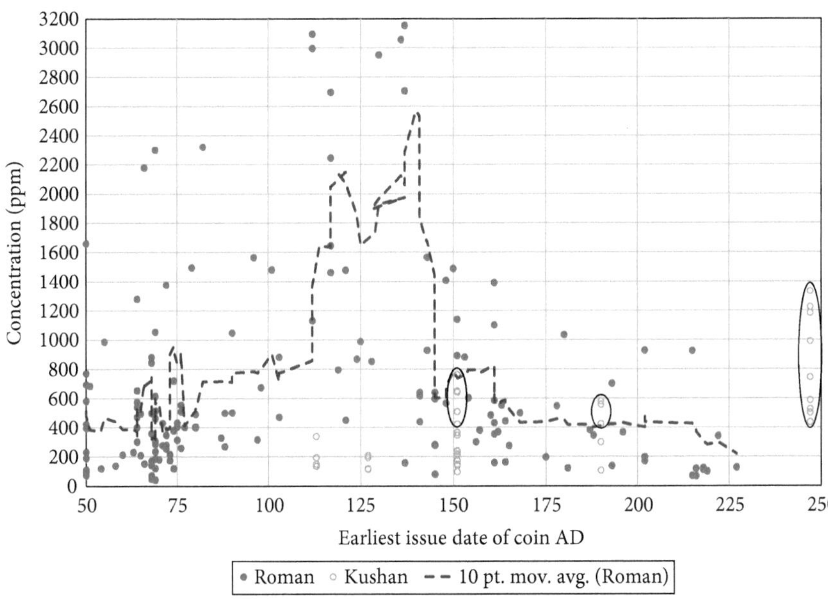

Fig. 13.4a. The concentration of iron in Roman and Kushan gold. Relatively high-iron Kushan gold (>400 ppm) is ringed and plotted in Figure 13.4b. A ten-point moving average is provided for the Roman data.

[37] Table 13.3, nos 151, 154, 157, 259, 260, 163–4, 166, and 168–76.

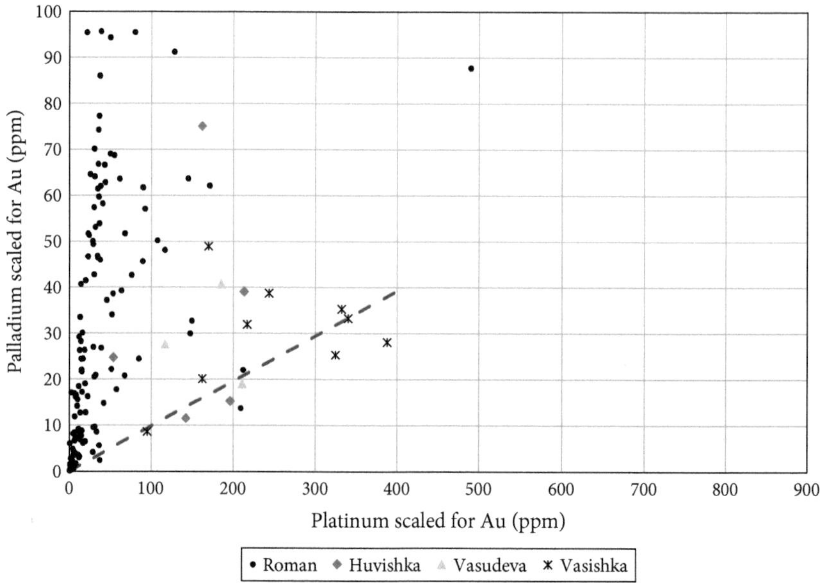

Fig. 13.4b. The platinum and palladium concentration of Roman *aurei* compared to the high-iron Kushan gold ringed in Figure 13.4a.

From *c*. AD 100 to 165 Roman gold has a relatively distinctive chemical 'fingerprint'. During this time the Roman state appears to have been intensely exploiting gold-telluride ores for its gold.[38] These are a particularly uncommon ore type,[39] but they are abundant in the Roman gold-mining regions of Dalmatia and Dacia which appear to have been worked at this time.[40] For the first two-thirds of the second century, this causes a consistent elevation of tellurium in Roman gold (Fig. 13.5a). Generally, it contains barely appreciable levels of tellurium, so an increase to a few ppm is a significant 'spike'. Similarly, the vast majority of the Kushan gold coins analysed contain almost no tellurium—a median concentration of 0.12 ppm—which is to be expected given the rarity of gold-telluride ores. Under Huvishka, Vasudeva I, and Vasishka, however, a handful of coins break from the pack and contain small, but noticeable, increases in tellurium.[41] It is improbable that a local telluride source was contributing a trickle of gold that was somehow exclusively used to make certain issues of coins for well over a century. Instead, it is much more probable that this is a result of recycled, mid-second-century, tellurium-rich *aurei* making their way into the Kushan gold stock. Given

[38] Green and Smythe (2021).
[39] Boyle (1979); Hauptmann, Rehren, and Pernicka (1995); Morteani (1995); Constantinescu *et al.* (2010a: 1036–7).
[40] Jurković (1995); Tămaş *et al.* (2006); Constantinescu *et al.* (2010b); Baron *et al.* (2011); Cauuet and Tamas (2012).
[41] Table 13.3, nos 157, 259, 167–8, 171, and 174.

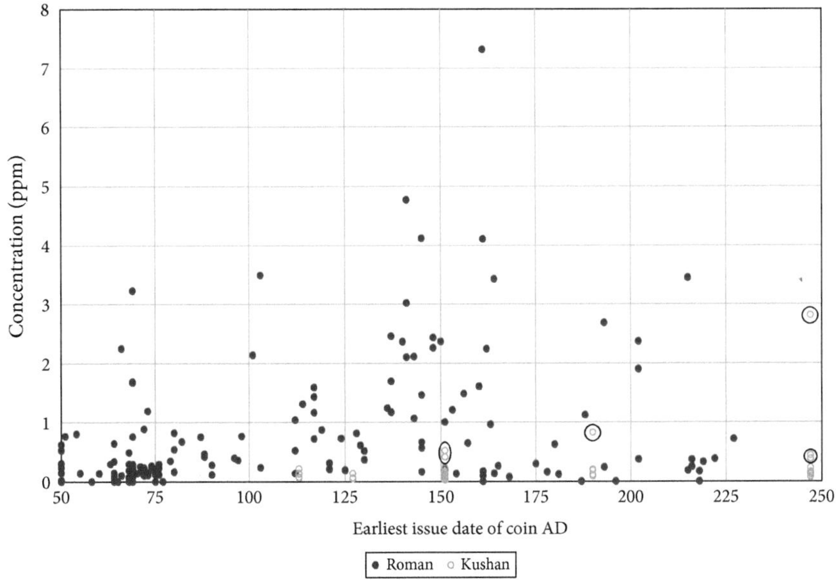

Fig. 13.5a. The concentration of tellurium in Roman and Kushan gold. Relatively high-tellurium Kushan gold (>0.3 ppm) is ringed and plotted in Figure 13.5b.

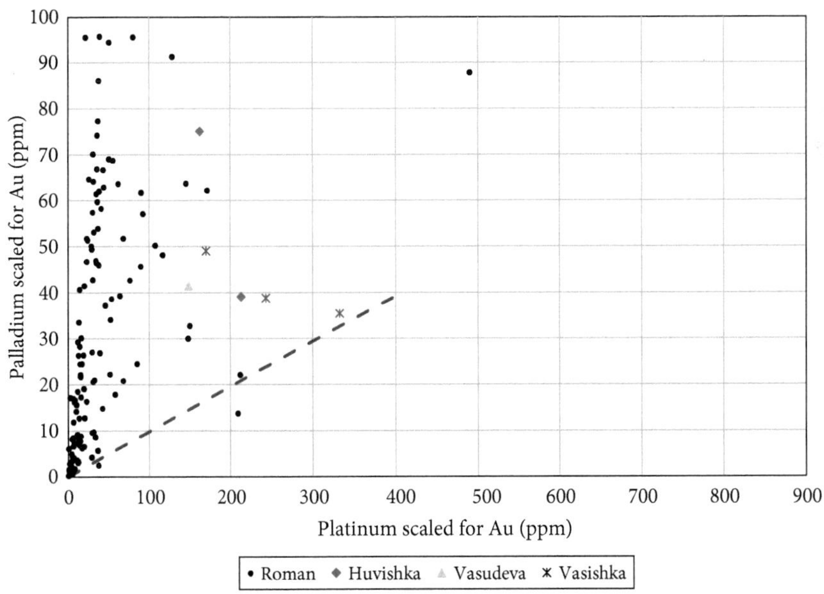

Fig. 13.5b. The platinum and palladium concentration of Roman *aurei* compared to the high-tellurium Kushan gold ringed in Figure 13.5a.

that tellurium barely survives the Roman refining process, for appreciable quantities to then survive the Kushan recycling and manufacturing process we would expect that a large proportion of Roman gold was used to make these coins. When their platinum and palladium content is plotted (Fig. 13.5b), this does appear to be the case: the median Pt:Pd ratio is only *c.* 7.5:1 and the median concentration of platinum is *c.* 150 ppm. This is even clearer for the two coins of Vasudeva I and Vasishka, with noticeable spikes in tellurium (Table 13.3, nos 167 and 171): they are almost on top of the Roman data.

Finally, the exploitation of the gold-tellurides in Dacia brings with it an associated 'spike' in antimony.[42] From *c.* AD 125 to 165, antimony in Roman gold ranges from *c.* 5 ppm to 30 ppm, with much lower concentrations seen outside this time range—with the exception of a small peak around the AD 68/9 Civil Wars (Fig. 13.6a). As this increased antimony is largely confined to the mid-second century, we should not expect to see large 'spikes' in antimony under Huvishka or Vasudeva even if they were recycling lots of Roman gold. We have to assume there was a substantial time lag between an *aureus* being minted at Rome and it being available for recycling in modern-day Afghanistan. However, these coins should make up some proportion of what was available to Huvishka and Vasudeva in the late second and early third centuries, so we should expect to see a slight increase in antimony if Roman *aurei* were a significant Kushan gold source. To some extent this can be observed. Huvishka and Vasudeva both have clusters of coins containing elevated concentrations of antimony (*c* .2–4 ppm), and coins of Vasishka reach as high as 12 ppm. Coins containing greater than 2 ppm of antimony are all ringed on Figure 13.6a.[43] When their platinum and palladium content is plotted (Fig. 13.6b), once again their 'more Roman' PGE profile is evident: they have a median platinum concentration of *c.* 140 ppm and a median Pt:Pd ratio of *c.* 9:1. We would expect a good degree of overlap between the 'higher-tellurium' and 'higher-antimony' Kushan gold coins given that elevated concentrations of antimony in first- and second-century Roman gold are largely confined to the time when the tellurium- and antimony-rich Dacian gold source was exploited. Indeed, this is also the case. The six Kushan gold coins selected for their higher tellurium concentration were also selected for their higher antimony content; crucially this includes the much higher-tellurium coins of Vasudeva I and Vasishka (Table 13.3, nos 167 and 171).

The overlap between the PGE and 'trace element fingerprint' methodologies is, broadly speaking, quite good. Twenty-nine gold coins produced under Huvishka, Vasudeva I, and Vasishka were sampled. The 10 coins with the lowest Pt:Pd ratios were all picked out three or more times by the 'fingerprint' metrics.[44] Fifteen of the 29 gold coins sampled were on the 'Roman side' of the dashed line,

[42] Green and Smythe (2021). [43] Table 13.3, nos 151, 154, 157, 259, 163–72, and 174–6.
[44] A Pt:Pd ratio of less than *c.* 10:1.

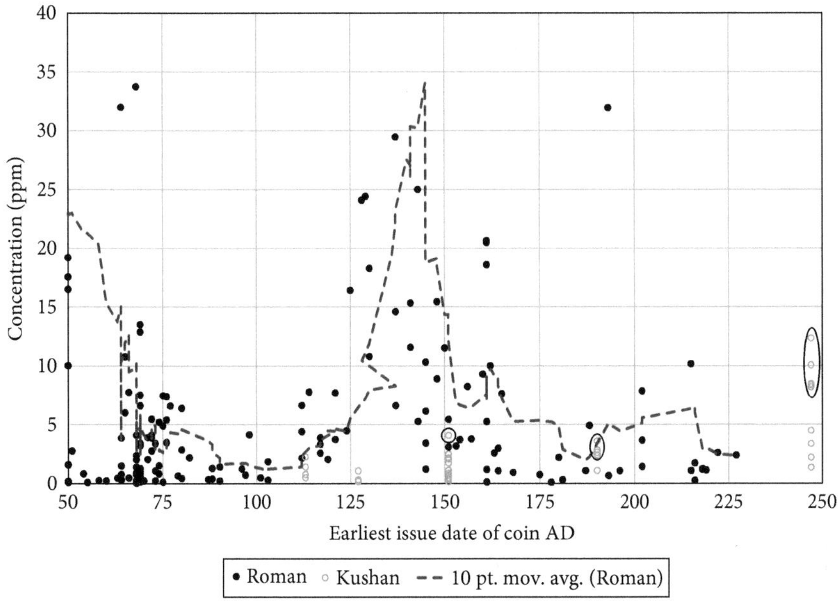

Fig. 13.6a. The concentration of antimony in Roman and Kushan gold. Relatively high-antimony Kushan gold (>2 ppm) is ringed and plotted in Figure 13.6b. A ten-point moving average is provided for the Roman data.

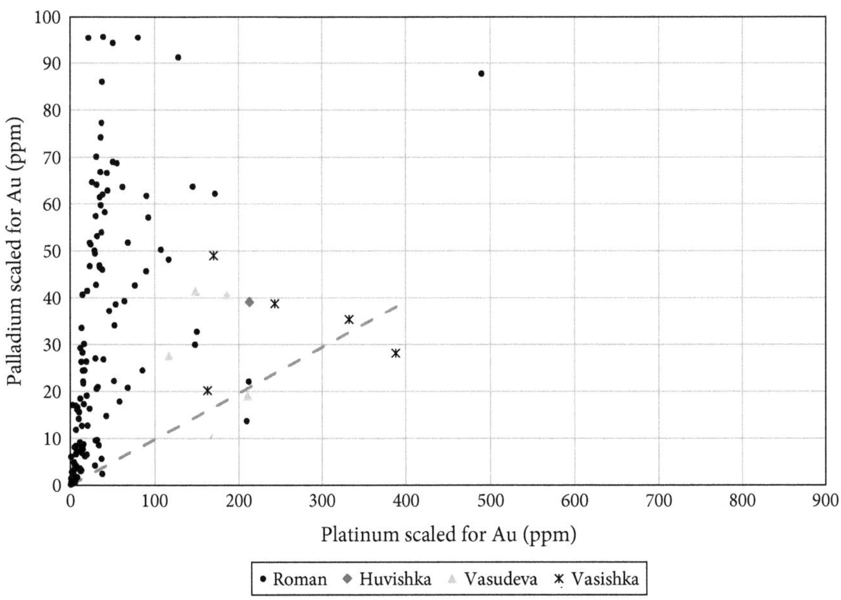

Fig. 13.6b. The platinum and palladium concentration of Roman *aurei* compared to the high-antimony Kushan gold ringed in Figure 13.6a.

based on their PGE profiles: a platinum concentration of ≤200 ppm and Pt:Pd ratio of less than 19:1. Of these 15, 12 featured in two or more of the 'fingerprint' metrics, with ten featuring in three or more. Ten of the 11 coins the 'fingerprint' metric picked out three or more times had a 'more Roman' PGE profile. The outlying coin of Vasishka (Table 13.3, no. 174) had a Pt:Pd ratio of *c.* 12:1 but a—slightly elevated—platinum concentration of *c.* 250 ppm. This cluster of coins produced under Vasishka containing *c.* 250 ppm of platinum was picked out by the antimony and iron metrics, but their PGE profile does not quite fit with the rest of the 'more Roman' material. Without a better understanding of potential Kushan gold sources it is difficult really to say whether this is a product of containing a smaller proportion of recycled Roman gold or is an artefact of their original source.

Considering all the chemical evidence detailed above, we can now be quite confident in proposing that the use of recycled Roman gold was one of the factors depressing the Pt:Pd ratio of the gold produced under Huvishka, Vasudeva I, and Vasishka. While recycled Roman gold was certainly not the dominant source of this later Kushan gold—the platinum concentrations and Pt:Pd ratios are still far too high—it was most probably a significant one.

CONCLUSION

It is clear that Kushan gold coinage contains far too much platinum for Roman gold to ever have been its exclusive metal source. It is also improbable that recycled Roman gold was even a notable metal source, compared to the exploitation of local sources, when Kushan gold coinages were first struck. Under Wima Kadphises and Kanishka I most gold coins show essentially no evidence for significant influxes of Roman metal. Nonetheless, one coin of Wima Kadphises analysed—providing it is genuine—seems to have been made entirely from a 'European' gold source, so some recycling of imported, probably Roman, material clearly was happening at this early stage.

A clear chronological shift can be observed under Huvishka and his successors. Kushan gold now had both a lower platinum content and platinum-to-palladium ratio, appearing to have a platinum group element profile that had shifted noticeably closer to the Roman material analysed. While some of this may well be explained by a change in local source, the much lower Pt:Pd ratios are probably better explained by platinum-rich local gold sources being 'diluted' with recycled Roman gold. Given that the vast majority of the Kushan gold with a 'more Roman' platinum and palladium profile *also* contained many of the same trace element markers as did contemporary *aurei*, we can be confident in proposing that an influx of significant quantities of recycled Roman gold was the cause of the shift in the PGE profile of Kushan gold coinage.

Table 13.2. The major and trace element composition of 159 *aurei* issued between AD 50 and 227 held by the Ashmolean Museum.

Coin Number	HCR	Reign	Reference	Dates	Mint
44	88409	Claudius I	RIC I^2 80	50–4	Lugdunum
45	88427	Claudius I	RIC I^2 76	50–4	Lugdunum
46	88419	Claudius I	RIC I^2 76	50–4	Lugdunum
47	88407	Claudius I	RIC I^2 80	50–4	Lugdunum
48	88392	Claudius I	RIC I^2 53	50–4	Lugdunum
49	88426	Claudius I	RIC I^2 78	50–4	Lugdunum
50	88408	Claudius I	RIC I^2 80	50–4	Lugdunum
51	88418	Claudius I	RIC I^2 82	50–4	Lugdunum
52	88390	Claudius I	RIC I^2 59	50–1	Lugdunum
53	88410	Claudius I	RIC I^2 80	50–4	Lugdunum
54	88425	Claudius I	RIC I^2 76	50–4	Lugdunum
55	88386	Claudius I	RIC I^2 61	51–2	Lugdunum
56	88513	Nero	RIC I^2 3	54–4	Lugdunum
57	88517	Nero	RIC I^2 6	55	Lugdunum
58	88521	Nero	RIC I^2 16	58–9	Lugdunum
59	88527	Nero	RIC I^2 23	60–1	Lugdunum
60	88534	Nero	RIC I^2 40	63–4	Lugdunum
61	88545	Nero	RIC I^2 50	64–5	Rome
62	88548	Nero	RIC I^2 52	64–5	Rome
63	88543	Nero	RIC I^2 48	64–5	Rome
64	88536	Nero	RIC I^2 44	64–5	Rome
65	88547	Nero	RIC I^2 52	64–5	Rome
66	88540	Nero	RIC I^2 46	64–5	Rome
67	88546	Nero	RIC I^2 52	64–5	Rome

(*Continued*)

Table 13.2. (Continued)

Coin Number	HCR	Reign	Reference	Dates	Mint
68	88562	Nero	RIC I^2 59	65–6	Rome
69	88563	Nero	RIC I^2 59	65–6	Rome
70	88556	Nero	RIC I^2 63	66–7	Rome
71	88553	Nero	RIC I^2 63	66–7	Rome
72	87135	Galba	RIC I^2 63	68–9	Rome
73	88875	Galba	RIC I^2 164	68–9	Rome
74	88872	Galba	RIC I^2 203	68–9	Rome
75	88874	Galba	RIC I^2 169	68–9	Rome
76	88893	Galba	RIC I^2 215	68–9	Rome
77	87136	Galba	RIC I^2 51	68–9	Tarraco
78	88894	Galba	RIC I^2 148	68–9	Rome
79	87115	Galba	RIC I^2 1 var.	68–9	Tarraco
80	87153	Galba	RIC I^2 119	68–9	Narbo
81	89100	Vespasian	RIC II, 1^2 1	69–70	Rome
82	89048	Vitellius	RIC II, 1^2 11	69	Tarraco
83	89329	Vespasian	RIC II, 1^2 1295	69–70	Tarraco
84	88985	Otho	RIC II, 1^2 9	69	Rome
85	89006	Vitellius	RIC II, 1^2 89	69	Rome
86	89017	Vitellius	RIC II, 1^2 94	69	Rome
87	88983	Otho	RIC II, 1^2 9	69	Rome
88	89029	Vitellius	RIC II, 1^2 85	69	Rome
89	88984	Otho	RIC II, 1^2 9	69	Rome
90	89361	Vespasian	BMCRE II.75	69–79	Uncertain
91	88986	Otho	RIC II, 1^2 9	69	Rome
92	88980	Otho	RIC II, 1^2 22 var.	69	Rome
93	89088	Vespasian	RIC II, 1^2 24	70	Rome
94	89332	Vespasian	RIC II, 1^2 1110	71	Lugdunum
95	89333	Vespasian	RIC II, 1^2 1114	71	Lugdunum

96	89134	Vespasian	RIC II, 1^2 358	72–3	Rome
97	89142	Vespasian	RIC II, 1^2 361	72–3	Rome
98	89143	Vespasian	RIC II, 1^2 361	72–3	Rome
99	89144	Vespasian	RIC II, 1^2 361	72–3	Rome
100	89161	Vespasian	RIC II, 1^2 551	73–3	Rome
101	89162	Vespasian	RIC II, 1^2 555	73	Rome
102	89166	Vespasian	RIC II, 1^2 540	73	Rome
103	89220	Vespasian	RIC II, 1^2 696	74	Rome
104	89198	Vespasian	RIC II, 1^2 707	74	Rome
105	89200	Vespasian	RIC II, 1^2 707	74	Rome
106	89202	Vespasian	RIC II, 1^2 787	75	Rome
107	89208	Vespasian	RIC II, 1^2 769	75	Rome
108	89199	Vespasian	RIC II, 1^2 775	75	Rome
109	89229	Vespasian	RIC II, 1^2 859	76	Rome
110	89234	Vespasian	RIC II, 1^2 875	76	Rome
111	89235	Vespasian	RIC II, 1^2 875	76	Rome
112	89264	Vespasian	RIC II, 1^2 954	77–8	Rome
113	89713	Titus	RIC II, 1^2 17	79–9	Rome
114	89795	Titus	RIC II, 1^2 358	80–1	Rome
115	89771	Titus	RIC II, 1^2 265	80–1	Rome
116	89737	Titus	RIC II, 1^2 117	80	Rome
117	89989	Domitian	RIC II, 1^2 143	82–3	Rome
118	90046	Domitian	RIC II, 1^2 520	87	Rome
119	90177	Domitian	RIC II, 1^2 680	88–9	Rome
120	90068	Domitian	RIC II, 1^2 561	88	Rome
121	90118	Domitian	RIC II, 1^2 697	90–1	Rome
122	90116	Domitian	RIC II, 1^2 695	90–1	Rome
123	24036	Nerva	RIC II 3	96	Rome
124	24053	Nerva	RIC II 15	97	Rome
125	90993	Trajan	RIC II 821	98–117	Rome
126	90495	Trajan	RIC II 49	101–2	Rome
127	90527	Trajan	RIC II 90	103–11	Rome
128	90642	Trajan	RIC II 207	103–11	Rome

(Continued)

Table 13.2. (Continued)

Coin Number	HCR	Reign	Reference	Dates	Mint
129	90690	Trajan	RIC II 275	112–14	Rome
130	90708	Trajan	RIC II 294	112–14	Rome
131	90673	Trajan	RIC III 253	112–14	Rome
132	90724	Trajan	RIC II 319	114	Rome
133	91021	Hadrian	RIC II, 3^2 2448	117–18	Rome
134	91020	Hadrian	RIC II, 3^2 29	117	Rome
135	91014	Hadrian	RIC II, 3^2 50	117	Rome
136	91035	Hadrian	RIC II, 3^2 120	117	Rome
137	91048	Hadrian	RIC II, 3^2 508	121–3	Rome
138	91092	Hadrian	RIC II, 3^2 201	119–20	Rome
139	91054	Hadrian	RIC II, 3^2 586	121–3	Rome
140	91230	Hadrian	RIC II, 3^2 711	124–5	Rome
141	91228	Hadrian	RIC II, 3^2 781	125–7	Rome
142	91247	Hadrian	RIC II, 3^2 1061	129–30	Rome
143	91395	Hadrian	RIC II, 3^2 1477	130–3	Rome
144	91377	Hadrian	RIC II, 3^2 2366	137–8	Rome
145	91274	Hadrian	RIC II, 3^2 934	128–9	Rome
146	91431	Hadrian	RIC II, 3^2 1565	130–3	Rome
147	91322	Hadrian	RIC II, 3^2 2210	136	Rome
148	91495	Hadrian	RIC II, 3^2 2647 var. (denarius type)	137	Rome
149	91506	Hadrian	RIC II, 3^2 2624	137	Rome
150	92395	Antoninus Pius	RIC III 75C	140–3	Rome
151	91075	Antoninus Pius	RIC III 349Aa	141	Rome
152	91076	Antoninus Pius	RIC III 352A	141	Rome
153	91077	Antoninus Pius	RIC III 356A	141	Rome
154	92397	Antoninus Pius	RIC III 113	143–4	Rome
155	92396	Antoninus Pius	RIC III 109C	143–4	Rome
156	92399	Antoninus Pius	RIC III 147D	145–61	Rome

157	92281	Antoninus Pius	RIC III 432A	145–60	Rome
158	91080	Antoninus Pius	RIC III 503Ba	145–61	Rome
159	91079	Antoninus Pius	RIC III 501	145–61	Rome
160	91078	Antoninus Pius	RIC III 494A	145–61	Rome
161	92291	Antoninus Pius	RIC III 445Ac	148–9	Rome
162	92401	Antoninus Pius	RIC III 177D	148–9	Rome
163	92402	Antoninus Pius	RIC III 199A	150–1	Rome
164	92403	Antoninus Pius	RIC III 213	151–2	Rome
165	92404	Antoninus Pius	RIC III 213	151–2	Rome
166	92405	Antoninus Pius	RIC III 233D	153–4	Rome
167	92307	Antoninus Pius	RIC III 464A	154–5	Rome
168	92312	Antoninus Pius	RIC III 469A	156–7	Rome
169	91073	Antoninus Pius	RIC III 279C	157–8	Rome
170	91074	Antoninus Pius	RIC III 313A	160–1	Rome
171	116609	Lucius Verus	RIC III 470	161–2	Rome
172	116616	Marcus Aurelius	RIC III 717	161–76	Rome
173	116611	Lucius Verus	RIC III 487	161–2	Rome
174	116615	Marcus Aurelius	RIC III 704	161–76	Rome
175	116610	Lucius Verus	RIC III 472	161–2	Rome
176	116608	Marcus Aurelius	RIC III 435	161–80	Rome
177	116605	Marcus Aurelius	RIC III 77	162–3	Rome
178	116612	Lucius Verus	RIC III 499	163	Rome
179	116606	Marcus Aurelius	RIC III 127	164–5	Rome
180	116617	Marcus Aurelius	RIC III 783	164–80	Rome
181	116613	Lucius Verus	RIC III 551	165–6	Rome
182	116607	Marcus Aurelius	RIC III 184	168	Rome
183	116614	Marcus Aurelius	RIC III 616	175–6	Rome
184	116622	Commodus	RIC III 287	178–91	Rome
185	116621	Commodus	RIC III 275	180	Rome
186	116618	Commodus	RIC III 40	181–2	Rome
187	116619	Commodus	RIC III 164	187–8	Rome
188	116620	Commodus	RIC III 179	188–9	Rome
189	116623	Pertinax	RIC IV 11	193	Rome

(Continued)

Table 13.2. (Continued)

Coin Number	HCR	Reign	Reference	Dates	Mint
190	62916	Septimius Severus	RIC IV 536	193–6	Rome
191	63118	Septimius Severus	RIC IV 3 (Caracalla)	196	Rome
192	62651	Septimius Severus	RIC IV 267B	202–10	Rome
193	62504	Septimius Severus	RIC IV 181C	202	Rome
194	62694	Septimius Severus	RIC IV 311	202–10	Rome
195	63527	Caracalla	RIC IV 265F	215	Rome
196	63526	Caracalla	RIC IV 264E	215	Rome
197	63576	Caracalla	RIC IV 280A	216–17	Rome
198	63575	Caracalla	RIC IV 281C	216–17	Rome
199	64452	Elagabalus	RIC IV 151d	218–22	Rome
200	64303	Elagabalus	RIC IV 57d	218–22	Rome
201	64233	Elagabalus	RIC IV 26d	219	Rome
202	64827	Severus Alexander	RIC IV 142d	222–8	Rome
203	64735	Severus Alexander	RIC IV 60d	227	Rome

		XRF			LA-ICP-MS						
Coin number	HCR	XRF Au (%)	XRF Ag (%)	XRF Cu (%)	Fe (ppm)	Ni (ppm)	Cu (ppm)	Sb (ppm)	Te (ppm)	Pt (ppm)	Pd (ppm)
44	88409	99.65	0.35	*	423	3.8	387	1.6	0.2	5.0	7.8
45	88427	99.79	0.21	*	1660	17.3	329	1.6	0.4	9.0	4.2
46	88419	99.58	0.28	0.14	190	5.0	2120	17.6	*	12.0	10.0
47	88407	99.74	0.22	0.11	73	0.6	156	0.2	0.0	17.0	43.8
48	88392	99.83	0.17	*	396	10.5	625	*	10.0	41.3	10.2
49	88426	99.77	0.19	*	770	12.6	179	49.9	0.8	36.7	17.1
50	88408	99.64	0.28	0.12	230	5.9	1358	16.5	*	30.4	28.4
51	88418	99.83	0.17	*	583	7.3	537	19.2	*	73.9	26.2
52	88390	99.70	0.30	*	694	11.2	546	113.2	0.7	128.0	47.8
53	88410	99.75	0.25	*	95	2.5	20	0.1	*	8.9	3.4
54	88425	99.85	0.15	*	110	2.6	26	0.2	0.3	1.6	0.8
55	88386	99.71	0.29	*	684	6.6	78	2.8	1.0	10.5	3.2
56	88513	99.83	0.17	*	119	2.0	82	0.8	1.1	3.3	2.2
57	88517	99.81	0.19	*	985	2.9	56	0.1	0.2	5.2	5.4
58	88521	99.45	0.55	*	138	1.7	22	0.3	*	2.1	1.0
59	88527	99.22	0.78	*	213	1.5	263	0.2	0.2	28.3	30.6
60	88534	99.75	0.21	*	231	4.7	34	0.5	0.4	5.6	1.8
61	88545	99.26	0.74	*	399	6.0	443	32.0	0.1	9.1	8.5
62	88548	99.23	0.37	0.13	472	2.6	1053	0.3	0.4	9.1	3.4
63	88543	98.90	1.10	*	574	4.4	93	0.4	*	4.9	3.9
64	88536	99.36	0.53	0.12	301	1.5	1493	0.8	*	23.4	12.4
65	88547	98.96	1.04	*	653	2.4	497	3.9	0.1	31.0	43.9
66	88540	99.15	0.77	0.11	1279	20.1	3994	62.9	0.8	41.8	15.6
67	88546	99.02	0.85	0.13	541	4.0	1195	1.5	0.2	85.9	23.0
68	88562	99.57	0.38	0.13	209	4.4	203	10.8	*	31.9	51.2
69	88563	99.76	0.24	*	495	5.7	417	6.0	*	71.8	20.9

(*Continued*)

Table 13.2. (Continued)

		XRF			LA-ICP-MS						
Coin number	HCR	XRF Au (%)	XRF Ag (%)	XRF Cu (%)	Fe (ppm)	Ni (ppm)	Cu (ppm)	Sb (ppm)	Te (ppm)	Pt (ppm)	Pd (ppm)
70	88556	98.99	0.79	0.13	2176	5.0	1016	7.8	3.0	2.0	7.9
71	88553	99.78	0.22	*	151	2.5	292	0.5	0.1	54.4	23.7
72	87135	98.61	1.39	*	842	5.8	138	4.1	*	0.7	0.7
73	88875	99.48	0.52	*	358	2.6	547	2.4	0.1	10.0	12.1
74	88872	99.50	0.41	*	498	1.5	318	2.0	0.6	14.9	12.1
75	88874	99.61	0.39	*	881	3.2	472	0.9	0.4	27.3	21.5
76	88893	98.82	0.83	0.34	140	1.5	4259	1.4	*	49.5	29.2
77	87136	99.59	0.41	*	172	1.4	182	0.3	*	50.6	183.2
78	88894	98.67	0.57	0.76	70	1.3	8191	0.8	0.1	392.0	40.2
79	87115	89.33	4.92	5.75	47	10.7	54760	33.8	0.2	333.7	216.7
80	87153	99.80	0.20	*	64	1.0	5	0.0	0.1	1.2	0.7
81	89100	99.42	0.58	*	305	1.7	198	0.2	4.2	0.5	2.8
82	89048	98.67	1.20	0.12	615	2.7	235	3.4	0.2	8.0	7.2
83	89329	97.23	2.77	*	120	2.4	157	7.5	0.1	4.2	1.6
84	88985	99.75	0.25	*	2299	4.1	210	6.6	2.2	3.6	1.6
85	89006	99.19	0.74	0.10	515	2.1	1065	3.2	2.2	27.6	28.2
86	89017	99.06	0.72	0.21	1053	2.3	2051	1.0	*	27.7	21.3
87	88983	99.53	0.47	*	465	1.4	545	1.3	0.2	35.2	28.8
88	89029	99.56	0.44	*	234	1.8	714	0.9	0.4	71.6	65.6
89	88984	98.52	1.14	0.34	286	2.4	1236	0.3	1.0	102.6	41.8
90	89361	93.92	4.02	2.06	42	2.0	22978	0.6	0.2	93.2	22.1
91	88986	83.66	10.94	5.40	185	12.0	60990	12.9	0.2	42.8	17.7
92	88980	99.27	0.65	0.12	464	5.2	255	13.5	0.3	1721.7	47.6
93	89088	97.50	2.50	*	180	1.7	106	0.2	0.2	1.4	0.6
94	89332	98.19	1.81	*	276	2.4	602	2.1	0.3	15.9	19.0
95	89333	97.75	1.95	0.31	429	3.6	2362	3.9	0.2	28.7	27.4

96	89134	99.17	0.65	0.27	1375	2.1	706	2.8	1.2	11.9	10.1
97	89142	99.06	0.81	0.13	347	2.8	1291	4.1	0.2	24.2	19.6
98	89143	99.10	0.79	0.12	253	2.4	835	5.5	0.3	19.2	23.6
99	89144	98.77	1.10	0.13	279	2.9	1082	3.9	0.1	23.2	22.7
100	89161	99.00	1.00	*	175	2.3	95	0.2	0.1	2.3	0.4
101	89162	99.54	0.46	*	216	2.9	105	3.4	0.2	10.5	15.4
102	89166	99.31	0.51	0.17	5440	24.9	171	1.1	1.6	6.1	7.4
103	89220	99.08	0.88	0.14	720	5.6	106	1.5	0.3	9.4	13.4
104	89198	99.50	0.50	*	120	2.1	44	0.8	0.3	7.7	6.5
105	89200	99.42	0.53	0.13	377	3.4	289	5.2	0.3	20.3	29.6
106	89202	99.49	0.51	*	432	2.8	49	0.1	0.1	2.1	0.6
107	89208	99.50	0.50	*	405	3.3	222	4.9	0.3	18.2	21.4
108	89199	99.50	0.36	0.13	314	3.4	200	7.5	*	23.9	26.3
109	89229	99.66	0.34	*	258	3.1	243	3.5	0.1	24.5	32.2
110	89234	99.51	0.42	0.10	508	3.9	331	7.4	0.4	28.6	34.0
111	89235	99.60	0.40	*	554	3.3	259	5.4	0.3	29.9	39.5
112	89264	99.56	0.44	*	400	3.9	202	6.6	*	35.0	50.1
113	89713	99.66	0.34	*	1495	2.6	206	0.7	0.5	3.9	2.1
114	89795	99.67	0.33	*	406	4.6	225	0.4	0.2	29.3	35.5
115	89771	97.31	2.17	0.51	398	3.7	5444	6.4	0.7	17.8	7.5
116	89737	99.50	0.41	0.14	492	4.6	318	2.9	1.1	129.7	280.9
117	89989	99.82	0.18	*	2321	5.4	108	2.2	0.9	124.6	61.4
118	90046	99.71	0.29	*	328	5.8	61	0.4	1.0	10.6	5.8
119	90177	99.69	0.23	0.13	269	2.7	368	0.4	0.6	11.3	13.0
120	90068	99.65	0.35	*	499	2.8	463	1.3	0.5	48.4	83.1
121	90118	99.59	0.37	0.12	502	2.3	537	0.2	0.2	11.6	11.2
122	90116	99.71	0.29	*	1047	*	459	1.4	0.4	15.3	8.8
123	24036	99.68	0.32	*	1565	2.3	466	1.2	0.5	30.1	21.1
124	24053	99.74	0.26	*	316	3.5	233	0.7	0.5	29.4	24.7
125	90993	99.39	0.61	*	674	4.1	422	4.1	1.0	18.3	23.7
126	90495	99.57	0.39	0.13	1480	8.9	230	0.5	2.8	25.7	9.6
127	90527	99.79	0.21	*	471	3.3	162	0.3	0.3	24.9	4.4

(*Continued*)

Table 13.2. (Continued)

		XRF			LA-ICP-MS						
Coin number	HCR	XRF Au (%)	XRF Ag (%)	XRF Cu (%)	Fe (ppm)	Ni (ppm)	Cu (ppm)	Sb (ppm)	Te (ppm)	Pt (ppm)	Pd (ppm)
128	90642	99.66	0.34	*	881	2.9	218	1.9	4.6	38.7	51.9
129	90690	99.72	0.28	*	1129	*	104	2.2	0.2	4.4	0.4
130	90708	99.77	0.23	*	2994	2.1	49	6.6	0.7	29.7	1.1
131	90673	99.68	0.28	*	3092	*	70	4.4	1.4	44.3	31.5
132	90724	99.60	0.40	*	3840	6.5	65	7.8	1.7	2.7	1.1
133	91021	99.33	0.67	*	1461	2.2	43	3.9	1.9	12.8	13.8
134	91020	99.38	0.62	*	2695	2.3	40	3.3	0.9	8.5	1.7
135	91014	99.29	0.71	*	1643	3.8	354	2.6	1.5	48.5	81.4
136	91035	99.45	0.55	*	2243	1.4	35	3.9	2.1	12.4	7.9
137	91048	98.17	1.83	*	1477	2.5	40	7.7	1.1	20.7	66.1
138	91092	98.58	1.42	*	794	3.0	86	2.1	0.3	10.0	1.5
139	91054	99.51	0.49	*	451	2.0	400	3.7	0.4	25.1	24.4
140	91230	98.99	1.01	*	867	*	216	4.5	1.0	23.4	4.4
141	91228	99.45	0.37	0.15	986	2.9	46	16.4	0.2	12.2	4.0
142	91247	99.54	0.46	*	4721	3.3	108	24.4	1.1	24.3	9.5
143	91395	99.66	0.27	0.12	3392	2.6	97	10.8	0.8	3.9	3.7
144	91377	99.61	0.39	*	3150	4.3	146	6.6	0.5	34.5	30.6
145	91274	99.52	0.48	*	851	2.2	21	24.1	0.7	26.6	3.9
146	91431	99.54	0.46	*	2949	3.7	96	18.3	1.6	33.7	6.8
147	91322	99.13	0.39	0.57	3054	5.9	34	82.7	2.2	1.4	0.3
148	91495	90.18	5.89	3.93	156	16.2	35984	29.5	3.2	54.3	9.6
149	91506	99.49	0.51	*	2703	4.1	56	14.6	1.5	72.2	28.3
150	92395	99.50	0.50	*	3685	7.0	509	47.5	3.1	61.1	19.6
151	91075	98.60	1.40	*	639	2.4	298	11.6	6.3	2.0	0.9
152	91076	99.69	0.31	*	616	2.2	138	15.3	2.8	1.3	1.3

153	91077	99.65	0.35	*	440	3.3	33	53.0	4.0	15.3	3.0
154	92397	99.73	0.27	*	1565	4.0	360	5.3	2.8	0.9	0.3
155	92396	99.69	0.23	0.12	928	3.0	184	25.0	1.4	13.3	11.2
156	92399	99.63	0.30	*	640	3.5	26	55.9	5.4	13.4	2.8
157	92281	99.68	0.27	*	281	2.2	52	6.1	0.7	16.0	5.9
158	91080	99.66	0.34	*	275	1.6	272	10.3	1.9	22.7	23.0
159	91079	98.81	1.19	*	596	3.5	29	3.4	0.9	167.5	6.3
160	91078	98.93	1.00	0.11	80	1.2	499	1.2	0.2	0.2	0.1
161	92291	98.86	1.14	*	566	2.2	371	15.5	3.2	1.9	0.2
162	92401	97.96	2.04	*	1408	7.5	96	8.9	3.0	6.7	7.6
163	92402	98.42	1.58	*	1488	2.9	168	11.5	3.1	10.7	102.1
164	92403	99.62	0.38	*	1138	1.9	244	5.5	1.3	1.2	53.9
165	92404	99.78	0.22	*	892	2.1	110	3.1	0.3	2.1	0.7
166	92405	99.82	0.18	*	881	3.3	21	3.2	1.6	31.1	12.3
167	92307	99.46	0.54	*	603	1.7	260	3.7	0.2	51.3	18.0
168	92312	98.81	1.19	*	300	1.2	145	8.3	1.9	1.1	0.1
169	91073	97.01	2.99	*	379	2.4	788	3.8	0.8	29.1	2.6
170	91074	99.32	0.68	*	485	2.1	488	9.3	2.1	9.9	3.9
171	116609	99.73	0.27	*	585	3.2	176	18.6	9.6	3.3	0.9
172	116616	99.66	0.34	*	1392	4.8	705	20.5	14.0	46.3	8.2
173	116611	99.71	0.16	*	158	2.4	7	0.1	0.1	285.5	1419.0
174	116615	99.49	0.51	*	354	1.6	47	1.2	*	125.2	914.6
175	116610	99.63	0.37	*	1100	4.3	92	5.3	0.2	169.7	10.1
176	116608	99.83	0.17	*	432	12.1	223	20.7	5.4	0.7	0.2
177	116605	99.77	0.23	*	369	2.9	184	10.0	3.0	4.0	0.2
178	116612	99.83	0.17	*	553	3.7	344	2.6	1.3	5.0	3.0
179	116606	99.45	0.55	*	444	3.8	122	3.0	4.5	22.9	1.9
180	116617	99.44	0.56	*	161	1.6	101	1.1	0.2	116.0	29.2
181	116613	99.30	0.70	*	273	27.2	162	7.6	0.3	1.2	0.3
182	116607	99.37	0.63	*	499	1.6	317	0.9	0.1	189.7	1064.4
183	116614	99.46	0.54	*	196	1.2	95	0.8	0.4	118.1	13.8
184	116622	99.64	0.36	*	546	3.3	32	0.1	0.2	0.8	0.6

(Continued)

Table 13.2. (Continued)

		XRF			LA-ICP-MS						
Coin number	HCR	XRF Au (%)	XRF Ag (%)	XRF Cu (%)	Fe (ppm)	Ni (ppm)	Cu (ppm)	Sb (ppm)	Te (ppm)	Pt (ppm)	Pd (ppm)
185	116621	99.71	0.29	*	1033	3.7	141	2.2	0.8	7.9	1.7
186	116618	99.70	0.30	*	120	1.5	172	0.3	0.2	68.2	11.2
187	116619	99.64	0.32	0.10	381	4.8	231	1.1	*	119.7	15.0
188	116620	99.45	0.46	0.25	344	3.6	967	4.9	1.5	6.3	0.8
189	116623	99.70	0.26	0.11	700	3.3	481	32.0	3.5	11.7	3.5
190	62916	99.57	0.43	*	137	1.9	465	0.7	0.3	40.3	43.3
191	63118	99.67	0.33	*	365	2.2	342	1.1	*	66.4	65.7
192	62651	99.81	0.19	*	169	2.6	191	7.9	3.1	9.4	1.4
193	62504	99.65	0.35	*	926	2.1	388	3.7	2.5	107.2	61.6
194	62694	99.84	0.16	*	196	1.5	202	1.4	0.5	1.0	0.2
195	63527	98.92	0.86	0.23	923	3.5	1785	10.2	4.5	11.3	18.7
196	63526	99.75	0.20	*	68	*	142	1.1	0.2	136.9	28.5
197	63576	99.70	0.30	*	67	*	133	1.7	0.3	5.8	3.3
198	63575	99.68	0.28	*	116	*	59	0.3	0.5	612.0	2496.9
199	64452	99.65	0.35	*	110	2.5	468	1.3	0.2	40.3	31.7
200	64303	99.65	0.35	*	121	2.1	434	1.2	*	47.6	51.3
201	64233	99.59	0.29	0.14	99	1.6	443	1.1	0.4	64.2	43.8
202	64827	99.49	0.51	*	341	2.1	360	2.6	0.5	24.8	29.4
203	64735	99.36	0.48	0.16	125	3.9	545	2.4	0.9	32.4	26.7

The LA-ICP-MS data are the raw, unscaled data and should be viewed as semi-quantitative in their current state. Coin numbering follows Green (2021), the original source of the data. Heberden Coin Room (HCR) accession numbers have been provided (https://hcr.ashmus.ox.ac.uk/coin/hcr#####). Coins are listed by reign only.

Table 13.3. The major and/or trace element composition of 39 Kushan gold coins issued between *c.* AD 113 and *c.* AD 265 held by the Ashmolean Museum.

Coin Number	HCR	Ruler	Göbl (1984)	Date (*c.*)	Mint
143	87009	Wima Kadphises	11	113–27	Balkh
144	87010	Wima Kadphises	18	113–27	Balkh
145	87011	Wima Kadphises	18S	113–27	Balkh
146	87012	Wima Kadphises	9	113–27	Balkh
257	83557	Wima Kadphises	18	113–27	Balkh
258	83558	Wima Kadphises	9	113–27	Balkh
147	87007	Kanishka I	41	127–51	Balkh
148	87008	Kanishka I	34	127–51	Balkh
149	87006	Kanishka I	80	127–51	Gandhara
150	87005	Kanishka I	51	127–51	Balkh
151	87001	Huvishka	285	151–90	Balkh
152	87002	Huvishka	219	151–90	Balkh
153	87003	Huvishka	342	151–90	Gandhara
154	87004	Huvishka	150	151–90	Balkh
155	86999	Huvishka	290	151–90	Gandhara
156	87000	Huvishka	311	151–90	Gandhara
157	86996	Huvishka	253	151–90	Balkh
158	86997	Huvishka	141	151–90	Balkh
159	86998	Huvishka	142	151–90	Balkh
160	86993	Huvishka	166	151–90	Balkh
161	86994	Huvishka	157	151–90	Balkh
162	86995	Huvishka	371	151–90	Gandhara
259	86943	Huvishka	325var.	151–90	Gandhara
260	86944	Huvishka	325var.	151–90	Gandhara

(*Continued*)

Table 13.3. (Continued)

Coin Number	HCR	Ruler	Göbl (1984)	Date (*c.*)	Mint
261	86945	Huvishka	326	151–90	Gandhara
163	86988	Vasudeva I	503	190–230	Balkh
164	86989	Vasudeva I	503	190–230	Balkh
165	86990	Vasudeva I	509	190–230	Balkh
166	86991	Vasudeva I	509	190–230	Balkh
167	86992	Vasudeva I	505	190–230	Balkh
168	86984	Vasishka	557	247–65	Main mint (Gandhara)
169	86985	Vasishka	556	247–65	Main mint (Gandhara)
170	86986	Vasishka	556	247–65	Main mint (Gandhara)
171	86987	Vasishka	559	247–65	Main mint (Gandhara)
172	86980	Vasishka	621	247–65	Subsidiary mint
173	86981	Vasishka	621	247–65	Subsidiary mint
174	86982	Vasishka	621var.	247–65	Subsidiary mint
175	86983	Vasishka	624	247–65	Subsidiary mint
176	86972	Vasishka	556	247–65	Main mint (Gandhara)

		XRF			LA-ICP-MS						
Coin number	HCR	XRF Au (%)	XRF Ag (%)	XRF Cu (%)	Fe (ppm)	Ni (ppm)	Cu (ppm)	Sb (ppm)	Te (ppm)	Pt (ppm)	Pd (ppm)
143	87009	99.37	0.44	0.20	*	*	*	*	*	*	*
144	87010	98.22	1.12	0.66	133	5.0	6713	0.5	0.1	387.4	9.5
145	87011	98.73	0.80	0.47	*	*	*	*	*	*	*
146	87012	99.12	0.50	0.37	335	6.1	3656	2.3	0.1	411.5	6.1
257	83557	98.84	0.73	0.31	191	7.0	3084	0.7	0.1	528.9	31.0
258	83558	99.24	0.76	*	148	6.4	13	1.4	0.2	0.4	0.1
147	87007	98.34	1.10	0.56	190	6.2	6771	1.1	0.1	365.0	6.7
148	87008	98.34	1.12	0.55	111	4.3	6264	0.3	0.1	371.1	10.9
149	87006	98.27	1.15	0.53	202	3.5	5372	0.2	0.1	648.7	10.5
150	87005	98.54	1.02	0.43	116	2.5	5687	0.2	0.1	370.1	6.9
151	87001	88.59	8.35	3.06	376	10.1	22503	2.2	0.2	126.6	3.9
152	87002	96.84	2.36	0.80	232	2.1	10554	0.3	0.1	151.1	8.3
153	87003	99.17	0.67	0.16	171	3.5	2948	0.1	0.1	113.6	4.6
154	87004	97.05	1.93	1.02	495	5.0	11393	2.1	0.2	38.6	9.1
155	86999	98.44	1.21	0.35	232	2.8	3499	0.4	0.1	287.0	12.7
156	87000	97.48	1.84	0.68	337	9.4	7964	0.5	0.1	458.3	11.0
157	86996	96.60	2.83	0.57	736	2.5	6416	2.0	0.4	117.8	31.8
158	86997	98.48	1.24	0.26	138	5.1	2724	0.3	0.0	205.8	9.5
159	86998	96.01	3.18	0.81	142	12.6	8728	0.4	0.1	289.3	14.5
160	86993	98.31	1.41	0.28	215	3.0	2587	0.4	0.1	217.4	7.4
161	86994	98.54	1.19	0.27	96	1.9	2896	0.7	0.0	94.2	5.5
162	86995	96.31	2.98	0.71	204	7.8	16484	1.7	0.1	438.5	14.4
259	86943	96.10	2.70	1.20	630	9.8	12426	3.8	0.5	163.6	23.7
260	86944	96.07	2.93	1.00	638	10.3	10677	0.8	0.0	110.1	7.0
261	86945	95.84	2.76	1.40	358	18.6	14290	1.0	0.0	262.1	15.4
163	86988	96.36	2.76	0.84	409	7.3	9681	2.5	0.2	134.9	18.8
164	86989	96.61	2.31	1.08	560	7.9	11920	2.3	0.2	85.2	13.1

(Continued)

Table 13.3. (Continued)

		XRF			LA-ICP-MS						
Coin number	HCR	XRF Au (%)	XRF Ag (%)	XRF Cu (%)	Fe (ppm)	Ni (ppm)	Cu (ppm)	Sb (ppm)	Te (ppm)	Pt (ppm)	Pd (ppm)
165	86990	95.99	3.06	0.95	287	9.9	12089	1.0	0.1	215.0	9.5
166	86991	96.00	3.03	0.98	536	9.7	9564	3.4	0.1	153.0	9.8
167	86992	97.31	1.89	0.80	102	3.9	9180	2.8	0.8	115.1	14.2
168	86984	89.59	7.40	2.88	887	36.9	34355	10.8	0.3	165.0	19.1
169	86985	91.90	5.66	2.44	402	13.8	28299	2.0	0.1	150.9	16.5
170	86986	91.03	6.83	2.14	1075	22.2	24622	7.3	0.2	267.8	14.7
171	86987	91.51	5.64	2.85	481	10.8	25560	7.5	2.4	117.9	26.4
172	86980	94.25	5.26	0.50	1153	20.5	15647	4.1	0.1	67.5	4.8
173	86981	94.76	3.70	1.54	555	10.3	14880	1.2	0.1	244.2	18.8
174	86982	84.96	10.21	4.82	1131	18.6	49580	7.0	0.4	215.0	18.0
175	86983	94.36	4.49	1.15	701	7.3	8166	9.2	0.1	117.1	11.4
176	86972	92.20	4.82	2.99	461	47.6	29442	3.0	0.1	230.3	14.1

The LA-ICP-MS data are the raw, unscaled data and should be viewed as semi-quantitative in their current state. Coin numbering follows the analytical numbers given to the coins as part of the Determining the Flow of Gold across Ancient Asia, Africa and Europe project. Heberden Coin Room (HCR) accession numbers have been provided, (https://hcr.ashmus.ox.ac.uk/coin/hcr#####).

ACKNOWLEDGEMENTS

The author wishes to thank Duane Smythe and Aart Van der Waal at the University of Oxford's Department of Earth Sciences for their technical assistance when performing the Roman and Kushan experiments. Access to the LA-ICP-MS equipment was kindly granted by Prof. Bernie Wood.

ABBREVIATIONS

BMCRE II	Mattingly, H. and Carson, R.A.G. (1930). *Coins of the Roman Empire in the British Museum*, Vol. 2: *Vespasian to Domitian*. London.
RIC I^2	Sutherland, C. H. V. (1984). *The Roman Imperial Coinage*. Vol. 1 (rev. edition): *From 31 BC to AD 69*. London.
RIC II, 1^2	Carradice, I. A. and Buttrey, T. V. (2007). *The Roman Imperial Coinage* Vol. II—Part 1. *2nd fully rev. edition. From AD 69–96, Vespasian to Domitian*. London.
RIC II	Mattingly, H. and Sydenham, E. A. (1926). *The Roman Imperial Coinage* Vol. II: *Vespasian to Hadrian*. London.
RIC II, 3^2	Abdy, R. with Mittag, P. F. (2019). *Roman Imperial Coinage* II.3: *From AD 117 to AD 138. Hadrian*. London.
RIC III	Mattingly, H. and Sydenham, E. A. (1930). *The Roman Imperial Coinage* Vol. III: *Antoninus Pius to Commodus*. London.
RIC IV	Mattingly, H. and Sydenham, E. A. (1936–8). *The Roman Imperial Coinage* Vol. IV, *Part 1 (Pertinax to Geta) and Part 2 (Macrinus to Pupienus)*. London.

REFERENCES

Azarpay, G. (1970). 'The Kushan conference in Dushanbe', *Archaeology* 23.3: 254–7.

Baron, S., Tămaş, C. G., Cauuet, B., and Munoz, M. (2011). 'Lead isotope analyses of gold-silver ores from Roşia Montană (Romania): A first step of a metal provenance study of Roman mining activity in Alburnus Maior (Roman Dacia)', *Journal of Archaeological Science* 38.5: 1090–100.

Behrendt, K. A. (2007). *The Art of Gandhara in the Metropolitan Museum of Art*. New York and New Haven.

Benjamin, C. (2018). *Empires of Ancient Eurasia: The First Silk Roads Era, 100 BCE–250 CE* (New Approaches to Asian History). Cambridge.

Blet-Lemarquand, M. (2006). 'Analysis of Kushana gold coins: Debasement and provenance study', in F. De Romanis and S. Sorda (eds), *Dal denarius al dinar: l'orient e la moneta romana*. Rome, 155–71.

Blet-Lemarquand, M., Nieto-Pelletier, S., Téreygeol, F., and Suspène, A. (2017). 'Are platinum and palladium relevant tracers for ancient gold coins? Archaeometallurgical and archaeometric data to study an antique numismatic problem', in I. Montero Ruiz and A. Perea (eds), *Archaeometallurgy in Europe* 4. Madrid, 19–28.

Bocciarelli, D., Blet-Lemarquand, M., and Suspène, A. (2017). 'Les monnaies d'or des années 68-69 p.C. frappées dans les provinces occidentales: l'apport de l'étude pondérale et des analyses élémentaires', in L. Bricault, A. Burnett, V. Drost, and A. Suspène (eds), *Rome et les Provinces: Monnayage et Histoire. Mélanges offerts à Michel Amandry*. Bordeaux, 175–88.

Bojanovski, I. (1982). 'Antičko rudarstvo u unutrašnjosti provincije Dalmacije u svjetlu epigrafskih i numizmatičkih izvora', *Arheološki Radovi i Rasprave* 8–9: 89–120.

Boyle, R. W. (1979). *The Geochemistry of Gold and its Deposits* (Geological Survey of Canada Bulletin 280). Ottawa.

Bracey, R. (2017). 'The date of Kanishka since 1960', *Indian Historical Review* 44.1: 21–61.

Burnham, H. and Burnham, B. (2004). *Dolaucothi-Pumsaint: Survey and Excavations at a Roman Gold-Mining Complex, 1987–1999*. Oxford.

Butcher, K. and Ponting, M. (2015). 'The reforms of Trajan and the end of the Pre-Neronian denarius', *Annali dell'Istituto Italiano di Numismatica* 61: 21–43.

Butcher, K., Ponting, M., Evans, J., Pashley, V., and Somerfield, C. (2014). *The Metallurgy of Roman Silver Coinage: From the Reform of Nero to the Reform of Trajan*. Cambridge.

Cauuet, B. (2014). 'Gold and silver extraction in Alburnus Maior mines, Roman Dacia (Rosia Montana, Romania). Dynamics of exploitation and management of the mining space', in L. Fontes (ed.), *Paisagens Mineiras Antigas na Europa Ocidental. Investigação e Valorização Cultural*. Boticas, 81–104.

Cauuet, B. and Tamas, C. G. (2012). 'Les travaux miniers antiques de Rosia Montana (Roumanie). Apports croisés entre archéologie et géologie', in A. Orejas, C. Rico, and J. Sánchez Palencia (eds), *Mineria antigua: estudios regionales y temas de investigacion actual*. Madrid, 219–41.

Cech, B., Kühtreiber, T., Schindel, N., Lang, R., Emmerig, H., and Beyer, F. (2013). 'Ein römisches Goldbergbaurevier im "Karth", einer Landschaft südöstlich von Neunkirchen, Niederösterreich', *Römisches Österreich* 36: 1–94.

Constantinescu, B., Oberländer-Târnoveanu, E., Bugoi, R., Cojocaru, V., and Radtke, M. (2010a). 'The Sarmizegetusa bracelets', *Antiquity* 84.326: 1028–42.

Constantinescu, B., Pauna, C., Vasilescu, A., Constantin, F., Cristea-Stan, D., Popescu, G., and Neacsu, A. (2010b). 'Some applications of X-ray based elemental analysis methods for studies on Romanian gold minerals', *Romanian Reports in Physics* 62.1: 47–56.

Domergue, C. (2008). *Les mines antiques. La production de métaux aux époques grecque et romaine*. Paris.

Errington, E. (2017). *Charles Masson and the Buddhist Sites of Afghanistan: Explorations, Excavations, Collections 1832–1835*. London.

Glicksman, K. (2018). 'Metal mining in Roman Dalmatia', *Opuscula archaeologica* 39–40: 261–83.

Göbl, R. (1960). 'Roman patterns for Kushana coins', *Journal of the Numismatic Society of India* 22: 75–96.

Göbl, R. (1984). *System und Chronologie der Münzprägung des Kušānreiches*. Vienna.

Gostenčnik, K. (2016). 'Zum Metallhandwerk in der römischen Stadt "alt-Virunum" auf dem Magdalensberg', *Carinthia* I 206: 11–35.

Green, G. A. (2021). *Gold Coinage in the Roman World: Function and Production*. PhD thesis, University of Warwick.

Green, G. A. and Smythe, D. (2021). 'Tracing Dacian gold in Roman aurei', *Journal of Archaeological Science: Reports* 39: 103128, DOI: 10.1016/j.jasrep.2021.103128.

Green, G. A., Ishida, K., Domoney, K., Agoro, T., and Hillier, A. D. (2022). 'Negative muons reveal the economic chaos of Rome's AD 68/9 Civil Wars', *Archaeological and Anthropological Sciences* 14.9: 165, DOI: 10.1007/s12520-022-01631-1.

Hauptmann, A., Rehren, T., and Pernicka, E. (1995). 'The composition of gold from the ancient mining district of Verespatak/Roşia Montană, Romania', in G. Morteani and J. P. Northover (eds), *Prehistoric Gold in Europe: Mines, Metallurgy, and Manufacture*. Dordrecht, 369–81.

Hirt, A. (2010). *Imperial Mines and Quarries in the Roman World: Organizational Aspects, 27 BC–AD 235*. Oxford.

Hirt, A. (2020). 'Gold and silver mining in the Roman Empire', in K. Butcher (ed.), *Debasement: Manipulation of Coin Standards in Pre-Modern Monetary Systems*. Oxford, 111–24.

Jongeward, D. (2003). *Buddhist Art of Pakistan and Afghanistan: The Royal Ontario Museum Collection of Gandhara Sculpture* (South Asian studies papers). Toronto.

Jongeward, D., Cribb, J., and Donovan, P. (2015). *Kushan, Kushano-Sasanian, and Kidarite Coins: A Catalogue of Coins from the American Numismatic Society*. New York.

Jurković, I. (1995). 'Bakovici: The bigest gold deposit of Bosnia and Herzegovina', *Rudarsko-geološko-naftni zbornik* 7: 1–15.

Lim, S. Y. (2018). *Mining under Empire: Exploiting the Metal Resources of Roman Dacia*. Oxford.

McKerrell, H. and Stevenson, R. B. K. (1972). 'Some analysis of Anglo-Saxon and associated Oriental silver coinage', in E. T. Hall and D. M. Metcalf (eds), *Methods of Chemical and Metallurgical Investigation of Ancient Coinage: A Symposium Held by the Royal Numismatic Society in London on 9–11 December 1970*. London, 195–209.

Morteani, G. (1995). 'Mineral economics, mineralogy, geochemistry and structure of gold deposits: An overview', in G. Morteani and J. P. Northover (eds), *Prehistoric Gold in Europe: Mines, Metallurgy, and Manufacture*. Dordrecht, 97–113.

Pernicka, E. and Bachman, H.-G. (1983). 'Archaeometallurgische Untersuchungen zur antiken Silbergewinnung in Laurion', *Erzmetall* 36: 592–7.

Pollard, A. M., Bray, P., Gosden, C., Wilson, A., and Hamerow, H. (2015). 'Characterising copper-based metals in Britain in the first millennium AD: A preliminary quantification of metal flow and recycling', *Antiquity* 89.345: 697–713.

Redentor, A. (2010). 'Aproximação a um esboço social da área mineira romana da Serra da Padrela (Tresminas e Campo de Jales)', in C. M. Braz Martins (ed.), *Mineração e povoamento na antiguidade no Alto Trás-os-Montes occidental*. Porto, 121–62.

Redondo Vega, J., Alonso-Herrero, E., Santos-González, J., González-Gutiérrez, R. B., and Gómez-Villar, A. (2015). 'La Balouta exhumed karst: A Roman gold-mine-derived landscape within the Las Médulas UNESCO World Heritage Site (Spain)', *International Journal of Speleology* 44.3: 267–76.

Resano, M., García-Ruiz, E., and Vanhaecke, F. (2010). 'Laser ablation-inductively coupled plasma mass spectrometry in archaeometric research', *Mass Spectrometry Reviews* 29.1: 55–78.

Rosenfield, J. M. (1967). *The Dynastic Arts of the Kushans* (California Studies in the History of Art). Berkeley.

Rtveladze, E. V. (1994). 'Kampir-Tepe: Structures, written documents, and coins', *Bulletin of the Asia Institute* 8: 141–54.

Sánchez-Palencia, F. J., Fernández-Posse, M. D., Manzano, J. F., and Orejas, A. (1990). 'La zona arqueológica de las Médulas (1988-89)', *Archivo español de arqueología* 63.161: 249–64.

Sánchez-Palencia, F. J., Romero, D., and Beltrán, A. (2018). 'Geoarqueología del oro en la zona minera de Pino del Oro (Zamora)', in C. Rico and A. Orejas (eds), *Los metales preciosos: De la extracción a la acuñación (Antigüedad—Edad Media)* (Mélanges de la Casa de Velázquez 48-1). Madrid, 63–87.

Sarianidi, V. I. (1980). 'The Treasure of Golden Hill', *American Journal of Archaeology* 84.2: 125–31.

Tămaş, C., Bailly, L., Ghergari, L., O'Connor, G., and Minuţ, A. (2006). 'New occurrences of tellurides and argyrodite in Roşia Montană, Apuseni Mountains, Romania, and their metallogenic significance', *The Canadian Mineralogist* 44: 367–83.

Thorley, J. (1979). 'The Roman Empire and the Kushans', *Greece & Rome* 26.2: 181–90.

Wahl, J. (1993). 'Três Minas. Vorbericht über die archäologischen Ausgrabungen im Bereich des römischen Goldbergwerke 1986/7', in H. Steuer and U. Zimmermann (eds), *Montanarchäologie in Europa. Berichte zum Internationalen Kolloquium "Frühe Erzgewinnung und Verhüttung in Europa" in Freiburg im Breisgau vom 4.–7. Okt. 1990*. Sigmaringen, 123–52.

Zwalf, W. (1996). *A Catalogue of the Gandhāra Sculpture in the British Museum*. London.

George A. Green, *Chemical Evidence for the Recycling of Roman Gold in the Kushan Empire* In: *Roman Coin Hoards Across Frontiers*. Edited by: Benjamin D. R. Hellings, Marguerite Spoerri Butcher, and Chris Howgego, Oxford University Press. © Oxford University Press 2026. DOI: 10.1093/9780198986478.003.0013

14

The Export of Coin from the Roman Empire and the Imperial Economy: Critical Remarks on Select Textual Sources

Bernhard E. Woytek

The use and deposition of Roman coinage beyond the Empire's frontiers is attested through various sources across the Republican and Imperial periods—most importantly through the numismatic material itself, which not only gives a general idea of the remarkable scale of the phenomenon but also allows for some more specific conclusions. For example, it enables us to recognize preferences for certain metals and denominations in specific export zones in certain periods,[1] and to identify geographical areas in which particular practices regarding the use of Roman coins may be observed.[2] However, coin finds of course do not provide us with information on the economic mechanisms that led to the export of Roman coinage, nor do they shed light on the historical contexts in which it occurred.

In order to learn about these aspects the historian obviously turns to textual sources. In the 2008 conference publication on *Roman Coins Outside the Empire*—a point of reference for the present volume,[3] both in scope and content—an article by Peter Kehne deals with the contribution of ancient texts to our understanding of the outflow of Roman currency from the *Imperium Romanum*. Kehne cautiously called his piece 'Eine Problemskizze' in the subtitle, and justly so. While the contribution is valuable especially for its substantial bibliography that makes up about half of the paper, the text itself is somewhat disjointed and does not really seem to do justice to the phenomenon it is supposed to cover. In general, Kehne is perhaps overly pessimistic about the potential of ancient texts for the elucidation of the topic. Moreover, while his article takes into account the considerable time span from the first to the fifth centuries AD, it focuses on Barbaricum,

[1] See, for European Barbaricum, Voß and Wigg-Wolf (2017: 112–18), and, for India, Turner (1989: 11–16). Note especially the switch from silver to gold in the material exported to India.

[2] See, for example, Zapolska and Dymowski (2021).

[3] Bursche, Ciołek, and Wolters (2008).

thereby excluding the outflow of Roman coin to other regions of the ancient world, especially to South Asia.

A different and more global approach has been chosen for the present chapter. In its first three sections, three different categories of ancient coin export will be studied. Each will be illustrated with a few examples from the textual sources, both literary and documentary, though without any claim to exhaustiveness. I will analyse modern attempts at categorizing and modelling the outflow of Roman coins and propose to look at the agency behind different types of Roman coin export. It is also my aim to contextualize the study of coin export within the larger debate about the budget of the Roman state and the development of its trade balance. In the concluding section of the chapter, I will compare the potential increase of coin outflow over time with general changes to the Roman currency during the Principate, thereby aiming at a better assessment of ancient and modern interpretations of the dynamics involved in both developments. It is worth asking the question whether these changes were interdependent.

CROSS-BORDER TRADE

Usually, political boundaries do not prevent commercial activity across borders. The northern frontier of the Roman Empire is a well-researched case in point. The entire first part of Mortimer Wheeler's epoch-making monograph *Rome Beyond the Imperial Frontiers* is dedicated to Rome's trade with free Germany,[4] and the importance of the subject has been evident to researchers across the globe ever since.[5] A quick glance at distribution maps of archaeological finds of Roman products in central and northern Europe makes it clear that the distances from the *limes* were often considerable. While inner-Germanic trade connections must have played an important role in the distribution of these items, direct Romano-Germanic economic relations were clearly responsible for getting them outside the Empire. These trade relations evidently covered a wide spectrum, from small-scale cross-border transactions to ambitious longer-distance expeditions by more adventurous entrepreneurs from the Empire.[6]

In the present context, I would like to focus on the former category, which is described in paragraph 5 of Tacitus' *Germania*. This passage of the work, so well known among numismatists, has attracted considerable scholarly attention in recent times; however, some of the interpretations advanced call for comment. The text runs as follows:

[4] Wheeler (1954: 7–94).

[5] The massive increase in the material evidence available for study since the 1950s has, of course, caused a shift in the approach to the topic; see Voß and Wigg-Wolf (2017: 108–9) on Wheeler's legacy in that respect.

[6] See Wolters (1986: 84) on this point.

Est videre apud illos [sc. Germanos] argentea vasa, legatis et principibus eorum muneri data, non in alia vilitate quam quae humo finguntur; quamquam proximi ob usum commerciorum aurum et argentum in pretio habent formasque quasdam nostrae pecuniae agnoscunt atque eligunt. interiores simplicius et antiquius permutatione mercium utuntur. pecuniam probant veterem et diu notam, serratos, bigatosque. argentum quoque magis quam aurum sequuntur, nulla affectatione animi, sed quia numerus argenteorum facilior usui est promiscua ac vilia mercantibus.[7]

You may see among them [*sc.* the *Germani*] vessels of silver, which have been presented to their envoys and chieftains, held as cheap as pots of clay. Those near the border, however, on account of commercial contacts [*sc.* with us], value gold and silver and are familiar with—and show preference for—some kinds of our money. The tribes of the interior use the simpler and more ancient practice of the barter of commodities. They like the old and well-known money, coins with a serrated edge and two horses. They likewise prefer silver to gold, not from any special liking, but because a number of silver pieces is more convenient for buying cheap and common articles.[8]

In this passage, Tacitus evidently contrasts the *proximi*—those living 'next to' the Romans and their Empire—with the *interiores*. The former were accustomed to using Roman gold and silver coins, because the contact zone between *Imperium* and Barbaricum was part of the Roman monetary sphere, while those living further away, in inner Germany, were part of the barter economy zone. As Jerzy Kolendo pointed out in a major contribution on this passage, this dichotomy is, of course, the result of a simplification of an infinitely more complex economic reality. It follows a thought pattern typical of ancient chorography (and attested in two further passages of the *Germania*) whereby the degree of civilization of a barbarian people was determined by the geographical distance of its dwelling place from the zone of (Mediterranean) high culture.[9]

One of the most recent papers on this passage, by Sven Günther (who did not cite Kolendo's excellent article), unfortunately endorses a misinterpretation of Tacitus' text. According to Günther, the final part of the passage quoted above, beginning with '*pecuniam probant veterem et diu notam*', should refer specifically to the *interiores*—despite the fact that Tacitus, in the preceding sentence, expressly defined them as practising barter. Günther therefore saw himself forced to conclude that Tacitus conceptualized 'ein Paradoxon sondergleichen' by establishing

[7] For a critical review of modern editions and minor variations regarding the punctuation of this passage, see Günther (2020: 569–70). There are no significant manuscript variants to the text.

[8] In the present chapter, English translations of passages in ancient authors are based on those published in Loeb Classical Library editions, with changes and adaptations by the author.

[9] Kolendo (2008: 368–9).

that the Germanic tribes of the interior 'bartered' in Roman Republican silver coins, thus effectively establishing something like a zone of stable money circulation and at the same time a 'better functioning economic system' than the tribes near the *limes*.[10] Needless to say, it is Günther's interpretation that is paradoxical, not the text written by Tacitus.

In reality, through his use of the word '*pecunia*' in '*pecuniam probant veterem et diu notam*', Tacitus resumes the terminology in the phrase *formasque quasdam nostrae pecuniae agnoscunt atque eligunt* (just before the sentence about the *interiores*), thereby referring to his description of the *proximi*, next to the border. His mention of their preference for old and well-known coins is merely an explicative 'postscript', defining which pieces exactly the *proximi* knew, appreciated, and therefore 'selected' (*eligunt*).

Which coins (or coin types) did they prefer? Tacitus reports that they privileged silver coins over gold, because they were better suited to the types of transactions they conducted. Tacitus here paints the picture of barbarians carrying out small-scale purchases of cheap goods—we are evidently not in the sphere of wholesale merchants or high finance here. The author also specifies that they were looking to obtain *serrati* and *bigati*. The term *serrati* is unambiguous: it refers to Roman Republican *denarii* with a serrated edge. Coins of this type were produced from the third century BC (*RRC* 79/1) to the first alongside *denarii* on conventional flans. The last issue to exhibit a serrated flan is that of the moneyer L. Roscius Fabatus, best known for its elaborate system of control marks and struck around 60 BC (*RRC* 412/1).

The term *bigati* has been interpreted in different ways in scholarship and therefore needs to be discussed in greater detail here. The *locus classicus* is Pliny's explanation of the types and names of Roman Republican silver coins in his *Natural History* (33.46): *notae argenti fuere bigae atque quadrigae; inde bigati quadrigatique dicti* ('the images on the silver were *bigae* and *quadrigae*, whence they were called *bigati* and *quadrigati*'). As is well known, the reverse types of the drachms and didrachms of the final series of Rome's so-called Romano-Campanian silver show Jupiter in a chariot drawn by four horses, driven by Victory.[11] The passage in Pliny has plausibly been connected with these silver coins of the pre-*denarius* phase, which is why they are commonly known as *quadrigati* in scholarship today. The reverse type of these *quadrigati* was copied, with a slight variation, on *denarii* around 144 BC.[12] In the following decades, *quadrigae* of various kinds sometimes featured on the reverse of *denarii*, too; these may have been called *quadrigati* in antiquity as well, but are not normally referred to in this way

[10] 'Im Endeffekt haben also die *interiores* ein weitaus besser funktionierendes Wirtschaftssystem, das auf einem geschlossenen und vertrauensbasierten... Geldkreislauf beruht': Günther (2020: 579).

[11] *RRC* 28/3–4; 29/3–4; 30–4; 42/1.

[12] *RRC* 221/1.

in present-day numismatics.[13] By analogy, the *communis opinio* explains the term *bigati* as denoting silver coins depicting a chariot drawn by two animals on their reverse: this is, for example, the definition provided by Wilhelm Kubitschek in his entry on 'Bigati' in Pauly-Wissowa's *Realencyclopädie*.[14]

However, as perceptively observed by Kubitschek in the same entry, several passages in Livy point to a more generic use of the word, as a synonym of *denarius*.[15] This conclusion was later embraced by Kurt Regling and Michael Crawford.[16] It may seem a bit unexpected insofar as the chariot drawn by a *biga* was not the original type of the *denarius* when this new denomination was introduced, probably shortly before 211 BC. Originally, the reverse of the *denarius* (and its half and quarter) was adorned by the Dioscuri galloping to the right, with couched spears; the chariot and *biga* of horses was introduced about twenty years later, in the first decade of the second century BC.[17] From that period onwards, both reverse types continued to be struck side by side on *denarii* for a few decades.[18] Charles Seltman, in a short and little-cited 1944 paper on the subject, therefore pointed out that '*biga* ... means "a pair of horses", usually, but not necessarily always, harnessed to a chariot'. He elegantly concluded that the original *denarius* featuring the Dioscuri on horseback might very well have been called a *bigatus* by contemporaries as well, 'for the twin horses are what catch the eye more than their riders'.[19]

It was necessary to recall earlier scholarship on the term *bigatus*, because as recently as 2022 John Melville Jones published a short note in which he advocates a radically different explanation.[20] Astonishingly, he chose to revive Leslie Neatby's (1951) interpretation, according to which Livy used the word *bigatus* to denote not a *denarius* but the silver coin conventionally known as the *victoriatus*—since the latter supposedly functioned as a half *quadrigatus*.[21] This conjecture is impossible to accept, and it should never have been disinterred. In formulating it, Neatby focused too narrowly on Livy, paying no attention whatsoever to the passage in Pliny quoted above, which says that *bigati* were named after their coin image (*N.H.* 33.46), or to the equally unambiguous testimony of Festus, according to which the term derives 'from the image of their engraving'.[22] This

[13] See, however, Regling (1970b, originally 1930: 541).

[14] See Kubitschek (1897: 467): 'Bezeichnung von Denaren der römischen Republik, genommen von dem Gepräge...: der Darstellung einer auf einem Zweigespann daherfahrenden Gottheit.'

[15] See Kubitschek (1897: 467): 'geradezu mit Denar gleichbedeutend verwendet', with reference to Livy 23.15.15 and 34.10.4 (*bigati*); 33.23.9, 34.46.2 and 36.21.11 (*argentum bigatum*).

[16] 'bei Liv.... einfach für Denarius gebraucht': Regling (1970a, originally 1930: 74). 'Livy in my view uses bigati as a synonym for denarii; he does not mean by them explicitly denarii with biga types': Crawford (1974: 630).

[17] See *RRC* 133/3, 136/1 (reverse: Luna in a *biga* of horses; both dated to 194–190 BC by Crawford), etc.

[18] For a concise overview of the typological developments, see Woytek (2012: 325–6).

[19] For both quotes, see Seltman (1944: 79).

[20] Melville Jones (2022: 4).

[21] Neatby (1951: 242–3).

[22] Festus s.v. *Grave aes* (p. 87 L.): *Item nummi quadrigati et bigati a figura caelaturae dicti.*

statement is simply not compatible with an identification of the *victoriatus* as Livy's *bigatus*: *victoriati* show the head of Jupiter and the eponymous Victory crowning a trophy. Furthermore, Melville Jones in his paper wrongly asserts that '*denarii* with a biga as their reverse type did not begin to be minted until about 157/156 B.C.'[23] Around this time, Victory first appears in a *biga* on Roman *denarii*,[24] but Luna in a chariot was used as a reverse type about forty years earlier, on Crawford's chronology, as already noted.

To sum up, in the passage of his *Germania* cited above, Tacitus stated that the Germans had a preference for Roman Republican silver *denarii* of an archaic phenotype—*serrati* were not produced after the first half of the first century BC—and with very traditional images: the heyday of *denarii* with two horses was the end of the third and the second century BC, before the astonishing diversity in the Republican *denarius* typology set in, from the 130s BC onwards.[25] Hence, Seltman's interpretation of the phrase *serratos, bigatosque* in Tacitus as denoting 'the whole of the silver coinage of the Roman Republic' after the introduction of the *denarius* seems to go a bit too far; rather, it should be understood to mean 'older Republican *denarii*'.[26]

Ever since Mommsen,[27] this passage in Tacitus' *Germania* has been interpreted against the backdrop of Nero's reform of the precious metal currency in *c.* AD 64,[28] in view of the text's early Trajanic publication date.[29] However, as emphasized by Jerzy Kolendo, it is essential to take the chronology of the source of Tacitus for this piece of information into account as well. If it was borrowed directly from the *Bellorum Germaniae libri XX* by Pliny the Elder, as Kolendo assumes (following Eduard Norden), it is impossible that a reference to Nero's reform was intended in the source text, since Pliny published this work already in the 50s.[30] Although it would theoretically still be conceivable that Tacitus used the information given by his source in order to voice thinly veiled criticism of the reduced *denarius* standard of the post-Neronian period, there is little to suggest this interpretation. The primary purpose of the passage of the *Germania* in question manifestly is to stress the otherness of the German tribes as compared to the Romans, not to criticize Roman Imperial monetary policy.[31]

Reinhard Wolters recently re-examined the passage in the light of his in-depth study of the important *denarius* hoard of Niederlangen.[32] This hoard of 62 Roman silver coins closes with an IMP CAESAR *denarius* of Octavian.[33] Its structure is

[23] Melville Jones (2022: 3).
[24] See *RRC* 197/1a–b.
[25] Woytek (2018: 360–5).
[26] Seltman (1944: 80–1).
[27] 'Mit Recht also bemerkt Tacitus in seiner im J(ahre) 98 abgefassten Schilderung von Germanien, dass die Deutschen den republikanischen Denar dem neronischen vorzögen': Mommsen (1860: 771).
[28] For which see Butcher and Ponting (2014: 201–38).
[29] See, e.g., Kubitschek (1897: 468), Regling (1970a, originally 1930), and Dymowski (2016: 130); for further proponents of this interpretation see Wolters (1999: 383–4).
[30] Kolendo (2008: 364–5 and especially 370–1).
[31] Wolters (2021: 420).
[32] *RRCH* 452; Lockyear (2007: 281, no. 402).
[33] *RIC* I (2nd edition) Augustus 264.

most unusual in that it contains no fewer than 41 *serrati*.[34] The deposit may therefore be evidence for a targeted selection and deposition of *serrati* on the right bank of the Lower Rhine in the valley of the river Ems, 20 km north of the city of Meppen, Lower Saxony, in north-western Germany. It may perhaps have been closed before the Roman occupation of German territory,[35] although we cannot be sure when exactly the hoard was buried. More generally, Wolters plausibly suspects that the influx of legionary *denarii* of Mark Antony—produced in huge quantities in Greece in 32/31 BC—into the west may have prompted the practice to preferentially select *serrati* and other older Republican issues.[36] We now know that Antony's legionary *denarii* (*RRC* 544) have an average fineness of *c.* 83% and are therefore much baser than earlier Republican silver coins.[37] Furthermore, Wolters hypothesizes that the source of Tacitus (*Germ.* 5) goes back to the period before the Roman occupation (that is, before the campaigns of Drusus the Elder from 12 to 9 BC).[38]

The present section focuses on the Roman cross-border trade with Germanic tribes because it is a very well-known phenomenon that generates a lot of discussion in scholarship. However, it is just one example of short-distance commercial relations across frontiers that will have occurred on most land and river borders of the Roman Empire. In general, these trade connections depended on the agency of private people—merchants and entrepreneurs whose activity not only contributed to familiarizing their trade partners with Roman coins but was also instrumental in supplying regions across the borders with Roman currency. Private agency was also the main driving force behind another economic activity resulting in Roman coin export: overseas trade, especially with Arabia, India, and Ceylon.

LONG-DISTANCE TRADE

The importance of Rome's eastern trade has long been discussed among historians of the ancient economy, not least because two corresponding passages in Pliny's

[34] Lockyear (2007: 170) underlines the 'exceptionally archaic profile' of this hoard.

[35] For this suggestion see Wolters (2021: 419).

[36] Wolters (2021: 420). Already Dymowski (2016: 130) had conjectured that the passage in Tacitus may perhaps reflect the Germans' rejection of Antony's legionary *denarii*.

[37] See Butcher and Ponting (2014: 161–4), who also demonstrate that the weight of Antony's legionary silver coins seems to have been somewhat lower than that of earlier Republican *denarii*.

[38] See Wolters (2021: 420). This should not, however, be taken to mean that Tacitus consulted a textual source older than Pliny the Elder. Pliny, it is true, seems to have gathered information for his *Bella Germaniae* during his presence on the Rhine in Claudian times, but practices related to selecting coins he described—perhaps because reported to him by locals—may well have been much older. The knowledge that *serrati* and *bigati* were always a safe choice (as compared, for example, to the largest issue of Mark Antony) may have been handed down over two generations and conveyed to Pliny while he was in Germany.

Naturalis Historia provide seemingly precise information about a drain of capital that the *imperium* had to face annually as a consequence of its trade with Arabia, India, and China.

The first passage deals with India alone (*N.H.* 6.101):

> *Nec pigebit totum cursum ab Aegypto exponere, nunc primum certa notitia patescente: digna res, nullo anno minus HS* $|\overline{D}|$ *imperii nostri exhauriente India et merces remittente quae apud nos centiplicato veneant.*
>
> It will not be out of place to set out the entire (sea-)route (*sc.* to India) from Egypt, now that reliable knowledge on it is available for the first time. It is a subject worthy of consideration, because in no year India drains our empire of less than 50 million *sestertii*,[39] giving back goods in exchange which are sold among us at one hundred times their cost.

A corresponding text in Book XII provides a total for the capital drain to Arabia, China, and India (*N.H.* 12.84):

> *Verum Arabiae etiamnum felicius mare est. ex illo namque margaritas mittit. minimaque computatione miliens centena milia sestertium annis omnibus India et Seres et paeninsula illa imperio nostro adimunt. tanti nobis deliciae et feminae constant.*
>
> But it is the sea of Arabia that has even a still greater right to be called 'happy', for it is this that furnishes us with pearls. At the very lowest computation, India, the Seres, and the Arabian Peninsula withdraw from our empire one hundred millions of *sestertii* every year—so dearly do we pay for our luxury and our women.

These passages have given rise to wildly differing interpretations. To start with, scholars disagree in their overall assessment of the numbers given by Pliny. While Arnold Hugh Martin Jones noted that 'these are not very astronomical figures', referring to the senatorial census as a comparandum,[40] Richard Duncan-Jones felt that 'Pliny's figures appear very high, and are evidently more indicative than exact. Nevertheless, loss of precious metal through trade was real'.[41] Moses Finley, for his part, was extremely sceptical regarding the validity of the figures in general, labelling them as 'dubious'.[42] Indeed, the numbers given by Pliny—50 million

[39] The only textual variation in the manuscripts is $|\overline{DL}|$, which would stand for 55 million *sestertii*, but the numeral printed in the text above has been preferred by editors since 1904; see the conspectus in Brodersen (1996: 274).

[40] 'The minimum property qualification for a senator was a million sesterces, and many were far richer': Jones (1974: 144).

[41] Duncan-Jones (1994: 103–4).

[42] See Finley (1999: 132). By contrast, Wilson (2007: 110) regarded them as 'plausible'.

sestertii for India and twice the sum, 100 million, for the combined total of the drain to India, China, and Arabia—do not inspire confidence. They were regarded as rounded by some scholars,[43] in view of the qualifications '*nullo anno minus*' and '*minima... computatione*', but it cannot even be excluded that we are dealing with largely stylized monetary valuations,[44] which are not helpful for quantifying Rome's eastern trade at all.[45] The suspicion that the latter may be the case is to some extent fuelled by the third numeric indication in the passages cited above, in which the figure 100 features again: Pliny's contention that the retail price of goods from India was a hundred times their cost.

Federico De Romanis recently examined the case of black pepper imported from India, for which Pliny (*N.H.* 12.28) indicates a retail price of four *denarii* (16 *sestertii*) per Roman pound, presumably for the city of Rome, which gives a price of 1,520 *sestertii* per Egyptian talent.[46] Sadly, there are no data about the cost of *piper nigrum* in India in Roman times, but a comparative analysis of the price levels of pepper in the Kingdom of Cochin (Malabar Coast) and in Lisbon in the sixteenth century suggests a ratio of 1:13 or 1:14. Therefore, it is plausible to regard Pliny's indication of a hundredfold mark-up of the price as merely hyperbolic, as proposed by De Romanis.[47]

In his classic book *The Ancient Economy*, first published in 1973, Finley rightly insisted on the aspect that Pliny's remarks regarding an enormous cash outflow for luxury items 'are moral in their implication'.[48] Paul Veyne developed Finley's remark further by contextualizing these passages within Pliny's general ideas about the capital flows in a state's economy. His ideal was clearly self-sufficiency, much like in an estate run by a paterfamilias who took care to produce almost everything that his family needed and to sell the surplus. Cato the Elder's much-quoted motto (*Agr.* 2.7) best sums up this traditional approach: *patrem familias vendacem, non emacem esse oportet* ('The head of a household should have the selling habit, not the buying habit').

This brings us to the next key point. It is often assumed that Pliny indicates a strongly negative trade balance in these two passages.[49] However, as convincingly

[43] See, for example, Veyne (1979: 214): 'un chiffre rond'.

[44] For which see Scheidel (1996).

[45] 'Pliny's HS 100 million for the annual drain of bullion eastwards' is 'difficult to accept literally': Duncan-Jones (1994: 111–12).

[46] See De Romanis (2020: 103, 266, and 294).

[47] De Romanis (2020: 266–7). The comment on the mark-up by Saller (2022: 95) is inconclusive.

[48] Thus Finley (1999: 132). For Pliny's economic thinking in general, see now Saller (2022), especially ch. 5 ('Pliny's Economic Observations and Reasoning', 84–113). He points out: 'The condemnation of luxury is perhaps the most consistent theme throughout the *Natural History*' (2022: 55; see also 56–8 for examples). Regarding Pliny's understanding of the economics of trade, Saller concludes that 'the conflation of the moral with the economic leaves the [*sc.* Pliny's] analysis fragmentary and superficial': Saller (2022: 96). See also the chapter on 'Roman moralism and the eastern commerce' in Young (2001: 205–7).

[49] Compare Raschke (1978: 636), who speaks of 'the annual quantity of the balance of payments deficit in Rome's trade with the East', and Duncan-Jones (1994: 112): 'It is unlikely that an empire with large armies to pay could have afforded such a high net loss'.

pointed out by Veyne, this is not strictly true. Pliny here focuses exclusively on the money leaving the Roman Empire each year and disregards the annual capital inflow, simply because he is taking a moral stance. His intention is not to provide economic historians with accurate figures to work with but to denounce what he regards as an immoral development of Roman society.[50]

All of the above makes it clear that what are perhaps the two most famous literary passages about Rome's India trade in fact do not provide us with helpful information about the flows of capital involved in it. At the same time, the preoccupation in previous scholarship to ascertain where exactly Pliny got his figures from, and which his official sources were,[51] appears somewhat misguided, from this point of view. The overall scepticism regarding the testimony of Pliny voiced by Manfred Raschke in his monumental overview of Rome's eastern trade seems well founded. He flatly denied that the passages discussed above enabled any quantitative assessment.[52]

When Raschke's contribution to *ANRW* was published in 1978, nobody could know that a few years later a papyrus transforming our knowledge of Rome's India trade would come to light: *P. Vindob.* G 40.822, a document acquired for the papyrus collection of the Austrian National Library by its then director Hermann Harrauer, who also published the *editio princeps* of the document in 1985, together with his friend and colleague Pieter J. Sijpesteijn.[53] Unlike the passages in Pliny, this papyrus—often referred to as the 'Muziris papyrus'—which does not bear a date but is paleographically dated approximately to the mid-second century AD[54] contains reliable numerical data that give a better idea of the sums of money involved in Rome's eastern trade.

Due to the extremely fragmentary state of the text it took decades of papyrological and historical research work to unravel at least some of its secrets, although many points remain controversial. Among the scholars who made substantial

[50] 'Le chiffre de cent millions n'est pas la différence entre les sorties et les rentrées d'or: il représente les seules sorties.... Pline n'a pas oublié les exportations: il ne veut pas les connaître. Il considère qu'elles vont de soi, tandis que les importations, elles, sont contre nature, elles sont...un scandale': Veyne (1979: 212). Howgego (1992: 5–6) endorsed the main points made by Veyne, although he correctly added that 'it is unreasonable to deny that any net outflow took place'. This remark is directed against Veyne (1979: 213): 'Bref, le témoignage de Pline ne signifie pas que l'hémorragie d'or ait existé'.

[51] 'Il est certain que le chiffre est induit des recettes de la douane romaine (*portorium*) en Syrie et en Égypte': Veyne (1979: 214); see also Young (2001: 210).

[52] 'Thus, both Roman bureaucratic practice and the surviving records from Egypt itself indicate that it would have been impossible for the Elder Pliny to obtain any accurate figures.... What has long been regarded by many as unimpeachable statistical evidence thus disappears. It is not my purpose to deny that Rome had an adverse balance of trade with India...but merely to indicate that we have no way of calculating its approximate size. Pliny's figures are thus also not reliable as to their geographic division, to the Seres, to India, and Arabia': Raschke (1978: 636–7). It appears irresponsible by Young to use the figure of 100 million *sestertii* as a basis for further calculations (2001: 210–11), despite the fact that he had acknowledged its unreliability himself just a few pages earlier (2001: 203).

[53] Harrauer and Sijpesteijn (1985).

[54] De Romanis (2020: 2). Morelli (2011: 199) dated the piece 'al II secolo d.C.' without narrowing down the date.

contributions to the current understanding of the papyrus, whether through better readings of the difficult text, improving upon those of the first edition, or through new interpretations, Gerhard Thür, Dominic Rathbone, Federico Morelli, and Federico De Romanis must be singled out.[55]

The papyrus bears two different texts on the recto and verso respectively, written in two different hands. The recto side, containing one column of text, preserves part of a loan contract in support of a commercial trip from Egypt to southern India and back. The main destination of the business expedition was Muziris, which is named in the contract (col. ii, line 12).[56] Muziris is also known from various ancient literary sources as one of the foremost trading bases on the west coast of southern India.[57] The part of the contract that has come down to us deals just with the concluding legs of the return journey: the transport of the goods purchased in India across the Egyptian desert, from a Red Sea port (probably Berenice) to Coptos on the Nile, where they were put into interim storage in a customs warehouse, and finally the river transfer of the cargo from Coptos to Alexandria, where the goods were to be stored in a warehouse for payment of a 25% tax, the *τετάρτη*, on which we shall say more below.

The verso side, on which just one and a half columns of text (of originally at least three) are preserved, contains highly complex calculations regarding the value of the cargo imported from India, transported on a ship called the *Hermapollon* (col. iii, line 28), for tax purposes. The preserved part of the text names three of the products concerned: Gangetic nard, (entire tusks of) 'sound' ivory—apparently meaning 'of good quality'—and *schidai*. This otherwise unattested term was understood in different ways but is probably to be interpreted as a type of ivory of lesser quality. Building on an interpretation by Rathbone, De Romanis suggests that it may refer to 'fragments that are regularly trimmed from the tusks of captive elephants'.[58] In total, however, the ship's cargo contained six different products. Of the three products unnamed in the preserved part of the text, the most important, doubtless, was pepper,[59] clearly accounting for the lion's share of the *Hermapollon*'s load, while the remaining two may have been malabathron and, perhaps, tortoiseshell, according to De Romanis.[60]

[55] See Thür (1987); Rathbone (2000); Morelli (2011, fundamental for significant corrections to the text); De Romanis (2020).

[56] The numbering of the columns of the papyrus in this contribution follows De Romanis (2020).

[57] Compare, for example, Pliny (*N.H.* 6.104), who reports for the harbour of Ocelis in Arabia: *inde vento Hippalo navigant diebus XL ad primum emporium Indiae Muzirim* ('from there they sail to the first trading centre of India, Muziris, in forty days, taking advantage of the Hippalus wind'). In this passage, Pliny goes on to mention several disadvantages of Muziris for western traders: pirates, dearth of goods (*neque est abundans mercibus*), and the distance of the anchoring place from the mainland. Muziris is also mentioned in the *Periplus Maris Erythraei* 53–4 as well as in Ptolemy 7.1.8 (Stückelberger and Graßhoff [2017: 688–9]) and 8.26.4 (Stückelberger and Graßhoff [2017: 892–3]).

[58] De Romanis (2020: 220). The term seems to be derived from the verb *σχίζω* ('to split, divide, cut').

[59] As convincingly argued by Morelli (2011: 222–5); see also De Romanis (2020: 236–45).

[60] De Romanis (2020: 245–50).

Lines 27–29 of col. iii on the verso side are perhaps the most significant of the entire text from a Roman economic historian's point of view. They give a grand total for the fiscal value of three-quarters of the ship's entire cargo,[61] in the currency of Roman Egypt: 1,151 talents and 5,852 drachmas.[62] This is explained by the fact that an import tax of one-quarter (25%) had already been deducted by the time this text was drafted. It therefore becomes possible to calculate the total fiscal value of the commodities imported to the Roman Empire from Muziris: 1,535 talents and 5,802⅔ drachmas. This equals 9 million and 215,802⅔ drachmas—or the same amount of *sestertii* in the Imperial currency, since the Egyptian tetradrachm and the Roman *denarius* (and, consequently, the drachma and *sestertius*) were equivalent from Tiberius onwards.[63]

It is not possible to go into detail here regarding the interpretation of the potential procedure followed in the tax payment for the cargo. But it is necessary to contextualize the information preserved in the document, in order to be able to appreciate the importance of the Indian trade for the Roman Imperial economy. First and foremost, the papyrus provides additional evidence that the volume of goods transferred to Egypt, and, for the major part, thence redistributed to other parts of the Empire, was substantial. The size of the ship mentioned in the Muziris papyrus and the weight of its cargo have recently become a point of contention. It is now commonly acknowledged that pepper must have formed the bulk of the freight. While the papyrologist Morelli concluded that the *Hermapollon* carried *c.* 4,411 talents of pepper (equalling *c.* 139 tons), which points to a total for the ship's cargo of a bit more than 180 tons,[64] Federico De Romanis recently proposed a surprising alternative reconstruction. According to him, the total weight of the goods transported would have been no less than *c.* 635 tons, of which pepper accounted for more than 550 tons.[65] This hypothesis is fundamentally based on an alternative reading and restoration of a number in col. ii, line 20 of the verso side of the papyrus, where the actual weight of the three-quarter portion of the *Hermapollon*'s pepper cargo seems to be recorded. The amount of talents given in this difficult passage was read as]'*Γτη* (= 3,308) by Morelli,[66] while De Romanis proposed to add more than 10,000 extra talents by reconstructing the number as *α*]'*Γφ*[(= between 13,500 and 13,600).[67] This reconstruction has met with staunch criticism by Dominic Rathbone, who pointed out that Morelli's reading must be the correct one.[68] Indeed, the overall size of the cargo assumed by

[61] As established by Rathbone (2000: 45).
[62] Morelli (2011: 214) was the first to correctly read the numerals: (*τάλαντα*) *Ἀρνα* (*δραχμαὶ*) *Ἐωνβ*.
[63] Mitthof (2009); Butcher and Ponting (2014: 618 and 658).
[64] Morelli (2011: 227–8).
[65] De Romanis (2020: 249).
[66] Morelli (2011: 208 and 212).
[67] De Romanis (2020: 242).
[68] Rathbone (2021: 449–50). My thanks to Dominic Rathbone for informing me about the main points of his review before it was published. Also, I am grateful to Federico Morelli for confirming that he stands by his original readings and regards the overall reconstruction proposed by De Romanis as highly problematic.

De Romanis seems rather implausible for two reasons. First, research on Roman cargo ships of the late Roman Republic and the early Empire has shown that the so-called *μυριοφόροι*—merchant ships of large tonnage—normally had a transport capacity of between 330 and 500–600 tons.[69] In view of these figures, the *Hermapollon* as imagined by De Romanis would have been a ship of truly colossal size, much larger than average, which is *a priori* not too probable.[70] More importantly, De Romanis himself pointed out that just eight or nine ships of such a huge dimension would have been enough to transport the total of the annual pepper production of all South Malabar, as estimated in the Early Modern period.[71] It seems doubtful whether Roman traders would have taken the considerable risk of transporting such a high percentage of the total of pepper available in a certain region in any given year on a single ship. Hence, Morelli's figures fit better with general considerations and should stand.

Despite the new evidence provided by the papyrus, we are still in the dark regarding the overall volume of Rome's India trade in the second century AD, because it is unknown how many shiploads like the one mentioned in the Muziris papyrus arrived in the Empire in that period. In order to get hold of a suitable multiplier, it is tempting to turn to the well-known testimony of Strabo (2.5.12 [p. 118 C.]) on the number of Roman merchant ships going to India in 26/25 BC:

> *ὅτε γοῦν Γάλλος ἐπῆρχε τῆς Αἰγύπτου, συνόντες αὐτῷ καὶ συναναβάντες μέχρι Συήνης καὶ τῶν Αἰθιοπικῶν ὅρων ἱστοροῦμεν, ὅτι καὶ ἑκατὸν καὶ εἴκοσι νῆες πλέοιεν ἐκ Μυὸς ὅρμου πρὸς τὴν Ἰνδικήν, πρότερον ἐπὶ τῶν Πτολεμαϊκῶν βασιλέων ὀλίγων παντάπασι θαρρούντων πλεῖν καὶ τὸν Ἰνδικὸν ἐμπορεύεσθαι φόρτον.*
>
> When Gallus was prefect of Egypt, I was with him and accompanied him up the Nile, as far as Syene and the frontiers of Ethiopia, and I learned that about 120 ships sail from Myos Hormos to India, while in the time of the Ptolemaic kings hardly anyone would venture to sail and trade in Indian goods.

In this passage, Strabo's main concern obviously is to underline the Augustan boom in the India trade, as compared to the Ptolemaic period. However, we have no information about the average cargo of these Augustan ships, nor about the size of the India fleet in the second century, when the Muziris papyrus was written.[72] In fact, the development of the Red Sea trade from the beginning of the

[69] See Pomey and Tchernia (1978: 250); ancient ships with a transport capacity of 1,300 tons and more, for which there is very sporadic evidence in the philological sources, must have been absolutely exceptional; see Pomey and Tchernia (1978: 245–6).

[70] Rathbone (2021: 458), by contrast, plausibly assumes that 'the Hermapollon...was probably of 300 to 400 tonnes burden'.

[71] De Romanis (2020: 254–5).

[72] The treatment of the problem by De Romanis is marred by his assumption of an enormous 'technological and organizational leap implied by a ship like the *Hermapollon*', as compared to the ships of the Augustan period, which he believes to have carried 100 tons each at most (2020: 255; cf.

Principate to the third century is poorly understood.[73] Strabo's testimony is therefore not of much help in the present context.

It is evident that the purchase of huge quantities of Indian goods by traders from the Roman Empire, as exemplified by the Muziris papyrus, was made possible by a significant export of Roman precious metal currency. Unfortunately, the absence of price data for India in the Roman period precludes any type of model calculation for the cost incurred by the traders in Muziris, on the basis of the evidence provided by the papyrus. By contrast, it is possible to perform calculations at the other end of the route, in Egypt. In this context, another passage in Strabo (17.1.13 [p. 798 C.]) plays a crucial role:

> *νῦν δὲ καὶ στόλοι μεγάλοι στέλλονται μέχρι τῆς Ἰνδικῆς καὶ τῶν ἄκρων τῶν Αἰθιοπικῶν, ἐξ ὧν ὁ πολυτιμότατος κομίζεται φόρτος εἰς τὴν Αἴγυπτον, κἀντεῦθεν πάλιν εἰς τοὺς ἄλλους ἐκπέμπεται τόπους, ὥστε τὰ τέλη διπλάσια συνάγεται τὰ μὲν εἰσαγωγικὰ τὰ δὲ ἐξαγωγικά: τῶν δὲ βαρυτίμων βαρέα καὶ τὰ τέλη.*
>
> But now even large fleets are despatched as far as India and the extremities of Ethiopia, from which the most valuable cargos are brought to Egypt, and thence sent forth again to the other regions, so that double duties are collected, on both import and export; and on goods that cost heavily the duty is also heavy.

It is beyond dispute that customs dues at the external frontier of the Roman Empire initially amounted to 25%—the *tetarte* mentioned in the Vienna papyrus, as cited above. After the time when this document was drafted, namely at some point between AD 174 and 227, this tax was halved to 12.5% (*octava*).[74] As for customs dues levied inside the *Imperium Romanum*, by contrast, current scholarly orthodoxy regards them as very low, most often just 2.5% (*quadragesima*), sometimes also 2%, or 5%, in what Richard Duncan-Jones called a 'very untidy' overall structure.[75] Against this traditional reconstruction, Federico De Romanis postulated that—at least in Egypt, from Augustus to the time of the Muziris papyrus, thus during the Early and High Principate—goods from India or Arabia that were re-exported to other parts of the Empire were subject to the same high customs rate of 25% twice, which would have resulted in an exceptionally high

also 318–19). His reconstruction of the volume of the Muziris cargo recorded in the papyrus, however, is highly dubious, as laid out above.

[73] For a few hints in the sources, see Sidebotham (1986: 37, 46) and Young (2001: 74–88), who believed that in the second century AD the India trade continued 'perhaps on a more limited scale than in the first century' (2001: 79); he saw evidence for a decline in commercial activities in the Red Sea in the Severan period and for 'a marked downturn in the later third century' (2001: 82).

[74] Duncan-Jones (2006: 5).

[75] Duncan-Jones (2006: 4), with detailed references to the classic treatment by De Laet (1949). For customs dues of just 2.5% inside the Empire, see also Freyberg (1988: 56–60, esp. 58) and particularly France (2001) (*quadragesima Galliarum*).

overall tariff of 43.75% for these goods.[76] Central to his hypothesis is Strabo's wording 'τὰ τέλη διπλάσια' in the passage cited above, in which the geographer emphasizes the high amount of the tariffs. De Romanis takes these words to mean that 'double duties' (of the same amount) were levied, and not that duties—potentially of different percentages—were levied 'twice' (= 'δίς').[77] While this interpretation may *prima vista* seem tempting, this passage alone is certainly not enough to support his bold assumption—notably in the absence of clear documentary evidence for a double customs tariff of 25% in Egypt.[78]

In any case, it is highly instructive to calculate the customs duties that the merchant responsible for the cargo of the *Hermapollon* incurred. The overall fiscal value of the Indian goods of more than 9.2 million drachmas/*sestertii* resulted in an import duty alone of more than 2.3 million *sestertii*—for just a single ship! Extremely high sums also seem to be recorded for the customs house at Palmyra, where the *tetarte* on eastern goods entering the *Imperium* via caravan routes through the desert was levied.[79]

Richard Duncan-Jones rightly highlighted the fiscal importance of customs dues for the Roman Empire in general, which he regarded as 'one of the principal sources of Rome's revenue' that 'contributed very heavily to public finances'.[80] More recently, Andrew Wilson studied the significance of the *maris Rubri vectigal* (Plin. *N.H.* 6.84), in a paper dealing with state interest in Indo-Mediterranean trade. Wilson argues persuasively that, for example, the Roman state's extraordinary investments in the infrastructure of Red Sea routes may partly be explained by the enormous customs revenue that the state derived from the trade with Arabia, the African coast, and India, which clearly must have been of strategic importance to the Empire.[81] This income is often underestimated in overall calculations of the Roman Imperial state's budget. Wilson used the import duty of the *Hermapollon*, as calculated above, very effectively to demonstrate that, by way of example, one hundred cargos of the same value could have provided the state with tax revenue equivalent to about one-third of the estimated annual army costs of the second century.[82] This calculation does not even take into account the customs dues occasioned by the onward transport of the goods to other provinces of the Empire.[83]

The gigantic revenue of the state from the Red Sea trade, as estimated on the basis of the figures in the Muziris papyrus, is at odds with the picture emerging from literary sources. In the latter, the India trade primarily appears as a strain on

[76] De Romanis (2020: 291). [77] De Romanis (2020: 289).
[78] Thus also Rathbone (2021: 452–3), in greater detail.
[79] See De Romanis (2020: 320), with further bibliography. [80] Duncan-Jones (2006: 12).
[81] Wilson (2015: 23–4). The same point is also made by Young (2001: 69, 89, 207).
[82] Wilson (2015: 22–31, esp. 23). See also Cobb (2018: 115–16). On modern estimates of army costs, see Wolters (1999: 222–5).
[83] Wilson (2015: 24–5).

the Roman economy. Apart from the famous passages in Pliny discussed above, a fictitious letter by Tiberius to the Senate comes to mind, which we read in Tacitus' *Annales*, under the year AD 22. Among the chief symptoms of the growing luxury in Rome, Tacitus (3.53.4) has the emperor write that *lapidum causa pecuniae nostrae ad externas aut hostilis gentis transferuntur* ('for the sake of jewels our money is transported to alien or hostile peoples'). While this export of coin certainly took place, it is also essential to acknowledge that, from Augustus onwards, the Roman state relied heavily on revenues from the Egyptian customs duties and that the *maris Rubri vectigal* must have represented a sizable part of its overall income.

In the context of this divergent perspective, it is necessary to return to the question of agency in the eastern trade, briefly alluded to above. In general, there is no doubt that private entrepreneurs were responsible for conducting the expeditions in the Indo-Mediterranean trade.[84] Perhaps the most informative source at our disposal for how exactly these trips played out is the *Periplus Maris Erythraei*, a Greek-language merchants' handbook for the eastern trade, written in the mid-first century AD. This text is especially precious for the detailed lists it contains of the goods traded in the various *emporia* along the route. It is reassuring to see that the products named in the preserved parts of the Muziris papyrus—Gangetic nard and ivory—are listed among the prime export products of the region in the *Periplus* (56), alongside pepper, malabathron, and a few others. The list of the goods most in demand in the same region (Muziris/Nelkynda) according to the *Periplus* is headed by προηγουμένως χρήματα πλεῖστα ('above all a lot of money', 56). Metals are listed separately in the same passage: χαλκός, κασσίτερος, μόλιβος ('copper, tin, lead').[85] As for coined money, Muziris is by no means the only port of India for which the author of the *Periplus* recommends bringing it along: it is also mentioned for Barbarikon (39: χρῆμα), and in the instructions for Barygaza he indicates that Roman gold and silver coinage should be exported there because it 'commands an exchange at some profit against the local currency' (49: δηνάριον χρυσοῦν καὶ ἀργυροῦν, ἔχον ἀλλαγὴν καὶ ἐπικέρδειάν τινα πρὸς τὸ ἐντόπιον νόμισμα). While here Roman money was imported merely in order to be exchanged profitably against Indian coins, it was clearly used directly to buy goods in other ports; the Roman trade on-site involved both purchase and barter.[86]

It is therefore easy to see why in a second- or third-century Tamil poem, westerners—clearly traders from Roman Egypt—are described as 'arriving with gold and departing with pepper', on 'beautiful vessels'.[87] The Roman India trade

[84] 'Rome's trade with the East was a matter of private enterprise': Casson (1989: 32, n. 46).
[85] On the problem of the Roman trade in metals with India, see Casson (1989: 27–9).
[86] Casson (1989: 29–31).
[87] See Casson (1989: 296) and De Romanis (2020: 139), with references.

involved the export of huge quantities of Roman precious metal coinage to the subcontinent,[88] not by the Roman state but by private entrepreneurs. As Roman coin finds in India show, it was the Roman Imperial currency, not the coinage of the Alexandria mint, that was in demand in India and that was exported there.

Since the Roman Imperial currency had only very limited circulation in the province of Egypt, almost all the gold and silver coins for the India trade first had to be transported to Alexandria, whence they then needed to be sent on, up the Nile, to the Red Sea for shipping to India. The practical aspects of these cash transfers are not well understood. Dario Nappo has recently re-examined a group of documentary ostraca from Berenice on the Red Sea, which he proposed to reinterpret as evidence for the transfer of Roman coin across the eastern desert.[89] These texts are part of the so-called dossier of Sarapion in *O.Berenice*, dating to the second half of the first century AD.[90] The ostraca were used as *laissez-passer* by merchants who wanted to export goods from Egypt; they seem to have been issued in Coptos and were received by officials in Berenice on the Red Sea coast. Several ostraca from the group record the transport of large quantities of containers abbreviated as *μαρσιπ*(...): between five and 235 of them; in a few cases they are labelled as 'double' *marsip*(...).[91] Following the original resolution of the abbreviation proposed by the editors,[92] Nappo interpreted it to denote *μαρσίπ*(*πια*) and hypothesized that these bags were standard-sized sealed money bags (*μαρσίππια ἐσφραγισμένα*), all of the same weight, which would have simplified the handling of the valuable load.[93] However, the ostracon *P.Bagnall* 11 from Xeron Pelagos, dated 24 July AD 96, mentions *μαρσίππους διπλοῦς δέκα καὶ ἁπλοῦν ἕνα* (lines 3–4). As pointed out by Hélène Cuvigny in her commentary on this text,[94] the abbreviation on the ostraca of the dossier of Sarapion should therefore be resolved *μάρσιπ*(*ποι*), instead of *μαρσίπ*(*πια*), in the light of this new evidence. In all probability, the word does not refer to money purses but to 'bags' containing unknown commodities.[95] Hence, the supposed textual evidence for the transport of coined money through the Egyptian desert seems to vanish in the sand.

When the traders returned to Egypt, it was the Roman state's turn to cash in. As to the approach adopted by the state to realize the dues, various models may be envisaged. In principle, the *tetarte* could, of course, be paid in kind, and indeed

[88] Wilson (2007: 110). [89] Nappo (2017: 561–5).

[90] On this dossier, see Bagnall, Helms, and Verhoogt (2005: 62–4). New texts from the dossier have subsequently come to light; see, e.g., *O.Berenice* 4 (Ast, Bagnall, and Vanderheyden [2022]), nos 517–21.

[91] Nappo refers to *O.Berenice* II (= Bagnall, Helms, and Verhoogt [2005]), nos 159f., 162f., 165f., 170, 172–4, 177, and 182.

[92] See Bagnall, Helms, and Verhoogt (2005: 63). [93] Nappo (2017: 564–5).

[94] Cuvigny (2021, vol. 2: 368–71). The ostracon was originally published in 2012.

[95] The resolution *μάρσιπ*(*ποι*) is now also endorsed by the editors of *O.Berenice* 4; see Ast, Bagnall, and Vanderheyden (2022: § 61).

there is Late Antique evidence from Egypt for this procedure with regard to pepper and other spices.[96] This option may also have been chosen earlier, and the procedure, of course, made it necessary for the state to auction off the goods it had obtained. There is evidence in Pliny (*N.H.* 12.123) for the *fiscus* selling *balsamum*. While the Roman authorities were thus clearly involved in the resale of commodities sometimes, we should perhaps be cautious in envisaging the state as 'the largest single dealer in luxury goods in the dockside markets of Alexandria' in general.[97] If De Romanis is right in contending that, at the time of the Muziris papyrus in the mid-second century, merchants preferred to pay in cash because they wanted to take advantage of higher market prices in Alexandria themselves,[98] the picture changes drastically.

Furthermore, the overall reconstruction is somewhat complicated by the fact that the *maris Rubri vectigal* was not levied directly by the Roman *fiscus* but farmed out, as we know from Pliny.[99] The *societas publicanorum* responsible for it was presided by an arabarch (or παραλήμπτης τῆς Ἐρυθρᾶς θαλάσσης), of whom about ten are attested for Egypt so far in total.[100] They worked with a team of officers responsible for collecting not only the official customs dues for importing the goods into the Empire (the *tetarte*) but also a surcharge, mentioned in the Muziris papyrus (verso, col. iii, lines 11–12). The arabarchs were high-ranking business personalities, usually from the elite of Alexandria. De Romanis contends that one of the signatories to the loan contract preserved on the recto of the papyrus—the lender who financed the expedition to Muziris—was the very same person who, as *paralemptes*, was responsible for the collection of the *tetarte* in Egypt after the trip had been successfully concluded.[101] If this was indeed the case, and if it was indeed a recurring constellation, as De Romanis surmises, these arabarchs would have been the true key players in the Red Sea trade. By putting their money in maritime loans through which they were financing the expeditions to India, they would have been creditors of (groups of) merchants, while being at the same time debtors to the Imperial *fiscus*, from which they had farmed the right to collect the *tetarte*, which would have ensured that their sphere of influence was considerable. As has been pointed out above, several of the surprising hypotheses formulated by De Romanis in his book are unprovable or problematic: unfortunately, it seems that this interpretation will not stand the test of time either.[102]

96 For the evidence (fourth century AD and 649), see De Romanis (2020: 277–81), in great detail; Rathbone (2021: 453).

97 Wilson (2015: 24).

98 De Romanis (2020: 277 and 282).

99 Plin. *N.H.* 6.84 (*Anni Plocami, qui maris Rubri vectigal a fisco redemerat, libertus*...).

100 See De Romanis (2020: 300–2). For critical comments on his reconstruction, see Rathbone (2021: 461, n. 40).

101 De Romanis (2020: 308–12).

102 Compare the reservations of Rathbone (2021: 461).

In sum, Rome's eastern trade may be modelled as an outflow of private money (and privately owned goods) from the Empire, which was used to generate a subsequent inflow of privately owned 'luxury' goods,[103] mainly via the Syrian and Egyptian borders. The Roman *fiscus* then acquired 25% (or more) of the fiscal value of these commodities, so that the Roman state profited greatly from these privately organized commercial enterprises.

ROMAN STATE PAYMENTS TO PEOPLES ACROSS THE *LIMES* AND THE EMPIRE'S BUDGET

While Roman trade (whether over a short or a long distance) was carried out through private agency and involved private funds, another major drain concerned money from government sources that was exported directly by officials of the state: payments to the 'barbarians' used as an instrument in Rome's foreign policy. It is often not possible to reconstruct precisely from which funds these payments were drawn, due to the nature of our sources. Over the course of the Roman Imperial period the demarcation lines between the private property of the emperor on the one hand and the various funds of the *populus Romanus Quiritium* on the other became increasingly blurred anyway.

It is essential to realize that these payments could be made in several different forms and that they came with many different designations. Various researchers have therefore tried to classify Roman payments to peoples in central, northern, and eastern Europe attested in the literary sources. Developing a typology of coin exports helps with 'modelling' this aspect of the relationship between the Romans and their barbarian neighbours. In preparing the present chapter, the in-depth analysis provided by Aleksander Bursche has proved more useful than the brief overview given by Peter Kehne.[104] Problems of terminology are, of course, ubiquitous. As pointed out by Bursche, for example, the term 'subsidies', frequently used in English-language scholarship, is by its very nature somewhat vague and in reality covers various types of payment.[105] Be that as it may, the main types of coin outflow distinguished by Bursche include army pay for barbarian soldiers fighting in Roman auxiliary forces; single payments and periodic payments (*annua munera*) to peoples across the borders; the ransoming of captives; the *annonae foederaticae* of Late Antiquity; and, finally, diplomatic gifts.[106]

[103] For a re-evaluation of the categories of goods imported from the east, not all of which were strictly luxury items in the modern sense of the word (such as silk or jewels), see, for example, Young (2001: 14–18). He points out that some of the commodities were of religious significance, such as frankincense and myrrh, while others were also used for medicinal purposes (especially spices such as, for instance, malabathron).

[104] Bursche (1996: 101–23); Kehne (2008: 79–80).

[105] Bursche (1996: 110, n. 77).

[106] See Bursche (1996: 121) for a tabular overview.

Chronology is crucial, and it has caused scholarly controversy in the present context. It is beyond dispute that by the Trajanic period the practice of transferring large sums of money to peoples across the frontiers for political purposes had been well established. In his *Panegyric*, Pliny the Younger contrasted Trajan's supposedly restrictive policy in that respect with his predecessors' approach,[107] and Tacitus, in the *Germania*, famously wrote that the tribes of the Marcomanni and Quadi were supported 'more often by Roman money' than Roman arms.[108] More generally, he stated that the Germans had become used to receiving money as a gift, under Roman influence (*Germ.* 15.3):

> *Gaudent praecipue finitimarum gentium donis, quae non modo a singulis, sed et publice mittuntur, electi equi, magna arma, phalerae torquesque; iam et pecuniam accipere docuimus.*
>
> They are particularly delighted by gifts from neighbouring peoples, which are sent not only by individuals but also at the public expense, such as choice steeds, heavy armour, trappings, and neck chains. We have now taught them to accept money also.

In one of the classic contributions on the subject, Colin Douglas Gordon carefully analysed the development of Roman 'subsidies', as he called them in the title of his paper. He traced forerunners of the phenomenon to the Roman Republican period and remarked that 'with the stabilization of the frontiers under Augustus and his successors... the whole policy of subsidization was put on a well-organized basis'.[109] Gordon was heavily criticized for this by Peter Kehne, who accused him of inadequate source criticism and a failure to differentiate between disparate phenomena.[110] On closer examination, however, Kehne's criticism turns out to be too harsh. In fact, Gordon did not argue for 'eine durchorganisierte, kontinuierliche Subsidienpolitik Roms zum Zwecke der äußeren Reichsverteidigung', 'von Augustus an', as Kehne stated, but merely pointed to a steady development during the Julio-Claudian period. There can be no doubt that, over the course of the first century AD, the Roman state did indeed start transferring money to Barbaricum on a large scale.[111]

[107] *Paneg.* 12.2: *accipimus obsides ergo, non emimus: nec ingentibus damnis immensisque muneribus paciscimur, ut vicerimus. rogant, supplicant; largimur, negamus, utrumque ex imperii maiestate* ('Hence, we now accept hostages instead of buying them: and we do not make agreements on the basis of huge losses and enormous gifts, in order to keep up the appearance of victory. They ask for peace and implore us; we grant or deny it, either way according to the dignity of our empire').

[108] *Germ.* 42.2: *raro armis nostris, saepius pecunia iuvantur.*

[109] Gordon (1949: 60).

[110] Kehne (2008: 78).

[111] For a comprehensive collection of sources, see Wolters (1986: 85).

A key element of Gordon's paper is his observation of a paradigm shift in Rome's use of money for its foreign policy during the Marcomannic Wars:[112]

> In these wars from AD 167–180, an important change came over Roman policy. For the first time Rome was forced to use subsidies in default of any other secure defence. Hitherto subsidies had been a cheap and, on the whole, efficient expedient; now the barbarians were in a position to demand them and Rome in no position to refuse.[113]

It is instructive to read Michael Stahl's thorough analysis of the diplomatic contacts of Marcus Aurelius and Commodus with the tribes and groups north of the Danube *limes* against this background. Stahl dedicates a specific chapter of his article to the crucial role payments played in these two emperors' foreign policy in this area.[114] He rightly draws attention to the fact that Rome faced very heterogeneous groups of Germanic negotiating partners: large tribal societies with complex internal structures on the one hand, such as the Marcomanni, Quadi, Jazygi, Naristi, and Buri; and more dynamic, but not necessarily ethnically homogeneous groups on the other, which were held together merely by their allegiance to a charismatic leader, to whom they had sworn an oath of loyalty. Cassius Dio names several of these warrior leaders, and the case of Tarbos may serve as an illustration of the double bind of 'pay or fight' the Romans encountered, as described by Gordon in the passage quoted above. The leader is introduced by Dio as 'the chief Tarbos, who came into Dacia and demanded money, threatening war if he would not get it'.[115] Michael Stahl shows that, for the Romans, groups that were held together by 'Kriegsgefolgschaft' were especially difficult to deal with, and that payments of money directly to their leaders were often the only way to neutralize them, or to use the military potential of some of these groups against others.[116] In such cases Stahl interprets the payments as personal gifts to the respective leaders. Roman coins enhanced their status, because they allowed them to acquire prestigious objects (often of Roman manufacture, such as tableware or weapons), which in turn they could redistribute among their tribesmen and followers in order to strengthen their position.[117]

[112] The period of the Marcomannic Wars is widely regarded as a watershed among archaeologists, too: cf. Voß and Wigg-Wolf (2017: 111 and 117) and especially Erdrich, who states that 'nach einer Unterbrechung von über 60 Jahren setzt…verstärkt ab etwa 170 n. Chr. ein kräftiger Zufluß römischer Funde in das Untersuchungsgebiet ein': Erdrich (2001: 120; see also 127).

[113] Gordon (1949: 63).

[114] Stahl (1989: 296–8).

[115] *Τάρβον δυνάστην…ἐς τε τὴν Δακίαν ἐλθόντα καὶ ἀργύριον αἰτοῦντα, ἀπειλοῦντά τε πολεμήσειν εἰ μὴ λάβοι* (Cass. Dio 71.1.1; vol. 3, pp. 252–3 Boiss.).

[116] 'Geldzahlungen…waren das einzige Mittel, eine außenpolitische Verbindung mit solchen Partnern herzustellen': Stahl (1989: 296–7).

[117] See Stahl (1989: 297–8).

The injection of huge amounts of monetary subsidies into northern continental Europe by the Roman state from the Julio-Claudian period onwards must also have been a boost for the commercial relationships between Roman traders and their clients and partners in *Germania magna*. Apart from the sums that the Roman *negotiatores* paid for goods of German origin (like amber, slaves, women's hair, feathers, etc.), the subsidies sent by the Roman state were another crucial source of Roman coinage for the Germans, as pointed out a long time ago by Reinhard Wolters.[118] The availability of considerable quantities of Roman money offered them the opportunity to purchase large amounts of high-quality goods produced in the Empire, attested through archaeological finds in free Germany.[119]

The accounts of Cassius Dio and Herodianus contain several passages in which payments to the barbarians in order to 'buy peace' are mentioned for the first half of the third century. We will not discuss them in detail here,[120] except for Dio 78.17.3 (vol. 3, p. 421 Boiss.). In this passage, the historian has Macrinus criticize his predecessor Caracalla's extraordinarily high expenditure on this budget item:

> *αὐτὸν* (*sc.* *τὸν Καράκαλλον*) *τὸ δημόσιον ἰσχυρῶς τῇ τῶν χρημάτων* <*τῶν*> *τοῖς βαρβάροις διδομένων αὐξήσει βεβαρηκέναι ἔφη* (*sc.* *ὁ Μακρῖνος*)· *ἰσάριθμα γὰρ αὐτὰ τῇ τῶν στρατευομένων μισθοφορᾷ εἶναι.*
>
> (*Sc.* Macrinus) said that he (*sc.* Caracalla) had added an immense burden to the public treasury by increasing the amount of money given to the barbarians: for it was equal to the pay of the soldiers under arms (he said).

Chris Howgego and Aleksander Bursche rightly sounded a call for caution regarding the reliability of this passage because it seems tendentious.[121] The text still does command some interest, since it is the only source potentially enabling us to estimate at least the order of magnitude of the Imperial expenses for subsidies sent northwards. This obviously depends on our ability to assess the expenditure for military pay under Caracalla. It is universally acknowledged that army pay was the largest single item in the Roman state's budget by far, perhaps accounting for two-thirds of the total.[122] We know from Herodian (4.4.7) that Caracalla had increased the pay of his soldiers by 50%; this pay rise came after a doubling under his father, Septimius Severus. In absolute numbers, the most reliable modern reconstruction by Michael Speidel proposes an increase from

[118] Wolters (1986: 87).

[119] For bibliographical references on current developments in archaeological research on this topic, see Voß and Wigg-Wolf (2017: 121).

[120] For a critical survey, see Bursche (1996: 106–9).

[121] 'presumably…rhetorical overstatement' (Howgego [1992: 5]); 'should be treated with reserve' (Bursche [1996: 109]).

[122] Thus Wolters (1999: 223).

2,400 to 3,600 *sestertii* per year for a legionary under Caracalla (AD 212).[123] While varying estimates have been provided for the total army costs under Caracalla, Kehne's figure of about 500 million sesterces is definitely too low in view of the Severan military cost explosion.[124] Duncan-Jones proposed a range of *c.* 1.13–1.19 billion *sestertii* for AD 215,[125] while Wolters envisaged up to 1.6 billion *sestertii* in a point estimate, of which 720 million was just for the legions.[126] While none of these figures can be precise, they allow for a glimpse at the scale of state expenditure for army pay under the Severans. As for the claim regarding the subsidies being as high as the army expenses, put into Macrinus' mouth by Cassius Dio, it is probably fair to say that it sounds fantastic. Still, there is, of course, no way of knowing exactly how much money was spent under that title. The mere fact that Dio ascribed the claim to Macrinus makes it clear, in my opinion, that Duncan-Jones's estimate of 100–150 million *sestertii* per year for Caracalla's Imperial household costs, his gifts, and external subsidies paid by him must be ridiculously low.[127]

By the time of the Severan dynasty the days when the Germans were said to prefer silver over gold (as in Tacitus, *Germ.* 5.3) were long gone. The main medium of payment was apparently *aurei*, and indeed the sums transferred may often have been so large that it would have been utterly impractical to use any other denomination.[128] This preference for gold coins is reflected in literary sources for payments to barbarians in the late second and early third centuries AD,[129] and it continued into Late Antiquity, when gold, of course, remained the metal of choice for subsidies.

Questions of audience targeting have been discussed in recent decades in Roman Imperial numismatics, with a focus on the potential type selection for certain denominations—thus possibly for certain strata of Roman society[130]—or for particular geographical areas within the Empire.[131] *A priori*, it seems plausible to assume that the reverse typology of the export coinage was not specifically attuned to the non-Roman recipients. As has recently been observed,[132] to peoples across the frontiers (and, of course, not only to them) the most significant

[123] See, most recently, Speidel (2014: 56), in confirmation of his original treatment of the problem.

[124] Kehne (2008: 81).

[125] Duncan-Jones (1994: 45).

[126] Wolters (1999: 223).

[127] Duncan-Jones (1994: 45). He acknowledges, though, that subsidies 'had clearly become high' in the Severan period.

[128] For the difficulties involved in reconciling this picture emerging from the literary sources with the archaeological evidence, see Wolters (1999: 388).

[129] See, for example, Cass. Dio 73.6.1 (vol. 3, p. 310 Boiss.), referring to AD 193, and Cass. Dio 77.14.3–4 (vol. 3, p. 391 Boiss.), on which see below (Caracalla).

[130] See Metcalf (1993).

[131] See van Heesch (2018: 432, 436–7 and 440) for a specific selection of the types—and, in one case, a specific choice of legend—of the base metal coinage produced in Lyon for circulation in Gaul under Nero.

[132] Voß and Wigg-Wolf (2017: 121).

feature of Roman coins by far was—unsurprisingly—the Imperial effigy.[133] When pierced Roman coins, medallions, or pieces with a loop attached are found in Barbaricum, they are usually perforated or mounted in such a way that the head of the emperor was upright when the piece was displayed.[134] This raises all sorts of questions about what exactly the Imperial portrait meant to people across central and eastern Europe or in India, but these cannot be answered here. What matters in our context is that, in this perspective, all Roman precious metal coins were suited for export.

The obsession with the Imperial image is particularly evident in a group of numismatic objects that have been attracting a great deal of scholarly attention, especially since the 1990s: uniface gold pieces from the first half of the fourth century AD featuring the busts of Constantine the Great (AD 306–37) or one of his sons (Constantine II, Crispus, Constans, or Constantius II) wearing a helmet, a radiate crown, a diadem, or a laurel wreath, encircled by their name and title in the legend (Fig. 14.1). As a rule, these objects most unusually either have a completely plain reverse or, more often, just show a central dot, apart from the dotted border. The latest pieces of the group, struck in the names of Constantius II (AD 337–61) and Constans (AD 337–50) as Augusti, feature mint signatures of Trier, Siscia, Thessalonica, or Aquileia on an otherwise plain reverse: they were all produced in Europe. These objects were all about Imperial heads. This is additionally highlighted by the fact that most of them have come down to us with a loop (at the position of 12 o'clock), and some additionally with two suspension loops above the head; these 'medallions' were clearly worn on chains or sewn onto a leather or textile backing. Georges Depeyrot provided a corpus of 45 pieces of this

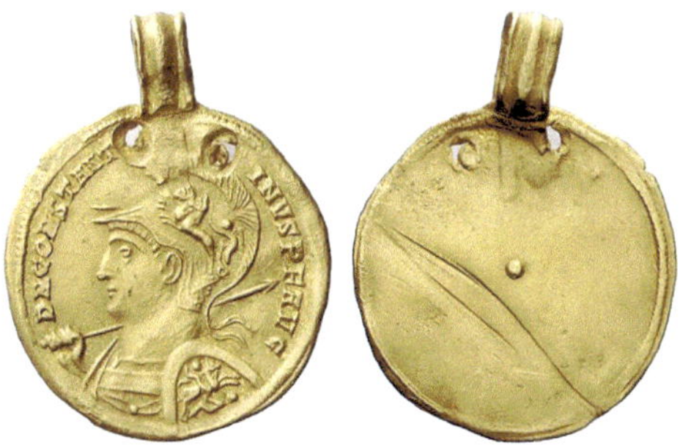

Fig. 14.1. Constantine I the Great (AD 307–37): gold 'medallion', pierced twice (from the obv.) and looped (at 12 h). Numismatica Ars Classica 72 (16 May 2013), lot no. 1708 (4.14 g; max. diameter of the flan 22 mm). Depeyrot (1996: 168, type no. 11). © Numismatica Ars Classica NAC AG.

[133] For a comprehensive collection of source texts documenting that the portrait was the quintessential element of the design of Roman Imperial coins to contemporary observers, see Crawford (1983: 55–6) and Wolters (1999: 309–11).

[134] On this point, see Voß and Wigg-Wolf (2017: 121).

kind which he dated to the years 318–40.[135] He concluded that these objects were not produced for circulation but that they 'ont été préparés pour des distributions liées aux divers *donativa* lors des campagnes militaires'.[136] When Nick Holmes published a variety of the group not known to Depeyrot from the collections of the National Museum of Scotland, he suggested that these issues may have been 'military merit awards of some sort—badges of status or recognition of achievement or valour'.[137]

Recently, Roger Bland re-examined the evidence pertaining to this peculiar class of objects in his publication of one such piece from Cumbria in northern England and three from Ireland; he also republished the specimen discussed by Holmes, which he proposes to identify with a specimen found in Birrens (Scotland) around 1725.[138] Hence, four of these five pieces were unearthed outside the Roman Empire, and one close to its northern frontier. Taken together with two pieces already catalogued by Depeyrot, which are now known to have been discovered in Brestiv in western Ukraine, and one found in Jutland (Denmark),[139] this means that the majority of these 'medallions' with an attested provenance come from outside the Roman Empire.[140] Bland also confirms that the pieces could not have been intended as ordinary currency, since the wide range of weights (also among the non-looped and non-holed specimens) indicates that they were apparently not struck to consistent weight standards. Metallurgical analyses of two of the Irish specimens showed a purity comparable to contemporary *solidi* though, at 95% and 96% gold respectively.[141] While agreeing that these objects were produced to be worn, Bland denies that they could possibly have been handed out to regular Roman troops and proposes two possible alternative interpretations. According to him, these gold 'medallions' may have been used for paying (or rather 'rewarding') the leaders of troops recruited from barbarian settlers inside the Empire, the so-called *laeti*.[142] They were undoubtedly in touch with their relatives living across the borders and therefore had open channels of communication to Barbaricum, which might explain why

[135] Depeyrot (1996). For some additions to the corpus from the coin trade, see Beyeler (2011: 31, n. 110) and Bland (2012: 218, n. 7). Several new pieces have appeared more recently; see, e.g., NAC 72 (16 May 2013), no. 1708 (4.14 g; looped, two holes); Jacquier 47 (21 September 2019), nos 1580–1 (4.84 and 3.81 g; both neither looped nor perforated); Schulman 365 (22 October 2020), no. 1556 (3.34 g; loop removed); Leu Numismatik 10 (24 October 2021), no. 2374 (3.79 g; neither looped nor perforated); Hess-Divo 340 (1 June 2022), no. 106 (4.82 g; neither looped nor perforated).

[136] Depeyrot (1996: 165).

[137] Holmes (2004: 235).

[138] Bland (2012: 223, no. 3); this is not unlikely, although the 1727 engraving of the object republished by Bland (2012: 219, fig. 3a) shows it with a slightly different obverse legend and no hole—possibly in an attempt to make the piece look nicer.

[139] See Depeyrot (1996: 169, nos 18a–b), with the correction regarding the findspot reported by Bland (2012: 218, n. 12), and Depeyrot (1996: 165, no. 3).

[140] Apart from the specimen in Cumbria, just three have been reported from Imperial territory, namely from France, Thrace, and the former Yugoslavia; see Bland (2012: 218).

[141] Bland (2012: 221).

[142] On whom see Jones (1964, vol. 2: 620, and vol. 3: 186–7).

some of the pieces ended up there. Alternatively, Bland suggests that the objects may have been produced as subsidies specifically for barbarian tribes. In both cases, their singular uniface design may have been selected with the barbarians' well-known preference for converting Roman coinage into jewellery in mind.[143]

Unfortunately, the vast majority of these 'medallions' are unprovenanced, because they are known exclusively from the coin trade, so that our understanding of the distribution of findspots is insufficient. Nevertheless, it seems necessary to discuss them in the present context, since there is a strong likelihood that they were connected with the barbarian world one way or another. If Bland's reconstruction is correct, they would probably be the only group of ancient Roman numismatic objects that were designed by the authorities specifically for export across the frontiers. However, it was clearly a short-lived experiment, which did not even last a generation.

COIN EXPORT AND THE DEVELOPMENT OF THE ROMAN CURRENCY

By the Severan period, it seems to have become evident to a wider Roman public that the payment of subsidies to peoples beyond the border of the Empire, in principle a long-established practice, had turned into a problem. A comment by Cassius Dio about Caracalla is enlightening in this respect.

> *ὅτι πολλοὶ καὶ τῶν παρ᾽αὐτῷ τῷ ὠκεανῷ περὶ τὰς τοῦ Ἄλβιδος ἐκβολὰς οἰκούντων ἐπρεσβεύσαντο πρὸς αὐτὸν* (*sc.* *τὸν Καράκαλλον*) *φιλίαν αἰτοῦντες, ἵνα χρήματα λάβωσιν. ἐπειδὴ γὰρ οὕτως ἐπεπράγει, συχνοὶ αὐτῷ ἐπέθεντο πολεμήσειν ἀπειλοῦντες, οἷς πᾶσι συνέθετο. καὶ γὰρ εἰ καὶ παρὰ γνώμην αὐτοῖς ἐλέγετο, ἀλλ᾽ὁρῶντες τοὺς χρυσοῦς ἐδολοῦντο· ἀληθεῖς γὰρ τοὺς χρυσοῦς αὐτοῖς ἐδωρεῖτο. τοῖς δὲ δὴ Ῥωμαίοις κίβδηλον καὶ τὸ ἀργύριον καὶ τὸ χρυσίον παρεῖχεν· τὸ μὲν γὰρ ἐκ μολίβδου καταργυρούμενον, τὸ δὲ ἐκ χαλκοῦ καταχρυσούμενον ἐσκευάζετο.*[144]
>
> Many also of the people living close to the ocean itself, near the mouths of the Albis, sent envoys to him (*sc.* Caracalla) asking for his friendship, just in order to get money. Because when he had done as they desired, many attacked him, threatening to make war, and yet he came to terms with all of them. For even though the terms proposed were contrary to their wishes, when they saw the gold pieces they were captivated: the gold coins that he gave them were genuine. By contrast, the silver and the gold coinage he supplied the Romans with was spurious; for he manufactured the one kind out of lead plated with silver and the other out of copper plated with gold.

[143] Bland (2012: 222). [144] Cass. Dio 77.14.3–4 (vol. 3, p. 391 Boissevain).

This passage is full of stereotypes—barbarians are not only insidious but also avaricious—and factual errors.[145] The Roman mint did not officially produce fourré *aurei* and *denarii* made of copper and lead under Caracalla in order to put them into circulation in the Empire, while reserving pure gold coins for export. Despite these shortcomings, the paragraph remains highly instructive. Although Cassius Dio got the technical facts completely wrong, his text provides a near-contemporary record that the emperor's reforms of the Imperial currency were perceived as damaging his subjects, the coin users. In AD 215, Caracalla had reduced the target weight of the standard gold coin, the *aureus*, by almost 10%, from *c.* 7.2 to 6.5 g.[146] The new lower standard seems to have been 50 to the Roman pound; the gold coins' traditional purity, however, was maintained.[147] Around the same time he introduced a new silver coin with a larger diameter than the traditional *denarius*, but struck from the same (debased) silver alloy as the latter: i.e. about 46% fine, the standard introduced for *denarii* by his father, Septimius Severus, around AD 194.[148] This new silver coin was typologically differentiated from the old *denarii* by the emperor's headgear—a radiate crown, after which the new denomination is often called 'radiate' in English-language scholarship, while another name used for it by numismatists, especially in the German-speaking world, is 'Antoninianus'. Irritatingly, the coin's official ancient name is not evident from the literary sources.[149] This could perhaps be the reason why Theodor Mommsen, in his little-read first comprehensive treatment of Roman Imperial monetary history, advanced the idea that it may simply have been called *denarius*, just like the denomination that it was eventually going to replace.[150]

Its weight was about one and a half times that of the Roman standard silver coin that Caracalla had inherited from his predecessors and continued to strike himself. Hence, the new larger silver pieces must have been worth more. However, their precise tariffing is nowhere expressly stated in our written sources either, which is why modern assumptions regarding its exchange value range from 1¼[151] to 2 *denarii*. The latter opinion, developed by Mommsen in his *Geschichte des römischen Münzwesens*, which was published nine years after his first

145 See Howgego (1992: 6) on this point.

146 See Bland (1996: 68 and 94, fig. 7).

147 Callu *et al.* (1985: 83, nos 36–7) published the results of metallurgical analyses of two *aurei* of Caracalla's sole reign, which had a fineness of 99.4% and 99.8% respectively.

148 See Butcher, Ponting, and Chandler (1997: 25).

149 Eckhel (1792: XXVII) therefore avoided referring to the denomination by a specific name, but simply called it '*novum monetae argenteae genus*'. For the hypothesis that Caracalla's new denomination was called *bicharactus*, see Weiser (2023: 31–2). This interpretation was justly criticized by Strobel (2015: 160–2); the problematic term *bicharacta* (*pecunia*) is attested in the inscription I.Aph. 230, dated to AD 301.

150 Mommsen (1851: 256–7). This passage needs to be added to the otherwise exhaustive and most useful survey of the history of scholarship on this denomination provided by Butcher (2015: 187–200).

151 Thus Hultsch (1882: 322).

treatment of the topic,[152] was subsequently endorsed by Harold Mattingly,[153] among many others, and has proved the most popular to this day. If it is correct, this would mean that under Caracalla the fiscal administration tried to enforce a significant overvaluation of the new silver denomination,[154] which would tie in with the apparent unrest among the coin users, who felt that the new coins were 'tricky money', as we learn from Cassius Dio. Among the arguments in favour of Mommsen's 'two-*denarius* hypothesis' a parallel in the gold coinage may be cited: Caracalla introduced not only a new silver coin but also a larger gold coin of about the same module as the new silver pieces and bearing, just like them, a radiate bust of the emperor on the obverse. The recorded weights of the rare pieces of this kind indicate that they were double *aurei*, so-called *biniones*.[155] Still, this is not definite proof of the exchange value of the silver coins, and the monetary history of Caracalla's reign and the later Severan period in general clearly calls for a new in-depth investigation.

The second, and perhaps more important, point emerging from the passage in Cassius Dio cited above is the juxtaposition of Caracalla's tampering with the Imperial coinage and his subsidies to barbarian peoples. This is evidence that, to some contemporaries, the overall situation under Caracalla seemed a slippery slope: extremely high army costs that had more than doubled within less than a generation, a considerable outflow of cash in view of the payments to peoples across the frontiers, and at the same time currency manipulations that seemed to disadvantage coin users. We must be clear that the moralizing attitude ever-present in ancient texts dealing with the export of Roman coins to India, as discussed in the second section of this chapter, is in evidence in passages dealing with payments to barbarian tribes as well. The text under examination illustrates this tendency. Regardless, it would be unjustified to deny the existence of a factual basis for pertinent moralizing remarks in the sources.

Mommsen's first major contribution to Roman Imperial numismatics, in which he first tackled the problem of Caracalla's new coinage, was published under the suggestive title 'Über den Verfall des römischen Münzwesens in der Kaiserzeit'.[156] In this work, he famously concluded a section reassuming the results of some

[152] Mommsen (1860: 828). Here Mommsen also adopted the name 'Antoninianus' for the denomination, borrowed from the *Historia Augusta* (*Quadr. Tyr.* 15.8). However, in this text, it has nothing to do with the silver coin introduced by Caracalla. The *Historia Augusta* uses the term for gold coins as well, as Menadier (1914: 46–8) already recognized; it must be a fantasy of the *Historia Augusta*'s author.

[153] *BMCRE* 5, part 1, p. xviii.

[154] This is the solution also preferred by Bland (1996: 74–9).

[155] For gold coins of this type Bland (1996: 68, n. 26) recorded three individual weights of 13.36 g (British Museum: *BMCRE* 5, Caracalla 21, in the name of Julia Domna; worn and pierced), 13.35 g (Kunsthistorisches Museum, Vienna: see *BMCRE* 5, part 2, p. 457, note to Caracalla 141), and 13.02 g (British Museum: *BMCRE* 5, Caracalla 157). One may add the specimen auctioned by Rodolfo Ratto, 8 February 1928 (Collections Morcom, Hands, Wertheim, etc.), no. 3445 (12.60 g; worn), of the same reverse type as the Vienna piece. See also Weiser (2023: 29, n. 140). 1/25 of a Roman pound corresponds to *c.* 13.1 g.

[156] 'About the decline of the Roman monetary system in the Imperial period': Mommsen (1851).

metallurgical analyses of Roman silver coins with the adage, 'Wo die Geschichte schweigt oder lügt, reden die Münzen'.[157] It therefore is Mommsen's legacy that the monetary history of Rome in the Principate has subsequently often been framed as a story about debasement, decline, and ultimately collapse, as Kevin Butcher recently demonstrated in a most stimulating essay. The progressive reduction of the silver bullion content of the Roman standard 'silver' coin from almost 100% to under 5% in the period from Nero to the mid-third century AD and then on to Diocletian was interpreted as mirroring the history of the Roman state, which was supposed to have gone from its prime almost to bankruptcy—economically, but also to some extent politically, within two centuries and a half.[158] In Mommsen's opinion, this development was driven by the denomination introduced by Caracalla.[159]

It is perfectly legitimate and even necessary to examine the question whether the nexus between the drain of coinage to Barbaricum and the debasement of coinage that the passage in Cassius Dio hints at really existed. Was the relationship between high expenditure for subsidies and a lowering of the standards of the coinage a causal one? This question is even more pressing now that recent research on the metallurgy of Roman silver coinage has cautioned us against all too simple fiscal explanations of the changes to the *denarius* in the first and early second centuries AD.[160] While some of these changes clearly were profitable to the state, it has been pointed out that they may in fact have been partly occasioned by the authorities' desire to renew and homogenize the silver coinage in circulation and, at the same time, to integrate provincial coinages with the *denarius*.[161]

A brief review of some modern interpretations of the larger economic implications of Roman coin export to the 'barbarian' world reveals a curious dichotomy. While some scholars hold that it had most serious consequences, others tend to minimize its impact. Let us give two examples from opposite ends of the spectrum. In his classic account of the Roman monetary history of the third century AD, Jean-Pierre Callu was unambiguous: 'Cette hémorragie (*sc.* the outflow of gold to Barbaricum) a de graves conséquences. À cause de sa raréfaction, l'or monte. Cette poussée se justifie également par les nouvelles émissions de mauvaise monnaie, pour combler le déficit'.[162] Filippo Carlà, in a more recent book on the economy in Late Antiquity, takes a completely different stand: 'La teoria secondo cui la fuga dell'oro sarebbe stata un gravissimo problema, causa di un drenaggio costante e pernicioso per le casse imperiali . . . è pertanto da rigettare

[157] 'Where history remains silent or lies, the coins speak': Mommsen (1851: 309).

[158] Butcher (2015: 184–5, with fig. 1).

[159] Mommsen (1860: 830).

[160] These interpretations quite understandably pervaded earlier scholarship and remain attractive in some cases; see, for example, Wolters (1999: 403).

[161] Butcher and Ponting (2014: 699–700).

[162] Callu (1969: 313).

completamente'.[163] 'In effetti...l'uscita di metallo prezioso...non sembra essere così rilevante'.[164]

One cannot help but wonder if these interpretations may have been determined at least to some extent by the coin material of the respective periods. Callu, working on a century characterized by silver coins that were subject to significant, continuous debasement, which was ultimately stabilized at a very low silver bullion level, and by gold coins of changing standards—sometimes affected by debasement of their alloy, too—was prepared to acknowledge an impact on coinage by the outflow of gold to foreign lands.[165] Carlà, by contrast, who focused on the period between the fourth and seventh centuries, when the Roman monetary system had been reshaped through the introduction of the stable gold *solidus*, saw no significant problems. The truth, as so often, probably lies somewhere in the middle.

ACKNOWLEDGEMENTS

I am grateful to Chris Howgego for the invitation to speak at the 'Crossing Frontiers' conference in Oxford and to Andrew Wilson (Oxford), Andrew Burnett (London), Eivind Heldaas Seland (Bergen), and David Wigg-Wolf (Frankfurt/Main) for their helpful questions and remarks both during the discussion and *per litteras electronicas* after the event. Thanks are also due to Walter Scheidel (Stanford) for discussing problems of the Roman customs system with me, to Reinhard Wolters (Vienna) for advising me on current research on the contacts between the Roman Empire and Germanic peoples, and to Federico Morelli (Vienna), Dominic Rathbone (London), and Thomas Kruse (Vienna) for their kind help and advice in papyrological matters.

ABBREVIATIONS

BMCRE 5	Mattingly H. (1975). *Coins of the Roman Empire in the British Museum*. Vol. V: *Pertinax to Elagabalus*. 2nd Edition (prepared by R. A. G. Carson and P. V. Hill), 2 parts. London.
RIC I (2nd edition)	Sutherland, C. H. V. (1984). *The Roman Imperial Coinage*. Vol. 1 (rev. edition): *From 31 BC to AD 69*. London.
RRC	see Crawford (1974).
RRCH	Crawford, M. H. (1969). *Roman Republican Coin Hoards* (Royal Numismatic Society Special Publications 4). London.

[163] Carlà (2009: 272). [164] Carlà (2009: 363).

[165] Bursche (2013: 161–4) hypothesized that the capture of the Roman Imperial gold reserves by the Goths in the Battle of Abritus (AD 251), when Trajan Decius and his son Herennius Etruscus lost their lives, may have contributed to the drop in weight and fineness of Roman gold coinage under Decius' successors. This provides a structural parallel to Callu's reasoning. Note that the outflow of Roman coinage as booty is beyond the scope of the present chapter.

REFERENCES

Ast, R., Bagnall, R. S., and Vanderheyden, L. (2022). 'O.Berenike 4. Ostraka from the Port of Berenike', *Pylon* 1, https://doi.org/10.48631/pylon.2022.1.89358 (accessed 11 April 2023).

Bagnall, R. S., Helms, C., and Verhoogt, A. M. F. W. (2005). *Documents from Berenike. Vol. 2: Texts from the 1999–2001 Seasons* (Papyrologica Bruxellensia 33). Brussels.

Beyeler, M. (2011). *Geschenke des Kaisers. Studien zur Chronologie, zu den Empfängern und zu den Gegenständen der kaiserlichen Vergabungen im 4. Jahrhundert n. Chr.* (Klio Beihefte N. F. 18). Berlin.

Bland, R. (1996). 'The development of gold and silver coin denominations A.D. 193–253', in C. E. King and D. G. Wigg (eds), *Coin Finds and Coin Use in the Roman World. The Thirteenth Oxford Symposium on Coinage and Monetary History, 25.–27. 3. 1993. A NATO Advanced Research Workshop* (Studien zu Fundmünzen der Antike 10). Berlin, 63–100.

Bland, R. (2012). 'Gold for the Barbarians? Uniface gold medallions of the house of Constantine found in Britain and Ireland', *Britannia* 43: 217–25.

Brodersen, K. (trans. and ed.) (1996). *C. Plinius Secundus d. Ä. Naturkunde. Lateinisch-deutsch. Buch VI. Geographie: Asien*. Darmstadt.

Bursche, A. (1996). *Later Roman-Barbarian Contacts in Central Europe: Numismatic Evidence. Spätrömische Münzfunde aus Mitteleuropa. Ein Beitrag zur Geschichte der Beziehungen zwischen Rom und dem Barbaricum im 3. und 4. Jh. n. Chr.* (Studien zu Fundmünzen der Antike 11). Berlin.

Bursche, A. (2013). 'The battle of Abritus, the imperial treasury and aurei in Barbaricum', *Numismatic Chronicle* 173: 151–70.

Bursche, A., Ciołek, R., and Wolters, R. (eds) (2008). *Roman Coins Outside the Empire: Ways and Phases, Contexts and Functions. Proceedings of the ESF/SCH Exploratory Workshop Radziwiłł Palace, Nieborów (Poland) 3–6 September 2005* (Collection Moneta 82). Wetteren.

Butcher, K. (2015). 'Debasement and the decline of Rome', in R. Bland and D. Calomino (eds), *Studies in Ancient Coinage in Honour of Andrew Burnett*. London, 181–205.

Butcher, K. and Ponting, M. (2014). *The Metallurgy of Roman Silver Coinage: From the Reform of Nero to the Reform of Trajan*. Cambridge.

Butcher, K. and Ponting, M., with Chandler, G. (1997). 'A study of the chemical composition of Roman silver coinage, A.D. 196–197', *American Journal of Numismatics, Second Series* 9: 17–36.

Callu, J.-P. (1969). *La politique monétaire des empereurs romains de 238 à 311* (Bibliothèque des Écoles françaises d'Athènes et de Rome 214). Paris.

Callu, J.-P., Brenot, C., Barrandon, J.-N., and Poirier, J. (1985). 'Aureus obryziacus', in C. Morrisson, C. Brenot, J.-N. Barrandon, J.-P. Callu, J. Poirier, and R. Halleux, *L'or monnayé I. Purification et altérations de Rome à Byzance* (Cahiers Ernest-Babelon 2). Paris, 81–111.

Carlà, F. (2009). *L'oro nella tarda antichità: aspetti economici e sociali*. Turin.

Casson, L. (1989). *The Periplus Maris Erythraei: Text with Introduction, Translation, and Commentary*. Princeton.

Ciołek, R. and Chowaniec, R. (eds) (2021). *Aleksanderia. Studies on Items, Ideas and History Dedicated to Professor Aleksander Bursche on the Occasion of his 65th Birthday*. Wiesbaden.

Cobb, M. A. (2018). *Rome and the Indian Ocean Trade from Augustus to the Early Third Century* CE (Mnemosyne Supplements 418). Leiden and Boston.

Crawford, M. H. (1974). *Roman Republican Coinage*. (2 vols). Cambridge.

Crawford, M. H. (1983). 'Roman imperial coin types and the formation of public opinion', in C. N. L. Brooke, B. H. I. H. Stewart, J. G. Pollard, and T. R. Volk (eds), *Studies in Numismatic Method Presented to Philip Grierson*. Cambridge, 47–64.

Cuvigny, H. (2021). *Rome in Egypt's Eastern Desert: Edited with an Introduction by Roger S. Bagnall*. Vol. 2. New York.

De Laet, S. J. (1949). *Portorium. Étude sur l'organisation douanière chez les Romains, surtout à l'époque du haut-empire* (Rijksuniversiteit te Gent. Werken uitgegeven door de Faculteit van de Wijsbegeerte en Letteren 105). Bruges.

De Romanis, F. (2020). *The Indo-Roman Pepper Trade and the Muziris Papyrus*. Oxford.

Depeyrot, G. (1996). 'Les médaillons d'or unifaces du quatrième siècle (318–340)', in T. Hackens and G. Moucharte (eds), *Italiam fato profugi Hesperinaque venerunt litora. Numismatic Studies Dedicated to Vladimir and Elvira Eliza Clain-Stefanelli* (Numismatica Lovaniensia 12). Louvain-la-Neuve, 163–70.

Duncan-Jones, R. (1994). *Money and Government in the Roman Empire*. Cambridge.

Duncan-Jones, R. P. (2006). 'Roman customs dues: a comparative view', *Latomus* 65: 3–16.

Dymowski, A. (2016). *Nummi serrati, bigati et alii: Coins of the Roman Republic in East-Central Europe North of the Sudetes and the Carpathians*. Warsaw.

Eckhel, I. (1792). *Doctrina numorum veterum*. Vol. 1: *continens prolegomena generalia, tum numos Hispaniae, Galliae, Britanniae, Germaniae, Italiae cum insulis*. Vienna.

Erdrich, M. (2001). *Rom und die Barbaren. Das Verhältnis zwischen dem Imperium Romanum und den germanischen Stämmen vor seiner Nordwestgrenze von der späten römischen Republik bis zum Gallischen Sonderreich* (Römisch-Germanische Forschungen 58). Mainz am Rhein.

Finley, M. I. (1999). *The Ancient Economy: Updated Edition with a Foreword by Ian Morris* (1st edition 1973). Berkeley, Los Angeles, and London.

France, J. (2001). *Quadragesima Galliarum. L'organisation douanière des provinces alpestres, gauloises et germaniques de l'Empire romain (Ier siècle av. J.-C.—IIIe siècle ap. J.-C.)* (Collection de l'École française de Rome 278). Rome.

Freyberg, H.-U. von (1988). *Kapitalverkehr und Handel im römischen Kaiserreich (27 v. Chr.–235 n. Chr.)* (Schriftenreihe des Instituts für Allgemeine Wirtschaftsforschung der Albert-Ludwigs-Universität Freiburg i. Br. 32). Freiburg im Breisgau.

Gordon, C. D. (1949). 'Subsidies in Roman imperial defence', *Phoenix* 3: 60–9.

Günther, S. (2020). 'Die Germanen und das Geld. Anmerkungen zu Tac. Germ. 5,3', *Gymnasium* 127: 569–80.

Harrauer, H. and Sijpesteijn, P. J. (1985). 'Ein neues Dokument zu Roms Indienhandel. P.Vindob. G 40822', *Anzeiger der phil.-hist. Klasse der Österreichischen Akademie der Wissenschaften* 122: 124–55.

Holmes, N. M. McQ. (2004). 'A uniface gold medallion of Constantine II', *Numismatic Chronicle* 164: 233–5.

Howgego, C. (1992). 'The supply and use of money in the Roman world 200 B.C. to A.D. 300', *Journal of Roman Studies* 82: 1–31.

Hultsch, F. (1882). *Griechische und römische Metrologie. Zweite Bearbeitung.* Berlin.

Iossif, P. P., de Callataÿ, F., and Veymiers, R. (eds) (2018). *ΤΥΠΟΙ. Greek and Roman Coins Seen Through Their Images: Noble Issuers, Humble Users? Proceedings of the International Conference Organized by the Belgian and French Schools at Athens, 26–28 September 2012* (Série Histoire 3). Liège.

Jones, A. H. M. (1964). *The Later Roman Empire 284–602: A Social and Administrative Survey.* (3 vols). Oxford.

Jones, A. H. M. (1974). *The Roman Economy: Studies in Ancient Economic and Administrative History* (ed. P. A. Brunt). Oxford.

Kehne, P. (2008). 'Auskünfte antiker Schriftquellen zu Umständen und Größenordnungen des Abflusses römischer Münzen ins *Barbaricum* vom 1.–5. Jahrhundert n. Chr. – Eine Problemskizze', in Bursche, Ciołek, and Wolters (2008), 75–88.

Kolendo, J. (2008). 'Die Germania des Tacitus und die Funktion römischer Münzen im *Barbaricum*', in Bursche, Ciołek, and Wolters (2008), 363–75.

Kubitschek, W. (1897). 'Bigati', *Paulys Realencyclopädie der classischen Altertumswissenschaft. Neue Bearbeitung* vol. III.1: cols 467–8. Stuttgart.

Lockyear, C. (2007). *Patterns and Process in Late Roman Republican Coin Hoards, 157–2 BC* (BAR International Series 1733). Oxford.

Melville Jones, J. (2022). 'The meaning of *bigati* in Livy's history of Rome', *Gazette Numismatique Suisse* 72.285: 3–4.

Menadier, K. (1914). 'Die Münzen und das Münzwesen bei den Scriptores Historiae Augustae', *Zeitschrift für Numismatik* 31: 1–144.

Metcalf, W. E. (1993). 'Whose liberalitas? Propaganda and audience in the early Roman empire', *Rivista Italiana di Numismatica* 95: 337–46.

Mitthof, F. (2009). 'Das Wertverhältnis des alexandrinischen Billon-Tetradrachmons zur Reichswährung unter Augustus und Tiberius', *Chiron* 39: 193–208.

Mommsen, T. (1851). 'Über den Verfall des römischen Münzwesens in der Kaiserzeit', *Berichte über die Verhandlungen der Königlich Sächsischen Gesellschaft der Wissenschaften zu Leipzig. Philologisch-historische Classe* 3: 180–312.

Mommsen, T. (1860). *Geschichte des römischen Münzwesens.* Berlin.

Morelli, F. (2011). 'Dal Mar Rosso ad Alessandria. Il *verso* (ma anche il *recto*) del 'papiro di Muziris' (SB XVIII 13167)', *Tyche* 26: 199–233.

Nappo, D. (2017). 'Money and flows of coinage in the Red Sea trade', in A. Wilson and A. Bowman (eds), *Trade, Commerce, and the State in the Roman World*. Oxford, 557–78.

Neatby, L. H. (1951). 'The "Bigatus"', *American Journal of Archaeology* 55: 241–4.

Pomey, P. and Tchernia, A. (1978). 'Le tonnage maximum des navires de commerce romains', *Archaeonautica* 2: 233–51.

Raschke, M. G. (1978). 'New studies in Roman commerce with the East', *Aufstieg und Niedergang der Römischen Welt* vol. II.9.2: 604–1361.

Rathbone, D. (2000). 'The 'Muziris' papyrus (SB XVIII 13167): financing Roman trade with India', *Bulletin de la Société d'Archéologie d'Alexandrie* 46 (= *Alexandrian Studies II in Honour of Mostafa el-Abbadi*): 39–50.

Rathbone, D. (2021). 'Too much pepper?' Review of De Romanis (2020), *Topoi* 24.2: 439–65.

Regling, K. (1970a). 'Bigatus', in Schrötter (1970), 74.

Regling, K. (1970b). 'Quadrigatus', in Schrötter (1970), 541.

Saller, R. P. (2022). *Pliny's Roman Economy: Natural History, Innovation, and Growth*. Princeton and Oxford.

Scheidel, W. (1996). 'Finances, Figures and Fiction', *Classical Quarterly* 46: 222–38.

Schrötter, F. von (ed.) (1970). *Wörterbuch der Münzkunde. Zweite, unveränderte Auflage* (1st edition 1930). Berlin.

Seltman, C. (1944). '*Argentum Oscense* and *bigati*', *Numismatic Chronicle (Sixth series)* 4: 77–82.

Sidebotham, S. E. (1986). *Roman Economic Policy in the Erythra Thalassa 30 B.C.–A.D. 217* (Mnemosyne Supplements 91). Leiden.

Speidel, M. A. (2014). 'Roman army pay scales revisited: responses and answers', in M. Reddé (ed.), *De l'or pour les braves! Soldes, armées et circulation monétaire dans le monde romain. Actes de la table ronde organisée par l'UMR 8210 (AnHiMa) à l'Institut national d'histoire de l'art (12–13 septembre 2013)* (Scripta Antiqua 69). Bordeaux, 53–62.

Stahl, M. (1989). 'Zwischen Abgrenzung und Integration: Die Verträge der Kaiser Mark Aurel und Commodus mit den Völkern jenseits der Donau', *Chiron* 19: 289–317.

Strobel, K. (2015). 'Die Aufwertung des Jahres 301 n. Chr. und ihre epigraphische Dokumentation in Aphrodisias (Karien). Ein Beitrag zur tetrarchischen Währungspolitik', *Tyche* 30: 145–72.

Stückelberger, A. and Graßhoff, G. (eds) (2017). *Klaudios Ptolemaios. Handbuch der Geographie. Griechisch—Deutsch. Einleitung, Text und Übersetzung, Index. 2. Teil: Buch 5–8 und Indices. 2. Auflage*. Basle.

Thür, G. (1987). 'Hypotheken-Urkunde eines Seedarlehens für eine Reise nach Muziris und Apographe für die Tetarte in Alexandreia (zu P. Vindob.G. 40.822)', *Tyche* 2: 229–45.

Turner, P. J. (1989). *Roman Coins from India* (Institute of Archaeology, UCL, Occasional Publications 12 = Royal Numismatic Society Special Publications 22). London.

van Heesch, J. (2018). 'Coin images in imperial Rome: The case of the emperor Nero', in Iossif, de Callataÿ, and Veymiers (2018), 429–45.

Veyne, P. (1979). 'Rome devant la prétendue fuite de l'or: mercantilisme ou politique disciplinaire ?', *Annales. Économies, Sociétés, Civilisations* 34.2: 211–44.

Voß, H.-U. and Wigg-Wolf, D. (2017). 'Romans and Roman finds in the central European *Barbaricum*: A new view on Romano-Germanic relations?', in S. González Sánchez and A. Guglielmini (eds), *Romans and Barbarians Beyond the Frontiers: Archaeology, Ideology and Identities in the North* (TRAC Themes in Roman Archaeology 1). Oxford and Philadelphia, 105–24.

Weiser, W. (2023). *Die Geldwährung des römischen Reiches. Untersuchungen zu den Münzsystemen der mittleren und späten Kaiserzeit. Aus dem Nachlass herausgegeben von Johannes Heinrichs und Werner Eck* (Antiquitas Reihe 1: Abhandlungen zur Alten Geschichte, 79). Bonn.

Wheeler, M. (1954). *Rome Beyond the Imperial Frontiers*. London.

Wilson, A. (2007). 'The metal supply of the Roman empire', in E. Papi (ed.), *Supplying Rome and the Empire. The Proceedings of an International Seminar Held at Siena – Certosa di Pontignano on May 2–4, 2004 on Rome, the Provinces, Production and Distribution* (Journal of Roman Archaeology Supplementary Series 69). Portsmouth, RI, 109–25.

Wilson, A. (2015). 'Red Sea trade and the state', in F. De Romanis and M. Maiuro (eds), *Across the Ocean: Nine Essays on Indo-Mediterranean Trade*. Leiden and Boston, 13–32.

Wolters, R. (1986). Review of J. Kunow, *Der römische Import in der Germania libera bis zu den Markomannenkriegen. Studien zu Bronze- und Glasgefäßen*, Neumünster 1983, *Münstersche Beiträge zur Antiken Handelsgeschichte* 5.1: 80–7.

Wolters, R. (1999). *Nummi signati. Untersuchungen zur römischen Münzprägung und Geldwirtschaft* (Vestigia 49). Munich.

Wolters, R. (2021). 'The *serrati* of Niederlangen and Tacitus' Germania', in Ciołek and Chowaniec (2021), 415–22.

Woytek, B. (2012). 'The denarius coinage of the Roman Republic', in W. E. Metcalf (ed.), *The Oxford Handbook of Greek and Roman Coinage*. Oxford and New York, 315–34.

Woytek, B. E. (2018). 'The depth of knowledge and the speed of thought: The imagery of Roman Republican coins and the contemporary audience', in Iossif, de Callataÿ, and Veymiers (2018), 355–87.

Young, G. K. (2001). *Rome's Eastern Trade: International Commerce and Imperial Policy, 31* BC–AD *305*. London and New York.

Zapolska, A. and Dymowski, A. (2021). 'Roman Imperial bronze coins from the 1st–3rd centuries AD on the southern and eastern Baltic coast', in Ciołek and Chowaniec (2021), 429–34.

Bernhard E. Woytek, *The Export of Coin from the Roman Empire and the Imperial Economy: Critical Remarks on Select Textual Sources* In: *Roman Coin Hoards Across Frontiers*. Edited by: Benjamin D. R. Hellings, Marguerite Spoerri Butcher, and Chris Howgego, Oxford University Press.
DOI: 10.1093/9780198986478.003.0014

General Index

Hoard Index

Hoards with details available online through the Coin Hoards of the Roman Empire project (https://chre.ashmus.ox.ac.uk/) are listed with their CHRE numbers. Hoards that fall outside the scope of the project, or that await publication, are listed by name only, unless they are comprised in *IGCH* (Thompson, M., Mørkholm, O., and Kraay, C. M. (1973). *An Inventory of Greek Coin Hoards*. New York).